1936: A CRUCIAL YEAR IN BRITISH POLTICS

COMPLETE REPRINTS OF SIX KEY ISSUES FROM 1936 OF THE WEEKLY NEWSPAPER OF THE BRITISH UNION OF FASCISTS.

CODA
BOOKS LTD

Published by Coda Books Ltd,
Unit 1, Cutlers Farm Business Centre, Edstone,
Wootton Wawen, Henley in Arden,
Warwickshire, B95 6DJ
www.codabooks.com

ISBN: 978-1-906783-76-1

CONTENTS

INTRODUCTION

You hold in your hands a unique piece of the history of the 20th Century. Action was one of a small group of ultra-nationalist publications produced in Britain in the thirties; only one complete set of Action survives today. The six complete editions reproduced here are all from 1936 and are taken from the master copy set retained by the printers. They represent an intriguing insight into a fascinating episode in the political and social history of the United Kingdom at a portentous moment.

Action was published in 222 editions between February 1936 and June 1940 under the direction of Oswald Mosley. Mosley is today viewed as a figure of the extreme right although he himself always denied that the politics of his movement were right wing, describing himself as essentially left wing in his political orientation. However, it is difficult, if not impossible, for a modern reader to comprehend the British Union of Fascists in any other light. If one examines the Mosley claim at literal face value there was clearly some measure of justification for this statement. In common with Hitler's National Socialist Workers Party there were a number of genuinely socialist initiatives which formed the political creed and much of what you will read in these pages would be equally at home in the pages of the left wing press. However, as a result of their nationalist and racist policies, the historical consensus has placed Hitler and Mussolini firmly on the right of the political spectrum and by association Mosley will forever be an iconic figure representing the most identifiable figure on the extreme right wing of British politics.

Sir Oswald Mosley, an ardent admirer of Mussolini, established the British Union of Fascists in 1932 as a

Oswald Mosley pictured in London in 1936, shortly before Parliament ordered a ban on the wearing of political uniforms.

nationalist alternative to the three mainstream political parties in Britain. Mosley had a chequered political history and was the youngest elected Conservative MP before crossing the floor in 1922, joining first the Labour Party and, shortly afterwards, the Independent Labour Party. During the twenties his exceptional political skills were soon recognised and he became a minister in Ramsay MacDonald's Labour government where he was especially anxious to tackle the problem of rising unemployment. In 1930 he issued his 'Mosley Memorandum' a Keynesian programme of policies designed to tackle the mass unemployment problem. The plan was deemed to be too expensive and rather speculative and as a consequence in early 1931 the entire scheme was rejected. Faced with the rejection Mosley impetuously resigned from the party. With nowhere left to go in the political mainstream Mosley immediately formed the New Party, it's populist policies were based on his memorandum; but, despite winning 16% of the vote at a by-election in Ashton-under-Lyne in early 1931, the party failed to ever achieve any electoral success.

Over the course of 1931 The New Party became increasingly influenced by Mussolini's model of fascism. Mosley had first hand experience of the new political phenomenon as a result of his January 1931 visit to meet Benito Mussolini in Italy. Mosley's own conversion to fascism was rapidly confirmed. He was so impressed by Mussolini he wound up the New Party in April, but shrewdly preserved its youth movement, which would come to form the core of the British Union of Fascists.

It is interesting to note that small parties on the extremes of the political spectrum tend to be the most outward looking. In the thirties the left looked to the Soviet Union and the right to Germany, Italy and latterly Spain. This trend was especially marked in the extremist parties as in an essentially conservative society like the UK there were insufficient numbers to produce critical mass and the small parties had to look overseas for inspiration funding and support. Having set his sights on emulating Il Duce Mosley spent the summer of 1932 writing a British fascist programme, *The Greater Britain*, and this work formed the basis of policy of the British Union of Fascists, which was officially launched in October 1932. Mosley, known to his followers as *"The Leader"*, completely modelled his leadership style on Benito Mussolini and the BUF as a whole on Mussolini's National Fascist Party in Italy. Mosley went as far as to adopt the Italian Fascists' black uniform for his members, earning them the nickname *"The Blackshirts"*. The BUF was anti-communist and protectionist, and proposed replacing parliamentary democracy with executives elected to represent specific industries, trades or other professional interest groups – a system very similar to the corporatism of the Italian fascists. Unlike the Italian system however, British fascist corporatism planned to replace the House of Lords with elected executives drawn from major industries, the clergy, and colonies. The House of Commons was to be reduced to allow for a faster, *"less factionist"* democracy. The BUF's programme and ultra-nationalist ideology were as outlined in Mosley's *The Greater Britain* and later upon A. Raven Thompson's *The Coming Corporate State* (1938). Many BUF policies were built on isolationism, prohibiting trade outside an insulated British Empire. Mosley's system aimed to protect the British economy from the fluctuations of the world market, especially from the worst effects which were witnessed during the Great Depression, and thereby prevent "cheap slave competition from abroad."

With the hungry thirties underway, the BUF was an instant success on the streets and soon claimed 50,000 members.

In the years before the creation of *Action* there was some support for the BUF in the mainstream press. The *Daily Mail* was an early supporter, running the now famous headline *"Hurrah for the Blackshirts!"* Despite strong concerted resistance from anti-fascists, including the local

Benito Mussolini and Adolf Hitler during Mussolini's official visit to Munich in 1937. Hitler was a guest at Mosley's wedding in 1936.

Jewish community, the Labour Party, the Independent Labour Party and the Communist Party of Great Britain, the BUF found a strong following in the East End of London where in the London County Council elections of March 1937 it obtained reasonably successful results in Bethnal Green, Shoreditch and Limehouse. The BUF polled almost 8,000 votes, although none of its candidates were actually elected. It is important to note that the BUF never stood in a General Election. Having lost the funding of newspaper magnate Lord Rothermere that it had previously enjoyed, at the 1935 General Election the party urged voters to abstain, calling for "Fascism Next Time". There was never to be a "next time", as the next General Election was not held until July 1945 by which time the Second World War in Europe had ended and fascism was considered to be beyond the pale.

Towards the middle of the 1930s, the BUF's violent activities and its staunch alignment with Hitler's Nazi Party began to alienate some supporters, particularly from the middle class, and membership rapidly decreased. This trend was exacerbated by the continuing violence at BUF rallies. At the party rally in London, in 1934, BUF stewards violently ejected anti-fascist disrupters, with one protester claiming to have lost an eye. This was the final straw for the conservative forces that had been lending their support and led the *Daily Mail* to withdraw its backing for the movement. The level of violence shown at the rally shocked many, with the effect of turning all parties against the BUF and contributing to anti-fascist support. As one observer remarked *"I came to the conclusion that Mosley was a political maniac, and that all decent English people must combine to kill his movement"*. The reaction to the Olympia rally can be illustrated in the growth in British Communist parties from 1935 onwards.

With lack of electoral success, the party drew away from mainstream politics and under the growing influence of Adolf Hitler and the NSDAP adopted policies of extreme anti-Semitism, which began to take root from 1934-1935. This was unpalatable to many British supporters and led to the resignation of members such as Dr. Robert Forgan. The provocative anti-Semitic policies also provided a rallying point for political opponents. This was particularly marked in London and led to serious, often violent, conflict, which aped the excesses of the street battles being played out in Germany between the SA and the communists. The culmination of these tensions was the infamous "Battle of Cable Street" in October 1936, when over 100,000 opposing demonstrators successfully prevented the BUF from marching through London's East End. The riot was to prove a turning point in the fortunes of the movement.

Even before the Cable Street events the BUF had been in decline with numbers dipping to below 8,000 by the end of 1935. The British Union of Fascists shared the ultra-nationalist and anti-democratic stance echoed by Hitler and Mussolini that marked them apart from the mainstream parties. Unfortunately for Mosley there was very little in common between Britain and either Germany or Italy. Both of which were relatively young nations which were the products of the nation building process which had swept Europe in the nineteenth century. The immaturity of German and Italian constitutions was in marked contrast

Oswald Mosley with members of the British Union of Fascists.

to the UK where a variety of factors including the relative stability of democratic institutions, the long established assimilation of Jews into British society, the maturity of the widely accepted constitution, it's democratic tradition and the lack of a strong, threatening Communist movement all made it difficult for fascism to succeed. In a settled and innately conservative society such as Britain there was no real appetite for a revolutionary brand of politics. However, thanks to the sinister profile of the tiny party the government was still sufficiently concerned over the quasi-military antics of the BUF to pass the Public Order Act 1936, which banned political uniforms and required police consent for political marches. This act was designed to hinder BUF activity by stripping it of the glamour which many members felt was attached to the wearing of a smart uniform. It worked; and this measure above all others signalled the end of the movement.

From 1936 onwards-mass BUF rallies were held in "mufti" attracting large crowds but it is uncontestable that the wearing of a uniform and the associated marching and public preening were a major draw for a certain type of mentality. BUF members shared a desire for order and a willingness to subjugate themselves to state authority. The uniform was an outward sign of that willingness and it also signalled a strong bond with their European counterparts who were on the march across a large swathe of European countries.

Despite his excesses Mosley was an astute politician and he accurately predicted the outbreak of World War II. In the years building up to the war the BUF enjoyed brief success on the back of their "Peace Campaign" to prevent conflict with Germany. Sympathy for the organization evaporated rapidly as war with the Axis approached. The BUF was finally banned in 1940 and Mosley was jailed for the duration of the war along with 740 other fascists. After the war, Mosley made several unsuccessful attempts to revive his brand of fascism, notably in the Union Movement.

The weekly newspaper published by The British Union of Fascists was a rare phenomenon. Unlike many political publications of the day which were crudely produced on the rudimentary copying processes available in the thirties *Action* was an elegantly conceived and stylishly realised production. It had to be. *Action* was an attempt to counter the growing influence of *The Daily Worker* a newspaper produced by the forces of the left which championed the politics of Stalin's Soviet Union. The first edition of *The Daily Worker* was produced on 1st January 1930.

By January 1934 the first eight page long issue of the *The Daily Worker* was produced. Thanks to its mainstream style *The Daily Worker* had succeeded in finding it's way into the newsagents of Britain and circulation was rising. Today the paper is known as *The Morning Star* it remains the organ Central Committee of the Communist Party of Great Britain. It was widely held that at the time that *The Daily Worker* received £2000 pounds per month from "Moscow", and that Moscow directed the paper to print anti-war stories in order to prevent Britain re-arming.

Faced with the growing influence of *The Daily Worker* the nationalists in Britain needed it's own publication. Mosley had lost the support of *The Daily Mail* in 1934 and the vacuum needed to be filled. *Action* was the solution. It was intended to be funded by advertising. One of the intriguing aspects of the printers set is the surviving dummy issue that anticipated a great deal of space being given over to advertising. The hoped for advertising deluge never materialised and most ads are for BUF rallies and BUF publications. This shortfall in revenues had serious consequences as it starved the paper of much needed funds and financing such an expensive publication was always a struggle for Mosley.

Somehow the paper managed to survive and the 1936 editions are particularly notable as they contain numerous examples of the thoughts and outpouring of William Joyce - Lord Haw-Haw. In 1932 Joyce joined the BUF and swiftly

William Joyce (Lord Haw-Haw).

became a leading speaker, praised for his power of oratory. The journalist and novelist Cecil Roberts described a speech given by Joyce - *"Thin, pale, intense, he had not been speaking many minutes before we were electrified by this man ... so terrifying in its dynamic force, so vituperative, so vitriolic."*

In 1934 Joyce was promoted to the BUF's director of propaganda and later appointed deputy leader. As well as being a gifted speaker, Joyce gained the reputation of a savage brawler. His violent rhetoric and willingness to physically confront anti-fascist elements head-on played no small part in further marginalising the BUF. It was Joyce who spearheaded the BUF's policy shift from campaigning for economic revival through corporatism to a focus on anti-Semitism.

Also in 1936 Joyce was instrumental in changing the name of the BUF to the rather cumbersome "British Union of Fascists and National Socialists". In 1936, he stood as a party candidate in the 1937 elections to London County Council. Joyce was eventually sacked from his paid position when Mosley drastically reduced the BUF staff shortly after the failed 1937 elections. Although Joyce had been deputy leader of the BUF from 1933 and an effective fighter and orator, Mosley snubbed him in his autobiography and later denounced him as a traitor on account of his wartime activities.

As the reader will no doubt note the 1936 issues are rife with anti-Semitic sentiment. After 1937, the party turned its focus away from anti-Semitism and towards activism, opposing a war with Nazi Germany - a policy which *Action* had advocated even earlier, championing the peace movement in 1936 as can be seen in the examples reproduced here. Although Mosley himself was never a committed anti-Semite even with Joyce gone it was too late to change course, in any event Mosley did very little to change matters preferring to exploit anti-Semitic sentiment for political gain.

A. K. Chesterton, the original editor of Action.

During the first year of its life the paper was edited by A. K. Chesterton cousin of the famous author G. K. Chesterton. G. K. was a harsh critic of his cousin's activities and despised the Mosleyites whom he memorably described as "the solemn fools of Teutonism". A. K. Chesterton was originally a staff writer for the *Stratford Herald* and later became editor of the *Torquay Times*. He was a great lover of Shakespeare and was asked to write the speech for the Prince of Wales opening the newly remodelled Stratford Theatre. In the thirties he moved to London and lived near the headquarters of Oswald Mosley's British Union of Fascists. Chesterton took to dropping by to join in the heated political debates which were a feature of life in that hot house environment. By late 1933 he had become so enthused and joined the movement. He soon became the director of publicity and propaganda and was also chief organiser for the Midlands. His tenure at the helm of *Action* was to prove brief. In 1936, alcoholism and overwork led to a nervous breakdown. Chesterton consulted a German neurologist and during 1936 to 1937 lived in Germany. After returning to Britain he was appointed editor of the weekly BUF magazine *The Blackshirt*. This position provided a pulpit for his increasingly anti-Semitic rhetoric. A. K. Chesterton left the BUF in 1938 disillusioned and worn down; nonetheless he continued to be active in far-right politics. He continued to be active by joining the Nordic League.

The six complete editions of *Action* re-printed here provide a fascinating glimpse into the British version of nationalist politics in 1936 at a time when such sentiments enjoyed real currency throughout Europe. A complete re-print of all 222 editions is currently available and it is to be hoped that they will provide a fascinating primary source reference for historians, sociologists, students of politics and general readers and further our understanding of an all too often overlooked chapter of British political history.

Bob Carruthers
May 2011

ACTION, Friday, February 21, 1936

No. 1 [REGISTERED AT THE G.P.O. AS A NEWSPAPER.] "BRITAIN FIRST" FEBRUARY 21, 1936

FOR KING AND PEOPLE

PEACE OR WAR?

By OSWALD MOSLEY

(SEE PAGE 9)

Back to 1914 Diplomacy

NATIONS PREPARING FOR WAR

"Nearly every day for a week Mr. Baldwin has smoked his pipe at meetings of the Cabinet Defence Committee," says the "News Review." His grave political blunders compelled even Sir Austen Chamberlain to rebuke him last week.

Soviet troops on the march. Warlike speeches by their leaders are arousing in them a lust for war. Communism, they vow, will overcome all capitalist countries.

Marshal Tucachevsky, the Soviet Vice-Minister of Defence. He came to London for King George's funeral and then "stayed a few days to see the country." Actually, he was visiting British armament factories. Trotsky called him "the glory and pride of the revolution."

Mr. Anthony Eden, the British Foreign Minister, is closely associated with the policy of M. Litvinoff, the Soviet architect of war.

Japanese guns at the moment are resting, but Soviet aggressiveness in the Far East may well cause them to become active.

These men, and millions more, paid with their lives for the blunders of pre-war politicians. German, British and French soldiers were slaughtered by the tens of thousands in a war that was to end war.

French officers on manoeuvres. The politicians of France are in alliance with the Soviet. In 1914 France was dragged into war by Russia and to-day she is in danger of suffering a similar fate.

Is Our Generation to be Sacrificed once more to the Blunders of the Politicians?

"ALL'S WELL WITH ENGLAND!"

A WEEKLY ANTHOLOGY

Compiled by "LUCIFER"

Shadow Over Mayfair.

"It will be some time before the West End resumes its normal life and gaiety, but last week signs of returning activity manifested themselves.

"It was more a matter of personal disinclination than any question of convention that prevented people visiting cabarets and the livelier restaurants. A quiet dinner in a grill-room and a cinema afterwards fitted in more to the Mayfair mood of the moment, and the resultant early hours and absence of night-life was probably very beneficial."—Miss Peeps in the "Bystander."

* * *

But We Still Carry On.

"The usual ermine-coated, orchid-ed, 'twenty-four shillings a stall' audience; the usual barrage of flash-light photographers—'Just a minute, Lady Hornby'; and 'If you please, Lord Moore!'

"A queue of autograph hunters, celebrity spotters, and film fans, half-way down the Strand; all the looking-on public who get a kick out of other people's lives."—Same page in the "Bystander."

* * *

The Active Life.

"During his two-weeks' visit there last month he managed to include a double execution at Sing-Sing . . . an investigation of a ten-cent dance-hall and a flying visit to Boston to interview the big noises of Christian Science."—"Bystander."

* * *

"Formidable Problems!"

"Almost a thousand applicants, all eligible for presentation, had to be refused last year simply because it was impossible to issue further invitations. . . . As the number of applications to attend Courts in the reign of a new sovereign is likely to be far greater than in ordinary times, Lord Cromer's department will be faced with formidable problems a few months hence!"—"Tatler."

* * *

Charity Begins at Home.

"The second night of Cochran's revue, 'Follow the Sun,' was arranged by Mrs. Anthony de Rothschild and Mrs. Israel Sieff for the Women's Appeal for the German Jews. Over £7,000 was collected by the performance, and the stalls and dress circle of the theatre were sold out at ten and five guineas. Lady Scarsdale, resplendent in a chinchilla cape, was in the audience, and so was Lady Oxford, who gave a spirited and witty criticism of the rumba, with appropriate actions, to a few friends in the interval.

"Lady Granville, who was one of the vice-presidents, brought a small party, and Mrs. Simon Marks was in a box. Her husband is at present in New York, hoping to raise additional funds for this charity, which needs £30,000 to further its work of transporting the young Jews to Palestine."—"Tatler."

* * *

Our Suffering Sur-Tax Payers.

"The weather there is apparently lovely, the place is packed, our Austrian friend Charlie from the Ritz is a 'wow' at the Sporting Club at supper-time. There is a new kind of double roulette, at which you have a twelve-hundred-to-one chance.

"The Marquess of Cholmondeley is enlarging his villa; Count Sala is building a new one; Lady Eva Wemyss has rented the lovely 'Mauresque' from Mr. Somerset Maugham; Mrs. Stanley R. Smith won a million gold francs one night and lost it the next."—"Bystander."

* * *

These Stirring Times!

"To say that French women are not suitably clad for games is to proclaim yourself five years behind the times. These stirring times!"—"Sketch."

* * *

Portrait of a Nobleman.

"This association with the Renaissance manifests itself in many other ways. Lord Tredegar has written three or four books of elegant poetry, one of which, 'The Eel,' has been translated into three languages. He is very fond of swimming—another Renaissance characteristic—and he keeps an aviary and a menagerie. . . . An exact example of his exotic life may be found in the circumstances of his succession to the title two years ago. He was in a New York millionaire's yacht off Venezuela when Prince Paul of Greece heard the wireless bulletin and informed him that he was now the new peer. . . . He . . . does everything he can for his tenants in Bow and Bromley, most of which he owns."—From "After You, Who . . . ?" in the "Bystander."

* * *

The European Crisis.

"I'm open to correction, but I'd say that King Boris had the bluest eyes of any King in Europe."—"Tatler."

* * *

Pigging It!

"'I designed the whole of my own house in Hollywood and the *decor* of each room. There are 25 rooms.'

"She turned to her husband, sunk in his big overcoat on the opposite seat.

"'What *style* would you say the house was, dear?' (She says '*style*' in the French manner, having a way of dropping French words and phrases into her conversation—'"Mutiny on the Bounty" is so full of British *esprit*'—when speaking to her husband, who has, during the years he has spent in Hollywood, acquired a Californian accent.)

"Miss Bennett talks with a distinct, rather deep voice, turning her enormous eyes full on you when she is speaking. Her good-looking husband says little, but sits hunched up in his coat, absent-mindedly making faces into the collar. His hobby is making colour pictures in remote parts of the world, and he is now what he calls 'recuperating' after completing one in Indo-China."—From the "Daily Mail," February 13, in an interview with Miss Constance Bennett, the film star.

* * *

We're in the Money.

"I should love to tell you the name of the English Duchess who figures in the best story of the week. But obviously I cannot.

"It is about her conversation with a friend on the subject of the clumsiness of her husband the Duke.

"'He came in last night,' she said, 'just as I had finished dressing for dinner and sat straight down on my tiara.'

"'Good heavens,' was the reply, 'what did you do?'

"'Oh,' said the Duchess quite unconcerned, 'I just took another out of the cupboard.'"—From the "Sunday Graphic," February 16.

* * *

Going Native.

"Fashion in nail varnish is decidedly paler. Apart from the fact that it tones delightfully with mauves and black, it beautifies the hands when so many darker shades show up their cold-weather defects.

"A particularly lovely shade has a trace of mauve in its depths so that it harmonises with a blond or medium lipstick and all shades of mauve and violet in your gowns.

"It is called Sunrise, and in the manicure salons the deeper shades of burgundy and rust are tucked away."—From the "Sunday Dispatch," February 16.

* * *

The Voice of the Charmers.

That the Webbs' "Soviet Communism" is a great book all are agreed. Catching something of the grandeur of its theme, it brings home to the reader a realisation of the vastness of the Russian experiment. It is impossible not to be infected by the excitement that glows beneath the austere sentences of the authors. Perceptibly, as one reads, one's pulse beats faster, for almost it seems as if the dead weight of human inertia and apathy might be overcome—is, indeed, being overcome—as if the bad old world were being made afresh. Doubts arise only to be charmed away. The Webbs, indeed, like Plato, lay a spell upon their reader, so that while the voices of the charmers are still speaking, he has no choice but to submit. It is only afterwards that reflection sets in.—From an article by C. E. M. Joad on "The Reappearance of Sin in Russia," in the "New Statesman and Nation."

THE OTHER SIDE OF THE PICTURE

Tragedy of Surplus Labour

THE HOPELESS THOUSANDS OF LANCASHIRE

ABANDON Lancashire! Remove from the county those thousands who wait hopefully amid demoralising idleness for the revival of the cotton industry.

And that is all the Ministry of Labour can apparently say.

Mr. S. Warrington, Divisional Controller, Ministry of Labour, in an address to a group of the Manchester Statistical Society, summed up his examination of the North-Western unemployment figures and revealed the gravity of the position.

The fall in unemployment from the peak figure of 696,000 in September, 1931, continued with some consistency until recently. The encouraging downward trend has become slower, and Lancashire knows that the number now unemployed can never hope to be reabsorbed until some drastic economic changes are made nationally and imperially in the control of the industry.

Workless Without Hope

"Surplus labour" is the description used by Mr. Warrington in his reference to the workless for whom the staple industry of a once great county offers no further hope.

Surplus labour! In an age of potential plenty and existing want; in an age when the genius and power of science have been harnessed to the production of man's requirements; in an age when in the streets of the great cotton county itself the children of trained cotton operatives are seen in pathetic rags, lacking the clothes which their parents could produce.

Surplus labour! In December of 1935 there were 404,000 on the live register of Lancashire, Cheshire, and Cumberland. What to do with them? The Ministry of Labour can make an analysis. The Ministry can discover that "there is a large surplus of labour in the North-Western Division at the present time, which is not likely to be absorbed into employment in the division, at any rate in the near future." And the Ministry can go no further.

There in all its hopelessness is the position. Hundreds of thousands of people must wait impotently on an impotent Government until, "at any rate," beyond "the near future."

Look Elsewhere for Help

"The North-West must," says Mr. Warrington, "look to other parts of the country for help in absorbing North-Western workpeople into employment."

Presumably, if the steel factories and mines of industrial Britain find themselves through some mistake of National Government plunged into prosperity, the hands which tended the spindle will guide the lathe or load the bucket.

Nor are the people of Lancashire favourable to this suggested method of transporting the misery of the cotton county to some other part of England.

They know that Lancashire's goods are needed and that markets could be secured by a Government of honesty and determination, and one can understand the reluctance which Mr. Warrington found among skilled women operatives when transference to domestic posts in other areas was suggested.

Transference Not Possible

In only a small percentage of cases is transference possible even if desirable. Unemployment bears more hardly upon older than upon younger people, and such evidence as is at present available suggests that this position is more likely to intensify than to lessen. More than 35 per cent. of the unemployed men (on an analysis made in May, 1935) were over 45, and nearly 45 per cent. were over 35.

As the Ministry Controller pointed out, much of the surplus labour in the division consists of workpeople with long years of experience in particular occupations. Though it may seem to be obvious to others that openings for their skill no longer exist, it is difficult for the workpeople concerned to realise it. The pull is all against making a plunge into the unknown, even if suitable openings offer; and openings for which past experience in a declining industry fits are, in the modern world, few or non-existent.

Eighteen Persons to the House

OVERCROWDING IN NEWCASTLE

AT a Ministry of Health inquiry into seven clearance orders made by Newcastle City Council, held last week, it was revealed that 215 persons are living in twelve houses at Newcastle.

Mr. J. Atkinson, Deputy Town Clerk, said the order included Millers-hill, City-road, where there were twelve houses containing sixty-three separate holdings, with 215 inhabitants. The seven orders involved fifty-six houses and affected 598 people, comprising 178 families.

At the St. Mary's-place scheme there were seventy people in five houses. There was one water-tap for seventeen people and no sinks.

Similar conditions were stated to exist at other of the areas scheduled in the clearance orders. Representatives of several owners lodged objections to the proposed demolition.

The Ministry Inspector is to make his report after viewing the property.

Thirteen People Living in One Room

THIRTEEN people sleeping in one room. No electric light; nothing but paraffin lamps burning in a smoky, airless, and cramped surroundings. Children huddled together in beds which can never be properly aired or tended. Always the risk of infection and disease.

No, this is not a picture of life amid the chaos and failure of any foreign land, nor a scene to be encountered among some animally barbaric race.

This is Longton, fifth of the Five Towns, sphere of one of Britain's important industries.

30,000 Want Homes

TEN per cent. of the houses in the town are overcrowded. Thirty thousand men, women, and children are in need of fresh accommodation.

In Stoke itself 4,000 people are waiting for Corporation houses. But the Corporation can do no more than slowly clear the slums. Four thousand people want cheap, habitable houses. The Government offers no subsidy for the necessary building except in relation to slum clearance schemes.

These people demand decent homes. They are of the race which made Britain great; of the blood of those who gave us the legacy of a mighty and wealthy Empire and those who live in Mayfair or sleep at the Savoy.

Reduced Grants Depopulate Rhondda

LACK OF WORK DRIVING PEOPLE AWAY

THE false hopes raised by the Government in the distressed areas of South Wales with regard to the promise of new industries have had an appalling effect upon the population. Rather than even ameliorating conditions, the special areas have been further impoverished by the reduction of Government grants for social services. When the first grant period started there were a hundred and fifty thousand population in the Rhondda, and the grant for social services was £96,283. When the second period came more than 14,000 people had been transferred to the more populous and overcrowded districts around London on temporary work schemes. The consequence was that although the Rhondda had to provide exactly the same social services, the grant was reduced by over eleven thousand pounds, because of the temporary transference of these working people. And the grant continues to drop.

Men of action would have seen that work was provided in the Rhondda area, and also would see to it that the many brilliant youngsters who are at present shut out of training for Civil Service posts were given training to enable them to qualify. Under the present system parents who are unable to provide their youngsters with the training have no chance whatever of seeing their lads get an opportunity to qualify for such posts. The endeavour of the juvenile training centres is all directed to training the lads in manual and physical exercises.

LITVINOFF

Bolshevism: Defender of Civilisation?

A Page of Imperial & Foreign Affairs
Edited by
ROBERT GORDON-CANNING

R. GORDON-CANNING

By R. GORDON-CANNING

SELDOM, I expect, has any nine-month period in the history of European diplomacy been so rich in changes of a kaleidoscopic nature as those months between the Stresa Conference in April, 1935, and February, 1936, which saw the ratification of the Franco-Soviet Pact in Paris. From out of the funeral procession for the late King-Emperor has emerged a triumphant Litvinoff. The Stresa Conference on the surface, if no deeper, represented a united front between Italy, France, and Great Britain against "so-called" "breakers of peace." The Danubian Conference vanished into thin air, the Anglo-German Naval Agreement appeared from nowhere, and the outbreak of hostilities in Ethiopia smashed in a few weeks whatever agreement had been made at Stresa.

★ ★ ★

Out of Cold Storage

THIS Conference was the beginning of yet another attempt to encircle Germany, but failed, as had all previous attempts. Then, in desperation, France brought out of cold storage the Franco-Soviet Pact for ratification, and Litvinoff, taking full advantage of the dissension between the Stresa friends, began to forge a new steel ring round the German frontiers, with France, Czechoslovakia, and Rumania.

The funeral of King George saw the culminating point of this policy attained with the presence of Litvinoff and Marshal Tukhachevsky in London, feted by Eden, Baldwin, and others; so, with the friendly assurances of the British Government with regard to these various pacts, Litvinoff has changed European policy from one of defence against Soviet Russia to one of attack against Nazi Germany. The result is that Europe is once again divided into two hostile camps as before 1914, with all nations feverishly arming themselves. In fact, the League has brought insecurity in place of security.

★ ★ ★

Forestalling the League

THE Franco-Soviet pact stands for "the rendering of *immediate* assistance" in the event of the territory of either being attacked from land, sea, or air. This clause forestalls the legal finding of the League, signifying that there will be no delay, while the League gives a unanimous decision as to who is the aggressor.

The vicious situation in which Europe finds itself to-day is the direct consequence of the Treaty of Versailles, and the actions of successive French Governments. Germany, trampled on and degraded, has arisen Phoenix-like under Herr Hitler's leadership to assert her right to live free and to exist as a nation. No League was able to accomplish this against French and British opposition, so Germany acted and became strong of her own accord. France to-day discovers that her policy of frustration towards Germany has achieved the reverse of what she hoped, and in consequence, finding also the League by no means a "security," returns to the old pre-war system of alliances under the post-war names of defensive pacts, and the use of Russia against Germany.

★ ★ ★

European Suicide

EUROPE to-day confronts a position analogous to, but worse than, that of 1914. France and Great Britain are prepared to employ the declared enemy of their empires and their civilisations, Soviet Russia, against a vital and cultured nation like Germany, which has stamped out Communism in its own territories.

Such a situation leads direct to chaos, to the suicide of Europe, to the abnegation of civilisation, and to the vindication of Bolshevism.

How to act in order to escape this fate? Offer Germany the hand of friendship and equality; give her an opportunity to obtain raw materials without breaking her currency, and help her to defend Western civilisation against Communism.

If Great Britain and Germany are found on opposite sides in another European War it will be the death-knell for both, and of Western culture.

The Isle of Cloves and Palaces

By F. C.

ZANZIBAR, the Pearl of the Indian Ocean, is not often in the news. The population usually is peacefully picking and drying cloves, of which trade they possess almost a monopoly. Only in Zanzibar and the near-by dependent Pemba Island will the clove tree grow to perfection. The tree is a species of myrtle, and the clove is the flower. Copra, which is made from the coco-nut, is also an important industry. The recent riots were a protest against the new law to prevent the adulteration of copra.

The island is governed by a Sultan and the British Resident, assisted by a nominated Legislative Council. For generations every Sultan on his accession has built himself a palace; so along the coast and inland there are many palaces, in beautiful settings, now abandoned and falling into slow decay.

★ ★ ★

Drink Licence Please?

THE majority of the population are Arabs and Swahilis, who belong to the Mohammedan faith, and consequently practise entire abstinence from intoxicating liquors. The Government makes sure that the Faithful keep this abstinence by issuing drink licences, price two rupees each, to Christians and other infidels. There is no drinking test before the application for a licence is granted. It is the same size as a driving licence, and to avoid disappointment on a hot day it should not be left at home! The licence exempts the holder from the obligation of teetotalism, and if he abuses the exemption the licence may be withdrawn for six months, or longer, at the discretion of the British Resident.

★ ★ ★

A Native Wedding

THE Mohammedans ask Christians to their festivals. It is an exhilirating experience to be, at night, one of a few Europeans in the midst of some twenty thousand men who are intoning responses to the imam. Together with another Englishman the writer received an invitation to a wedding. The bride might have been in Timbuctoo; anyhow, she was not to be seen. The bridegroom evidently had thought hard on the best method of entertaining two Englishmen. In a conspicuous position were placed two chairs, the rest of the guests being seated on carpets; between the two chairs was placed a small table, and on the table were two glasses, a siphon of soda-water, and a bottle of whisky.

The Arabs, who form the upper classes and farmers, are docile and trusted; they habitually by right carry swords, which often are sheathed in chased silver scabbards. What has made them even think of rioting in an island where the prestige of the white man is so high? Perhaps the supposed successful resistance of the Abyssinians to a white race has changed their ideas. News travels swiftly in Africa, and becomes distorted. It may be that from drum to drum, and by word of mouth, the rumour is spreading that the white man after all is not invincible. There are ominous signs elsewhere of grave unrest.

RED ARTILLERY PASSING THROUGH MOSCOW

Getting Ready for the Yankee Elections

THE State primaries for the coming American Presidential campaign begin in April and continue until June. At the moment the Republican Party have no outstanding personality to put up against Roosevelt.

Seventy-year-old Senator Borah is competing, and is to-day supposed to be supported by the Jewish and Radical elements in the Republican Party.

This chivalrous and gentlemanly campaign for the honour of being the next President of the United States will be fought with more than customary venom then those preceding, and there is no doubt that Postmaster General Farley will spend money freely in order to secure success for Roosevelt.

This election for the Presidency of the United States is another fine example of the methods of modern democracy.

★ ★ ★

AS statistics become available, the people of this country are discovering that the foreign policy of their Government is having its effect upon their economic well-being.

Figures now available show that the Empire is also suffering under the sanctions boomerang, for Newfoundland has lost a market for 150,000 cwt. of dried cod. A large proportion of the catch is left unsold, and prices are falling rapidly.

★ ★ ★

RECLINING in an armchair of that most loyal spinster Ellen Wilkinson, the Marxist Indian Congress Leader Jawaharlal Nehru informs the British Press that he is out to put an end to the Government of India Act, and also to turn all Indians into industrialists. This lawyer of eloquence and elegance is an out-and-out Socialist and a defender of the poor. At least, so he says.

★ ★ ★

FURTHER troubles and riots have occurred during the last month in Syria, in which many Arabs have been shot and many imprisoned.

The economic and political situation in Syria has long been in direct opposition to that which was intended at the establishment of the Mandate, but one hears no voices of protest raised at Geneva on behalf of the Syrian Arabs, and of Syria, a land of infinitely greater civilisation than Ethiopia.

★ ★ ★

IN Italy workers are able on "Theatrical Saturdays" to attend the finest operatic and dramatic performances at prices within the reach of the poorest. These "Saturdays" have proved immensely popular, and the Rome Opera House gave last "Saturday" its seats over to the workers for a performance at prices not exceeding 1s. 8d.

★ ★ ★

WHILE the Italian armies are freeing Abyssinian slaves by the tens of thousands, and in consequence of which are suffering from international boycott, the Soviet Government, staunch supporters of liberty and the League, are employing 200,000 men, women, and children in forced labour gangs, euphemistic term for slaves, to complete the doubling of the railway line between Lake Baikal and the Manchurian Frontier.

★ ★ ★

IN Egypt Lord Kitchener brought in the Five-Feddan Law in 1912 in order to save the fellah from starvation. To-day the High Commissioner for Palestine intends to enact a similar law for this country in order to protect the poor Arab peasant from the same evil.

Jewish bodies both in Palestine and in other countries are declaiming and agitating against the passage of such a law on the grounds that it will create a further obstacle in the way of establishing a Jewish State in Palestine; and they say that this claim takes prior consideration to that of the welfare of the Arab population, and that even the starvation and unemployment of Arabs must not be allowed to interfere.

★ ★ ★

M. TANNERY, Governor of the Bank of France, inquires of Dr. Schacht for information regarding the political intentions of Herr Hitler, at a meeting of the Governors of the Central Banks at Basle.

Is this in the province of bankers? Apparently!

By A. K. Chesterton . . .

Should the British Empire Be Disestablished?

PROGRESSIVE people—staunch democrats who wish to make a contribution to their time in keeping with its spirit—are convinced that the day has come for the dis-establishment of the British Empire.

* * *

Their belief rests upon their observation of the happy lot of their fellow citizens in the British Isles. They see them in true perspective, as a fortunate race of men with so much room at home that they require none for expansion overseas; possessing such abundance of raw materials at their doorstep that there is no need to go abroad for them; enjoying the sound of their own industries working at full blast and the sight of the extensive cultivation of their own soil; inhabiting a land of song and laughter in which joy rules supreme because of the lack of all material cares.

Contemplating this delightful spectacle of prosperity, progressive people ask themselves, most properly, whether in a world otherwise completely civilised it is right for Britain to retain an Empire, especially since there are so many other well-disposed nations which have a greater claim to our Imperial heritage than we.

* *

IF circumstances were other than they are; if Britain were not a vast tract of territory but a small and over populated island; if we were not economically self-contained and if our industries and our agriculture were not straining every nerve to keep pace with the effective demand of the home consumer; if our fellow-countrymen were not all handsomely fed, and clothed, and housed, and replete with the amenities of modern life—then, of course, the case for Imperial dismemberment would not be so strong, and in that event the patriots who are now the advocates of this policy would not dream of pressing it upon us.

In view of the reality of the British millennium, however, their arguments are unanswerable, and if logical reinforcements were required the rest of the world, so much more advanced in humanitarianism than we are, would very soon supply them.

* *

THERE is France, for instance — large-hearted, pacific, beautiful France, only awaiting for the opportunity to bestow French Africa and Indo-China upon well-loved neighbours. Let France be our true exemplar.

There are Germany and Italy, nobly resigned to a dearth of raw materials, scorning to assert their national claims to live.

Then there is Russia, scrapping all her arms, relinquishing her foreign propaganda, happy to die if only her death can give life in greater abundance to the capitalist countries so dear to her heart.

Finally, to the west there is America, owning allegiance to the highest ideals; and to the east there is Japan, withdrawing from the scramble for territory, relinquishing markets which do not belong to her, assisting the national aspirations of China by every means in her power, and demanding a quantitative maximum of naval armaments sufficient only to protect fishing smacks from the sharks and rebellious oysters of the sea.

* * *

IN this splendid world, wherein every humanitarian value is asserted to the exclusion of every other value, the people of Britain—fat, prosperous, and overfed—simply dare not continue with a policy of selfishness and greed.

Progressive politicians such as Lansbury are not alone in imploring the citizens of Britain to rise to heights of sublime sacrifice. They have behind them the unanimous support of the financiers. The City of London recognises the perils which beset a nation if it bows down in worship of Mammon, and, rather than allow the British people to experience these perils, they have shown the most selfless devotion possible in allowing themselves to risk the contamination of gold by collecting all the British money they can lay their hands on, and sending it abroad to finance our competitors against us in all the markets of the world.

* * *

THE reason is clear. These high-souled financiers desire that the people of Britain shall exalt only the things of the spirit, spurning the temptations of wealth and turning from the dangerous pride which Imperial possessions may stir within them. And so there is strong and aristocratic support for the modern, progressive movement of Empire disestablishment.

Already an inspiring start has been made by the surrender of India, and nothing could be more encouraging than the fact that the first steps to this end—the setting up of the new provinces of Sind and Orissa—brought upon the Government the congratulations of all the parties in the House, which shows how worthy the politicians have proved themselves of the trust reposed in them by their mentors, besides demonstrating their superb readiness to sacrifice party advantages to the lofty cause of giving away the power and the territories which previous generations of Britons most selfishly died to uphold.

* * *

THAT the virtual abandonment of India will be a triumphant success is assured by many factors, not least among them being the high degree of literacy and administrative skill of the Indian people, to say nothing of the age-long harmony which unites all races, creeds, and castes in that vast sub-continent. The truly remarkable affinity and brotherly love between Moslem and Hindu, for example, has shone for centuries as a beacon before men, presenting them with a sublime object-lesson of the joy of religious tolerance, co-operation, and unfaltering good-will.

India off our hands, we shall be free to distribute the rest of the British Empire in any way that seems most equitable to our politicians in consultation with their financial advisers, and it is devoutly to be hoped that we shall not stop short at the gift of the overseas possessions when our title to our own land is not a thing to be stressed in an age of practical altruism.

* * *

KENT may go to Paraguay, Lancashire to Latvia, Devon to Poland, and Surrey to Haile Selassie and all these gestures shall be accounted part of the new Imperial theme, which has no trafficking with memories of Clive or Rhodes, or the Empire's million warrior dead, but which is that far higher thing—the translation into practical politics of the swelling Lansbury heart and the irrigation of the desert of international relationships by the ever-flowing Lansbury tears.

Leave us Throgmorton Street and Whitechapel as the last flaming citadels of the British spirit, and who among us will regret the passing of the rest into abler, wiser, greasier hands?

GEORGE LANSBURY kicking away. In this picture he has just kicked away a football. He now appears to be anxious to kick away the Empire!

WANTED: FAIR PLAY FOR YOUTH

By Anne Brock Griggs

IN their election manifesto, the Government undertook to raise the school-leaving age to fifteen, with a right to exemption between fourteen and fifteen for "beneficial employment."

In the Bill which shortly will come before the House of Commons, exemption will be granted "in any circumstances in which the authorities consider . . . that exemption is justifiable." In other words, we shall be exactly where we are. Without a maintenance grant the Bill is a farce. Even the self-sacrifice of mothers cannot achieve the impossible, and numbers of families will be unable to keep their children at school without aid.

In spite of the fact that the exemption loopholes are condemned by educationists all over the country, in the face of humanity, or even common sense, the juggernaut of Government proceeds with the Bill.

Among the local authorities who have already applied for power to raise the leaving age to fifteen, exemptions have ranged between 70 and 90 per cent. In fact our best and brightest children will be deprived of their birthright and pitched into the turmoil of industry to help support their homes because their parents have committed the crime of poverty.

What is beneficial employment? Under the Act it is not even made to coincide with bona-fide apprenticeship. Is it "beneficial" for a lad of fourteen to go down the pit, or into the mill, or into a blind alley occupation, because his parents need the few shillings a week that he can earn; later, when he requires a man's wages, to be thrown into unemployment without the equipment of a trade?

THE CASE FOR GIRLS

In the case of girls, if their assistance is urgently needed in the home, they may have exemption at fourteen. Their education may be broken off at a critical stage of their development, that they may share in drudgery too heavy for their years; to "mother" younger brothers and sisters, deprived of schooling because they are poor.

As long ago as 1930, Oswald Mosley, when speaking in the House of Commons and advocating the raising of the school age to relieve unemployment, estimated that it would give work to 150,000 adults annually. The Fascist policy has no room for half-measures. We regard the raising of the school age as vital, not only for the sake of our children, who must be trained for future citizenship, but also for the welfare of the community as a whole. Good schooling must be available for all children irrespective of the parents' income. The ability of the child to benefit should be the only test of education.

The present policy amounts in effect to exploiting the young and penalising adult workers, whose jobs are threatened by an influx of juvenile labour.

Pressure will be brought upon the authorities by poor families who desperately need the assistance of the small wage which their child can earn. Is it better for them to stay at school, cramming knowledge on an empty stomach, or to be fed and untutored? In all except the most stricken areas, the problem will be decided by the majority whose children will continue to face the world at fourteen.

SANCTIONS HAVE FAILED

"Sanctions have failed," writes Sir Arnold Wilson, M.P., in an account in "The Observer" of his recent visit to Italy and interview with Signor Mussolini.

"Irreparable damage is being done, not the least being the apparent attempt to join hands with the Soviet Government, through its alliance with France, in a vain attempt to save not peace, but the League.

"Sanctions are hurting Italy; they are hurting France and Great Britain, too.

"German coal has taken the place of British coal. We shall not recover this market. German and Austrian goods are replacing British goods, and the public and shopkeepers alike vow that the change is permanent.

TRADE WILL NOT RETURN

"Trade prohibitions have given a renewed fillip to the demand for economic self-sufficiency. From these developments we, who depend more than any other nation on international trade, are bound to suffer."

Sir Arnold asked Signor Mussolini whether trade would return to its old channels when League committees reverted to the task of peacemaking, so rudely disturbed by the action of the two remaining Parliamentary democracies of Europe, and when sanctions ceased to operate.

"No," the Duce said, "that cannot be.

"We have spent and are spending too much in creating fresh channels to take the place of those that you have taken the lead in diverting. We cannot abandon the mines we are opening, the great plants we are erecting, the long-term contracts we are making.

PUBLIC OPINION AROUSED

"We have relied, more than most countries, on the normal avenues of international trade: these, once choked, cannot quickly be opened. Public opinion has been aroused.

"We shall not soon forget the language used by your statesmen. You have turned a colonial war into what may yet be a world-wide disaster.

"We cannot forget the blood and treasure we poured out in the Great War, nor put away from us the remembrance of 670,000 dead. Have you so soon forgotten?"

As a direct result of Britain's attitude, he told Sir Arnold, "much Ethiopian and some Italian blood has been needlessly shed. You have prolonged the war; a great responsibility lies on you.

NO DESIGNS ON BRITISH INTERESTS

"I have repeatedly assured the British Government," he said in answer to a direct question, "that we harbour no designs against any British interest in Africa. The development of our interests in Ethiopia should create no divergent, but common, interests with Great Britain."

"This claim," writes Sir Arnold, "seems to me to be well-founded. If Italy assumes heavy liabilities east of Suez she must help us in all circumstances to keep open the Canal."

Commenting upon the feeling in Italy, Sir Arnold, who points out that all foreign newspapers are on sale in Italy and the situation is freely and openly commented upon, says, "What principally excites resentment is the attempt of successive Foreign Secretaries to distinguish between Signor Mussolini and the Italian people. We tried it with Lenin and later with Mussolini (in 1923) and failed. We tried it again with Herr Hitler and failed.

MUSSOLINI WILL REMAIN

"Mussolini will remain at the helm till the hand of death removes him; he is in the prime of life and—notwithstanding rumours—in perfect bodily and mental health."

"Is it not time," he said to Sir Arnold, "that the British people realised that their present attitude implicitly condemns all that is greatest in their history. Do you really believe that you should, in the past, have left the savage world to its own devices, in the New World, in the Antipodes, Africa, and Asia?"

THE FARMERS' DIARY

THE POTATO OUTLOOK

"Do Not Overplant"

FARMING IN SOUTH WALES

(By Our Agricultural Correspondent)

THE Potato Marketing Board is to be thanked for a booklet it has published, showing the acreage by counties, of each variety grown by registered producers in 1934 and 1935, and the total acreage that was under the crop in the United Kingdom.

According to the Board's figures in 1934 there were 546,000 acres of potatoes cultivated by registered producers, and in 1935 there were 518,000 acres. These figures differ somewhat from those issued by the Ministry of Agriculture, for in the former case very few growers of less than one acre are registered, and in the latter the figures are those for farms of one acre or more of land.

From the figures available we see that potato growing in Great Britain as a whole has declined by 29,000 acres, or 5.1 per cent. This, of course, can be attributed to the years of bad prices suffered by growers, when imports were so heavy and prices so low that many thousands of tons were left to rot in the clamps, or were fed to stock.

I can well remember friends of mine being offered potatoes for nothing if they would fetch them away from the farms, and that such a state of things should obtain is, I consider, a reflection on the way in which those in power neglect our natural resources, for surely there must be scientific means available whereby potatoes could be processed for use in various forms of industry, and also for pig food.

A Word of Advice

THE Board has been wise to issue a warning recently against excessive planting this season, realising that the better prices that were obtained last year were mainly due to the shortage of the crop. Any over-planting in excess of national requirements might result in a serious drop in prices.

As we all know, potato imports are subject to quantitative regulations and during 1935 we imported 191,000 tons, compared with 154,000 tons in 1934, probably the increase being due to the shortage of the crop here.

However, when we remember that in the week ending February 1 this year we imported 122,102 cwt. of potatoes, and of these 48,584 came from our old friend, Denmark, and 22,637 cwt. from the Netherlands, it would seem to the ordinary observer that our growers might well put in more acres, for thus we should be safe (if there is a shortage) from having to increase our imports, while if the crop is abundant we might then think seriously of cutting down these imports much more drastically.

As Denmark and the Netherlands are also our chief rivals in the bacon industry it would appear that they are finding the production of pigs and potatoes more profitable than do our growers and pig breeders.

Both these industries employ much labour and are worthy of all the encouragement we can give them, and without doubt the Potato Board is doing its best for growers. But there is always the Board of Trade to consider.

Farming in South Wales

I WAS interested to learn that the Leader had been speaking in South Wales, that being a part of the country I used frequently to visit on work connected with agriculture some years ago.

I have vivid recollections of the Royal Show at Cardiff in 1919, the Bath and West at Swansea in 1923, the Royal Welsh Shows at Carmarthen, Bridgend, Cardiff, and other places, and many of the smaller Welsh one-day shows in that part of the Principality.

I shall never forget, in the early years after the War, seeing the miners in their thousands turn out and thoroughly enjoy the events. Many of them with whom I had conversation showed great knowledge of agriculture and live-stock breeding and were not slow to pick out the various points in the exhibits.

Wales has made a wonderful effort to improve her live stock, and for years she has been famous for her herds of Shorthorns, Herefords, and in the North for her national breed of Welsh black cattle. For flavour of mutton and hardiness there are few breeds to equal the Welsh Mountain sheep, to say nothing of the Kerry Hills. Then, too, the Welsh white pig is eminently suitable for bacon, and had there been more money behind the Breed Society we should have heard a great deal more about the breed.

Of late years Wales has become much more of a dairying country, but I feel sure that if only we could get the beef industry fairly on its legs we should again see a more plentiful supply of those excellent beef stores, so well known a feature at the markets in years gone past. Knowing South Wales in prosperity, and revisiting it in adversity, I marvel at the pluck shown by the miners and industrial workers generally, and also that of the farmers who depend for their living on the purchasing power of the industrialists.

The Sugar Beet Industry

MOST arable farmers will feel thankful that the Sugar Beet Bill should soon become law, for there can be no two opinions as to the value of the crop for keeping land under cultivation and workers employed that otherwise would have been stood down; again, it has kept the price of sugar low to the consumer, and, despite what is sometimes said and written, sugar is very necessary in our diet.

Anyone who knew anything of agriculture realised at once that it was merely fatuous of the Greene Report Committee to suggest that beet growers should take up an alternative crop. There is no such crop. Had the beet-growers of East Anglia all turned their attention to milk production, what the state of that already over-burdened industry would be now one cannot conceive. There are still several points that require settling ere those engaged in the industry can feel satisfied, and one of them, and a very important point, too, is the redistribution of factories. While the present number of factories are sufficient to deal with all the beet that is grown, here is grave dissatisfaction that they are not distributed more evenly in districts that have a large area of beet. Thus the South, South-West, and Western portions of the country have to send their beet too far for it to be a really economic proposition at present prices per ton, while Wales has no factory at all.

The proposal for a flat rate for carriage has not commended itself to the majority of growers in the Eastern and North-Eastern counties, which are well served by factories; but if this flat rate is not to come in future years, then it is essential that factories should be moved to cater for the growers who are now at a grave disadvantage by being so distant.

We want to see fair play for all growers, and justice throughout this new and vital industry.

Hope Deferred . . . !

IF ever a body of men had to nourish their minds and pockets on "Hope Deferred" the breeders of beef and beef store cattle are those men. We get nothing to encourage us from the Government, only promises that the position is being kept in mind, while of late we have heard rumours that it will not be easy to overhaul the existing arrangement with Argentina.

Then to pin faith to "gentlemen's" agreements when our cattle industry is perishing before our eyes is but foolishness . . . some might call it by a stronger name.

Meanwhile each month sees our supplies of suitable beef stores steadily dwindling, and breeders are not encouraged to keep up the supply, especially when they know that there is always a sale for dairying heifers, who carry a useful bag and look like being heavy producers.

VALUE OF SUGAR BEET INDUSTRY

MR. ELLIOT SAYS INDUSTRY NEEDS PROTECTION

IN moving the Second Reading of the Sugar Industry Reorganisation Bill, Mr. Walter Elliot, Minister of Agriculture, gave clear and sufficient reasons for the Government proposals for reorganising the industry by the amalgamation of the beet sugar companies into a single corporation, to be known as the British Sugar Corporation, Limited.

This proposal was the direct outcome of due consideration of the Greene Report. While Government adopted the Report's proposals for drastic economies and reorganisation, they rejected the recommendation that the industry should be closed down altogether.

LARGE NUMBER EMPLOYED

One of the principal reasons for continuing the sugar beet industry was the employment, direct and indirect, that it afforded throughout the country for some hundreds of thousands of men.

The extinction of this industry would affect every agriculturist, and the introduction of an alternative crop would deeply affect many thousands of agricultural labourers or small agricultural producers. There is no other crop to which the men or the acres concerned could be turned.

Beet sugar can only be produced in this or any other country through Government assistance. In this country such assistance has been reduced from 7s. 3d. per cwt. in 1934 to 5s. 6d. in 1935, and it will be 4s. 9d. in 1936. The direct charge was reduced from just under half a million in 1934-35 to two and three-quarter million in 1935-36.

This subsidy has been described by Opposition Members of the House as an outrageous ramp, but we have to realise that without this subsidy we should have to pay far more for our sugar. As it is, sugar in Britain is cheaper than in most other countries, standing at about 2¼d. per lb. In other countries prices range from 3d. to 7d.

Mr. Elliot stated that every industry now required and obtained protection against world competition, and that this country was becoming the world's market where every agricultural product was sold more cheaply than in its country of origin. He went on to say that it was desirable to use the world's surpluses, and to admit rather than to dam out the world flow of trade.

MR. ELLIOT'S TWO VOICES

Mr. Elliot speaks with two voices. On the one hand he strongly advocates the support of a British industry, but for which he admits that the Eastern Counties would be another depressed area, and at the same time he emphasises the admittance of the world's surplus production. In other words, he supports sugar beet but condemns the residue of the agricultural industry in Britain to ruin through foreign competition.

Every utterance of Ministers makes it more clear that the National Government have no intention of taking any steps to improve the lot of British farmers.

Grass For Milk Production

INCALCULABLE BENEFIT FROM SCIENTIFIC DRYING

The "Morning Post" of January 9, 1936, published an interesting article from its agricultural correspondent, in which valuable information is given on the subject of drying grass for milk production.

It is stated that, from experience already obtained on farms where dryers have been installed for drying grass for milk production, an increase in permanent employment of one man per fifty acres of land for hay would appear to be a fair estimate.

The Minister of Agriculture returns give approximately six million acres of grass and clover for hay per annum. If this acreage were developed by cultivation, fertilisation, and drying, it would therefore employ an additional 120,000 men, This would at the same time confer enormous benefit on the agricultural engineering industry, as the machinery and equipment cost would average about £5 per acre, which would result in an order for some £30,000,000 for that industry.

In addition to this, allowing one ton of coke per acre for drying, six million tons of coke would be required per annum. The **(Continued at foot of preceding column.)**

(Continued from next column.)

fertiliser industry as well would benefit, and about 600,000 tons of fertiliser would be required.

NOTHING IS DONE

Such are the possibilities of grassland improvement. It seems so easy, so obvious, so much a matter of course. And yet nothing is done, or, for that matter, likely to be done by our National Government with its international proclivities. As the "Morning Post" pertinently remarks, "the only possible drawback to this development may possibly lie, in the eyes of some politicians, that it might take place at home instead of abroad"—which sums up the situation pretty shrewdly.

SUCCESSFUL FARMING IN DENMARK

£20,000,000 FAVOURABLE TRADE BALANCE WITH BRITAIN

TWO recent publications on Denmark, the report of the Agricultural Council and "Denmark in 1935," afford interesting information as to the co-operation and organisation of the agricultural industry in Denmark which has raised production both in quality and quantity with such marked success.

The Government has contributed in no small degree to the success of the Danish farmers, and, to judge by the favourable balance of trade with this country, has succeeded in providing them with a market for their produce, in marked contradistinction to the British Government, which certainly provides farmers with Marketing Boards but gives the market to the Danes.

Farming properties in Denmark number about 204,000 and employ 1,200,000 people. In Britain we have twenty-five million acres employing only 741,000 workers.

CO-OPERATION AND RESEARCH

The high standard of living of the Danish workers refutes the contention that agricultural development in this country would reduce the standard of living. The main factor of success in Denmark appears to be co-operation aided with technical research, to which the Government has given great assistance, with the result that wheat production has increased during the last sixty years from 17.4 cwt. per acre to 23 cwt. per acre. Potatoes have increased during the same period from 47 cwt. per acre to 132 cwt. per acre.

Continual experiments are being carried out at four experimental stations to determine the merits of farmyard manure and artificials, and to ascertain the correct proportions of the kinds of fertilisers suitable for the various kinds of soil. Artificials have given much larger crops than farmyard manure on clay and sandy soil.

HUGE EXPORTS TO BRITAIN

Danish imports from Britain have increased from £10,700,000 in 1929 to £13,350,000 in 1934, but Danish total exports to this country stand at £32,875,000, the great bulk of which is farm produce—a balance of nearly £20,000,000 in favour of Denmark.

The "Morning Post's" Agricultural Correspondent states that "no one wishes to decry the value of such Danish trade as we can get, but we must not lose sight of the fact that we have a much more valuable and expanding market at home."

The Trade Agreement with Denmark comes up for reconsideration in the near future, and it is of vital consequence to British agriculture that the interests of the farmers should be made paramount. Other countries with whom our agreements are about to expire are putting forth every effort to show their value to our manufacturers, and British farmers must not lose this opportunity to press for due consideration, or they will be left behind again.

Anglo-Egyptian Treaty

NEGOTIATIONS are taking place in an attempt to frame an Anglo-Egyptian Treaty to settle the four outstanding points:—

(a) Defence of Egypt against aggression.

(b) Defence of Empire communications.

(c) Defence of foreign interests in Egypt.

(d) Sudan.

It is also hoped to make Egypt a member of the League of Nations. Whatever may be the value to Egypt of this membership it appears to have been somewhat delayed, considering the history of Egypt compared with that of at least half of the member States in the League.

No great confidence is to be found in Cairo for the result of these negotiations, and the moment seems particularly inopportune to embark upon fresh negotiations in view of the unbalanced situation both in the Mediterranean and in Abyssinia. But apparently while the National Government refuses to listen to the voices of patriotism at home, it is always prepared to accede to the boisterous requests of students, and to yield before the threat of riot.

BOOK OF THE WEEK

BRANCKER—MAN OF ACTION

By BLACKBIRD

("*Sir Sefton Brancker.*" *By Norman McMillan. Published by William Heinemann, Ltd. Price 21s.*)

THE Brancker family is an old Dorset one, which dates from 1560.

The name probably is of Dutch origin. There was certainly the spirit of the old Dutch seafaring adventurers in Air Vice-Marshal Sir Sefton Brancker's make-up. The family inter-married from time to time with Germans, and in Brancker was to be found all the best characteristics of the British, Germans, and Dutch. As these three nations are the world's leading airfarers, it is not difficult to see how Brancker was able to reach the position he occupied in the hearts of the whole aviation world.

The first half of the book is written by Brancker himself and was intended for publication after he had ceased to be a Government servant.

His sympathy was always with the genuine worker no matter of what rank, which accounts for the fact that when, during the war, certain Labour troubles arose which were stirred up by paid agitators, Brancker was always able to get the men back to work by talking to them as man to man and showing them that he had an honest understanding of their point of view and a genuine desire to right their wrongs, at no matter what trouble to himself.

* * *

OF Kitchener, Brancker says: "Lord Kitchener was an enormous asset to the R.F.C. He instinctively understood aviation and realised fully its vast possibilities. . . . He was much harassed by endless quibblings of the Cabinet at this time, and I remember him bursting out to me one day that you never knew where you were with these damned politicians!"

He wrote to Trenchard in 1916 of Parliamentary and Press interference:—

> I get more and more impressed with the rottenness of our system, our institutions, and a large proportion of our people every day. The Bosche will beat us yet unless we can hang our politicians, burn our newspapers, and have a dictatorship.

What Brancker hoped for in 1916 may come true after twenty years.

* * *

THE second half of the book is devoted to Brancker's life in civil aviation and has been pieced together skilfully by Captain McMillan. Unfortunately, Brancker left very few papers which deal with this phase of his life, and so we are unable to obtain quite the vivid impression which we get of his service career.

Aviation took up the greater part of his life from one moment in December, 1910, when his sergeant-major in Calcutta came into his room and said: "Beg pardon, sir, but they've just disembarked some aeroplanes at the dock." Brancker says: "I was up and away as quick as I could go, and arrived at the docks to find an expedition dispatched by the British and Colonial Aeroplane Company of Bristol half-way ashore."

The ill-fated R101 carried Brancker to his death

This sentence is typical of all of Brancker's career.

Captain McMillan gives a vivid and realistic account of Brancker's last hours and the fight of the great airship against storm and tempest over Southern England and Northern France until, out of control, she finally hit a ridge at Beauvais and went up in flames. Eight men escaped, but Brancker, with forty-five others, perished. He left a gap in aviation that has never been filled.

Captain McMillan deserves our thanks for having presented Brancker's personality to us in this vivid book, which must be read and re-read by all. Let Brancker be an example to us when our time comes.

BOOKS IN SHORT

"Life Errant." By Cicely Hamilton. (Dent. 10s. 6d.)

Miss Hamilton is to be thanked for an interesting and sincere book on events of pre-war and present days. Stage and war-time experiences make excellent reading. Wonderful insight into Jewish problem in Germany.

* * *

"Proletarian Pilgrimage." By John Paton. (Routledge. 10s. 6d.)

A graphic and witty slice of real life in the early part of the twentieth century, telling of a youth with a sense of humour making his way in the world.

* * *

"Keir Hardie." By Hamilton Fyfe. (Duckworth, 2s.)

A book about the life, character, and work of Keir Hardie. A high principled, tough son of a Scottish miner, who had no sympathy with the MacDonald types.

FILM OF THE WEEK

'THINGS TO COME'

By MAURICE BRADDELL

★

THE H. G. Wells film "Things to Come," produced by Alexander Korda, is presented at the Leicester Square Theatre this week.

The chief importance of this film lies not so much in the story which it tells, or the work which Mr. Wells has put into it, as to the effect which this masterpiece of big canvas painting will have upon the British film industry at large.

A Scene from the Film.

Mr. Alexander Korda spent the better part of two years and nearly half a million pounds on this picture. But all the money did not go solely to the making of the picture, but to building the necessary studios, collecting the necessary staff from all four corners of the globe, and experimenting in new forms of trick work. The result is a magnificent spectacle portrayed with that rare combination of intelligence and imagination which characterises all Mr. Korda's work.

* * *

The story reminds one that Mr. Wells before the Great War wrote a book called "War in the Air." In it he foretold the Great War, and drew a picture of Zeppelins bombing New York with such devastating effect that they brought to a complete standstill the entire life of civilisation. The scene has been somewhat repeated in "Things to Come."

One cannot help reflecting that in the war of 1914-1918 things happened on a scale far larger than Mr. Wells had imagined in his "War in the Air." Events necessitated an organisation even more stupendous than Mr. Wells had foreseen. It did not end in the destruction of civilisation; rather can it be said that it advanced civilisation four or five generations at a bound.

And here again one feels that in "Things to Come" Mr. Wells is merely repeating his pessimistic prognostications.

Mr. Wells clearly has no warm feeling towards the dictators of Europe or Fascism itself. He portrays Fascism upon the screen in travesty. There is nothing more than local robber barons with their gangs fighting for the possession of coalfields in the hills of South Wales.

His leader, whom he calls Boss, does not bear any resemblance to either Hitler or Mussolini, and yet there is a very definite attempt on the part of the author to caricature these two men in the small, but childish figure of the leader of Everytown. It will be observed that there is no sort of policy attached to this leader's ruling of the town. He is much more like a tiny pirate than the man who restored the self-respect of the Germans, or the other man who raised decadent Italy to the position of a first-class power in modern Europe.

* * *

Nevertheless, in watching this film, one sits amazed at the whole achievement from a purely film point of view. All congratulations must go to the British workmen and technicians who toiled night and day to perfect to the smallest detail the scenes, the sets, the models, the skies, the research, and all the work that goes in all its forms to the construction of a really magnificent film.

British people can truly be proud of the fact that they have produced a picture which shows all the technical finish of Hollywood, combined with a much higher level of intelligence.

PLAY OF THE WEEK

COWARD AS A GIANT *among Dwarfs*

IT is amusing to read in "Antony" that young Viscount Knebworth in desperate seriousness once led a crusade to save the *jeunesse dorée* from the Noel Coward dragon. Later he wrote to a fellow crusader in surprise to record his discovery that the dragon, if it did devour people, gobbled up the people most meet to be devoured. At the same time he hastened to affirm that Coward was not a great artist.

The controversy as to whether or not any contemporary is a great artist belongs to the ancient and solemn order which embraced the polemics as to how many angels could comfortably inhabit a pin's head. These discussions lack criteria.

But Antony Knebworth was right when he discovered that Coward gives proper direction to his shafts of derision. At the time when their sober, conventional elders were laughing bitterly at the Bright Young Things, one of the Bright Young Things brilliantly turned the tables on the elders by exposing them as a most deserving target for bitter laughter. He mocked their huntin', their shootin', their fishin'. He showed them up as freaks. And he lashed their morality for the empty, cruel, bourgeois thing that it is. At that time it did seem as though there was a streak of greatness in Noel Coward.

Gertrude Lawrence

* * *

NOW, after a lapse of years, his more mature plays are before the British public. They have been running in a one-act series at the Phoenix Theatre, and, to judge by three of them, "Hands Across the Sea," "Fumed Oak," and "Shadow Play," their author has decided to take the ready cash of entertainment-values and renounce whatever there may be of credit in the profundities.

The first reveals Mayfair repaying honest hospitality received in Malaya, forgetting the visitors' names, and skating with graceful embarrassment over the *contretemps*. Just that. It is an exquisitely observed little piece of portraiture, but nothing in it matters to a single soul.

* * *

"FUMED OAK" carries us a trifle nearer to the heart of things by bringing the scene from Mayfair to Clapham, where a humble man has long endured a beastly wife, a beastly child, a beastly mother-in-law; surreptitiously saved five hundred pounds; taken a couple of whiskeys and sodas, and arrived home to enjoy the ecstasies of telling the lot of them what he thinks, prior to disappearing into the blue.

This is an extremely good playlet, although its theme suggests more of wish-fulfilment than of actuality.

* * *

THE third play is a piece of tinsel artifice, meretricious in its sentiment and incredibly clumsy in its mechanism. We are back in Mayfair, where young husband arrives to ask young wife to divorce him. Young wife has taken too much sleeping-dope, and what follows is her dream. Noel Coward and Gertrude Lawrence croon, jazz, and clod-hop their way back through the past; and when they return, then young husband no longer wishes to divorce young wife, and we have as much as the author can give us in the way of a "happy ever afterwards." We do not care very much, one way or the other.

The acting of Gertrude Lawrence in all three plays, and of Noel Coward in the second, is beyond praise, while the supporting company does no violence to the tenuity of its tasks. In the third play Coward is as grotesque as the part he fills.

The totality of impression is disappointment. The author does not fulfil his promise. Suave, witty, shrewdly observant, almost always deft, though sometimes fatuous, Noel Coward proves himself a giant of this age of dwarfs only to the extent that the popular dance-band leader proves himself a giant. And in the world of modern art it is with such giants that the victory lies. The Press doth fawn upon them, and the people gladly pay.

A. K. C.

TOPIC OF THE WEEK

DEFENCE ORGANISATION

THE Cabinet met on Monday to consider a report of the Special Committee of Defence which for many weeks past had been examining proposals for strengthening the Defence Services. The Government proposals are expected to be published in a White Paper early in March, and they will be keenly debated in both the House of Lords and in the House of Commons. The subject is expected to dominate Parliamentary time during the whole of the present session.

The inadequate arrangements for the defence of Great Britain and of the British Empire have thus at last become a problem of political importance, demanding urgent and vigorous action on the part of the Government. British foreign policy in recent years has been conducted in a spirit of irresponsible pugnacity, while at the same time the defensive system of the country, it is now generally admitted, is in a pa lous state.

Grave Danger

ALL the Powers, excepting Britain, are re-arming with a vigour that exceeds anything seen in pre-war days. In those days, Great Britain, while adopting a non-provocative foreign policy, took great care to be the supreme power on the seas, and at the same time developed an army which, though small, was amazingly efficient when judged by the military knowledge available at that period. To-day Britain finds herself caught up in a hot-bed of international intrigue, mainly operated from Geneva.

The League of Nations, before the autumn of 1934, was a comparatively harmless organisation, but after Litvinoff persuaded the League to accept the Soviet as a member of the Geneva organisation, he set the pace with a series of vast intrigues that to-day has b ought about a situation of grave danger.

War in April

ON the Continent, it is being freely prophesied that another European war will break out in April. "This date," wrote G. K. Chesterton, a few days ago, "coincides approximately with the beginning of the rains in Abyssinia and with the opening of the campaigning season for Russia."

We mention this rumour because floating dates of the same kind have turned out accurate in the past.

Our own British statesmen have adopted a policy that has fallen in with the wishes of M. Litvinoff. We remember in this country, and no doubt it is remembered even more vividly on the Continent, how, recently Mr. Baldwin declared that "Great Britain's frontier was no longer the white cliffs of Dover, but was on the Rhine."

Such a declaration to Britain, and to Europe, obviously meant that, in the event of future Continental wars, Britain would have to defend the left bank of the Rhine, just as, in the past, she had to defend the cliffs of Dover.

Not a Ship, Not a Gun

AGAIN, we all remember how, not so many weeks ago, in a dispute between the League of Nations and Italy—a dispute in which the British people had no part—Great Britain sent her fleet and a large air force into the Mediterranean, and the garrisons in Egypt, Malta, and Aden were all greatly strengthened.

All this the British Government did on its own initiative. It was not asked to do so by the League of Nations, and nor did any other country take similar action. We bear in mind the famous declaration of Sir Samuel Hoare on December 19, 1935:

"Not a ship, not a machine, not a man has been moved by any other member State."

So, rightly or wrongly, the British Government has been taking an active part in affairs which cannot be said, by any stretch of the imagination, to be a main concern of the British Empire.

Whether or not one agrees that the possibility of war is near, there must be general agreement that a foreign policy which runs the grave risk of offending great Powers must entail as a corollary a policy of strength in armaments so that the country can defend itself if called upon to do so.

The Facts Revealed

WHAT are the facts? They are fairly well known. Rear-Admiral Sir Murray Sueter, in the House of Commons last week, reminded the country of the blunders of the pre-war and war period, of how the Germans had the monopoly of aerial reconnaissance in the North Sea; of how torpedo-dropping aeroplanes were developed too late to be of any service during the war; of how the Admiralty refused to build aircraft carriers; of how Sir Ian Hamilton was sent to the Dardanelles without any war plans from the War Staff, and of how the Committee of Imperial Defence shelved problems instead of solving them.

What was perhaps more important was the revelation of the helplessness of the Fleet against air-craft. The Fleet, said Rear-Admiral Sueter, could not stay at Malta a minute in the event of a Mediterranean war. Gibraltar was not safe; nor were Devonport, Portsmouth, Chatham, and Sheerness. And, he might have added, nor was Woolwich Arsenal!

A Known Weakness

IT is not as though the Government were not aware of the weakness of Britain's defensive organisation. On the contrary, leading spokesmen of the Government have boasted of our weakness. Take, for instance, Mr. Baldwin's words in the House of Commons on March 12 last year. He said:

"Our Air Force is still only fifth among the air forces of the world. . . .

"I think the House ought to realise that in the Navy the personnel fell from 102,000 eight years ago to 89,000 two years ago, and the First Lord of the Admiralty, in introducing the estimates, said that that was a lower figure of personnel than had existed in this country for forty years.

"The Army . . . has probably suffered more than any other Service from the drastic cuts that have been made. In 1932 the annual training of the Territorials could not take place and the field training for the Regular Army had to be cut down.

"Since 1914—and no one pretended that our Army was too large for pre-war needs—even since then nine cavalry regiments have been disbanded, twenty-one infantry battalions, sixty-one batteries and companies of artilleries, twenty-one companies of engineers, one hundred and one battalions of special reserve, and three battalions of colonial and native troops."

A Committee By Any Other Name

MANY schemes are put forward for improving the machinery of administration whereby the defences of this country could be adequately maintained. There are those who advocate a Minister of Defence, and there are others who want another Committee similar to that of the Committee for Imperial Defence. The Committee of Imperial Defence was set up by Mr. Balfour, when Prime Minister, soon after the Boer War. The Prime Minister of the day always presides over its deliberations and it is now generally agreed that the system it represents has been a failure. Some people suggest that calling the old Committee for Imperial Defence by the new name of "Council of Defence" would be useful. Changing names, however, does not seem, to us, to be much good. The machine, of course, depends on the men. The men who operate the present machinery of government have neither the energy to make the present machine work at full power, nor to scrap it and create a new machine.

Take, for instance, the question of money to meet the needs of the time. The Government is "considering" a proposal to raise a sum, said to be between £200,000,000 and £450,000,000 within the next six years by means of a loan.

★ ★ ★

Mosley's Proposal

YET it was so long ago as July 12, 1934, that Sir Oswald Mosley, when speaking at Brighton, advocated a National Defence Loan for three purposes, namely:—

1. To give Britain immediate air strength.
2. To modernise and mechanise our Army.
3. To put the Fleet in proper condition to defend our trade routes.

Meanwhile Mr. Montagu Norman, the Governor of the Bank of England, and Mr. Neville Chamberlain, Chancellor of the Exchequer, are wrangling behind the scenes as to the best method of raising money. The Government, no doubt, pleads that even if it had raised the money it would not know how to spend it.

That, then, is the position now before Parliament and before the country. Defences have been neglected, the Government has been dilatory; for weeks they have been "considering" the position; they are not yet decided on a programme to overtake arrears of work, and they are not agreed on the way to raise the money.

THE FARMERS' FRIEND

TACTICS OF THE FINANCIERS

By HENRY J. GIBBS

SINCE the war British farmers dependent solely upon the meat trade have been practically ruined by Argentine meat. The home market, which always consumed the vast bulk of their produce, was swamped with chilled meat imported from Argentine to such an extent that a report upon meat marketing, issued by the Ministry of Fisheries and Agriculture, was forced to admit that these imports had nearly killed the home industry. Dwindling markets resulted in decreased output and increased prices and unemployment. The average wage of a farm labourer to-day is 30s.

Whatever tentative proposals the Government put forward to back up the wild promises it made to agriculture during the last two elections have proved utterly useless, as Lord Halifax admitted, at York in January, when he said, "It is true in a sense that in the matter of beef British agriculture has been hampered by the existence of trade agreements with Argentina"

This was further borne out by the news that of 476,777 tons of meat sold in Smithfield last year 35.7 per cent. came from the Argentine.

In view of this, it is interesting to note who profits by selling chilled foreign meat to the agricultural isles of Britain.

The largest concern is the £12,000,000 Union Cold Storage Company, which possesses a monopoly of Argentine meat through its ramifications, extending from ranches, cold storage plants, shipping company, to retail butchers' shops dispensing meat to the British public.

In producing, transporting and storing meat, the company owns or controls:—

The Blue Star Line, Anglo-Argentine Cold Storage Company, Argentine Meat Company, International Export Company, Empire Meat Company, Pure Ice Company, Union Cartage Company, Blackfriars Lighterage and Cartage Company, British and Argentine Meat Company, British Beef Company, Commercial Properties, Ltd.

This vast organisation is backed upon the distributive side by:—

C. Kingston, Ltd.; Donald Cook and Son, Ltd. (Cook's Farm Eggs); Eastman's, Ltd.; G. Wiseman's, Ltd.; J. H. Dewhurst, Ltd.; Lonsdale and Thompson, Ltd.; Proprietors of Fletchers (Meat Importers), Ltd.; R. C. Hammett, Ltd.; W. Weddell, Ltd.

Upon the board sit Lord Vestey, his brother Sir E. H. Vestey, R. and J. M. Sing, and W. G. Bundey.

The long list of investors include such patriotic concerns as the Army and Navy Investment Trust; the Britannic Assurance Company; the Eagle Star and British Dominions Insurance; the Royal London Mutual; the Scottish Insurance Corporation and the Bank of Scotland; the London and Manchester Insurance companies; Foreign, American, and Investments Trust; the Rochdale Equitable Pioneers Society (the first co-operative society in England); the Westminster Bank, and others; while private shareholders include Miss Doris Cadbury, Miss Agnes Rowney, W. M. Wills, and others.

It is interesting to note that all these concerns assisted in the "Buy British" campaign of a few years ago.

AIR MAIL SERVICE

Leaving Air Commerce to the Foreigner

MAJOR TRYON, the P.M.G., stated in the House of Commons that during 1935 a sum of £60,000 was paid to French and German postal administrations for the carriage of British air mail to South America.

The trail across the South Atlantic was originally blazed by a British aeroplane with a British engine in 1922, and yet we have allowed other countries to develop the vast air mail possibilities of the route to South America. We should remember that if we are to gain supremacy on the air commerce routes which we have on the sea we have not **only** to think in terms of Empire communications. Our air routes must be world wide. We shall lose valuable trade if we leave the routes to the great capital cities of the world which lay outside our Empire to foreign concerns to develop.

CONSERVATIVE CURIO

BUT A "LEAGUE OF NATIONS FREETRADER"

THE Rochdale Conservatives have recently held a school for their women supporters, and after reading the speeches one wonders how they dare to call themselves Conservatives. They have as their candidate a young man, brilliant in many ways, just new from the University. He calls himself a Conservative supporter of the National Government, and he is so eager to save the League of Nations that he threw out this suggestion:—

> That we should offer to those who are members of the League freedom of trade within the British Empire.

The real Conservatives are aghast, and it is possible that the candidate, Mr. Gordon Murray, will hear more about this wonderful gesture of his. Mr. Gordon Murray is a true Baldwinite, for he is a Socialist without the courage of his convictions. We shall watch Rochdale and see whether those who have fought for honesty in politics in the past will make their candidate find his real political level. He ought not to be in the Conservative Party.

Cotton-workers' Concert Party

GAY BROADCAST PROMISED FOR MARCH

THE rattle of looms and spinning mules, the smoking mill chimneys and the "depression" will all be forgotten for a brief hour in Lancashire on March 12 when King Cotton—represented by a talented band of millworkers—goes on the air from the North Regional broadcasting station.

Fifteen turns will be heard in the variety programme from Cottonopolis, and to Bolton—the centre of the fine cotton spinning industry—has fallen the honour of providing two-thirds of the talent.

There is a surprising assortment of entertainment among the performers.

The Florence Terracian Band, which is composed of members, or prospective members, of one family, will give selections on their piano-accordions; Mr. Harry Dean, a ring-jobber, will provide light patter. Others in the programme will contribute whistling, banjo, concertina, mouth-organ, and singing acts.

Increase in Durham's Poor Relief

ESTIMATED £82,636 MORE NEXT YEAR

PRELIMINARY estimates published by Durham County Council show that the estimated net cost to the rate for poor relief in the coming financial year is £1,334,694, an increase of £82,636 over the current year.

The weekly bill for ordinary outdoor relief in County Durham has increased from £11,564 in 1931 to £17,479 now, a weekly increase of nearly £6,000 in five years.

The publication of the estimates has again aroused a demand for assistance from the National Exchequer. While the average rate for poor relief throughout the country is about 2s. 7d. in the £, it is between 9s. and 10s. in County Durham.

Leaders of all parties have expressed the view that there can be little hope of industrial revival in the district so long as the local authorities are left to shoulder this financial burden unassisted.

MEN WITHOUT CLOTHES

Suits Shared by Brothers

THERE are men in Britain who have but one suit of clothes. They are rich compared with the thousands who would not be able to appear in public were it not for the good offices of the Personal Service League to provide them with articles of clothing.

Broadcasting an appeal on behalf of the League, Mrs. Marsham told stories of almost incredible hardship.

She told of men who are unable to go out because of having to share a suit with their brothers, and of men who had waited for months, even years, for a job, and then could not start work because they had no clothes.

"ACTION" challenges the mood of defeat which to-day assails the British spirit. It attacks those who accept this mood and represent it as progressive. What they speak is not the language of progress, but the simpering lisp of decay.

New ideas dominate the more alert nations. Unless Britain is receptive to them, she will be crushed out of existence in the financial stampede to exploit cheap labour in Central Europe and the East. A virile British Empire, proclaiming national ideals above the corrupt values of the moneylenders, would stand athwart the sinister path of international finance. That is why demoralising factors are being so assiduously fostered.

We believe in the British race. Our people have the brains and sinew of greatness. Their energy created the Empire, though to-day it is betrayed. They are the world's finest workers, though to-day two millions of them are idle. They shall yet forge a future eclipsing their splendid past.

★ ★ ★

Britain First

FIRST they must find a Government to place their interests before those of the foreign lending-house and the foreign bondholder. Their interests have been abominably neglected.

Recent history is littered with broken promises, scrapped policies, betrayals of every kind—every measure a half-measure, playing with problems of vital urgency. Housing Acts give bonuses to vested interests, but the slums remain. Tariffs for the British farmer's protection enable the foreigner to charge more for less value, but the British farmer continues unprotected.

Poverty amidst plenty is perpetuated so that the wealth of the few may increase.

"Action" urges "Britain First"—first preference for our own products and second for those of Empire. Replacing smash-and-grab economics with corporate planning, we can solve distributive problems and ensure high standards of living for all.

Opposed equally to the Capitalist Internationale and to that of Communism, we are loyal to our King and Country, passionately proud of our people and determined that they shall prevail.

★ ★ ★

Ruthless Surgery

IN this place will appear each week a survey of current events and of tendencies which in the belief of "Action" indicate the rapid disintegration of the British Empire and of the British people. It will not be required of us that we should attempt to find a mellow style or strike a reassuring note. This is no time either for *belles lettres* or for the Utopian policies of the *flaneur.*

Those who dislike bitter reading will find only too many journals anxious to dose them with sweet-tasting palliatives. The only remedy in which we have faith is the surgery which will cut from Britain the cancer of her decay.

WE shall attack not only decay, but those who organise and grow fat on it. We shall attack many of the leading men of the day, not because of what they are (which is negligible), but because of what they do; because of the lead they give to mad-dog activities which end in hatred and war; because of their muddling incompetence which creates economic chaos at home; because of their subservience to vested interests which brings a mighty Empire to defeat; and because of their abuse of public trust to further their own paltry careers. We hope to expedite the day when Britain is restored to her ancient grandeur, once again greatly to live and greatly to achieve.

A CRY FROM LANCASHIRE : ELLIOT DEFINES THE GOVERNMENT'S POLICY

★ ★ ★

Cheating the British Farmer

MR. WALTER ELLIOT has again defined the Government's policy on food imports. After telling Parliament that this country is "more and more becoming the world's surplus market," he went on to say that in order to secure cheap food they had rejected the solution of agricultural tariffs "raised to a point which would enable the grower to produce at his own price."

"We wish to use the world surplus and admit, rather than dam out, the world flow of trade," he said, with unblushing candour.

The excuse about cheap food happens to be sheer humbug, camouflaging the assertion of international financial interests at the expense of the British farmer. Moreover, shutting out cheap foreign imports need not necessitate monopolist prices, as will be proved when Britain possesses a Government strong enough to deal with the profiteering parasites who cheat both producer and consumer.

★ ★ ★

School Exemption

THE Association of Education Committees found little good to say of the exception clause in the Bill to raise the school-leaving age, observing that the Government had ignored the experience and knowledge of expert administrators. That is not surprising, since the experts—free from all considerations of vote-catching—were able to give disinterested advice, which is the last thing to commend itself to politicians.

Although the clause was rejected by a huge majority, support for it was forthcoming from the Mayor of Mossley on the amazing ground that there has always been a demand for juveniles in the cotton industry.

Instead of suporting the Bill, it would have done the Mayor more credit if he had swept Lancashire in a crusade against a *laissez-faire* capitalism, which thus starves the adult while exploiting the young.

The Bill is a typical democratic measure, calculated to offend none; certain to injure all.

Downwards, Ever Downwards !

DURING 1935 Britain increased her imports from Egypt by 3 per cent. and sold that country 3 per cent. less goods. We now take from Egypt 34 per cent. of her total exports, and yet provide her with only 21.5 per cent. of her total imports.

Japan, on the other hand, has decreased her imports from Egypt to 5 per cent of the latter's trade and increased her exports to 13.8 per cent.

Thus are years of British help in the development of Egypt receiving their scurvy reward! And the British Government is now preparing for still further adventures in its policy of "scuttle," to mock the courage and enterprise of the past.

Equipping the Economic Foe

MR. W. E. CLUCAS, presiding at the annual meeting of the Manchester Chamber of Commerce, pointed out that many of the important markets from which Japan is driving our goods are either countries within the British Empire or countries which have every reason to place a high value on their commercial relations with Britain.

"In these circumstances," he said, "we are entitled to look to our own Government to pursue with even greater energy and despatch than in the past, the policy of securing fairer conditions for our trade as compared with that of Japan."

The words "even greater" are grimly amusing when one contemplates the desolated area of Lancashire.

Mr. Clucas will "look to the Government" in vain until such time as the British people refuse any longer to tolerate the tyranny of the dictatorship of High Finance, which uses the politicians as puppets to dawdle and temporise, while money and machines are sent overseas posthaste still further to equip the coolie labourers in their economic war against Lancashire.

★ ★ ★

The Eden Manner

THE "News Chronicle," with a due sense of appreciation, records an interesting story of Eden in Russia.

Stalin questioned him about the salaries of British Cabinet Ministers, and, when he was told, remarked that he thought the money was wasted—for which view, incidentally, there is a good deal to be said.

By way of illustration Stalin indicated Comrade Kalinin, who was present. "He is our President, and he doesn't get more than £36 a month."

Mr. Eden took a look at M. Kalinin. "Really!" he replied, "I don't expect he would get much more in England."

If this story is true it is legitimate to ask whether the British Foreign Secretary is naturally polite or whether he merely endeavoured to fit more harmoniously into the Muscovite landscape by appearing to be.

ADDING INSULT TO INJURY

WAR OR PEACE?

The Line-Up In Europe

By OSWALD MOSLEY

LITHUANIA
EAST PRUSSIA
BERLIN
GERMANY
POLAND
FRANCE
CZECHO-SLOVAKIA
RUSSIA
AUSTRIA
HUNGARY
RUMANIA

THE ENCIRCLEMENT OF GERMANY

France has thrown Europe into a state of turmoil by lining up with the Soviet. Her policy is the revival of the Balance of Power, a policy that has always led to war.

Czecho-Slovakia has concluded a pact with the Soviet which will give the Russians the use of air-bases within bombing distance of Berlin.

WAR does not come suddenly and without reason. The causes of war operate over a long period before war actually occurs. These causes are invariably unnoticed by the general public until the last moment.

When the public awake it is usually too late. This danger of public apathy to the causes of war was never greater than at the present time. Decisions are now being taken by the Government, and policies are being adopted of the gravest character. If unchallenged, they may irrevocably determine the destinies of Europe and of the British Empire in a new and greater world catastrophe. Let us, therefore, briefly review the trends of present policy.

The central fact is the conclusion of a virtual alliance between Britain, France, and Soviet Russia. The object of that alliance is the encirclement of the Fascist countries of Germany and Italy. In the case of France and Russia, the alliance is now open and avowed in the Franco-Soviet Pact.

Feting Mr. Litvinoff

IN the case of Britain, the open aspects of the matter have proceeded no further than the recent feting of Mr. Litvinoff by the Government of this country; the close association between Mr. Litvinoff and Mr. Eden during the latter's recent visit to Moscow; the collaboration of Mr. Eden and Mr. Litvinoff against Italy at Geneva; and the protracted stay of the Soviet War Minister in this country after the King's funeral.

Further, the co-operation of the British and French Governments in the face of Germany is ever closer, and without the signature of any formal pact, makes Britain, in practice, a third party to the Franco-Soviet alliance. In addition, the satellites of France in Europe have entered into ever-closer military association with the Soviet. Czechoslovakia concluded a pact with the Soviet last June, under which Soviet air bases can be erected in the former country with the only conceivable object of bombing Berlin.

Such is the Line-Up

SUCH is the line-up between the Soviet and the remaining Democratic countries. On the other side, Germany and Poland grow closer together under the threat of Soviet aggression. Italy, isolated and assailed by League sanctions, draws within the same orbit. Japan, equally denied any outlet for her national aspirations in territory remote from the British Empire in the Far East, also joins the ranks of nations repressed and circumscribed.

In fact, the last six months of British policy has recreated in Europe, in a yet more dangerous form, the system of the Balance of Power which brought the world to catastrophe in 1914 and which the League of Nations was designed for ever to abolish.

Stripped of Defence

THIS ineptitude has been perpetrated at a time when the policy of successive democratic Governments has stripped Britain of effective defence, and she enters the resultant armament race a slow starter and heavily handicapped.

If disaster to Britain and the world was malevolently planned it would be difficult to create a more dangerous situation than this achievement of sheer bungling inspired by panic. For the foreign policy of the present Government, and even more, the policy of the Socialists, is dominated by fear and hatred alone.

These politicians fear and hate a new world creed which threatens their system and their careers with destruction. It sweeps Europe with the force of a religious revival. At home in British form and character of British growth and inspiration it assails their corrupt citadel.

Abroad, in all nations, the new world conquers the old and the politicians pass with the passing of the old world. So Fascism at

M. Titulescu, Prime Minister of Roumania. His Government has just placed an order with France for armaments to the approximate value of £10,000,000.

home and abroad must be fought by every means, fair or foul, that they possess. We care not for the attacks they make on Fascism in Britain; from every attack we come back the stronger. But we are concerned with their use of the might of British Empire and their gambling with the life of the British Empire in pursuit of their vendetta abroad.

Whom Do They Serve?

IT will be said by many that I overstate the case, and that these men whom I denounce do not serve their own fears and their own vendetta but rather serve the interests of Britain. In answer to that view let us inquire what British interests they serve.

Do they serve British interests by losing the century-old friendship of Italy because she enters a territory where no British interests are affected in precisely the manner by which we founded the British Empire? Is it really a British interest to save Abyssinia whose armed bands, according to the Governor of Kenya Colony, had for years crossed the frontiers of British territory and carried our subjects into slavery? Was the League of Nations really founded as a bulwark to protect slavery and barbarism or is all this cant about the League merely an excuse for intervention against a Fascist country? What British interest is served by joining the Soviet against Germany? Germany, stripped of natural outlet and encompassed by Soviet aggression, may be driven in the end to expand or explode. None will deny that in British and European interests it is better that she go East than that she should go West.

It is better that she should expand at the expense of the Soviet than that she should turn again toward Alsace-Lorraine. What British interest does the Government serve by protecting the frontiers of the Soviet so much more strenuously than they have ever defended the frontiers of Britain? The same Government that surrendered India in 1935 is exerting itself to defend the Soviet in 1936.

An Outlet For Japan

WHAT British interest is served by joining the Soviet against Japan? That country too must expand or explode. In Northern China, north of the Yang-tse, no material British interest is affected. In that bandit-ridden territory Japan can find an outlet for her goods and population in the founding of an empire comparable to our work in India.

By accepting that fact we could exclude Japanese goods from India and the Crown Colonies and would relieve Japanese pressure on the Pacific, which threatens Australia and New Zealand. No British interests are affected by the entry of Japan into Northern China, but the interests and political influence of the Soviet are affected. So Lancashire and Yorkshire may not be saved by the removal of their most dangerous competitor and Australia and New Zealand may not be relieved from a growing menace.

A Political Vendetta

WHEN we review the circumstances of the Soviet alliance we cannot escape the conclusion that the Government policy is animated not by British interest, but by a political vendetta. They are prepared even to use the Soviet against Fascism and National Socialism. Because they use the Soviet they depend on the Soviet and are drawn into its support even in the remotest Oriental adventures. Every true British interest demands a policy exactly the opposite.

Italy and Japan should be free to expand where no British or Empire interest is adversely affected. Germany should be welcomed as a friend in the great bulwark of European civilisation against the disruptive Soviet barbarism. Then, at last, collective security will become a reality on the sure basis of a collective spirit.

Then, at last, a League of National States, united in universal Fascism, will secure and build the world civilisation of the future. For the international League of Nations, like the Holy Alliance before it, has succeeded in perverting to exactly the opposite conclusion the purpose for which it was founded.

Our generation was sacrificed to bring to an end the Balance of Power which divided European civilisation into two armed and hostile camps. The avowed purpose of the League of Nations was to consecrate that sacrifice in a new world system. But from this League mockery of prelates and politicians emerges the old system in a yet more hideous and fatal form. Again our generation is challenged to save the ideal of which the old men cheat us once again. Shall Europe be divided or united? Shall it be War or Peace? It is not yet too late, but the nation must be roused. Forward in Fascism while time remains.

Speaking Personally

By E. D. Randall

IN our day, probably more than in any other, the immediate future is perplexed and obscure. It is our fate to have been born into one of history's most dynamic, most restless and changeful periods, when all old certainties are challenged and old systems of values melted into the seething universal flux.

★

Which?

THIS age is at once marvellous and terrible. It may be that we are destined to see the long-awaited dawn of the Age of Leisure—a golden time when poverty, slavery, disease, and misery, all brutal evils which have troubled man from the beginning of his communal relationship, fade from the world like a bad dream that is ended. . . . Or it may be that we are fated to be blown to pieces in some hideous new war, tortured and maimed and maddened with fearful scientific things, products of some white-walled shining-clean laboratory, or beautiful symmetrical fat or gaunt things piled in lofty halls, like empty cathedrals, dim and silent.

★

"The Country of the Blind"

MR. H. G. WELLS, who has a pleasantly romantic turn of mind (by whose agency, in earlier days, he entertained the public with Kipps and Mr. Lewisham), encouraged by the success attending upon one or two frankly fantastic tales of the future, desired to win larger honours by assuming the impressive rôle of "Historian of the Ages to Come."

Mr. Wells made no secret of the fact that he has always entertained a dogged ambition to be regarded as a high-class intellectual —like Aldous Huxley, perhaps, or Wyndham Lewis—only more so. For while they content themselves with being loftily and entertainingly satirical of the world we live in, he decided to apply his richest inventive faculties to writing a detailed history of the world to come.

But a great many admirers of the fiction of his earlier career have reason to deplore the older and wealthier and portentously prophetic Wells.

It is the tragedy of a man who has too frequently mistaken his imagination for his intelligence.

★

"Advanced" Archaism

I FOUND it amusing the other night to analyse the audience which the loud ballyhoo for "The Dog Beneath The Skin" had attracted to the Westminster Theatre. Reports that the play was very "advanced" intellectualist satire of a strong Left-Wing flavour had naturally brought troops of smirking dishevelled "progressives" out of Bloomsbury, and rumours that it was a biting parody of Hitlerism had inevitably filled the more expensive seats with the type of Jew whom the non-Jew finds most physically repugnant.

Actually, however, the play is positively archaic in form. The accompanying chorus who interpret the theme of the play speak in blank verse or glittering satiric couplets reminiscent of the eighteenth century, while the poetic comment of the speech-chorus, the symbolic gestures and dances against the most rudimentary scenery, might have derived inspiration from the Attic theatre of Greek days.

★

. . . And Very Funny

THERE can be no doubt that the text of the play is brilliant, and contains some magnificent verse. As jocular superficial satire on the society of our day the whole production is clever and very funny.

Its propaganda message is pleasantly obscure. At the very end of the play there is a dramatic exhortation by the Dog (having discarded the skin), which seems to deprecate individualism.

"As individuals you are all pretty lousy," seems to be his opinion; "it is only as organic elements of a living society that you are worth while."

And these remarks are addressed as much to the audience as to the players, who represent characteristic types of British Democratic society. (At one point the Chorus gently questions the audience: "Can you honestly say that a small voice in your heart has never whispered, 'I am the nicest person in this room?'")

★

The Lunatic Democrats

THE one scene which could possibly be regarded as deliberately anti-Fascist (it represents a coterie of raving lunatics dressed in black or brown shirts and waving small flags, who screech and gibber like a cage of excited monkeys) is so completely distraught and hysterical that I find it hard to believe it is intelligently intended as a parody of Fascism itself, but rather a parody of the startled Social-Democratic nightmare notion of Fascism.

★

Officialdom versus the Artist

MR. HAROLD SPEED, the artist, in a recent interview with the "Evening Standard," reveals the details of the gross and stupid mismanagement by London officialdom of Gilbert's design for Eros, who is made to perch at a very uncomfortable and dangerous angle, with one foot on a wriggling fish, in the middle of Piccadilly. The statue acts as the central pivot on which the whole of London solemnly swings, like an immense and ugly top.

Had the artist's original delightful conception been followed (the young love-god, cast in glittering aluminium, delicately poised amid cascades of clear water, leaping and rippling into a series of wide, graceful bowls), the fountain would have been a thing of grace and beauty in the heart of London, instead of the grotesque and grimy monument it is to-day. The unfeeling disfiguration of his design broke Gilbert's heart, and remains a disgraceful indictment of the uncouth Philistinism of London officialdom.

Victim of the "Uncouth" Philistine.

★

Hidden Rodin Masterpiece

FAR too many other instances could be cited of this depraved lack of taste and discrimination in the authorities responsible for the adornment of our public places—the boorish desecration of precious works of art, the callous relegation of fine statues and pictures to dark and grimy corners, hidden from the light and the public eye.

As a single instance, Rodin's magnificent group, "The Burghers of Calais"—a possession of which London should be proud, one of the major achievements of his incomparable genius—is hidden away in a corner of some gardens by the Houses of Parliament, stuck on the top of a massive and monstrous plinth. The group is thrust up almost against the elaborate Gothic imagery and stone filigree of the Victoria Tower, a background quite unsuited to the Impressionist style of Rodin's group, and in any case the figures lose their outline entirely against the grey stone wall of intricate carvings behind. I suppose very few Londoners indeed would know where to find this masterpiece, although it is one of the most famous in Europe.

★

Dictatorship of Mediocrity

I HOPE that one of the first actions of a yet to be created Ministry of Culture (whose responsibility it will be to protect the artist from the democratic *dictatorship of mediocrity*, and the public from the despotism of powerful little men with commercial souls) will be to take down this wonderful sculptured group from its present gross and dizzy Governmental plinth, and put it in some more suitable position where the sunlight can get at it and people can see it without craning their necks and blinking their eyes.

TORPEDOED IN PEACE TIME

THE following experience, which must have been almost unique and might have been more unpleasant, took place about 1896 or 1897 when, a midshipman in a battleship of the Mediterranean Fleet, I was in charge of the steam pinnace with a crew of four men.

The scene was the coast of Greece on a bitterly cold morning, and our duty was the towing of a target for torpedo practice. It should be explained that for this purpose, instead of the "war" head with the explosive charge, torpedoes are fitted with a "dummy" head—otherwise this story would not have been written.

One or two runs had been made and torpedoes fired at the target, which, of course, was towed some distance astern, when one of the men remarked that it looked as if the next was coming rather close. As most people now know, the course of a "tin fish" is shown by the air bubbles appearing on the surface. The accuracy of his observation was soon apparent. In fact, it was quickly realised that *we* were going to be hit, and not the target.

"Stand By to Swim"

THE men, I should mention, were very keen on having a new type of steamboat, which had been supplied to some ships, and the next remark was to the effect that their wish was about to materialise! However, there was no time to lose, and I gave the order "Off coats and boots, and stand by to swim," at the same time hastily removing my heavy overcoat, sea-boots, etc.; the stoker, meanwhile, raking out the fire, as a boiler explosion appeared possible.

All this was a matter of minutes, and then we got it clean amidships, luckily without anybody being hit, and the boat began to fill.

Things Began to Hum

ON board the ship, as soon as it was seen what was going to happen, things began to hum. A cutter was quickly manned and pulled towards us like mad, towing a grass line, which was paid out from the ship.

The torpedo officer, a rather corpulent and good-humoured man, who had by some error pressed the wrong firing key in the conning tower, was, I was told afterwards, hoping for the best and whistling to keep his spirits up, as it looked, of course, as if we were in for serious injury, or a watery grave.

However, just as our boat was sinking under us the cutter arrived, the grass line was hastily made fast in the bows, and down she went, while we clambered into the cutter.

Our safe return to the ship was greeted with a certain amount of hilarity, but the face of the torpedo officer was an interesting study of anxiety mixed with relief.

Orders were at once given for salving the pinnace. Divers were sent down, the work being carried on throughout the night and, to the blasting of the hopes of the men for one of the new type boats, our sunken craft was raised to the surface, hoisted on board, repaired, and within a fortnight was running again.

Happened to King George

SINCE the above was written our great and well-beloved King George the Fifth has passed away, and, on looking at an account in "The Times" of January 21, of his early life in the Navy, it is seen that my experience was an almost exact recurrence of what happened to His late Majesty when a midshipman in H.M.S. Bacchante, of which the following is a description, taken from the journal of Canon Dalton, tutor to the Princes:—

"June 4, 1881.—Albany.—Exercised running Whitehead torpedoes at a spar, which was towed astern of the whaler with George in charge. The second torpedo that was fired, when it hit the water, deflected 3 deg. to 5 deg. to the left, and ran along the surface and, striking the whaler, ran clean through the port side of the boat, and remained there as a plug fast wedged in the air-cases which it had penetrated. The boat at once filled but, being a lifeboat, kept afloat, and was towed alongside with the torpedo still sticking in it, by Captain Durrant in his galley. The torpedo was then extracted and the boat hoisted up. It was a lucky thing that nobody's legs were broken."

J. H. A.

PUZZLING THE POST OFFICE

Decoding Freak Addresses Is Not Even A One Man Job

PRACTICAL jokers frequently amuse themselves by inventing freak addresses with which to puzzle the Post Office.

Hundreds of envelopes, addressed in shorthand, Russian characters, reversed handwriting, and even picture puzzles, are sent through the post, and in practically every case are delivered to their correct destinations with a minimum of delay. And it does not even require a special department to handle "freak" envelope addressers

"Most sorters are accustomed to this sort of thing," a G.P.O. official told an "Action" correspondent, "and are able to decode the addresses with little difficulty.

"If the signs employed are too obscure, and the addresses cannot be decoded locally, then the letters are forwarded at once to the Returned Letter Section—more commonly called the 'dead letter office.' Here the envelopes are very carefully scrutinised, and in most cases the puzzles set us by the public are solved.

"Generally speaking, the local sorters work so efficiently that the Returned Letter Section does not receive sufficient puzzles to keep one man employed in solving them all day long."

To test the sorters, our correspondent enclosed the manuscript of this article in an envelope addressed with a picture-puzzle. The letters "Acti" were written above the word "Sanctuary," and followed by a crude sketch of a house and a church. This was intended to read: "Acti **on,** Sanctuary Buildings." The word "Smith," written in large letters, followed by "St.," implied "**Great** Smith Street." The postal district was indicated by the weathervane on top of the church.

And the Post Office sorters promptly solved the puzzle and delivered the goods.

A WOMAN'S OUTLOOK

One of the modern house models designed by a woman architect on view at the Women Architects Exhibition at the Building Centre.

WHAT DO YOU THINK?

Give Us Sunshine Homes

IN these columns, week by week, I shall comment upon current topics, both political and social. My views may not be yours, but they are subjects which most of us have thought about, and upon which each of us must sooner or later form an opinion. In another part of this page we shall deal with matters relating to the home, in which we do not lose sight of the relationship between our homes and the larger landscape of the State.

Will you write and tell me what *you* think, and suggest topics for discussion in our columns. Letters of general interest will be published. You may wish to write about housing, or the city of the future, factory conditions, or it may be diet; perhaps the method by which you organise your daily life may be of interest to others.

If you are a business woman, how do you arrange your housekeeping? Perhaps you are interested in your child's upbringing, not only from the point of view of the individual, but also remembering that he or she must take a place as a citizen in the future.

On these or any subject which occurs to you I shall welcome your ideas, and only through your co-operation as readers shall we be able to talk of the matters which really concern us.

★ ★ ★

"Shadow or Sunshine"

FIRST let me talk about the shadow. I will mention one of many similar cases, which is that of a family whose home is condemned. They must immediately leave it and seek for other premises. For a year before this, however, they have lived with only three sides of their back bedroom standing, with only a curtain of sacks to protect them from wind and rain.

Foreign visitors to our country laugh at us when we say we live at a high standard; frequently they consider it is a very low one! In fact, one woman visitor, recently, who came from a country where they have abolished their slums, gave it as her opinion that in our country the problem was insoluble, as we are starting too late.

★ ★ ★

Better Late Than Never

MY answer to that is—better late than never. Admittedly the problem is a huge one, but it can be solved. Too much of our building at present is unregulated and of a type which will produce more slums in the future. Wide powers under a national scheme are vital if slum clearance is to be carried through. Actually, to clear slums is not the costly business generally supposed if one takes a long view. For example, a State guaranteed loan to be invested in well-designed houses and flats

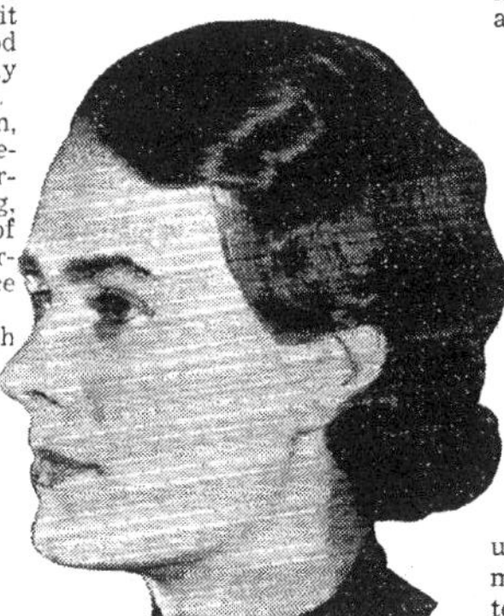

ANNE BROCK-GRIGGS, who Edits our Women's Page

might even be repaid in forty years, and at the same time admit of low rents.

★ ★ ★

The Growing House

EXPERT planning and good design will ensure that every flat or house has its share of sunshine, that they are easily run and pleasant to the eye. An interesting development lately is the "growing house," which is built up by a unit system. That is to say, it begins very small—just for two! Then as the family grows nurseries, sun balconies, and bedrooms can be added, **provided the income grows also.**

By the way, women might do well to impress on their architect friends that when they design family flats for towns to remember the unfortunate mother and to provide her flat with a wrought-iron balcony where the baby may have its airing. Too many flats are built nowadays without these useful appendages.

Therefore, give us sunshine homes for our people. We can't afford the slums.

★ ★ ★

"Britain Builds Bonny Babies"

WHEN food is short in the family budget not only is it usually the mother who has to rack her brains in an endeavour to make her slender purse cater for the needs of a growing family, but also she is the one who usually goes without in order that her children may have enough.

We have a Government which considers that an adult can live upon 4s. 10½d. per week as a minimum diet. They are thus willing to destroy the real wealth of the nation in a penny-wise-pound-foolish economy. The appalling misery among the unemployed in the depressed areas has been pointed out by many doctors. The mothers are anaemic, their children under-nourished. It has been shown that to give them an adequate diet (particularly for expectant mothers) would cost 5s. a week in addition to their meagre normal diet.

★ ★ ★

Storing Up Ill-Health

IT is obvious that neither the unemployment relief nor the starvation wages which prevail in many trades are enough to provide a nourishing diet. While millions are existing on the poverty line or below it, we are laying up a store of ill-health for the future which will be too heavy a bill for us to pay. We must raise the standard of living for the people so that their wages are high enough to absorb the products of industry, of which the science of the twentieth century can provide an abundance.

★ ★ ★

Two Sides of the Picture

We began with oysters on side dishes, then turtle soup, for which two turtles were killed, accompanied by old milk punch. The baron of beef, cooked forty-eight hours previously, and boar's head were then served after being piped in by two of Mr. Dolmetsch's players.

Norfolk turkeys, ice pudding, maids of honour, and a savoury completed the menu. Champagne, port, and old brandy were served at the appropriate stages.—(From the "Sunday Times.")

Robert A. Burgess was found dead in a gas-filled room. It was revealed at the inquest that he had been unemployed for nearly four years. The doctor stated that the body was emaciated as a result of prolonged under-nourishment.—(News item.)

A STORY TOLD BY A WAITRESS

AN orchestra—a very weary crew, with the exception of a perspiring conductor—thumped out a so-called "hot number" amid the glaring decorative banalities of one of the popular London cafés. The music came to a sudden end, and they mopped their brows, covered their instruments, and walked off the dais.

The National Anthem was not played. I controlled myself with an effort.

The waitress who presented me with a cheque seemed a quiet, pleasant-looking girl, but very tired, which was understandable, for it was after midnight. When I said how hard the girls worked she was very glad to talk.

"We work nine hours a day, sometimes on very late shifts, as this place is always open," I was told, "but during very busy periods, and once a week, generally on a Sunday, twelve hours, from noon until midnight."

12s. 6d. a Week

Casually, I remarked that I supposed the wages compensated for the hours. Then I received a shock. She told me that the wages were 12s. 6d. per week, less insurance.

Gratuities? Oh, yes; these were permitted, but the average person who patronises these places can ill-afford to tip lavishly or at all.

"Of course," she finished, "it's better than nothing."

Thousands Similar

The case I have quoted is typical and not singular. There are thousands of women in a similar position.

A Government of authority and action is needed—a Government which can offer to the women of this country a promise and a hope that the sweating of their sex in the hands of Jewish commercialism will be prevented by the strictest authority of the State.

With such a hope the women of Britain will fight until this menace shall be crushed, as it, with every foul means its gold can obtain, has tried to crush the Britain they hold as sacred. They will fight until the day when every English man and woman can sing once more: "Britons never shall be slaves," and know that they sing the truth.

DINAH PARKINSON.

WHAT OTHER WOMEN ARE DOING

Beautiful Work at Women Architects' Exhibition

By Rosalind Raby

Women architects do not confine their talents to the designing of houses and flats. Drawings, models, and photographs of offices, laundries, a nursery school, and even a private zoo are among the exhibits at the Building Centre, New Bond-street, where the work of women architects is on view.

The excellent combination of utility and beauty seen in the reconstruction work done on old houses leads one to speculate that the special sphere of influence of the feminine artist will be that of interior planning. Such work involves much intricate detail, a fact which will be appreciated by anyone who has lived and worked in a badly built or badly converted house or flat.

The best-known woman architect represented is Miss Elizabeth Scott, A.R.I.B.A., who, it will be remembered, won the competition open to men and women architects in England and America with her design for the Shakespeare Memorial Theatre.

I was particularly interested in the work of Miss Reavell, A.R.I.B.A., who was responsible for the designs used for a village settlement in Northumberland. This includes a number of houses on small holdings and also village shops, school, hall, etc. The work of Miss Gillian Harrison, F.R.I.B.A., free from any of those deplorable pseudo-Gothic or pseudo-Tudor tendencies, showed purity of line and real beauty.

The number of registered women architects in this country is given as only 130, and it is to be hoped that women architects will, in increasing numbers, take their place in designing the school, the factory, and the home of the future.

Eve at the Fair

AT its coming of age this year, the British Industries Fair is pre-eminently a woman's fair.

The exhibitors, it is true, are mostly men, but the exhibits, at the White City and Olympia at least, are mainly calculated to attract the woman buyer, an added proof of the immense purchasing power woman wields today.

The most interesting, as well as the largest, exhibit is the textiles section at the White City. It is a definite challenge to our competitors, and a proof that, for beauty of design, quality of material, and skill in workmanship, Britain is still supreme.

The "Judy" fabrics specially attracted me. I was told that "Judy" had grown up, that mother as well as daughter could now wear a frock in these dainty fabrics. And here was the cotton queen of Manchester to show how charming they could look!

★ ★ ★

FURNISHING FABRICS

FOR skill in workmanship the prize must go to the furnishing fabrics, many of them reproductions of old embroideries, paintings, hand-weaves, etc., executed in fast colours, vying with the beauty of the original. Two of the most attractive exhibits were those of the "Old Bleach" Irish linens, and the many designs, both old fashioned and modern, of the "Eton Rural Fabrics."

The furnishing section, second largest at the Fair, was less interesting. There was too much of the meretricious type of furniture we are accustomed to see in the advertisements of the hire-purchase firms, and too little that, to borrow an Americanism, is content to "be itself."

Let us hope that the generation which considers no piece of furniture complete without an entirely gratuitous specimen of machine moulding, and that a touch of gilt or a highly polished veneer can conceal the fact that the piece is in itself merely shoddy, will soon give place to a generation which will put its faith in beauty of line and skill in craftsmanship.

At present our skilled cabinet makers are on the dole or have turned to other crafts.

We have certain advantages, however, over the past. Beds continue to improve, and the comfortable divan type seems to have come to stay. Chromium furniture was conspicuous by its absence, but there were many attractive examples of basket furniture.

★ ★ ★

THE CINDERELLA OF THE FAIR

ON another stall is the Cinderella of the Fair, a section called the North-East Development Board, which has as its object the introduction of new light industries into the North-East. A list of those already started includes such diverse requirements as fishing flies and cough mixture (or can we trace a natural sequence).

The Commissioner for the Special Areas reported last week on the failure of new enterprises to develop this area. It is to be hoped that this section will produce results for the men and women of Tyneside.

I made a vow with myself as I left the Fair to buy British—because it's best!

A. R. R.

By

John Emery

John Emery, Editor of our Industrial Feature, in this brilliant article tells his readers of a new hybrid group.

IN making my bow to readers of "Action," I think it only fair to warn you in advance what to expect. My job week by week will be to record the activities of the great trade union leaders in their strenuous efforts to raise the standards of life for their members.

Frequently, I know, there will be no efforts to record, in which case the "Emery" at the top of the page will be used to rub some of the rust from the creaking machine. It will be a fair summary of the work, however, neither hesitating to give praise for honest service nor sharp criticism when the service fails.

I hope the notes will be neither dull nor pedantic. I have, I am told, a sense of humour, but this humour, I know, takes perverse turns, and sometimes I laugh loudest just at the time when Labour leaders feel I should be taking them seriously. If that ever happens, I hope you will never think I have become cynical. For, take it from me, I am not cynical. The only thing that makes life worth while for me in its richer and deeper aspects is the passionate belief that some day in my lifetime a man, or group of men, will sweep poverty from Britain, and with it all the shams and humbugs which befoul English public life.

Having introduced myself, I wish to record a piece of news which, whilst it may not be thrilling, is news, and may be amusing.

* * *

"They Be All There"

BEFORE these notes see the light of day another great political and industrial organisation may be launched in Britain.

Now, most organisations which play at the game of politics are funny. This will be no exception. It is an organisation composed of bright lads from all the political parties and from the T.U.C. I know most of the men who will be bright shining lights of the new party or group, and all have this in common—they are most frightfully anxious that something should be done to improve Britain, provided they are not asked to do the improving themselves. That, indeed, will be the guiding principle of the new group—they will advise and guide and counsel, but the moment any of its members suggest doing anything—out he will go.

Now in such an organisation you would naturally expect to find Lord Allen of Hurtwood, Sir Arthur Pugh, and Mr. Harold MacMillan, and in *any* sort of organisation you would expect to find Mr. John Bromley. Well, you have guessed right the first time—they are all there. So is Sir Walter Layton.

* * *

A Hybrid Group

NOW I want you to trace with me the ramifications of this hybrid group.

Through Harold MacMillan they become indirectly linked up with Lord Melchett and his Industrial Reorganisation League. Through Sir Arthur Pugh and Mr. Bromley they get linked up indirectly with the T.U.C., and you get a revived Mond-Turner Committee.

Not much advance there, you will say. But wait a minute.

Through Mr. Bromley they get linked up indirectly with the Communist Party, because Mr. Bromley's Executive has announced that they want the Communist Party inside the Labour Party. As the Archbishop of York is also in the group, the Communist Party will probably try to secure affiliation to the Church of England, and so there you beautifully are! The only other point is—is there one single fundamental problem under the sun on which these men are agreed?

* * *

HOW long can Mr. Bevin's top-heavy union last? This is the question now being discussed in inner Labour circles.

It is prompted by the many unofficial strikes amongst the union members which

"Mr. Ernest Brown is a Minister because he has a louder voice than anybody else in Britain."

Mr. Bevin is obviously quite powerless to direct or control. These men pay their union dues regularly; they have grievances which lie unattended for months. (In the Smithfield fiasco the men stated they had waited eight months.) When, in sheer exasperation, the men take action it is an unofficial strike.

Now the advantage of an unofficial strike to the union is that the men receive no strike pay. They fight their battle alone and unaided. Sometimes they secure concessions and, of course, in the annual report of the union these wage gains are trumpeted abroad as being secured as a result of powerful trade union organisation.

* * *

Big Flare Up Soon

NOW this sort of thing cannot go on indefinitely. Men are becoming too intelligent to continue paying into a union that not only refuses to help them in their battles but openly opposes them. There will be a big flare up soon, and Mr. Bevin may be obliged to leave his office to quell the flames instead of having it done by a junior official.

And here lies the cause of the trouble. In a ramshackle union such as this, composed of almost every type of worker willing to pay a subscription, there is no such thing as a properly conducted ballot for the election of officials for each trade. Consequently, the man sent to negotiate settlements frequently knows nothing whatever of the work on which he is sent to talk.

If it is a safe, spectacular thing, Mr. Bevin will go himself. If it looks risky somebody else is sent whom the men have never seen and who cannot even talk the language of the trade.

That is why one or two glib-tongued men in the Smithfield strike got the ear of the public, whilst the little office boy was paid not the slightest attention.

And it will not be forgotten that union men were driving the meat supplies which eventually broke the strike.

* * *

Trifling With Lives

AND now I must passionately protest against this Government trifling with the lives of miners. It is four months since they decided to appoint a Royal Commission to inquire into the terrible toll of death and mutilation that goes on in British mines.

Last year 1,073 were killed and 132,895 were injured.

In face of these appalling figures the Government appoints a Commission, then waits nearly four months for its first meeting; the Commission sits for a few days and then retires for a week. That, of course, is typical of Government speed, except when they decide to increase the salary of Mr. Thomas for curing unemployment. That goes through with a bang.

The only thing that has emerged from the Commission so far is the terrible confession that the Mines Department can only wring its hands and confess its disappointment that there are still so many accidents.

* * *

Accidents Preventable

THIS is not enough. The Mines Department knows perfectly well that most accidents are preventable.

With proper ventilation there never need be accumulations of gas, as gas is lighter than air and would be driven before it.

The whole thing is a sham. This Commission can tell the Government nothing that it doesn't know now. Every fact is known. One would think mining was a new industry. The Gresford pit disaster so shocked the public conscience that it had to do something, and this is what we get.

The Secretary for Mines should be a skilled mining engineer. Instead, look back over the list and you will find the Department has been used as a job for Party hacks.

The first Minister of Mines was a Master of Foxhounds. Mr. Shinwell was a tailor. Mr. Ernest Brown is a Minister because he had a louder voice than anybody in Britain. This trifling with death and mutilation must cease.

* * *

P.S.—If in my notes I get mixed with the titles of Labour leaders I hope they will forgive me.

Labour Man Expelled from Party

EX-ALDERMAN TO APPEAL

(From Our Bolton Correspondent)

A PIQUANT position may arise in connection with the appeal to the executive of the National Labour Party of ex-Alderman Samuel Lomax against his expulsion from the Party, and his deposition from the Aldermanic Bench by the Bolton Labour Party for alleged breaches of Party discipline, and his opposition to an official Labour candidate at a Bolton Council by-election which cost the Labour Party a safe seat.

Ex-Alderman Lomax is confident that his appeal to the National Executive against his expulsion and deposition will succeed, and that feeling is shared by other members of the local Labour Party who were present at an inquiry into ex-Alderman Lomax's case conducted at Bolton by Mr. F. O. Roberts, of the National Executive.

I have good authority for stating that if the National Executive decide against ex-Alderman Lomax's expulsion, their decision may be resisted by the local Labour Party, who may refuse to reinstate ex-Alderman Lomax, writes an "Action" representative.

The Bolton Labour Party would then render themselves liable to disaffiliation for a breach of Party discipline.

We await developments with interest.

LANCASHIRE WAITS ON INDIA

WHAT WILL THE TARIFF BOARD DECIDE?

(From Our Manchester Correspondent)

ON the decision of the Indian Tariff Board depends the prospects for the Lancashire cotton industry. Everybody in Lancashire—raw cotton importers, manufacturers, merchants, shippers, and operatives—are eagerly awaiting the findings of the Tariff Board on the question of the future duties to be placed on Lancashire cotton and rayon goods entering India.

The present tariff is 25 per cent., and the minimum reduction traders are expecting is 5 per cent. Cable advices received from some of the leading merchant houses in Bombay and Calcutta indicate that the reduction might be 7½ per cent., and in one or two well-informed quarters the opinion has been expressed that the rates will be cut by 10 per cent., leaving the duty 15 per cent.

Lancashire's Biggest Market

INDIA is Lancashire's biggest export market, and the welfare of hundreds of firms and thousands of operatives depends upon the cotton trade between the two countries.

Should a reduction in the tariffs take place it can be safely predicted that manufacturers in Blackburn, Burnley, Preston, and other weaving centres who cater for the India market will experience a period of brisk trade. The important factor is that lower duties will enable Lancashire cloths to be sold cheaper and thereby compete more effectively against Japan.

More Indian Cotton Used

LANCASHIRE, during the past two years, has done everything she can to encourage India to treat this country better, and one practicable and very important step has been the big increase in the use of Indian cotton by the spinning mills. The Lancashire Indian Cotton Committee is constantly pushing forward the sale of Indian cotton, and on this account alone Lancashire is entitled to expect reasonable treatment from India.

It is expected that the decision of the Indian Government will be made known before the end of the month.

School Scheme Too Advanced?

SUNDERLAND EDUCATIONAL SYSTEM CHANGE

BIG changes in the local educational system have been decided upon by the new Socialist majority on Sunderland Town Council.

The Council has decided to remit the fees of the Bede Collegiate Secondary School, to increase special place awards from 50 per cent. to 100 per cent., to provide text books free, and to make graded maintenance allowances.

The scheme has been strongly opposed by the Moderate members of the Council, who have pointed out that the proposal to make maintenance grants from the age of eleven is even more advanced than the scheme operated by the Durham County Council.

Scottish Bank Employees Protest at Low Wages

BANKERS in Scotland are again up in arms about the low pay they receive for their work. At the present moment sundry meetings are being held in various centres, but shortly a mass meeting will be held in Edinburgh of members of the Royal Bank of Scotland, the bank which is responsible for the dissatisfaction.

Mr. D. Hood Wilson, secretary of the Scottish Bankers' Association, said that after eight years of service the average wage of members of the Royal Bank of Scotland is £120 a year. Men in some other banks have £160 a year after the same length of service

He further says that after sixteen years of service in the Royal Bank men receive £260 a year, while in another bank for the same service the salary is £360 a year.

VESTED INTERESTS IN ASSURANCE

Does The Public Receive a Fair Deal?

The general public is not aware of the conditions which prevail in the Life Assurance world in this country to-day owing to vested interests and the out-of-date methods still in use by most English and Scottish companies.

The system which was adopted many years ago and is at present generally in use is to pay commission to solicitors and bankers for life assurance business introduced by them to the Life Company, and it can be said with truth that 80 per cent. to 90 per cent. of solicitors and bankers receive commission from Life Assurance companies.

These professional gentlemen favour four or five companies, and it is only natural that the major portion of life business is placed with the company offering the most favourable terms, irrespective of the client's needs.

COMMISSIONS FOR BANKS

The Big-Five Banks give permission to their bank managers to transact life business on behalf of their customers with certain life companies whose directors are often also directors of the bank. In some cases the commission paid by the life company is not the personal profit of the bank manager, but goes into the coffers of the bank, thus enriching capitalistic institutions at the expense of the legitimate representative of a life company.

In many instances, however, the bank manager profits personally by commission he receives through introducing life business to a company.

SOLICITORS AS AGENTS

This scandalous system prevails amongst solicitors also. The client wants a mortgage; a marriage settlement is being arranged; an annuity is required; a hundred and one reasons are made the excuse to arrange life assurance for the client. Granted that life assurance is necessary in a great many cases of solicitors' business, there are too many cases when it is not necessary and only arranged for the benefit of the solicitor's pocket. The solicitor demands his commission. Sometimes he informs the client that he will get commission on the life assurance and that he will forgo his fee in this connection.

Most times, however, the client pays a fee without knowing that the solicitor has also received commission.

Most life companies depend on the introduction of life business by solicitors and bankers and employ "inspectors" on a small salary to call on these professional gentlemen. In competition, commission terms are increased.

The Big-Five Banks have a list of Assurance companies with whom the bank manager is allowed to transact business. Any company preferred to the listed companies has to be dealt with in secret by the bank manager. The commission cheque is so manoeuvred that the bank manager's account with his own bank does not show this transaction with a forbidden company.

This iniquitous "solicitors and bankers scandal" affects two classes of people. (1) the insuring public, and (2) the legitimate Life Assurance agent. The insuring public does not receive fair treatment under this system. He trusts his banker or solicitor and is usually betrayed.

True, all life companies will pay a claim at death or at the maturity date on Endowment polices. But this is simply the Alpha of Life Assurance.

THE AGENT'S LOSS

The agent has no protection. He may have spent weeks dealing with the client; may have spent pounds in travelling expenses; have made numerous calculations and comparisons, and gone to untold trouble for the client—to learn that a solicitor or bank manager has stepped in, arranged the policy for his client, and robbed him barefacedly of his well-earned commission.

All his work has gone for nothing. The client may have been perfectly honest and innocent in the matter and believed that the agent would receive his recognised commission. But a life company does not pay commission twice. And it is practically impossible to nail down a powerful solicitor or bank manager. They will refuse to divulge information and proof that they have interfered in the case is practically impossible to obtain except through the courts, which is too expensive a method to entertain.

The companies do not support the agent as they have got the business in any case.

HEALTH IN ITALIAN EAST AFRICA

Excellent Conditions

Professor Aldo Castellani, Health Commissioner for Italian East Africa, upon returning to Asmara after his third tour of inspection on the Eritrean front, made a statement to the Press on health conditions of the troops and the civilians, both Italian and native.

He said health conditions were excellent and denied reports published in the foreign Press of epidemics of cholera, plague, and other diseases alleged to have broken out among the troops and gave out the following figures on cases of tropical diseases in Eritrea and the occupied territories from July 1 to December 31.

There was not a single case of cholera or plague. There were a few cases of dengue fever at Massawa, this disease being common to all ports on the Red Sea and the Indian Ocean and was rarely fatal. Out of a total of thousands of troops and workers, both Italian and native, there have been thirty-eight cases of typhoid fever and one hundred and forty-two of malaria.

Of small-pox there was none among the whites, but six cases among the natives, none of which proved fatal, and of amoebic dysentry, fifteen cases. Of cerebro-spinal meningitis there was one case among whites and ten cases among natives, none of which caused death. Of tropical fever there were three cases among whites and twenty-four among natives.

Professor Castellani formally denied that sick soldiers and civilians were sent to hospital at Rhodes, or that 20,000 beds had been prepared for them. In fact, he added, not a single patient had been sent to Rhodes, where, in any case, the local hospital could only provide one hundred and twenty beds.

BAD YEAR FOR TRAWLERS

Lowestoft trawlermen experienced one of the worst years of recent times during 1935. It is stated that the total value of their catch over the twelve months showed a decrease of over £100,000 on the figure of 1934.

"An escaped bullock spent a night in the rectory grounds at Balham. 'He has done damage in the garden which it will take a year to put right,' said the Rev. Canon W. C. J. Thompson."—Evening paper.

The damage now long done by certain Bishops running amok in the international garden will take much longer that that to remedy.

A VERITABLE EDEN

Godlessness and Cruelty in Russia

The following appeared in the "Manchester Guardian" for February 10:—

> The Society of Militant Godless has been celebrating its tenth anniversary, and at a congress attended by a thousand delegates, Mr. Emelyan Yaroslavsky, the president of the society, boasted that already half the population of the Soviet Union was atheist.
>
> Yaroslavsky warned the meeting, however, that 40,000 communities still maintained churches and that 34 per cent. of the collective farmers and a larger number of individualist farmers persisted in their religious practices.

And these godless atheists are the people with whom our Mr. Eden dines and sings "God Save the King"!

In the same issue of the "Manchester Guardian" appears a letter describing the horrible suffering endured by political prisoners banished to Siberia.

The writer, who signs himself "For Freedom," says:—

> Prisoners are usually sentenced without trial, and sentences are often renewed by administrative order and without trial or even without rearrest—a departure from pre-revolutionary practice.

Several letters from political prisoners are quoted by the writer, describing the awful privations and cruelties to which those men whose only crime is that they disagree with the policy and methods of Mr. Eden's friends, Stalin and Co.

Banishment to Siberia is their lot. There, conditions are ghastly. Snow dominates their lives for six months of the year. Fuel and food are scarce. Solitary confinement as a punishment is common.

And yet we receive M. Litvinoff over here as the representative of the country which is responsible for these crimes. Mr. Eden fetes him and his representatives are taken for a tour round our armament firms to buy weapons so that Soviet Russia may build up an army and air force to spread its "civilisation" over Western Europe.

BAD AGRICULTURAL SCHEMES

"We will not have agriculture treated as the Cinderella of the industrial fabric," declared Mr. H. Ramsbottom, M.P., Parliamentary Secretary to the Minister of Agriculture and Fisheries, when addressing the Colchester branch of the N.F.U., recently.

Mr. John Garton, chairman of the Essex branch, said that all realised they had got to have a pig scheme, but they were equally confident that such a scheme as they had was no good to anyone. He asked if it was likely that any scheme would be successful when those who would not contract got better money than those who did contract. Agriculture could never be prosperous in this country without Government help and protection, because other countries could produce more cheaply, while many Continental countries were selling their produce at high prices in their own country, and their surplus came here at "any price."

THE SANCTIONS BOOMERANG

Newfoundland Fishers Suffer

Once again sanctions have proved how injurious they can be to British interests. This time, it is the fishing industry of Newfoundland that suffers.

The Newfoundlanders have lost nearly 80 per cent. of their sales of dried cod normally sent to Italy.

Over one-fifth of the average catch of one and a quarter million cwt. was, in pre-sanctionist times, sent to Italian buyers. Now, huge quantities are lying unsold while exporters are faced with the prospect of having to sell at a loss.

The result—a glut in the home market, consequent depression in prices, and, inevitably, a slump in employment figures among the fisherfolk. It seems that sanctions against Italy are hurting everyone except the Italians.

Our Society Girls.

"Society girls are taking their stage careers very seriously. Following Miss Penelope Dudley Ward's example, Lady Caroline Paget has joined the Repertory Company at Oxford, and from all accounts shows great promise.

"Then there is Miss Sarah Churchill, who is in the chorus of C. B. Cochran's new show, 'Follow the Sun.' She is a good-looking girl, with regular features, but isn't as gaily impertinent as the average chorus girl."—From the "Bystander," February 15.

RADIO-HOMING SYSTEM FOR AIR LINERS

Why Britain Lags Behind

In the House of Commons on February 12 Mrs. Tate asked Sir Philip Sassoon whether it is the intention of the Air Ministry to install at Croydon an up-to-date and efficient system of wireless control and a radio beam homing system such as has been in successful operation elsewhere for some time.

Sir Philip replied that the system at Croydon has been continuously modified in order to keep it abreast of the latest developments.

Sir Philip would have done well to add the words "as understood by the Air Ministry," for it is well known that the Croydon wireless system lags a long way behind developments abroad. One would also remind him of that absurd and useless 120 ft. mast erected on the aerodrome a year or so ago, which, although implored to do so on account of its danger to navigators, the Air Ministry failed to remove until a foreign air liner hit it and killed the occupants.

TO BE USED AT HESTON

For a long while now radio beam homing systems have been used with great success at many continental aerodromes, and such a device is now being installed at Heston.

On this subject Sir Philip said that his information was that such a device has not yet passed the experimental stage and that pilots are not willing to trust themselves to it in fog.

Of course the device is not yet out of the experimental stage. Nor are aeroplanes, but still they are used. If the Air Ministry would be more progressive over devices to aid flying we should not lag behind other nations as we do.

OUTPOSTS OF EMPIRE

THE KHYBER PASS

FOR centuries the Khyber Pass has formed the Gateway to India from the distant north, and gives direct communication to Kabul via Jalalabad, and so to the Oxus and Russia-in-Asia.

The Pass, thirty miles long, cuts clean through the tumbled mass of hills which form the North-Western Frontier of India, the age-long home of the Afridis and other wild tribes; brave, treacherous, and utterly undependable, but proud of their desolate country and zealous for the honour of their women. A magnificent race of men, hardy, to endure the most terrible privations which no white man could withstand.

Every man is armed, for in this land of feuds life itself depends on quickness and accuracy. Formerly they had to depend on rifles stolen from the British, but nowadays rifles are made in native factories on the road to Kohat and elsewhere.

Bare and Desolate Country

THE country consists of tumbled masses of hills bare and desolate. On either hand gaunt peaks rise to Heaven as if threatening the rash intruder. In the valleys nestle the villages with their patches of crops.

The Pass is traversed by a camel road, a motor road, and the railway, which extends as far as Landi Khana, within a mile of the frontier. It twists and turns through the hills, climbing the steep gradients, and plunging down the ravines till it lands you, with a triumphant snort, at the terminus.

Such an important gateway is well guarded. There is a fort at Jamrud, just outside the southern entrance, another battalion in well-defended barracks some ten miles within the Pass, several battalions and mountain batteries at Landi Kotal, and, finally, a battalion at Landi Khana. These posts are guarded by surrounding blockhouses.

Camel Caravans

IT is an interesting sight to see the camel caravans swinging through the Pass on their way from Kabul to Peshawar bearing fruit, hides, and carpets from the far-distant Bolshevik countries of the north. They stay the night in the great serai at Landi Kotal and reach Peshawar the following day.

In former days they provided the chief means of livelihood for the tribes, who extorted tribute for their safe conduct. This fact was recognised by the Indian Government, who now pay the tribes an annual subsidy in place of former tribute.

Houses in the Pass are really little forts, each with its watch tower, occupied by armed men at night, who fire without warning on all who are rash enough to approach, for it is considered that no one moves about at night for any good purpose.

Family Vendettas

IT often happens that a man has not dared to go outside his house for many years for fear of being shot by a member of a hostile family. I heard of one case of a feud which was finally settled for good and all by the introduction of a Mills grenade in the family council of the opposing family. There was no more family and no more feud. It is a lawless land, where a man must fend for himself and take his life in his hand when he walks abroad. As Kipling says:—

> The bullet flying down the Pass
> That whistles clear—all flesh is grass.

H. E. CROCKER.

OUR SHORT STORY

By

ARTHUR MARSDEN

THE cohort, shrunk to a mere century, lay where the Long Wall ran down into the sea. The icy gale, whipping the crests of the waves to stinging spray, set the men shivering in their ragged cloaks, buffeting the dank smoke of their cooking-fires to monstrous shapes racing among the dunes. Flavius, the centurion on whom the command had devolved, a tall young man clad in battered half-armour and short tunic, peered out grimly over the waste of tossing waters.

"The wind has gone eastward . . . . They will come soon!"

Claudius Drusus turned on him. For all his drawn, haggard features, by contrast he was almost a dandy; slender, effeminate, his garments gaudy despite their travel-stains.

"Flavius"—his voice trembled with some scarce-suppressed emotion — "Flavius, again I tell you that to stay is madness. . . . You must withdraw while there is time. With my own eyes I have seen the legions leaving. The whole southland is filled with men marching to the coast!" His gaze swept the weary groups of soldiers with contemptuous pity—"How can you, and these, hope to check the Winged Hats alone?"

The centurion's jaw set.

"My duty is to watch the sea-mark. . . . I have received no orders to retire!"

"Orders—Bah!" Claudius sneered impatiently. "Man, I tell you, it is impossible for orders to get through . . . the land behind you is empty of troops. You have been guarding the Wall's end so long, you don't realise what's happening. Britain's like a cheese crawling with maggots—rotten with rebellion and decay. Barbarians are breaking in everywhere. The folk who hate us are rising—dour, swift-stabbing Picts, and the sly, dark little men. . . . And Rome to-day needs her every son to defend her own walls!"

HE paused, drew a deep sobbing breath.

"The things I have seen as I made my way North; horrors unbelievable in this once peaceful land—the perils I have endured! Think, if of nothing else, of my sister Cornelia, whom you love, for whose sake I came. Like all the noble families, we are leaving England. . . . She made me swear I would not return without you. Flavius, in a month we could be in Rome! Our house has power and influence; you would be able to forsake this grim mode of life, and live in luxury and peace. I. . . . I cannot bear fighting, I am not a man of war. . . ."

Flavius looked at him oddly. Then his clear eyes gazed beyond, like those of one who dreamed. He said slowly:—

"The soft south has changed you, Claudius Drusus. I love Cornelia greatly, and I love life. . . . But you, nephew of the Emperor, should understand. I follow the old ways, my family has dwelt in Britain these two hundred years—we are rooted in her soil. Besides"—he pointed to the dim outline of the Standard on the dune above him, scarce to be seen through the driving mist—"the very fact that the Eagle is still planted there, yet holds in check the dark hordes massing to the north. While it remains there are still unravaged homes here in the shadow of the Wall. Such is the power of the very name of Rome, the power that holds the fortunes of this land in trust. That power stands firm!"

"Firm!"—Claudius laughed bitterly—"Firm as that Eagle, trembling in the wind; as those shifting sands, swirling about your feet! Face realities, man—the Empire's finished! Forget these useless, outworn loyalties, or we both die! I won't let your stubborn madness sacrifice our lives. Consent or I'll address your soldiers, I'll tell them the truth, I'll tell ——"

"Stop!"

FLAVIUS'S eyes were blazing, his hand on the hilt of his broad, short sword, as he beat down the other's words. His brain was working rapidly. His men were nearly worn out with fighting and hardship, with the ceaseless vigil against forays. For all that they were mostly British Romans, sturdy provincials of the great, old breed, untainted by the general rot, he knew the almost intolerable strain they were enduring, how thin a wall of faith and discipline held them from panic now. Knew, too, how disastrous the effect would be, if they saw one of the great House of Drusus yammering his fears.

Yet he could not strike Cornelia's brother down . . .

"Dare that," he said more quietly, "and you die! . . . But I'll make a bargain with you!" He smiled grimly—"You say the Empire has become as these shifting sands? Very well, then, I swear by Mithras I will leave, the cohort will withdraw—when that standard falls!"

CLAUDIUS gazed upwards once again. The Eagle shook still more with the buffet of the storm. Sand-particles stung against his face. Some of the fear fled from his eyes, was succeeded by a cynical craftiness. So this was how Flavius would save his pride. . . .

"That will be to-night," he said. "With the wind strengthening from the East, nothing planted in sand can stand. Nothing at all!"

. . . .

Darkness came. Vague rumour had spread among the soldiers, for a few had caught snatches of Claudius's wild words, and watchful eyes peered anxiously through the gloom. Claudius slept fitfully in Flavius's tent, imagining the howl of the Winged Hats in every clamour of the storm, feverishly praying that the standard soon might fall. Yet at dawn the winged symbol still stood, glaring defiance at the sea

FOR Claudius the day was a tense agony of waiting. As the hours dragged by, time and again his eyes sought the wild horizon for the dread sea-rovers; time and again they went to the Eagle swaying on the dunes. The imperturbable calm of Flavius, the disciplined routine of the cohort, his growing sense of his own smallness in the scheme of things, enraged and bewildered him. The men even laughed and jested as if they were in some safe, walled city, the poor, block-headed fools; sang songs that offended his delicate ears. There were no baths, no theatres, no scented slave-girls—only the hungry shore and the drear land stretching out behind.

Bitterly he cursed his action in coming here—not that he had dreamed, when he started, of the awful venture it would be. He thought longingly of the suave, luxurious life of the capital, where he had spent most of his life, for though he and Flavius had been school-fellows, they had gone very different ways; of the sweet, decadent dissipations introduced by the cunning Eastern folk, which he and the other patrician youths had so much enjoyed. They had followed the witty, dilettante philosophers who sneered at Empire and the old virtues. "Leave such crudities," they said, "to the provincials!" It had not been fashionable to learn the arts of war, from the very thought of struggle his soul recoiled. What nonsense to talk of "trust," and Imperial honour . . . what weight had duty against his precious life. If he had dared, he would have fled now by himself, but he knew there was scarce a chance of retracing his way south through the disordered country alone.

As the day dwindled, far to the north and west the gathering Picts moved on the heather-clad hillsides like thin clouds . . . . But they did not cross the Wall. Night came once more, a howling turmoil; yet the watch-fires still flickered on the dunes. . . .

With the first grey light, trumpets shrilled their alarm above the noise of wind and water. Shields flashed dully in the sunrise. . . . The cohort was standing to its arms. With a sick fear Claudius awoke to realisation, and thrust from the tent. Far out, just discernible through the flying spindrift, lean, high-prowed craft were racing for the shore.

The Winged Hats had come!

THE thought pounded terror in his brain. Blundering among the forming ranks, he sought Flavius, clutched at him as he buckled on his armour—"Flavius! Flavius! We must save ourselves now!"

Flavius stared down at him. He seemed remote, taller; his head, like an eagle's, held high and proud.

"Remember you are a Roman! Remember our bargain!" was all he said, and turned to the disposition of his men.

Hopelessly Claudius stared up at the Standard. Still it stood, defying the laws of chance. . . . How swiftly those dread dragon-sails were coming in! Then, as panic destroyed the last vestige of his pride, a new idea came, lending a crazy courage.

Flavius had indeed sworn to flee—*if* the Eagle fell! There was a chance yet to save them all!

With drawn sword he scrambled up the dune. "I am Claudius Drusus, nephew of the Emperor—Make way!" he shouted to the guard who would have barred his path, hacked the man down. Then he was tugging at the bronze staff, striving with frantic strength to uproot the Eagle.

It would not move. The sand was soft and yielding, yet it would not move! Horribly he realised. With a whimper he fell upon his knees, digging desperately at the base with his broad, short blade, till it struck on something hard, snapped short. He was suddenly aware of strange, dreadful war-cries, of Flavius by his side with naked sword.

"It will not fall!" he screamed. "It will not fall!"

FLAVIUS gazed down. His eyes held contempt and anger, a flame of courage and a light unquenchable. Above the turmoil his voice rang stern and strong, a triumphal paean, a proud, prophetic chant

"Nay, Claudius. For you forgot one thing, and while you slept, I saw to it! Beneath the sands that shift with every wind, the heart of Britain is of rock, firm and immovable. That banner stands, based in good stone, held fast by Roman mortar. So stands the Imperial spirit, e'en though the Eagles fall!"

His sword drove home, and Claudius' whine was stilled. Long prows leapt snarling up the shore. The Winged Hats swept inland like a cloud. Proud, disciplined, undaunted, the cohort met the onslaught.

For a little while the air was filled with the noise of fighting men.

TALES OF A SWADDY

MUCH as the average citizen welcomes the modernisation of the British Army, many ex-cavalrymen will regret the passing of their "long-faced pals."

Armoured cars can never replace the old "Esprit de Horse" of the famous Cavalry regiments. Men will recount affectionate tales of "raw" riding-school days, rides through trackless deserts, steaming jungle, rocky hills, hours spent in the saddle on dear old B.8— you know the blighter that used to waggle his near fore when you said "Salaam" —(where is he now?), or "Houdini," the strawberry roan who could get loose from four shackles and two short chains in a minute, or "Mary," the drum horse, not so innocent as she looked, and a thousand others—all to be scrapped. One cannot imagine men of the future ex-army lovingly talking about "dear old BYE.1," the car that could do fifty to the gallon, or such-like inane achievement. We must march with the times, however, but how the devil an armoured car will manage in some places I've been to—why, what about that time when we dragged a nice new armoured car from a marsh during Lucknow manoeuvres—but that's another yarn. What I want to know is—if I am called to serve in the regiment again, am I to saddle a tank or fit an engine to a private charger? 'Cos, verily, I was trained to ride a HORSE.

W. A. C.

SPORT

By OUR STAFF OF EXPERTS

BOXING

RATHER an eventful seven days. The big fog, and last, but not least, Jock McAvoy, the Rochdale middle-weight, gets down to it in preparation for lifting the world cruiser-weight championship from John Henry Lewis, the American negro.

McAvoy has captured the imagination of the fight fans in "God's Own Country," and is confidently expected to beat Lewis, even by the Americans themselves. Jock is a fine two-fisted fighter, and should hold the cruiser-weight crown for a considerable time. Meanwhile, he intends to engage in several contests to help his training along. This is a very good idea, and one which our heavyweights would do well to adopt. Many boxers feel that too much work in the gymnasium is apt to bore them and make them stale, while a contest or two, besides relieving the tedium of ordinary preparation, serves to key them up for the "great occasion."

Petersen Again

AS far as London is concerned, there are no big fights fixed for the next month or so. Petersen is keeping quiet, and as Harvey is just getting over an operation for tonsilitis he is unlikely to make any plans for a few weeks yet. Despite his narrow victory over Harvey, Petersen is still the "top liner" in Great Britain, and two or three promoters are angling for his services. The trouble seems to be the absence of any reasonably attractive opponent, although Neusel and Bob Olin are searching for fights. It will be remembered that during the days of "Pa" Petersen when Olin was the cruiser-champ., he (Olin) turned down a very substantial offer to fight Petersen in London. It is unlikely that the two will meet now, for the good and sufficient reason that Olin, shorn of his championship, is no longer attractive either to Petersen or the Great British Public.

Strange Rulings

TOMMY LOUGHRAN (another distinguished visitor) seems to have been very unfortunate in this country. I was not present at Leicester when Ben Foord won on points, but I am assured by a friend that the referee's decision was a very dubious one. It sems rather peculiar that Loughran's last two fights have ended with somewhat strange rulings. Ronnie James, the Swansea boy (who impressed competent judges very favourably on his last appearance), is due to fight Maurice Holtzer, the French Hebrew, at the Albert Hall, on March 20. I think it is rather unwise to match James with the experienced Holtzer so early in his career, but it may turn out all right. We shall see.

Real Control Wanted

THERE is a distinct feeling in certain circles that all is not well in the world of boxing administration. The fistic art has most certainly ceased to exist as a reasonable sport, and except for the amateurs, it has developed into a rather unhealthy racket. To the layman, it seems utterly incomprehensible that men should fight to fill the pockets of Jewish racketeers. The British Boxing Board of Control seems to control nothing except a wearisome series of eliminating contests to provide challengers for existing champions. It seems incapable of controlling small promoters who scandalously underpay young or unknown fighters. Many a good lad has been ruined both physically and morally by these leeches who spin wonderful stories of success to follow if the lad will only put himself in their hands. The lad usually lands up as a racecourse tout, or in the workhouse. There are too many openings for grafters in the somewhat loose organisation of boxing. 'Nuff said.

ICE HOCKEY

GREAT BRITAIN'S magnificent display on the ice at Garmisch should result in increased attendances at the various ice hockey jamborees throughout the country. It has given a tremendous fillip to the sport which, although new over here, has already achieved an immense following.

The big fly in the ointment is the provision of sufficient players of class to make the game attractive. We can't go on importing players from Canada for the rest of our lives; we must somehow make the sport accessible to all. Moreover, the regulations regarding professionalism must be clarified. As far as one can gather, ice hockey in this country is supposed to be entirely amateur. In the same breath, the information is imparted that the majority of the players with first-class sides are Canadians. Are they so wealthy that they can afford to leave their homes and come over here simply to play hockey? How were they persuaded to leave their clubs on the other side? What inducements were offered, if any?

Clean-up Wanted

ICE hockey, as a sport and a spectacle, has come to stay. It might as well be laid down immediately by the responsible body that the sport must be clean, straightforward, and free from any suspicion. Unless rules are made, and adhered to, it is no earthly use having a Board of Control. As it is, the people who are willing to pay their two bobs to see the game are wondering how the thing is run. The fact that a team (or teams) is owned by one man, or a syndicate for that matter gives rise to a lot of unpleasant suspicions. The fact is that most Englishmen are somewhat antagonistic to sport being turned into a commercial undertaking. When that happens it ceases to be sport and becomes a rather sordid racket in which both players and public are exploited to the advantage of unscrupulous "business men."

No one would quarrel with professional ice hockey. Any sensible person realises that any game at all, which excites public interest and financial support, must be played by the best exponents possible, and that it should not be the prerogative of the wealthy alone, but everyone quarrels with the idea of shamateurism, there is something underhand about it. Perhaps someone will explain what is going to be done about it. It is about time that the whole question was dealt with in the full glare of publicity.

SOCCER

WITH two drawn matches to be replayed before a clear-cut sixth round fixture list can be shown, the task of forecasting the teams to enter the semi-final appears full of pitfalls.

Whichever team wins the West London Derby, and I think Chelsea should come out on top, will have a hard job in the next round against Derby County. The County forward line is one of their strong points, and it should prove a little too good for either Fulham or Chelsea, even though operating away from home.

If Arsenal accounts for Newcastle, they stand a good chance of passing into the semi-final at the expense of Barnsley. In spite of only fair displays being given by the Gunners recently, I cannot see Barnsley setting the roof alight at Highbury.

Sheffield United have the choice of ground against Tottenham, and should prove semi-finalists. The Grimsby v. Middlesbrough match is quite a different proposition, but the manner in which the Fishermen accounted for Manchester City last Saturday can only make me give them the vote.

Rough Play

THE controversy on this subject has been brought to a head by the recent serious incident, and is causing many heart-burns in some strongholds of the game; especially in the manner in which it is drifting from its original idea of recreation and entertainment. The F.A. and the authorities to which the player is subordinate must face up to the position, introduce more drastic measures for control, and insist that the game be played in the spirit it was meant to be.

It is also necessary for some referees to tighten up their disciplinary control. They are generally blamed for a game being allowed to revert into a "dog fight," and in some of the matches I have attended this season a stricter control has certainly been warranted. That referees have a very difficult job to do is admitted, but it is time that the few players who resort to unfair tactics, and who are generally known, should not be treated so leniently as they have been in the past.

Beware of Commercialism

COMMERCIALISATION has developed competition to a very elastic degree, and players are being forced into an outlook no farther than their weekly pay envelopes. Soccer is in danger of becoming more and more a fight for possession, and less and less one of skill and control, where brains count for more than muscle. It is all very well to say that more people pay to-day for the present type of game—such a cry is only true when a better alternative is obtainable.

Generally, the players are a decent and fair-minded crowd of fellows, and would look forward to a little relief from the competition which is forcing the game down. Clubs can easily sort out the players who are known to be unfair and kick them out; and if the F.A. come down with a heavy hand on future offenders a considerable step will have been taken in making the public believe that football is not played solely from the point of view of financial profit.

Spurs Late Staff

MANAGER PERCY SMITH and Captain Tommy Meads are not finding Third Division football with Notts County a bed of roses. Tommy is one of the fittest, fairest, and most wholehearted half-backs who ever kicked a football, and we cricketers with whom he used to play and delight with some fast batsmenship can only wish him the best of luck, and say we hope once again to see him on the White Hart-lane playing-fields out-Jessoping Jessop, or sending up those peculiar spinners of his.

RUGGER

I AM creditably informed that at least two changes are to be made in the English Rugby Union side to meet Scotland. Against Ireland there seems to have been a distinct weakness in the centre, and it will come as no surprise to see two new faces among the three-quarters for the Calcutta Cup match. It is believed that experiments may be made with a view to next year's possibilities. In the Rugby League, Liverpool Stanley continued their winning way with a 17-10 victory over Wigan. It seems rather strange to see what used to be the old Wigan Highfield Club beating the brilliant Wigan combination. The Stanley seem to have settled down well at Edge Hill, Liverpool, after their disastrous "floodlight" experiment at White City. They are receiving excellent support, and are a good tip for the championship this season.

CRICKET

Those Matting Wickets

TALKING of cricket (a few more lumps of coal, please), the matting wickets of New Zealand seem suited to the spin bowling of Sims and Baxter, who have done quite well out there.

Sometimes this type of wicket is not all it should be. I remember, on one occasion in Cologne during a Rhine Army League match, playing against the R.A.S.C. on a mat wicket which had been laid on a fairly loose bed of fine cinder. I had not taken a wicket during the first four overs when a badly pitched ball six inches outside the leg stump bounced immediately behind the batsman's heels and disconcertingly came in and took the middle one. My conscience still pricks me as ball after ball was pitched as near as possible to that same spot, and I came out with an analysis of seven for 23, and received a considerable amount of praise to which I was not entitled. If, by any chance, any of my opponents on that day read this paragraph, I hope they will forgive me.

BILLIARDS

Our Young Veterans

IT is extraordinary how Tom Reece, at sixty-two, appears to be playing as well as ever; and, combined with the performances of Sidney Smith, the final result of the Gold Cup tournament seems to be almost as difficult to forecast as before it began; but I still favour the chances of Joe Davis. Tom Newman is not displaying the confidence and form he showed when winning it last season, and if Inman wins by his obstructionist tactics I can only parody a well-known remark of his to a certain judge after a match with Reece, by saying that "Inman should have been hanged and the cup given to Joe Chambers."

SKATING

Partenkirchen

AS expected, Sonja Henie retained her championship at Garmisch, but Cecilia Colledge, our representative, gave her a very hard fight. The difference in age and experience between the two makes the performance of Miss Colledge a meritorious one, and there appears very little doubt that we possess a future world's champion. Well done, Cecilia!

LAWN TENNIS

IT is good to hear that F. J. Perry's back strain is on the mend. You may remember that in the final of the U.S.A. singles championships against Wilmer Allison, Perry fell on his racket and severely damaged his back. He went on playing, both in the States and later in Australia and never gave it a chance to heal. Eventually he took advice, ceased playing, and underwent treatment, with a successful outcome. He has now resumed play.

His first big test will come in May, when he will play in the British Hard Court Championship at Bournemouth. Here we shall probably see a Perry-Austin final. Although most people believe that Perry is in a class by himself, there is really little to choose between him and Austin. I would not be surprised to see Austin beat him. The latter is steadily gaining in stamina as the years go on, as those who saw his great five-set match in which he beat Allison in the Challenge Round of the Davis Cup know.

With these two players, and with Hughes and Tuckey as our doubles pair, and with such players as Hare and Wilde in reserve, our chances of retaining the Davis Cup are bright. I fancy Germany and not the U.S.A. will be our challengers this year.

Happy Lancashire Weavers

By a Lancashire Correspondent

THE Lancashire weavers live in plain, square stone houses, set monotonously in rows.

They pay from seven shillings a week upwards in rent. This is a lot of money when the total family income is 35s. a week, and there are four, five, or even six mouths to be fed.

I know of one case where 35s. a week has to feed, clothe, and shelter a family of eight. But let us not talk of that. I have never understood how it could be done.

When you enter one of these houses for the first time you are struck by the defiant cleanness of it. Blackleaded fender and oven-door; hearth-rug shaken and brushed; dustless mantelpiece. It is the ineradicable nature of a Lancashire woman to wash, polish, and brush until her house is shining and speckless, and she goes on doing it when there is not enough food in the house and the blackleaded grate is without coal. If ever she stops cleaning then the end has come.

* * *

She works in a mill all day, if she is lucky, and cleans in the evening or in the early morning. She gets up at an incredibly early hour. When she is angry her tongue is sharp and shrill, and you had better look out. When the gentler emotions fill her—gladness, gratitude, relief—she is without words to express herself, and falls silent.

In the old days a woman who went out weaving earned a regular and adequate wage, and with planned and disciplined expenditure (so much set aside for this, so much for that) she got at least twenty shillingsworth of value for every pound she spent. But now she has, somehow, to get about thirty shillingsworth of value out of a pound, and it is hard work.

For example take the case of Annie and Joe, her husband, who are friends of mine. Annie is just over thirty, and she has borne Joe two children. When Joe married Annie soon after the War he was earning enough to keep her—earning it at a mill very like the mill which Annie left on the day before their wedding.

When the second child came in 1929—the year when the slump was hovering over Lancashire, ready to swoop—Annie decided to go back to the mill to "help out." Their first child was then five years old, and was going to school. Annie therefore had to find somebody to "mind the children."

This minding of children while their mothers are at work is a regular and understood solution to an otherwise insoluble problem in Lancashire, where women can earn as much as men can and sometimes more. The minding is done by elderly neighbours, generally those who have "gone past" working at the mill, whose own children are grown up and have left home. The charges for minding vary, of course, with the ages of the children and the prosperity of the times. When Annie first went to work she paid twelve and six a week to the woman who gave her little boy his mid-day dinner between school hours every day except Saturday and Sunday and looked after the baby from seven o'clock in the morning, when Annie deposited her, swapped in thick shawls, until five o'clock in the evening, when she called on her way home from the mill.

Gracie Fields with girls from Lancashire in her film "Sing As We Go."

Both Annie and Joe were then on four looms, and were getting on famously. But soon things got from bad to worse.

Six hard, unbelievably hard years have passed since then. Annie looks older than she is, and paler than she ought to be. Joe has grown silent and grumpy. But they still live in the seven shillings a week house; Annie still at the mill; but now they do not have to pay money for minding the children. Joe does it. He is out of work.

Joe gets his unemployment relief, less what the Means Test takes off because of Annie's wages. And Annie is now on two looms, which means that she works just as long but draws only half of what she used to get.

* * *

She said to me, in an accent I dare not try to reproduce: "What makes me mad is to think that if I was out of work I could probably get a bit more off the dole than I get for working. Only I daren't chuck up my job. Last week a fellow at our mill chucked his job and went on relief, and the manager telephoned the employment exchange and told them. In the end he came back. They've got you both ways, you see."

In the grey hill-street where Annie and Joe live they are regarded as an average lucky family. Annie does not deny that there are any amount of worse cases. "I suppose," she says, with the bitter philosophy of Lancashire. "I suppose we've a lot to be thankful for."

POLITICS AND MUSIC

By Pelham White

THE statement often quoted by leading musicians that they do not mix politics with their art, is rather out of place when the well-known musician, Spike Hughes, writing under the title, "I Am A Misguided Idealist," in the February number of "Rhythm," states: "Why do any of us care what happens to anybody? What has Fascism and Nazism to do with us? Or the wages of miners? Or depressed areas so long as we don't live in them?

"It is just an instinctive preference for freedom, tolerance, fairness, and happiness as the case may be!"

In other words, Spike Hughes's argument sounds remarkably like the "Lullaby of Love" issuing forth from the mouth of a snake. Spike's idea of "happiness" seems to be, as long as I am O.K. why worry about my neighbour. His "concern" for the "depressed areas" exists just as long as he himself does not have to give up his "champagne suppers" and go and live in them . . .

★ ★ ★

He Should Know Better

SPIKE should know better than to jibe at miners' wages. His wages are far in excess of a score of miners together—and earned in the comfortable manner of "striking the ivories," not by striking coal from the mine-face in an atmosphere of sweat and toil. Spike has not yet experienced the "delights" of a miner's life, or the wages they earn—so he should not comment.

Another choice excerpt from the article reads: "My dislike of Nazism is a common human dislike of intolerance and prejudice against other common human beings."

Well! well! . . . Spike in his superb inconsistency should look up the meaning of the word intolerance and learn it.

★ ★ ★

"Tramp, Tramp, The Boys Are Marching"

IT appears to me that this song fits the present plight of British musicians.

A friend of mine, who has just returned from touring the North and Wales, tells me that the belief that British people do not make good musicians is all "apple sauce." While up North he heard some remarkable acts, bands, and soloists all composed of British musicians, who, were they in "Big Time" down here, would soon become famous and overshadow "Swinger" Rubenstein, so that he would go out of "bithness"—which is just what "Ruby" knows and "keeps the clamp on" for.

It is just this alien monopoly that puts our boys out of the best jobs. The Jewish managers of musicians' agencies see to it that the imported Als and Eddies get all the "cream," while our lads must be content with the "skim" when the former are feeling charitable.

Manchester's Seven Wise Men

STOPPING WORK ON RINGWAY AIRPORT

RECOMMENDATIONS of Manchester's "Seven Wise Men," the members of a sub-committee appointed to seek ways and means of keeping down rates, are likely to meet with fierce opposition at the Council's annual Budget meeting.

The "axe" committee have suggested: (a) Curtailment of expenditure on new arterial highways; (b) shelving of Art Gallery scheme for garden site in Piccadilly; (c) nothing but bare necessities for new airport at Ringway; (d) and complete abandonment, for five years at least, of any proposals to build tube railways under the city or to cover the River Irwell to make additional motor-coach accommodation.

The Art Gallery, tube, and river-covering schemes are not likely to be deeply lamented, but the Ringway suggestion will meet with strong opposition.

It is pointed out that, already, contracts let at Ringway—which must be completed—are equivalent to an additional farthing rate. The building of the "trimmings"—clubhouse, additional hangars, and mechanics' quarters—will only add another farthing. Meanwhile, aero experts from Holland, Germany, and France have all condemned the existing aerodrome at Barton as unsuitable for the landing of heavy machines. So—if the Wise Men have their way—Manchester, which should have been the first city to own its aerodrome, is to be out of the beaten track of the big air liners.

Flashes From The Ether

By THE PATIENT LISTENER

GEORGE ROBEY on the radio on a Sunday! Sir John Reith, I am surprised at you! Things are coming to a pretty pass when the B.B.C. allows us to laugh on a Sunday. Of course, I know George was there just to amuse **and** instruct us, and we were highly amused and most ably instructed. He let us into a few secrets of how he enjoys testing his audience for laughs, and how he enjoys making the audience do all the work while he just stands still and looks at them with pained surprise. He mentioned that a promising writer, one Will Shakespeare of Stratford, had written a very good play in which he (George) had recently appeared. He mentioned the amazing fact that in three years' time he (George) will be seventy.

If the B.B.C. do much more of this sort of thing the advertisement charges on the foreign stations with Anglo-Yiddish output will have to be reduced from lack of listeners.

The Saturday-night programmes are not what they were a year ago. Then we used to have a whole Saturday evening with something worth listening to (we expect to be amused and entertained on Saturdays) from 6 p.m. until midnight.

Now we have the curate's-egg-like Saturday magazine and an occasional music-hall programme, or a wishy-washy substitute. After that we have the Second News, in which we have at least four times since December been told that Makale has been taken by the Abyssinians (the last three times they must have captured it from themselves). Surely the B.B.C. are not so stupid as not to know, after four months, that the Abyssinian communiqués and anything that emanates from Addis Ababa is all sheer bunk.

After the news we get wishy-wash from most stations until 11 p.m. Then, on alternate Saturdays, we get Henry Hall's Hour, which, to my childish mind at any rate, is worth hearing for the cross talk of Haver and Lee. On the other Saturdays we get a dance band which, though usually competent, is just one of the dance bands which we get on other nights.

The serial called "The Spy at Rippingham" is just sheer utter tripe. It could have been made quite funny, but is not even silly enough to be funny. I wonder if the B.B.C. really thinks that boys at a public school talk and think like the boys of Rippingham? Actually, in real life, boys, in whatever walk of life, talk and think much the same, and yet each in his class, divided by the social barriers, thinks the other type to be utterly different from himself. And the B.B.C. seems to be helping to foster this delusion.

Printed by ARGUS PRESS, LTD., Temple Avenue and Tudor Street, London, E.C.4, England, and published by ACTION PRESS, LTD., Sanctuary Buildings, Gt. Smith Street, London, S.W.1, England. All inquiries regarding advertisements should be addressed to the Sole Agents, C. ROWLEY, LTD., 5 and 6, Avenue Chambers, Southampton Row, London, W.C.1, England. Telephone: Holborn 2807.

ACTION, Thursday, March 12, 1936

ACTION

2d No. 4 [REGISTERED AT THE G.P.O. AS A NEWSPAPER.] "BRITAIN FIRST" MARCH 12, 1936

FOR KING AND PEOPLE

R.S.4

The Story of the News Chronicle

See page 4

PEACE WITH GERMANY

COLOGNE
Rhineland town, which welcomed the German soldiers with festivity and enthusiasm, recognising that the new Germany had established her sovereignty.

Along her frontiers Germany has seen her neighbours erect immense fortifications such as the gun emplacement below.

GERMANY WILL NEVER BREAK THE PEACE OF EUROPE

—Declared the German Chancellor before the Reichstag on Saturday

Can the Allied Powers object to-day when Hitler sends the glorious manhood of the new Germany into Rhineland?

Senegalese Soldiers. After the war France committed a crime against civilisation, policing the Rhine with coloured troops.

EUROPE'S GREAT OPPORTUNITY: *Read Oswald Mosley on page 9*

"ALL'S WELL WITH ENGLAND!"

THEIR ENGLAND

You're Lovely To Look At!

Lord Sefton, Mr. Anthony Eden, and Sir John Milbanke. Suggest to them that they have anything so terrifying as an influence on women's fashions and they would blush uneasily. But these gentlemen have something in common that women not only notice but covet: style. Easy indifferent tailored style.

They have their wardrobes down to a system—a series of classics flawlessly suited to their days. And this, too, is desirable to a modern woman, whose busy life grows more and more comparable with a man's. So desirable that she turns copy-cat and steals their dress ideas. All this has nothing to do with Marlene Dietrich's pants, but with practical, tailored fashions for daylight and dark.

So the newspaper photos of Mr. Eden send us to the shops looking for Rose Valois's black homburg and a velvet-collared Chesterfield.—"Vogue," February 5.

By Appointment to Mr. Eden?

The International Private Gentleman's Tailor of Repute. Expert designer and cutter. Latest styles warranted.—H. Sanit, 56, St. George's-street, London, E.1.—"Daily Worker," March 5.

Have WE No Need?

Two hundred Putney, London, schoolgirls are knitting scarves for Abyssinian warriors.—"Sunday Express," March 8.

Lucky Dogs

A dachshund was among the guests—I rather think he belonged to the bride. This Sherlock Holmes piece of deduction is based on the fact, my dear Watson, that he

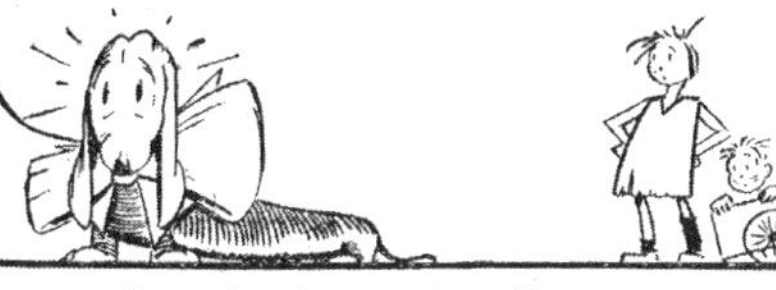

wore a collar of white satin ribbon decorated with orange blossom.—"Tatler," March 4.

The Great Awakening

The world is as it is because there are so many people exactly like us, and the sooner we put ourselves on the mat the better. There is no other way out.—The Rev. Dick Sheppard in the "Sunday Express," March 8.

Intellectual Pursuits

I have always wanted to keep grass-snakes, but have been debarred by the stinking fluid they exude for self-protection, and for this reason have had to content myself with the little slow-worm.—David Garnett in "New Statesman," March 7.

Personally, I prefer Fred Astaire's voice to Ginger Rogers's, but if you feel the other way, get the "Piccolino" and "Cheek to Cheek."—Edward Sackville-West in "New Statesman," March 7.

Riches Not Respected!

There were high jinks at the Embassy Club the other night. A young millionaire was requested by a head waiter to leave the club. I do not think that he had done anything worse than a little mild "trucking" on a corner of the floor.

But the Embassy is conservative, and I remember it frowning on a mild Charleston I did when the dance was new to England.—"Sunday Dispatch," March 1.

Their Idea of Work!

From now on all the lovelies and would-be lovelies will be watching shows, choosing models, fitting and fitting and fitting. . . . Let us hope the results will justify the really "hard" work this involves!

Cocktail parties go on and on. . . .

Also at this party were the Inchiquins and M. and Mme. Slavko Grouitch. Lord Inchiquin is one of the many peers who have taken up "business" as a means of livelihood.—"Tatler," March 4.

The Universal Aunt

I think the situation was admirably put the other day by one of the representatives of one of the smaller Powers in Europe who had read some account of what this country was proposing to do with its defence forces. "That comes as a relief because we know that Britain is one of the police forces of the world."—"New Statesman and Nation," March 7.

Mr. Bonar Law, in a letter published in "The Times" on October 7, 1922, wrote:—"The course of action for our Government seems to me clear: **We cannot alone act as the policemen of the world.**"

Society Intellectuals

This was bad luck, because it is the most attractive of all Riviera tournaments, with its excellent canteen facilities at the adjoining hotel, or where the coloured statuette of a black page guards fat fishes swimming round a pool in the tree-darkened courtyard. Why do fishes swim around and around and not to and fro?—"Sketch," March 4.

The Lioness of Judah

The dignified white dress which Mrs. Simon Marks wears for Sunday galas is a young Londoner's spring creation.—"Sketch," March 4.

Oxford Proceeds

Tricycling, on the other hand, may leap back into its old social position any day; though the Oxford Tricycle Club, founded

a year or two ago, has failed temporarily, we're told, for lack of sponges—the special kind of small sponge kept in the tool-bag and used for cleaning the celluloid collar which has to be worn with tricycles.—"Bystander," March 4.

The Test of a Party

One of the prettiest women in the room was Mrs. Philip Kindersley, just back from New York and Mexico, and looking like a child in a white satin dress and a longer, looser coiffure than of yore. She arrived with the Mark Ostrers (whom we had seen at the theatre with Miss Jessie Matthews and her husband), Lord Oranmore and Browne, her sister, Mrs. Brinsley Plunket, and Mr. A. C. Blumenthall (Blumey), who is at every worth-while party.—"Bystander," March 4.

Geese are Important—to Geese!

We writing chaps are so proud of the improved social conditions of the profession—all the best people are in it: bishops and actresses and jockeys, politicians and debutantes and boxers, peers and Mayfair hostesses and big business men, and practically everybody important.—"Bystander," March 4.

OUR ENGLAND

"All shall serve the State and none the Faction;

"All shall work and thus enrich their country and themselves;

"Opportunity shall be open to all, but privilege to none;

"Great position shall be conceded only to great talent;

"Reward shall be accorded only to service;

"Poverty shall be abolished by the power of modern science released within the organised State;

"The barriers of class shall be destroyed and the energies of every citizen devoted to the service of the British nation, which, by the effort and sacrifice of our fathers has existed gloriously for centuries before this transient generation, and which by our own exertions shall be raised to its highest destiny—the Greater Britain of Fascism." *From "Code of British Union of Fascists."*

THE OTHER ENGLAND

British Farmers!

When Alfred Finch, a farmer, of Wallasea, an island in the Thames Estuary, answered a rate summons at Southend today he told the Bench that he had been so reduced by various charges on his farm that he could only earn his living by knitting stockings.

The balance of rates owing to the Rochford District Council, Essex, was 19s. 8d. and the Bench sentenced Finch to one day's imprisonment which meant that he was free at the rising of the court and that the debt was wiped out.

Finch said that his farm, which was heavily mortgaged, was forty-six acres in extent but, in order to pay mortgage interest, tithes, and sea wall charges, he had to sell the whole of his stock. He hadn't even a cow or a truss of hay.

It took Mr. Finch the rest of the day to get back to his lonely island home.—"Manchester Evening News," March 5.

Two Fleets Cease Fishing

Despite desperate last-minute efforts to save the situation, yesterday saw the end of the Gamecock and Red Star fishing trawler fleets, of Hull.

A mortgage running into tens of thousands of pounds crippled the companies involved, and they have gone into voluntary liquidation.

On an average, the fleets provided a thousand boxes of fish a day for the fish markets.

Crews of forty-seven trawlers and eight fish carriers—about six hundred men—will lose their jobs, together with shore staffs which bring the total to well over one thousand men.—"Sunday Pictorial," March 8.

Workhouse Luxury

The issue of sweets to women and children in L.C.C. institutions is to be increased from two ounces to four ounces a week.

Male inmates who do not smoke, and desire to have sweets, will also have an increase. But, reports a committee, the number of these men is small.—"Sunday Pictorial," March 8.

Making Criminals

A recent criminal case ended in the passing of a sentence of five years' penal servitude. An innocent wife and three young children were left penniless in consequence.

Why do we allow retributive "justice" to punish the innocent for the sake of the guilty? Can we find no better way?

Not only is there hardship and suffering for the innocent under the present method, but the mother has either to tell the children the truth about their father and so lower him in their eyes or else must lie to them. School and social life become almost impossible, and probably three new criminals are made.—"Yorkshire Weekly Post," February 29.

More Existence

Sir,—Here are a few suggestions and hints to vary Mr. Minton's diet. He spends 1s. 6½d. on bread, margarine and cheese. The 2s. 5d. spent on tinned food and mustard-and-cress might be used as follows:

	s. d.
Sunday. ½ lb. roast brisket of beef ...	5½
Monday. 2 oz. boiled ham	3
Tuesday. Beef and potato pie, hot ...	3
Wednesday. Fish (3d.) and chips (1d.), hot	4
Thursday. ¼ lb. potted meat	4½
Friday. Beef and potato pie, hot	3
Saturday. ¼ lb. brawn (or fish and chips, 4d., hot)	2
Extras	
½ lb. cream crackers or ginger biscuits or 1 lb. dates	3
1 banana or 1 bar plain chocolate, spread or grated on the bread and margarine	1
	2 5

He could buy the roast brisket, ham, and brawn at a "Cooked Foods" shop on Saturday. Confectioners sell pies hot from the oven before noon; they also sell potted meat the latter half of the week. Fish and chips are sold at noon on Wednesdays and Saturdays.—M. W. S., Filey.—"New Statesman and Nation," March 7.

Is this Prosperity?

The census of weavers' wages in Barnoldswick for the week ended February 15 shows that out of 2,610 members of the Weavers' Association, 468 drew less than 30s., while 427 received an amount not exceeding 35s.

The analysed returns are grouped as follows:—

Wages.	No.	Percentage.
Under 30s.	468	17.931
30s.—35s.	427	16.36
35s.—40s.	316	12.107
40s.—45s.	242	9.272
45s.—50s.	102	3.908
Over 50s.	18	.688

During the standard week, 342 members were either sick or unemployed, 44 were employed at Colne, and seven at Skipton. There were 282 blank returns, and 362 cards were not handed in.—"Northern Daily Telegraph," February 28.

While Mayfair Revels

A MOTHER WITH SIX CHILDREN.

Income	32s. 6d.
Rent	22s. 8d.
Coal	2s. 1d.
To Live	7s. 9d.

At Stratford Police Court to-day an Ilford mother was charged with attempting to commit suicide.

For over twelve months, it was stated, she had been trying to clothe and feed herself and six children on 7s. 9d. a week. Her husband, who had been ill for several months, died last November.

She is Mrs. Violet Baker, aged 35, of Beehive-lane, Ilford, E.

Inspector William Smith said the woman's husband died in November last after a long illness. She was receiving 32s. 6d. a week, and of that, 22s. 8d. went in rent. Then she had to pay 2s. 1d. for coal, and was left with 7s. 9d. to feed and clothe herself and six children.

England's "Vile Record."

England's "vile record" in the treatment of children during the last century was advanced by Canon F. W. Green, of Norwich, as evidence of the fact that English people do not naturally love children.

"Historically, I can find no records in other countries to equal ours in the public and declared treatment of children from the beginning of the industrial revolution to the end of the Factory and Education Acts," declared Canon Green.—"Catholic Herald," March 6.

A SPECTRE IS HAUNTING EUROPE

By H. J. GIBBS

MR. GIBBS, who is the author of "The Spectre of Communism," to be published shortly, investigates M. Stalin's declaration that Soviet Russia is not working for world revolution in the light of Communist policy and activities.

IN an interview with the editor of the New York "World Telegram" recently M. Stalin, Boss of Bolshevism, replying to a question whether the Soviet Union would force its theories upon other nations, said: "There is no justification for that fear. If those to whom you refer believe that the people of the Soviet Union have any desire to alter the face of things by force or change the established order in surrounding states by force, they are entirely mistaken." Replying to a later question, as to whether the Soviet Union had changed its plans for creating world revolution, Stalin answered: "We have never had any such plan or intention."

Future generations will undoubtedly refer to the story of "The Three Bears" in the singular tense: it is difficult to picture even the vivid imaginations of the Grimm brothers or Hans Andersen rising to such heights. As it is, the proof reveals Stalin as one of two things—either a man who does not know what is going on in his Party propaganda, or an abject liar.

The Third International publishes a fortnightly magazine, "Communist International," a journal published in six languages and reaching the majority of the Communist parties in forty-nine countries where the International has its branches. In the issue for March 1, 1934, under the heading, "Theses for Instructors," this magazine stated:—

"Fifteen years ago, on March 4, 1919, in Red Moscow, the First Congress, under Lenin's leadership, established the *Communist International*—the new International Working Men's Association. The fifteenth anniversary of the Communist International is the fifteenth anniversary of the *United World Communist Party*." (Their italics.)

In the same issue, William Rust, Communist in England, wrote another article, commencing, "The formation of the Communist Party of Great Britain arose out of the direct assistance given by the Communist International and the personal intervention of Comrade Lenin.

"The Twelfth Congress of the Communist Party (of Great Britain) calls upon the workers of Britain to help build up a mass Communist Party by joining its ranks and hastening to forward the revolutionary solution of the crisis." (Extract from the published resolutions of the Congress.)

M. Stalin

Prior to the C.I. meeting last August, a Plenum of the Executive Committee of the Communist International was held which claimed, "The example of Bolshevism is the example of proletarian internationalism. . . . The Plenum of the E.C.C.I. obliges all sections of the Communist International to be on their guard at every turn of events, and to exert every effort, without losing a moment, for the revolutionary preparation of the proletariat for the impending decisive battles for power."

The published "Programme of the Communist International" refers to armed insurrection against the State as "the highest form of revolutionary activity. . ."

In an unguarded moment Lenin once said, "We only succeeded in winning thanks to the profound disagreement between imperialist Powers. . . . Hence our policy—to render wherever possible disagreement between imperialist Powers, or to make such agreement temporarily impossible."

Communists throughout the world—members of "our" parties, as the International calls them—are constantly being called to follow the lessons of the Russian Bolsheviks and "our glorious Chinese Soviets" (*vide* any delegate to the Seventh World Congress of the C.I. last summer).

What an opportunity is afforded Litvinov and his Third International masters, the international financiers, in the present situation. We should not forget that Litvinov was Lord President in Office to the Council of the League of Nations during the months following the Wal-Wal incident; that he is afraid of a pact between Germany and Japan, the penetration of the Caucasus and the occupation of Vladivostock that the Manifesto of the Communist Party says, "The Communists disdain to conceal their views and aims. They openly declare that their ends can be attained only by the forcible overthrow of all existing social conditions"; that it is this thought which is in the mind of all delegates who are feted in Moscow (otherwise, why should they assemble there); that Russian money founded the Communist Press in England; that millions have been butchered in Russia and China, in South America, Uruguay, and Spain; that the French Communist United Front was organised on direct instructions from Moscow, as is every other such attempt to thus gain power; all in pursuit of the ends of the Third International.

Well might the Manifesto open its preface with the words, "A spectre is haunting Europe—the spectre of Communism." That spectre overshadows every nation to-day, whether its feet be in Moscow or Geneva, and stretches most blackly over the British Empire. Our futile Foreign Office nabobs play directly into its hands, therefore it is the task of every Englishman to give the lie to M. Stalin's pretensions.

A significant sentence in "The Programme of the Communist International" absolutely denies M. Stalin: "*The successful struggle of the Communist International for the dictatorship of the proletariat pre-supposes the existence* in every country *of a compact Communist Party,* hardened in the struggle, disciplined, centralised, and closely linked up with the masses."

DICTATORSHIP

WHEN the Government proposed to set up a Legislative Council in Palestine a most interesting debate took place in the House of Lords. Lord Melchett and others opposed the measure on the grounds that, as the Arabs were more numerous, they would hold the majority all the time, and it was suggested that the Government should wait a few years before taking action.

Presumably, this is in order that the Jews may become a majority in the country before that time. Thus, because it is against Jewish interests, the "democratic" Government of Britain refuses to bestow the doubtful blessing of democracy upon the inhabitants of Palestine, who must be at least as capable of self-government as are the Indians.

M. HENRY TORRÈS, the Jewish Lawyer who has negotiated the notorious Franco-Soviet Pact.

PARTY FIRST, COUNTRY LAST, IN U.S.A.

THE President seeks from Congress a sum of £227,400,000 in new taxation, leaving to the latter the method for raising this sum. At the same time Franklin Roosevelt has announced a further income tax on corporations to the tune of £30,000,000. During the next sixteen months more than £2,000,000,000 has to be found by the Treasury to meet deficit expenditures, veterans' payments, and necessary refunding operations.

This is all very awkward for the New Deal and Roosevelt in a year of Presidential election. In consequence the methods for raising these enormous sums will not be based upon the general welfare of the Union, but upon how to forfeit the least number of votes in the Presidential election. Everywhere is to be found the same tendency where the old democratic party system still exists—party first, country last

THE National Debt, from being nineteen millions when Roosevelt was elected, will be, early in 1937, in the vicinity of thirty-five billions. The banks hold to-day eighteen billions of bonds and Treasury notes, of which at least twelve billions represent "deposit credits" and can be checked against for the creation of an equivalent amount of deposit currency. The basis has, therefore, been laid for currency inflation.

Unemployed in the United States have risen in a month by 1,229,000, according to figures for January. They now number 12,626,000. This was roughly the number of unemployed when Mr. Roosevelt was elected President. While millions of men and women are seeking jobs, child labour, which Roosevelt claimed to have abolished during the heyday of the National Recovery Administration, is sweeping back again. According to a survey by the Children's Bureau, it shows a 58 per cent. increase throughout the nation since the Supreme Court killed the N.R.A. last May.

IS Leadership extinct in America? a writer asks, and goes on to state:—

". . . The lowering of American standards has been done not only to the promiscuous influx of foreign immigrants who have helped to draw Americans down to European standards, not only to selfish yellow journalists, who, by pandering to the lowest elements in human nature, have increased their circulation and bank accounts and undermined American character, *but to leadership that has followed instead of leading.*"

This seems to be very similar to that from which we suffer in Great Britain, and the U.S.A. appear to be a long way off establishing that position of moral superiority of which Franklin Roosevelt spoke after signing the Neutrality Resolution of Congress.

HITLER WANTS PEACE

The "News Chronicle" publishes the following, and we have pleasure in reproducing it without comment:—

HERR HITLER has repeatedly referred in his public utterances to a rapprochement with France. These are some extracts from his speeches and interviews:

"Germany is ready to undertake further international security obligations if all nations for their part are equally ready. Germany is ready to dissolve her whole military system and to destroy the small remnant of weapons remaining to her, if neighbour nations will do the same."—In the Reichstag, May 17, 1933.

"The history of the past 150 years should, in its changing course, have taught the two nations (Germany and France) that essential and enduring changes are no more to be gained by the sacrifice of blood. It would be a mighty happening for all humanity if these two nations of Europe would banish, once and for all, force from their common life."—In a broadcast following Germany's withdrawal from the League, October 15, 1933.

"We want to be friends with Europe. We are also prepared to treat with France. The election takes place (in Germany) only to show the whole world that when I declare we want peace and reconciliation with our former opponents the whole people agrees with us."—At Cologne, October 26, 1933.

"When the Saar territory is returned to Germany there is nothing which could oppose Germany to France. If I were told what I could accomplish for France I would gladly do it."—In an interview with a French journalist, November 23, 1933.

"France fears for her security. No one in Germany wants to threaten it and we are ready to do anything to prove this."—In the Reichstag, January 30, 1934.

"Let us hope that our great neighbour is ready, together with us, to seek peace. It must be possible for two nations to grasp hands and to remove all the obstacles in the way of peace."—In the Saar, March 1, 1935.

"This age-old quarrel (between France and Germany) will take its place with forgotten follies and bitterness some day. Europe cannot have a peace worthy of the name until it does."—In an interview with an American journalist, May 10, 1935.

"The blood spilt on the European Continent in the last 300 years is out of all proportion to the results gained by each nation. At the end of it all, France remains France, Germany remains Germany, Poland remains Poland, and Italy remains Italy."—In the Reichstag, May 21, 1935.

OUR PRESS LORDS—No. 2

THE NEWS CHRONICLE

By John Beckett

THE "News Chronicle" is the sole survivor of the countless attempts to found an influential morning National Liberal newspaper. It has always been an extraordinary feature of British Radicalism and Democracy that it found its own Press unattractive and could never be persuaded to pay the piper for the tune it wished played. This is probably a reason why, for all its sound and fury, it never gets that particular tune.

The subject of this week's article was born on June 2, 1930, as the result of an unlovely alliance between the "Daily News" and the "Daily Chronicle." If there is anything in heredity it is not, therefore, surprising that while there is no trace of the sturdy, if narrow-minded, radicalism of the early part of this century, the paper's chief claim to personality is a vicious and old-maidish carping at any idea born outside Bloomsbury and later than 1914.

Early Career of Parents

BOTH parents had enjoyed inglorious careers up to their joint dissolution in the effort of giving birth to their peculiar child. The "Daily News" sprang into notoriety during the Boer War. In spite of its connection with radicalism, its owners did not see eye to eye with Mr. Lloyd George, and were bought out by a group including Lloyd George, G. Cadbury (Quaker chocolate), R. C. Lehmann, H. Samuel, and Leon.

From then until 1915 the larger shareholders included: Sir C. E. Schwann, M. G. Schunck, Roscoe Brunner, Baron Swaythling (né Samuel Montagu), J. Rowntree, and T. P. Ritzema. Mr. Heine Simonis was a prominent director then.

About the same time the "Daily Chronicle" was obtained by the Lloyd George group, but great financial difficulties were encountered until extra capital was found by Lord Reading (né Rufus Isaacs), and two prominent Indian industrialists, Sir D. Yule and Sir T. S. Catto. Prominent shareholders were Schroeder, Sauman, Goldberg, Sir J. Cory, Schwabe, Auchenloss, Wolf, and Wertheim.

Queer Bedfellows

THIS long connection between Liberalism and Jewry seems odd in view of the fact that the Jews are generally acknowledged to be the most illiberal race in the world. The only feasible explanation appears to be that while Jewry is most illiberal, Liberalism is noted for its gullibility, and, therefore, like the T.U.C. and Messrs. Odhams, internationalism covers a multitude of sins.

At any rate, we will now proceed to a closer examination of the offspring, where we shall find that the happy association still continues.

K.Z.G. Ltd.

THIS company was formed under the auspices of Mr. Heymann Binder in 1930, for the purpose of taking over the existing two papers and combining them under the title of the "News Chronicle." Mr. Binder is associated with Lloyds Bank and fourteen South American companies, and is in close association with Lord Bearsted (né Samuel), Sir Robert Waley Cohen, and Mr. F. A. Szarvasy (largely interested in Hungarian coal-mines and the "Daily Mail").

The two groups who now obtained control of the joint production, which later changed its name to The News Chronicle, Ltd., were The News and Westminster, Ltd. and United Newspapers, Ltd. Two groups of directors were appointed, and the fact that the share capital was restricted to £1,000 shows clearly that it was not intended that any but a small group of selected people should control this means of approach to the public ear. In the last list available in 1935 the directors and sole shareholders were shown as J. L. Cadbury, Sir W. T. Layton, J. B. Morrell, B. H. Binder, and Camille Akerman. These directors were appointed by the two previously quoted controlling groups.

The Hidden Hand

IN order to find where the real interest lies it is necessary to investigate the two controlling companies. The News and Westminster, Ltd., presents few difficulties; it represents the Radical, pacifist side of the partnership. It is almost entirely owned and controlled by the Cadburys.

United Newspapers are far more involved. On first examination we merely find that the majority of shares are owned by The Daily Chronicle Investment Corporation, the directors of which are B. H. Binder, Camille Akerman, and Sir H. B. Grotrian. The total capital of this company is £3,050,000, and its short list of large shareholders includes:—

American Investment and General Trust.
American Trust Co.
J. Auchencloss.
Barclay's Nominees.
Baring's Nominees.
Britannic Assurance.
S. Christopherson.
H. L. Cohen.
Albert Goldberg.
Northern American Trust.
Prudential Assurance Co.
Marquis of Reading (né Isaacs).
J. P. Rudolf.
Trans. Oceanic Trust, Ltd.
Franklyn Thomasson.

But the most interesting of its shareholders is the General Investors and Trustees, Ltd., which holds a controlling interest of one million shares.

Journey's End

NOW we are in sight of our goal. The "News Chronicle" is controlled by United Newspapers; United Newspapers are controlled by the Daily Chronicle Investment Corporation, and the Daily Chronicle Investment Corporation is controlled by General Investors and Trustees, Ltd.

Mr. Lloyd George

When we find who controls General Investors and Trustees we shall know where this freedom of the Press, which excites so much controversy, really resides.

The directors of this coy but important company are G. T. Moody, W. C. Cripps (a famous name in the annals of our post-war glory), E. Davenport, H. Kahn, Felix Rose (né Rosenheim), and Maurice Stern. The Jewish population of Britain is 0.6 per cent.

When we turn to the list of shareholders outside banks and insurance companies, who are well represented, there are few British names amongst them. A short list of large shareholders includes:

American Trust.
Alphonse Beer.
Board of Guardians and Trustees for Jewish Poor.
P. M. Boase.
L. B. Burton.
Baron De Longeueil.
P. J. Franks.
O. E. d'Avigdor Goldsmid.
J. H. Guld.
Emmanuel Harris.
Jewish Memorial Council.
C. Joorgensen.
Alphonse Joseph.
C. Kahn.
London Jewish Hospital.
Sebag Montefiore.
G. A. Newgass.
H. Nieltenius.
J. Pollitzer.
F. Rose (Rosenheim).
Mrs. Sauman.
F. Schottler.
Maurice Stern.
Benno Stoneham.
C. Wurtzburg.

Mr. John Beckett

"Britain First" and one of Britain's most priceless possessions, we are told, is the Freedom of the Press. The British people will be certain that their interests will be well looked after by the "News Chronicle" now they know who its owners really are.

Where Their Heart is . . .

IN conclusion, let us glance for a moment at the other investments of the Jewish Guardians, the Jewish Council, Messrs. Rose, Kahn, Stern, and their fellow investors. In addition to their interest in the "News Chronicle" they have over half-a-million invested in Foreign Stocks and Bonds.

Truly we may rest happy in the knowledge that no necessary facts that the British people should know can escape our notice when Messrs. Abrahams, Elias, Isaacs, Cohn, Marks, Kahn, Rosenheim, and Stern have such imposing interests in our two newspaper fighters for Freedom, Equality, and Justice—the "Herald" and the "News Chronicle."

NEXT WEEK

THE BEAVERBROOK PRESS

GERMANY AND ITALY

Although many National newspapers purport to give Herr Hitler's speech to the Reichstag in full, not one of them suggests that he made any reference to the position of Italy or that he condemned the policy of sanctions. Yet the truth has leaked out by the back door, for the Rome correspondent of the "Observer" writes:—

> "Herr Hitler's speech has made a tremendous impression in Italy. . . . The reference to Italy's need for colonies and the condemnation of sanctions are, of course, approved."

At a time like this it is vital that the public should know the truth, and the whole truth, even a paper that has always opposed sanctions omits this vital passage from Hitler's speech. Is there a conspiracy to conceal from the British people the growing friendship and solidarity of the two Fascist nations against the Powers of internationalism?

At the beginning of his anti-sanctions campaign Mr. Garvin did not disguise his regret that the international situation had appointed Herr Hitler as the arbiter of Europe's destiny, and the leading article in the issue of March 8 is far from friendly towards Germany in its tone. If only Mr. Garvin would bring to the German situation the same realism as he has shown towards the Italian, he would be performing a great service to the British people.

WHAT OF THE FUTURE?

IS YOUR OLD AGE SECURE?

THIS question is the nightmare which haunts all clerical workers, men and women, except those employed by the Government, insurance companies, banks, and other firms who are wise and humane enough to provide for the comfortable retirement of their employees at a reasonable age.

What is going to happen to me when I no longer have the only real capital I possess—my youth and health? is the bugbear which frightens these people from their early middle age onwards, and casts a shadow over their lives. The basis of a healthy and happy community is security. What security have they?

Many lack the initiative to strike out, or the responsibility of some relative prevents them taking the risk; and so they go on, feeling confident that they will achieve something whilst they are still young; but when they reach middle age their daily dread is whether they will be replaced by someone younger with the latest smart ideas at less wages. Will they be turned adrift, with the meagre pittance of 10s. per week, for which they pay all their working lives, allowed them under the National Health Insurance scheme, and which would be taken away from them should they be compelled to enter a poor-law institution through bad health or the lack of anyone to take care of them in their old age?

The Single Woman

THE economic conditions prevailing to-day, which prevent most men of their class from marrying at a reasonably early age, bar women from entering the sphere in which the normal woman is happiest. Apart from the financial side of this question, lack of family life, which is really the foundation of any country, and the fact that men and women who are the victims of these circumstances feel they are being deprived of their just due, is not only a loss, but a canker that is slowly destroying the morale of our country.

A Serious Problem

WITH a little careful thought and planning the old-age problem could be avoided. Either the fund which, in connection with the National Health Insurance Act, affords a pension of 10s. per week at sixty-five must be extended, or the State should have a separate superannuation fund into which every man and woman should pay from the moment they commence work. The contributions in the beginning should be very small—a few pence—increasing with their wages. The scheme should be framed in such a way as to prevent loss of benefits through unemployment or illness, and enable retirement at the latest at sixty, with a pension of about £3 per week.

The fact that institutions and firms of the type mentioned earlier in this article do provide for their staffs in this way without any great loss to themselves proves that it can be done

Pension Scheme

THE Government is believed to have a scheme in mind, but is it comprehensive enough to ensure adequate protection? It could be extended to be so at little or no cost to the State. In fact, the benefits that would accrue by reason of the increased purchasing power and happiness of this vast section of the population, and the additional employment created by its withdrawal from the labour market, also the expense saved the Public Assistance Committees who grudgingly dole out pittances to them, would be of enormous advantage to the country as a whole and the taxpayers.

Provision can be made for old age through insurance companies, but the financial circumstances of this class of worker, and the fear of loss of their savings, should they be unable to maintain the premiums, deter them from taking advantage of these facilities.

In any case, the welfare and happiness of the citizens who elect it is a duty which any good Government should fulfil.

A. G.

THE BRITISH COUNTRYSIDE

"BIG BUSINESS" AND AGRICULTURE

Would the Industry Benefit?

DUMPED EGGS FLOODING MARKETS

(By Our Agricultural Correspondent)

EVERYONE who has had any connection with agriculture values the opinion of Sir Daniel Hall, and we feel in hearty agreement with him when he tells us that small-holders should specialise in one branch of farming, and more especially those who have had no previous experience of farming.

I do not think, however, that everyone will agree with him when he states that the 300-acre farm has become almost as weak an economic unit as the small-holding, or when he says that he would like to see Big Business attracted to the land.

Another speaker, in Mr. E. P. Weller when he recently addressed the Chartered Surveyors' Institution, also touched on this theme, his idea being that Joint Stock Companies could be formed to work the land. Yet another well-known speaker, Sir John Orr, also talked Big Business in a recent broadcast, but he wished his schemes to be financed by increasing the income tax.

Is it not strange that the ideas on so-called benefits to agriculture all mean "taking something from someone else" here at home?

Why is it also that no one seems able to come forward with really sound suggestions other than those that spell increased taxation, when it must be so fully realised that the already crushing burden of taxation is lowering the purchasing power of thousands all over the country, and lowering their standard of living as well?

Some Criticisms

I HESITATE to rush in where angels fear to tread, but it does seem to me that before we hand over our land and its productive power to companies, we should first of all try the policy advocated by Fascists—that of shutting out completely all food products that can be produced at home or in the Empire. That policy would soon right matters on the land, and there would be no need then to talk of Big Business taking over farming, three-hundred-acre farms being uneconomical, or of depleting the purchasing power of a great number of the people by increasing taxation.

Many present-day economists neglect the simple fact that you can settle as many men on the land as you like, and they can produce all the foodstuff we need; but unless the people possess purchasing power, the extra produce can never be consumed, nor will producers get a paying price until purchasing power is increased **and foreign imports severely checked.**

Most of us have seen something of large farming undertakings by companies, and especially in the years just after the War, but if you look round to-day you won't find many of those companies in existence, and I very much question whether they benefit agriculture at all.

The Crushing Hand

BIG Business possesses a somewhat crushing hand on small men: it wishes to make profits—naturally—but when business is slack or things do not go just right, the first thing to be cut is the number of hands employed, and the next thing is the wages. This would be nothing less than a disaster if it were applied to agriculture. Big Business would think in terms of thousands of acres and hundreds of villages and farmsteads, and I cannot think the nation would benefit by displacing men already settled on the land, and by breaking up individual farming operations to make way for colossal schemes.

Moreover, would the land be any better cultivated than it is at the present time? I think not. Again, if Big Business takes a hand farms would be run as cheaply as possible, and hundreds of men would be scrapped to make way for mechanisation. I doubt, too, if there would be the good feeling displayed between employer and worker that obtains to-day on the majority of farms, for I know only too well that many a farmer has dipped deeply into his capital to retain men on his farms, because he has hated to throw valued and trusted workers out of employment.

This feeling was just as strong between the landowner and his tenants, and you cannot tell me that Big Business would feel any sentiment towards those over whom it had closed its fist.

Lastly, Big Business might not be composed of purely **British Financiers,** and we certainly do **not** want aliens to get a grip of our agricultural land and the great industry itself.

Dumping Eggs

EVERYONE connected with poultry farming must feel alarmed at the large numbers of imported eggs that are finding their way to these shores, and at a time when poultry farmers have to be prepared for their great seasonal increase in production.

For the week ended Feb. 26 we imported no less than 430,837 gt. hundreds, as compared with 389,760 gt. hundreds the week before. No less than 180,896 gt. hundreds came from Denmark; 57,046 from the Irish Free State, 38,626 from Belgium, and 32,106 from Roumania. On top of this (thanks to the absurd and dangerous sanctions) Jugoslavia is to be allowed to export to this country 25,000,000 eggs free of duty, and 20,000 cwt. of chickens, paying only a duty of 1d. per pound, instead of the usual 3d. per pound.

Unless these were correct statements of fact as proved by figures, I could hardly credit any responsible Government being so foolish as to filch away their living from a hard-working body of agriculturists who **could** and **would** supply all the eggs, poultry, and processed products of this branch of the industry. There are thousands of acres available for the production of eggs and poultry in this country, plenty of men only too willing to start, and thousands of men already in the business, and to the latter these ever-rising imports come as a deadly blow.

There are more poultry farms and poultry kept in Lancashire (I believe) than in any other part of the country. The cotton tragedy has been bad enough for Lancastrians, so what will their poultry producers say to yet another deadly blow?

Presumably, the Government will do nothing unless the poultry industry is willing to submit to another of these absurd marketing schemes, which very obviously the industry itself **does not want.**

Why should poultry farmers be coerced into a scheme in this way when we have been told time and time again that British agriculture must be made to pay? You will not make this important branch of agriculture pay by opening the ports to these huge importations of foreign eggs.

Planning Production

I WAS glad to read recently a letter signed by men whose names are household words in agriculture, calling attention to the fact that if expansion of agriculture in the interests of national defence is to be undertaken, it is no good putting off such an expansion until a time of actual warfare.

Some of us (myself included) have been advocating expansion as a means of defence for more years since the war than we care to remember, but so far with no result. We realised how very close to disaster through food shortage we were in 1917 and 1918, and next time, we felt, there might be no escape.

Yet the acreage under our essential bread cereal wheat has fallen and fallen, and despite what some tell us, it is **bread** we need to support life, for all other foodstuffs, necessary though they may be, are but adjuncts to bread. Shall we wake up in time and **act?** There is no time to lose, for it is an axiom in farming that we should be planning our future wheat acreage now while this year's wheat is still growing. Let us know the proposals without delay, for during the next few months much land that is poor and now under grass can be made fit for the plough and thus for wheat by folding poultry, pigs, or sheep upon it.

Only those who have seen the effects of poultry dressing on land, where they have been folded or kept on the slatted floor-house system, can realise the immense amount of nitrogen they leave behind them on the land, and this nitrogen is an essential fertiliser for wheat.

I will not dwell on the way in which pigs and sheep benefit the land, for Fascists know already my ideas on this subject.

In a Sussex Lane.

SIR OSWALD MOSLEY'S LETTER TO SIR JOHN SIMON

Sir Oswald Mosley has sent the following letter to Sir John Simon, the Home Secretary:

Dear Sir,—

With reference to your statements concerning Fascism and Jewry in the Parliamentary debate of Thursday, March 5, I should be obliged if you would be so good as further to elucidate certain matters. If I do not misunderstand your observations, you enunciated principles which appear to be novel to the Government of Britain and the previous interpretation of British law. Further explanation from the Minister responsible for the maintenance of law and order and from such a high legal authority may, therefore, be of interest not only to this organisation, but to British citizens in general.

I will defer to another occasion a reply to the attack upon Fascist principles and organisation which you combined with the spokesman of the Labour Party to deliver. Also, I certainly do not dispute your statement that anyone guilty of an act of violence should be prosecuted. So far from condoning such conduct, this organisation informed the Commissioner of Police on February 15 last, that any member so guilty would be expelled from the organisation, and offered any co-operation within our power to bring such conduct to an end if, in fact, it existed.

My only comment on this subject is that you omitted to mention in Parliamentary debate that 293 persons have been convicted in the Courts of this country for offences against Fascists in the years 1934 and 1935, and that over 20 per cent. of these were definitely Jewish, although the Jewish community represents only .6 per cent of the total population.

It is, however, the object of this letter to request further elucidation of those passages in your speech which appear, at least to some readers, to suggest that it is illegal in public speech to attack Jews or the conduct of Jews in this country.

If you mean to imply that it is illegal to incite others to commit acts of violence, no one will dispute you. If you mean to imply that it is illegal in public speech to attack Jews or the conduct of Jews in Britain, I strongly dispute it as introducing an entirely new principle to British Government and law We have as much right to attack Jews in public speech as Mr. Lloyd George had the right to attack landlords when Chancellor of the Exchequer in the pre-war Liberal Government, of which you were Home Secretary.

We have as much right to attack Jews as members of the Labour Party have the right to attack anyone who possesses capital, to say nothing of their advocacy of class war. We have far more right to attack Jews than Communists and some members of the Labour Party have the right to attack the Crown. I have observed the vilest attacks on the Royal Family published by the Communist Party which have been the subject of no action or prosecution whatsoever, although they were clearly quite illegal.

You appeared to suggest in your speech that Jews were the only people in this country immune from criticism or from attack in public speech. If you did not mean to suggest that, it is only proper that the matter should be made clear. It is only fair to you that it should be made clear, as any suggestion from you that Jews alone were immune from criticism in this country would provide the strangest possible justification for the Fascist complaint against Jewry and its relationship with the older Parties of the State.

Yours faithfully,

(Signed) O. MOSLEY.

Rt. Hon. SIR JOHN SIMON, K.C., M.P.,
Secretary of State for Home Affairs.

THE FILM OF THE WEEK

THE FIGHTING MILKMAN

"THE MILKY WAY" (now at the Carlton) is the funniest film I have seen for a long time. Unlike Chaplin, Harold Lloyd has adapted his fooling to the talkies.

It is pleasant to see the large, round spectacles and dazzling grin on the screen again. After so much dramatic realism and satirical complexity, it is good to lay back and relax in the luxury of easy laughter. We have had our fill of emotional intensity translated into celluloid, and there is deep relief in this expansive unreality.

Lloyd, wisely, has not thrust himself forward or surrounded himself with nonentities for the sake of contrast. It is to his credit that Adolphe Menjou and a whole team of competent and well-known actors can play big parts beside him without lessening his effect.

THE story is just another amusing farce on the boxing racket. Harold begins as a meek and unassuming milkman, affectionately devoted to Agnes, his cart-horse, but gets mixed up in a scuffle with the middle-weight champion of the world—who has been unwisely celebrating in his manager's absence—and inadvertently knocks him out. Sensation-hunting American journalists are very soon rampaging in Harold's track, and the incident immediately flares into the news. He becomes a fighter in a big way in consequence, the manager of the disgraced champion having decided on a strategy, by which humanitarian Harold—desperately needing funds for Agnes, who is expecting a happy event—is signed on in a number of faked matches. All the fights end victoriously for Harold after the first round—by secret arrangement between his opponents and the manager—and the vast crowd seems highly satisfied and delighted. In fact, Harold becomes a popular hero, and soon learns that the most innocent eccentricities have a high publicity value in modern America, where reputations thrive on idiosyncrasy.

ADOLPHE MENJOU carries the film smoothly over the lapses inevitable to slap-stick. The last vestiges of the romantic French accent which delighted audiences in the early talkies have long since disappeared. Those who admired the dashing Continental villain or gallant of earlier soft-whispering dramas will hardly recognise him as the bullying, scheming manager who raves and shouts his way through this film. Only in glimpses do we see the old Menjou.

Lionel Standing, with his massive blunt head, and deep-throated croak, makes a most convincing thug.

Dorothy Wilson, as Polly Pringle, sometimes looks sweet in this film, but more often merely inane.

E. D. R.

THE PLAY OF THE WEEK

RED NIGHT

IT is one of the tragedies of play production that a play which reads colourfully in manuscript form is often disappointing in actual production, and a part which sounds like an actor's dream becomes commonplace to his audience. This play may have been chosen solely on its merits as a play, but the impression left on the mind of the audience is that it is propaganda of the most fervent kind.

It is a play for pacifists setting out once again in lurid detail the havoc caused to men's minds and bodies by the modern form of the lasting primitive need of man for battle. Played as it is with descriptive realism, the difficulty is to understand why it appeals as only another demand for peace in the modern manner of overstatement and exhibitionism.

Perhaps the first reason why it just fails to carry conviction lies in the fact that so devastating and outside man's experience were the war years that the post war generation is unable even to comprehend, much less paint, their bitter tragedy.

The reaction of men who have once heard the menacing squeal of a shell at too close range is not, we feel, truthfully portrayed here. Perhaps these spectacles of disgust and grime have been done so well and so truthfully by the cinema that no stage production can hope more sharply to point the moral, and can only be an anti-climax. Whatever the reason, although bleeding corpses are a commonplace of this stage, and the producers do not blench at a prolonged and bloody death in the last act, the play does not convey to us horror in its characters, but only a deep boredom. The players seem to skate superficially over the real abyss of terror.

The humour to which the squalor of war conditions lends itself is excellently brought out by John Mills, David Markham, and Alick Hayes. That excellent actor, Mr. Robert Donat, seemed to find the part of the private whose moral is gradually undermined by war conditions a little unwieldy.

There are three changes of scene in the last two acts of this play, and in the first act, one. The second scene of the second act, changed only in order that the audience may be harrowed by the verbal description of the death of a soldier, and, although the changes are very swift, they seem unnecessarily to hold up production. The play is a pale shadow of "Journey's End," which brings home to us the fact that, whether we seek peace by disarmament or rearmament we do seek it, and the time for exhibition and pictured horror is over. We know these things. We have seen them again and again in pictures and the maimed bodies of men in the street. We want to know how to prevent them.

A. C.

THE BOOK OF THE WEEK

WHITHER BRITISH FARMING?

"So Long to Learn." By Doreen Wallace. (Collins. 7s. 6d.)

THIS story of the betrayal of our greatest industry, agriculture, is not fiction, it is the truth; a social document of the highest importance.

It is the story of Mary Mayhew, who married "Squire" Edward Bartley, a man twenty years older than herself, rather than be separated from the Suffolk farm she loved so dearly, and of her unfulfilled love for Justin Ardwell (brilliantly and refreshingly handled this episode), who took up farming after the war because he had "two pieces of shrapnel wandering about in his head," and the story of English earth during the past eighteen years.

Blackshirts in Tithe War.

Season by season, from early spring when a livid green fire creeps along the branches, until the bleak days of winter, when sullen lowering clouds etch the bare outline of gaunt trees and hidden life thrives beneath the black soil, we follow the author until her life absorbs us. So consummate is the artistry she employs, so great her gift for revealing what is a hidden book to most city-dwellers, that even the trivial, everyday things of the little farming community become matters of extreme importance and high adventure.

IN the early days of her marriage we follow Mary through the betrayal of the Agricultural Act, witness her frustration of working on the land as she had before her father retired and went to Birmingham, the end of the semi-prosperous years following the war, into the depression of British farming, which began in the middle '20's and goes on until this day.

There is beauty:

"Fine dry weather had coloured the trees without stripping them; the willows of Tod's Folly were in pale golden and silver lace, and the large loose twirling leaves of the poplar were discs of pure yellow, save at the top, where the tree still wore the bright clear green of spring. . . ."

And uncommon commonsense:

"'I thought you were a Socialist,' said Mary.

"'. . . They're as lop-sided as the Conservatives.'

"'Don't they want to level out the classes, perhaps?'

"'I doubt it. No top-dog and no under-dog? That isn't their notion of a Socialist State. They want the one who's on top now to be underfoot as soon as may be, so that the present under-dog may do some face-grinding for a change. . . .'"

SELDOM has the plight of our farming centres been dealt with such honesty. I must call attention to the description relating the arrival of a column of two hundred policemen on a farm where impounded stock, waiting to be collected by the bailiff, lies side by side with a party of camping Blackshirts:

"The column marched on, across the meadow now, to the stackyard, under a fire of more or less good-humoured impertinences. Some of the ears under the tall blue helmets grew red. . . .

"The inspector stalked into the stackyard, where the Blackshirts were busy about the daily chores of campers, and, approaching Enton (the Blackshirt leader), read something from a paper, and signed to two minions. 'Arrested!' breathed the crowd. Enton went quietly—excessively quiet, indeed. . . . And so did the eighteen others whom the police succeeded in arresting. It was such a lengthy business that several of their mates managed to slip away behind the buildings, and they must have warned the outlying scouts, who never turned up at all.

"So that was the game—to get rid of the Blackshirts before the arrival of the Company! On what charge the arrests were made the crowd did not know. It booed and jeered heartily, and had a good laugh out of the amusing spectacle of large bobbies, two by two, removing medium-sized Blackshirts one by one. . . ."

The whole ungodly business of tithes is told with power and sincerity. This unjust levy, the portion of the Levites—but that is Miss Wallace's story. And how she tells it!

Miss Wallace has told the plain truth about agriculture in an absorbing and compelling style. It moves, it breathes *it feels,* the plight of farming in its hour of desertion by the Government. A fine achievement, which I heartily recommend to all.

H. J. G.

By OUR POLITICAL CORRESPONDENT

Foreword

IN case any of the readers of this column obtain the impression from the heading that we are opposed to Parliament in any and every sense, let me hasten to reassure them that they are wrong. We oppose the present archaic method of governing the country as expressed in the existing Parliament, because it permits minorities to so obstruct the work of Government that it becomes impossible to implement the will of the people by legislation. Parliament's procedure belongs to another century; the majority of its occupants are equally obsolete, and that is why they cling with leech-like tenacity to its forms and ceremonies

A Mockery of Poverty

MONDAY, business opened with another debate on the Distressed Areas.

Mr. Dalton, a tall, typical working man, son of Canon Dalton, and product of Eton and Cambridge, opened for the Opposition. The matter of his speech was sound. No one disputes the continued stagnation and its demoralising effects. There is little or no improvement, although the Special Commissioner stated in his report that the registered unemployed declined last year by 26,000. This decline in unemployment, however, is offset by the fact that 22,000 persons migrated in search of work elsewhere. In Cumberland and in Durham there was an increase in unemployment. Votes of Censure on the Government, debates on Unemployment, have contained the same figures, the same arguments, the same charges of callous indifference and inefficiency. The Government have always replied that things are looking up, prosperity is just round the corner, and that they are doing all they can to improve conditions in these areas. They have appointed a Special Commissioner; they have given him £2,000,000 to spend, they have appealed to all charitably-disposed men and women to assist them. What more can a Government do? No one can expect them to take off their coats and put in real hard work.

Mr. MacDonald Replied

THERE is no one who possesses the faculty of saying nothing in such long, high-falutin', windy, and meaningless phrases. He rebuked Mr. Dalton in his most pontifical manner when he said that the Special Areas have been too much the subject of political capital. He poured regal opprobrium on employers for their failure to respond to the appeal to build factories and start industries, and so help to get out of the mess. He promised that all plans anyone thought of would have the Government's earnest consideration, until a member, exasperated beyond control with his asinine complacency, got up in his place and said, "For God's sake man, sit down. This is a serious problem."

Unemployment

TUESDAY'S debate was similar in substance.

Mr. Clynes moved to reduce the vote by £100; a polite method of criticising the Government on a specific issue.

Sir A. M. Samuel made a shrewd hit when he said that the Clyneses of the Party appealed to the employers to open new industries in the Distressed Areas while the Cripps element denounce capitalists and threaten them with confiscation of their profits.

The attractive member for Wallsend, Miss Ward, who twice defeated the ill-starred Miss "Maggie" Bondfield, had several criticisms to make of the Government's inaction. Her chief complaint was the refusal to consider suggestions which have been put before them over a number of years to improve conditions. "We find it so difficult," she said, "to get a definite negative or affirmative answer from the Government," and ended by exhorting them to "make up their minds to give us a specific declaration of policy."

Mr. Boothby, formerly one of the bright young men of the Tory Party, but now a little soured and cynical through lack of recognition, commiserated and handed Miss Ward some advice culled from painful Parliamentary experience. He told her that "if from any speech delivered she begins to see results from any Government in office within five or ten years, she will be fortunate.

The Cranks' Day

PRIVATE members had a day out on Wednesday, and that young and fortunate Mr. Taylor, the Conservative member for Eastbourne, whose first Parliamentary contest resulted in his unopposed return, moved a resolution urging the Government to achieve a further reduction in the appalling death roll from road accidents. His suggestion that a uniform policy of constructing, surfacing, maintaining, signalling, and lighting the principal roads is commendable, but with the tremendous multiplicity of authorities uniformity of anything is a dream. Germany has overcome this disability by centring road authority into one office with one man in control. There can be no progress until this happens here.

Dr. Salter, the temperance fanatic, made his usual speech on the dangers of motorists taking alcohol when driving, and although it is difficult usually to agree with him, some of the facts adduced from scientific inquiry appeared impressive. Mr. Hore-Belisha, the smug and persistent self-advertiser, was at his oiliest when rolling out impressive figures. He informed the House that in 1910 there were 30,000 fatal and non-fatal accidents. The annual total ascended until in 1934 it reached 200,000. During the late King's reign the casualties were in excess of 2,500,000! Democracy's inability to deal with a problem before it becomes a curse is typically shown in his statement: "So quickly has this development occurred—it covers but the space of a generation—that the engineers and surveyors have not been able to evolve the means of assuring free flow of traffic in conditions of method and safety."

Morrison Frightened

THURSDAY we had the Home Office vote, which the Opposition turned into an anti-Fascist United Front field day. Herbert Morrison, the perky, ambitious little cockney Socialist, repeated the usual half-truths, and innuendoes relating to Fascist activities in the East End, and begged the support of the Government to suppress these terrible fellows. Sir John Simon, the Home Secretary, and another pillar of the United anti-Fascist Front, was all solicitation for his Jewish friends. But did not mention the attacks on Fascists which during the years 1934 and 1935 resulted in 293 convictions, over 20 per cent. of whom were definitely Jews

This Freedom

ON Friday again the private member came into his own when Mr. Gledhill moved the second reading of his own Bill to stabilise hours of opening of public-houses and to restrict bogus drinking clubs. Sir John Simon was in action again and told the House that the Bill did not deal adequately with the problem and that it was time something was done. He promised that the Government would introduce a Drink Bill next session.

IN BRIEF

ST. IVES SOCIETY OF ARTISTS

Fascist Artist Among Exhibitors

A new exhibition of pictures by the Saint Ives Society of Artists is always an event one anticipates with great pleasure. Thus, I was particularly pleased recently to have received an invitation to a private view of the Spring Exhibition at the Porthmeor Gallery at St. Ives, Cornwall.

Works by such famous artists as Lamorna Birch, R.A., Julius Olsson, R.A., and Stanhope Forbes, R.A., were included. Frank Brangwyn's "Notre Dame, Paris," drew a considerable crowd, and there were two good examples of the work of the late Adrian Stokes, R.A.

Three excellent examples of the work of a member of the British Union of Fascists, Herbert Truman, were on view. Of these "Pudding Bag Lane" was a pleasing picture of this quaintly-named locality in St. Ives, while in "French Crab Boats," the artist showed his ability to place a fresh and original interpretation on this familiar scene.

Many people are unaware that Mr. J. Millar Watt, a prominent exhibitor, whose wife was also exhibiting, as well as being an outstanding artist, is the creator of that delightful figure "Pop" of the "Daily Sketch."

R. J. A.-H.

VEILLE D'ARMES (Eve of Battle) — Studio One

Strong sea drama in the full-hearted French manner. All the elements of celluloid drama are here, in a long intense struggle of emotions . . . jealous suspicions, lovely innocence compromised, taut suspense, floods of tears, blind heroism, and noble abasement to duty . . . battle at sea, bombardment, torpedos, explosions heroic captain staggering through flame and smoke, with scarred and blackened face and tear-dimmed eyes crying to the rescued crew from the bridge as the ship sinks, "*Courage, mes enfants! Courage!*"

Victor Francen, as the captain passionately devoted to his honour and his wife, acts with fervour and conviction, and Signoret makes a magnificent Admiral. Mme. Anabella, as the captain's beautiful young wife, who eventually risks her honour as a woman to save his honour as a captain, has lovely eyes and an appealing mouth.

One feels over-familiar with the story, and, as I saw it, the film is far too long. Once or twice, when I thought it had finished, it started all over again. It is as typically Continental as any I have seen —a whirl of terrific emotion, spiced with the merest delicate hint of scandal.

It will be worth while to watch the programmes of this new cinema. E. D. R.

'FRISCO KID — Regal Cinema Marble Arch

The story of San Francisco and its Barbary Coast is another of those rich, colourful incidents of early American history, in which the extremes of conventional morality meet and vanquish the extremes of vice and corruption. **'Frisco Kid,** at the Regal cinema, is Hollywood's latest version. It is a swiftly moving picture, competently produced and providing good entertainment value. The almost unattractive but vital James Cagney gives a brilliant performance as the tough sailor to whom environment has given a dog-eat-dog philosophy, and the whole cast, dressing, and production show a workmanlike and probably truthful picture of these sordid, brilliant times. Love interest by Margaret Lindsay.

If half of the programme at this cinema is very good entertainment, it is an unhappy fact that in this and other cinemas so much must be endured before the last and best half of the programme is reached. **Paddy O'Day** is the other picture, starring Jane Withers, America's horrible child become a Little Eva, with a touch of mitigating endearing jollity. Here is the extension of the Coogan period at its most cloying, with the eager little emigre from Ireland, whose mother, of course, has died before the child reaches the shores of the new land. Here is all the unimaginative "courage" of childhood sentimentalised. Here is embarrassment upon embarrassment and affront upon affront.

A. C.

FOLLOW THE SUN — Adelphi

Follow the Sun is likely to dissatisfy, though not bore, those who cannot enjoy good dancing, lyrics, and lavish colour; for

(Continued in preceding column.)

(Continued from next column.)

it consists of a series of sketches, mainly ballets and dancing acts.

The title sketch is by no means the best, although the theme-song is good. "Love is a Dancing Thing" is a delectable affair, with bewitching colours and a bewitching tune. Of the rest "The First Shoot" stands out conspicuously, and many will prefer it to "Love is a Dancing Thing." It is really excellent, and contains Osbert Sitwell's ballet, with more marvellous scenery and more enchanting dresses.

The rest are for the most part humourous, although songs and dances again predominate. There are one or two fantastic and quaint sketches, and of these "Sleigh Bells," reminding one of a Dickens chimera amid the snow, is deserving of mention.

In this spectacle of spectacles (to use a cliché) Cochran has shown that, in addition to showing-off personal genius, he can, by a touch, transform the banal into something approaching the marvellous

L. L.

FREE ADVICE BUREAU

Everyone has difficult technical points cropping up.
What sort of a car shall I buy? Does the "So-and-So" use much petrol?
How many miles will "This or That" do before it gives trouble?
Write to "ACTION." We'll tell you.
If your Benefit has been unfairly stopped; if your landlord is making things difficult; if you are tangled up over legal questions; write to "ACTION," we'll tell you.
"ACTION" WANTS TO HELP YOU.

THIS WEEK'S QUERIES

INDUSTRIAL

Mrs. S., London.—The house in which she is living is to be pulled down, and she asks what is the position with regard to suitable alternative accommodation.

A.—It is presumed that the house is to be pulled down under a Clearance Scheme, and therefore the Local Authority must find suitable alternative accommodation. If any house is not suitable on the grounds you mention, you should see the Local Authorities and put your case to them.

MOTORING

Last year I bought a 1933 Ford Tudor 8 h.p., and can only do 25-30 miles per gallon (although they are supposed to do 35-40). If I use National Mixture the car will stop about every ten miles, then be all right again after about ten miles. Do you think this is sticking valves, as it does a few back-fires before stopping? This trouble does not occur with cheap petrol.

There is also a dead spot in the carburettor. When throttle is depressed about ¾ inch the engine stops, and when pressed another ¼ inch the engine is racing badly, consequently, when starting off or changing gear (on an incline especially) the engine has to be revving quickly, which will be bad for the crown wheel in back axle.

I have had the car at the local Ford agents to overhaul the ignition and petrol appliances, and they have not improved it. Is there anything you can suggest? The engine is rather heavy on oil, but I do not think it is quite to the stage yet of requiring a rebore.

A.—As you have had your ignition checked and petrol supply overhauled, your trouble cannot be coil, plugs, or petrol starvation.

There remain (a) valves, as you suggest, (b) mixture. If the trouble were valves, you would probably get no better results with heavier fuel than No. 1. Back-fires through carburettor or explosions in silencer generally indicate too weak a mixture, and this would account for excessive consumption as well. Stopping after ten miles would indicate that the trouble develops when the engine gets properly heated up and the metal expands. It looks as if there was an air leak somewhere in the induction system, which only becomes noticeable when the engine is heated up. This would also account for "flat-spot" in acceleration, and especially for "racing," which is almost always due to excessive air. The trouble would be less marked with No. 3 petrol, which is heavier and oilier than the more volatile No. 1.

I suggest that you overhaul all joints in induction pipe between carburettor and cylinder. If these are sound, then cylinder head gasket may be faulty, especially in a car some years old. See that cylinder head nuts are screwed down tightly: if found loose, remove head and insert new gasket. If all these fail, then the air leak is most likely a crack in valve seating or excessive wear in valve stems, both of which would necessitate a new cylinder block, though in the former case I have known a cure effected by pouring a full tin of "Never-leak" into the radiator.

If the valves were replaced in the wrong guides last time engine was decarbonised, this would cause the trouble, as the Ford valves are not interchangeable.

LEGAL

A.—It is a little difficult to advise on this question without knowing the contents of the Policy or whether it is an ordinary or Industrial Policy.

In view of the smallness of the premium, it would appear that it must be an Industrial Policy, in which case it is governed by the Industrial Insurance Act of 1934. Assuming this to be so, the company cannot in law refuse to issue a fully paid-up policy after the first year's premiums have been paid, no matter that the age of the person whose life was insured.

If the company refuses, a complaint should be made to the Industrial Commissioner.

Action
EDITORIAL OFFICES—
SANCTUARY BUILDINGS, GREAT SMITH STREET, LONDON S.W.1.
Telephone : Victoria 9083 (six lines)

ON another page Mr. William Joyce deals with the absurd debate in the House of Commons on alleged Jew-baiting. Mr. Herbert Morrison, conspicuously silent on his own past record of virulent class-warfare in speech and social-climbing in practice, basked in the limelight and protection that the House of Commons so gladly extends to democratic non-entities posturing in statesmanlike garb.

Even Mr. Morrison, however, was put in the shade by Sir John Simon, who was described so well by Mr. Winston Churchill as a great man on small matters and a small man on great ones. Both Sir John Simon and Mr. Morrison were at their greatest in this debate, and it will be now interesting to see what reply they will make to the moderate and reasonable letter addressed to them on this matter by Sir Oswald Mosley.

Jewish Violence

A MUCH more serious aspect of th situation, however, is shown in the reports that are beginning to creep in a diluted form into the local and provincial Press of a fresh outbreak of violence by Jews and Communists against unoffending disciplined men and women preaching, as they have every right to preach, the political doctrine in which they believe, from as far apart as Scotland, Lancashire, and London. During the last week it has been obvious that a systematic campaign of violence against Fascist speakers runs hand in hand with the apparently innocuous babbling at Westminster.

We learn in the Lancashire Press that a Mr. Revett, while holding a meeting at Warrington, was attacked by members of the audience armed with chairs, and badly injured. The sight of one of his eyes was in jeopardy for several days, and a steward who went to protect him was attacked and had to receive medical treatment. At Camden Town another report describes a crowd of over 100 Communists and Jews attacking a small party of Blackshirts. One Blackshirt was hit over the head with a milk bottle, and at the time of writing was still in hospital, and a number of others were injured.

At Willesden in London Mr. Raven Thomson, a well-known philosopher, while attempting to address an indoor meeting, was attacked by a gang who picked up chairs and sang the Internationale. The Fascist headquarters have reports of over twenty meetings attacked since this debate took place, and a considerable number of members injured by their opponents' use of weapons.

The Conspiracy of Silence

VERY little publicity has been given in the Press to the figures our political correspondent quotes this week, showing the enormous number of attacks upon Fascists in the early part of 1935 and the very high percentage of Jews convicted in the courts for this class of offence. As we write, we have on our desk a copy of a leaflet being broadcast in London showing M. Blum in bandages, stating that Sir Oswald Mosley is holding a meeting at the Albert Hall on March 22, insidiously encouraging violence in every line, and winding up with the usual slogan to "Smash the Blackshirts."

Whatever the nation's opinion may be of the policy of the British Union of Fascists, we are certain that the overwhelming majority of the people of this country believe that any organised section of British public opinion has the right to express that opinion in halls rented for the purpose without being subjected to this deliberate organised hooliganism.

The crime the Fascists seem to commit is that like the worm they turn when trodden upon, whereas the Conservative, lower even than the worm, apologises to its interrupters and closes its meetings. It is probably true to say that the British Union of Fascists is the only non-Communist organisation daring to hold meetings to proclaim a patriotic British policy in many of the most Jew and Communist-ridden localities.

The Sacred Beast

IN view of these facts, which are now made known in the Jewish-controlled Press, and the further fact that not one single case has been brought forward of any attack made by Fascists upon Jewish or Communist meetings, decent citizens may have good grounds for believing that at Westminster the Jew is a sacred beast to his henchmen, and to wonder what hidden hand there can be which keeps our politicians silent about these continued attacks upon British men and women, and even gives them the courage and impudence to endeavour to paint the attacker as the innocent person who is being baited.

CORRESPONDENCE

CHANCE FOR GAS COMPANIES

An article was published in yesterday's "Sunday Dispatch" on "Homes with Electricity to be Raided."

The persons responsible for this raid do not understand the financial position of the ordinary householder. Why charge the householder with the cost of re-wiring, etc., when the electrical installation in the house is owned by the landlord, and for which the tenant pays rent, and, under the present system, a very exorbitant one?

Again, the faults in any of the systems would be due to the landlord failing to keep the equipment in proper order, or in the case of faulty installation due to cheap labour and material.

I would estimate that at least 70 per cent. of the householders would be unable to pay the charges, and, where possible, will resort to gas or paraffin lighting.

What a prospect is in store for the buyers of houses under the instalment plan, where so many of the houses are "jerry-built," and what a chance for the gas companies to increase their customers! G. H. SMITH.

Hove, March 2, 1936.

ACT BEFORE IT IS TOO LATE

It is time that all honest, serious thinking citizens should pause and consider, before it is too late, which national leaders are likeliest to be honest patriots working to preserve peace and avoid the unspeakable horrors of another world war?

Will they choose a man of the calibre of those two great national leaders who have themselves risen from serving in the ranks in the horrors of the last great war to be the saviours of their countries, beloved and followed by the vast majority of their fellow countrymen? Or will they have a man of the same old corrupt democratic gangs of political imbeciles who were directly responsible for the last war, although remarkably few of them have had any personal experience of what war means?

I know well, of course, that all our howling hypocrites of the League of Nathan's Jewnion will shriek in answer:

"*Italy the Aggressor!*"

I say to them, you are unholy howling liars. You know, and we all know well enough, that Italy was not the aggressor. The barbarous slave-raiding tyrants of Abyssinia were the true aggressors, and if England and France had been governed by Christian gentlemen, instead of by corrupt and infamous political charlatans in the pay of the international bankers, England and France, with the backing of their respective peoples, would have joined hands in helping Italy when she asked them to in putting down the slave trade, and thereby would have saved already much bloodshed and thousands of precious lives.

Abyssinia flouted the League of Nations in its Geneva Sanhedrim for years, long before Italy took action, and Eden, Baldwin, and the whole National Government gang know it.

Well may your correspondent Admiral Martin dub this invention of the Devil "The League of Rogues." ALEX. SCRYMGEOUR.

Olympic Games 1936
Impressions of Garmisch

By EMERSON BAINBRIDGE

I HAVE just returned from Garmisch Parten-Kirchen where Germany is acting as hosts for this year's Olympic Games. This duty she performs with all the Nordic enthusiasm for athletic sports, coupled with the dignity and spirit of National Socialism.

In deed as well as in words she gave all comers a "Hearty Welcome."

I will not attempt to describe the actual matches and feats of strength that took place, as these have already been amply recorded in the newspapers, as well as efficiently broadcast; but rather I should like to give a general impression of the Olympiad, paying special attention to the opening and closing ceremonies.

On the platform of the station at Munich, which was gaily decorated with all shapes and sizes of swastika and Olympic flags, burst forth from loud-speakers the stirring sounds of martial music, and these strains also enlivened the squares and Sports-platz of Garmisch Parten-Kirchen. There the streets were flanked by the long red banners of the Third Reich, and on every house appeared the emblem of the New Germany.

THE opening ceremony took place in a very welcome, if uncomfortable, blizzard, as three days previously the weather conditions were "no snow, raining."

Reich Chancellor Adolf Hitler, accompanied by Dr. Goebbels and other members of his staff, was acclaimed with tumultuous "Heils" by the crowd, who then sang vociferously "Deutschland, Deutschland" and the Horst Wessel song.

After a short speech the Leader declared the Games open.

The Olympic fire was kindled on a high pylon, and the massed bands of the Air Force played the Olympic hymn.

Then the teams from each country, headed by their flags, filed past, most of them, including the British team, giving the Nazi salute. This brought terrific applause from the crowd, special enthusiasm being accorded the fellow-Germans in the Austrian team. The Italian Fascisti looked particularly smart in their black and blue-shirted uniforms.

Herr Hitler could not leave the Ski Stadium until at least twenty minutes after the ceremony, owing to the repeated cheering of the crowds which had thronged the arena.

DURING the whole week the good fellowship, well-being, and happiness of the new Germany was apparent.

In vain could one search for those suppressed people, spied upon by police, and suffering from every kind of butter, egg, and other food shortage, described *ad nauseam* by our Jew-ridden Press.

On the contrary, the "Strength through Joy" organisation had erected a large hall which was crammed every night. Good food and quantities of beer were consumed at very small cost, and were enjoyed alike by local inhabitants and Labour Corps.

In addition, two large orchestras, one in Bavarian costume, and troupes of singers and dancers were provided as entertainment. A likewise spirit of good cheer permeated the Gasthofs and cafés.

Keen interest was shown in the sporting events, and those unfortunate enough not to get tickets were able to listen to the almost continuous Olympic broadcast from Munich. The German crowd, although terrifically keen that their own side should win, never lost an opportunity of cheering the good play of their opponents.

Herr Hitler and General Göering attended several of the sporting events.

Wherever the Chancellor appeared the closely packed crowds and deafening cheering proved that love for the saviour of their country is genuine, deep, and immense in the hearts of the German people.

THE closing ceremony was truly fine. Although good weather had persisted throughout the ten days, that morning gave overcast skies and drizzle, but by four o'clock the sun had appeared, and soon the mountains were flushed with the setting rays.

The great crowd watching the final of the Ski events at Garmisch.

The flags filed past. They were followed by the prize-winning teams, including the British Ice-Hockey team which got a great ovation.

The teams formed up in the middle of the arena and the Olympic hymn was played to the accompaniment of gun fire. The Reich Sports Minister took up his place opposite the grandstand and gave out the prize medals. As each team received its token, the national anthem of the country was played, and artillery bellowed on the mountain side above the arena.

Everyone gave the Nazi salute during the rendering of these anthems and the sight of the entire audience with their arms stretched out in the traditional gesture of friendship was particularly stirring.

Flares were lit in various parts of the Ski Stadium and the five rings of the Olympic sign on the ski jumps became circles of fire. Suddenly the Olympic flag was hauled down, and was dragged behind eight skiers down the slope of the jump, and at this moment the Olympic fire was extinguished. The troops who lined the arena lit torches, and these flared all round and on both sides of the high ski jumps. At this moment fireworks were lit above the jumps and searchlights played in the sky. It was a magnificent finish to a great ceremony.

This ended the ten days at Garmisch Parten-Kirchen.

MACDONALD DEFENCE MINISTER?

This proposal is a most excellent joke, but one of his Labour Governments gave us two still better ones. These were the spectacle of the Cabinet Minister, Mr. Ammon, former Conscientious Objector, with exemption on grounds of national importance, voting for the retention of the death penalty for cowardice, and Mr. Emanuel Shinwell, holding an Admiralty post, when he had helped foster discontent on Clydeside during the late War and possessed from workshop experience the indisputable right to dance, if he so choose, the tailor's hornpipe.

PEACE WITH GERMANY

THE WAY OUT FOR EUROPE

by

OSWALD MOSLEY

The German Leader's speech and the resumption of full German sovereignty throughout Germany should, in my view, be accepted by the British people as the best thing that has occurred in European affairs since the war.

Whether it proves in the result to be the best or the worst thing that has yet happened in European relationships depends on whether or not the steady will to Peace of the British people is maintained. At one stroke this speech and this action restores German sovereignty over her own territory, and thereby removes the inferiority under which Germany has laboured since 1918. So long as that repression prevailed war was ever likely to recur—now it is gone. The will of Hitler and of a Germany reborn has regained Germany's place among the nations. Having regained that place she offers the nations Peace in concrete terms, together with a limitation of Armaments. If this new basis of friendship is accepted Peace can be built for the first time on a sure foundation.

On the other hand, if Great Britain is commanded by the panic of France, and still more by the corrupt interests within this country who seek war with Germany, a greater catastrophe than mankind has yet known may well confront us. Whether Europe has Peace or disaster rests upon the will and determination of the British people, for their own will to Peace is their only safety to-day. Therefore, let all patriots make felt that will to keep the Peace. Let us declare with unequivocal determination that the closest friendship and association between Britain and Germany should be the fixed object of British policy, and is the best guarantee of European Peace.

Politicians and lawyers dispute legal points while men act. The mass of our people see with simple but clear vision certain eternal truths. Treaties founded on injustice cannot endure. Alliance between civilisation and barbarism can lead only to world disaster. Friendship between the civilised powers of Europe is the only basis of European Peace. Let us, therefore, accept that friendship when it is offered, and so maintain the Peace of the world.

This alone is realism, and this alone is Peace.

Rhinelanders welcome German troops.

THERE SHALL BE PEACE

I believe this straightforward desire for peace and friendship with Germany represents the view of the overwhelming majority of the British people to-day. Let us examine the contrary view which is freely stated in the National Press and dominates the older Parties of the State.

They say that Germany has violated the Locarno Treaty. Germany replies that France had already violated that Treaty by her alliance with the barbarous Soviet to encircle Germany. The British people have never been concerned with hair-splitting legalities when they were faced with realities. Whatever be the legal merits of that dispute our people prefer the reality of peace when it is offered to a legal argument which may end in blows. But none can deny that France has been fully warned of the possible consequences of her alliance with the Soviet.

It was inevitable that this alliance would be regarded by Germany as an attempt to encircle her. Any such attempt traverses completely not only the spirit, but in some respects the letter of the Locarno Treaty. The ill-omened Pact between France and the Soviet lies at the root of the present trouble.

Only three weeks ago in these columns I denounced the virtual alliance between the Democratic Governments of France and Britain and the Communist Government of Russia. This alliance between civilisation and barbarism was bound to produce dangerous reactions in Europe. It has produced its inevitable result in a shorter time than anyone could foretell. We are thus faced with a sequence of events tragically characteristic of the diplomacy from which this country now suffers. (1) The Soviet alliance violated Locarno and jeopardised all amicable arrangement with Germany; (2) Germany consequently repudiated Locarno; (3) Mr. Eden made a statement on Monday last in the House of Commons which twists Locarno into a unilateral alliance with France. He stated in the House of Commons that if Germany attacked France we were "in honour bound" to go to the assistance of France. Not one word was said by Mr. Eden concerning the contingency of France attacking Germany, which is the more likely event in view of the great concentration of French troops on the frontier. Yet the Locarno Treaty, on whose behalf Mr. Eden claims to speak, provided for both contingencies.

The simple answer of the mass of the British people is that they consider themselves in "honour bound" to defend one country alone, and that country is their own land of Great Britain. Locarno is dead, and that, too, is one of the best things that has happened for a long time past. All the old Parties combined to support that Treaty; I am proud to recall that at the time I opposed it with a small minority. It was one of the most dangerous instruments which ever emanated even from the confused intelligence of Sir Austen Chamberlain. It was so loosely drawn and so vague in all its terms that Britain was involved in unlimited commitments of which the British people were totally unaware.

OUR COMMITMENTS

In regard to the Franco-German frontier, it was understood to mean that Britain and Italy would come to the assistance of France if she was attacked by Germany and vice-versa if Germany was attacked by France. But fully to understand the Locarno Treaty it is necessary to read it in conjunction with the French treaties with her other allies in Europe.

For instance, if war broke out between Poland and Germany France retained liberty to march to the assistance of her ally without previous reference to Great Britain, to the League of Nations, or to any authority except herself. She was to be judge and executioner in her own cause. In the event, however, of France being defeated Britain was involved.

If France invaded Germany in support of Poland and was repulsed by Germany she could appeal for British assistance when in the consequent fighting German troops crossed the French frontier. It was thus possible at any time for France to frame up an "incident" between Germany and one of her allies and then to declare Germany the aggressor and to attack Germany. But in the event of France getting the worst of it she could claim that Locarno had been violated when German troops crossed her frontier and could then demand the intervention of Britain on her behalf.

A CONSTANT DANGER

The Treaty of Locarno, in fact, has been a standing menace to the Peace of Britain and of the world for the last decade. Now at last we have an opportunity to rid ourselves of that danger and to build instead a stable Peace resting on the clear-cut terms of Hitler's offer. Demilitarised zones on each side of the Franco-German frontier enable the ambiguous question of aggression at last to be clearly determined. Precise definition can then limit and clarify the obligations of all. An Air Pact in the West, which is now offered by Germany, has long been the ardent desire of the British people, and will be the biggest single factor in removing the fear and suspicion which is a prime cause of war. Above all, the return of Germany to European affairs as an equal among the nations provides an enduring basis for peace. On that basis of equal friendship in days to come the movements of modern manhood in Britain and in Germany together will build the abiding Peace of Europe.

Mr. BALDWIN
"Britain's frontiers are on the Rhine."

Owing to the Important Nature of the German Proposals dealt with here Sir Oswald Mosley's article on

THE BRITISH FARMER AND THE ARGENTINE

has been held over until NEXT WEEK

SEARCHLIGHT OVER BRITAIN

DIRECTED BY WILLIAM JOYCE

HIS MAJESTY'S visit to Glasgow was marked by the practical patriotism characteristic of our Royal Family. A monarch so experienced as ours could not be satisfied with a conducted inspection of the great liner, which had provided the official reason for his presence. He wanted to see Glasgow as it was. He went to the poorest quarters of the city and saw, not for the first time, the living tragedy of poverty and squalor. He spoke out in royal fashion; and if the days of the Divine Right are gone, the power of a King's human feeling for his people is with us; and the greatest loyalty which we can pay to our Sovereign is to work for the well-being of his people.

TO the debate in the House of Commons on March 5, in which the Home Secretary elevated Jewry to the rank of a sacrosanct caste, unmentionable by ordinary mortals, adequate reference must await the result of the correspondence which Sir Oswald Mosley has begun with the Home Office; but one of Sir John Simon's observations deserves special notice because it is so highly relevant to the questions which are often addressed to Fascists concerning freedom of speech. Quoth the famous lawyer: "It is all very well for some people to say 'It was only words,' but there are occasions when words produce very serious action, for which the speakers must be held responsible."

Are there now? We are at last being instructed that there is some connection between words and deeds. As we have clearly explained, the British Union of Fascists neither uses nor sanctions illegal or unconstitutional methods. Our purpose is not to break the law, but to make the law in the interests of the people and against the interests of their enemies.

Yet we must ponder on Sir John's pontifical announcement. Surely social democracy has accorded freedom of speech on the sole assumption that no form of speech could ever conceivably lead to any action.

We have always held that Communist attacks on the monarchy were calculated to promote action so grave as to be treasonable. We urged that the Communist appeal to the "workers" to drive the Blackshirts out of Hyde Park and drown them in a sea of "shock-brigaders" was intended to lead to criminal action. A learned magistrate held otherwise.

Only when some speaker refers to the dominant power of Jewry do the cunning lawyers seek a formula to forbid speech on the ground that it does lead to action. There is no Social Democrat who will not murder his principles one thousand times over rather than permit a single word to be breathed against Jews.

MR. HERBERT MORRISON'S performance was even more remarkable than Sir John Simon's. This good democrat, whose present theme is "No Free Speech against Judah," made a number of impudent observations concerning Mr. John Beckett. Several times he referred to this Fascist, with his eighteen years' political experience, as a person of no importance. Morrison himself could never fill the King's Hall in Hackney as did Beckett. Moreover, when this apostle of Judah commanded a Labour Council in Hackney, his organisation lost every seat at the end of three years.

Mr. William Joyce, whose face bears a scar made by a Jewish attack with a razor, is well qualified to write on this subject.

His main criticism of Mr. Beckett's speech was that it enunciated two principles: one that Jews are not and cannot be English; the other that the Jews have no right as aliens to do work which keeps British people out of employment.

These propositions are axiomatically true; but the truth is proverbially bitter to certain classes of persons.

BEFORE me as I write, I have a copy of a letter written by an Englishman resident in the East End to the Home Secretary. He describes how his son was slashed by Jewish razormen for having been present at a Fascist meeting. Mr. Greenland writes: "The British people of this district are insulted daily by this race which you seem so ready to champion, and the police of Stoke Newington, no doubt inspired by your attitude, allow foreigners hardly able to speak our language to sell revolutionary papers in the street unchecked while British street traders are threatened with arrest." With further reference to the Jews he writes: "The only violence suffered by them has been brought about by their own overbearing and insulting behaviour."

For long months the Fascists were weak in the East End. Ambush, injury, beating, and slashing was the fate of any Fascist who walked the streets alone at night. No protection was granted to them.

Not by violence, but by law and constitutional action, the streets of the East End must be made free for the English people.

SOON we shall learn if the Social Democrats, at the behest of Judah, will impose a ban on the freedom of speech which they profess to revere. The Press is controlled by Jews; the kinema belongs to them; but the minds and hearts of the British people, the tongues and voices of the British race, are gaining freedom every day; and this last attempt at suppression calls for a retribution in proportion to the offence.

LET the Gods weep, the light of Heaven grow dim, and the deep red rose turn ashen pale: for the Ostrers' "Sunday Referee" has had the astounding effrontery, the nefarious impertinence, to declare that in order to smash Germany we must help Italy to make a "satisfactory peace." But that is not all!

These Jewish nationals have the impudence to state, "Italy is basically friendly to this country, and that must not be overlooked." Week after week, month after month, this Hebrew journal has printed the foulest and vilest insults against Mussolini. In every possible way its editorial sought to hold up the Italian leader to ridicule and hatred. Now the Jews want to use him against Germany; they dare to flatter him; their thick hypocrisy must choke them!

OXFORD has once again extinguished itself. The famous old University of Heidelberg extended to British universities an invitation to send delegates to its 550th birthday celebrations.

At once Professor Gilbert Murray held counsel with his academic gangsters and thugs. These desperate young fellows came to the conclusion that no delegate ought to be sent. Jews, their spies reported, had been excluded from Heidelberg; now Jews "rush in where Pansies have their bed." Indeed, Oxford is to-day overrun with Jews. Jewish power grows to the extent that the good old University has degenerated into a Kosher Joint. Perhaps, then, it is not surprising that Heidelberg should be considered unapproachable by the people of the City of Refuge.

It is nevertheless worthy to be recorded that Cambridge accepted the invitation at once, and will accordingly be represented. Thus the responsibility of assisting a good understanding in Europe has been discharged, and the University which on this occasion represents Britain in Germany is entitled to be regarded as representative of our own people.

"ALL Lancashire," announces the "Manchester Guardian" of March 2, "anticipated that when the Finance Member introduced the Indian Budget last Friday some lightening of the tariff on her manufactures would be announced, but nothing of the kind occurred. . . . As Sir William Clare Lees points out, there is real anxiety lest the good work that is being done in encouraging the use of Indian cotton in Lancashire should be set back because of a lack of faith in India's desire for co-operation."

This canting rubbish would scarce be worthy of quotation were it not that the "Manchester Guardian" has for so many years been identified with the cause of Imperial disintegration. Why should Lancashire anticipate anything when the Congressmen, to whom our politicians have confided the sovereignty of India, have taken every opportunity to proclaim their hatred of Britain and their intention of closing Indian markets to Lancashire? Who on earth, except a lunatic or a person completely ignorant of India, could for one moment suppose that the babus and fakirs who defeated the British Government have any desire to co-operate with us?

A View of Oxford

Lancashire Members of Parliament are now piteously begging that some consideration should be given to Lancashire; but surely they knew that the Swarijist Movement in India was built and maintained by International Finance precisely in order that Lancashire labour might be displaced by slave labour. Likewise, they must know that the time to protest was during the debate on the Indian White Paper, which could have been rejected if Lancashire M.P.s had opposed it.

The Leader of the British Union of Fascists predicted clearly and accurately to great Northern audiences the course which events would take. The people of Lancashire must feel the need of representatives who will fight; their present Members did not fight; and this tardy whining will not atone for their cowardice at the time when they could have acted with decisive effect.

MR. SERGE RUBINSTEIN is a financier whom the public cannot afford to ignore; it is, therefore, not unfortunate that he should receive occasional notice in the Press.

On this occasion, he appears as managing director of the Chosen Corporation, which seems to be involved in some little difficulty with its auditors. Apparently the London books of the company have been audited up to December 31, 1935. The boards of the subsidiary companies requested that their affairs might be similarly examined. With respect to these concerns, however, shareholders have been informed that instructions were subsequently varied by Mr. Serge Rubinstein, who gave orders to the office in Japan of the chartered accountants that the date of the audit should be up to September 30, 1935, instead of up to December 31, 1935.

The chartered accountants write to the Chosen Corporation as follows: ". . . . the investigations must embrace the subsidiaries and must coincide as to date. . . . we have failed, despite repeated and urgent requests, to obtain the necessary authorities of the required information."

Mr. Rubinstein is not at present in Great Britain, whence, it will be recalled, he came from France, for business reasons.

MEMBERS of the House of Commons have been indulging in further criticism of their assembly, its methods and its procedure. Miss Ward, Conservative member for Wallsend, on March 3, in a manner reminiscent of Alice in her more plaintive mood, reflected, "All of us on both sides of the House have put forward over a period of years a large number of suggestions; we find it so difficult to get a definite or affirmative answer."

Mr. Boothby, in a style truly worthy of the March Hare, observed: "If from any speech delivered in this House she begins to see results from any Government in office within five or ten years after it has been delivered, she will be fortunate."

Whether Mr. Boothby's suggestions will be acceptable to the Fascist Government of the day it is not our purpose to discuss: but by 1943 a Fascist Government will have been in power for a period sufficiently long to extract from Mr. Boothby suggestions of value.

THE REARMAMENT BURLESQUE

By R. GORDON-CANNING

THESE lovers of peace in words, yet hounds of war in action of meddling mischievousness, these Baldwins, MacDonalds, and Edens have at last under the guise of "collective security" placed before the British public a plan for re-armament. After years of criminal neglect, in which the Navy, Army, and Air Force have been reduced to the last extremity of armed ineffectuality, these Ministers of the Crown, infatuated with inactivity except for occasional stentorian denunciations of friendly nations, produce what "trust me" Baldwin is pleased to call a plan "to repair deficiencies."

This is the lucidity of language to which we are accustomed in our politicians—to repair something which does not exist—and the plan in general outline appears to be as nebulous as Mr. Baldwin's words. The plan is divided into naval, military, aerial, and industrial compartments, but, as is only to be expected, agriculture and the storing of food supplies have been altogether neglected, and the population of the British Isles still faces the possibility of starvation. In fact, the whole scheme savours of the burlesque which will turn into drama.

The Navy

THE building of two capital ships cannot be begun until 1937, so that the battle fleet is not going to be in a position to fight a modern action until 1939, while the addition to the cruiser strength will give Great Britain only fifty effective ships to cover the vast mileage of sea routes of Europe.

No reference has been made to "fuel," one of the most important considerations in naval policy, and training is still apparently for reasons of economy to be carried out at half-speed. There is to be an increase of 6,000 men, which is a most necessary addition to the personnel, as our capital ships are only three-quarters manned.

The Army

HERE the chief step is an extensive mechanisation and an increase of four new battalions. Nothing, however, has been said as to how these new battalions are going to be recruited and how the old establishment of the regular Army is going to be brought up to strength. In 1935 this was 152,200, and there was a shortage of 10,000. In 1936, 26,500 men will leave the Colonies, and therefore there will be required during 1936 42,500 recruits. In 1935 there were only 19,594! The establishment of the Territorial Army was in January 1, 1936, 128,300; there is here a deficiency of over 40,000 recruits.

Recently a memorandum was addressed to commanding officers suggesting that discipline was too strict, that the men should be more pampered, and that on leaving the Colonies the men should be given better character records! The usual method of social democracy in difficulty—bribery, softness, refusal to face the issue. Since 1914 the Army has been reduced by twenty-one battalions, and at present our regular military forces at home number only 115,000 men. Under the rearmament plan no steps are being taken to recondition the Territorial forces, but only to improve its "inadequate equipment and training."

The Royal Air Force

THE principal function of the R.A.F. is recognised as being "to provide an effective deterrent to any attack upon the vital interests of this country situated at home or overseas." Here the plan shows probably its greatest inadequacy. It is difficult to compare respective air forces by numbers alone, as quality, both in machine and pilot, count heavily in aerial warfare. But the numerical extension for the Empire is limited to 400, of which 250 go to the First-line Air Force, bringing the total of the latter up to 1,750.

This number surely must appear totally inadequate when one regards the number, modernity, and trained pilots in Germany, Russia, Italy, and France. This plan for expansion of the Air Force will in no sense bring us into line with the above-mentioned powers, giving us 2,500 aeroplanes compared with the 4,000 of Russia and Germany and Italy. Besides, how will this expansion take place when the addition authorised last May has not been nearly completed, only twenty-one out of seventy-one new squadrons having been formed.

The rate of progress under this first increase does not mean that our ratio of strength ascends, but, if anything, rather deteriorates in comparison with the growing forces of other countries, and according to a report of the Royal Air Force estimate in "The Times" of March 7, 1936, the White Paper expansion will not begin until the financial year 1937-38. Again, in comparison with the U.S.A. our Fleet Air Arm is weak, being 181 compared to 475.

Beyond aeroplanes there is the question of pilots, aerodromes and ground organisation. Under the air plan outlined in the White Paper, it appears that the British public will still be at the mercy of Continental Powers and that the National Government in this action, as in so many others, does nothing really decisive, but merely produces palliatives and temporary expedients.

The preparation for industrial organisation in time of war is probably the most progressive step taken by such retrogressive minds, but unfortunately opportunity is still going to be there for undue profit and speculation at the expense of the public.

That most peace-loving country, the U.S., even under democratic Franklin Roosevelt, is spending £180,000,000 in 1935-36 Budget on armaments, while that of Great Britain was only £104,000,000.

As usual the National Government, with its facilities for propaganda, flourish their rearmament plans as ones which will bring security from attack to the British Empire. To those outside this party clique the plan appears definitely inadequate, and nothing but a burlesque of what should be planned and put into operation without a moment's delay.

THE HUNGRY THIRTIES

By ANNE BROCK GRIGGS

THE 1930's—in which the suicides rose to nearly 9,000 in 1933, as against 6,000 in 1925. The figures for 1934-1935 are not yet published, but to judge by the tragedies almost daily reported in the Press, they will remain grimly high, these "prosperity" suicides.

We read last week of a mother of six children who tried to take her life. For a year she had struggled to feed and clothe them on 7s. 9d. per week (all that was left after the rent and coal were paid). "She was in a distressed and delicate condition owing to her hardship." She felt that by taking her own life and that of the children "we should be so much better off." On the same page we read of the annihilation of a family whose father had been unemployed for a year.

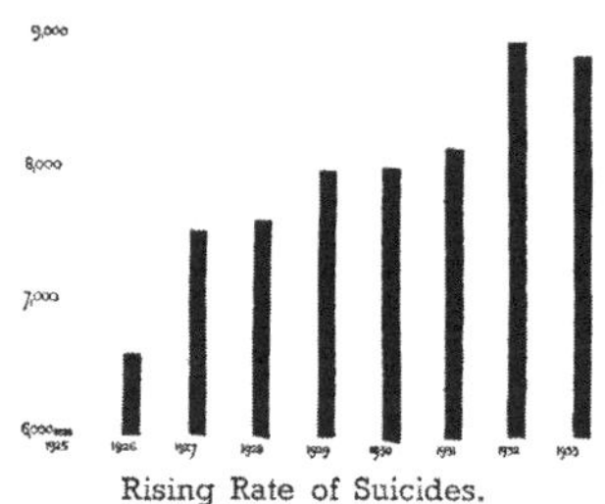

Rising Rate of Suicides.

What is Malnutrition?

THE number suffering from malnutrition, we are told, remains "surprisingly small." The fact is that malnutrition among school children has risen from 9.5 per thousand in 1925 to 13 per thousand in 1934. But the refined phraseology of Whitehall reports shrinks from such a crude term as hunger and draws a subtle distinction between malnutrition and undernourishment. Adding the number of children malnourished to those merely undernourished, we have the figure of 26 per thousand, or 2.6 per cent.

The Palliatives of Democracy

BETWEEN 1931 and 1933 the number of children receiving free meals has doubled, and those receiving milk both free and on payment increased five times. This increase is a true measure of the poverty in the country. While it has prevented the deterioration in health from being an alarming one indeed, such measures are not a substitute for the living wage and good home to which every British family is entitled. King Edward, after his tour of the Queen Mary, with her luxury suites and her synagogue for patrons, visited the homes of the men who built her. There he saw for himself the squalid houses of some of his subjects in the slums of Glasgow.

M.P.s Get Down to the Problem

WHILE so many families are short of the valuable nourishment given by milk, M.P.s are scratching their heads over the forty millions surplus pints of milk a month. We have a surplus! Democracy's latest self-denying ordinance is to offer families in the depressed areas the chance to buy at 2d. a pint some of this surplus at present sold to the manufacturers at 1½d. Good bithness! or a sardonic jest. Thousands yearly are ending their lives after a vain struggle against poverty and hunger, yet we have surplus milk, surplus money; and the fact emerges, after cold-blooded perusal of statistics, that the childless homes of Britain can afford enough milk for health, but where there are children to rear milk is too expensive.

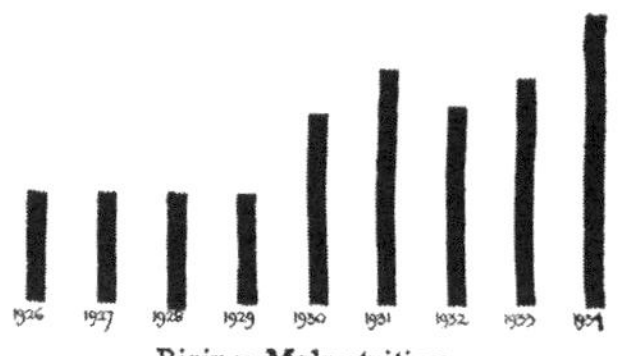

Rising Malnutrition.

In default of a constructive plan, Government must subsidise. A reorganisation committee is already sitting like a broody hen. The results are to be seen in May. But as the matter is "very complicated," a long-term policy to save the health of Britain is once more deferred.

When we feel complacent let us remember the despair of the hungry, and let these "unimpeachable witnesses" speak.

THE PROPHET

"ENGLAND, which they knew . . . to be the free dumping ground for all the refuse of other nations who liked to come, for though many questions might be asked, they need not be answered, or could be answered very indifferently by proxy.

"In this way England had become overrun with an undesirable foreign element, for in the height of her prosperity she gave all a welcome, blind to the possibility that harm would come, and that though she held the zenith of the world, there might come a setting. Spain, Greece, Russia, Turkey, and other Powers had long sunk below the horizon, and to oblivion, and already many of England's foreign possessions had passed to the stranger, for England had loved the perfumed air and the lap of luxury too much to protest—till the power to protest was lost. Her children had been pampered and pauperised till they expected all things to come to them without effort, and rather than work for their needs they had bartered England's honour for a downy bed; and the time had come when other nations could do just as they liked if it was done pleasantly and insidiously and caused no inconvenience."

This extract is not, as one might think, from a speech by Oswald Mosley in 1936, but is from a book, "Through the Sun in an Airship," written by John Mastin, a well-known botanist, in 1909.

As the title of the book indicates, it is a futuristic dream of the H. G. Wells type, but it is hardly necessary to point out how much of this prophecy has already come true.

GOOD LITTLE CITIZENS

By JENNY LINTON

THE school was breaking up. The children had gathered in the big hall to say prayers. They stood in neat rows with eyes closed and hands clasped. At their feet lay their little possessions; pennies, bags of sweets, and toys.

One felt with a rush of emotion how simple and innocent were their lives; how far removed from the stern realities of adult existence.

There is a great responsibility both in school and in the home in the wise upbringing of the child. Most healthy children have only fleeting glimpses of such angelic tendencies as those I have described above.

THE child is father of the man. Do we realise this in these days when the child is very often master of the man.

A child who has discovered that he can nearly always get his own way will grow up into a difficult adult. He will expect an unfair compromise from life.

Parental authority or control is supposed to be sadly lacking these days and one continually hears of the problem of the spoilt or the only child. This is not to be taken too seriously. Families tend to be smaller and children are soon made conscious of themselves as personalities. If this is developed in a sane manner, it is all to the good, but a child with a strong will and latent powers of a dominating personality can soon have its parents nicely on a string.

How few children have such surroundings?

I HAVE seen children who have not long before started school coming along hand in hand with their mothers, and as the child has shown some disinclination to attend school one has to witness the amazing spectacle of the mother in tears and the child standing by quite calmly with an expression "see what I can do!"

A sensible teacher soon transports him inside where he is instructed in the first gentle elements of discipline. The wise parent at this stage leaves the child to the care and experience of the teacher; but there is the ill-controlled and over-anxious type who are always ready to take up the cudgels on behalf of their offspring. A child thus encouraged has little chance to develop a character of its own.

AFFAIRS IN SPAIN

ALTHOUGH a majority of votes in Spain was cast for the Centre and Right Parties, the Left group, consisting of Republicans, Socialists, and Communists, has gained the majority of seats with 259 against 194. Señor Gil Robles, who is in no sense a Fascist, but a die-hard Parliamentarian, still commands the largest party with ninety-five members (Socialists 88, and Communists 12). Nevertheless, the Red processions held in Madrid on Saturday last demanded his head.

Spain and France are only at the beginning of their troubles, Soviet influence is permeating everywhere.

INDUSTRIAL NOTES

By JOHN EMERY

Socialists and War— Parliamentary Yes-Men Labour M.P.s Making Discoveries

The Socialist War Front

LABOUR'S wrangle on rearmament has worked out according to time-honoured plan. All the conflicting elements expressed their views. Everybody, except the faithful mutts who provide the leaders' salaries, know that those views are poles apart, but the "Daily Herald," true to form, tells the faithful mutts that there was absolute unanimity.

The actual unanimity is that George Lansbury and Dr. Salter will have no weapons at all. Instead of a front line fleet of war and air ships, George prefers a fleet of missionaries (preferably Church of England), who will go forth as evangelists to effect a change of heart.

Sir Stafford Cripps, on the other hand, will use any war to achieve the social revolution.

Dr. Dalton thunders because we do not impose sanctions on Italy, which might mean war.

A. V. Alexander bleats that we are spending too much on armaments. Then there is the large section which is quite keen to go to war with Italy, provided we go armed only with bows and arrows.

These prattling politicians have no real say in the business at all.

They oppose the Government proposals because the Parliamentary system would burst if the opposition did not oppose. If Mr. Baldwin says "To-morrow will be a fine day," Mr. Attlee would be bound to rise in his place, congratulate the Prime Minister on making the best of a bad case, and then move a vote of censure on the Government because they had failed to make provision against rain.

The Yes-Men

THE only men who can say "Yea" or "Nay" to the Government are the trade union leaders. A million speeches can be made in Parliament, but battleships and aeroplanes are not built in Parliament; they are built on the Clyde, the Tyne, and elsewhere.

The trade union leaders would not allow a single speech to be made against re-armament if they believed for one moment that the speeches could prevent the building of ships.

The only effective way to prevent re-armament is to refuse to build the ships. Have you ever heard one trade union leader even hint that they would not be built? That is the test of their sincerity in opposing rearmament.

So the Parliamentarians will talk; each will explain his own muddled views, and the trade union leaders will send their unemployed men back to the machine-shop and the shipyard. Union membership will rise again, the spectre of bank overdrafts and economy in travelling expenses will vanish once again, and the "Daily Herald" will say there is perfect unanimity.

But when the ships are built and the men once again on the street—what then? Trade union leaders have not even begun to think of that; they live from day to day.

A Live Man

THE one live man in the Mine Workers' Federation, Mr. Jim Griffiths, is just about to be ruined for all effective purposes. He is fairly certain to be elected to Parliament in the by-election at Llanelly, and that will be the end of him. In choosing Griffiths, South Wales Miners' Federation has reversed its age-long policy. Up till now it has been the custom when a man had proved himself absolutely incapable of rendering any useful service in mining organisation he was sent to Parliament. The local leaders usually felt he would do no good there, but equally they felt he could do no harm.

All that is to be changed, because Mr. Griffiths is perhaps the only member of the executive of the Mine Workers' Federation who is not only intelligent, but is also alive.

Now the Coalowners' Association for ten years has had a rooted objection to meeting anybody who was alive. But since Mr. Ebby Edwards and Mr. Joseph Jones came to power in the Federation the whole atmosphere has changed. Mr. Edwards stated scores of times that he and his colleagues were quite harmless and were only too anxious to co-operate with the coalowners. But the owners were still suspicious, they felt in their bones that the miners were still a fighting race, and not until the past two months, when they began to meet Mr. Edwards and Mr. Jones face to face, were they reassured.

Now they can meet round the table, and the owners only surprise at the whole business is that they should ever have thought of the present Miners' Federation as being anything but nice, tame English gentlemen.

Pukka Sahibs!

OTHER unions which are behaving like perfect gentlemen are the three railway unions. They are still seeking the restoration of cuts imposed in the industrial crisis of 1931-32, but they are in no hurry about it. Part of the cut was restored in 1934, but even then the N.U.R. executive had not thought of making any move until resolutions began to pour in from their branches asking them to convene a special delegate conference.

Unable to resist the pressure of their members, the executive had to move. They went through all the formal motions of calling the three executives together and agreeing to make a joint claim, but with little hope of getting anything and with much less desire to fight if their claim was refused. But, having made their claim, they met the three rail companies, argued for about six weeks, and then to their surprise and relief were given part restoration without having to do anything about it.

A fresh application was made at the beginning of this year for full restoration of the cuts; one meeting has been held, but although nearly two months have elapsed since that meeting, nothing further has been done, and at the time of writing there is not the remotest indication that the union leaders intend to do anything further.

I know, of course, a meeting will be held some day. It will adjourn again, and the newspapers will record that the negotiations have reached a critical stage.

Then one day in midsummer there will be Press photographs of the rail managers shaking hands with the union leaders; they will be smiling sheepishly at each other, and the Press caption will be, "Common sense triumphs over force."

Meantime, the shockingly paid rail workers are still awaiting their lost wages. The cuts could be restored to-morrow, as the relief in rates granted to the railways equals all that the railwaymen are likely to get out of the negotiations.

Life Saving

I NOTICE that several Labour M.P.s have discovered that there is an industrial disease known as silicosis. They have actually been asking questions about it in the House of Commons. For this sudden spurt of activity we have to thank a woman journalist, Miss Louise Morgan, whose articles on this deadly disease in the mining and pottery districts seem to have shamed the M.P.s. Their interest will not be long maintained, however, as silicosis has been killing miners by the score for years with scarcely a protest from miners' M.P.s. They must have seen its deadly effects and it is only now when it has become a topic that their interest has been quickened.

When they have stopped discussing sanctions and whether pubs should be kept open half an hour later at night, I hope they will turn their attention to that new safety device against fire damp explosions known as the Ringrose lamp.

I have not forgotten how Mr. Joseph Jones, the miners' president, sought to make Party capital following the terrible Gresford pit explosion when two hundred and sixty-five miners were suffocated and whose bodies still lie sealed up in the death pit in North Wales.

Mr. Jones made great play of the fact that this lamp which he said had been available in 1928 had not been used. He blamed the Conservative Minister of Mines because he had not compelled its introduction, but Mr. Jones conveniently forgot that two Labour Ministers for Mines, Mr. Shinwell and Mr. (now Sir) Ben Turner, had failed to compel its introduction during the tenure of the Labour Government between 1929 and 1931. Well, the Mines Department is now satisfied that the Ringrose lamp can detect collections of gas in time to withdraw the men from the danger zone. Will the miners' leaders see to it that the lamp is introduced into every fiery mine?

Love of Labour Lost

THE one hopeful feature in the whole industrial situation is that just as the leaders get older and sleepier, the men themselves are waking up.

The next few years will be years of serious industrial unrest. One reason is that the workers have tolerated low wages and poverty in the midst of plenty because their leaders had buoyed them up with the belief that a Labour Government would come to their rescue.

They know now that that is a vain dream. The intelligent amongst them see their political leaders shaping their policy in the hope of capturing those comfortable, smug people who think they are doing something revolutionary when they join the League of Nations Union.

In doing this the Labour Party is alienating its own enthusiasts, and the League of Nations Union votes for Mr. Baldwin as before. Having lost hope from Labour political action the workers are now swinging to industrial action.

And the older generation of trade union leaders cannot understand it. They have no sympathy with the young and hate nothing so much as action. They have been used for years to the comfortable routine of a union car calling for them in the morning. A chauffeur at the wheel opens the door and tucks them in and the answering of a few routine letters constituted the day's work. That period is over. It is when trade becomes busy that the workers get on to their hind legs and demand things. And they will not wait for months whilst their leaders play about showing what skilled negotiators they are and how reasonable and statesmanlike.

No Cause for Alarm

"THE slight variations," says the British Medical Journal, referring to the increase from 1925-34, "are not of significance. They do not, in fact, imply any real increase in malnutrition." These returns being quoted in a "Health of the School Child" report illustrate the delicate shrinking of Whitehall from statistical proof.

In such districts as Lancashire and South Wales, the Rhondda, and Cardiff, one-fifth of the children are classified as short of nourishment.

In many homes fresh milk, first in the list of protective foods, is never bought at all. Not only shortage of food, but lack of sleep and rest, and existence in a home harrowed by the anxiety of unemployment, all prevent the proper development of the child, and lead to the condition known as malnutrition, of which the Medical Officer of Health for Lancashire reports a rise last year of 25 per cent.

AN INVITATION

Write to us, telling us how you think "Action" can be improved. Our address is:—

SANCTUARY BUILDINGS
GREAT SMITH STREET
S.W.1.

Sanctionist Press Blackens the Name of Britain

By
A. K. CHESTERTON

MARSHAL BADOGLIO in recent weeks has done more than defeat the Ethiopian forces. His achievements have led to the rout of the rabble Press army which the British Sanctionists have mobilised against the Italian nation. Each of the great thrusts south, east, and west of Makale has helped to expose newspaper absurdities, repulse newspaper lies, and show up the newspaper prophets as a pack of mendacious hacks.

"Blackshirts can't win battles," screamed "Reynolds's Illustrated News" in January, proceeding to state, in its own epic language: "Badoglio is in a bit of a pickle. If he exclusively employs his best troops, the native Askaris, for 'shock' work, he creates discontent among these fighters. If he employs his own men, whether regular or Blackshirt, he gets beaten."

It is now known that in the recent fighting the Italian white troops were entrusted with most of the storm work, and suffered four casualties to every one suffered by the equally valiant Askaris. Owing to our "glorious democratic liberties," however, it is possible to defame brave men with impunity, and in the pestilential world of modern journalism there is no such thing as the *amende honorable*.

Mere Lies

ON January 1 the "News Chronicle"—of all Sanctionist papers by far the most shrill-voiced, loutish, and hysterical—asserted that the Italian armies in the north had surrendered four thousand square miles of conquered territory, and added: "The war seems to have collapsed dramatically."

Soon after the beginning of the New Year this stupid sheet informed its readers: "Advance in the immediate future is impossible." It went on to talk about "gigantic blunders now realised; Dictator looks for face-saving peace plan," together with a report about "Reverses in Abyssinia, desertions in the South Tyrol, depression in Italy."

The same tune was played by the "Daily Express": "The campaign has gone badly enough for the Italians already. . . . No big drive is possible," it declared only a few weeks ago.

The "Daily Herald," not to be outdone, announced in December: "The Italian invaders of Abyssinia are to-day everywhere on the defensive. It is no longer a question of how far they can pursue a conquering march: it is a question of whether they can hold their line against Abyssinian attack. The initiative has definitely passed to the Abyssinians. Abyssinian morale is high. Italian morale is obviously badly shaken. . . ."

Moonstruck Gossip

"A TERGO," of the "Sunday Referee," that indefatigable garnerer of moonstruck gossip, reported in December: "Italy is on the brink of catastrophe. A push from the inside, delivered by the growing anti-Mussolini forces, or a push from the outside with the tightening of the oil sanction—and over she goes. . . . Mussolini is a desperate man. . . . I learn on good authority that he is in a condition bordering on breakdown."

Amidst this welter of ludicrous reports and sham prophecies, all crammed with the snarling bitterness of small and frightened men, there was only one note of compassion. It came from the large heart of Lord Castlerosse. After lecturing the Italians, telling them that they were making "a terrible and desperate mistake," he went on to say: "How sadly do I write this of our late ally. I would that it were otherwise, and the world could see as I see, for in my eyes constantly is the vision and conception of peace. Therein lies beauty, love, and contentment. . . ."

These noble utterances of a noble, high-souled peer ought surely to have proved the last straw to the poor, misguided Italians.

The Sanctionists Militant

THE net result to date of the offensive conducted by the Sanctionist Press is that the Italian forces, on the day after they were reported to be hemmed in at Makale and receiving their food by aeroplane, began the offensive which smashed the power of the three Abyssinian generals of the northern front and gave the lie direct

Mr. A. K. Chesterton

to the grotesque story of their siege and impending downfall.

That is why I say that more than the Ethiopian armies have been smashed by Italy, the entire conspiracy of Sanctionist lies stands uncovered as the leprous thing that it is. The difference between the two wars now in progress is thrown into the sharpest relief.

One war is being conducted on the actual field of battle, which is always a field of honour, in that those who fight upon it offer to back their causes with their lives. The unspeakable Amharic barbarians at least prove themselves men when they stand their ground awaiting the onslaught of guns and death.

But those whose services are enlisted in the other war—the war on the Sanctionist front—make no such proud offerings in support of their cause, which is best upheld, not by the qualities of manhood, but by all the characteristics that manhood most profoundly loathes.

Their weapons are belittlements and lies. Secure in their Fleet Street funk-holes, they can use their weapons with a rapturous zeal, knowing that their own precious flesh is never likely to be exposed to jagged lumps of red-hot iron.

Gutter-snipers

IT is their proud task to befoul the fair reputation of Italy in the minds of the British people, not simply by condemning an action which they profess not to like, not simply by casting the most unwarrantable aspersions on the courage of the Italian soldiers, but by the employment against the Italian Leader of every device of insult and distortion in their well-stocked armoury of abuse.

There is little to suggest honour in the sight of these little grubs being paid to fling their gutter-snipe sneers at the immense figure of Mussolini, whose achievement it has been to shake a frenzied mob once again into a great and self-respecting nation.

The "Daily Herald," whose every appearance is a reminder of the grotesque Socialist compromise, refers in these words to a man not born for compromise:—

"It is at last being realised that this 'greatest figure of his sphere and time' is a mixture of madman and gangster and intriguer and bombastic actor . . . a saw-dust Caesar."

Most dignified utterances, these! A gesture of peace to the Italian nation, who venerate their leader.

It is left to the "Sunday Referee," though, to let the very high-smelling cat out of the bag. It proves, what we have always known, that the Sanctionists care nothing whatsoever for the Abyssinians or for the ethics of Mussolini's action with regard to them. In concert with other journals, it turned screaming against France when the French made a move to establish peace, which the Sanctionists claim to be their sole desire. The "Sunday Referee" described the French move as the "incorrigible M. Laval's latest peace intrigues!"

That Britain should be so foully misrepresented by the hyenas of its Press is a national disgrace. When Fascism comes to power in this country immediate steps will be taken against newspapers which have forgotten the very name of British honour, and which delight to present the heroic British race as being cast in their own rat-like image.

The River Forth from the air.

FORTH BRIDGE SCANDAL

SHAMELESS WESTMINSTER TREATMENT OF SCOTTISH NEEDS

By R. A. PLATHEN

THE idea of bridging the River Forth at Queensferry, to provide an extension of the Great North Road and to open a way between Edinburgh and the North, was originated in 1923 by Mr. J. Inglis Ker, F.R.S. Edinburgh.

Twelve years of patient research and careful inquiry by men of integrity, enjoying the confidence of a widely representative community and acting unselfishly in the interests of a large part of Scotland, are disposed of by the Minister of Transport in a letter to the Town Clerk of Edinburgh, in which he turns down the whole proposition.

Committee of Inquiry

THE apparently prohibitive cost caused a shock and local interest waned, until the energy of the directors of the Leith Chamber of Commerce brought about the formation of a Committee of Inquiry. Under the leadership of Major J. MacDonald Smith, chairman of Leith Chamber of Commerce, this committee diligently investigated the proposals from every possible angle, including alternative suggestions involving less capital expenditure.

In 1931 the committee published their reports and findings. The economic situation at the time discouraged any attempt to carry the matter further.

By 1933, however, the national situation had so far improved to permit of the question being opened again. An enlarged Joint Committee of Inquiry, embracing, in addition to the bodies already mentioned, also the Automobile Association, Edinburgh; Leith Shipowners' Society; Royal Scottish Automobile Club, Glasgow; and the Publicity Club of Edinburgh, took the matter in hand.

The Focal Point

THE committee of 1931 had found that the construction of a road bridge "was the final solution of the problem." The committee of 1933 regarded it as "the ideal means of vehicular traffic crossing the Forth."

For instance, it was shown that while there is a population of only 94,000 within an eleven miles radius of Stirling Bridge, which at present carries the bulk of the road traffic to the North, a bridge at Queensferry would serve a population of 680,000 within the same compass.

A Great Saving

THE added convenience and the time and mileage saved were demonstrated by the following figures:—

	Via Queens-ferry.	Via Stir-ling.	Miles Saved.
Edinburgh—Kirkcaldy ...	25	74½	49½
" —Dunfermline	15½	56½	41½
" —Perth	43½	69½	26
Linlithgow—Kirkcaldy ...	25½	57½	32

In predicting the traffic to be carried by the proposed bridge, the committee had no proper basis on which to work, and were obliged to extend their inquiries over a wide sphere. They took into account the figures of the Government road traffic census, and made allowances for local and through traffic. It was estimated that the daily crossings would range from 6-8,000 up to 12,000, as the public adjusted themselves to the new facilities.

The Financial Aspect

THE financial aspect of the scheme can best be described in the words of their memorandum:—

The question of financing the construction and upkeep of a road bridge is recognised to be of the utmost importance, but in the light of all the foregoing it is submitted:

1. That this scheme is one of necessary road improvement coming within the resources of the Road Fund for the provision of capital expenditure, or, alternatively, to be met as outlined hereunder.

2. That construction is justified by either means on account of the abnormal times through which the country is passing. Unemployment is so great that men and construction plant are standing idle. The scheme has undoubted support from the standpoint of traffic value, and it is pregnant with the highest form of reproductive utility.

3. It is a self-supporting proposition capable, from its own revenue, of freeing itself within a reasonable period.

Grant Refused

FINALLY, the scheme was presented to the Minister of Transport with an application for a grant of £3,250,000 from the Road Fund. His reply was:

"The Minister . . . is not convinced on the information now before him that the project possesses sufficient justification. . . ."

In the light of the submissions made, Mr. Hore-Belisha's reply is an insult to the intelligence and integrity of the public bodies that have given the matter such careful and conscientious consideration.

What greater justification can there be than (1) the needs of a great and growing industrial and agricultural population; (2) the convenience of thousands of road users; (3) the saving of time and distance, often enabling business to be transacted in a day where more time is required under present conditions; (4) the establishment of a connection between two sections of the Great North Road, built at enormous expense and now linked only by a very inadequate and expensive ferry service; (5) the contribution towards a reduction in unemployment and the restoration, possibly, of hundreds of families to standards which have been denied them for years; (6) the recovery of expenditure, capital or otherwise, through the payment of tolls?

Economic Aspects

THE economic aspects of the scheme have already been made known to the Minister in so far as the financial estimates are based on the Survey and Report of the Government's agents who investigated the technical feasibility of the project, and on traffic predictable from calculations made with the Government's Road Traffic Census of 1931.

Mr. Hore-Belisha is reported as having stated in the House of Commons on February 19 last, "I have merely asked for evidence that this project is justified on traffic grounds."

Responsible men, elected by the people to represent their interests, have found that a road bridge is essential to the welfare of the community and the development of the land. They are justified in expecting assistance from the Road Fund created for such purposes.

The Minister of Transport has all the relevant material before him.

He could serve the community. He seems to prefer to serve the interests vested in the present inadequate facilities.

OUR SHORT STORY

STATELY SHIP

BY FRANK H. SHAW

JOE LEAROYD was just out of his time and a journeyman rivetter when it was arranged to build the Colossus at Starkley; and along with a few hundred others like himself, he applied for work at the shipbuilding yard—which wasn't much of a yard at best. But for reasons best known to themselves the future owners of the Colossus had given the contract to Smythe and Wetherby, in face of keen competition.

Starkley was, as its best friends admitted, a one-horse spot, and its name best described it. It was stark and forlorn and ugly; but once the keelplates of the Colossus were laid, a rugged beauty of purposeful utility began to inform the district.

Prosperity was begotten and the rattle of the rivetting hammers set up a song that, the years were to prove, grew into a thunderous chorus of achievement, re-echoing round the world; for the Colossus was the fore-runner of a noble fleet of ships whose bows tore all the seven seas into gleaming foam.

JOE LEAROYD put all he knew into his job, once he was taken on at Smythe and Wetherby's. He was a good craftsman, who believed in going a yard or two along the second mile; and in a way a sense of gratitude possessed him; since securing steady employment made it possible for him to put a long-cherished plan into execution, whereby he was able to marry Mary Roberts, whose people gave themselves airs, because they kept the general shop. Joe hoped in time to become a foreman; Mary spurred him on to dream that in a far-off distant day he would rise to the giddy rank of yard-manager.

NOT only Joe worked hard at the Colossus: a few hundred other grimy, muscular men, not much given to smiling or light badinage, did the same. These iron men of the North sang hymns as a recreation, or attended clandestine cock-fights; but they were undoubtedly craftsmen; and out of their single-minded zeal the Colossus grew to be a ship of infinite beauty: a picture of a ship, about which artists raved, naming her the lineal descendant of the white-winged beauties which had made England's sea-history a triumphant paean.

It was, for all the world, as if the single-minded efforts of that hard-bitten army had inspired the Colossus with a something approximating a soul. On her first voyage she made history by hurrying through a snorting Atlantic gale to bring rescue to seven hundred panic-stricken people aboard a blazing Italian liner.

No other ship could have stayed the course in the same short time; but the Colossus did it, with margin enough to save the terrified emigrants a night in an open boat with a temperature running down towards zero. A lot of the women had young babies, who must have died of exposure.

JOE LEAROYD was proud when he read the accounts in the newspapers, because he felt—every man in Starkley felt the same—that he had borne a hand in that phenomenal rescue. It was the staunchness of their handiwork that enabled the Colossus to endure the Atlantic rigours; and that same craftsmanship enabled the great and lovely ship to capture the record for speed and hold it during many years.

Naturally enough, other ships were ordered from the Starkley yards. The prosperity, begun when the Colossus's keel-plates were laid, continued unabated; enhanced, rather. Ship after ship left the ways—proud ships, humble ships, but all of them were characterised by a certain quality of workmanship that made them renowned the wide world over. And in most of these stately bottoms Joe Learoyd bore a share.

MARY made him a good wife in her quiet, unemotional way. She was proud of his capabilities, because she had endured the scoffings of her family when she, a tradesman's daughter, decided to throw in her lot with an artisan; but Joe was made foreman at a surprisingly early age; and a foreman with Smythe and Wetherby was a person of no little importance. The time came when Mary, then nursing her fourth child, was given a little maid-of-all-work, which was more than her mother had ever had. There was a piano in the Learoyd parlour on which Mary used to batter out hymns which the children sang in ragged, shrill voices.

When the war broke out Joe Learoyd felt it his duty to go and fight for England, and his six children—to say nothing of Mary herself.

But he was told that he was indispensable: any man could fire a rifle or dig a trench or throw a bomb; but not every man could help to build warships fit to keep the enemy from violating England's coasts. Furthermore, it was pointed out: think of the wages of a head-foreman in a premier shipbuilding yard as compared with those of a middle-aged private in the Northern Fusiliers, which was the local regiment!

Joe, reading of things done here and there the world over, gritted his teeth and longed for the satisfaction of personal retaliation; but when he heard that the Cockatrice—he was pretty nearly completely in charge of her building—had sunk two submarines to her own cheek, he began to see reason. His eldest son became of an age sufficient to allow him to represent the family in uniform before the Armistice was called; he was a sergeant and a V.C., when one of the last bullets fired in the war struck him down fatally. During all the troubled years Starkley worked well: ship after fighting ship left the launching ways, to go out and do battle for Britain's honour and safety. The stately Colossus carried uncounted legions of warriors to most parts of the world as a transport, until she was converted into a hospital ship and turned from conquest to a work of healing.

THERE was no shadow of doubt that the Colossus had made Starkley's name. Why, the world over, a Starkley-built ship meant a ship as near perfection as human skill could make her. And owing to the loss of tonnage during hostilities and the need to replace such casualties, the building yards at Starkley remained active for quite a while after the world's bugles sang truce.

But then it was discovered that there was not enough trade to keep ships fully employed. A period of heavy depression set in; every harbour in the country filled with idle, rusting tonnage—Starkley ships amongst them. Orders fell off: folks had no money remaining to spend on expensive travel.

Foreign countries, driven to utilise their own resources when British yards were too busily employed to court their commissions, found themselves able to supply their own needs.

The prosperity that had made Starkley blossom faded away into gaunt distress. Unemployment grew rife. Joe had trained his sons to become expert shipbuilding men; but expert as they were there was presently no work for them to lay their skilled hands to. One or two, already married to wives who had not learnt Mary's canny thriftiness, left the district to seek occupation in the more promising South.

Feeling that the slump could not long endure, Joe and Mary lived much as they had lived from the beginning. They found themselves able to assist their daughters when their husbands fell idle and were compelled—bitter-hearted, for they were a proud breed—to draw unemployment pay.

"THINGS'LL tak' up yet," surmised Joe, as he had surmised in his young manhood when a rainy morning docked him of a quarter day's pay. "This sort o' thing never lasts, owd lass."

But it did last. It presently became necessary to dispose of the piano, on which Joe could play fit to stir the strings of the soul. It was sold in a glutted market. Other items of furnishing followed. Bitterly, Joe was compelled to draw unemployment pay for his own part.

The great cranes and gantries at Smythe and Wetherby's rusted forlornly; the ways were overgrown; the river silted up. Gaunt want reared its spectre head on that grim coast. Years of it persisted; and all the heart-felt services in the chapels seemed in vain.

Starkley became a derelict area, officially listed as such. Smythe and Wetherby, after making desperate efforts to survive, went under. The one-time sturdy workers became thin and peevish. A new generation was growing up with no future ahead of it. Well-meant schemes of relief could only mitigate, not cure, the ever-growing malady.

"GOD, oh, God, send *work*!" Joe Learoyd prayed. He saw his sons lose heart and drift away with revolutionary blasphemies on their lips. He saw their sons idle, with no chance to learn a trade to fill their mouths with food.

"It'll tak' up yet," he tried to console Mary, herself pallid and gaunt and underfed, because she had a trick of sparing food from their meagre supply to fill even hungrier mouths than their own. "Trust i' God, owd lass—He'll ne'er let Starkley down!"

"Ay, lad, I'm trustin'—I'm trustin'—hard," agreed Mary. "But it fair racks me to see them lads a mouchin' around doin' nowt."

"It'll tak' up, Mary."

AND then the whisper went the rounds, kindling extinguished fires in staring eyes, flushing parchment-yellow cheeks. Starkley was to waken from her long coma at last. The Colossus, that had made the district's fame, was coming back, on her last forlorn voyage; coming back to be broken up, her period of usefulness at an end. Their lovely ship: their pride—to be torn piecemeal as a carcase in a knacker's yard!

She came, stripped to her naked hide, and men deplored her lonely wistfulness; she the most beautiful ship the East Coast had ever launched. But room was made for her; and for the first time for a handful of years the steam-whistle blew, summoning hungry men from idleness to toil. Joe Learoyd answered that call—not as a foreman, but as a labourer; for there were foremen enough and to spare. In common with a couple of hundred needy men he was given employment—he became again a man.

"IT'S a pity," deplored Jim Formby, placing the chisel against a rivet-head for Joe's sledge to strike the first blow that should result in the stately Colossus's extermination as a ship. "Her 'at we slaved at to make a lovely thing!"

"Ay, mebbe!" said Joe, and there was a half-forgotten ring in his burred voice. "Mebbe! I druv this identical rivet mysen. But—this ain't her end, by no means, Jim. Mebbe it's hunger makes me fey; but—things'll tak' up yet—and likely you'n me'll see this steel start to build a bonnier ship nor her. Th' Lord's wunnerful way o' manifestin' Himsel'—likely this is one such. Likely prosperity an' health's come back to Starkley along wi' th' ship she built. To my mind, we that was so proud o' th' owd Colossus'll yet go down on our knees an' call blessin's on her name!"

CAPT. FRANK SHAW has been well known as a writer of sea and air stories for the last 40 years. As far back as 1900 he was writing stories foretelling the Great War. He went to sea early and served before the mast. During the War he served as a balloon officer with the R.F.C.

SPORT

By A. G. FINDLEY

ATHLETICS

Cross Country

ON Saturday the National Cross Country Championship will be held at Alderley Edge, Cheshire, and a great struggle is expected between the leaders to fill the first nine places, in view of the fact that from these will be chosen the English team for the International Race at Blackpool on March 28.

Jack Holden, who has won three International Championships, will be competing. He has yet to win a national title, but I expect something better from him on this occasion, as he has already won the two chief events of this season. Very little information is forthcoming from the northerners, but it will not be a surprise if they fill five of the first nine places.

Sam Ferris, the marathon champion, is now on his way to India, and is, unfortunately, definitely out of the Olympic arena.

Lovelock's Rival

WHILE Jack Lovelock has been fighting his way to victory in the Hospitals Boxing competition, his chief rival on the track, Glen Cunningham, has been having a bad spell.

He seems to be losing his form, and the Americans are getting worried, as they have to find a team for the Olympic Games next August.

In the last few weeks Cunningham has twice lost on indoor tracks. First Joe Mangan and Gene Venzke finished in front of him at Manhattan, and Venzke beat him again a week or so later.

Is It Staleness?

IT seems that Cunningham is passing through the bad spell which similarly affected Lovelock last season, when the latter lost to Wooderson.

At one time there was a doubt about Lovelock appearing at Berlin, but there now seems to be every likelihood that he will be there. The leg injury he received in Oxford Rugby does not now trouble him much, and he is getting back to fitness.

FOOTBALL

This Pool Business

I HEAR that a certain individual from Ireland has written a letter to a well-known goalkeeper suggesting that, when playing at home, he should let through one or two "soft" ones. The writer states that he intends backing all away teams on his coupon, and that there will be "thousands in it for them." Of course, the goalkeeper concerned referred the letter to his directorate, who, in turn, reported to the Football League.

Although this sounds a little fantastic, it helps to prove there is a possibility of the danger of bribery entering into football, based on the large individual prizes offered by the present Pools.

It also strengthens my suggestion made two weeks ago, that pool betting should be officially controlled by the Football Association. The pool promoters say they are not interested in "who" wins the prizes offered—that is where the danger lies; their disinterestedness of the game itself. If controlled officially, a great deal of information would be available for use of the F.A., which would help them to detect any underhand work attempted. The prizes should be made smaller and more numerous; this, in itself, would minimise danger of bribery.

Arsenal v. Huddersfield

AT Highbury last Saturday Huddersfield sprang a surprise by taking a point from the Gunners. Only a week previously Blackburn drew at Huddersfield, and the Rovers are the present wooden spooonists.

The stage seemed set for a home victory as Arsenal had a fairly strong team out, but the forwards were not so sure as usual.

Huddersfield crossed over with the lead, and after a ding-dong struggle in the second half the persistence of the home forwards enabled them to draw level.

The goal scored by the Huddersfield leader was about the only shot he had. The game more or less developed on defensive lines, and a considerable amount of spoiling and kicking out was done by the Huddersfield defenders. During this half Young, the centre-half, outshone stopper Roberts.

The "save-at-any-cost" policy of Huddersfield was negatived a few minutes from the end by a brilliant goal from Bastin from the edge of the penalty area.

Watching Brief of Grimsby

IT was interesting to hear that George Allison and Abe Jones, of the Arsenal, were at Wolverhampton last Saturday watching Grimsby, their Semi-Final opponents. They did not see much. League games and Cup games are things apart, and Grimsby can certainly show more thrust than they did in this game.

It seems rather peculiar to say that if Grimsby do not arrive on the Wembley road they will have lost money on the Cup. The postponement of League fixtures is the cause, and they have received a claim for £650 from Bolton for compensation, and are expecting similar claims from Middlesbrough, Wolves and Sunderland.

While the position is only fair to the clubs applying for compensation, it appears a little hard on the club who is forced to pay for success in the Cup. Perhaps the Football Association could do something in the matter, from the large resources they themselves have obtained from that source.

Football Shorts

"PROUD Preston" are out to make an effort to prove their title. After being without a manager for four years, they are trying to obtain one of the best-known in first-class football.

Aston Villa have enough players on their books to run five professional teams.

Arsenal are still looking for a first-class goalkeeper. Peter McWilliam was at Fulham last week to watch Fairhurst, of Bury. Fulham scored seven times, so Fairhurst can consider himself an unlucky young man.

Ball, the Luton centre-forward, was called before his directors recently—to receive thanks for his sportsmanship. That's the stuff, Luton!

Aston Villa's League position looks like costing Massie and Cummings their Scottish caps at the Wembley International.

Dawson, Simpson, Smith and McPhail, of the Rangers, appear to be the only certainties for the Scottish team against England.

Bath City are to make another attempt to gain admission to the Football League.

Falling gates have caused Notts County to make it known they are willing to talk business about several of their players.

OLYMPIC GAMES

AS a large amount of propaganda and ballyhoo has been given to the Olympic Games to be held in Germany; and as some people are finding it easy to suggest sinister motives behind Germany's effort in sport, extracts from a letter to the Press by the captain of the British Olympic figure-skating team, who was also attaché to Mr. Evan Hunter and Lord Aberdare—jointly responsible for the British delegation—would not be out of place.

"Sport in Germany . . . is producing in the young a sense of duty, a respect for discipline, a realisation of their obligations to their country, and that by them and their behaviour is their country judged. Were this spirit inculcated even a little into our young athletes, many of whom seem to imagine that as soon as they are out of their own country any sort of behaviour is permissible, nothing but good could come of it.

CRICKET

The Don Still Flows

AT Adelaide, Bradman reduced batting to mere mechanics, cracked on 100 runs in forty minutes, and hit up a South Australian record of 356.

When Bradman was over here we were told he was a sick man. Or so they said. He proved in the Tests how wrong these people were.

Up to two years ago he was a very serious Bradman, but since that time he has changed and is considerably more care-free. It is suggested that the reason for this change was the young Sydney girl he married, and that she altered his mental outlook and made him understand that cricket was only a game; the advice acted like a tonic.

Since Bradman has been with South Australia, young Badcock has improved considerably under his influence, as witness recent scores.

What about England's young men? We have some coming along, but not enough. There is Hardstaff, of Notts, Read, of Essex, E. R. T. Holmes, and others. Herbert Sutcliffe believes that Hutton, of Yorkshire, is the future master batsman; it looks an accurate prophecy.

An incident in the Arsenal v. Huddersfield match

BOXING

McAvoy's Match

ALTHOUGH Jock McAvoy is a first-class fighter, I am a little sceptical about the outcome of his fight with Petersen in April at Earl's Court. McAvoy is a middle-weight, and, no matter how good he is, the odds should be in favour of the heavier man. Len Harvey, who is a light heavyweight, will confirm this. If McAvoy does confound us with a win, he will certainly earn the title of being called "an extraordinary boxer."

Wednesday of this week saw a show by ten talented boxers at the Albert Hall in aid of the Jewish Fund, in front of a packed and glittering house. It is a pity that some of the punch-drunk, ex-five-bob-a-fight pugilists were not resurrected from the scrapheap and given the "honour" of also helping this fund.

Can anybody tell me why these periodical displays are so well advertised, "house full" notices exhibited, with programmes composed of fighters of championship rank, when one hardly ever hears of a similar display for the benefit of an English charity? Perhaps the nationality of the greater number of promoters and managers has some bearing on the question?

RADIO FLASHES

By BLUEBIRD

I SUPPOSE it is because of the association with Canon Sheppard that I have always imagined that anything emanating from St. Martin-in-the-Field must be tainted with that cleric's special brand of sob-stuff pacifism. His moans and groans on behalf of Abyssinians and his diatribes against manliness stir in one such feelings of repulsion that I now never listen to him if I have any choice.

But on Sunday evening I happened to listen to the sermon from St. Martin's by the Vicar, the Rev. Pat McCormick. To my surprise, I heard a manly sermon, preaching pure Fascism. I rather wondered whether Mr. McCormick knew that he was preaching true Fascism, and whether the knowledge that he was preaching Fascism was or is news to him. Fascism really is what every true Britisher believes in his heart, and were it not that Fascism is deliberately misrepresented by its enemies, Mosley would already be in power in Britain to-day.

After the service and the usual silliness which is called "news," there was a splendid popular concert from Eastbourne, marred only by a singer called Mavis Bennett-Levin, who even succeeded in making one of the Christopher Robin songs sound sloppy!

Earlier in the evening the B.B.C. put over a very fine performance of "Henry VIII." Every part was played superbly well.

In the afternoon I had listened to a concert from Radio-Normandie. In the space of about an hour there were at least four technical breakdowns. Whatever are the shortcomings of our B.B.C. on the programme side, it does seem to be almost perfect on the mechanical side. This is to be expected, as it is built of British material entirely, which statement is not true of the programme side. It is all the sadder, therefore, that the skill of British engineers should be used for propaganda which, to say the least, is not always in the best interests of Britain.

The "Spy at Rippingham" fizzled out with a futile ending. The great joy of a "twopenny blood" is that it always has a sensational if improbable ending. This serial had a flat ending with no point in it, and one that was quite impossible.

But I suppose that to the B.B.C. whose officials seem to believe implicitly the Addis Ababa communiques and give them out as gospel truth, the story may have sounded quite sensible.

I have never heard a more revoltingly sanctimonious tone than that adopted by the announcer who read the B.B.C.'s story of the alleged bombing of the British ambulance in Abyssinia.

I tuned-in once or twice during Saturday night to the German rejoicings over the Rhineland affair. Our own B.B.C. rises well to a solemn occasion, but they do not know how to put over a joyful occasion. The Germans do. One could hear the spontaneous cheering and rejoicings in the streets, and the singing of patriotic songs. At 11 p.m. the broadcast from the streets stopped suddenly, and there burst forth the gloriously triumphant strains of the overture to the "Mastersingers." It was magnificently done. Incidentally, when the B.B.C. Orchestra, Section E (doesn't it sound dull), played the same overture on Sunday evening it sounded merely ordinary.

I had intended to advise my readers to listen to Mr. Ivor McClure's talk on aviation on March 2, but, unfortunately, I forgot. Mr. McClure always combines humour and common sense, and this talk was no exception. He was most exhilarating. He began by telling us that flying was very dangerous, and then proceeded, by recounting an episode of a cloud flight, to explain how absolutely safe flying can be if the right precautions are taken.

Mr. George Robey again broadcasts on Friday and Saturday. He is likely to be as amusing and instructive, in a different manner, as Mr. McClure.

BEHIND THE NEWS

Alien Over-crowding

SOMEBODY, somewhere, once said that there was an unemployment problem involving some two million British men and women, many hundred thousands of black-coated workers and agricultural labourers were without relief, the value of wages had gone down because cost of living had soared up.

Knowing how "National" our Government is, we must have said good-bye to all that, for, in 1934, 373,965 aliens entered this country. Last year 404,014 foreign ex-subjects, mostly Jews from Germany, sought asylum in United Kingdom. During first two months of 1936 the average rate of last year has been maintained, if not exceeded.

London and Manchester are principal sufferers. In Bloomsbury, Limehouse, and Soho thousands of aliens are herded into houses. In Manchester, Cheetham Hill district, there are nearly four long streets filled with Jews from Germany. Manchester waterproof garment factories are overrun with aliens, yet British workers find it difficult to get employment. A weekly newspaper in German starts publication this month.

During past three years a million aliens have come to England seeking asylum, while unemployed Britons are constantly being taken to one—the rate of inmates to our mental homes has also increased during past three years.

How long, O Simon, how long?

The Vultures Gather

"VETERAN brothers-in-arms, looking forward to bigger and better booming, met last week in a discreet hotel at Cannes on the French Riviera. Bethlehem Steel represented America; Krupp, Germany; Vickers, Britain; and Schneider and Skoda, France and Czecho-Slovakia.

"'Authoritative sources,' said that Sir Basil Zaharoff, dark angel of the underworld would come out of his burrow at nearby Monte Carlo to join the secret session."—"News-Week."

Communists Mostly Yiddish

IN Moscow Roosevelt has been called "the first Communist President of the U.S.A." Bernard Shaw recently dubbed Roosevelt as a Communist.

In the Fish Report to Congress, January, 1931, it is stated:—

"A large percentage of all known Communistic district organisers are of Jewish origin. The largest daily American Communist newspaper is published in New York in Yiddish."

Big Increase in U.S.A. Workless

UNITED STATES unemployment figures for January: 12,626,000, showing increase of 1,229,000 in one month.

Although Roosevelt claimed to have done away with child labour under National Recovery Administration, Children's Bureau records 58 per cent. increase in child labour since last May, when the Supreme Court squashed N.R.A. While millions of adults vainly seek work.

Alberta's Social Credit Budget

THE first Budget presented by the Social Credit Government of Alberta has sadly disappointed voters who were promised an effortless monthly income of £5 a head. Its main feature is substantially increased taxation. Income tax is increased to provide 85 per cent. more revenue and a new 2 per cent. sales tax is introduced. The Budget provides for a total deficit of £509,800 in the coming year.

South Wales Coal Trade Worsens

MR. R. FINLAY GIBSON, Secretary of Monmouthshire and South Wales Coal Owners, paints black picture of declining coal trade. Production and exports, he said, were lower in 1935 than in the previous twelve months. Decrease in production during the year amounted to 156,084 tons, and in exports 670,951 tons.

Conditions in the foreign trade in 1935 were the worst for nine years. Exports from the Bristol Channel to Italy fell by 870,000 tons; to France, 79,000 tons. Exports in January and February of this year were about £400,000 less than in the same period last year.

Mr. Marchbank Celebrates

ACCORDING to a newspaper, Mr. John Marchbank recently held what is amusingly described as a "Victory Dinner" to celebrate the result of Sir Oswald Mosley's libel action against him. Found guilty in the High Court of a grave offence, not everybody would claim it as a legal victory. But it seems Mr. Marchbank and his friends had felt so certain of defeat and "financial ruin" that the result was a delightful surprise. Certainly, those who saw him in the box and heard his evidence will not be surprised that Mr. Marchbank should feel a very deep relief when the case was over.

Among the guests at this happy party of friends—"which testified to the sympathy

Mr. John Marchbank

felt with Mr. Marchbank and his wife in the anxiety they had been through"—were many bitter enemies of Fascism, including Sir Walter Citrine, Mr. Arthur Greenwood, M.P., and Mr. Joseph Henderson, M.P., in whose Social-Democratic bonnets the Fascist bee buzzes and stings most violently.

The Tithe War

SUFFOLK has had a stirring "call to battle."

It was made at a mass meeting of tithepayers at Ipswich, when the following resolution was passed amid enthusiasm:

"That this meeting of tithepayers, whilst appreciating the fact that to some extent their contentions are upheld in the report of the Royal Commission, at the same time considers that not even the Commission's proposals, much less those of the Government, in any way represent elementary justice to tithepayers, and should be strenuously opposed."

The occasion was the annual meeting of the Suffolk Tithepayers' Association. In presenting the report, the secretary (Mr. P. J. Butler) said that progress had been hindered by the Government's delay in issuing the report of the Royal Commission. Now that the report had appeared tithepayers could claim to have reached the most critical stage in their struggle.

The President congratulated tithepayers in Suffolk on the splendid fight they had put up.

"Suffolk has been right in the forefront from the start," he declared.

He added that the new proposals would bring to the countryside, not peace, but a sword; not harmony, but striving, bitterness, and contention.

"I say to the Government and to the Church that this industry through long years has been patient—patient when it meant sacrifice and loss. The sands have run out and there can be no peace unless they are prepared to concede to us elementary justice."

Red Gold

MR. G. WARD PRICE, the well-known journalist who has never tired in his efforts to expose the underground machinations of the Soviet—who will forget his exposure of the Communist plans in the "Sunday Dispatch" after the Battle of Olympia?—has turned his searchlight on Spain, and in a recent article in the "Daily Mail" informs us that the Moscow payroll in Madrid amounts to just over £40,000 a year.

He then goes on to give an account of how that money is spent, and shows how £2,500 is spent each month in subsidising newspapers. £816 goes to sixty-eight Communist party officials in Spain, who receive a wage of £12 per month, and £300 per month is used for "special propaganda purposes." Presumably this means the firearms which the Red comrades of Spain have not scrupled to use.

If the Soviet spends £40,000 a year on a country like Spain, how much more must it expend on a "valuable" country like Great Britain?

The Time Has Come . . .

THE time has come, the Government said, to talk of many things . . . Last week, amidst a welter of discussion upon moustaches, bail, ex-convicts, health resorts, and watering places (oh, la, la!), Mexican cigarettes, linoleum and floorcloth, Hyde Park lighting, and other important national matters, the Government found time to talk of Air Raid Precautions.

One Hon. Member set the ball rolling by asking the Home Secretary whether he will arrange for members to attend a demonstration of the gas-mask to be used by civilians.

The Under-Secretary of State for the Home Department replied: "When the design of the respirator referred to is finally settled, I hope that Hon. Members will not merely attend, but will also test for themselves the efficacy of the respirator in various concentrations of poison gases."

The Hon. Member for the Scotland Division of Liverpool, then asked a really unkind question. He asked, "Is there any intention of using the apparatus in this House?"

JEWS ATTACK BRITONS

THREE CONVICTED ON POLICE EVIDENCE

ALLEGATIONS of "incitement to violence" on the part of Fascists were strongly denied by Manchester police officers at the resumed hearing to-day of charges against three men who were accused of an attack on Blackshirts, assault on the police, attempted rescue, and wilful damage to a tramcar window.

Officer after officer spoke of the peaceful attitude of Blackshirts when they left a meeting at Cheetham Public Hall (in the heart of Manchester Jewry) on February 27, and the prosecution produced a large stone and a metal knuckle-duster said to have been flung at the tramcar by one or other of the defendants.

The charges were brought against Reuben Craft, aged twenty-two, of Broughton-street, Cheetham; Joshua Davidson, aged twenty-one, of Bignor-street, Cheetham; and Louis Black, aged thirty-one, of George-street, Broughton. All three were charged with behaving in a disorderly manner, whereby a breach of the peace might have been caused; Craft was accused, in addition, of wilful damage to a tramcar window to the extent of 15s., by flinging a stone through it, and with assaulting P.C. Kendrick; Black was further accused of obstructing the police in the execution of their duty by attempting to rescue Craft from police custody; and Davidson was further charged with assaulting P.C. Parker by kicking him in the stomach.

Prosecuting, Mr. G. M. Fearnley, of the Town Clerk's Department, said both the Fascist meeting and a protest meeting against it, held on a nearby croft, were quite peaceful, and it was only when there was a rush for a tramcar, after a number of Blackshirts had boarded it, that the trouble began. He alleged that the crowd, which had apparently come largely from the protest meeting, completely blocked the tramcar, and that they started a free fight on the tramcar platform. The police interfered, and then occurred the incidents which he thought had amply justified the charges being brought.

During police evidence in support of the charges, one officer denied that there was any sort of row started by the Fascist element. He said the Blackshirts who had boarded the tramcar had their backs turned when the assault on the car took place, amid cries of "Down with the Blackshirts." He also denied that a woman who was with the Blackshirts screamed out: "Down with the dirty —— Sheenies."

Sergeant Green was more emphatic in these denials. He declared that there was no doubt it was the Jewish element which started the row.

Mr. Hinchcliffe was suggesting that the "Blackshirts had come to the wrong district to be awkward," when the police sergeant said if he had seen any Blackshirts creating a row he would have interfered and probably taken them into custody.

The Stipendiary Magistrate (Mr. J. Wellesley Orr) observed: Why should you assume that they would not arrest Fascists? The police would arrest anyone if they caused a disturbance. The police have nothing to do with political opinions.

Mr. Hinchcliffe: I am only saying that my men in this mêlée got more than they gave. We say that the Fascists shouted: "Wipe these so-and-so Jews off the face of the earth."

The police sergeant said he heard no remark of that kind. On the other hand, Davidson was inciting the crowd to pull the Fascists off the car.

According to later police evidence, the stone produced was thrown through the tramcar window by Craft, and the knuckle-duster produced (which Mr. Hinchcliffe denied was ever in the possession of any of the defendants) was thrown by Davidson, being picked up after it had struck the back of the tramcar.

Another officer said there were no inflammatory speeches about Jews at the Fascists' meeting.

A tram guard said the behaviour of the Blackshirts when they boarded the tramcar was quite normal.

Each of the defendants denied all the charges and declared that they were themselves set upon and badly mauled by Blackshirts.

Craft was fined 20s. for assaulting the officer, and 20s. and the cost of the damage to the car window. Davidson was fined 20s. for kicking another officer, and Black was also fined 20s. for attempting to rescue a prisoner.

Printed by ARGUS PRESS, LTD., Temple Avenue and Tudor Street, London, E.C.4, England, and published by ACTION PRESS, LTD., Sanctuary Buildings, Gt. Smith Street, London, S.W.1, England. All inquiries regarding advertisements should be addressed to the Advertisement Manager, ACTION PRESS, LTD., Sanctuary Buildings, Great Smith Street, Westminster, S.W.1. Telephone: Victoria 9083 (6 lines).

No. 17 [REGISTERED AT THE G.P.O. AS A NEWSPAPER.] "BRITAIN FIRST" JUNE 11, 1936

FOR KING AND PEOPLE

R.S.17

FOUNDATIONS OF FASCISM

By **MARSHAL BADOGLIO**

See page 6

HEART OF AN EMPIRE

London's East End, claimed by the Socialists as a "Red Stronghold," gave a wonderful reception to Sir Oswald Mosley, Leader of the British Union of Fascists, on Sunday.

Blackshirts marched through East London amid scenes of unparalleled enthusiasm. People crowded the pavements, leant from windows; hundreds saluted the Blackshirt standards as they passed.

"It is your last opportunity to drive Fascism out of the East End," screamed a Communist speaker to a crowd round a platform in Victoria Park. But neither Red violence nor Red oratory prevailed, and the "last opportunity" passed and was lost.

Never before has the East End witnessed such scenes. Over 100,000 people crowded Victoria Park and cheered Sir Oswald. To the Blackshirts the demonstration was more than an immense and successful rally. Held on the anniversary of the great indoor meeting at Olympia in 1934 it symbolised the triumph of the Blackshirt Movement over the violence of Red hooliganism. In the two years since the Olympia meeting Fascism has won the hearts of the people. How great that victory has been was seen on Sunday when a huge crowd listened to Sir Oswald with an attention such as is seldom accorded to speakers at open-air meetings.

The lethargy and cowardice of Conservatism left the East End to the Socialists: the failure and betrayal of Socialism has discredited forever the so-called leaders of the working classes. Sunday's demonstration proved that although Conservatism has run away and Socialism has collapsed, Fascism can still arouse in the hearts of the people a great enthusiasm for the cause of Britain.

The Blackshirts' column, over half a mile in length, included men and women members of the Blackshirt Movement, the majority of them wearing black shirts. Members of the Youth Movement, also marched. Throughout the march the Fascists received an enthusiastic and friendly reception, which reached its peak on their arrival at the Park. When they left, a dense mass of people crowded round the head of the column cheering and saluting Sir Oswald.

Part of the huge crowd at Victoria Park.

EAST LONDON TRIUMPH—See page 7

The World, The Flesh— and Financial Democracy

A Weekly Review of Men and Events

By WILLIAM JOYCE

EAST London is a place where the English people are poor and where, to men and women of lesser courage, life would present a drab and sordid, unrelieved monotony. Indeed, those of our people who do not understand the meaning of poverty must wonder how the English people in the East End manage to live at all.

On Sunday it was evident not only that the people were alive, but that in them had been reborn that spirit of vitality which has made the British Empire. For, as Sir Oswald Mosley, at the head of his Blackshirts, marched to his gigantic meeting in Victoria Park, he was accorded by these simple English men and women who lined the streets a triumph which, in its spontaneity and plain sincerity, must have been nobler than any triumph given by the ancient Romans to their victorious leaders.

Out of every side street little children came running, and shouting, as they ran, "Up, the Blackshirts!" I thought, as I saw them, of the day when they would maintain the achievements of National Socialism being won and to be won by Sir Oswald Mosley.

History in broad and general is not lacking in irony, but the grimness of its humour is not always so apparent in so short a period as two years.

A Famous Victory

JUNE 7, the day selected for the great East End demonstration, was the second anniversary of Olympia, but it was not of Olympia that I thought. No more trenchant contrast have I ever known than that between the Hyde Park rally of September, 1934, and this greater rally which the Blackshirts have just held. It must be admitted that in Hyde Park there were thousands of people who were prevented by the Jewish Red Front from hearing a word the speakers said.

Enormous as was the crowd in Victoria Park, the interruption was negligible, and every word that the National Socialist leader said was clearly heard.

Those who attended the Hyde Park rally will remember that immense forces of police were used to keep apart the Blackshirts and their enemies. On this occasion, as the Fascist column moved through the East End, it was accompanied by few police, whilst thousands of men who did not belong to the Movement walked alongside the column ready to avenge even the slightest look that threatened the colours with insult.

The attempt was made at one point during the meeting by some hooligans to rush the great crowd which was listening to Sir Oswald Mosley. Had the attempt been successful many women and children must have been seriously hurt, but the mounted police dealt rapidly and skilfully with the situation, so that tens of thousands who were listening intently were unaware that any disturbance had occurred.

At Hyde Park the Blackshirts held their own. In the East End on Sunday they swept the enemy out of sight, if not out of existence. Ironical it is that London's most fashionable park should have its lesson to learn from a less celebrated but more necessary ground, where the people have reason to know the value of the little fresh air that is allowed to them.

The Red Front would have done better if they had stayed away altogether. As it was, they only showed their weakness.

Another Ostrich

IT is a serious breach of etiquette to mention by name a certain vile manifestation of the Communist aspiration to literature which is allowed by the present Government to insult each day the majesty of the Crown, but this sheet, probably fabricated from the skin of a Jewish ass, has hitherto maintained that all Fascist demonstrations have failed, thanks to the indignation of the "angry workers." This time, however, it does not even pretend to describe the vast demonstration of English National Socialism against Jewish money power and the Communist sub-man.

There is, however, a most amusing reference to the operation by some person who attended what he was pleased to call a "Peace Demonstration" held elsewhere. He caught sight of the Blackshirt column and these are his words: "Dressed in their black uniforms with their special storm troopers decked out with peaked caps and knee boots, they presented a very unwholesome and ugly spectacle. It was good to get back to the Square where the finest representatives of British youth were listening to the speeches." Good to get back to the Square, forsooth! I bet it was.

But I hope one day to publish on this page a photograph of what the Communist scribe calls the "finest representatives of British youth," who have always given me the impression either of scrofula and anæmia, or of Jewry in emulsion. All Blackshirts must have received the greatest encouragement of their career of so great a demonstration showing them so clearly those our friends whom they would wish to have as friends and those our enemies whose enmity is necessary to the saving of Britain.

RELATIVITY. Commander Oliver Locker-Lampson befriending the Communist Jew Einstein who fled from Germany.

A Weather Cock

FOR many years Commander Oliver Locker-Lampson has tried to interest the public, and for some time he succeeded when he appeared as an opponent of Bolshevism. To-day, however, one might imagine that he had entertained for the Bolshevists, whom he once abused, a lifelong regard. The little invective of which he is capable is now directed entirely against the man who saved Germany from Communism. Having ceased, however, to interest, he attempts to entertain. And if he cannot be entertaining, he does not fail to be egregious.

We have often wondered why with shotgun he stood on guard outside Einstein's residence, and we were assured it was not because the Professor might be desirous of escaping; and as nobody proposed to deliver a physical assault on the Jewish president of the Anti-Imperialist League, we almost wondered whether the Commander had not been infected with the Hebraic love of ostentation.

At last he has given us an explanation of his conduct. Speaking at Ealing recently, he said: "I may have a great deal of Jewish blood in me, and there are a great many other people who must have. Really, I think I must have Jewish blood in me because I am so much more clever than the average Englishmen." Who would care to dispute this masterly analysis? But the English will prefer their stupidity to the condescendng patronage of the arrogant oriental peddler.

Exodus or Genesis

THE City of Leeds possesses a very large Jewish population. It is probably a fact that every fourth person you meet in the streets will belong to the once chosen race. This foreign element has heard already the rumbling of National Socialist revolution, but it does not yet with sufficient clarity realise the nature of the situation which is developing in England to-day. For it has had the effrontery to attempt to impose its distorted and obscene travesty of culture on the white people, whose forbears owned the city.

RELATIVITY. Commander Locker-Lampson addressing an anti-Communist meeting at Albert Hall.

The proposal is, in a word, to include a living representative of Epstein's hideous statue "Genesis" in a carnival to be held in the city. The Lord Mayor comments, "It sounds gruesome. We do not want anything of that nature in Leeds." The Vicar of Leeds drily and mildly remarks, "I shall be surprised if they can find a woman of that shape."

Again and again on the films, on the stage, and in every kind of spectacle which presents the opportunity, the Jewish submen strive to insult the white woman. The psychology of the Jew is, of course, that he believes that he can buy everything; that he trys to buy everything, and that when he finds there is something which he cannot buy he hates and loathes it, and strives to cover it with ridicule.

Such is the secret of unnatural bestiality exemplified in the so-called modern Jewish art, which, in a few years' time will have become so ancient as to have passed from human memory and human ken.

FRANCE—The Arrival of "Kerensky"!

A Page of Imperial & Foreign Affairs *Edited by* ROBERT GORDON-CANNING

By R. GORDON-CANNING, M.C.

ON Thursday, June 4, M. Leon Blum, of German-Jewish extraction, enjoyed the doubtful honour of being France's first Socialist Prime Minister. From Sarraut and his fellow Radicals the new Prime Minister has inherited neither a pleasant political present nor any gift of fragrant roses from the French electorate. On the one hand M. Blum finds an empty Treasury and on the other a "mixed grill" of political parties as his support in government—neither one nor the other a concrete foundation on which to erect the crazy superstructure of Socialist doctrine.

Financial Position

THE national income has fallen over the past five years from 250,000,000,000 to 160,000,000,000 francs. The Bank of France has advanced £133,000,000 to the Treasury during the last few weeks. The deficit for the budget of 1936 is over £200,000,000, and the limit for Treasury bonds has been raised by the Sarraut Government from 15,000,000,000 francs to 21,000,000,000 francs for the purposes of financing rearmament. This limit is again about to be reached.

At the very moment Blum takes up his long-desired office the French peasant withdraws his savings as quickly as possible to his stocking, and the French investor changes to foreign currency and securities. Each day for many weeks on an average £1,000,000 of gold has been leaving France (from May 29 to June 5 it is believed that £40,000,000 was withdrawn) and the franc begin its big decline, first by centimes, which will soon become francs if immediate steps are not taken to control an agreed revaluation.

But is this feasible with a Government made up of such divergent political, economic, and financial principles as those of the Radicals, Socialists, and Communists? In such circumstances action, swift, decisive, and controlled, is an impossibility. A dozen different currents fight against one another, chaos intervenes, until one firm hand, one courageous directing hand, is given the task of producing order. Both Communism and Financial Democracy are proved producers of chaos, while national Socialism and Fascism have created order and union where none existed before.

The Political Situation

M. BLUM has a solid group of 146 Socialist Deputies behind him, on his right a group of Radical-Socialists, and on his left a block of eighty Communists. With this heterogeneous team the great blessed heaven of Socialistic dreams is going to be inaugurated for the French people. Unhappily for this Jewish Prime Minister, the real masters of the situation are the C.G.T., similar to the trade union leaders in Great Britain, and the Communists under Maurice Thorez and Jacques Duclos; both the groups have refused to accept the responsibility of entering the Government.

THOREZ, the French Communist Leader

The leaders of these organisations are under the direct orders of Moscow and, having obeyed the first instructions to form a "Common Front" for electoral purposes, are now commanded by the same power to "right-about turn" and to create disunion and disorder. This virulent Jew, who one day shouted to the French deputies opposed to him, "I hate you!" has, with the approach of responsibility, become weak and pusillanimous like our Snowdens and MacDonalds, and has already attempted to placate the bankers, the U.S.A., and the Communists. Like them, he will be hauled down to dusty futility by these clashing and hostile forces.

Blum and his fellow-Socialist Deputies are not going to enjoy for long the plentitude of political power; their tenure of office will be short and violent. Between the powers of international finance and revolutionary Communism the tepid theorists of Socialism are but stepping stones for the furtherance of the particular aims of these two destructive and greedy forces.

The Stay-in Strikes

THE Communist leaders, obeying their orders from Soviet Russia, immediately set about forming "Soviets" throughout industrial France after the recent success of the Left at the polls. The outbreak of strikes is the first result of these Soviets. As in Italy, as in Russia, as in Spain, so in France the electoral victory of the Left has been inaugurated with a series of powerful, highly organised strikes spreading through a wide distribution of industries.

In 1924 similar occurrences on a small scale took place in Great Britain, while this year the recent Belgian election results have caused similar strikes to take place in Antwerp. The Communist leaders, that is, the real active minds, take control. The orthodox, respectable Socialists and prosperous trade-union leaders are entirely ignored.

These strikes which have occurred during the last week in France have been conducted, as far as strikes can be, with order. Violence, cruelty, and murder, however, are only waiting on the doorstep of M. Blum. Blum puts his head out of the window and broadcasts promises. The workers await fulfilment.

If these Fascist principles for labour welfare do not become law within a week or so, there will be riot and pillage and scenes equal to anything seen during the French Revolution of 1789, and to those which have recently taken place and are continuing to-day in Spain. Is there a sufficiently loyal, patriotic, and unselfish body prepared to confront the impending terror?

Is the Croix de Feu organised sufficiently to take over the government, to crush the Moscow-paid Communist leaders, to give the French industrial workers and peasants a fair deal, to withstand the financial presence of Jewish finance and their equally rapacious Gentile co-partners, who have for so long under financial democracy been at *liberty* to defraud and to impoverish the mass of the people?

Widespread Net

ABOUT 800,000 workers, so far (June 7), have participated in these stay-in-strikes, and, to show the widespread net of Communistic control, these strikes have covered the metallurgical, transport, chemical, building, laundry, provision and gas industries. The "Populaire" of June 5, 1936, gave a list of fifty-three strikes as having been settled to the satisfaction of the workers, and of 254 new strikes, sixty-nine in Paris, 114 in the suburbs of Paris. The "News Chronicle" of June 5, 1936, in its leading article states that these strikes are not a "revolutionary movement."

This is correct in so far that it could be said, probably with truth, that the mass of the French workers are not fundamentally revolutionary Communists, but incorrect, in that an active minority is revolutionary in the most extreme form, and organises the majority, an easy prey, under their bad working conditions, under years of deflation and a 35 per cent. fall in wages, to mass support of Communism.

A scene in the French strikes

The demands of the strikers are for an increase in wages, collective contracts in industries, holidays with pay, and a 40-hour working week. To show the malignity of Communist, Radical Socialists, and Socialist leaders, who form a "common front" to fight against Fascism, as the enemy of the working classes, the Italian worker has for several years enjoyed most of these benefits for which the French worker to-day strikes. The 40-hour week has been in existence nearly two years in Italy, and the Italian Charter of Labour, enacted in 1926, was one of the most advanced pieces of legislation ever granted to the workers of any country.

These leaders are not out to benefit the workers but to secure political power for themselves and a minority, and to dupe in their own ways the mass of the voters as they have always been betrayed under financial and socialistic forms of democracy.

Thorez is, as all Communist leaders, out to bring about a class war; the first statement in the programme recently drawn up by the Communist party in France reads, "no class collaboration, transformation of imperialist war into civil war; defence of the Soviet union in all cases and by all means."

Paradoxical Element

IN spite of the apparent victory for Socialism and Communism in the recent elections, there is one paradoxical element which was noted by d'Ormesson, writing in "Le Temps" under the heading of "La victoire du Fascism." In the programme of these Left Wing parties appeared a national appeal—the key point of Fascist doctrine—"pour la France, libre, forte, et heureuse." d'Ormesson points out that the French people demand action, demand a halt to corruption and repeated large-scaled financial-political scandals; therefore they vote for a revolutionary doctrine.

It is not a hatred of Fascism which, our Attlees here and Daladiers over there imagine, made the French vote for the extreme Left, but the desire for a change from a parliamentary régime which has brought them nothing but evil and is obviously worn out and corrupt. Blum must fail for he is not master of the situation, and a revolution cannot be carried out by a combination of groups holding divergent views.

There are to-day at least three bodies who govern France. The Socialists, the Communists, and the Confédération Générale du Travail led by M. Jouhaux. The decisive hour for France is rapidly approaching. Either a French form of Fascist revolution must intervene and take control, or a further and even swifter fall to the chaos of Soviet government under Communism must eventualise.

From a British point of view there can be no doubt that the political results achieved by a "Common Front" in Spain and in France will procure affiliation of the Communist and I.L.P. parties with the Labour party in this country. The Amalgamated Engineering Union as recently as Saturday last passed a resolution whereby the above groups should be unified. From this point of a "United Front," the real issue of Fascism v. Communism becomes clear and takes precedence. Conservative, Liberal, and Socialist in all countries will fade into the background or become merely museum pieces, like the costumes and carriages of former times. Financial democracy swollen with putrescent gases everywhere explodes. France, one of the worst of sufferers, is about to throw off this corruption, and turns in despair to Communism because there seems to be no other alternative.

Leon Blum

AS a Jew he possesses the characteristics of that race, tenacity of purpose and a plethora of patience. Thus after years of struggle he finds himself as Prime Minister of France. But as a Jew, he possesses the weaknesses of that race, the inferiority complex and the impossibility to conceive on a grand scale with the spirit of man.

The Jewish fraternity will be prominent under Blum's régime. At a dinner given recently to him there were present well-known American Jews, such as Jess Strauss and Jacob Schurman. The two hundred rich families who are going to be made to disgorge their wealth do not include such Jewish families as Schwab d'Hericourt Patenôtre, Dreyfus, Seligman and others.

Will there arise a racial issue in France?

During the first phase of the Dreyfus case, Nationalists were opposed to Jewry. Will the French people submit to a Government formed by Blum, associated with many other Jews? After the Socialist meeting in the Avenue Wagram, while the "Internationale" was being hurled upon the ears of French citizens in one quarter, in another, at the Gare St. Lazare, was to be heard; "à bas les Juifs."

Not many months ago, M. Laval was asked at Geneva if M. Mandel might form the next French Ministry. His reply was, "What, a Jew? Why the pavements of Paris would rise up to protest!"

It was, then, not unexpected to read of a Nationalist deputy inquiring in the Chambre des Députés whether "this ancient Gallo-Roman country is now to be governed by a Jew?" And again "how can a peasant nation like France be governed by a Jew?"

As regards the foreign policy of France, Blum stands for an agreement with Germany, but is hostile to Italy. His violent Communist supporters are not in accord, regarding Hitler and Germany as the arch-opponents of Soviet government.

M. Blum certainly begins his presidency of Government with a prickly pear, not in his hand, but in his mouth. On every occasion he speaks he will find a fresh thorn embedded in his tongue, and his situation will become even more hopeless, particularly as each thorn will be impregnated with the poison of a "friend!"

One cannot pity him. The fruit is of his own choice! And, in revolutions, the guinea pigs must be devoured by the hyenas of Communism or the eagles of Fascism.

But what of France, M. Blum? Must she be your mouse which must suffer vivisection from the knife of your Socialistic theories?

THE BRITISH COUNTRYSIDE

IMPORTATION OF RED POTATOES & CHINESE EGGS MUST STOP

First Place for British Producers

(By Our Agricultural Correspondent.)

ARE we never going to be clear of these foreign importations of foodstuffs? It would appear not, judging by figures that lie before me as I write.

Last year was a poor year, so far as the potato crop was concerned, and not only in this country but abroad also. Yet, realising this, we still find the Potato Board intent on limiting the acreage of production at home, for there are not a great number of farmers who feel inclined to pay the levy of £5 per acre if they wish to start out as potato growers, and so we are again left to the vagaries of the British climate to decide whether even heavier imports of potatoes will not have to be made from foreign sources next spring. Of course, we may have a bumper crop, but, on the other hand, we may not; and as potatoes can be put to so many other uses than merely being used for human consumption, one cannot but question the wisdom of limitation of area at home.

In April we imported 42,941 tons of potatoes, as compared with 11,891 in that month 1935, and of this amount 16,640 tons came from Spain, a country that has now gone "Red," so home growers are deprived of an opportunity to satisfy the full needs of their fellow countrymen that Bolshie growers in Spain may profit! Over 14,000 tons came from the Netherlands, and this part of Europe seems singularly favoured, for it supplies no mean percentage of our bacon, hams, butter, and dairy produce generally, as well as potatoes. Yet acres and acres of fertile land lie waiting to be cultivated in this country by men who are second to none in skill.

British Eggs for British Consumers

ALL is not well with the poultry industry; we hear of far too many of the small producers who, after a gallant fight against odds, have had to relinquish the uneven contest, but the lot of poultry farmers generally will not be improved by any sort of compulsory marketing scheme, which is only designed to take away the liberty of the producer and to bring the most efficient producers to the level of those who are not so efficient.

I admire the enterprise of our contemporary, the "Farmers' Weekly," in instituting a ballot of egg producers in this country, when 79,583 votes were polled, the result of the ballot being that 66,630 votes (or 83.58 per cent.) were given for increased tariffs without a marketing scheme of any kind, and only 3.57 per cent. polled in favour of the compulsory scheme that is now being suggested.

This shows very strongly the opinion throughout the country, and proves that, given adequate protection, British poultry farmers feel that they are quite capable of making things pay without the creation of pin-pricking regulations, devastating levies, and hoards of officials.

Drastic action is called for to prohibit the importation of liquid eggs from Russia and China (amongst other countries), there is a chance of creating a new industry in that line here, or, to be correct, to expand the limited amount of liquid eggs produced here. At the present time pastry-cooks and bakers, who must have liquid eggs are driven to buy these cheap imported eggs because they cannot get enough of the home-produced article in tinned form, and they cannot spare the time to crack their own eggs. Home producers of eggs cannot compete with the flood of eggs in liquid form from abroad, but if those eggs were prohibited, then there would be an incentive to manufacturers to expand this industry and supply all that is required.

Fascists, you must realise that in 1934-35 the output of eggs in this country declined, and we produced only 3,108,000,000 hen eggs and 62,000,000 duck eggs, compared with 3,154,000,000 and 64,000,000 respectively in 1933-34.

Fertilising the Land

THIS decline may not seem much to worry about, but I have seen so often a small decline turn into a positive rush downhill ere it can be checked.

Our poultry farmers only need to be encouraged by keeping out foreign eggs in shell or in liquid form, but it is not much encouragement to import 131,340 Great Hundreds from Poland, 79,573 Great Hundreds from Denmark, 67,373 Great Hundreds from the Netherlands, 42,423 from Rumania, and 17,937 from China in one week, which happened in the week ended May 27, when 483,371 Great Hundreds were imported, or less, mark you, than the colossal total of 600,583 Great Hundreds imported in the previous week.

Yet poultry not only provide eggs and meat, but fertilise the land when kept either on the slatted floor house system or folded, and after a very few years of treatment with poultry, or with pigs, running the poor, waste grass-land, such land would, in very many instances, be fit to plough and to grow crops.

Much of our land cries aloud for fertilisers, but so often from lack of liquid capital farmers cannot afford to purchase as much as their land is really in need of. In all cases manures may bring a dividend in the shape of bigger and better crops, but it has to be waited for. Fertilisation by means of poultry, pigs, and sheep is another matter, for they are bringing in money all the time they are performing this useful service.

Shortage of Labour

A SOMEWHAT lengthy tour en route for various agricultural shows took me right through the West—those glorious counties of Hampshire, Wiltshire, Berks, Somerset, Gloucestershire, Monmouth, and Glamorgan; later on through Worcestershire, and still further into Bucks, Middlesex, Herts, Suffolk, Essex, and into Cambridgeshire. On all sides I learned of a shortage of labour, which shortage is serious, but would be infinitely more so were it not for the increased use of mechanical appliances.

I was told that the younger generation do not seem to care for work on the land, although many of them are keen on learning the use of the latest mechanical devices. There is certainly no unemployment in agricultural villages, but the sad part of it is that the younger men are drifting away from the land, and often find their way into blind-alley occupations. Wages, although much higher than before (war years excepted) are not high enough to keep the young men on the land, and in many villages there is a shortage of dwellings for young folk who wish to marry and settle down.

There is also a shortage of casual labour in many places, and though a certain number of gipsies are available for root-hoeing and like tasks, yet there is room for more, and . . . they are not forthcoming.

The Royal Counties Show

BY the time these lines are in print we shall all be eagerly looking forward to the opening of the Great Combined Show of the Royal Counties, Sussex County and Hackney Horse Societies, which takes place at Worthing on June 15 to 18. No such huge show has ever before been held in Sussex, and representatives of all our most famous breeds of horses, cattle, sheep, pigs, goats, and poultry will be on view. The educational side of this great exhibition is not being neglected, and rural industries, the work of the various County Council Education Committees and Young Farmers' Clubs will prove a delight to those who study this side of agriculture. Horticulture and forestry exhibits will attract many, and gradually efforts are being made to create a love of trees amongst the younger generation, for there is danger in that direction that the beauty and beneficial action of trees may be forgotten by the young brought up in an atmosphere of bricks and mortar and ribbon development.

This should be a great show and a link between town and country.

Orchards in full blossom on the East Kent Coast. A typical landscape showing the beauties of the English countryside as seen from an aeroplane.

FASCISM IN OUR VILLAGE

VI.—Peter Davey has a Nasty Jar

IT was later than usual when we gathered round at the Dog and Duck the other night. Uncle Tom Cobleigh was already seated in his chair with a full tankard at his side. He hardly looked up from his paper when we came in and never noticed anything amiss when 'Arry 'Awke, in an absent-minded way that will get him into trouble one of these days, lifted the old man's tankard and took a hearty swig at the beer. We talked of one thing and another, and presently one of us asked the old man's opinion.

"Butter," he replied, without looking up.

"What did you say, Uncle Tom?" I asked, as we hadn't been talking about butter.

"I said butter," he replied, looking up for the first time.

"Don't you understand English? Not that the butter's English by that token, for it's Japanese."

"What's Japanese butter got to do with us, Mr Cobleigh?" asked Peter Davey, who does a bit of dairying at his farm.

"It's got a lot to do with you, Peter Davey," replied Old Tom Cobleigh. "You make butter, don't you, but can you sell it at a price that pays you for making it? Tell me that."

"Well, no, I can't; that is to say, not at what you might call a fair price," replied Peter, slowly. "What with all this Danish butter coming into the country, not to mention the butter that comes in from Australia and New Zealand, it's very difficult to make it pay."

"It will be worse still," announced Old Tom, "if what they say in the paper is true. You'll have to face Japanese butter, Peter, and you know what that means."

"Is that what it says there?" asked Peter, looking flabbergasted.

Japanese Butter

"YES, it's all here. I'll tell you about it. Fifty tons of Japanese butter have just been landed in England. The Japanese Government help the farming industry out there in Japan, and now they are out to try and capture the English butter market, so you look out, Peter. You'll be up against the yellow coolie and dairymaid, sure as eggs is eggs." The old man paused. "And that's what your National Government, who we voted for last Election, has done for us," and he turned to the table and reached for his tankard.

"Who's been at my beer?" he roared, glaring at each of us in turn. "That tankard was full just now, and I swear I haven't even put my lips to it. One of you swiped it. Was it you, 'Arry 'Awke? You're that absent-minded you'd drink anyone's beer."

"Very sorry, I'm sure," said 'Arry 'Awke, sheepishly. "I can't think how I came to make such a silly mistake. Here, Tam, bring Mr. Cobleigh another tankard and put it down to me."

Mollified by this generosity, Uncle Tom calmed down, and took a long pull at the fresh tankard at his elbow.

Jan Stewer now up and spoke.

"What you have said is all very well, Mr. Cobleigh, about the farmer getting

good prices, but if prices are to be raised how am I and the other labourers to buy food at all? It is hard enough to buy food with our wages of thirty-one shillings, and if you are going to put prices up by keeping out cheap foreign foodstuffs, we shan't be able to buy any food at all, and what will Mr. Mosley do then?"

"I don't quite know how that works out, Jan" replied Uncle Tom, slowly scratching his head. "I know there is an answer but I shall be seeing that young Blackshirt in a day or two and I'll get the answer from him and let you know. Good night all."

And Tam once more turned us out into the night.

H. E. CROCKER.

The WORLD OF LABOUR

By JOHN EMERY

The Great Exposure—Deluded French Workers—A Change in the Unions

THINGS are moving rapidly to a crisis in every part of the world. With dramatic suddenness the thoughts of man have been swinging completely away from the old game of politics, and he is now facing realities. Never again will babbling, futile windbags keep nations enslaved to poverty amidst plenty. The day of the man of talk is finished; it is now the day of the man of action.

Within two years we have seen every single politician who passed for a statesman, utterly discredited. In all countries they have also been proved to be corrupt and dishonest. Events are proving that by the very nature of the political game, only the unscrupulous, the vain, and the grafter could succeed.

No man of courage and real pride of character could play the old political game. He either revolted and got out, or made himself so unpleasant that everybody said he was a failure and had no real ability. A John Wheatley or an Oswald Mosley could never fit into a political Labour Cabinet. Jimmy Thomas and Mr. Clynes could.

The Internationale

THINKING men have no illusions left about the old gang. Ability to talk on any subject for hours will no longer be accepted as leadership. In France M. Blum tries the same tricks of oratory as were practised by Mr. Ramsay MacDonald. The French workers have just elected M. Blum in the hope that he would do something for them. Instead, M. Blum has only one message to deliver, and it is to the financiers, who know no country, no patriotism, and whose god is dividend.

M. Blum spoke soft words to them. They had nothing to fear from him. He, by God, was a statesman. They would have their ducats and their pound of flesh, too. And while he was still wining and dining and strutting and posing for the camera-men, something happened. Groups of workmen who saw a world teeming with wealth and starvation everywhere, said to M. Blum that an intelligent country could get along without international financiers, but it couldn't get along without people to produce the real wealth.

And M. Blum, who had hoped to get his photo in the newspapers every day, like Mr. MacDonald and Mr. Lloyd George, for whom life was just one long reception, now finds that the French workers mean business—they want something done for themselves and for their children.

Primrose Poseurs

BUT the events in France and Britain have proved that all are discredited. The honest-man pose of slashing Stanley is destroyed for ever. Nobody believes in him to-day. The Budget leakages have been the last straw, and the movement which is led with vigour to-day and can organise the anger and disappointment will win.

The most striking thing in all this debacle is that official Labour gains not one single new adherent. In Peckham, with all the might of the party machine, and all the alleged organising genius of Mr. Herbert Morrison thrown into the division, the candidate receives fewer votes than did John Beckett when he fought and won in spite of the Labour leaders. The explanation is that Labour has now no message of hope for anyone. For years they have been preaching the same gospel as Mr. Baldwin, Mr. MacDonald, and Lord Robert Cecil, and no intelligent person can see the remotest difference in any of them.

The Communist Party, which should have had a clear-cut message to-day, has achieved the united front with every reactionary politician in Britain. In France they cannot support the strikers because it might weaken the hands of M. Blum. The men who were paid from Moscow to foment revolution must now be paid to prevent it.

Psychological Momentum

IN Britain to-day there is a great rank-and-file movement waiting for somebody to organise it into a fighting force. The Labour Party cannot do it, the Communist Party daren't do it in case it disturbs the calm of Geneva, and Mr. Maxton hasn't the will. The best evidence that the movement exists was supplied at the Conference of the A.E.U. Never in my experience has a ruling executive been so rebuffed and so humiliated. In fact it only needed an official of the union to recommend a policy to ensure its being defeated. The delegates seemed to feel instinctively that anything supported by their leaders must be wrong. That feeling is not confined to the engineers, nor did the humiliation take place because the A.E.U. leaders are more dull and stupid or dishonest than other Labour leaders. Mr. Little and Mr. Smith compare quite favourably with any of the others. If, therefore, they find themselves discredited, how long will the others last? Sir Walter Citrine is finished, and will probably end up in the City, whilst Mr. Bevin is shaking, and a few more strikes would see a complete crash of his top-heavy edifice. Ask yourselves who is left and you will find there is nobody.

The Old Gang

THE fact is that almost unnoticed a complete revolution has taken place inside the trade union movement itself.

All the old platform tricksters have vanished. And they were platform tricksters. There was old Ben Turner who, when he wanted to put across a particularly bad settlement, always flourished his New Testament in the air and swore by that that it was a good one.

Jimmy Thomas had an even better trick. When he went to face a hostile audience of railwaymen he always took with him two or three old doddering men long since past work. They were placed in prominent seats on the platform, and Mr. Thomas always expressed his delight and surprise at the sight of these old workmates and workers for the union. Old Tom and Old Bill were held up to the audience for exhibition. Mr. Thomas would say, "Ah, Bill, when you and I started this union things were different—what struggles, what trials." The tears would begin to flow, and then Mr. Thomas made his real speech and got away with it every time. But now both the good and the bad old leaders have gone. Ben Tillett, John Hill, Arthur Pugh, Walkden, Purcell, Sexton, have all vanished.

Whence the Inspiration?

OF the older gang there remains only Mr. George Hicks, but nobody, of course, could take this big good-natured fellow seriously. Mr. Hicks, it may be remembered, led the great movement for Peace in Industry, which culminated in the Mond-Turner agreement. That was in 1926, but by 1927 Mr. Hicks had started a new movement against Peace in Industry. Well, I ask you.

And so in Britain to-day we find that of 12,000,000 insured workers only 4,000,000 are in any union at all, and these four million are without a single leader of any kind, either in the political Labour movement or the industrial side.

Who in heaven's name could work up any enthusiasm for Major Attlee? What or whom could the Major inspire? Who in all Britain would die fighting for Mr. Herbert Morrison, and who stupid enough to repose blind faith in Hugh Dalton? And yet these 4,000,000 must have a leader — they like 'em.

Much more important is the fact that in a very short time the situation will demand leadership. The man of courage who knows what he wants and goes steadily to his goal will always win, whilst the vacillating politicians are calling their committees together.

They won in Russia, Italy, and Germany. It will be France and Britain next, because the political system in these countries is as rotten and corrupt as it was in Russia, Italy, and Germany.

Comrade Blum among his Communist friends giving the Communist Salute

Fascism or War?

SOCIALISTS in all countries never cease to proclaim their horror of Fascism, not so much because of its political theories—concerning which they display abysmal ignorance—but because they say that Fascism means war. It would be interesting to know if these pacific war-provokers in various countries, including our own, have read General von Blomberg's recent speech on the subject of war. Here are two extracts well worthy of attention by them and indeed by British Fascists and National-Socialists as well:

"We Germans need attach no new honours to our already glorious banners and standards, but we need peace to finally establish the National Socialist Revolution.

"The hope and desire of the New Germany is that war, as the medium of politics and the moulder of the fates of nations, shall disappear."

Trade Union Leaders Foment Foreign Subversion

ONE might have thought that British trade union leaders would have their hands full in assisting the millions of British workers thrown out of work by the capitalist system they profess to combat, or else helping the underpaid employed in their struggle for better conditions. This is not so, however.

Mr. J. C. Little, president of the Amalgamated Engineering Union, has been describing to his colleagues at their Morecambe conference the great work which is being carried on by a body of revolutionaries in Germany, who "were planning the overthrow of Herr Hitler."

£15,000, he stated, was distributed in Berlin alone last Christmas by this underground organisation, and the funds were being collected from trade unionists in five countries, including Britain.

We feel inclined to accept with reserve his statement that "the new movement consisted entirely of Germans." We had an impression that 99 per cent. of Germans were in favour of National Socialism, and that the only body who wished to destroy it were of quite a different race.

In any case, however, Mr. Little's suggestion that the hard-won pence of British workers should be employed to finance revolutionary plots in foreign countries is not likely to endear him to the wives and children of unemployed trade unionists in the depressed areas.

Black Treachery

A DISGUSTING example of treachery has just been afforded by the Hackney Socialist Council, which has decided that, in future, all their employees who are members of the Territorial Army shall lose their wages whilst they are in camp. Here we see in combination the poisonous malice of the International Socialist and the demented idiocy of the International Socialist mind.

The International Socialists were howling but a few days ago for the use of armed force against the Italian people, and yet they have decided to penalise the man who fulfils the elementary duty of citizenship, which requires that the citizen should be able to defend his land.

Moreover, I would request all readers to ask their Socialist acquaintances what they think of a Socialist Council which refuses to pay its employees during their annual holiday? Accustomed as we are to public scandals, we can think of no viler example of hypocrisy than that which has been given by the body of Socialists which not only penalises its employees, but dictates to them how they may not spend their own time. Yet these hypocrites would level the charge of dictatorship against Fascism.

Canada Wakes Up

A CANADIAN newspaper of May 15 states that during a session of a Committee of the Quebec Legislature spectators suddenly jumped up and cried, "Down with the Jews!" Both in Montreal and in Quebec there is a considerable increase of active anti-semitism due to the usual tendencies of Jewish industrialists and politicians.

THE FOUNDATIONS OF FASCISM

Italy's Part In The Great War

By MARSHAL BADOGLIO

BY a strange whim of fate it is decreed that the nations of the world shall not advance in progress or in power, or in their own moral or material welfare, except by passing through the fiery ordeal of war.

This fate of humanity does not allow of enduring peace merely because the human race wishes it to do so. On the contrary, it frequently insists that it shall be a prize dearly paid for. All nations are, during the cycle of their existence, confronted with the tempests of battle, unless they choose to decay or slip towards the abyss of disintegration.

In the case of the individual, it is the same. A man only gains the moral force requisite to make him worthy of the name of man after being tested and tried on the battlefield of life. For the sinews of the body are not hardened but by exposure to the elements or the discipline of labour.

It is struggles which transform the calibre, both mental and moral, of nations, just as hammer and fire temper metal.

Great War Lessons

WHEN the world-war broke out in 1914 a few far-seeing persons, who to Italy's good fortune seem to spring up at crises in her history, realised, when they saw the political horizon in flames, that it was incumbent on Italy also to take her part in the conflict.

These individuals realised the historic necessity for intervention, and understood that it was not possible for Italy to remain a passive spectator.

The sparks kindled in the soul of Benito Mussolini, though flaring at first in isolation, gave rise finally to a veritable conflagration in the hearts and souls of the people, reawakening in them the valorous instincts handed down from foregoing generations and reviving the traditions of the Renaissance.

The young men, the great poets, and the men of affairs came little by little, by their reasoning powers and their intuitions, to see that, in order to be an adherent of the "New Life" and to conquer the "Primate," it was necessary for Italy to fight. Italy had to show to the world that she was capable of fighting and of enduring in order to attain, at the cost of war, the ends that constituted her ideal.

The War, it was announced, was to be waged in the interests of liberty and to defend the rights of nations. It was, therefore, the duty of Italy, the eldest daughter of Rome, to contend for these ideals and the rights given birth to by the genius of her race and disseminated by her throughout the world.

Unity Through Strife

THE independence of Italy had been won some fifty years earlier by the spirit and unanimous determination of the Italian people. Every district and province had provided its heroes, but, so far, there had been no great war waged by all Italians conjointly. After weighing up the cost of this fresh undertaking, Italy, with her eyes open, decided to confront the world with this proof of her moral unity.

The War, which enlisted the whole of the Italians under the banners of a single army, may be said to have created a soul in their fatherland, and it also swept away at one stroke and through a common sacrifice the last remaining vestiges of regionalism, and also the new Utopias of international alliances. It swept away, also, every vestige of subservience to foreign influences, whether in the intellectual, the economic, or the industrial life of the nation, and it saw the inception of the great martial prestige of the New Italy.

This new aspect shown by Fascist Italy was begotten by the War. The trials Italy had to undergo as the War advanced were out of all comparison with those experienced on any other fighting front. These operations took place on Alpine heights and passes popularly regarded as inaccessible. Thither the guns were dragged up and there our soldiers fought, surrounded by glaciers and avalanches. The Italian élan confronted our age-long enemy in a series of sanguinary battles waged in swift succession and without respite on the flinty slopes of the Carso and the Sabotino, on the ridges of the Ortigaro and the Grapea, as well as on the plains. Our soldiers contested and won this rough, inhospitable terrain metre by metre and launched their offensives more than ten times. In each of these colossal engagements, which lasted for several days, wave after wave of our infantry followed each other, marching over the dead bodies of their already fallen comrades.

The flower of our nation took part in this War—veterans already turning grey, young men called up before conscription, volunteers from beyond the sea, and also from other lands, some of whom fought in the front line and fell into the hands of the enemy, though they all ascended the scaffold, so to speak, like the martyrs of the Renaissance.

Field Marshal Pietro Badoglio

Twentieth Century Renaissance

THE tenacity of the army chiefs and the valour of the men demonstrated to the world at large that the splendid traditions of Italy still survive intact in the present generation and that our children do no discredit to the notable achievements of their forefathers. The foot-soldiers of Italy were the authentic descendants of the soldier-peasants who founded the world-empire of Rome and imprinted on the world the ineffaceable stamp of the Latin civilisation, which is the product of calculation, of conscience, and of discipline.

Italy had embarked on the War fired by the irresistible enthusiasm of the people, but gravely handicapped in her military equipment and lack of resources, but what Italy lacked in resources was made up for by the spirit of sacrifice evinced by her fighting forces. Then it was that Italy revealed herself to the world in a new light and enhanced her reputation among other nations when they witnessed her power of self-organisation. Throughout the War, Italy gained prestige for her name as a result of the intelligence, tenacity, and energy she manifested. She overhauled her military organisation completely and recreated her industry. Not only did she rebuild what had been destroyed, but she also multiplied her armament and her resources on a scale to which history so far offers no parallel.

In certain departments of her organising and constructive work, Italy, which has reared so many pioneers in the sciences and the arts and has nurtured so many indefatigable workers, evinced her mastery and even superiority as compared with nations richer in resources and experiences, thereby giving proof of her full efficiency in every branch of social, intellectual and productive activity. The War episode raised Italy to her proper rank as a Great Power and rearoused in her the energies she manifested two thousand years ago. Thus one of the most ancient peoples of the world has been transformed into a nation quivering with the most modern vitality. The country owes everlasting gratitude to all who have contributed to its greatness.

RADIO FLASHES

By BLUEBIRD

RATHER a trying week on the whole. I was severely frowned on by the Editor for occupying three columns last week when I only ought to have occupied two, and the Assistant Editor looked at me in the morning with a razor in his hand. But, apparently, he was only going to sharpen a pencil or shave or something. In other words, I must be briefer, and, being the soul of wit, I will.

Then somebody in Bristol writes in to say I am futile. But I do at least try to get it out of my system every week.

But the last straw was the discovery that we have been nourishing a viper in our bosom, or, at any rate, are harbouring a newsfinch in our pages. Did you read the scurrilous attack on me by Blackbird last week! Blackbird indeed! A newsfinch with soul of black.

But I do not believe in vulgar brawls with the unworthy. I must just tell you, though, that I read in the "Daily Express" the other day that a blackbird has a reputation for being quaite a naice bird because it has such a lot to say. Actually it is quite a useless bird, because it goes to bed so early that it misses all the slugs and bugs it is supposed to eat. These get up and dress just after the slothful blackbird has gone to bed. [This correspondence has ceased!—"Bluebird."]

That Holiday Variety

MOST people seem to agree with me that the programmes broadcast by the B.B.C. as their contribution to the Whitsun Holiday fun were a disgrace. Of course, those wealthy English people, such as the Maschwitz family, who select our holiday fun, can afford to go rushing all over the world on the money we listeners pay them. So, presumably, they imagine that at holiday time all the rest of the listening public can afford to do the same.

Why cannot we have someone in charge of variety who understands the taste of the Englishman, the Scotsman, the Welshman, and the Irishman. Each of these has different tastes in humour and entertainment. The original B.B.C. before it became Jew-ridden, understood this and planned the country into regions with separate transmitters and studios to each region.

The present rulers of the B.B.C. are unable to grasp this essential fact, with the result that during many important listening hours, half the stations are closed down and the rest all transmit the same programme. The Saturday evening variety programmes, which have now reached a very low standard, are put out to the whole country on all National transmitters with even more flat and wishy-washy alternatives on the Regionals.

And it looks as though we shall have to wait for Fascism before variety will be controlled by someone who understands the British taste.

The Jew shows his hand

WHAT must be the most shameful incident in the career of the B.B.C. occurred on Thursday evening.

You will remember that the ex-Negus was permitted to come to British territory provided that he promised not to engage in the spreading of propaganda in any way. Of course no one in his senses expected this poor creature to keep his promise, and therefore no one is in the least surprised that he has broken his word.

But few people would have expected the Government-sponsored B.B.C. to assist this creature to spread his foul propaganda. And yet on Thursday, in the second news bulletin, the newsfinch read a statement by this fugitive from justice. The newsfinch, by the way, being partly ostrich, still calls him "the Emperor of Abyssinia."

The statement, which was read in full, was sheer anti-Italian propaganda and must obviously have done much towards widening the breach between Italy and England, which the B.B.C. should do its utmost to heal. It will be interesting to see if anyone has the guts to raise this question in Parliament.

It is high time that the B.B.C. altered its motto to read "Nation shall speak only unto nations approved in writing by the Learned Elders of Zion."

After reading the so-called "Emperor's" proclamation, the newsfinch gave such a sorrowful and loving sigh. The pathos (or was it bathos?) was almost too much for the stupid bird.

An Opportunity

IF the B.B.C. loves the ex-Negus so dearly, why does it not do something practical for him. Why not give him the job of corner-man in the forthcoming all-Jewish concert party. No doubt Mr. Selassie would be glad to add to the swag even the pittance the B.B.C. pays. And being a foreigner, Mr. Selassie would naturally be up in the four-figure class.

When hundreds of thousands of British boys are giving their pennies to King George's Jubilee Fund, why, I wonder, was it necessary to broadcast the fact that a few Jewish boys have also contributed. Considering that they are for the moment resident in our country and will, presumably benefit from the fund, surely it is a disgrace that so very few Jewish boys have contributed. But I suppose there is news value in a Jew making a voluntary contribution.

On Sunday I listened in Victoria Park, East London, to Sir Oswald Mosley's great speech. I guarantee that more people listened to that speech than listen to the broadcast speeches of our reigning politicians. It was a speech to which any Englishman would have been proud to listen. And yet the Jew-ridden B.B.C. prefers to broadcast speeches by the "Emperor of Abyssinia."

Real News

ON returning from Victoria Park I tuned in to the Rome broadcasting station for the English bulletin, which is now given on Sundays.

I was amazed and pleased to hear an accurate description of the meeting given, and also a number of extracts from Sir Oswald's great speech.

Although I did not get home in time to hear the B.B.C. newsfinch, I would bet that not a word was heard of this great gathering of Britishers, but I feel sure that we were told all about what was happening in France and Palestine.

GOOD NEWS

Those who have been exasperated by the concealments, misrepresentation, and distortions of Fascist news by the B.B.C. news-finches will be interested to hear that regular times have now been arranged for broadcasts of news bulletins in English from Rome.

These will be given on Sunday nights between 9.35 and 10.15 p.m., according to convenience of programme arrangements. The exact time will be announced at 7.20 p.m. on Saturdays. The bulletins will be transmitted by Rome 420.8m., Naples 272m., Bari No. 1 283m., and also from 2RO on the short wavelength on 25.4 and/or 31.13m.

You may remember that the newsfinch told us last week that the Italians were not allowed to hear anything of the success of the Queen Mary. This is a deliberate lie, as full details of her runs have been broadcast. One of these days the newsfinch will be choked by his own words.

And he should remember what happened to Ananias, especially when there is all that electricity about. One of these days a transmitter will turn on a newsfinch, and then we shall have roast parrot, and all be poisoned.

Like the Queen Mary

SO they are going to make Broadcasting House twice its present size. Soon it will be able to hold twice its present quantity of red tape, and there will be twice the number of newsfinches twice the size of the present ones, which will be twice as poisonous.

There are to be enormous studios about twice the size of the Jewish picture palace, and no doubt we shall be told about the number of railway engines that can run up and down the lift shafts, and the number of double-decker motor-buses that can be packed in the studio. And, of course, there will be a Synagogue.

I expect the place will contain twice as many officials, and I am willing to bet the design will be given to a Jew and a Jewish firm will build it.

But what we really need is a place about half the size of the present building, and about one-tenth of the present officials, and just a few people to arrange our entertainment for us. But that could only happen in a dream.

IN THE HEART OF AN EMPIRE

Great East London Welcome To Sir Oswald Mosley

By Anne Cutmore

THE narrow streets of Bethnal Green straggle across East London, hidden like a shameful secret behind the City's facade of wealth. The tiny box-like houses lining them were hastily flung up years ago, without thought, without plan, without consideration of beauty or regard to health, to accommodate the unhappy population which manufactures the City's goods. The people who inhabit them, many bitter in spirit and weary of living on the edge of starvation, are yet too used to their condition to question its justice.

They are oppressed by poverty and deprivation and blinded by custom. Humiliated from their birth by the conditions in which they live, they do not question, and only occasionally, goaded too far, break into rebellion as damaging to themselves as it is futile and barren in result.

Months of Fascist propaganda has brought into the lives of these unhappy people the promise of release, and the promise of a just Government— a Government which will not admit the sovereignty of wealth, but only that of ability. Their reaction to that promise was demonstrated last Sunday, when the Leader of the British Union of Fascists, Sir Oswald Mosley, marched at the head of some two thousand Blackshirts and many hundreds of others through the narrow streets of Bethnal Green to Victoria Park, and there spoke to the people.

The People's Man

HE had been told many times that the East End of London was closed to him. The people, fed by the daily Press, were led to believe that he and his policy were antagonistic to their interests—those interests which have never been considered by any Party yet. They had been told to distrust him. Yet when he joined the ranks the people closed about him cheering. Each man wanted to be near him. Hundreds jostled to walk in step with him as he marched.

The possessor of a baronetcy created in the seventeenth century, he walked through those narrow streets — a fine man, the one man in all England who would not condone her betrayal, who has through fifteen years of Parliamentary life, in speeches and still more in his acts, been consistently the friend of the underdog.

He had refused high position and honour because the working people whom he represented and for whom he fought were being betrayed. And now he leads a militant army of those working men to the positions which they have earned, in a country of which we may be proud again.

Westminster to Victoria Park

THE impressively long column swept past Westminster Abbey on its seven-mile march through London. "What are it?" queried a Dane, as the colours pass. "Ah! Good men. Good men." They are good men. They are men who realise the desperate need of the country for strong leadership, and they are ready unquestioningly to accept the leadership of Oswald Mosley because he has proved the strength of his determination to oppose the forces of corruption threatening the country.

In Victoria Park he speaks from the top of a van to over a hundred thousand people congregated about it. This has been called the stronghold of Communism. Yet the people listen and cheer. There is a self-conscious effort to sing the "Internationale," and there are a few impudent pointless questions.

For the most part, however, the meeting is quiet and orderly, and the people listen in silence punctuated by bursts of cheering. The speaker touches upon the vexed and misrepresented European question . . . ". . . and then Germany, whom we fought before and will not fight again, France when Socialism collapses—and it will collapse—and then we shall have the four great countries of Europe Fascist, and together that block of great European nations will guarantee the peace of mankind."

His care, however, is nearer home. "What a tragedy it is that in an age which should be an age of plenty we have low wages, we have bad houses, we have unemployment. These problems could be solved once the Government looks after British interests instead of looking after foreign interests, and once you give to the Government the power to act."

Led by Sir Oswald, the men march out of the Park, and along the mean streets, lined with people. In the Blackshirt ranks are men who saw service in the last war, and some of them bear its marks. There are boys who have grown up under its shadow, and under the threat of unemployment, and there are men of position and substance. The differences are levelled up. Onlookers cheer as the Leader passes, and a woman throws a flower from a window.

Here, in Bethnal Green, where unemployment is rife and necessity sets the standard of living, where, they say, the Blackshirts were afraid to come, Oswald Mosley held one of the most triumphant meetings of his career.

The Colours after Passing Sir Oswald at the Saluting Point on the Embankment

THE FALLACY OF EXPORTS

Kenneth Smith Analyses Our Trade Figures.

THE catastrophe of the world slump which practically wiped out world trade appears to have wiped out what little intelligence many of our leading lights possessed at the same time.

Mr. W. Favill Tuke, at the annual meeting of Barclays Bank, said:

"Unfortunately, there is still much unemployment . . . and . . . the solution of this grievous problem is to be found in that increase in our overseas trade which the spirit of economic self-sufficiency is making so difficult. Upon a satisfactory revival in international trade depends, not only the raising of our own standard of living, but also that of other countries . . ."

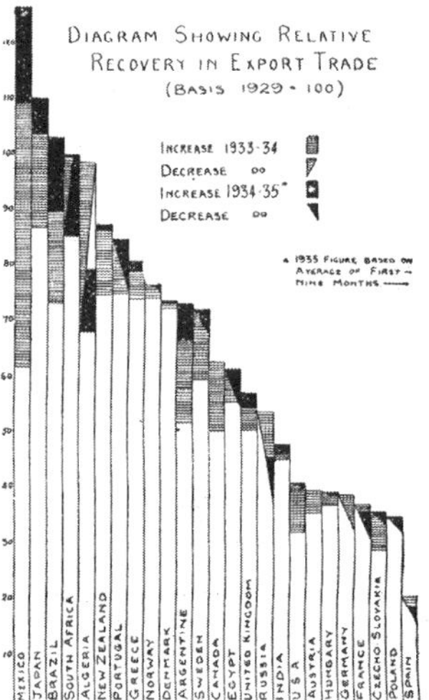

A glance at the accompanying diagram shows how ill-founded are our hopes of a recovery in our export trade. Of the twenty-five countries shown twelve show a decline during the first nine months of 1935, and two more show no improvement. Mexico, Japan, Brazil, and South Africa alone have reached or exceeded the 1929 level, and the Argentine is showing promising signs.

Thirty Years On

AT our present rate of recovery we should achieve our 1929 level (when we had about one million unemployed) by about 1963. We can, however, look forward to three slumps before that date, and if, as Mr. Tuke believes, "the solution of this grievous problem is to be found in that increase in our overseas trade upon whose revival depends, not only the raising of our own standards, but also those of other countries," our unemployed can be truly thankful that there exists in Great Britain that "statesmanship and leadership of a high order" upon which Mr. Tuke insists.

The Real Solution

"AS a great and powerful nation offering a large market for the products of other countries, we have widespread influence." Britain is the happy dumping ground for the products of any foreign blackleg unfortunate enough to live in a backward country run by international finance.

The influence of that large market shall be used to encourage reciprocal trading by the inflexible application of our slogan "Britain buys from those who buy from Britain." As a highly industrialised country capable of producing all the manufactured goods we require, and of enormously increasing our agricultural output, the foreigner can find a fresh customer and the financier a more friendly atmosphere in order to put our own British workers back to work.

It is a big enough task for any statesman and leader to raise our own standards without troubling his head about "those of other countries."

With Mr. Tuke we "feel justified in believing that a way will be found," but not in poking our noses into the business of any country but our own.

That way is the orderly and disciplined march to power of National Socialism, determined to sweep away every obstacle to a Greater Britain.

SMASHING THE SHOPKEEPER

THE Tobacco Trades Association was formed in 1931 to protect the various interests of those traders and manufacturers engaged in the tobacco industry. One of the first things it did was to try to stop the then extensive operation of coupon trading, which was lowering the quality of the product sold to the public, on account of the huge sums which rival concerns were spending on free gifts. Up to 1933, most leading brands of cigarettes were sold purely on the strength of the gifts offered, and so fierce had competition become, that many manufacturers had difficulty in keeping pace with the scheme, when it was considered that the value of the gift to the smoker was as much, or more, than the profit allowed to the trader.

It was only towards the end of 1933, after a Bill had interminably been talked out in Parliament, that any action was taken as far as the general public and retail trade was concerned.

Coupons and Freedom

NOW comes the interesting point. From this time a gradual elimination of gift schemes and coupon trading took place, but a "bombshell" was dropped, when it was discovered that the manufacturers had so manipulated things to their own ends, that the individual trader was to be prevented from handling any coupon lines.

That the manufacturers had every right to combine among themselves to stop gifts when they chose, is not disputed. But to use this combination to coerce the trader into agreeing to further their ends, is wrong in principle, and as a result has been bitterly resented by the trader who feels that he is the scapegoat led into the desert. A form of agreement was forced upon the trader, whereby he undertook, after a given date, not to purchase, supply or sell goods containing coupons, and not to have *any trade relations* with firms manufacturing or handling coupon goods.

This may not sound so serious to the average person not connected with the tobacco trade, but it amounted to a flagrant attempt by the vested interests controlling the tobacco supply market, to put the small trader and shopkeeper "on the spot." It meant boycott and ruin to the small man, who had to close his door.

Tobacconists Hard Hit

WHAT happened was that the T.T.A. virtually tried to establish an "equalisation fund." Every wholesaler was called upon in advance to pay one guinea, and every retailer who had dealt direct with a manufacturer had to pay 5s.

What really happened was that a sum above the required figure was obtained by this means, and no signatory to the agreement ever saw the balance sheet! It would be interesting to know how this money was spent.

The proof is there—it is time the traders took action with the Fascist Movement to protect the interests of the small man against the ruthless methods of the Vested Interests and Chain Stores. H. P. W.

Action

EDITORIAL OFFICES—
SANCTUARY BUILDINGS,
GREAT SMITH STREET,
LONDON S.W.1.
Telephone: Victoria 9084 (six lines)
Editor: JOHN BECKETT

The Drums Come Nearer

IF you were standing anywhere along a seven mile route, stretching from the Houses of Parliament to Victoria Park in the heart of East London, your ears would have caught the distant heavy rolling of the drums. Gradually, as the beating grew louder, the head of a purposeful column, with gay colours flying, would come into sight, and then for what seemed an endless period, file after file of steady marching men, broken by large colour parties, flanked by motor cyclists and accompanied on each pavement by a stream of followers, would pass by.

Over two thousand uniformed men, more than five hundred uniformed women, a contingent, seemingly endless, of men and women in civilian clothes were marching this long route, while at least another two thousand walked at the side or joined in at various stages of the journey. At a minimum figure, ten thousand followed Mosley to Victoria Park and more than a hundred thousand waited for him inside, excluding the massed East London Blackshirts who also waited inside the Park.

An Historic Event

THIS is an unheard of phenomenon in England. After weeks of Press booming, after thousands of pounds being spent in advertising, the old Parties would rub their eyes in amazement were they to succeed in gathering a quarter of this number of people together. The Fascist demonstration was boycotted by the Press, a few pounds spent on posters and handbills was all the advertisement it received. It should be pointed out that all the advertisement was paid for. Far more important than printed publicity was the work done by the active members of the Blackshirt Movement in London. More important even than that, was the hope that Fascism has raised in the minds of the present generation and the love that a great Leader has aroused in their hearts.

Some papers have alleged that this huge army was raised by special trains and coaches from all over the country. Let us break a rule of this journal and use bold type to contradict this lie. **Of all those thousands, everyone had made his, or her, own arrangement for arrival. Not one fare was paid and the parade, with the exception of a few dozen provincial visitors, entirely a march of the London Blackshirts.**

The Aftermath

LONDON witnessed the greatest spontaneous demonstration in modern times, yet the kept Press of the financiers hardly mentioned this huge event. Had one of Mr. Baldwin's nepotic pets, or some undistinguished ex-member of the disastrous Labour Government addressed ten deaf dowagers in the parish hall at Diddlecombe far greater space would have been given to the event.

On one fringe of the huge crowd a small band of Jews and Communists attempted to create a riot. They were promptly dealt with, but two Fascists repelling the attack were arrested in common with seven of the attackers. Almost every paper reported fighting in Victoria Park and one used a heading "Fascist Arrested." Several published photographs of a Fascist in the hands of the police. So small was the event in comparison with the size of the demonstration, that few members of the audience knew that it had occurred. Yet reporters and photographers, unable to describe or picture that stirring march and great spell-bound audience, could find it and give it publicity.

It is said that men may be known by their friends. If it is equally true that we may be judged by our enemies, then Sir Oswald Mosley and his Movement are to be congratulated upon the hatred and malice which Fleet Street displays towards them.

CORRESPONDENCE . . .

COMING EVENTS . . .

I was at a dinner, at which J. H. Thomas was in the chair, a few days before the Budget leakage was made known. He told a story of a parrot who, having said "Cats!!" to a fox terrier, crawled back to its cage, very much hors de combat, with the remark: "I know what's the matter with me. I open my bloody mouth too much!"

W. A. BELLAMY.

BRITAIN FIRST

May I be allowed to congratulate you on having presented to the British peoples your grand policy of "Britain First" in your most excellent journal. When such men as you have in YOUR party, and whose main policy is "Britain First," *that* is the party for any right-thinking Englishman. My late father served in H.M. Forces during the war and I myself volunteered and joined the Army at the age of 15½ years of age. As an ex-Service man who has studied foreign politcal affairs, I can assure you that I did not want any more "Locarnos" or Moudania (1921) treaties. The Moudania Treaty, signed on the ancient site of Troy, was an everlasting blow to British prestige in the Near East, and only for the tact and fine judgment of (then) Sir Horace Rumbold, our Ambassador in Constantinople, the gallant Consul Sir Henry Lamb, and our fine statesmanly Commander-in-Chief of the Allied forces in Turkey (i.e., General Sir Charles Harington, K.C.B., D.S.O.) was anything done to raise British prestige in that sphere of the world.

When I came home from India in 1924 I found tub-thumpers in Hyde Park, Trafalgar-square, and elsewhere shouting "Hands off Ghandi" (the gent that gave me many a restless night in India!), "Hands off Russia," "Hands off China," in fact, I was so fed up on one particularly pathetic occasion that I turned to a bored police inspector and said, "What about hands off Great Britain?" and his reply was, "They would have a blue fit if you suggested such an awful tragedy!"

It seems very tragic that the average Englishman cannot help his fellow-men MORE, than to try to help other peoples (especially peoples that would never dream of helping us!). Wishing the Leader and all members of the only truly "Britain First" party every success in the future.

STILL A PATRIOT AND PROUD OF IT.

CORNER MAN

Are we not taking "bluff" ex-King Haile too seriously? Why not give him a jazz-band and his son a mouth-organ, and send them both to Palestine to earn their living? I feel sure that the Jew, Larry Adler, would provide the latter with free instruction.

Alternatively, perhaps Ras "Prince" Monolulu would consent to take them into partnership.

In any case, time will hang pretty heavily upon their hands when their "turn" for the stunt Press is over.

CUTHBERT REAVELY.

BRIDISH DANCE BANDS

After reading "Bluebird's" article on the Queen Mary, it may interest your readers to compare the salaries of musicians on the world's most luxurious liner with London's better class hotels. One hotel pays three bands of approximately 12 musicians each . .an average of £15 per man, per week. They receive . .extra (?) for broadcasts, and a substantial . .extra for gramophone records.

The Queen Mary bandsmen receive £16 per month. No records and perhaps a little from broadcasts which would be better left out, especially on the American side, where criticism of a British band which can't be very good may be severe. This ship, with all the luxury of a first-class hotel, pays third-rate Palais-de-Danse salaries. The band will be worth more than its fee, owing to the hard times.

Incidentally, the pioneers of British dance music were the white men, Bobbie Hinds, Debroy Somers, Jack Hylton, Ramon Newton, Percy Macky, Percy Bush, etc., but no Jews. The Jews, true to their character, soon copied the original brains. Where are those originals now? Some still going, but not so very strong. Jews we have in plenty, Harry Roy, Lew Stone, Ambrose, Joe Loss, Harry Leader, Lew Preager, Geraldo, Jan Ralfini, Louis Levy, etc.

The decline of the Christians was not through their inferiority, but Jewish shareholders used their influence for their brother Englishmen, providing these Englishmen had the desired profile and astrakhan hair.—How long yet?

BANDSMAN.

SMASH "BLUEBIRD"

May I express my congratulations on the great "job" you have made of the "Blackshirt." Opinion amongst several here is that "Action" fails to reach an equivalently high standard.

"Bluebird" continues to disgust us with his piffling radio flashes. It is a pity that he can't be short-circuited. No rational person will object to convinced condemnation, but spiteful, cheap, or ranting diatribes only disgust. Instance, John Emery on Thomas, and the sickening Mr. Baldwin with his "chief admirer." Such a reference to the Leader in a Tory or Labour paper would have invited and doubtless got reproof. "Action" becomes a rather highbrow "Daily Worker" on weeks like that.

Bristol. JOHN N. P. I. MOUNTJOY.

NEWS-FINCH HELPS FASCISM

May I, a new reader of "Action," congratulate "Bluebird" on the very amusing "Radio Flashes." Only don't be too hard on the "news-finch"—he is doing some good, in spite of himself!

From the beginning of the war in Africa I had my doubts about him. It was all too bad to be true. The tragedy in his voice was almost comic and I simply couldn't swallow his bulletins. Thank heaven for a sensible English speaker at Radio Roma, who squared things for me.

I found my interest in Italy growing—followed interest in Mussolini—then Fascism—then *British* Fascism. (What a vision!) Finally, I joined the Union.

So you see, I owe my conversion from Toryism to Fascism largely to your "news-finch."

I wish your articles a wide circulation; they will do good!

F. E. HAYES.

"WAR-MONGERING BISHOPS"

I wonder how many Fascist actors and Shakespeare lovers have noticed the remarkable and very apt passage in the "Second Part of King Henry IV.," Act IV., Scene I., where the Earl of Westmoreland addresses the Archbishop of York, thus:—

". . . You, lord Archbishop,
Whose see is by a civil peace maintain'd,
Whose beard the silver hand of peace hath touch'd,
Whose learning and good letters peace hath tutor'd,
Whose white investments figure innocence,
The dove and very blessed spirit of peace,
Wherefore do you so ill translate yourself,
Out of the speech of peace that bears such grace,
Into the harsh and boisterous tongue of war;
Turning your books to graves, your ink to blood,
Your pens to lances and your tongue divine
To a loud trumpet and a point of war?"

This much may be said of the Lord Archbishop of York of that time, that he did not hesitate to change his mitre for a casque, his vestments for a coat of mail, his pastoral hook for a battle mace, and personally take his place in the van of battle.

The military activity of his present-day successor would consist, of course, in knitting socks and "keeping the home fires burning"!

H. GEE.

A REAL NEED

I think every edition of "Action" becomes better and better, and its sound commonsense and decent British honest contents must surely tell in the long run.

In fact, in view of the vacuous political matter, and the frankly dangerous political literature current, the paper of "Action" in its cleanly real British patriotic decency, comes like a breath of clear moorland air in an atmosphere which stinks with all manner of decadent treachery and foulness.

GILBERT B. HAY.

DISCIPLINE TELLS

I am not a Fascist as there are some things I cannot quite "swallow," but I should like to say how impressed I was with the East London rally. As the meeting broke up I was in a crowd to watch them go by. I heard filthy talk from, I suppose, Communist girls, accompanied by equally disgraceful gestures. I heard "Hebrew gentlemen" use nice terms of your "Blackshirt girls, but I never heard a bad expression back. I was so glad they kept their heads. Also in a crowd two girls made out a boy was struck by a Blackshirt which was a lie."

F. J. TAYLOR.

HYSTERIA

At a women's peace meeting held recently against Fascism and War, four hysterical females demanded action against Italy for daring to bring civilisation to Ethiopia, against Germany for reoccupying her own territory and in case Austria may one day join her Germanic brothers in an all-German Reich (terrible thing when Germans want to live with Germans), and then against Japan whose ambitions in China may annoy the comrades in the U.S.S.R. Having decided to have four wars on their hands, and also to disarm and place our trust in the League of Nations, the "Peace" demonstrators decided that they might as well have a war with the Blackshirts, so along come the friends of Russia and attempt to prevent a Fascist meeting being held.

As I rather object to spend the rest of my life fighting first one nation, then another (unless I am killed fighting without arms which our militant pacifists deny us), I prefer to march with Mosley and put Britain first.

I. F. P.

PRAISE

I am exceedingly obliged to you for the bundles of newspapers which we are putting to good use in this district with the hope that the Movement will gain sympathy and support.

If you are not too overwhelmed with praise for the later numbers of "Action," I should like to add my share. Certainly it gets better and better, and is now a paper to be really proud of.

Greenford. J. L. PETINGALE.

FINANCIAL DEMOCRACY IN DECAY

A. K. Chesterton Deals with the Decadent Condition of British Politics

IN the galloping putrescence of democratic society there seems to be no obscene stench which its Press will refuse to acclaim as an Elysian perfume.

It was not to be expected that the newspapers would have handled the Thomas affair in the way it should have been handled—as an altogether disgraceful business calling not only for the exemplary punishment of those implicated, but even more for a thorough investigation into the whole system of financial-democracy which breeds this and every other kind of corruption as part of its everyday routine. Press interests are too closely related to the existing scheme of things to have justified that expectation.

But few of us imagined that the newspapers would have had the audacious humbug to turn this unsavoury scandal, opening up as it did a sore for our contemplation and shame, into an opportunity for bidding its readers rejoice at the honour of British public life. Our institutions are indeed far gone in depravity when pestilence has to be heralded as health and when muck has to be decked out in the snow-white robes of purity.

Moral Inverts

THE "national" newspapers have been unanimous in taking this line, each one frantically concerned to minimise the enormity of the offence and to show that in any event one or two personal aberrations do not reflect upon the generally accepted standards of conduct both in the Cabinet and in the City of London.

"If the individual is condemned the system is justified," declared the "News Chronicle." Although the system is expressly designed to encourage the individual in every conceivable sort of corrupt ramp it is naturally the first thought of this lamentable sheet to assert that it must be held above reproach. "The system is watertight," asserted the "Star" in bland and even comic negation of the proven leakage.

"I am not concerned with that, Neville," said "Jim" at the Budget Enquiry

The "Daily Express" was even lyrical: "It is a blessed country where scandals of this kind are so rare. . . . The handling of this case, painful to many holding high authority, sets a seal again upon the integrity of politics in Britain." No less nauseating was the "Daily Herald," which found in the report of the Tribunal "a magnificent vindication of the reputation of political life," and referred with pride to "our public, our parliamentary, and our judicial traditions." And, of course, the "Daily Telegraph" did not lag behind in this abominable campaign to interpret shame in terms of national self-congratulation, endeavouring to give the public the impression that the last occasion when the "spotless reputation" of British statesmen suffered challenge was the Melville case—one hundred and thirty years ago!

The time has come to give the lie direct to all these attempts to represent the British Parliamentary system as incorruptible and a shining light before men. Without fear of contradiction from anybody in possession of the facts I assert that the edifice of financial democracy is rotten with turpitude and graft.

"Mac"

Many Kinds of Bribes

IT does not require evidence of monetary bribes to establish a charge of general political venality. The appeal to a democrat's vanity may prove much more difficult for him to resist than any appeal to his pocket. Years ago, strictly in this non-criminal but deplorable sense, we knew that J. H. Thomas had surrendered his political soul, as we knew that Ramsay MacDonald, Philip Snowden, and other alleged Socialists had done the same thing. They were not bought for cash in the way of a direct bribe, but they were no less certainly bought by the glittering prizes of the *beau monde* to which they had raised themselves upon the patient shoulders of the poor—the prizes of power and prestige and flattery; the opportunity to live in beautiful houses, to wear the best clothes, and to consort with Duchesses.

How can it be said that Snowden was not influenced by his surroundings when he earned the plaudits of the City as an orthodox Budgeteer, and thereafter cast derision on the whole of his life's struggle for the working class by taking his place in the Lords?

The MacDonald Motor

HOW can it be said that MacDonald was not affected in the same way when he began to use every contrivance to keep himself in power, no matter at what price, and when he did not hesitate to accept a costly motor-car and 30,000 industrial shares from a man upon whom he seized the first opportunity to confer a baronetcy?

It is well to remember MacDonald's Daimler and industrial shares, and to recall his explanation that it had nothing to do with Alexander Grant's subsequent elevation, as though it were easy for any Prime Minister in assessing honours claims not to be influenced by the fact that he had recently received so much assistance from one of the aspirants. Conduct of this order would never be tolerated in an age of strict decorum, and the fact that it was tolerated proves that it offended against neither the moral canons nor the political usages of the times.

These were all men who won popular favour and power by their championship of the claims of the oppressed against those of tyrannical vested interests, and the total result of their championship is that they held high office while the financial tyranny became more firmly entrenched at the expense of the masses, who continued to languish in insecurity and want. Remembering the solemn promises they made in return for the suffrage of the people, one can only affirm that the insuperable gulf between their promise and their performance is proof positive of the power of capitalist-democracy to corrupt the political soul of all save the grandest men. Such men do not tarry long in the spiritual bog of Party politics.

Big Business Politicians

IT is not the fake-Socialist alone who stands as a target for our contempt. The world of high politics is interpenetrated on every sector by the world of high finance, and Liberal and Conservative politicians have no need to resort to the baser crudities of corruption in order to hold and increase their personal wealth. They invest and speculate as a matter of course on the strength of their general knowledge. Moreover, in these transactions it is often clear that the City has nothing to teach them about financial technique, as was proved when certain prominent Liberal statesmen "milked" the old "Daily Chronicle" property with disastrous results for everybody except themselves.

While there was here no question of any official confidence being abused, the old-gang politicians have not always been above suspicion even in this, especially during the last fifty years of progressive Oriental infiltration into British political life.

There was, for instance, the Marconi business. While it is not my desire to re-open that old, fierce controversy, I am proud to recall that among decent Britons the memory of my distinguished kinsman, the late Cecil Chesterton, is held in a respect never to be achieved by the Godfrey Isaacs of the world, who secured his conviction on a charge of criminal libel. Whatever one may think of the verdict, one cannot blind oneself to the light it threw upon the intimate relationship between the political and financial wings of the Democratic system—a relationship that bestows no great credit on either.

Profits from Blood

THERE was also the very serious scandal of the disposal of war stock between 1919 and 1922. No sooner were the guns at peace than the Government set to work with feverish activity to destroy every atom of organisation for national production, in order that private enterprise might hold the field as before, without threat of challenge, and the consequent sales of national plant frequently constituted a first-class ramp. Gross favouritism was shown in many instances; private firms in other instances were equipped with huge surpluses of material for which they had not paid. Goods were resold as far as possible to the makers, while transactions were carried out in relation to plant in various parts of the world, whose value was not even known—"Contrary to the interests of the taxpayer," as was pointed out by the Select Committee on National Expenditure.

Thus were laid the foundations of that new Britain which was to be fit for heroes to live in!

Post-War Pestilence

IT cannot be said moreover, that the Labour Party initiated the practice of conducting brokerage in honours, for the scandal was rife during the war, and formed the subject of full-dress debates in both Houses during 1922. Since democratic politicians show so little respect for the honour of their country, it is not to be expected that they should show respect for their King, in whose name they elevated to the "nobility" almost any paltry coxcomb anxious to buy a title once awarded only for valour or for other great services to the State.

In the course of the two debates concrete instances were given of touting and trafficking in honours, the price ranging from £10,000 for a knighthood, to £40,000 for a baronetcy.

The Earl of Selborne declared: "It is not an exaggeration to say that immense sums of money continue to flow into the coffers of the political party in power at the moment. . . . I do not believe that these immense sums can continue to pass in complete secrecy, with no publicity, no responsibility, and personal corruption not ensue. . . ."

The Duke of Northumberland declared: "It is also remarkable how papers which have opposed the Government, and then turn round suddenly and support them, are immediately rewarded with honours for their proprietors and editors. . . . We find forty-nine Privy Councillors, Peers, Baronets, and Knights created since 1918, all of whom are either proprietors, principal shareholders, editors, managing directors, or chairmen of groups of newspapers."

Lieut.-Colonel Croft declared: "I mention two other cases. One is that of a man of great fortune who was appointed, or got himself appointed, representative on a tribunal for military service, and he used his position to gain exemption for his son and another very near relative . . . the gentleman was created a baronet on the recommendation of the Prime Minister. . . . In the third case the gentleman during the war was declared guilty of rendering false accounts. A judge and jury found him guilty of fraud. He was made a knight. . . . In this matter of the grant of honours, I submit, our country has been dishonoured."

Labour and "Honours"

THESE were but a few of the instances supporting the main indictment, and yet after many years the publicity given to a Mr. Maundy Gregory established the fact that the politicians are still very well content to carry on with this abominable system by which honours are bartered, so that party funds may keep them at the helm, faithfully serving their own wretched careers to the last.

The Labour Party, flaming with anger at such abuses, came to office determined to end them, and then promptly turned round and perpetuated them, placing special donations to its funds into a private account which were not shown in the Party balance-sheet. Among the chief contributors was the wealthy Jew, Bernhard Baron, whose son Mr. Ramsay MacDonald made a knight.

These are the scandals which have become public property. That many others have not seen the light is due to the truly magnificent façade which the democrats have built up to give a wholly meretricious appearance of respectability to their system. Behind the façade there is a riot of cynicism, intrigue, and graft. The public is rarely permitted a glimpse of what goes on here. Otherwise long ago it would have hurled to destruction a system of financial rampage and political chicanery which eats like a cancer into the heart of the British nation.

"David"

There can be no more temporising. Our country has been desperately wounded by the corrupt activities of finance, and from each wound there emerges the stench of political gangrene.

The self-seekers, the political bounders, the fawning yes-men—they must all be hounded out of public life. In their place, in the place of the men who accepted every reward of high office, the British people must set up the one great man who deliberately spurned those rewards rather than betray the nation and his own high honour—Oswald Mosley, leader of Fascism in Britain.

At heart we know that our people are fundamentally the least corruptible in the world. Their instinct will not fail them when the great hour strikes.

INTERNATIONALISM MEANS WAR

FOLLIES OF THE "SMASH FASCISM FRONT" EXPLAINED

By A. RAVEN THOMSON

A NUMBER of churches have exhibited the following remarkable placard:—

"*The new patriotism is internationalism.*"

Protests have naturally appeared in the Conservative Press but these entirely fail to grasp the significance of such an event. It is not enough to protest against the negative aspect of the statement. It is bad enough that we should be told to be no longer patriotic towards our own country, but it is far worse that we should be asked to be patriotic towards an internationalist system instead. Along that way can lie nothing but another series of World Wars!

It is highly ominous how our Christian Churchmen continue to preach war under the guise of peace. We have not forgotten the statement of the Archbishop of York. "It took one war to found the League of Nations, it may need another to establish its authority." Nor are we likely to forget the outburst of the Bishop of Durham so furiously applauded at the Convocation at Westminster, "Would that we could draw a sword and go and do battle for God's people." Quite the crusading spirit again! Except that Richard, the Lion-Hearted, would scarcely have done battle with Frederick Barbarossa on behalf of the Jews.

Our Western Mullahs

WE have long been accustomed to the Mahommedan Mullahs in the East preaching Holy Wars, which have cost our frontier forces many lives, but we scarcely expected to find similar fanatics filling our pulpits here in Christian Britain and threatening millions of British youth with a like fate. At least the Mullahs led their troops into action and often died riddled with bullets, a text from the Koran on their lips.

Our Bishops and Archbishops may be relied upon to urge greater and greater sacrifices to the "new patriotism" from the comfort and security of their palaces. And great will be the outcry if a bombing plane should happen to drop its cargo where it would do the cause of peace the most good.

Let us be quite clear about it. This "new patriotism" leads more directly into War than did the "old."

This "new patriotism" threatens world war whenever peace is disturbed in any quarter, whatever the cause and whether British interests are involved or not. All this in face of a complete inability to grapple with the real economic and political causes of war.

No more suicidal policy could be imagined, and no policy more contrary to the Christian doctrine of the Prince of Peace.

The Popular Front

IT would be serious enough if the only danger lay in being dragged into some local conflict, but "internationalism" is becoming increasingly aggressive, and, as is shown by the Bishop of Durham's statement, desires to interfere with the internal affairs of other countries. This is the worst aspect of the "new patriotism."

Marxist Socialism has always been internationalist, and has based its eventual success upon an international organisation of the "workers of the world." The Russian Army is known as the "Army of the World Revolution" in recognition of this fact.

Until the advent of Fascism this policy seemed successful enough in conflict with the capitalist system, which was in itself international, but the Fascist States now form great barriers to the Socialist International. Either the international method of advance must be abandoned, or these States must be destroyed. Thus does internationalism on the Socialist front lead to frustration or war.

Rather than abandon the international revolution the forces of world Marxism are marshalling against Fascism, determined to overthrow Mussolini and Hitler before the doctrines of Fascism spread.

For this reason Communism everywhere is abandoning its immediate revolutionary social purpose to form a Popular Front with Social-Democratic and even Liberal elements against Fascism, urging by every means possible a war of suppression against the Fascist States.

This is the truth behind the turgid flood of propaganda that has swirled through our newspapers during the past year. Fascism means war, because Internationalism will not tolerate the existence of Fascist States; just as Blackshirt meetings mean violence, because Communists cannot tolerate Blackshirt freedom of speech.

MIND BRITAIN'S BUSINESS

"Will No-one Rid Us Of These Turbulent Priests."

National Socialism

MUST all social betterment by revolutionary action be abandoned until Fascism is crushed? This would seem to be the argument of the international Marxist, who sees no possibility of social advance except on an international front. It is certainly the battlecry of the Jew, who sees in Internationalism the advantage of his widespread people.

There is no logical reason why social betterment must wait upon international action. There is no reason why each nation should not put its own house in order and solve its own problems for itself.

This is, in fact, the explanation of Fascism, which is a great National-Socialist effort of escape from intolerable conditions. It came to Italy and Germany first, because these countries found themselves in such a catastrophic state of breakdown in the respective capitalist depressions of 1922 and 1932, that they were compelled to resort to drastic national efforts of social reconstruction, and could not wait longer for the internationalist millennium.

Fascism is gathering force in Britain because there is a growing demand for a National-Socialist effort to grapple with the urgent social and economic problems of the day. People remember that Mosley was never interested in internationalism, but led the greatest effort of social betterment since the war under the last Labour Government, when the Labour Party turned down his proposals to find work for 800,000 men because they were resisted by the international bankers.

National-Socialism means peace, because it can attain its ends without interference with other countries, and because it sympathises with and recognises the national requirements of other countries. International Socialism means war, because it cannot attain its ends without interfering with other nations, and because it denies to these nations the economic and political satisfaction of their needs.

Britain within the next few years will have to make her choice between the "new patriotism" of internationalism with its inevitable bloodthirsty attack upon the national Fascist States of Italy and Germany, and the "new socialism" of nationalism determined to maintain peace for the reconstruction of Britain and the development of her Empire for the benefit of the British people.

Who will follow the bishops to battle, or Mosley to peace?

THE POLICY OF THE NEW FRENCH GOVERNMENT

(From Our Correspondent in France)

NEVER has the arrival of a new Ministry excited more interest than the Cabinet of the Second International and of Radical-Socialists which will be formed on June 5.

The future Ministers have been discussed somewhat as favourites for the Derby: Who will be the best for a place? Who will be Minister of the Interior? Will M. Chautemps or M. Delbos be in charge of Exterior Relations? Will M. Hérriot preside over the Chamber of Deputies, and if so can he manage the stairs that lead to the throne, for they are very narrow?

The factious, or Fascist Leagues, will be dissolved immediately, the Regency of the Bank reformed, a general amnesty will be accorded in favour of political prisoners, but it seems clear that this will only affect those who belong to the parties of the Left.

The decree laws passed during the Laval Ministry will be amended if not annulled.

M. Blum has promised, with a magic wand to restore prosperity, to redress injustice, and inspire youth with hope. Like Mr. Roosevelt in America, and M. van Zeeland in Belgium, he has a plan.

The Foreign Policy of the Front Populaire

HAVING settled the social questions, which are certainly dominated by the question of unemployment, M. Blum will secure peace in Europe by firmly supporting the League of Nations. He proposes progressive disarmament, reduction of military credits (this will help to supply the immediate needs of the Treasury), arbitration of international conflicts, revision of treaties. Really! It is indeed astonishing, for the Front Populaire promised something entirely new.

The President of the Council will be in favour of friendly relations with all countries—especially with Great Britain and the United States. The Americans are even encouraged to hope for a payment of the War debts, though these debts were denounced already both by England and France. The French have a special treaty with the Americans by which their debt to the United States depended on the German payments. (Cancelled by the Treaty of Lausanne.) M. Blum is not French, so he has forgotten. Yet the payment of the American debts was the policy of M. Hérriot. In this case, too, the Front Populaire shows no originality.

To say the real truth, all M. Blum's peaceful projects seem to make straight for a universal conflict. A distressing question arises—could the Israelites be interested in war? The international financiers might stand to gain; for many have no country to care for, no reputation to lose, no God to deny. As for the people who may think their own small fortunes are not at stake, they are utterly in the dark. Can one expect intelligence from those who are never tired of howling, *Les Soviets partout, Faites payer les riches*?

The Soviet Russians are only afraid of Germany—they are determined that their allies, the French, shall help them against Germany. Where could the French help but on the Rhine, which Mr. Baldwin has declared is the frontier of England?

Toleration

A RECENT leading article in the "North London Recorder" expressed "Intolerance of Intolerance" and demanded the right of all to express their views. After being assured that the journal was neither Jewish-owned nor Jewish-controlled, we read that it "will give every political organisation—whatever its colour—a fair hearing along with the rest."

The next sentence continued: "nor will it tolerate any organisation which aims at setting up a dictatorship—for that is something *no* self-respecting and independent country or newspaper will tolerate."

Democratic freedom of speech means, of course, absolute freedom for everybody—except those who do not agree with democracy. We imagine that Prohibition journals also give absolute freedom of expression to everybody—except those who like beer.

The "North London Recorder" was congratulated on its attitude the following week (May 29) by one of its Old English readers, Mr. Galinsky.

THE WARMONGERS

Germany's Enemies Want War

FOR six months Oswald Mosley has exposed the Geneva sanctions racket for what it was—an anti-Fascist ramp. The Covenant, which has been regarded as an interesting museum-piece by most of the world's Powers, has been galvanised into temporary life for use against Italy for the reason that Italy was Fascist and for that reason alone.

The democrats and the Communists have vigorously denied this, using much gaudy phraseology about sacred obligations and world peace; but a Jewish-controlled newspaper, as usual, lets the cat out of the bag.

In the "News Chronicle" of June 6 A. J. Cummings has written a remarkable article. While purporting to comment on the Government's attitude towards Geneva, the real purpose of the article is a demand for the intensification of sanctions to the point of war, and a reconstitution of the League on lines that will facilitate another future war against Germany.

"There is no reason," states Mr. Cummings, "why, even after Mussolini's temporary triumph, the League fight should not go on with unceasing vigour." What does this mean? That although no war exists, the League should be prepared to have one; and that the League is not concerned with existing facts or rights and wrongs, but merely with blind opposition to Fascist Italy.

That such an attitude is expected to characterise the League at all times becomes very clear from the next paragraph, where Mr. Cummings describes the statement issued recently by the so-called Council of Action for Peace and Reconstruction. The Council's plan, according to Mr. Cummings, has "the supreme merit that it makes no compromise with Italy."

Finally, he refers to the "Plan of Action" that the "News Chronicle" itself put forward a month ago: "To expel Italy from the League . . . develop through Geneva a much closer union of the peace-minded, League-minded nations (he means the anti-Fascist ones, including the Soviet); a union *involving clear and definite military commitments in the political field* . . . a League thus organised might soon begin to exercise immense authority and power and pave the way for a *final victory of democratic freedom over the tyranny of dictatorships.*"

The plan of Jewish finance acting through its mouthpiece of the Press emerges quite nakedly. The finance-ridden democracies of Britain and France are to combine with the bloodstained Soviet in a reconstituted League, "involving clear and definite commitments in the political field." If that means anything whatsoever, it means that war, far from being something we are to try to prevent, is to be openly advocated for the purpose of crushing the Fascist and National-Socialist régimes.

Mr. Cummings has perhaps stated the designs of Jewish finance a little more clearly than his employers would have wished.

MORE VERSE

A Modern Nursery Rhyme

A *READER sends us the following continuation of the verse printed under this heading some weeks ago.*

Haile Selassie, the conquering Jew,
Burned and tortured and robbed and slew,
Now he hasn't a crown to wear
He's coming to live near Grosvenor Square.

Friendly with Eden and Baldwin and Hoare,
What can any old Jew want more.
Eden calls on Monday morning,
On Tuesday Baldwin comes without warning.

On We'n'sday Sam'el Hoare turns up to tea;
Who could be so merry as we,
And when he's bored and wants some fun,
Off to dear Russia he only need run.

There he can torture, can flog and can slay,
Tho' there's no one to rob to-day.
If our gutter press tells us so true,
This need not bother the chocolate Jew.

When slaves chased him out of his stinking hold
He got away with all his gold.
So this cunning old conqu-ring Jew,
Burned 'em and tortured and robbed 'em and slew.

A. S.

THE CORPORATE STATE AND YOU

No. 5—THE TEXTILE WORKER

By A. Raven Thomson

IT was upon the basis of textile manufacture, especially cotton fabrics, that British industrial supremacy during the nineteenth century was founded. Manchester was then the centre of economic theory and commercial progress, and boasted "What Lancashire thinks to-day, England thinks to-morrow." A sad change has taken place to-day, when a Bill to scrap millions of spindles is before Parliament, and almost the entire cotton trade is lost to the Orient. Nor is the situation much brighter in Yorkshire, where Polish and Japanese competition is felt, and the bulk of the artificial silk trade has passed to Italy and Japan.

Alarming Figures

WHAT is the cause of this disastrous decline which threatens the very basis of British commercial life? The answer can be seen by the following round figures for the cotton trade (million square yards).

COTTON TRADE.

	Lancashire Exports.	Japanese Exports.	Indian Production
1913	7,000	200	1,000
1935	2,000	3,000	3,000

Thus, while the total consumption of cotton goods from these three sources remains the same, about 8,000 million square yards, the bulk is now manufactured out East, instead of in Lancashire. This is because of coolie labour, which is quite able to tend modern mass production machinery.

WAGES AND HOURS.

	Weekly wage.	Hours worked.
Lancashire	34s. 6d.	48
Japan	11s. 0d.	60
India	10s. 0d.	56

What possible chance has the Lancashire textile worker of competing with blackleg labour on this scale? The world has become so small that these sweated coolies might just as well be working in Bolton or Blackburn. In fact, they are actually better placed with regard to the tropical markets upon which Lancashire relies.

No Internationalist Solution

NEITHER of the two political parties of the State offers a remedy, as both are pledged to a policy of internationalism. So bankrupt of ideas is the Conservative Party that it actually proposes to scrap textile machinery and bury the decaying corpse of Lancashire's premier industry. It is hopeless to expect a finance-ridden Government like the present to resist the trend of industry out East, where higher dividends are to be made by exploiting coolie labour, while Lancashire men and women walk the streets in idleness.

The Socialists are no better, their one panacea being State ownership of an already bankrupt industry, without the slightest conception of how to win back markets from Oriental competition. Nothing would please the financiers more than for the State to take over the bankrupt mills of Lancashire and pay compensation to the present owners. This would be a classical example of leaving someone else to carry the baby.

An Empire Policy

FASCISM has the only remedy for the complete collapse of the textile industry. First, the Corporate State would endow the industry with self-governing powers within its own corporation, which would have separate woollen and cotton sections. This would enable it to carry through the many necessary measures of co-ordination and reorganisation without the financial resort of amalgamation or the Socialist one of nationalisation.

As the industry is so concerned with exports, it will not be sufficient for the Government merely to leave it to solve its own difficulties. Over-capitalisation in 1920 was a serious drawback, but the real causes of decline are nevertheless external. The textile worker will not look in vain to a Fascist Government for protection against coolie competition. Just as blacklegging within Britain will not be tolerated, neither will it be within the British Empire.

The textile corporation will be granted special privileges not only in supplying clothing to the home market, but also to Empire markets. The Government will exclude Japanese textiles from Empire markets, denouncing all treaties, such as the Congo Basin Treaty, which stand in the way. In India the 25 per cent. tariff against Lancashire goods will be removed, and steps taken to prevent the exploitation of Indian labour by unscrupulous financiers. Under such a firm policy there can be no doubt that present Lancashire exports can be doubled, and Yorkshire markets protected from the menace of Japanese competition which already threatens them.

Raw Materials

IN return for protected Imperial markets the Fascist Government will expect the Textile Corporation to obtain its raw materials from Imperial sources. At present much of our raw cotton comes from the United States and our wool from the Argentine, while a large part of the Indian cotton crop goes to Japan to be processed and returned to India as cotton goods. Lancashire will be expected to make use of Empire cotton, obtaining long staple cotton from Uganda and the Sudan, short staple from India. Yorkshire will be expected to use Australian wool, much of which at present goes to Japan.

By this means our textile industry will knit more closely the economic bonds of Empire, and extend the corporate concept from the Home Country to the Empire.

Wages and Conditions

AS an inevitable result of foreign coolie competition, especially in cotton goods, wages of textile workers have dropped, until the average wage in Lancashire is no more than 34s. 6d. a week, with many earning less than this. As long as Lancashire is exposed to this form of competition there can be no escape, short of ruinous subsidies. Internationalism will drag down the standard of the white worker to that of the coolie.

The Fascist policy of an insulated Empire will assure Lancashire an adequate market independent of Oriental competition, and it will be possible for cotton manufacturers to pay good wages and take their place in improving standards of life. What is more, the increased use of Empire raw materials will improve the standards of the native peoples who produce these materials and increase their purchases of textiles. So an ascending spiral of improving conditions and increasing production will take the place of the descending spiral of lower standards and declining markets which threatens to engulf Lancashire in its vortex. It is only through Empire co-operation that the British textile industry can recover its former national supremacy.

THE CREED OF ACTION.

"All shall serve the State and none the Faction;

"All shall work and thus enrich their country and themselves;

"Opportunity shall be open to all, but privilege to none;

"Great position shall be conceded only to great talent;

"Reward shall be accorded only to service;

"Poverty shall be abolished by the power of modern science released within the organised State;

"The barriers of class shall be destroyed and the energies of every citizen devoted to the service of the British nation, which, by the effort and sacrifice of our fathers has existed gloriously for centuries before this transient generation, and which by our own exertions shall be raised to its highest destiny—the Greater Britain of Fascism." *From "Code of British Union of Fascists."*

UNDER THE CONTROL TOWER

A Great Pioneer Celebrates A Jubilee

OTHER PIONEERS

By "BLACKBIRD"

ON June 3, the ever youthful and virile weekly, the "Aeroplane," produced a special issue to commemorate the first twenty-five years of its existence. I recommend everyone interested in the future of Britain in the air to buy this issue and read the somewhat hustled history compiled by its famous editor. For by understanding what happened in the past we can avoid making the same mistakes in the future. I well remember how, on June 8, 1911, a funny little paper, looking rather like the "Boy Scout" (another funny little paper of the period), and having some of the better and more vigorous characteristics of "John Bull," under Horatio Bottomley, arrived for me by post. At once I realised that here was a paper that was different from all other papers.

In the first place, it was so refreshingly amateur, and above all every page showed the hand of a forceful personality. And, indeed, they could hardly have done anything else. For practically every word was written and every photograph was taken by the hand of the editor, Charles Grey Grey himself, known throughout the aviation world as C. G. G.

No personality in the aviation world is so universally known and so universally liked and disliked by the same people at different times as C. G. Grey. But the fact that he has built up the "Aeroplane" from nothing to the most influential aviation paper in the world is a very great achievement.

A Rebel by Birth

AND owing to the fact that he is continuously in rebellion against incompetent authority he is not likely to receive the honours he has long deserved from an ungrateful country—at least, not until a Fascist Government comes to power.

Owing to his articles in the "Aeroplane," and particularly his recent ones on the Italo-Abyssinian war, I have often been asked whether C. G. Grey is a member of the B.U.F. He is not. And if you were to ask him if he was a Fascist he would certainly deny it.

But he would admit that he was a hundred per cent. Britisher, and cared only for the future of Britain as a strong and virile nation, and you would find that he, like all other true Britishers, holds views similar to those of the B.U.F. I rather doubt if he realises that his views are pure Fascism.

His outlook on life can be seen from this quotation from a letter he wrote to me a year or so ago:

"*You and I have one thing in common, that is that we have habitually been rebels against authority, not because we are naturally rebels, but because we have so much instinctive reverence for authority that we are driven to desperation by the fools whom God has been pleased to set in authority over us.*

"*You may remember the delightful remark of poor Peter Legh's father, old Major Gilbert Legh, Lord Newton's brother. He had been reproaching me with writing against the Government and had called me a Bolshie. I replied that I was not a Bolshie, but I was constitutionally a rebel against incompetent authority, and added that we had been beheaded for the same kind of rebellion generation after generation for centuries. He replied, 'Then all I can say is that they did not behead you enough.'*"

Since 1908

GREY has been writing on aviation since 1908, when, as a member of the staff of the "Autocar," he was sent to Paris to write up the world's first aero show.

Since that time he has come into intimate and close contact with everybody who is anybody in aviation. He is a very clear thinker and can visualise the trend of things aerial long before most people. At one time his theories used to be dismissed as "Grey's silly ideas." Then a few designers started taking them seriously, with consequent profit to themselves.

C. G. himself is one of the most exasperating people I know. At times he bullies his staff unmercifully, but would be horrified if he realised it. But he bullies himself more than anyone else. He is at times inconsiderate to everyone, but most of all to himself.

His staff at times loathe the sight of him and the rest of the time they adore him. One member of the staff has been with him for seventeen years.

When they cannot stand him any longer they leave. Some of them come back again. The rest, after expending their fury, are always welcomed back into the fold as sort of Old Aeroplanians, for C. G. is too great a soul ever to bear malice.

If he does have a quarrel with anyone he believes in getting it all over in one huge and glorious row. And then he forgets it.

Incorruptible

HE is quite incorruptible and cannot be bought. Once when he was adopting a policy which he himself believed was best for the future of British aviation, the aircraft industry thought otherwise. They attempted to muzzle him by threatening to withdraw advertisements. C. G. explained to his fellow-directors that he believed the course he was taking was the right one and he intended to stick to it, even though it might mean considerable personal loss. I know that in his own mind on that occasion he contemplated resigning, or even being asked to resign by the other directors. As it was, the other directors backed him up and the plot failed. Never since then has an attempt to coerce the "Aeroplane" succeeded.

By Courtesy of the "Aeroplane"

Maurice Farman "Longhorn," on which type many early R.F.C. pilots, including 2nd Lieut. Oswald Mosley, learned to fly

C. G. Grey has, during the twenty-five years as editor of the "Aeroplane," materially altered for the better the trend of things aerial, not only in Britain, but over all the world. May he long live to help to keep Britain first in the air.

Other Pioneers

ONE often comes across people in the B.U.F. who were in aviation in the early days. Sir Oswald Mosley, then a 2nd lieutenant, learnt to fly in May, 1915, in an old Maurice Farman "Longhorn" at Shoreham, where the present writer was a fellow pupil. The old "Longhorn," which is pictured here, was quite a nice aeroplane to fly. Its top speed was about 55 m.p.h. and its stalling speed was about 45 m.p.h., but it was about the easiest thing to land that was ever invented.

Many early Service people learned to fly on the old 504K Avro, the designer of which was A. V. Roe (now Sir Alliott Verdon-Roe), who has long been a member of the B.U.F.

When I was in the Croydon District Office of the B.U.F. recently I came across ex-Flight-Sergeant Baker, who was one of the old crowd of "ack-emmas" in the old R.F.C. before the War. If I remember rightly, Baker was one of the first to be raised to the rank of First Air Mechanic. He was at the old C.F.S. at Upavon, and after full war service he went to Kenley after the War until 1924. He has some wonderful stories to tell of the old days. He has now left the Service and is living in Croydon.

THIS FREEDOM

"We Fight for Freedom." By "A. Freeman." (Fascist Shilling Library. B.U.F. Publications, Ltd.)

THE need for such a fight is best proved by the fact that the author found it necessary to use a pseudonym, although he follows an honourable calling at the English Bar of Justice. That an officer of the Court should face certain victimisation and possible ruin through acknowledging membership of a patriotic organisation is an impressive impeachment of democratic liberty.

His legal qualifications enable him to illuminate, though hardly to elucidate, some of the inscrutable mysteries of D.O.R.A. and the petty tyrannies that cabin, crib, and confine the daily lives of what were once free Englishmen. His analysis is penetrating, but he uses no legalistic phraseology, writing, indeed, in the language appropriate to his subject — the language of common sense. Where the point at issue is too petty for his fierce indignation, he employs the whiplash of a biting wit. The description, for instance, of the film censorship as "an inverted Mr. Micawber, waiting for something to turn down," could hardly have been bettered. It would, however, be unfair to author and reader to quote at length the epigrams with which a fine piece of writing is pungently seasoned.

A large section of the book deals with the strictly personal freedom that we lack to-day — freedom in respect of what we shall see on stage or screen, what we shall read, where and when we may drink, dance, have a flutter, and other innocent pleasures that Mrs. Grundy frowns on.

But the broad issue of true liberty and its essential conditions is not allowed to be viewed out of perspective, and is treated in an original manner all the more striking for not emanating from an official Fascist thinking-shop. Mr. "Freeman" probably states, in a vivid and provocative manner, the thoughts of the ordinary Fascist-sympathiser or the plain Englishman who is Fascist at heart without knowing it.

He keeps off the grass of anything approaching doctrinaire economics, yet shows conclusively that the bases of all real freedom—economic security and a high standard of living—can never be established within a system of democratic internationalism, whose conception of freedom has extended the meaning of liberty into licensed lying, legalised exploitation, and legitimate pillage of the nation as a whole by the chartered profiteers of Lombard Street.

It is not necessary to be a Fascist to enjoy and appreciate this book. Would to heaven that some of our pontifical platform-knights, episcopal dragon-slayers, and self-appointed vigilantes of capitalism would read it and pipe down!

Fascism exposes and abolishes all rackets. Mr. "Freeman" has debunked the liberty-racket, which is an even fouler thing than the physical slums that Liberalism in the name of freedom built round the offices of the "Manchester Guardian."

J. A. M.

"Cock-Sparrow." By Oliver P. Bernard. (Jonathan Cape. 10s. 6d.)

THE author calls this "a true chronicle." It is also fairly obviously autobiographical, and the writer, during a varied and eventful career, has developed and preserved an affection and pity for his own youth which is made very obvious in the early chapters, and a little colours the whole book.

There is a vivid account of the sinking of the Lusitania, written from the passenger's viewpoint, in the early days of the war, and more than half the book is taken up with the writer's war service. It is an entertaining book of a varied and interesting life, and the writing is only very slightly self-conscious.

A. C.

'MODERN' FICTION

"A HOUSE OF WOMEN." By H. E. BATES. (Jonathan Cape, 7/6.)

BRITISH fiction of to-day stands at the cross-roads. Purposeless, lacking a single writer of consistent genius to point the way, it marks time, afraid to continue along the road of romantic prosody created by the masters of English literature, equally afraid to carve a new path for itself. Occasionally, amid the flood of books, we find one which leads to hope that the period of indecision has at last been ended by the emergence of a guiding spirit. Brett Young's "The House Under the Water," Linklater's "Juan in America," Huxley's "Point Counter-Point," Priestley's "Good Companions," and, possibly, Graves' "I, Claudius" all held out promise, but so far none of the authors has maintained this. A mixed bundle, these novels; it is doubtful whether any other age could have produced such contrasting subjects or divergent writing.

These books signify the indecision of the hour, from which emerges only one definite tendency, the development of the novel dealing with real people, united in their battle against the forces surging around them, divided and quarrelling among themselves when those forces become the conflict of their own emotions. Novels such as these have nothing in common with the cardboard passions of the "Society" or "modern" story; they are of the earth earthy, perhaps a little too earthy at times. Their writers tackle each set of events in their novels with a clinical precision.

In the vanguard of this movement stand three writers of exceptional ability, Doreen Wallace ("So Long to Learn"), Ann Bridges (a vastly different writer, but worthy of inclusion on account of "Pekin Picnic" and "Illyrian Spring"), and H. E. Bates.

Mr. Bates, who has already written several fine novels—notably, "Catherine Foster" and "The Fallow Land"—is the most clinical of any writers in this movement. In "A House of Women" he indulges his fancy with a surgical exactness that is almost horrifying.

Rosie, the attractive, desirable barmaid at the "Angel," in the full bloom of her many charms, marries Tom Jeffrey, a dour, egocentric though not unlikeable farmer, head of a family of rigid Methodists, in which the women—the old mother, Maudie and Ella, Tom's sex-starved sisters—dominate every move. Poor Rosie is bundled in amongst the women, finds her husband forever obsessed with crops and the land, her mother and sisters-in-law forever seeking to disparage her, a desire which reaches its culmination when they discover that Rosie is mother of an illegitimate daughter.

In her loneliness Rosie turns to Frankie, the younger son, a scared youth whom we perceive cares more for her charms than herself. Unfortunately for Rosie's hopes of escape to South Africa, Frankie is drowned.

The War intervenes. Tom leaves for the front. Maudie has an affair with Turk, Rosie's father. Lily, the daughter, marries a caricature of the parson. Tom returns a madman. Ella dies. Every fifty pages, with unremitting regularity, there is a death, a theft, a fire, or some tragedy.

This work has been hailed as demonstrative of Mr. Bates maturity as a writer. Certainly the writing itself marks a great improvement over his last book, but his timing of events is so regular as to become monotonous. Even the affair with Frankie is made sordid by its insistence upon the physical nature of their attraction.

The Late D. H. Lawrence—
A Bloomsbury Idol

The interesting thing about the book is not whether it is a good novel—that is not questioned; it most certainly is—but whether we need stories which revolve around a central point of physical passion. Apart from those incidents which the presence of a Censor prevents from inclusion, Mr. Bates has carefully described each sequence leading up to the inescapable culmination.

Is this really necessary? Since D. H. Lawrence, most writers have shown a terrific interest in this side of human nature. But it is becoming boring. There are more things to write about than passion; there are many facets of life which authors strangely ignore. It would appear that none of the members of this school of literature feels his work complete unless he details every step, every hand-touch, every look of physical prompting, revels in the exact description of every outward characteristic and inward craving.

This is to be deplored, and we must hope that by his next novel Mr. Bates will escape from the easy trap into which he has fallen.

H. J. G.

"Enter Mussolini." By Emilio Lussu. Observations and Adventures of an Anti-Fascist. English Translation. 1936. (Methuen. 7s. 6d.)

IN a preface to this book Wickham Steed says that he knows "of nothing better in all that has been written upon Italian Fascism." If British democrats rely upon this for an intellectual argument let them despair, for Fascism must prosper in spite of such social misfits as Signor Lussu.

The author presents a lightly connected panorama so interpreted as to show all Fascists, most democrats (all those who turned Fascist), some republicans, and most politicians as either brutal or cowardly. All who opppse Fascism are heroes, all who support it renegades; some even manage to be both in one day. Signor Lussu himself comes out all right; he is the hero of heroes, the man who opposed the Government, like all good democrats, because it was the Government.

Further, in democratic-republican Lussu's case, because it was a monarchical Government, too. Perhaps pro-republican Lussu would have written a different interpretation if Mussolini had formed a republican state.

This Mussolini must be a peculiar man, so cowardly, yet turning up at every crucial moment, and taking full responsibility upon himself. These cowardly Fascists, so lacking in courage that with every crisis they hide their blackshirt and badges, yet manage to grow stronger on each occasion in spite of the opposition of the whole population. "Truth is stranger than fiction," said someone. Truly this is stranger than truth or fiction; it is unbelievable.

Let Mr. Steed and all democrats take warning. Lussu makes one mistake in his whole tirade. It is contained in one sentence: "'That wretched aqueduct!' I said to myself" (page 138). An old man forced this admission, a non-Fascist member of the public. The village lacked water, and they had been waiting for an aqueduct for fifty years. "'I was a child,' said the man, 'when we were first promised an aqueduct, and now my hair is white, but still the water has not come.'" (Page 136.)

The Lussus had to be destroyed and Fascism had to be before the water came. Thus that short exclamation: "That wretched aqueduct!" contains a world of enmity and meaning.

F. C.

PATHOLOGY AS A HERESY

"I Am a Heretic." By "Vanoc II." (Peter Davies, Ltd. 6s.)

THIS book is the Marxist gospel according to Vanoc II., who once served under Ostrer auspices as the High Priest of dialectical materialism for Bloomsbury's intellectuals.

Its title is sufficiently self-important to suggest that there is no field of egotism in which its author would hesitate to wander, and so it proves, although the common denominator remains constant and there is nothing in heaven and earth which is not finally reduced to an unpleasant little Marxist smell.

The man is Marx-struck and Marx-bedazed. His chapter on the German Jew is headed "Ecce Homo," while his excursion into physics leads him to "only one certainty—namely, that the present scientific conflict will end with the victory of matter, or, better stated, of dialectical materialism." The encouraging thought here, I suggest, is that in the metamorphosis of matter even intellectual pus may ultimately be transformed into something rich and strange.

Even motor smashes are not motor smashes, but "only one aspect of the socialised murder of individuals by forces that cannot be contained in an outworn phase of society."

To such a mind every manifestation of vitality and health appears as decadence, Fascists are moronic reactionaries in the pay of capitalism. Naval officers and Rugby footballers are toughs. Generals are "repositories of sentimental hog-wash," discipline is "legalised terrorism," and Captain Scott's fine patriotism is seen as "almost to fall into the category of Oedipus complex."

At last I understand the tongs-and-incinerator attitude towards certain books. I am tempted to burn this volume, not because I disapprove of the writer's politics, which would make Stalin laugh uproariously, but because it seems to me to contain two hundred and thirteen pages of unrelieved nonsense.

I recommend it to all students interested in the pathology of Bloomsbury.

A. K. C.

FILMS OF THE WEEK

PASSION ON ICE

PETTICOAT FEVER
Metro-Goldwyn-Mayer

SO neatly are American cinema actresses divided into water-tight types that it is customary now to choose our entertainment not by the title of a picture but by the name of its starring players. The great mass of actresses are lovely ingenues, and so quickly do these young women with hearts of gold and gleaming smiles appear and disappear on the cinema screen that it is sometimes difficult to distinguish one from another. The pictures in which they appear are uniformly commonplace—films made during the cinema's work-a-day life for indiscriminate entertainment. Only five or six women, with poise and ability, have managed to become outstanding figures, and are recognisable as being very distinct and separate personalities, and to these are usually given costly films intended to shake the world of entertainment into recognition of the cinema's merits.

Myrna Loy is a beautiful young woman, whose repose of manner and finished style of acting has placed her, during the last five years, among the select company of Hollywood actresses whose work is entertaining and intelligent, quite irrespective of the picture in which it appears. "Petticoat Fever," in which she is playing opposite Robert Montgomery, is a trite and obvious piece of entertainment which is only saved by the delightful performances of its two stars. It was produced in London recently as a play but was not very successful, and was withdrawn after a short time. It is a thin, little story of a young wireless operator (British) with the improbable name of Dascom Dinsmore, who is marooned upon a lonely point in Labrador, and has been so marooned, without the society of women—or indeed any society but that of Eskimos and a pet polar bear—for two years.

Thus when a charming woman providentially crashes in her fiancé's aeroplane not three hundred yards from his hut, he follows the young lady with an almost improper haste to propose marriage.

The rest of the action is concerned with their last-minute rescues from the distressing fate of marrying the wrong person, and we leave them running cumbersomely over the ice to regain the hut in which (the producer seems to have overlooked this point) is Miss Winifred Shotter, a jilted lady, ice-bound for the next six months, and consequently in a position to make things a little trying for her ex-fiancé and his new bride. We should have liked this domestic difficulty cleared up, but Hollywood is often satisfied with very broad outlines and indications. Winifred Shotter, from the Aldwych farce company, very competently plays a thoroughly objectionable young woman, and Reginald Owen rather overplays the empty-headed British baronet. The polar bear was good.

The production is swift, and the conversation amusing in its deliberate offensiveness. Robert Montgomery is very decorative, and, between them, he and Miss Myrna Loy make the picture. A. C.

GEORGE HASSELL and WINIFRED SHOTTER.
"The Weaker Sex don't feel the cold."

THE UNGUARDED HOUR
Metro-Goldwyn-Mayer

THE virtues of this picture are excellent casting, a high level of acting, convincing sets, intelligent direction, and audibility which many recent "star" pictures have lacked.

Its chief fault is excessive length. Seventy minutes should have been enough; the extra 20 on the top emotional register tire the audience. Much time is wasted in the first half, which is badly needed later. Again, an "English adaptation" should be English, or American, not hybrid. American Court scenes are rollicking stuff; the Old Bailey is grave drama; a mixture induces laughs at the wrong moments. Neither should alleged English newspapers have splash headlines spelt in American, nor English generals say "necessairily." One need only hire an educated Englishman, a cheap enough commodity in these days, to attend to such details.

The moral of the story is Mr. Stephen Leacock's ancient jest: "Never begin to tell a lie until you can see your way through to the end of it." Both the rising young Attorney-General-designate (Mr. Franchot Tone, attractive, good actor) and his lady wife (Miss Loretta Young, competent, badly made-up) are blackmailed by the villain (Mr. Henry Daniell, a brilliant artist, rivalling Mr. Leslie Banks). The two family friends, the silly-ass-plus-bright-ideas man (Mr. Roland Young, just himself and delightful) and the old General turned Police Commissioner (Mr. Lewis Stone, I need say no more), attempt to help them out and succeed in convicting both.

The point of every scene is dramatic irony and the audience's knowing more than the characters. It is doubtful whether a whole play can be adequately hung on this device; even Euripides in all his experiments never tried it, and Mr. Fodor is no Euripides. J. A. M.

THE ROBBER SYMPHONY
Palace Theatre

THIS is a very interesting experiment in artistic production. Friedrich Feher has been successful in setting a film to the spirited and occasionally beautiful music which he composed as the basis of the show.

His success, however, is to some extent limited by the restriction of his appeal to those who can appreciate the beauties of the Alps and the humour of the Alpine peoples; for it is upon these two qualities that the very being of the film rests.

The plot is not very important and is obviously intended as a pretext for good music, beautiful singing, grand scenic effects, and a sustained subtle humour which could not be found very far from the shores of the Mediterranean.

The acting is uniformly good. Magda Sonja plays her part with exquisite feeling. Webster Booth has much too splendid a voice to be used as casually as it is used in this production; whilst Hans Feher possesses a histrionic sense which seems to render it impossible for him to make a mistake. The sound film technique has never yet succeeded in achieving perfect reproduction of music and the singing voice; but "The Robber Symphony" is, in this respect, the least disappointing presentation that has been offered to the public.

After reviewing the excellence of the photography, the skill of the players, and the competence of the music, we may wonder that so little rather than so much has been accomplished. I should like to see the experiment repeated with a more serious theme, but meanwhile would advise my friends to form a first-hand opinion of "The Robber Symphony." W. J.

PLAYS OF THE WEEK

THE TOTALITARIAN SHOW

GLAMOROUS NIGHT Coliseum
Written, Devised, and Composed by Ivor Novello

THIS is a generous entertainment. A twice-nightly musical show at popular prices suggests something suburban, if not economical. "Glamorous Night" is nothing of the kind. On the contrary, it is spectacular and as sophisticated as any "romantic musical play" has a right to be.

The trouble is that Mr. Novello has apparently determined that Mr. Noel Coward shall not possess the monopoly of what might almost be called the Totalitarian Show. This piece is really a sort of conjurer's hat, and you would be surprised at the things that come out of it, and how they are all woven into a two-hour miscellany without breaking the tenuous thread of an ultra-conventional story with an unconventional ending.

We begin with a street scene and a lovely blackout on a most unparliamentary remark for a hero to make to a would-be heroine. We wonder what is coming next, and when we wake up we are in the Balkans, with all the good old stuff, plots, royal mistresses, operettas, and tenors, a sinister minister, shooting, gipsies, uniforms, and the whole Ruritanian bag of tricks. Yes, and Mr. Novello is still not satisfied, for before the curtain falls we have had smart twentieth-century stuff aboard a cruising liner, ballet, spirituals, more attempted assassination, and grand old copper-bottomed Drury Lane melodrama, complete with bombs, bangs, screams, and a real sinking ship as large as life.

After recovering from these alarums and excursions and suitably restoring our shattered nerves, we have a rather calmer second act. We observe the English hero and his Ruritanian gipsy-princess-heroine hiking and considering the advisability of making love. The lady wants to play, but the young man is jealous of his honour (thank you, Mr. Novello, for defending the sex), and will not even have a "romp" until she promises to make an honest man of him, which she does in the next scene at a gipsy wedding. If only for this scene alone, the play would be worth while. It is perfectly beautiful and staged with sensitive and romantic charm: the singing is strangely moving, the costumes and lighting beyond cavil.

It is a pity that this magnificent scene could not have been made the finale instead of the gilded pasteboard of the usual "Court Ball," which provides a humdrum ending—though hero and heroine do indeed "part with such sweet sorrow" that no mawkish taste lingers, but only the pleasing titillation of the gentle satire that underlies the whole piece. Mr. Novello is having a quiet chuckle, we feel, at what we too often hear called "row-mance."

The music is pretty, with two haunting waltzes. Most of the players are adequate, if no more, but Mr. Fred Rivenhall's unctuous villain is delicious, and Miss Minnie Rayner can never fail us. Some people may like the colour of Miss Muriel Barron's hair as the gipsy-princess-singer. Mr. Barry Sinclair as the non-singing hero is quite lily-like.

MURIEL BARRON and BARRY SINCLAIR in "Glamorous Night."

The dances are a joy. All I need say is that it was entirely unnecessary for the programme to inform us that they had been "invented by Mr. Ralph Reader." His technique is unmistakable, and by some miracle he never repeats himself.

If you go to be entertained and not to pick holes, you will enjoy yourself very much at the Coliseum. J. A. M.

THE FUGITIVES By Walter Hackett
Apollo Theatre

THIS is an account of the adventures of Miss Belle Toots, the perfect lady's maid, who, pursuing her own sense of simple poetic justice, removes her employer's pearls to reimburse herself for having been cheated by that employer at cards. The reasoning is perfect, and the act is laudable. It is unfortunate that such simplicity and sweet reason should be regarded by the law without nice discrimination, but Belle finds herself, in the midst of a revolution in Spain, encumbered not only with a detective from Scotland Yard, but also with the costly national collection of jewels round which the revolution rages. Miss Marion Lorne's childish innocence carries her triumphantly through three acts to a triumphant, if hasty, marriage.

"The Fugitives" is a play in Mr. Walter Hackett's best style of light-hearted intrigue and confusion. Mr. Godfrey Tearle adds greatly to the charm of an entertaining play. A. C.

A MIXED BAG

TWO'S COMPANY
A Soskin-British and Dominions Picture

A PLEASANT light comedy of old vintage, but just the thing for summer time if you are in not too critical a mood.

An American traveller starts a feud with an English lord, from whom he has rented a manor. The American has a daughter (Mary Brian), the lord has a son (Patric Knowles). You can guess the rest.

The only entertaining feature of the film is the cross-talk between Gordon Harker, as the titled gentleman's major-domo, and the frozen-faced Ned Sparks, as the American's lawyer. They carry the fragile weight of the entire seventy-five minutes. Several of their lines are extremely good, as "If you want to make an Englishman happy when he's old, tell him a joke when he's young." One or two jokes are questionable, but we are getting used to bad taste.

Never at any time does the film justify the expense of bringing Miss Brian, Ned Sparks, and Harry Holman from Hollywood to play in it. H. G.

NIGHT MAIL
G.P.O. Film Unit

AN excellent documentary of the Scottish mail train. The photography is superb and the worker-actors perfectly natural. A trifle over-long, perhaps, but the audience was most appreciative. Technically lovely. S. M. W. B.

IN THE SOUP
Twickenham Films

THE title is painfully candid. Originally a farce, this has been toned down to a pale, light comedy pace. Ralph Lynn needs Tom Walls, although supported by six frantic and capable leads. Nelson Keys makes a lot of nothing and nearly steals the film, if that be a compliment. One day a producer will go mad or get drunk or something and give Keys a part worthy of his genius. There is one really funny sequence in which Ralph Lynn, as an idiotic barrister, pleads the wrong case in the wrong court in the wrong way. But as a whole the film has been manhandled from typewriter to megaphone. S. M. W. B.

MURDER ON A BRIDLE PATH
R.K.O. Radio

NOT for the discriminating, but tailor-made for the confirmed Saturday nighter. This is a good example of the "programme" film which Hollywood turns out in batches of fifty . . . capable all round . . . but which British studios seem incapable of producing or even attempting. An adequate cast, good camera-work, fair direction, and a business-like script. When will Elstree realise the steady profits from this type of production? If these replaced the quota offal, British film prestige would rise as a whole. Personally, I like James Gleason, and his team-work with Helen Broderick as a tough detective and his schoolmarm assistant is intelligent if not intellectual. S. M. W. B.

IN GALLERY TEN

By FRANK H. SHAW

PAUL ROGERS and Clem Potter thought enough of each other to be contemptuous of a girl. There were plenty of girls in Codringall. But Elsie Bright was the new teacher at the Council School and seemed different from the run of local wenches. She knew how to make the best of herself. So her arrival altered a lifelong friendship between two quite decent men.

Hewing upwards in Gallery 10, the flat of Paul's pick grazed Clem's shoulder, fetching a trickle of blood Both men were scarred from similar mishaps—it was nothing. Only, before, there hadn't been Elsie.

Paul was savagely dragged back. The candles in the two men's caps lit up their faces with a ghostly glimmer.

"You did that a-purpose, Paul Rogers," said Clem.

"You're a liar!" said Paul.

They went into action according to the habit of the Codringall men, who never know when they're licked. Paul's gorilla-like strength was matched by Clem's quickness Throughout the battle Elsie's name was never mentioned, but both understood why they really fought.

At exhaustion's point, both still game, Paul said: "You're beat; own to it!"

Clem spat on bleeding hands. "Come on, lad; I'm not right started yet," he grunted. Game as the terriers both walked, they were. They were hard at it again when the shift foreman came and told them not to make fools of themselves. They returned to work in silence; both worked bitterly, and labour eased their spleen.

"YOU'RE a mighty fine scrapper, Clem," Paul said, after a while. Blowing a blood-drip from his nose, Clem replied:

"You're none so bad yourself, Paul lad." On the edge of restoring the friendship Paul said: "I'm takin' Elsie to th' pictures to-night."

"The hell y'are!" Bitterness brewed up anew. The smaller Clem went to the wall. the truck-boy, coming for his load, thought a fall had happened. But presently Clem resumed work, though listlessly—as if his heart failed him. The train of trucks rattled away on its mile-long journey to the shaft.

"She's wettish," Paul said. "Them floods, I reckon." Clem refused the olive-branch.

"Elsie's a fine lass, owd lad."

"Shut yer mouth!" Battered to a standstill, he was still eager to sail in afresh. Paul, more placid, said evenly:

"Wenches, bein' as they are, 'tain't allus th' best man as get 'em, Clem."

"I walked her out last Sunday. We can't both wed th' lass," grunted Clem.

PREVIOUSLY there'd been no comparison between them; now each itched to prove himself the better. Neither knew what Elsie most required in her choice, she being different from such as the two had practised on.

"Harkee!" said Paul, suddenly. "What's that?" Both men knew it wasn't the rumble of distant shot-firing.

"Come on, Paul!" Clem shouldered his tools, grabbed the candle-box. Paul followed him down the gallery, the low roof of which caused them to bend nearly double. Their feet were in clayey mire. Only their cap-candles lighted them.

"On'y a bit of a fall," Paul said. But more water was in the mud than when they passed along to the coal-face a few hours before.

THE gallery was filled with the fall; splintered props stuck out. Most of the debris was rock in big chunks.

"Let's get agate," said Clem, driving into the mass. They faced disaster coolly, as usual, being miners, used to living with the menace of death at their shoulders.

After an hour of rock-cracking and tugging both realised the water was rising. There had been heavy floods in Codringall; the disused workings, long-sealed, were a danger-spot. This roof-fall made a breakwater, damming the leaks. There was nothing to fret about—yet. Before they knew, the relief gangs would be busy at the hither side. Neither Paul nor Clem knew the fall was hundreds of feet in extent; or that the water in the shaft was already a hundred feet deep above Gallery 10's entrance, and rising fast. Already a hundred men were dead.

ABOVE there were horror and activity. When the pit-siren screamed shawled women started for the pit-head, a few old men joining them. School being in, there were few children. The cage came up, discharged its human load, descended. The clatter of the pumps, working all-out, dominated other sounds. With water rising fast, all who lived must be brought up without delay.

The women kept their heads; someone started a hymn; many voices joined, the wind mocking the appeal. The mine manager drove up, asked questions, nodded. Extra pumps were coming; every pit was sending help. Rescue gangs were organising; but they could, as yet, do little. With the cage coming up monotonously, men stumbled into the pale daylight, were identified, questioned, wept over. Presently, school released, the children came scudding through the driving rain. Too many pumps were now on hand; the spares were sent to the old workings. Gangs worked like beavers to divert the swollen river.

Paul and Clem hewed on steadily. Knee-deep in water they were, unaware of what lay beyond the barrier. They were carrying the rock well up the gallery now, to give them room. Sometimes their candles flickered before shooting up more brightly. Sweat ran down their naked backs. When they listened for the knocks that should indicate succour, they heard only silence.

AFTER hours, Paul dropped his pick. "Quittin'?" Clem asked. Breathing was becoming difficult.

"No, hungry." He retrieved his meal-tin from the face; took out a hefty sandwich, washing it down with cold tea.

"Best eat easy," offered Clem. "In case it's a big fall."

"Mebbe we'd better." Paul returned the sandwich; but before closing the lid, "Have a bit?" he offered to Clem.

"I've got my own, lad." They resumed labour; the water now up to mid-thigh.

"Looks like we needn't ha' scrapped like we did over Elsie Bright. Sorry I knocked ye about a bit," said Paul.

"I give as good as I got, lad," said Clem, whose rancour was not yet all evaporated.

"Yer a grand little scrapper," grinned Paul, gap-toothed.

Later they saw their efforts were futile. Water rising still, the blows of their picks sounded still as solid as if they attacked virgin rock. They were fatigued, although trained to long spells of endurance in awkward positions.

"It'll be drier farther up," suggested Clem.

"There's another day to-morrow," agreed Paul.

They trudged back to the face, the water lessening as the road slanted upwards. It was fairly dry, warmish, too, by the coal-face. Squatting, they ate, but sparingly. It was Clem who suggested extinguishing the candles. "In case——" he said. In case the remaining air was used up too quickly.

IN the close darkness they discussed chances. Then they slept. The water whispered distantly. Clem stirred first, unaware how long he had slept. When he lit a candle he saw the water was lipping high, rustling in a sort of triumph. Knowing the gradient of the road he was aware further work at the fall was impossible. He shook Paul's cool shoulder.

"It don't look too good to me," he mentioned, yawning. Investigating, they found the water roof-high before they reached the fall.

"Reckon we're for it," said Clem.

"Not yet we aren't," said Paul. There were eight hundred feet of earth over them; only the geologists knew what lay between them and a sideways outlet. But the instinct for life clings tenaciously.

"Happen it'll tak' up yet." Paul quoted an ancient saying about Noah and a stubborn Yorkshireman.

"Ay, lad, happen it will," agreed Clem.

"Bein' as it is——" began Paul, "we might as well——"

He struck at the roof with his pick, but Clem gripped his arms and wrenched the tool clear.

"Who's a blinkin' coward now?" he demanded, eyes blazing. Pushing him away, Paul grabbed again at his pick.

"Nay, lad, I divvn't mean *that*!" he said. It had been known for trapped men, losing hope, to fetch down the roof in a rush, to make a quick finish. "You clear th' muck —I'll hew," he said. "Wi' th' water risin' this way, we might as well use up all th' air while we've got it."

He meant, he said, to carve a hole upwards, into which the water-compressed air, obeying nature, would collect. Thus they could still keep their heads free of the flood, even if the gallery filled to the coal-face. There was a supply of pit-props to hand, ready to support the new roof.

THIS sort of work was far from easy. But after a while Paul stood upright in an inverted pit of his own hewing. Clem relieved him and found it difficult, because of his lesser height, to continue. He wedged props in place, formed not only a foothold but a brace, and went on with better success. Time passed.

The air in the lessening space lacked life-giving quality; their working spells shortened. How long they had been caged they could not say: it seemed years—maybe it was only hours. They forgot the taste of food, enduring hunger-pangs; then grew indifferent, curiously, to all thought of staying their stomachs. The water increased, trapping them in their miniature shaft, where the compressed air threatened to burst their hearts. The water rose higher—higher. They had nothing on which to stand above the stealthy flood except the props braced from wall to wall. The water rose to Clem's breast, to his neck.

"This is it, then!" he said strangledly.

"Not it, lad," Paul said, hefting him to his own broad shoulders, giving him a better chance for life than he took himself.

Thus, with Paul's head and neck above water, and Clem's body in air-filled space, they incredibly waited. Neither admitting it, both prayed in a formless way. Paul said, with a gruff rumble:

"Another feller'll get yon lass, Clem; we wasted our time, an' all."

"Ay, lad." Clem's voice was weak, his head buzzed. An astonishing croak burst from Paul's lips.

"Th' water's none risin' no more!" he said. It was true. Better still, the water was falling. The pumps had won.

DAYS later two shadows of men emerged; incredibly Paul and Clem were alive. The rescue-gangs had cut through the fall in time.

Elsie Bright came to where the pair were laid on stretchers, ready for hospital. She went first to Clem.

"Thee go to Paul, lass; he's th' best," said Clem.

Paul reached a hand to find Clem's. "Nay, lad, wenches don't amount to much," he said; and the hands clasped with such firmness as remained.

THE GROUNDWORK OF MUSIC

IV.—HARMONY

WE have seen how, by the use of counterpoint, many strands of melody may be woven together to produce a pleasing or intriguing effect. It should be noted that, as Sibelius has said, the addition to a commonplace theme of another commonplace theme is in no way a virtue, and the whole is made not more interesting, but less interesting, by such addition.

In distinction to this a theme of no particular attraction can be enhanced and made luscious and seductive—or cold and hard—by the use of harmony. If counterpoint may be likened to the threads running through a tapestry, harmony dictates the resultant colours of the tapestry.

Music lovers are often puzzled to know how, when a composer has thought of a tune, he arrives at the bass notes and chords which harmonise his tune.

An Example

LET us take a piece of music in the key of C. It will be found that the majority of the notes of the melody belong to the scale of C. Well, every note of any scale can be harmonised by one of three "common chords"—i.e., the common chords on the key note, the fifth note of the scale, and the fourth note of the scale.

In our piece in the key of C the melody notes can therefore be harmonised by the common chords of C, G, and F. (A "common chord" consists of the sounds doh. mi, soh, sung upward from the note on which the chord is built.)

The "Hörst Wessel" song may be harmonised entirely by these three basic chords, though naturally the result is much more pleasing if an adventurous and wider choice of chords is used. The climaxes increase in power and the song itself glows with added tints.

SPORT

Edited by A. C. FINDLEY

CRICKET

Winter Sports

"WHAT a week," said both bowlers and batsmen at the close of play last Saturday night. I agree. With the exception of the bowlers, who had a happy time, the players have been forced to wear several sweaters to keep warm—they did not even stay long enough at the crease to warm up.

First, we had Larwood making hay of the Middlesex batsmen — Middlesex, in turn, made the Notts team look even worse, by spinning them out in the first innings, and fast bowling and bumping them out in the second for 41 runs, when Jim Smith took six of the wickets for 12.

It was stated that the Lord's wicket was the worst it has been for years, and it was due to the weather and not the leather-jackets.

It could not have been much better on Saturday, when the Middlesex skipper, R. W. V. Robins, by scoring 77 against Northants, saved the face of Middlesex, who had a total score of 192—quite respectable considering the state of the wicket.

The Indians were all out for 86 in their first innings against Yorkshire at Bradford, and of this total Major Nayudu compiled a very heroic and stubborn 41. They must think that the fates are unduly harsh to them, and that the English summer is a period to be experienced to be believed.

It is good to note that Wazir Ali, reputed to be India's best batsman, made a brilliant 85 not out on his first appearance for the tourists last week. He had been on the sick list during the previous part of their tour.

This Saturday a North v. South Test Trial begins at Lord's, and unofficially it will be used, like the matches against All India, as a means of sifting the wheat from the chaff, so that we can send a representative team to Australia next winter.

The teams picked to do duty in this game are quite good, but the selectors provided a surprise in choosing Warburton, a Lancashire League spare-time professional and bank clerk. I hope he turns out to be as big a success as Sidney Barnes when the latter was brought from League cricket to the Test field.

Averages

MAURICE LEYLAND, of Yorkshire, is now top of the batting averages with 87.25, and is followed by C. S. Dempster with 82.66 and Gimblett with 70.30.

Verity still maintains a good lead over the bowlers with 76 wickets for an average of 8.63. Although last week was a period favourable to bowlers, strangely enough Verity took less wickets than in any other week of the season. This puts him out of the running for the record of being the bowler to take the quickest 100 wickets in a season.

With the exception of Gover, the Surrey fast bowler, who has taken 67 wickets, Verity, however, appears almost certain to reach his 100 wickets weeks before anybody else.

LAWN TENNIS

The Wightman Cup

ON Friday and Saturday a team of British women opposes a team of American women in the annual match for the Wightman Cup at Wimbledon. Play starts at 2.30 p.m.

The contest consists of seven matches. There are five singles matches and two doubles. On paper we should easily win all five singles and at least one doubles. If our women play their usual game and do not get panicky, the match is theirs. The same has been the case in the last two years. But each time our women have been overcome with shyness like silly schoolgirls, and have let their side down. I shall not be in the least surprised if they do the same thing again unless they have been spurred to better things by remarks in private by their friends.

They should easily win. I expect they will lose. I hope I am wrong.

The Davis Cup

UNLESS a miracle happens, the inter-zone final of the Davis Cup will be fought between Germany and Australia, and it is most likely that for the first time in history Germany will be the challengers.

We are within a fortnight of the Wimbledon Tournament. The play of the Australians and the Germans will be watched with very special interest. I do not think Von Cramm will beat Perry on the fast Wimbledon surface.

Of the women, I shall be surprised if Kay Stammers does not win. I expect Helen Jacobs will be unlucky once again, in spite of the absence of Mrs. Moody.

OLYMPIC GAMES

Competitors' Equipment

THE equipment to be issued to male contestants for this year's games in Berlin will, to all intents and purposes, be the same as at previous Olympiads. It will consist of blue blazers and white trousers; but instead of straw and panama hats, which were worn at Amsterdam and Los Angeles, it has been decided to issue blue cricket caps with a Union Jack badge.

It is also possible that the Olympic badge, which up to the present has been a plain Union Jack, may be given a more elaborate design, embodying the Olympia Circles.

The equipment for women competitors has not yet been decided.

Sale of Seats

MUCH misunderstanding about the sale of seats for the Berlin Games has been caused by a mischievous rumour that they are now unobtainable. This is not so.

The Stadium passes, which admit to all the events in the main stadium, are sold out, but season tickets and daily tickets for the competitions in the different sports can still be bought by the public through the usual agencies.

HOW TO PLAY YOURSELF

Be Players, Not Spectators

CRICKET

By James Larratt

3.—LEG-SIDE STROKES AND THE CUTS

LEG-SIDE strokes can be divided into two sections, the first comprising the pushed or deflected shots, and the second aggressive shots requiring bodily power as well as accurate timing.

The two most important strokes in the first section are the leg glide or glance, and the push stroke.

The Glide.—The glide can be made either as a forward or back shot. To a well-pitched-up ball outside the leg stump you can lean forward and, with your bat held slightly crooked to the ball, deflect it to long leg. To the shorter-pitched ball you bring your left leg back, turning square to the ball, and again deflect it with a flick of your wrists, your bat held at an angle.

The Push Stroke.—The push stroke can be executed, just as the glide, either as a forward or back shot. You lean forward to the pitch of the ball and place it to the leg side with a straight bat, as in orthodox forward play. Playing back, you turn to face the ball and push it to an unoccupied part of the leg-side field.

The two most important of the aggressive leg-side strokes are the hook and the full-blooded leg hit.

The Hook.—This stroke is best made from the long hop on your wicket or on the leg side. You step back towards your wicket with your right foot, face the ball, and hit it hard with a horizontal bat to the on side. One of the most thrilling sights in cricket is that of a good batsman on a fast wicket hooking the ball off his nose to the leg boundary from a fierce bumping bowler. The beginner, however, will be well advised to essay this stroke only on slow wickets, which do not require such superlative quickness of eye.

The Leg Hit.—A half-volley outside the leg stump provides the opportunity for a glorious six. The leg hit, however, requires careful timing, especially if you are attempting to strike the ball from an upright position. The ball may also be met with a horizontal bat, which will lessen the risk of a mishit. For this stroke you bring your right knee to the ground, and swing your bat across the line of the ball's flight.

The Cuts.—There are two main cut strokes, the square and late cuts.

The square cut is used to the ball pitched short outside the off stump, and dispatched between gully and cover-point. You hit over the top of the ball, the right wrist turning over the left at the end of the stroke.

The late cut, as the name implies, is made as the ball is almost past the batsman, and is struck by a wrist chop, which sends the ball speeding on the ground towards third man.

Next week: Fielding.

LAWN TENNIS

By James Larratt

3.—THE SERVICE

THE success of your service depends upon ease of body position and stroke. The complicated twists and flourishes which are sometimes seen on tennis courts are unnecessary.

As for nearly every shot in tennis you should stand sideways to the net in executing the service. Your weight is distributed evenly, your left hand holding the ball, and the racket in your right hand, in readiness for your stroke.

The Stroke Analysed.—We can proceed from the preliminary stance to the actual stroke mechanism.

Throw the ball up to a point some five feet above and in front of your left eye. At the same time, transfer your weight to your right foot, swing the racket back and behind your right shoulder, and slightly turn your body, so that your left shoulder blade faces the net. These movements should take place without altering the original position of your feet.

As you strike the ball the arm should be extended upwards, so that at the moment of impact your arm and racket form a straight line, at the end of which the ball is met with the full face of the racket. At the same time, you must swing your body round and into the stroke, transferring your weight to your left foot, and following through, so that the racket completes its semi-circle and your right foot comes to the ground over the base line.

Remember, in order not to be foot-faulted, that both feet must be behind the line and your left foot on the ground at the moment of striking the ball.

An Accurate Service.—Many beginners make the mistake of trying to serve too fast. It is preferable to have a command of length and direction through a well-controlled service than to sacrifice accuracy for mere speed and spectacular effect and an occasional success. Two medium-paced services will pay you best, in which you are able to place the ball to your opponent's weakness. Later on you will develop speed with accuracy. Even then, you will be well advised to remember that studied variation is the strength of a good service. In the meantime, you will serve fewer double faults and conserve your energy better by taking pains to put your first service into court.

Next week: The Volleys, Lob, and Smash.

SWIMMING

By K. G. Green

2.—SIMPLIFIED METHODS

LAST week I gave an outline of the elementary essentials required by the beginner, and of how to acquire confidence. This week I propose to deal with the simplest stroke to begin with, namely, the breast stroke. Remember, above all, to avoid all hasty and erratic movement of the legs and arms, as this will only succeed in exhausting you and seriously impair your progress.

Breast Stoke.—Begin by drawing your elbows up to your sides, hands close to the chest, palms together, and facing downwards, and fingers tightly closed, to obtain the maximum purchase. Extend your arms forward, gradually turn your palms outwards, then bring slowly round to your sides in a sweeping movement. At the same time, draw your legs up with the knees turned outwards, and simultaneously with a forward sweep of the arms, throw your legs out sideways, bringing them slowly together.

Keep your feet loose at the ankles, and as they are brought together, give a slight flip of the feet to gain the necessary propulsion. New return again to the same position and repeat. Above all, do not overdo it for the first time, and stick to the old maxim that practice, and practice alone, makes perfect.

Next week: The Back Stroke.

BOXING

By 'Tommy' Moran

BOXING has been described as the noble art, and I think it is justified in claiming such a proud title because it demands the acme of physical fitness and personal endurance. Three hard rounds against a worthy opponent take more out of a man than a strenuous game of Rugby football, and for that reason the most iron discipline must be enforced if one aspires to honours.

A boxer must forego the pleasures of the ordinary man and practise the most stringent form of self-denial, only by doing so can the body be kept in a fit condition to combat against another man of equal weight with similar natural advantages. It has been said that boxers are born and not made. That is true only inasmuch as it applies to every other pastime. Individuals may be born to reveal genius in certain directions, but that does not mean that others cannot be taught to train themselves to compete against those fortunate few with natural inclinations.

I hope to be capable of conveying sufficient knowledge through these columns, at least to sow the seeds for those who desire to learn how to box. I frankly state thus early that three rounds with the gloves will teach more to aspirants than all the volumes that have ever been written, but I assure you that you will improve your ability by studying and practising the different punches and methods of attack and defence that I shall suggest to you.

I believe that a boxer should develop on natural lines, by which I mean that to model oneself entirely upon some champion of the past is a wrong thing to do. Some are natural fighters, others boxers, and although it is essential to have a knowledge of both, one should first of all develop the style that comes most naturally.

In a contest, if a man is being beaten at boxing, he should then go in and fight. On the other hand if his opponent is winning by fighting it is then policy to box him and keep him at a distance.

Thus we see that the successsful exponent of the game is the man who can adapt himself to either style, but in early tuition a good tutor will watch the natural inclinations of his pupil and develop them to perfection before attempting to teach him to do the things that, though necessary, are foreign to his nature.

It is wrong to assume that a good fighter is never a good boxer or vice versa, or that a man who is not orthodox can never be successful. There are many instances of men reaching the top of the tree who were hopelessly unorthodox, but they had developed to perfection their natural talents.

BEHIND THE NEWS

Edited by J. A. MacNab

The Light That Failed

POOR Sir Stafford Cripps is very upset. He just *cannot* get people to come and listen to him—not even in Hull.

His "Socialist League" held "a great meeting" at the Hull City Hall on March 1, when the Great Man Himself was to be the principal speaker. What a chance for the workers! Yet they didn't come.

The City Property Committee has done its best to console Sir Stafford. They were graciously pleased to agree to reduce the charge for the hall from £20 to £12. It was explained by Councillor Coult that after a Labour Party meeting in the hall

"*this meeting on March 1 was arranged as a counterblast. The 'star' invited was greater than either of ours —a man with a title, a man who could trim his sails to any audience, who could speak according to the crowd that came.*

"*But this time it was wet and the crowd did not come.*

"*It was a ghastly failure. And so the great party that governs this city applied to themselves for a reduction of rent.*

"*The charge is £20. The other people paid the charge and made no complaint. But apparently if your followers don't support your 'star' you can apply for a reduction of rent.*

"*A reduction of nearly 50 per cent. is recommended because you failed to get a crowd. It's a scandal. Suppose the boot had been on the other foot and our meeting had been a failure, you would have laughed such an application to scorn.*"

Last time the British Union of Fascists held a meeting in a large Hull hall, Mr. John Beckett deputised for Sir Oswald Mosley, who was ill. Not only was the hall packed, but hundreds had to be turned away.

Sir Stafford seems to be losing his glamorous attraction for the workers. Perhaps it's the result of talking too much about his intention of building a new Jerusalem.

Birrds of a Featherr

WE read that a movement has been started by some students of Edinburgh University to nominate Haile Selassie as a candidate for the now vacant Rectorial chair.

Well, why not? Their Parliamentary representative is Mr. Ramsay MacDonald. Mr. Selassie would make a suitable boy-friend for him. They each jumped the political ship when they saw it was sinking.

Half Lights

NO meeting has been arranged by the Balham and Tooting Conservative Association with regard to Sir Alfred Butt and the Budget leakage. When a "Manchester Guardian" reporter called at the H.Q. of the association they were indulging in that well-known Empire-building pursuit, a whist drive. "No meeting is pending or has been arranged," said Mr. Gladwell, the secretary. "We see Sir Alfred in quite a different light. He is one of us, and the affair has hardly been mentioned."

Aeroplanes v. Slave-Traders

FOR the first time in history aeroplanes are to be used to exterminate slavery. Routes habitually used by Abyssinian slave-traders will be patrolled by Italian aeroplanes to see that Badoglio's proclamation, abolishing the hideous traffic, is ruthlessly enforced. What Mr. Selassie could not or would not do in thirteen years Italy will complete in as many weeks. This is called Fascist brutality.

Beating Swords to Ploughshares

IN addition to this great work of civilisation, the economic development of Abyssinia for the benefit of white and black alike is to be hastened by the same agency. General Valle announces that not one of the seventy-nine newly-built airports in Ethiopia is to be closed. "On the contrary," he stated in a recent interview, "we intend to increase their number by building new 'air villages' near every important commercial centre so as to be able to solve the first problem of any colonisation scheme, that of securing regular, fast, and reliable transports."

Oxford Loses Yet Again

IT is announced that Mr. Anthony Eden is to receive from Oxford (no-flag-but-the-Red-Flag) University the degree of Doctor of Civil Law.

It was tactful of the University not to rub it in by conferring a degree in International Law.

THE DOCTOR of OXFORD

Lest We Forget

ON February 17, 1933, Mr. J. Maundy Gregory was summoned at Bow Street Police Court for having, on January 23, attempted to obtain from Lt.-Commander E. W. Leake £10,000 as an inducement for endeavouring to procure for him the grant of a dignity or title of honour contrary to the Honours (Prevention of Abuses) Act of 1925.

Lt.-Commander Leake, who had retired from the Navy in 1926, stated that previous to hearing from Gregory, a stranger approached him and told him some of the highest authorities in the country were desirous of him accepting some kind of honour, and that his name was very high up in the list. The suggestion was for a knighthood, and Mr. Gregory said that sinews would be necessary in order to open certain closed doors. It could be done, he added, for £10,000, but £12,000 would make it easier. Different prices of honours were discussed ranging over many years, and Gregory said he had been successful in arranging these matters for a considerable time. Lt.-Commander Leake reported the matter to the authorities, and told Gregory that he did not wish to continue the matter.

Gregory mentioned the New Year's Honours List, and said he knew it was then full, but that a supplementary list might be issued in February, otherwise Commander Leake's name would be on the June list, which was customarily published on the occasion of the King's birthday. At a further meeting later Gregory proposed another meeting at which, he said, a prominent Peer would be present. He wrote him a letter, asking him if he would meet him and this Peer at lunch at the Carlton. It was not necessary, Gregory said, to pay the whole of the money down, but they were satisfied with his credentials if he paid something on account.

On the second day of the trial Gregory changed his plea from Not Guilty to Guilty. The police declared that a number of complaints similar to this one had been recorded against Gregory. Birkett said in the difficult circumstances of this case it was difficult to do justice to Gregory and not do injustice elsewhere. He hoped that the magistrate would agree that the case would be amply met by a monetary penalty and the payment of costs. "I submit that would be a proper ending to this disturbing case," said Birkett.

The magistrate declared that the maximum fine would be inadequate to meet the facts of the case, but he did not propose to impose the maximum penalty allowed by the law, and sentenced Gregory to prison for two months in the second division and a fine of £50 and 50 guineas costs. Gregory's agent, Mr. Moffat, who was instrumental in him meeting Commander Leake, was mentioned by "The Morning Post" in 1922 as being concerned in the honours-selling business with a Mr. Harry Shaw under the name of Doorway Knights.

AN AUSTRALIAN VIEW

Dr. H. M. Moran, the Macquarie-street (Sydney) doctor who was an A.I.F. man and an international footballer, writes from Asmara, Eritrea—the date is March 20:

"I have been here a month, arriving in time to see the fever of the great victories which have made sure the northern front. . . .

"I went half-way up on the new road which these wonder-workers have built so quickly on the steep sides of Alaji. There I met a medical man who knew old Dr. Thomas Fiaschi, of Sydney, in the last war. It was Sunday, and he took me out to see where wretched Ethiopians were having their ills attended to by Italian medical officers in a sort of outdoor clinic on the side of the mountain. The dust of innumerable motor-lorries crawling along the newly-made road filled the air, for the troops were moving forward, in great spirit, to fresh victories near Quoram.

"I think the war here will shortly be over. The world will then realise that if any war in the world was justifiable this one was. I can only attribute the opposition to it among our British people to a complete ignorance of all the facts. The squalor and filth of the natives in upper Ethiopia are indescribable. I trust that the feeling between Australians and the Italians in Australia has again become warm and kindly. I feel strongly that anyone who does something to recreate the old friendship between Italian and British citizens is performing a great service to both countries. . . .

"Italy is more necessary than ever to European peace. And I know from personal contact that the Duce, in spite of all, is animated only by kind feelings towards the British race. It is up to us, then, to make a gesture to which the generous Italian people will not be slow in responding."—The "Sydney Bulletin," April 29, 1936.

Internationalism Only For Export

BLOOMSBURY and Whitechapel (and, of course, Oxford University) are behind the times. In Russia the "Internationale" is a back number. Its place has been taken by the new national anthem, dedicated to Rodina, "The Native Land." One verse of it reads:

We shall repulse every enemy, for we love our native land like a bride, and shall cherish her as a mother beloved.

This sounds a bit different from "Workers of the World, Unite," or "Arise, ye criminals of want." Evidently it has been decided to use, rather than attempt to crush, the feeling of nationalism and love of country which is indestructible among the human race. Indeed, this looks like Russia's first step in the direction of the inevitable National Socialism. Internationalism, materialism, and all the drab fustian of the nineteenth century must eventually give way to the creed of the modern age in some form. And the vital principle of the new creed is nationalism.

But Bloomsbury is still thinking in terms of the "Communist Manifesto" of 1844—ninety-two years out of date. It must be dreadful to be an Advanced Thinker—so delaying.

Soon Forgotten

THIS is an extract of an article published in "La Revue de Paris, 1928":

"M. René Blum, director of the Russian ballets at the Opera, Monte Carlo, published an article last week in an important Austrian daily paper, 'Neues Wiener Journal.' Herewith an interesting extract:—

"*We were five brothers, Leon was the second, I was the Benjamin of the family. None of us had the slightest idea what path we would follow in life—except Leon. He said: 'Ich werde Franzose.' It was confirmed in after years, now my brother Leon, who will be President of the French Council, has proved his fidelity.*"

Talking to the Americans at the Cercle Interallié, M. Blum regretted he could speak no other language but French.

America Again to the Rescue?

LAST week M. Blum received a visit from an agent of the famous American bank, *Kuhn Loeb and Co.*, at the Quai Bourbon. The rumour is floating that M. Blum is endeavouring to raise a loan of 10 milliard francs in the United States—to save the franc as Poincaré did, but by rather different methods.

Jews and The New Deal Administration

THE fact has been admitted by a prominent new dealer that "Karl Marx Professor" Felix Frankfurter, is the greatest political power in this country. Frankfurter has been a frequent visitor to the White House, and Roosevelt has expressed a vast admiration for the Jewish professor, a known international Red, who is the chief adviser of the administration.

All key jobs in the Labour Department, with the exception of one, are now held by Jews. An official telephone list of officials and their assistants shows seventy-three Jewish names out of about 270. The official contact directory of the W.P.A. lists 1,066 names, of which approximately 300 are Jewish. Through observation, a conservative estimate is that 40 per cent. of the employees of the National Archives are Jewish; forty-one of the names on the official personnel list of 139 have Jewish indications. Of the legal staffs of all departments and New Deal organisations in Washington, more than 35 per cent. are Jewish.

Strange News

From a correspondent at Washington we learn that Israel Moses Sieff, soon after his arrival in the U.S.A., held a secret conference up the Hudson River with Roosevelt, Frankfurter, and Filene, the two latter well-known Jewish controllers of the New Deal and famous for their Communistic tendencies.

It is significant that the Jewish-controlled Press in the United States have more or less suppressed all details of Sieff's visit to the U.S.A.

Telling the World

"WE shall never build our New Jerusalem by means of a Hitler, a Mussolini, or an Oswald Mosley."—Mr. Attlee at Blaise Castle, Bristol, June 1.

"If Russia is an expression of Communism, heaven help us!"—Mr. M. S. Davidson, Battersea delegate to the Socialist League Conference at Hanley, May 30.

"The fasces, the bundle of sticks, bound together with the axe, is generally accepted as the symbol of Fascism. It is much more than that, however. Most people think it is Italian, and of comparatively recent invention. Actually, it is as much of British as Italian origin."—The Mayor of Chiswick, in a recent Press interview.

"Abyssinia remains, therefore, an independent State, and Haile Selassie retains the throne which he has never abdicated." —"News Chronicle" leader, June 4.

"The leopard has not changed its spots. I have yet to learn that the Communist Party has removed from its constitution its avowed desire, not only to disrupt, but to destroy the Labour Party and the British Trade Union Movement."—Mr. J. Kaylor at the A.E.U. Annual Conference at Morecambe.

"There is a powerful feeling in this country against Fascism (and an equally powerful ignorance of the extent to which Fascism is achieving its essential purposes without any unnecessary display), but it has no central rallying point. Its natural rallying point is the Labour Party, if that party were not so busy rehearsing its funeral obsequies and handing itself wreaths—saying it with flowers in its hair."—Miss Storm Jameson in a letter in "Time and Tide."

"Some of us who, like myself, have lived in Abyssinia, away from Addis Ababa propaganda and intrigue, have seen the desperate condition of the subject races under Amharic domination. These are the greater portion of the population. If others could see the hopelessness expressed in every face of the conquered people more sympathy would, I think, be shown to Italian aspirations. They can achieve in a short time what the Emperor, with all his ambitions, could never have achieved in generations."—Mr. Philip Edwards in a letter in the "Daily Telegraph."

Printed by ARGUS PRESS, LTD., Temple Avenue and Tudor Street, London, E.C.4, England, and published by ACTION PRESS, LTD., Sanctuary Buildings, Gt. Smith Street, London, S.W.1, England. All enquiries regarding advertisements should be addressed to the Advertisement Manager, ACTION PRESS, LTD., Sanctuary Buildings, Gt. Smith Street, Westminster, S.W.1. Telephone: Victoria 9083 (6 lines).

ACTION, Thursday, July 23, 1936.

2d No. 23 [REGISTERED AT THE G.P.O. AS A NEWSPAPER.] "BRITAIN FIRST" JULY 23, 1936

FOR KING AND PEOPLE

R.S.23

INTERNATIONAL LABOUR OFFICE RAMP

See Page 9

MOSLEY AT MANCHESTER MUFTI RALLY

ALTHOUGH two successive Home Secretaries have declared that the wearing of Political Uniforms is perfectly legal the Manchester Watch Committee banned the British Union March last Sunday on the grounds that the wearing of Fascist Uniform was provocative. Sir Oswald Mosley replied by offering to hold the march and meeting in plain clothes.

Not even badges were worn, but in spite of wet weather over a thousand members and many thousands of the general public rallied. They marched through the rain and stood for nearly two hours listening to the Leader's speech. About 200 Jews and members of the Red Front attended and howled throughout the meeting. They used catapults and threw stones at the speaker.

The Manchester Watch Committee have proved two things which they did not desire to prove :

1. That successful demonstrations can be held by the British Union with or without uniform.
2. That the hooliganism of the Red Front has nothing to do with the wearing of uniforms.

The top half of the picture shows a part of the huge crowd gathered at Albert Croft to hear the Leader of the British Union. At the bottom is a section of members lined up prior to the march, and in the centre we show Sir Oswald as he inspected the parade.

The World, The Flesh—and Financial Democracy

A Weekly Review of Men and Events

By WILLIAM JOYCE

HUNDREDS of millions of people throughout the world were shocked to hear of the dastardly assault on our King. Nothing could bring to our own people so profound and horrible a shock as the thought that an attempt had been made on their Monarch's life.

McMahon, arrested after pointing a revolver at the King

The actual circumstances of the crime are not known at the time of writing; but what is known to every loyal subject of the Crown throughout the world is a feeling of the happiest relief that the danger should have been averted. Not only his own people, but the rulers of foreign States hastened to express their joy that such a man should have been spared.

Our Sovereign was quite unperturbed by the incident, nor could he be greatly moved by the event, for he is a soldier, and a soldier who possesses actual fighting experience. Upon his reign the greatest hopes have been based, and his people know that in him they have the living representative of Britain's greatness throughout the centuries. They are accustomed to think of him as the living symbol of our historical continuity. But, above all, they think of him as their friend and as a Prince who devoted years of his life to unremitting study of his people and their needs.

The Lesson

THAT he will be with us for many years we seem to know; and for this reason the shock was all the greater. Even now it is being said by many that neither valour nor virtue can secure a man from the attacks of a criminal lunatic. Whether this description does indeed apply to the assailant it is impossible for us to say at present; but the lesson of the sinister event is clear. Our Monarch, having been spared, we must stress continually and with ever-increasing emphasis, the duty of allegiance which every subject owes. We must tolerate no acts or language of a nature to propagate amongst criminal lunatics a desire to assault the King's person.

The law at present, however, stresses not the inviolability of the King's person, so much as the sacrosanct character of the Jews. The lowest type of alien is not only allowed, but even encouraged, to make speeches demanding the abolition of the monarchy with impunity. Sedition is preached day and night, and the Government not only allows it to be preached, but grants immunity to the ministers of evil.

The question pertinent to be asked at this juncture is, "Whence do the feeble-minded and the criminals draw their inspiration?" It is necessary only to review the constant attacks made upon the monarchy by aliens in our midst in order to understand how the irresponsible may rush into hideous crime, while the responsible enjoy the protection of the law and the favour of the politicians.

To amplify this theme is needless. For one awful moment our people feared that a great tragedy had happened. Then their fear was dispelled, and out of their relief will arise in even greater measure that noble sentiment of affection for the Crown which will endure so long as the English language is spoken.

Free Speech for Reds only

THE British Union recently held a meeting at Camden Town. It is part of the Union's policy to bring the message of National-Socialist patriotism to those districts where no speaker can obtain a hearing unless he is favoured by the Communist Party, or unless, like the Blackshirts, he is determined to face and overcome whatever opposition may arise.

Throughout the meeting a party of submen, Jewish in appearance, howled, shouted and made obscene gestures, and this obscenity reached its climax while the Fascists were singing the National Anthem. The vilest and filthiest insults were hurled at the Blackshirts throughout the meeting. But every member of the Union is instructed that the duty of preserving order on the streets belongs to the police, and, accordingly, regardless of the disgusting behaviour of the Red animals, the Blackshirts stood their ground, complied with every request that the police made, and did not attempt to retaliate against the Red mob which, from time to time, assaulted the police.

Never have I seen a clearer contrast than that of the Blackshirts standing silent, orderly, and dignified, while the monstrosities of the Gutter and the Ghetto were assaulting the police officers who have been so recently slandered in the House of Commons.

Baldwin Backs Argentina

THE Argentine still enjoys, in secure inviolability, the protection of the "National" Government. British agriculture is ruined because we take the whole of Argentine chilled beef, three-quarters of her frozen meat, and a fifth of her wheat, merely as a part of our imports from her, and yet in one year there has occurred a decrease of some 16 per cent. of Argentine purchases of cotton goods from the United Kingdom. As usual, the market which Lancashire loses is being gained by Japan. Nevertheless, we have to remember that the purpose of the Government is to help neither Lancashire nor the producer of British foodstuffs, for more clearly each day its purpose is revealed as the maintenance of Financial-Democracy even to the utter ruin of our people.

Destruction of Foodstuffs

DURING the past twelve months 12,000 tons of herring and fifty tons of other fish have been destroyed at Scottish ports. The Secretary for Scotland observed that he had no authority to take any official action with regard to this situation.

Kerstein, the Lawyer defending McMahon

When the bankers and Jewish usurers sit down to their banquets in the City of London, pass votes of confidence on each other, and receive the acclamations of a grateful Press, the man who does not know the meaning of starvation is deluded into believing that business is good. But the man who does know poverty, who has felt and seen starvation, will hold that this wanton destruction of foodstuffs would alone provide more than adequate grounds for a revolution to end the present system.

Again we would remind our readers that the Scottish herring industry appealed in vain for financial assistance, and this unanswered appeal was made at the time when it was proposed to raise a loan of half a million pounds for Abyssinia, and when the City of London, through France, was engaged in financing Soviet Russia.

FOUR QUESTIONS ANSWERED

As a regular reader of "The Blackshirt" and "Action," I should be grateful if you will answer my queries enumerated below in the columns of "Action." I am not a Fascist, but am interested in the Movement.

(1) First: On the question of Jews. When you come into power will you differentiate between Jews (British-born subjects) and British subjects of British parents? Will Jews (I refer to the decent, law-abiding Jew, not the riff-raff and international trickster) be under any disabilities?

(2) I am a Catholic, and as such my first allegiance is to my Church before all else. In a conflict between my Church and Fascism (should it ever arise) my duty would be with my Church, otherwise I would not be a true Catholic. What then?

(3) What is your attitude towards Birth Control? Is this doctrine to be allowed to be propagated *ad lib* by the enemies of my Church?

(4) What is your attitude towards the Irish question? Will you allow De Valera to declare a Republic?

Awaiting, with interest, your reply in "Action."

FEAR A' TEACH.

[The replies to the above letter are as follows:

(1) The British Union will treat the Jews, as they have constituted themselves, as a foreign community resident in Britain. They will not possess the vote or the right to Government Office, and in other particulars will be treated precisely as other aliens in Britain.

(2) The British Union do not believe that any clash between Christian and Fascist sentiments will arise, especially as Fascist Government will preserve the distinction between spiritual and secular affairs.

(3) Birth control is entirely a matter for the private conscience of the individual. The State will certainly encourage a higher birth-rate, but will not interfere with the private and intimate concerns of the family.

(4) The British Union will offer Ireland full and equal co-operation in Imperial development as one of the original homelands of the Empire. We do not believe that Ireland will abandon the Irish settlers in colonies and Dominions, not to speak of those in Britain. The declaration of a republic would, of course, involve the exclusion of Ireland from Empire co-operation, and the Irish in this country would be called upon to choose between allegiance to the British Crown and treatment as aliens subject to a foreign State.—ED.]

VIMY RIDGE
THE CANADIAN MEMORIAL

By CAPT. R. GORDON-CANNING, M.C.

THE Western battle front is studded with war memorials, now, nineteen years after the Battle of Vimy Ridge, the Battle of the Scarpe, or the Battle of Arras, as the British attack on April 9, 1917, is variously known, the greatest of all war memorials on this front is to be unveiled by His Majesty King Edward VIII. on July 26 in the presence of the President of the French Republic and eight thousand Canadian pilgrims.

The memorial personifies no glorification of war, no exultation in triumph, no trampling upon the defeated, but is meant to be in the words of the designer and sculptor—"a dignified protest against the futility of war." The accompanying photograph will give some idea of the simplicity and grandeur of this Canadian war memorial, standing upon a 235-foot base, with its two pylons representing France and Canada, rising to a height of 138 feet. Among the twenty figures grouped round the pylons are those representing Knowledge, Justice, Truth, and Peace.

The site of this memorial is but one of the many famous geographical features of war-time on the Western front which claimed for its ultimate conquest a heavy toll of French, British, and German lives. It is a lonely and desolate spot. Looking westward the hill of Notre Dame de Lorette with its "lighthouse" memorial to the French dead during the battles of 1915 is visible. Northward the battlefields of the Hohenzollern Redoubt, Fosse 9 and La Bassée; southward the Scarpe and Monchy-le-Preux; eastward the industrial plain of Douai with Lens in the foreground and its satellite villages.

The Torch of Empire

THE memorial which is to be unveiled is of more than ordinary interest to the British Union, representing as it does the culminating effort of the Canadian Corps, after months of heavy preliminary fighting and of minute tactical preparation in its final and victorious assault upon the crest of the Vimy Ridge. This memorial of a British cavalry regiment and a village. He recalled the walls of houses crumbling before one, the paved streets shooting upwards to the sky, horses falling, groaning, to the ground, great jets of blood spurting from their gaping wounds, and the men anxious, waiting. The officers promptly acting, to carry out their orders, amid the bewildering and awful noise. That is the scene that returned; but above all this terror and pain and shambles stood out clear, the human mind—master—beating back the monster "Chaos." This triumph of the mind in the midst of terror together with the comradeship of men are the two outstanding features and glories of modern war.

Was Prosperity Born Then?

BUT the smoking chimneys of the mining villages brought the writer back to the realities of the present day, and he wondered whether the men and families working these mines, and those in his own country in South Wales, Durham, and elsewhere, were any more prosperous and happier in consequence of that war? Whether a land fit for heroes had been created either in France or in Great Britain? Were not the same old cliques in political power; were there not the same extremes of wealth and poverty? Was not another European war threatening to make the world "safe for Democracy?"

Well may many of the spectators next Sunday ask of themselves, "Wherefore the sacrifice?" But the new world doctrine of National-Socialism steadily advances, breaking down the old vested interests. In Italy and Germany the mass of the people, and the manual workers, can now enjoy the liberty of economic security and the opportunity to indulge in many pleasures which were once only for the limited few.

This is the great task that awaits the British Union, which was born as a direct result of the War. The task not only to bring economic security to the British worker, but to cement the blood-links of the Empire and to bind the Imperial

The Canadian War Memorial on Vimy Ridge, which will be opened by The King on Sunday.

is a beacon of the torch of Empire; it is built upon soil rich in bones and blood of Imperial soldiers, and it is a personification of the blood-link of the British Empire and the magnificence of our Imperial heritage.

It is to be hoped that the feeling of shame will keep many of our political representatives and others from attending next Sunday's ceremony. Those who failed to do their duty in the war years but have since become heroes in other fields, those who have been privy to weakening the ties of Empire, and who have neglected in their international outlook the gifts of their forefathers, have no place here.

A few years ago the writer stood beside this memorial and watched the work of construction. Not far away—a few hundred yards—the battle-shocked soil lay as it had been in years gone by except that grass and weeds covered many of its wounds and the broken bodies of humanity had long since been gathered up and buried. As he looked towards Monchy-le-Preux his own small part in the battle came vividly back to him, with its days and nights of icy winds and snowstorms, the capture of Monchy, the shattering in a few minutes

nations in an unassailable unity. There can be no pride in Empire in the hearts of unemployed; there can be no reason in Empire if the interests of a foreign nation take precedence to those of a Dominion or of a Colony.

The Menin Gate memorial and now this Canadian memorial at Vimy represent the sacrifice and valour and loyalty of our Imperial citizens. Every portion of the Empire rallied to its defence in 1914 and gave without stint from the vaults of its foundations the pure gold of its finest manhood.

In the heart of every member of the British Union lies the wish to utilise this gold of the spirit, which will produce far greater wealth in return than all the gold bars from the mines of Johannesburg. And, as in the words of Roy Campbell:

> Old men have hunted beauty from our earth,
> Over the broken bodies of our youth,

so every member of the British Union must strive to hunt these old men, Conservative and Socialist, by all legitimate means, out of their seats of power into the night of obscurity. Then, and then only, will the British people regain their heritage, their respect, and their liberty.

THE NUISANCE OF DANZIG. Mr. Shaun Lester, the League of Nations Commissioner in Danzig, who likes Nazis to salute him.

JEWRY SHOULD PAY

THE High Commissioner of Palestine, Sir Arthur Wauchope, communicated the proposals for a Legislative Council to the Arab leaders on December 21, 1935, and to the Jewish leaders on the following day.

The Jewish organisations in Palestine rejected the proposals the same day. Their spokesman, Dr. Chaim Weizmann, president of the Zionist Organisation and of the Jewish Agency, said that under present conditions the proposals were contrary to the spirit of the mandate. This statement is not easy to understand, for the British Government is pledged to promote self-government in the mandated territory, and has declared several times their intention to set up a Legislative Council. Three years ago Sir Arthur Wauchope informed the League Mandates Commission that the necessary steps would be taken when local self-government had been brought into working order.

Jewish Pressure

JEWRY immediately commenced to work against the proposals of the High Commissioner. On January 31, the Secretary of State for the Colonies received a Jewish deputation, which was introduced by Sir Isidore Salmon, M.P. This deputation represented the following bodies:—The Zionist Federation of Great Britain and Ireland, the Jewish Agency for Palestine, the Palestine Foundation Fund of Great Britain and Ireland, the Jewish State Party of Great Britain and Ireland, the Peale Zion, the Board of Deputies of British Jews, and the Mizrachi Zionist Party of Great Britain and Ireland.

On February 4, Sir John Shuckburgh, Deputy Under-Secretary for the Colonies, received a deputation which represented the Council of the Agudas Israel of the United Kingdom, the Association of Rabbis, and the Pro-Palestine Fund.

Both these deputations expressed concern at the proposal to create a Legislative Council in Palestine. And on March 24, in a full dress debate in the House of Commons, all the friends of Jewry spoke up. Mr. J. H. Thomas, the Colonial Secretary, defended the Government's proposals. He since has fallen. In a leading article "The Times" said his speech would not remove misgivings and was no more convincing than were the arguments of the Government spokesman in the discussion in the House of Lords.

The Arabs

EVEN with the limitations proposed, the Arabs were ready to accept the setting up of the Legislative Council. In February the Arab parties sent in a memorandum to the Administration in Palestine which called for complete self-government, the cessation of Jewish immigration, and the prohibition of the sale of land to Jews. But they were prepared to accept the proposed Legislative Council as half a loaf. And only when even half a loaf seemed to have little prospects of being baked did the Arab leaders declare the strike.

But, in view of the Jewish opposition to the spirit of the mandate, an opposition which has made the Arabs say that they would prefer to pull down the house over their own heads than submit to further Jewish exploitation and domination, should not the vast wealth of Jewry pay for the moving of one British battalion after another into Palestine and for their maintenance? Why should British tax-payers again pay up to further the aims of Jewry, or pay for the results of Jewish policy?

F. C.

The Situation in Paris

THE season is no longer mentioned; the tourists have fled, and are not likely to encourage others to attempt to be diverted by the famous "semaine de Paris."

After the week of anarchy came a week of revolutionary agitation, which we know too well has not yet subsided.

It is clear now that the IVth International, that is to say, the Trotsky party, was active during the worst period of the strikes. Fear of being washed overboard by the most violent agitators finally induced the sinister Government to act. M. Blum announced that he would maintain order—a marvellous concession!

M. Salengro, Minister of the Interior, actually denounced *foreign agitators.* An important member of the Trotsky party, named Levacque was seen in France; a leading journalist of the party has been arrested.

It was interesting to learn that about the same time another extremist, whom Stalin had banished to Siberia, suddenly appeared in Belgium—Victor Serge. It is enough to convince the most doubting that the Bolchevik disease is catching.

It may seem strange also that there should be quarrels amongst the international parties. Yet Léon Blum, on hearing that "Vive Trotsky!" was graven on the walls of the *Samaritaine grand Magazin de nouveaute,* intimated that he was not pleased.

French Popular Opinion

"ANYONE is forced to admit that public opinion on the other side of the Channel is almost entirely for Germany and against us. Why?

"Because the English regard the war, the subsequent treaties, reparations—all that—as ancient history which bores them. 'The Rhineland is German,' says the man in the street. 'That is so obvious that you French evacuated it five years before the fixed date. Well, then, if it is German, why shouldn't Hitler occupy it?' For Heaven's sake don't talk to him about the Treaty of Versailles, which he has forgotten—or of Locarno, which he never knew much about, and which worries him, because it may one day draw him into a conflict with Germany!

"He dislikes all conflicts, and above all a war against a country for which he has racial sympathy and a real esteem."

"L'Homme Libre," Paris.

THE BRITISH COUNTRYSIDE

ANOTHER DISAPPOINTMENT FOR BEEF PRODUCERS

No Encouragement For "Quality" Animals

THE QUESTION OF IMPORTED BUTTER

(By Our Agricultural Correspondent.)

FULLY realising, as we Fascists do, the difficulties that lie in the path of anyone who makes an effort to improve the position of British beef producers, yet we, in common with a great number of farmers, feel sadly disappointed that all that has come of the much vaunted live-stock policy of the present Government is merely a small effort to avert the decline in production (which it will not do), and gives no assistance to what is needed most—increased production of beef. Again the Government have not instituted "standard" prices, which they had been advised to do, nor does the man who makes a speciality of the production of high quality beef receive anything extra for his trouble.

In connection with this, however, I understand that while Scottish farmers were

A beautiful piece of typical English Countryside in Sussex

keenly desirous that part of the subsidy should go to encourage the production of better quality beef, this suggestion was not acceptable to their English cousins.

Be that as it may, I cannot see how we are to compete with the good class chilled beef that is coming into this country while there is so much cow beef placed on the market. Moreover, the new rate of the levy-subsidy will hardly operate for at least another year.

More Delay

AS one who knows the live-stock industry pretty thoroughly, I submit that the beef and store producing side of it cannot bear any more delay.

For years it has just been "carrying-on" in the hope that things would in time improve. No such improvement has taken place, nor was it possible for it to take place while foreign beef poured into this country.

Now Mr. Elliot has told us that "the proposals to-day were not for a tariff on beef or a long-term policy. Detailed points would have to be worked out during the current summer."

Disheartening in the extreme, for while these "detailed points" are being worked out live-stock producers are at their wits' end how to carry on for, be it remembered, all through the summer, bullocks fattened on grass will be coming into the markets, and stores will be growing along to come into the yards in the autumn for the production of Christmas and winter beef.

Surely 'Tis Simple

TO the non-politician (and I count myself amongst these) the question is a simple one, although the answer may not be so simple.

Here in this country we once had a flourishing beef and store cattle industry, necessary not only for the production of good wholesome British meat, but also in a secondary way, but very important, for the production of the means to fertilise the land. While at the same time those producing beef did not produce milk and so helped to preserve the balance between these two branches of agriculture, which has now been rudely upset. It is acknowledged that the beef and store producing industry is necessary to the United Kingdom, but it has been killed by the growth of the import trade; therefore the simple solution of this problem would appear to be drastic limitation of beef imports from foreign countries not under the Flag, such limitation to take place gradually until the home industry was properly on its feet and could supply a great part of what was needed at home. Thus would production be increased, and after all increased production means more employment on the land and a higher state of fertility in our arable acres. A prosperous cattle trade means that those farmers who have been attracted from meat to milk would go back to producing meat, and thus we should be in a fair way towards obtaining a balanced agriculture, and thus prosperity would again return to our countryside.

Yet we still "wait and see," and while doing so good men, and true, are being placed in a position in which they are faced with bankruptcy.

Again Far Too Much Imported Butter

I HAVE just been wading through the figures (official) that bear on the question of dairy produce supplies in 1935. No mean task, either.

Now I want you to understand clearly that butter imports, by value, as in other recent years, were greater than those of any other single article of food imported into the United Kingdom during 1935.

We actually imported 9,609,000 cwt. of butter to the value of £39,338,000, although we are told that the year 1935 marked a check in the rising tide of United Kingdom butter imports, and for the first time since 1927 a decline was recorded. After all, this decline was but 1 per cent., but the gross imports then were in excess of any other previous year, and were 9 per cent. greater than in 1933.

Now, in connection with butter supplies, the chairman of the Milk Marketing Board has just made an important statement, and that is the Board intend to put up butter manufacturing plant in all areas where milk supplies in adequate amount are available, and that there will also be separating stations.

Producers, if they so desire, are to have their separated milk returned to them.

One may criticise the M.M.B., but here we can only praise this suggestion as being constructive and one likely to help the live-stock industry as well as those who desire to purchase home-produced butter. Many and many a time I have spoken with men who sell their milk under contract but would be thankful to obtain skimmed or separated milk for rearing calves or for feeding to pigs, yet, under the provisions of the M.M.B., they have been unable to obtain this wholesome home-produced feeding stuff. What I do so earnestly hope is that the M.M.B. will not allow vested interests to dictate to them where these butter-making factories and separating stations are to be set up, but will be guided by the needs of the various areas. There is a warning and a glaring example before them in the location of sugar beet factories where growers in the south, south-west, and west of England have suffered badly, although they were as well capable of growing beet as those more favoured counties that boast of factories that are redundant in numbers.

The whole country should be "zoned" by experts having no axe to grind, and fair play should be given to all.

What I should like to see, however, is more encouragement given to our farmhouse producers, for, after all, there is no butter turned out so well, or of such delicious flavour, as that made by the dairymaids of our farmsteads.

Our Fruit Growers

A BRIEF visit to Kent (that garden of England) has shown me that growers have again been up against the weather in more ways than one.

Early frosts, rain, and hail storms have damaged the fruit in many places, while in others no damage has been done. I learned that canners have been most busy of late, and as their stocks (owing to climatic conditions last year) are completely exhausted they are keenly anxious to replenish them by purchasing largely of the excellent fruit produced in Kent. Unfortunately, there is one snag. The greatest enemy to the canning industry, and thus to the producer, is the quantity of foreign peaches, pears, and pineapples that is imported, and upon which no effective tariff is placed. While these three fruits compete so heavily with British canned products the canners cannot give better prices for British fruit, which I understand they are ready and willing to do.

Thus the machinations of the foreigner intrude even into the peace and the profits of our most famous area for fruit growing.

How long? How long, we ask, will this state of affairs be tolerated?

FASCISM IN OUR VILLAGE

XII.—All About The Middlemen

DAN'L Whiddon turned up late the other night at the Dog and Duck, and didn't come in till Tam Pearce had brought round the tankards.

"I've been shopping over to Westbourne," he explained when at last he had settled down and had had a hearty pull at the tankard which Tam brought him.

"Thirsty work shopping," he remarked "and that basket weighs uncommon heavy."

"There's one thing that has always struck me as curious," remarked 'Arry 'Awke, "and that is the difference in the price you have to pay for anything in the shops and the price you get for that same thing if you grow it yourself. Cabbages, now, for example. You have to pay up to sixpence for a good one in the shops, and yet farmers can hardly sell them some seasons, or, if they do, they only get very low prices. What have your Fascists to say about that, Mr. Cobleigh?"

"Yes, that's true," replied Uncle Tom, "and the great difference in price is almost entirely due to the middlemen, who take all the profits from the farmer and put the price up against the housewife. Do away with all the middlemen that are not really wanted and you can reduce the price in the shops; at the same time, of course, you can afford to pay the farmer a higher price for his produce without raising prices against the consumer."

"Yes, I see that," interrupted Dan'l Whiddon, "but what will happen to the middlemen? They will lose their job won't they?"

"No, they won't" replied Uncle Tom, "for they will be given jobs in the distributing business where they will be really wanted. You see" he went on, "Mosley's idea is to get the foodstuffs as cheaply as possible from producer to consumer, and anything that stands in the way of that principle has to go, and that's where the middlemen, who are not really wanted, get off."

"Talking about that," remarked Peter Gurney, "I know a fisherman in Essex who told me that he can't bring his boat alongside because the only place for a deep water dock was taken for a swimming pool. Now he has to put his fish into a rowing boat which lands them on the beach, and then there is a man with a horse and cart to take them to the railway, only a few hundred yards away. Surely those extra men are not really wanted, are they?"

"No, of course not," replied Uncle Tom, "and if they had a Fascist Government they would have a deep water quay alongside the railway and load the fish straight from the boats into the train. But you cannot expect anything so sensible as that with our Modern Democracy," he added, draining his tankard.

"Modern Democracy is good," remarked Jan Stewer, with a broad grin "not but what there's a good deal in all that you say, Mr. Cobleigh."

Before we could finish the argument, Tam Pearce hustled us out in a way we didn't like and slammed the door on us. Democracy indeed. We'll give him democracy one of these days, if he treats us like that.—H. E. CROCKER.

THE WORLD OF LABOUR

PALE PINK POLLITT

By JOHN EMERY

The Disunited Popular Front—Harry Pollitt Fades To A Dull Pink

DEMOCRATS are getting good fun for their money these days. Apart from the joy of fighting for free speech and howling down Sir Oswald Mosley, the baiting of Sir Walter Citrine, and the fight as to who is to be Lord Mayor of Bradford, there are scores of other entertainments for the half-wits of the Labour Movement.

The chief diversion, however, is unquestionably the craze for a popular front.

This new game is being played quite a lot just now, both in the best and the worst circles.

Briefly, the proposal is that several groups who differ fundamentally on every issue under the sun should unite in one great popular movement.

The movement is being backed chiefly by Liberals, who see no hope of ever getting into parliament, and by Communists, who see no hope of getting anywhere.

The chief exponents of this proposal are Mr. Harry Pollitt and the gentlemen who draw their salaries from Liberal papers financed by oil and cocoa. Mr. Pollitt at one time advocated that the only hope of the workers was to seize power by force, and the fact that workers with bare fists were to take power from men who had machine guns, tanks, and aeroplanes, never deterred Mr. Pollitt from delivering passionate appeals asking the workers to revolt.

But something has come over Mr. Pollitt, and the story of Saul's conversion on the way to Damascus is a slow-motion affair compared to the conversion of Mr. Pollitt. Those of you who read your bible will remember that Saul required the voice of God direct from heaven to make him see the error of his ways. Mr. Pollitt needed nothing so powerful, he merely appeared on the same platform as the Moderator of the Church of Scotland since when he has been a changed man.

Lions and Lambs

NOW I am not going to suggest that one speech on the same platform as the Moderator enabled Mr. Pollitt to see the light. The fact that a disciple of the Prince of Peace and a disciple of the Class War were able to see eye to eye on the blessings to be derived from killing Italian workmen is, I know a wonderful manifestation of the power of the League of Nations. But the fact that Liberals who do not even believe in nationalising land, mines, and railways, and certainly not cocoa or oil, are now willing to join with Mr. Pollitt requires some other explanation than that of spiritual conversion.

The question naturally arises has the Liberal Party changed or has the Communist Party? Has Sir Walter Layton been swung over to the belief that the only hope of a solution of the poverty problem lies in the workers forcibly seizing power. If he hasn't, then has Mr. Pollitt been swung over to the belief that the only hope is by abolishing the safeguarding duties on gas mantles and safety razors? Those of us who are interested in trying to abolish poverty have a right to know why this fraternisation of lions and lambs. M. Kerensky was a typical Liberal, even a Radical, and we know the love which M. Lenin bore for M. Kerensky. There was a time, too, when Trotsky was anxious to press M. Kerensky to his bosom, but Kerensky thought better of it. He fled from his love.

Liberal-Communist Front

REMEMBERING all this, I have often wondered whether Mr. Pollitt really loves Lord Cowdray and Sir Walter Layton, and the man whom Mr. Kirkwood, M.P., used to call Dirty Davy.

If Mr. Pollitt still believes in the Social Revolution, he surely cannot hope to achieve it by an alliance with Mr. Lloyd George and Sir Archibald Sinclair. And Mr. Lloyd George surely cannot hope to preserve unadulterated Free Trade and the free play of private enterprise by allying with Mr. Pollitt and other Communist apostles.

But undoubtedly there the fact remains. Mr. Pollitt and his friends, who were such pure milk of the word of the Marxists that they couldn't work with Mr. James Maxton, are now ready and willing to work with Mr. Lloyd George, Sir Walter Citrine, and Mr. Ernest Bevin. The Communist paper each morning is full of stories showing the wonderful things which could be done if only the alleged progressive forces were united. The slogan, "Socialism is the hope of the world" is not quite abandoned, only there has been added to it a new one. The hope of Socialism is Mr. Lloyd George. I wonder what Lenin would think of it all. I wonder what Trotsky thinks of it all.

Mr. HARRY POLLITT,
"Willing to work with Citrine."

Happy Herb

ALL this may remain a mystery, but there is no doubt at all as to what Mr. Herbert Morrison thinks of it. Herbert is enjoying life once again. For a time Herbert was unhappy. People began to talk of him as a statesman chiefly because he was the Minister who had carried through a Transport Bill left him by his Tory predecessor.

When he became Prime Minister of London these same people expected him to do something big, and Herbert, who had never thought big in his life, because he had always been an office boy to Mr. MacDonald, had no idea where to begin. He had made good speeches on, "down with the slums, and up with the houses," and so he thought he would like to build a new bridge. If the people in the slums complained, he could always take them out and show them what a nice bridge he had built them. He appears to have abandoned all hope of pulling down the slums and is making precisely the same speeches on housing as the Moderates did before him—he is talking of the number of houses built since the war, but not one word of how many or how few have been built by him. The plain fact is now revealed that Herbert is always unhappy when he is expected to carry through any constructive legislation, and his real function in life is hunting witches.

A Question of Salaries

ACTUALLY this was the question on which Mr. Morrison's reputation was built. He can smell Communists at a hundred yards. Being clever at the game himself, he knows every trick and move of the Communist leaders, sometimes even before they know it themselves. And now, with this last despairing effort of the Communist Party to get inside the Labour Party, Mr. Morrison is in his element once again. Pitifully inadequate when trying to explain his failure on housing and his still harsh Public Assistance administration, he is a wonderful success when flaying the Communists. In this game of intrigue the Communists are babes in arms to Mr. Morrison. Words of wit and wisdom flow from his tongue and poisoned paragraphs from his pen. Not too harsh on the Liberals, with whom he says he has a great deal of sympathy, Mr. Morrison is merciless to poor Mr. Pollitt. He shows clearly that Mr. Pollitt draws his salary from the oppressed proletariat of Russia, whereas Mr. Morrison, as Secretary to the London Labour Party, has been able to draw his from the free, prosperous British working class. But, finally, Mr. Morrison shows why he will not associate with the Communist Party—he says quite openly that it would lose the Labour Party far more votes than they would gain.

The Fountain of Supply

HE is equally frank in his refusal to join with the Liberals in a United Front. He says it would be very difficult to get such a proposal carried in a British Labour Party Conference. Were it possible to carry it out without consulting the trade union delegates it would doubtless be done. But if this step were taken the unions might refuse to supply cash to make careers for men like Mr. Morrison, and he would be entirely dependent on the Lloyd George fund. All this would involve a struggle for leadership with Mr. Lloyd George, and Mr Morrison would find that, at the game of political intrigue, Mr. Lloyd George was no babe in arms.

The United Front, therefore, will not take place. Mr. Morrison is to go on alone trying to create a Labour majority. He believes he can capture the middle class. Poor man!

The handsome and dashing cavalier, Mr. Ramsay MacDonald, used to believe that, too, and if Mr. MacDonald, with his good looks and commanding figure, failed, what chance has Mr. Morrison?

Mr. Morrison has nothing to recommend him. The English middle class clearly love a lord. They might even be intrigued by a person not quite sure as to who his father actually was, for there is always the possibility that the father might have been a peer. Apart from Mr. Morrison's successes as a witch finder, I have never been impressed by his ability, but the man who believes that the English middle class will fall for the son of a policeman is not quite all there.

Almost a Campaign

AS I write these notes Labour is setting the stage for a delightful piece of organised hypocrisy.

They seem now to be assured that their hero, Haile Selassie, will not require to apply for parish relief and so they propose to devote a little attention to the unemployed of Britain. They are even threatening to get angry about the new Public Assistance regulations, and if they weren't all going away for their three months' holiday, they might even have a campaign about it.

Let us see first how much they are in earnest about this and how much is just humbug in the hope of catching votes.

In February of 1935 the first scales under the Public Assistance Commissioners were issued. Scarcely a Labour man in Parliament made the slightest fuss. They were gulled by the fact that each child was to receive 1s. more per week. Actually, the amount to be spent over all was to be less than in former years and obviously somebody had to be cut.

The qualifying clauses saw to that, but the Labour leaders, divorced from the working class, did not see through the qualifying clauses.

On the last Wednesday of the month the National Council of Labour held its monthly meeting at Transport House. The new scales were due to come into force on the week-end following the meeting, *but the National Council of Labour had not one single word to say about the scales, good, bad, or indifferent.*

The week-end the scales came into force the storm broke. It burst first in South Wales and swept the country from end to end. And the storm had been raging for nearly a fortnight before official Labour took a hand. They couldn't believe it at first, and then when they saw there might be votes from the storm, they began to denounce the scales of payment. *But the scales they were denouncing had passed through Parliament without a protest from a single Labour leader.*

Now see what happens. New scales of payment were introduced which actually increase the amount to be spent. And Labour leaders, who saw nothing wrong last year, are now righteously indignant that the scales are better than those which satisfied them last year. And here are the men who passed the Anomalies Bill and insisted on a Means Test when in office, now demanding its abolition.

Without the slightest hesitation I say the new zeal for the unemployed is just cant to capture votes.

(By Our Political Correspondent.)

AGRICULTURE occupied two days last week, but the farmer will get little consolation from this.

The Cattle Subsidy Bill was discussed, and the fate of British agriculture appeared to be at stake. The decision was never in doubt; Financial-Democracy had already decided. However well-intentioned Mr. Walter Elliot may once have been, international financiers and their Cabinet puppets were too strong. So much so that he now talks their own language. This cattle subsidy, he said, was necessary for two reasons: one, to improve consumption in these islands; and secondly, to throw no burden upon international trade.

They make international trade sound like some sacred incantation, which has up to now had the effect of blinding the people of this country to its real meaning. International trade and its essential corollary, international lending, is the life-blood of international finance and international usury. Dividends must be earned, so foreign foodstuffs and manufactures must come into this country.

Go into the House almost any day and you will never fail to hear either in question or debate some reference to the sacredness of foreign investments and dividends.

Financing Foreigners

LET anyone dare demand a loan to equip British industry, great measures for the relief of unemployment, etc., and the cry goes up that you must not divert money from its normal channels. But if Brazil, Argentina, or some Central European country desires to raise loans, they are oversubscribed. Since 1931, when we went off the Gold Standard, there has been an official ban on foreign flotations in order that our exchanges may retain some degree of stability; but the City of London has chafed at this restriction, and Mr. Neville Chamberlain, some few months ago, was forced to set up a Committee to implement the restoration of our age-old custom of financing our competitors.

Let no one suppose, however, that no British capital has gone abroad. Foreign stocks and shares have been purchased, balances have been transferred to banks in foreign countries, and other methods used to circumvent the edict of the Government.

All the Government protestations that they intend to restore prosperity to British agriculture must be false. There is only one choice if the farmer and the farm-worker are to come into their own—dividends on foreign investments must be sacrificed.

In its agricultural policy the Government has again come down on the side of the City of London, and the cattle subsidy is merely a sop to their conscience. Even Mr. Elliot, in whom the farmer at first had great faith, as he was that rara avis, a Minister with technical knowledge of his job, is uncertain for whose benefit the subsidy is given. On Monday he told the House that "the subsidy is now passing entirely to the producers," and then later on in the same speech he said: "This is a consumers' subsidy" — statements typical of the general muddle-headedness of the Government, and justly greeted with loud laughter.

The strangest factor in this debate to the observer is that in spite of the almost general condemnation of the Government's agricultural policy, no-one offered any intelligent alternative. No attempt was made to diagnose the causes of the wasting disease from which agriculture is suffering.

Serious Agricultural Decline

STATISTICS were reeled off; in 1921 the number of farm workers was 996,000; in 1935 it was 783,000—a decrease of 20 per cent. The price of fat cattle in 1925 was £2 12s. 7d. a cwt.; in 1935 the price fell to 31s. 10d.; and so on through the whole sorry story of Governmental treachery, and yet none proposes the obvious remedy.

Agricultural representatives expressed repugnance at subsidies, and appealed for fair play for the farmer. Admirable, but negative sentiments. The only hope for stockbreeding is elimination of foreign meat. But no Member of Parliament has the courage to fight for this.

The Socialist Opposition have no policy to offer except marketing boards. They are so obsessed with the demand for cheap foreign meat that they would flood the market and ruin agriculture. And having destroyed the market for the British farmer, they would offer him a marketing board!

The only intelligent observation came from Mr. George Hardie, who said: "If they wish that Scottish beef should be bought in Scotland they should see that the people get wages which will allow them to buy it." You have in these few words a concise summary of Fascist policy for the salvation of British agriculture—raise the standard of life of the industrial worker, and the solution is automatic. Only through the corporative organisation of industry, however, is this possible.

Runciman's Rousing Rubbish

ON Wednesday, Mr. Runciman, the High Priest of the Temple of International Finance, regaled the House with a veritable sunburst of optimism for the future of British industry. Britain, according to Runciman, is an economic Garden of Eden, with but two serpents—coal and cotton. With these two snakes in the grass eradicated, we shall reach the stage of full and unadulterated prosperity! He was lyrical in referring to the progress of the steel industry. Prospects are excellent. When housing demand fails, armaments will replace it. But Mr. Runciman has overlooked at least one important factor. Although our production of steel has reached record dimensions, the number of men required to produce it has gone down by some 40 per cent. What is he going to do about the men thrown out of employment through rationalisation? Industrial production has risen high above that of 1929, but nearly a million more men are unemployed. What has the Government to offer them?

It must have been particularly unpleasant to this Cobdenite disciple to admit that "progress has been remarkable in all industries supplying the home market." Two years ago, he was of the firm opinion that further progress in the home market was impossible, and that until international trading resumed its former dimensions there was no hope. There is not the slightest hope of a resumption of foreign trading on anything like its former scale. Local industrialisation, or economic nationalism, has struck roots deep into the industrial soil in all countries, and can never be eliminated.

Our future lies within the Empire and our policy and energies should be directed towards that end. Australia is of greater value to us than Argentina, even from the point of view of economic benefit. Investments in Argentina, according to the President of the Board of Trade, amount to £435,000,000, and dividends received amount to £8,500,000. In the case of Australia, we are officially informed that British investments amount to £524,000,000, and the revenue received from these investments amounts to £27,300,000. On a purely commercial basis alone, apart altogether from the fact that the country is peopled with our own flesh and blood, Australia is a much more desirable proposition than Argentina.

Our economic salvation lies not in making hopeless attempts to re-establish our former level of trade with foreign countries, but in concentration on our home and Empire markets. By these means we shall reconstitute the greatness Britain. Our improved trading figures show indisputably that Britain is capable of assuming her former leadership among the Powers, and only the inherent incapacity of democratic statesmanship to lead and to plan renders this impossible.—G. S.

RADIO FLASHES

ILL-MANNERED NEWS-FINCHES

By BLUEBIRD

ON Sunday morning we were given an excellent example of the manner in which the B.B.C. goes out of its way to annoy its listeners.

Many people on Sunday mornings tune in to the 10.30 a.m. weather forecast. I tuned in for this as usual at 10.30 a.m. The time signal went, and then there was a pause. Then began the peal of Bow Bells. This went on solidly without a single break for twenty-eight minutes! At 10.58 a.m., the weather-finch came on with the news, merely remarking that he was sorry he was so late.

We were not given a word of explanation. Surely this was our due. We might have been told that the Clerk of the Weather had overslept. Being human and Sunday morning, he would have been forgiven.

And, anyhow, surely there was no need to give us nearly half an hour of Bow Bells. Would Sir John Reith have thought it very wicked to give us a few jolly gramophone records to wile away the time? But it must have been extremely bad management on someone's part to cause this most important weather bulletin to be 28 minutes late.

Left in the Air

THOUGH I did not hear it myself, I am told there was further lack of consideration for listeners on Saturday afternoon. An extraordinary thrilling lawn tennis match between Australia and Germany was being broadcast. The match in question was a single between Quist and von Cramm. The players were about 5 all in the final set and the match had reached a very crucial point. At Wimbledon itself, excitement reached fever heat.

The B.B.C. curtly announced to its thrilled listeners that they were sorry and all that, but they had got to leave Wimbledon for the News Bulletin, as it was then 6 p.m.

Now that is all quite in order. The News is scheduled for 6 p.m. and it would be very wrong to keep everyone waiting. But what about the system of alternative programmes? Why have we got to have the news from the Droitwich National, the "Little" Nationals and the Regionals all at once?

Bad Taste from I.B.C.

HOW not to give a running commentary was demonstrated on Sunday afternoon by a news-tit belonging to the International Broadcasting Company from Radio-Normandie.

An account of a motor race at Deauville was being broadcast "by courtesy of" Somebody's patent bread. There was an accident in which Marcel Lehoux, the famous French driver, was killed, and Giuseppe Farina, the Italian, was injured. The news-tit told us there had been a most terrible accident. He said that the two cars had collided, and had jumped into the air and gone right over the line of spectators. How many had been killed or injured he was not going to tell us, as it might be too affecting for some listeners.

He certainly left us with the impression that one driver was dead, the other dying, and that there were many casualties, fatal and otherwise, among the spectators.

If he had given a simple straightforward account of what really had occurred and said that the accident actually happened at a point where there were no spectators it would all have been much less harrowing.

As it was, it was merely pandering to sensationalism.

Spanish Customs

OUR own news-finches do not seem yet to have recovered from the fall of their Abyssinian idol, or the alliance between their pet aversions, Germany and Italy. And they have not yet been able to make their minds up about Spain.

When we were hearing about the "woikers" being driven out of Barcelona I could not help thinking about the Woikers' "Olympic" Games which were to be staged there in "opposition" to the real show in Berlin. It crossed my mind that woikers appear to be having fun and games in Barcelona now, and one or two of them have probably broken records for everything from the 100 yards to the Marathon in their efforts to get out of Barcelona and indeed out of Spain.

Wasting Listeners' Time

ON Saturday night in the second news more than half the time was wasted by reports of absurd and meaningless speeches by Baldwin, Attlee, and silly little Eden. Baldwin said the usual speech and Attlee said the opposite, and the Eden urchin yapped as usual and ate a few more of his words.

After them we heard a few words of common sense from Sir Ian Hamilton, who urged us to make friends with Germany instead of playing the fool.

Finally, we were told with pride how Belisha had opened a new arterial road nine whole miles long in Cheshire. Then he had driven along it, and was trapped for exceeding the speed limit by a patent invisible ray!

Does not that whole incident sum up Belisha and his road policy? In the first place he ought to be opening trunk roads ninety miles long instead of fooling about with local affairs nine miles long.

And then having built an inadequate road for speeding he is far more interested in devices for preventing speeding.

Go away, Belisha, before Nemesis overtakes you, for Nemesis will not be stayed by invisible rays!

British Influence in B.B.C.

I ONLY heard the tail-end of the sermon by the Rev. P. B. Clayton of Toc H fame, but what I did hear was good. If we want peace, he told us, we must be strong enough to be able to enforce it. That seems definitely to be one down to Mr. Charles Siepmann, of Peace Week infamy.

According to that reliable fount of knowledge, Mr. Collie Knox, a faction, headed by Mr. Moray Maclaren, has arisen in the B.B.C. opposed to Siepmann and all his works. Good for Mr. Maclaren, and more power to his elbow. He appears to be for all things the British Union stands for, and seems to have the right idea about what should be done with Siepmann. But the Jews are there for definite propaganda purposes, and Maclaren will find he is up against a stiff proposition.

"The Ghost Train"

AS to entertainment of the week, "The Ghost Train" was thoroughly well done. The radio version was thrilling from beginning to end. The train noise did not seem quite so thrilling as when they were produced on the stage, but we get used to radio thrills and get blasé.

But why did Mr. Wellington, the programme arranger, have to put on "The Ghost Train" and the "White Coons" (with Stanley Holloway) at the same time on the National and the Regional?

On Friday night the dance band of Prince Pearl, alias Harry Roy, born Lipmann, was as dull and uninspired as ever. And we have been hearing Roy "step up to the microphone" and say good-night in his usual foolish and unwitty manner for years and years. It is time he made a new joke.

Variety on Saturday was fair. I thought that Bernard Hunter, a boy of fifteen, who sang songs, deserved further encouragement. He seemed to me to have real melody in his voice. He sang and did not try to croon.

In Henry Hall's Hour, Hall and a well-known composer (Ray someone or another whose name I forget) who wrote the "Birth of the Blues" and other well-known tunes, held a sort of mutual admiration society. Each thought the other's songs, singing, band, and boys were "simply grand." They got quite breathless about it.

Lohengrin and Tauber

A FINE performance of Lohengrin from Bayreuth on Sunday evening. The B.B.C. relayed too little of it, but as you could get it from most continental stations that did not matter much.

And on Sunday evening we had seventy-five minutes of Richard Tauber. This fine singer is, I believe, a Jew. This does not make him less pleasant to hear. I do not object to Harry Roy and Co. because they are Jews, but because they put out what I consider is bad stuff, whereas English bands, such as that of Jack Payne, are far better, but we do not hear them.

There is no one better than Tauber in his own line, and very few can even approach him. Therefore, let us hear him by all means.

I thought it was rather naughty of him to sing so little of "You Are My Heart's Delight," and in what little he did sing to give us a spot of vocal aerobatics that was suspiciously like crooning.

MOSLEY'S MANCHESTER RALLY

Lancashire Supporters of the British Union Teach Watch Committee a Stern Lesson

Described by THEO. LANG

Mosley speaking at Manchester

"WE can carry on our propaganda exactly the same whether we are in uniform or not," said Sir Oswald Mosley, Leader of the British Union of Fascists and National Socialists, in a statement to the Press at Manchester on Sunday night.

He had just returned from another great Lancashire triumph. He had marched through Manchester streets at the head of over a thousand members of the Union. At Albert Croft thousands of Lancashire people gathered despite threatening skies and downpours of rain.

Owing to objections raised by the Manchester Watch Committee, none of those taking part in the demonstration wore the familiar black shirt, but the event was as successful as any of the great events staged by the Union during the course of its activities in the North.

"A Man's a Man for a' that"

THE LEADER of the British Union himself wore a lounge suit, and not even a badge was worn by any of the marching men and women. Even the drummers wore ordinary clothes.

Yet all Manchester knew the Blackshirts were on the march.

Even if the crowds who stood on the pavements and braved the heavy rain had not seen the Union's standards and the Union Jack at the head of the long column, even if they had not recognised and acknowledged with shouts and salutes the familiar figure of Sir Oswald, they would have known the marchers were members of the British Union. The order and discipline of the march were of a nature associated in the public mind only with Blackshirt demonstrations.

To the democrat, leadership is impossible and discipline abhorrent. For those reasons democracy seeks to prevent the members of the British Union from wearing their uniform.

For those reasons the Manchester Watch Committee banned the march to the meeting. The Committee argued that a march of members wearing black shirts was provocative.

The Union's reply to this ban was a severe test to the sincerity of that argument. When a request for permission to hold a march of members not wearing the black shirt was presented to the Watch Committee they were beaten by their own arguments. The specious claim that they were frightened of "provocation" by the wearing of the black shirt was made only because they imagined that no march and no meeting could be held by the Union unless black shirts were worn.

"To-day's march and meeting has proved two things," said Mosley. "The first, that we can carry on our propaganda exactly the same whether we are in uniform or not. The second, that organised Socialist and Communist opposition is exactly the same whether we are in uniform or not.

Provocation Lie Exposed

"THE Red opposition to-day created far more disorder than at our recent march and demonstration in Victoria Park, East London, when all Blackshirts were in uniform and a crowd of 100,000 assembled without trouble. The Reds to-day also created more disorder than recently at Finsbury Park, North London, when all the Blackshirts were in uniform and a crowd of 50,000 assembled.

"In fact these experiences show that the attempts of our opponents, Conservative and Socialist alike, to excuse Red violence by our wearing of the Blackshirt uniform is sheer hypocrisy. To-day's experience also shows that even if they deprived us of the propaganda value of the black shirt in their efforts to arrest our progress we can carry on exactly the same and still draw great audiences to hear our case.

"The thousands who assembled on Albert Croft to-day heard our case with perfect attention and courtesy, but as usual at open-air meetings, a few hundred Reds did their ineffective best to prevent the audience hearing the speech by organised shouting and the throwing of missiles."

The Banner of Jewry

MOSLEY was recognised as soon as he appeared on the roof of the van and walked to the microphone. Cheer's rang out and hands were raised in the salute. He was recognised, too, by the crowd of howling Reds.

From my position on top of one of the vans I was amazed to find that the shrieking opposition was caused by about 150 whose choir-masters were obviously Jews who had made perfectly certain that their position should be to the rear of the "workers' front." Mosley began to speak, the "socialist terror" redoubled their efforts in the symphony of the "Russian International." But in spite of this they were drowned, firstly, by the use of the loud speaking equipment and, secondly, by the attitude of the majority of the audience who had come there to hear Mosley speak.

The antics adopted by the Socialists were amusing, they waved their "Daily Worker," they hoisted a Jew comrade on the shoulders of another to take a picture of the "workers" of Britain with their clenched fists raised. One can only imagine that the pictures of the faces betrayed would sell well in a bazaar in Cairo.

The Leader asked his audience to take a good look at this specimen. He was glad, he said, of the opportunity the Socialists were affording the crowd. They were showing a great Lancashire audience who their supporters were.

"Those are the people who want to govern England. We want to govern England by Englishmen," he declared, amid applause.

The Reds, with their howling and their violence, he said, were committing the greatest blunder they had ever committed in their fight against free speech and Fascism.

"The fact that our opponents are so afraid of our case being put is the best tribute that has been paid to our case. If they were capable of meeting us with reasoned argument they would do it. When they endeavour to prevent you hearing the case, then it proves to you people of Manchester that they cannot meet argument with argument and fact with fact."

In spite of every effort by Red hooligans, the Union had put its case at hundreds of meetings throughout the country, and to-day thousands of British men and women were in its ranks. The workers of Britain were turning to the new creed of National Socialism because they realised that there lay their only hope of building the Britain of their dreams.

The Reds howled and chanted, but the great majority of the crowd listened attentively to the speech.

Communist Confetti

OCCASIONALLY more tangible methods of interrupting the meeting than mere shouting and gesturing were attempted.

A Jew brandished an open razor. Missiles were thrown from certain quarters of the crowd. A half brick hurtled through the air. Directed at the speaker, it crashed against the van and inflicted a wound on the head of a member of the crowd.

"The Manchester Watch Committee said that if we held meetings in plain clothes," said Sir Oswald, "there would be no disorder from the Reds. You have to-day got the answer to that."

Literature inciting the Red hooligans to violence at that meeting had been circulated, and here they were, shouting at the top of their lungs, throwing bricks, using catapults, and doing everything they could to prevent the Blackshirt case being put. It was a splendid opportunity for the Manchester people to see the methods Socialism adopted against its opponents.

"It is because we love England and because you love England," he continued, "that every one of us here to-day, with the exception of that small alien minority, will soon be working with us to build the new England of our dreams. In this great audience are thousands of my brother Englishmen who have come here peacefully to hear our case, and only a small alien mob comes between Englishman and Englishman in an attempt to prevent that case being put."

"No one desires war," he declared, "but the old parties, Socialists and Tories and their bosses, the Jews. It is time we had a movement of Englishmen to call a halt to war and build the peace of the world."

A Section of the British Union Band in the Manchester March

Mosley in Uniform

Englishmen Stoned

WHEN Sir Oswald concluded his speech amid a burst of applause, the great crowd did not disperse. It stood while the National Anthem and the Fascist "Marching Song" were sung.

The Blackshirts reformed their column. Thousands pressed forward to greet Sir Oswald. Then, with their Leader once more at their head, the Blackshirts marched away from the scene of yet another Blackshirt triumph.

The Reds made their last attempt to give some evidence of their opposition. Bricks and stones were thrown in Sir Oswald's direction. A leaden bullet, fired from a strong catapult, smashed the window of one of the vans.

But the Blackshirt column marched through crowds of enthusiastic people back to the centre of Manchester. Rain swept the streets, but the crowds were not thinned by the downpour. Throughout the whole of the march people stood on the pavements, drew attention to Sir Oswald as he marched behind the standards, and watched the long column pass.

The thousands who went to Albert Croft, who responded with cheers when Sir Oswald declared "violence and intimidation never stopped Englishmen, and it is not going to stop you and I!" saw Fascist discipline at its best, and were able to compare its methods with those of the Jew-subsidised hooligans.

Action

PUBLISHED EVERY THURSDAY

EDITORIAL OFFICES—
SANCTUARY BUILDINGS, GREAT SMITH STREET, LONDON S.W.1.

Telephone: Victoria 9084 (five lines)

Editor: JOHN BECKETT

His Majesty the King

THE attack upon His Majesty is dealt with in more detail elsewhere, but it is fitting that we should express here the shock which the news of such an attempt had upon all King Edward's loyal subjects, and our relief that, thanks to police and public, the matter was dealt with so promptly and effectively.

The general chorus of indignation should not, however, blind us to the fact that there is a small and growing minority of people in this country, many of them importations, who do not share the national affection for a brave and devoted monarch. We ourselves have been at many meetings during the past two years where the singing of "God Save the King" is greeted with catcalls, howls of derision, and the chanting of that dismal dirge, the "Red Flag."

Even MacMahon is entitled to legal assistance, and we therefore can congratulate both the British legal profession and the man concerned on the fact that within half-an-hour of the news of the outrage, Mr. Kerstein was prominently in the headlines as the defending solicitor. Thus, what started as a tragedy finished as a kind of new instalment of the old story of the Kellys and the Cohens.

Warning From Spain

AS we write the fate of Spain appears to be in the balance. No one, least of all the unfortunate man in the street in Spain, knows what kind of a Government there will be to-morrow. For some years Red atrocities have brought forth armed reaction, and armed reaction has roused the Left to fresh atrocities. Whichever have been in power the lot of the masses has got worse and worse.

The lesson is clear. Reactionary government by a privileged class produces revolutionary conditions which Moscow is never slow to befriend and subsidise. This fomented trouble cannot be checked by armed measures alone. The causes must be removed and the troubles of the people cured, while the Jew and dupe leaders are placed firmly under restraint. That is why Italy and Germany have dealt successfully with their problems and Spain has failed. It would not appear from reading the British "kept" Press that we in this country are faced with a similar problem. Those who investigate conditions know, however, that it is very real.

Mob-rule

MOB-RULE, assault, the throwing of missiles, are becoming a common thing. The declared policy of the Communist Party of inuring the masses to street fighting has already begun. Those who resist and dare to defend themselves against the sub-men are haled before a Bench, abused by the magistrates, vilified by the Press, fined, bound over, and held up to public contempt.

We dare to prophesy that those who to-day are, by their silent support, encouraging "Red" violence, will before many moons have passed be regretting their conduct as emphatically as their counterparts in Spain are doing to-day.

There are no lack of Bela Kuns in the Ghettos of London, Leeds, and Manchester, while the policy of Government and Opposition alike creates steadily the atmosphere in which their poisonous propaganda spreads.

MALNUTRITION

May I be permitted to compliment Mrs. Anne Brock Griggs on her masterly summary of Dr. M'Gonigle's frank revelations of the ghastly poverty and consequent malnutrition still so prevalent in our country to-day?

The question of the slums is one that cannot be too strongly stressed and another—although a very different type of book—that I would recommend to all who would learn of the true state of the shameful heart of all of our big cities and towns is Joan Conquest's "With the Lid Off." Herein are related tales of slum life that are utterly incredible in their horror, but for which Miss Conquest vouches as being authentic, and that many of the incidents, such as the tragic case of the slum-girl burned to a terrible moving caricature of life because the streets were too narrow for the fire-engines to get near, come within her actual experience.

The author condemns in no uncertain terms the State and Church that allow the ghastly festering sores to continue in the midst of plenty, and sums up democratic government very ably through the medium of Hoot-me-Horn, the taxi-driver. "The country," he says, "votes a Party inter power at a Gineral Election, and Ministers have sce-lected to manage nashunal haffairs, sime as me old woman used ter knit me socks . . . Loike this 'ere:

"One row pearl.
One row plain,
Turn hit bally well
Hinside hout,
Hand start
Hall hover agine."

Yeovil. A. G. WOODGATE.

CORRESPONDENCE

A CASE FOR ENQUIRY

So Mr. Pritt, M.P., is concerned about Fascist activities in the East End. My daily paper, which usually gives about two lines to a Fascist meeting (if there is a disturbance), has favoured me with nearly half a page of the recent Parliamentary discussion on this menacing matter.

Hon. Members, however, were curiously reticent about the recent Red outbursts at Peckham, when Conservative meetings could not be held.

The age-old problem of the chicken and the egg arises, did the Reds first attack peaceful meetings of Fascist patriots or did the Fascists first organise their brutal battalions and then come out and terrorise the streets and their own meetings?

A public enquiry would speedily settle this controversy, but it would be just too bad for the newspapers to have to publish the evidence which such an enquiry would produce.

The B.U.F. might reasonably claim such an enquiry, but as it would in all probability double its membership as a result, it would be very interesting if such an enquiry were to be ordered by the present Government.

The worst feature of the matter is the apparent reluctance of the police to suppress a movement which dares to claim the right of freedom of thought and speech. Perhaps it is, when one has admitted the elementary justice of the matter, after all just a case of one disciplined body respecting the discipline of another, although political, body. Anyhow, any policeman will agree that, unlike the Reds and their sub-men, no police order or instructions have ever been disobeyed by the members of the B.U.F. But then only ex-Servicemen, of whom Sir Oswald Mosley is one, really understood what discipline stood for until this great patriot started to train the younger generation in this Spartan cult.

Is it not typical of the fatuous state of the present system of Parliament when Mr. A. P. Herbert, M.P., is allowed to make an exaggerated statement, carefully qualified by such expressions as "so I am told," and "so I am informed"? Would this sort of hearsay be accepted in any court of law?

OLD CONTEMPTIBLE.

"WHAT WOULD THE OIL COMBINES SAY?"

IT is not often that we get an admission from Conservative sources of the hidden power that sways Conservative policy; but the latest development of the Jarrow controversy has led Sir John Jarvis, the "adopter" of the town, into a remarkable statement.

The dispute began with an endeavour to obtain a large steel plant for Jarrow, which was very naturally resisted by the steel interests of Stockton.

By refusing structural steel for the new plant the Iron and Steel Federation has effectually scotched the Jarrow scheme, and as Sir John Jarvis plaintively remarks:

"The Iron and Steel Federation has its roots in all the financial and banking institutions in the City. They cannot be defied."

Sir John Jarvis

The use of the pronoun "they" is interesting. It refers not to the Federation, but to the "financial and banking institutions in the City," who, Sir John admits, "cannot be defied."

Oil Combine Adamant

THERE is in any case an alternative scheme for the site in question, which can be operated without harm to any existing industry in North-East England, indeed, with considerable benefit to the depressed collieries of Durham and Northumberland. This is the proposal to erect an "oil from coal" plant at Jarrow.

Unfortunately, as Sir John Jarvis says:

"That is not as simple as it sounds. These plants which are working are dependent on the rebate of the petrol duty for their profits. If a great new plant were installed and a large quantity of oil were produced—what would the oil combines say?"

It is not difficult to follow the trend of Sir John's thoughts. He is a business man and politician of some experience. He points out that the proposed plant would be entirely dependent upon the Exchequer maintaining the present rebate on petrol tax, and then goes on to suggest "what would the oil combines say?"

It doesn't matter a bit what they say, but what would they do? Obviously, Sir John fears that, with their power through "the financial and banking institutions in the City," who may not be defied, they might obtain the withdrawal of the rebate on the petrol tax, ruining the plant at Jarrow. As a good business man, Sir John Jarvis realises that no financial enterprise can afford to sink millions of pounds in a plant subject to the insecurity of protection by a Government dominated by alien financial interests opposed to the success of the enterprise.

"City" Interests First

SIR OSWALD MOSLEY has long since pointed out the impossibility of obtaining petrol from coal in the large quantities realisable by modern chemical research (Germany now makes over 50 per cent. of her own petrol requirements from coal) as long as the great oil combines dominate Government and have the power to flood the country with cheap petroleum products, even under cost. We had scarcely expected, however, such a direct confirmation of his views from the ranks of orthodox opinion, and we thank Sir John Jarvis for his candour.—A. R. T.

YOUTH IN GERMANY

My son, who has spent some months in a German University town, is full of enthusiasm over his experiences there. From what he says no young man or girl is lost there. The spirit of comradeship is developed to such an extent that no young man or girl, even coming to a strange town without a penny in his pocket, need despair. He can easily find food and shelter, and also work.

Young people who are not afraid of work can easily find a suitable job. The greatest marvel is the spirit of personal initiative and responsibility in which the young Germans are educated. The old habit of getting situations through good connections has completely vanished.

A young man, be he the son of a millionaire or of a labourer, has equal chances to rise. Once he is in an organisation he is given full freedom to do his work as he thinks best. If he is efficient, he is promoted, but if he fails he slides down the ladder and has to start anew. Further, young people are given many opportunities of visiting the nicest parts of the country absolutely free of any charges. Everybody works hard, but with joy and without worries, and full of hope for a brighter future.

K. LAW ROBINSON.

WASTEFUL HUMBUG AT GENEVA

The International Labour Conference of 1936

N. R. TEMPLE, WHO WAS PRESENT, DESCRIBES THE PROCEEDINGS

TELL any ordinary Englishman that you are just back from Geneva and he wants to know at once whether you witnessed the Antics of Anthony and Tantrums of Tafari. If you missed these exhibitionisms he loses interest in your visit—so closely have the League and all its ways and works come to be thought of as a monkey house rather than a serious performance.

In reality, although the League may, since Mussolini called its bluff, have lost much of its capacity for mischief, it is unfortunately not the only swarm of busybodies hived in Calvin's City. There is an organisation called the International Labour Office, which blossoms annually into an International Labour Conference, an assembly scarcely less fantastic than the League itself, and originating, like the League, in the Treaty of Versailles.

No one, and especially no Fascist, would object to an international organisation for collating and exchanging information on labour problems as on any others, if such an organisation were properly thought out. Much enlightenment would follow, for example, if the British public had better means of learning the material and moral benefits which have accrued to Italian labour for the establishment of Fascism, as set out in Mr. Loxon's article, "Renaissance," in the December Fascist Quarterly.

Labour Yes-Men

A RECENT much-advertised book with the weird title, "Yes and Albert Thomas," records the inception of the International Labour Organisation, in the perfervid imaginings of Albert Thomas, the Frenchman who was its first director, and whose "international" outlook swung it into a position where it is a menace to the working classes of every forward-looking nation, and is yet powerless to help (as he desired) the peoples of the backward States.

A word about its constitution is required to make its working understood. There is a governing body, parallel with the Council of the League of Nations, composed of permanent governmental representatives from eight chief industrial countries, with a floating population of additional members from the Governments of minor countries, from organisations of employers and employed—from so-called organisations of employed, one might say, as regards most countries represented.

The governing body meets each autumn. There is a permanent secretariat, parallel to the secretariat of the League, known as the International Labour Office. This collects statistics, drafts conventions, and otherwise busies itself throughout the year. It publishes reports, which are a standing joke among serious students of industrial affairs, by reason of their buoyant self-sufficiency and their cheery assumption that all information forwarded by members is of equal value. This polyglot team under its British director, Mr. H. B. Butler, who succeeded Monsieur Thomas, has the natural bias of its kind towards keeping the game going by any means.

Danger Ahead

SO far, though the performance involves cost to the taxpayers of Britain and those few member States which still keep up the formality of paying their subscriptions, no great harm is done. The annual "conference," corresponding in the "Labour" sphere to the Assembly of the League of Nations, is, however, quite another matter.

Not only were the two countries on the Continent of Europe, Germany and Italy, who have done most for the well-being of their workers, excluded from this year's conference in virtue of their position *vis-à-vis* the League, but from the point of view of Britain's interest the whole affair is vitiated by fundamental faults.

Build on rotten foundations, and your superstructure cannot fail to crack.

Before exploring the foundations let us, however, glance at the superstructure erected to hold legislative machinery for all the industries of all the world.

Discussion Only

THE I.L.O. produces draft Conventions which are placed before the Conference, much as a Government at home produces Bills for parliamentary discussion. This year, for example, there were Conventions for governing the hours of labour (a worthy object, indeed a Fascist object, Italy having pointed the way—as usual—to a forty-hour-week, without waiting for Geneva); for the safety of workers upon scaffolding and hoists; and for enforcing in industry an annual holiday with pay. All things which every Fascist would desire to further.

If a Convention is carried at Geneva, it cannot, of course, acquire legal force in any country until ratified by that country's Legislature; the constitution of the I.L.O., therefore, obliges the Government of each constituent State to bring before its Legislature within twelve months a Bill for ratifying whatever is passed as a Convention at Geneva.

If, for example, compulsory holidays with pay had been passed in 1936, every constituent Government, from China to Peru (both were members of the Conference), would have been bound to attempt to legislate to make it illegal to work twelve months without a holiday—a paid holiday at that.

International "Solidarity"

A GOOD thing, too—if anyone believed it was enforceable. But what chance is there that the coolie or the peon, in Asiatic rice fields or Peruvian jungles, will receive his annual paid holiday? What chance that Estonia and Ecuador, also members of the Conference, will enforce safety precautions in building work based (as was proposed) on the British Home Office requirements? The whole thing is a wicked farce.

It was, however, an article of faith with Albert Thomas and others of his kidney that "Labour," white or black or yellow, had identical interests in all countries, North and South and East and West, and that employers in all countries were equally the enemies of Labour. This iniquitous conception of the class war, cutting across national or racial divisions, is the first and greatest flaw in the foundations of the I.L.O., the second being the assumption, as in the League of Nations, that the votes of all countries must have equal value.

Britain Last Again

TAKE the latter first. The division list on any particular Convention shows (for instance) the Argentine, Australia, Austria, and Belgium, Canada, Chile, China, and Colombia—and so forth and so on, down to Uruguay, Venezuela, and Yugoslavia. This means that a Convention affecting British industry can be carried by Chinamen and Yugoslavs (not one of whom cares a curse for the British working man), and must thereupon be brought for ratification before our British Parliament, however damaging to our own people. To complete the picture of this first fundamental folly. Each Government has two votes, each employers' delegation and each workers' delegation one—four votes from every country. Thus, if the British employers and British workers should agree, as they might, on many topics, their votes could be neutralised by two Cuban votes bought by a Japanese competitor, or cast on the instructions of an anti-British Government.

Labour Leaders' Holidays

THE Conference is packed with delegates who turn up at the beginning and get upon the printed list of those attending, and then withdraw to enjoy the summer attractions of Geneva, until the time comes for voting at the end, when enough votes must be cast to keep the wheels in motion for another year.

Some Conventions must be carried to make a showing for the International Labour Office, whose staff canvasses the cafés and the corridors in search of votes.

Even this sorry farce is not the worst feature for the Briton. The most hideous feature follows from the conception of "capital" and "labour" as contesting forces in equal degree throughout the world. "Labour" in the political and international sphere is organised upon this basis, and the lead was taken in pressing on the Conference most of this year's draft Conventions by British so-called Labour leaders.

Geneva Reputations

THESE men would have been more surprised than anyone if some of the Conventions they were fathering had come to birth, but their pressure for this form of legislation has enabled them to pose upon the international stage as leaders of the united workers of the world—and thus (the serious matter) has forced the employers of the world, Britain included, into an uneasy alliance with the foreign employers' delegations, an unnatural opposition to all the workpeople's demands.

How uneasy this alliance was may be judged when it is realised that the Lancashire and Yorkshire textile employers, who equally with their workpeople are victims of international finance and Oriental competition, have by Genevan intrigues been brought into opposition concerted with the Bombay millowners and Japanese.

As one Oldham man was heard to say in the lobby of the Conference, "These Asiatics are my worst competitors. What am I doing here, acting with them against my own workpeople? I'd sooner pay six quid a week to my chaps in Lancashire than help to make a Jap or Parsee a millionaire."

In the same month, when the Conference was sitting, the Bombay millowners made a concession to the Bombay workers, in consequence of agitation, by raising the standard wage from fivepence to sevenpence a day.

And these are the people with whom British employers were obliged to act in unison by the operation of the "international" machine.

False Alliances

THE "reforms" at which the draft conventions aim could not possibly take effect in such countries, represented in the voting, as Siam and Ecuador. For the delegates from these industrially undeveloped States, Geneva is an annual outing at the public cost.

So it is for the self-styled representatives of Labour, in Great Britain and elsewhere, since the constituent Governments pay their hotel and travelling expenses.

Keeping the Wheels Turning

THE Government representatives from the non-industrial nations accordingly arrange with the officials of the International Labour Office to vote for at least a certain number of Conventions, in their common interest of keeping the machinery in motion. What Conventions are to pass depends on luck and cunning, upon lobbying, and the general irresponsibility of the Genevan mind.

To sum up the sorry business: many of the objects of these Conventions in themselves are excellent, and in accord with Fascist views—for example, the forty-hour week. But it is wrong that different parts of the Empire should be sending delegations which may act in opposition, with foreigners holding a casting vote between them; it is absurd that Iran, Irak, and Panama, Estonia, Siam, and Uruguay should have the same voting strength upon industrial conventions as the great industrial states. Worst of all, it is insufferable that an international organisation should force British employers into unholy wedlock with those of coolie countries.

British employers may be and often are willing to meet their workers at home in rational agreements, and in some trades are moving already towards a corporate organisation, once they can be relieved of the twin nightmares of foreign sweated competition and corrupt international finance.

Through corporate organisation lies the way to satisfactory conditions, in each country according to its circumstances and its national genius. To pretend a unity of interest between the Peruvian peon, the Chinese coolie, and the British working man is more than silly—in the results it produces at Geneva it is a crime against humanity and Britain.

The Huge New League of Nations Palace at Geneva

THE CORPORATE STATE AND YOU

No. 10.—THE LAWYER

By A. Raven Thomson

HERE we come to the first of the professions which are so well organised that they require no assistance to attain a corporate professional status. Indeed, many people complain that the legal profession is too well organised, too well equipped to defend its interests already. It has been termed the closest and most privileged trade union, protecting its ancient mysteries under a special professional jargon which compels the layman to seek legal guidance even in simple matters of law.

Codification of the Law

FASCIST government will codify the law in order that the layman may be better acquainted with the laws he is expected to obey. This codification will not be left entirely to lawyers, but will be carried out by the new legal corporation on which will be represented the layman as well as the lawyer. These laymen will insist upon the removal of all Norman French and "dog" Latin from our statute book and the reform of legal jargon until the laws are worded in language a twentieth century Englishman may be expected to understand.

Codification will apply not only to criminal but also to civil law and commercial practice. For example, standard forms of rental, hire purchase and other agreements will be laid down, and only such forms will be accepted in the Courts. This will act as a much-needed protection against unusual extortionate agreements which have been too complicated for understanding without expensive legal advice.

Simplification of Legal Practice

THIS may seem to lawyers to cut into their rights and privileges, throwing open knowledge of the law to all who can read and write, and reducing legal controversy to a minimum. Certainly this will be the result of drastic codification and simplification, but lawyers must recognise that they exist to perform a useful function. It is their task to interpret the law to the public, not to obscure and confuse it so that people must pay heavily to obtain "rulings" and simple legal guidance.

Legal actions will become less expensive when it is no longer a question of prolonged study of obscure legal precedents, but of the application of one or other of a few relevant paragraphs in a code of law. This will be a tremendous relief to litigants, and a certain knowledge of the actual law will reduce litigation to a minimum. It is uncertainty as to the law of complicated contracts and obscure precedents that leads to so much unnecessary and extremely expensive litigation. When the law is clear, the party in the wrong will obviously give way rather than fight a hopeless battle. Clarity in the law is a most necessary social reform.

Economic Justice

ALTHOUGH private litigation will be reduced to a minimum by a codification of the law, it does not follow that the bulk of the present legal profession will join the ranks of the unemployed. The organisation of the Corporate State will introduce a new code of economic justice. Every corporation will be empowered to pass by-laws governing commercial practice within its own industry, and regulating matters of wages and conditions of work. All these agreements between employers, workers, and consumers will bear legal sanction, unlike similar agreements to-day enforceable only by the anti-social weapon of the strike, and will be argued in case of dispute before an Industrial or Labour Court.

Here a new field of corporate law is opened to the ambitious young lawyer, who will find a higher satisfaction in the elucidation of public contract than in the bickering of private interests. In fact the law will take a different trend under Fascist government. It has existed merely to protect the bourgeois interests of private ownership. In future it will be concerned with social values, and Fascist equity will introduce the overriding principle of national well-being. It is in working out this relationship between national and individual rights that an unending vista of legal definition arises.

Corporate Law

FAR from depriving the legal profession of a livelihood Fascism must ultimately depend upon an extension of the legal faculty. The Corporate State implies the rule of law instead of the rule of might or of money. At present the law of the jungle largely prevails. It is a question of "eat or be eaten," with the great multiple combines of the Jewish financiers consuming their thousands.

This chaotic condition of lawlessness will end by the advent of the Corporate State, with the overriding legal principle in equity of the national welfare. No longer will it be permissible for the private owner or financial combine to pursue their own interests without concern for less powerful rivals, or for the stability of the economic order itself. All such interests, even the most powerful, will be subordinated to economic justice and to corporate law.

This immense extension of legal powers will require the loyal co-operation of the legal profession, as the guardians of the upright traditions of British justice. By setting lawyers free from the obscurity and confusion of present-day law by measures of codification and simplification, Fascism will enable them to take their part in the development of corporate law as the essential basis of the Corporate State.

THE CREED OF ACTION

"All shall serve the State and none the Faction;

"All shall work and thus enrich their country and themselves;

"Opportunity shall be open to all, but privilege to none;

"Great position shall be conceded only to great talent;

"Reward shall be accorded only to service;

"Poverty shall be abolished by the power of modern science released within the organised State;

"The barriers of class shall be destroyed and the energies of every citizen devoted to the service of the British nation, which, by the effort and sacrifice of our fathers has existed gloriously for centuries before this transient generation, and which by our own exertions shall be raised to its highest destiny—the Greater Britain of Fascism." *From "Code of British Union"*

MOTORING NOTES

THE NOT-YET OPEN ROAD

IT is not within the scope of this column to discuss those aspects of motoring which are adequately dealt with by our motoring Press. It will be our job to put forward the "Action" view-point upon topics concerning the motorist, the motor industry and all those things, directly or indirectly, tied up with this intriguing side of the nation's life and industry.

The importance of the motor and allied trades is not fully realised by a large number of people. An absurd and antiquated system of taxation, pettifogging regulations, and a hundred and one irritants liberally sprinkled upon the motoring community and the motor industry by the "horse and buggy" age legislators of our existing system, ensure adequate retardation of what should be one of the nation's greatest assets.

Having spent some considerable time in the North American Continent, where the car producer and user are regarded as human beings with the same qualities and the same weakness of his fellow-men, I feel deeply upon the subject.

In the U.S. and on the Continent some regulation of motor and traffic laws has ensured a fair deal for the pedestrian. An equal recognition that some measure of responsibility rests upon the pedestrian guarantees an equally fair deal for the road user.

Britain is to-day the second largest automobile-producing country in the world. At the same time British car taxation is the second highest in the world, ranking second only to Japan. It is to the credit of our producers that they have succeeded, in the face of super-taxation and stifling regulations, in forcing themselves into the enviable position that they hold to-day.

In spite of this, however, we cannot afford to crow. The typical British automobile is frankly not designed with maximum efficiency as the primary consideration. It is designed as a tax-dodging machine. Designed to work within the limitations of the most absurd taxation system in the world.

So long as that industry is hampered by artificialities we cannot hope to produce machines which are efficient in every sense of the word.

Because high taxation is restricting production we cannot hope to compete in price with the products of the foremost car-producing country—the U.S.A. Next week we will enlarge upon this subject, and will discuss the present taxation system and the Fascist alternative.—A. B.

UNDER THE CONTROL TOWER

THE KING'S FLIGHT

How To Tell A German Air Liner—And What To Tell Mr. Churchill

By "BLACKBIRD"

The Junkers tri-motor air liner, several of which fly to and from England daily and nightly

I WONDER why it is that the King's private aeroplane carries a registration number. The King's car carries no such distinguishing mark.

The machine he uses is a De Havilland Rapide, driven by two Gipsy engines. The Rapide is a faster version of the famous Dragon. It has wings which taper to a pronounced point and a fared-in or "trousered" undercarriage. It has a cruising speed of between 130 and 140 m.p.h., with a top speed of about 160 m.p.h. The cabin is fitted up to carry five people.

The King's pilot, Flight-Lieutenant E. H. Fielden, has just been appointed to the newly-created and romantic-sounding position of Captain of the King's Flight. He is known to everyone in aviation as "Mouse." He has had a long flying career, and his experiences are many and varied.

He has been pilot to the King since he, as Prince of Wales, took up regular flying in 1929. "Mouse" Fielden has many long flights to his credit, and has flown in many air races. Previously he served in the R.A.F.

For Scaremongers

ABOVE this article is a picture of the three - engined Junkers air - liner, which type plies daily, or rather several times daily, between England and Germany. I have shown this picture in order that Mr. Winston Churchill, M.P., Mr. Harry Day, M.P., Captain Harold Balfour, M.P., the staff of the "Daily Express," and others of similar kidney may be able to recognise this machine when they see it in the air.

My object in doing this is that whenever machines of this type pass over these gentlemen they will recognise them as German aeroplanes. My hope is that the recognition will cause several apoplectic strokes through succeeding frenzies of rage, after which a merciful Providence will prevent our further being troubled with their blatherings of spy-mania. (I wonder whether this is "incitement" on my part.)

Over Kenley

I DO not know what these gentry would have done had they been with me on a walk on Sunday. For when I was in the neighbourhood of what they would call the "strongly fortified aerial fortress of Kenley aerodrome," I saw a Junkers on its way into Croydon aerodrome, pass within photographic distance of Kenley.

I would not be telling the absolute truth if I were to say that I saw hordes of spies, complete with eagle eyes and cameras with telephoto lenses, looking out of the windows. Frankly, I didn't. But I feel sure that Mr. Churchill, Mr. Day, and Captain Balfour will feel quite sure that spies, eyes, and cameras were in full working order.

Actually, the weather was rather thick at the time and the Junkers was merely hanging about near Croydon aerodrome, waiting for the signal from the control officer to land. But I am sure that the machine circling round an R.A.F. aerodrome would seem *very* suspicious to the timid trio and others of similar mind. But then they shouldn't put Kenley within three miles of Croydon.

I should mention that, in addition, I saw French, Belgian, Dutch, and Swiss air liners doing the same thing. Every day German (and other) air liners actually cross our most sacred and secret heavily fortified coast line! They have to do this in order to enter or leave England. In doing so, they dare to pass over Captain Balfour's own constituency of Thanet, in which is situated Manston aerodrome. They then pass up the River Thames, passing over Eastchurch, Leysdown, and even near Sheerness and Chatham prohibited areas, to say nothing of Erith and Woolwich Arsenal, which are what are officially called "Explosive Areas."

An Explosive Area

MANY foreign air liners even dare to pass frequently over the private residence of Mr. Churchill itself, which must certainly be an "explosive area" on these occasions.

The real joke of the whole thing is that these naughty German air liners have been flying on this route with the full knowledge of the Air Ministry since 1925.

But the Timid Trio and Co. cannot, it would seem, recognise a German aeroplane when they see it. Their vast brains can only register the vast bulk of a Zeppelin. They know when they see a large rigid airship it must be a German, as no other country owns one. Hence their recent outbreak of squealing. But no sensible person worries.

SPECIAL INTERVIEW WITH FAMOUS BELGIAN STATESMAN

Count de Broqueville Expresses Strong Views To Our Brussels Correspondent

BRUSSELS!—The little Paris!—I have never been able to understand why it is so called. Nothing reminds me of Paris, neither its habits, its streets, nor its people, an entirely different type—heavier—steadier—a quite different race.

Order reigns in Brussels. The cafés are as busy as ever. People laughing and joking in the evening, sitting on the terrasse in front of a "demi."

The international Communistic agitators do not here find easy prey as in Paris—the Russian rouble has no power here.

The Aliens Department of the Brussels Police take good care that the international Jewish Communistic elements do not enjoy life.

In the street, particularly on the Boulevard Adolphe Max, much German is spoken. At first one feels surprised, but a brief examination of the physiognomies reveals that they are German emigrants of Jewish race. They have moved the Kurfurstendam from Berlin to Brussels. For how long?

Often foreigners are strikingly few, the whole of the fine Hotel Plaza, where in the past all was energy, gaiety, and life, is now deserted—silent as a grave.

"For this we have to thank the false reports of the British newspapers with their untrue stories of riots in Brussels," is the laconic remark of the manager.

Here in Belgium the workers have no desire for strikes. They long for and await a Leader bringing to them a programme not of destruction but of construction. They want good, clean living conditions and civilised wages.

The Count Speaks

COUNT DE BROQUEVILLE granted me an interview. For a great many years Prime Minister of Belgium, he has directed no fewer than seven different departments of State, and is still President of the Senate Commission on Armaments.

I asked the Count his opinion about universal suffrage, and he replied: "I make the same answer as I made forty years ago to Frère Orban, the illustrious statesman. Universal suffrage unorganised seems to me incompatible with a sound Parliamentary system. There must be corporative representation of the professions with effective restrictions, all the great national interests must be included, and the result, the triumph of competence through the real representation of the various interests which make for the greatness of the State. To-day we see the glorification of ignorance and incompetence. Unorganised universal suffrage must one day kill the Parliamentary system.

"'How long will it be before the nation understands that the present system benefits the politician to the detriment of the national interests?'

"Frère Orban pointed his finger to a street-sweeper. 'There you are. This is the man who perhaps to-morrow, by our Parliamentary system, may be given the same power as myself. I do not doubt that he is an honest man, but what of his competence to rule?'"

While listening I see on the desk Sir Oswald Mosley's book "Greater Britain," and over his desk a photograph of Mussolini. Am I not perhaps listening to a forerunner of Fascism?

Count de Broqueville continued. "Our statesmen do not understand, and it is their misfortune that the age in which we live belongs to youth. Youth has the enthusiasm which is necessary in the service of a great cause. Our present statesmen lack the spark of enthusiasm."

He himself is vibrating with fire and enthusiasm, and this at over seventy years of age.

We talk about the Peace Treaty of Versailles. The patchwork treaty that has endangered the peace of Europe since its creation.

He told me that, in his opinion, the Peace Treaty of Versailles was the work of well-intentioned people inspired, not, perhaps, by ignorance, but by "honest dreamers," against the realistic ideas which ought to, and must, govern the fate of nations. What did certain of these illustrious benefactors know of humanity—about European history—or the profound causes which had given the Continent of Europe its new face in 1919?

Were they in doubt as to the reasons,

The Royal Palace At Brussels

either historical or at least economical, which had kept together, in spite of the most cruel reverses, the Austro-Hungarian Empire?

Count de Broqueville continued:

Weak In Geography

"BRIAND assured me that in the field of geography certain members of the areopagus were as weak as they were in their knowledge of history." He was pointing to a large map—he had a broad smile. "Here you have the proof—Wilson, Clemenceau, and Lloyd George were looking for the River 'Danube.' They were looking for it in Russia and in Poland, and were surprised not to find it. He had to tell them that this river is called the 'Donau,' and passed through Vienna."

What further need to wonder why or how such geographic nonsense exists in the Treaty of Versailles?

Seventeen years have elapsed, but time has not altered the Count de Broqueville's opinion as to the Treaty. He does not believe that it can anywhere be honestly said that Versailles has enabled Europe to advance one step towards peace. . . . On the contrary. It was a noble gesture of the "idealistic dreamers" of the time.

The next point which we discussed was the question of disarmament. The dream of his political life; with great bitterness he confessed that, before the tragedy of Versailles, he had cherished great hopes. Since then, in his opinion, things have gone from bad to worse. We have to recognise that many mistakes have been made, principal amongst these "sanctions," on which he speaks with great indignation. He considered sanctions completely valueless unless Mr. Eden, who was the primary leader and prime mover for their imposition, had the courage to carry them through to the bitter end. It was all too elementary.

In his opinion, sanctions have again changed the political face of Europe. He quickly added: "I must apologise for my show of bitterness and indignation; for a moment I lost myself, but you will understand how my life was, and is, devoted to my country. I love it. And how I feel towards such ineffective and useless application of sanctions. I foresaw, and still see, the curse sanctions have proved, and will prove, in the politics and policy of Europe. I am deeply attached to England, but she has been our bad genius in this, the false policy of sanctions, and we have to pay dearly for it. The prestige of England has not increased."

The subject of our conversation changes. We are talking about the little man—the workman. One can feel in this Elder Statesman his deep love for the people, as well as his profound and sympathetic knowledge of their needs. "It is not the Government, which has to be directed by the people, and our people are far too intelligent to think otherwise—unfortunately; and this to my deep regret, the real interest of our people is not served by the falsehood of a Parliamentary system as we have it to-day.

Democracy!

INSTEAD of representing — like the "Etats Généraux" in the days of old—the great interests of the nation the present Parliamentary system represents only electoral interests, political passions, and childish personal quarrels."

He readily agreed with me that the light is penetrating into the minds of the people who are beginning to wonder what all the talk in Parliament has to do with the essential factor of the nation's welfare.

With emotion he spoke of the Belgian Dynasty, of the late King Albert, whom he served for so long. The nation will never know, he said, what it owes to its kings.

It is a pity that the Count de Broqueville does not write his memoirs. A man, during the years of the most terrible storm over Europe, has seen all the weaknesses . . . . has received the promises and . . . . who really knows so many mistakes which have been made. Who could be better qualified to give to the world such a written record?

The heavy cares and responsibilities which have so long rested upon him have not succeeded in extinguishing his fire, energy, and enthusiasm for his country; he retains his clear outlook. A deliberate act of his own alone has for the time arrested his political career.

But one can well believe when he says that should a major crisis again come to this country he would, in spite of his age, and all personal consideration, again take the helm of State, and you have but to look and listen to him to plainly see . . . . here is still the leader of the people whom he loves above all. . . .

The political life of the Count de Broqueville is not yet a closed book.

At the end of this profoundly enlightening and moving interview, which had extended well over two hours, I walked through the Boulevard du Régent, my mind struggling to retain the deep impression which the Count de Broqueville's views so ably expressed . . . . had left with me . . . . and then the sudden reaction! The first objects around me . . . . practically all the motor cars passing through this busy thoroughfare were American. . . . How is it that the great British motor industry has not conquered this market?

My next report will deal with the subject of the "Rexists."

THE SUEZ CANAL

AT the annual general meeting of the Suez Canal Company held in Paris on Monday, June 8, the chairman made a statement which should once and for all prove to the League of Nations Union and other anti-Fascist groups in this country that the closing of the Suez Canal against Italian ships would be illegal and a definite act of war.

The chairman said "The truth was quite simple." Article 1 of the International Convention of 1888, expressed and confirmed by the Treaty of Versailles, stated: "The Suez Maritime Canal should always be free and open, in time of war as in time of peace, to all merchants or war vessels without flag distinction. The canal was never to be used for the exercise or right of blockade."

Naturally

I GET very bored on looking at my old speeches, and I conclude everybody else does, naturally, as well."—Mr. Baldwin, at Wishaw, June 20.

TYNESIDE

T. P. Moran Pays Tribute To Its History

FEW people in any part of the civilised world can have suffered more from poverty than the people of Tyneside, and yet from this centre the whole world has derived the benefits of some of the finest technical brains known to history.

In the early days of the industrial revolution we had engineering establishments being erected all along the banks of this river, from which have emerged engineers and technicians who have revolutionised the industrial world.

Lord Armstrong startled the world with the development of water pressure, and his hydraulic cranes were capable of lifting 250 tons. Bridges weighing thousands of tons were made to swing round to allow ships to pass to and fro and even British Naval artillery responded to the same delicate pressure. It was in the workshops erected by Armstrong that rifling was introduced in guns of all calibres, and so, by creating greater velocity and accuracy, the distance that projectiles could be fired was considerably increased. A humble fitter, George Buckam, who was employed by this firm, not content with his daily labours, spent his leisure time at experimental work and at last perfected the screw breech block which is now used throughout the whole world for naval and military artillery.

Speed on Water

CHARLES PARSONS, another perhaps still more famous engineer, experimented constructively. The peoples of the world were aghast at the speed he attained on the vessel which is certainly one of the most famous that ever sailed out of Tyneside. The Turbinia, a small craft, little larger than a motor boat, was fitted with the first steam turbine by him. It tore through the seas at incredible speeds, the first, which by example brought millions of pounds to Britain and revolutionised world shipping.

One could continue adding to the achievements of the sons born midst the grime and smoke of this wonderful, dirty little river, but to what end? These brains had the assistance of millions of the world's most highly trained artisans, men of unassuming character who considered the wonderful results of their labour as being all in a day's work. During the nation's hour of need, when every sacrifice was demanded of every individual and admirals and generals were clamouring for munitions, brains and brawn of Tyneside's womanhood and manhood were devoted night and day to unceasing effort to satisfy the demand.

Saving Britain

GUNS, bombs, ships, shells, aeroplanes, and coal vomited from the old Tyne in a never-ending stream. Some of the finest ships that have ever added glory to the pages of Britain's history were built on Tyneside's slipways. Her artisans strained every nerve to turn out such superlative vessels as Agincourt, Malaya, Resolution, Furious, Courageous, Canada, Centaur, and Concord, followed by many other smaller craft—quite apart from repairs to injured warriors of the deep, in a relentless endeavour to serve the nation's needs—the Lion, Tiger, Invincible, Marlborough, and the Broke.

Thousands of willing hands applied themselves night and day to make these vessels seaworthy again. Millions of tons of coal poured into the holds of ships brought from collieries for miles around the river to keep our ships in action and to guarantee food to our populace.

Epilogue

WHAT a river, what men! The war ended and soon they came to realise that the only use the country could now find for them was to leave their skilled hands idle and to allow their bodies to waste through malnutrition. They struggled on in their efforts to survive and proved their skill by turning their endeavours to still other productions. Locomotives, paints, brushes, chemicals, every conceivable commodity was turned out in the efforts to keep alive their industrial prowess. But the odds were too heavy against them. Cheap commodities ruined their markets and as a result, derelict is now the unworthy title and reward that democracy bestows upon the district and its people.

Starving thousands, grasping the crumbs that a shameless Government allows as their only means of subsistence, fight for existence. With bodies wasting and brains decaying, their shipyards overgrown with weeds, and for miles around collieries closing down, the people are waiting patiently for the turn of the tide on this famous old river. Slowly, but surely, they are realising that the tide can only turn on the tide of Fascism.

Books  Read

AN IMPERIAL TRAGEDY

JAWAHARLAL NEHRU, AN AUTOBIOGRAPHY

The Bodley Head. 15s. Reviewed by John Beckett.

LIKE most Englishmen, I neither understand nor make friends with foreigners very easily, and true as that may be of fellow Europeans it is even more true of the so-called educated Indian, who seems to me to be the most trying and difficult of all human beings either to like or admire. Anti-Imperialists will at once decide that this shows some sort of a complex against persons who are difficult to rule. That, I am convinced, is untrue and unfair to both myself and the great majority of my fellow countrymen who experience the same feelings. The difficulty with the educated Indian is that he has usually lost the manliness of his more Asiatic brothers and acquired a superficial Western cunning, which, allied to his native hysteria, makes him well-nigh impossible to deal with on any recognised lines.

I had met Jawaharlal Nehru many years before I read his book and looked forward to its publication with pleasure. Implacable enemies as it seems he and I must be, I have rarely met a man for whom I had a greater personal respect or affection. If Nehru were typical of his race how simple the Indian problem would become. As he writes himself, almost regretfully:

"I owe too much to England in my mental make-up ever to feel wholly alien to her. Do what I will, I cannot get rid of the habits of mind and the standards and ways of judging other countries, as well as life generally. All my predilections (apart from the political plane) are in favour of England and the English people, and if I have become an uncompromising opponent of British rule in India, it is almost in spite of myself."

The history of the Nehrus, father and son, provides a tragic condemnation of the methods of British rule in India. This book is invaluable to the Fascist-minded, because just as we are determined to remain an Imperial race so should we be equally determined to understand the business of Imperialism. Motilal Nehru, the father, was a loyal friend of British rule for three-quarters of his life. The most die-hard Englishmen who knew him speak of his personal character in glowing terms.

Jawaharlal, the son, was sent to school, university, and Inner Temple in England. He began political work as chairman of the Allahabad Municipal Council, working with the British Government without question or doubt. Motilal Nehru died after sacrificing a large fortune and health itself in the fight against British rule; his wife, in her old age, was beaten with lathis and died as an after-result of her treatment. Jawaharlal, the son, has spent most of his adult life in prison, has been beaten on several occasions, has sacrificed a fortune and a brilliant career to fight against British rule.

Jawaharlal Nehru. "I have rarely met a man for whom I had greater respect."

From a considerable knowledge of both Motilal and Jawaharlal Nehru I know that this tragedy cannot be explained away by cheap personal accusations against them. Motilal was, and Jawaharlal is, fine and honest and disinterested, brave and prepared to make untold sacrifices for a cause in which they believe.

The security of Britain's hold upon India depends upon our understanding why men like this look upon us as their bitter enemy; and upon our learning to deal with such men. Surely we may find it easier to deal even with the brave and honest fanatic than with the self-seeking, slimy Indian politicians to whom British Governments have crawled on their bellies in the past.

The curse of British rule in India since the war has been due to two things, both of which Nehru brings out in this book: one consciously and the other unconsciously. In the chapter describing his work on the municipal council he shows the first clearly. British Government in India has been a debt collector's Government, as in every other part of the world. Britain has stood in India for the great vested interests and financiers. India had to be made safe for international finance, and the chief efforts of the machine have been directed to that end. British Government has been the bulwark of reaction. It is difficult to deny much of the following indictment:

"The British conception of ruling India was a police conception . . . . their public finance dealt with military expenditure, police, civil administration, interest on debt. The economic needs of the citizens were not looked after . . . . cultural and other needs, except for a tiny handful, were entirely neglected. The changing conceptions of public finance which brought free and universal education, improvement of public health, care of the poor and feeble-minded, insurance of workers against illness, old age, and unemployment, etc., in other countries, were almost entirely beyond the ken of the Government."

The second reason is that our Government has been not only reactionary, but also cowardly and vacillating in spirit. Tyranny is bad, but weak and vacillating tyranny has no friends at all.

In 1926 when the Nehrus were in London I saw something of their treatment by our own politicians. That visit was the turning point in Jawaharlal's life. He returned to India convinced that if Congress continued to fight for independence they would get it. Members of the Government made lavish promises and the Labour Opposition expressed complete sympathy. Men whom I heard assuring Nehru of their complete support were afterwards members of the Labour Government which, with Wedgwood Benn, an old "friend" of the Indian movement as Secretary for India, followed exactly upon Tory lines in their handling of the Indian problems. Nehru believed as a result of his talks with British politicians that they were a flabby crowd who would be bound to climb down if resolutely fought. Who shall say that he was wrong?

This magnificent autobiography is the swan song of Jawaharlal Nehru. Hopelessness, prison bars, and the lathi have killed a courageous, honest man who, properly treated, could have rendered great service to Britain. His sufferings will not have been in vain if this book is able to teach us the lesson we need to learn. An Imperial race must defend its subjects against exploitation and international usury; it must govern in an enlightened manner, recognising duties as well as rights; and it must govern firmly, leaving no room for doubt as to the reforms it will grant and the abuses it will not allow.

In spite of the magnificent record of many individual British administrators we cannot claim to have fulfilled these conditions during the past twenty years. Lathi charges and wholesale imprisonment are no substitutes for wisdom, courage, and firmness. Jawaharlal Nehru, for all his mistakes and wildness, does much to teach us this lesson.

THE QUEEN-EMPRESS

"Victoria of England." By Edith Sitwell. (Faber and Faber.)

MISS SITWELL has given us a book of supreme wit and charm. She has fully recognised the unfailing devotion of Queen Victoria that invariably placed the prestige and welfare of England far above personal happiness. And in the end, when, in her old age, she stood alone when death was near, she found, in the love of her country, a compensation for every sacrifice endured.

The Queen had never been beautiful. She was a small, homely woman, whose only claims to charm were her exquisite hands, her enchanting voice, and an amazing grace of carriage ("All the banners and all the brave music of the world seemed to have gone to make the walk of the Queen of England"), but she had a dignity, a courage and a sincerity which far surpassed mere physical beauty, and which eventually imposed her iron will on devoted Ministers and adoring subjects alike.

We who have witnessed the gradual undoing of all she had created, and who have seen the prestige of England brought low by incompetent Ministers and by a spineless intelligentsia, can only ask ourselves how long we—the heirs of her ideals—can bear the present powers of disruption?

The beginning of her reign saw the re-birth of the Fascist philosophy in England—dormant since the days of Elizabeth, though martyrs and the victims of the Chartist risings had proclaimed the rights of the people to decent surroundings and to some share of human happiness and political justice.

The finest, albeit the most terrifying, passage in Miss Sitwell's book is found in Chapter XIII., "March Past." The conditions described are so appalling that we can only congratulate the author on her strength of mind in bringing back to us the unspeakable sufferings of the workers in 1844. "No eye," writes a weaver of that day, "has seen, no ear heard, and no heart felt the half of the suffering those poor people endure."

At the present day we, who have seen for ourselves the conditions still prevailing in the slums of London and Manchester and in the bitter areas of the unemployed North, know how much has been left undone. There is a chapter in George Orwell's masterpiece, "The Clergyman's Daughter," describing a winter night spent by the prostitutes and destitute in Trafalgar-square, that for horror and degradation cannot be equalled.

The great Queen is dead and her Empire is threatened, but her spirit has descended on us. It is our right and privilege to carry on her work, to restore the prestige of Britain, for only in the greatness of our country, in the glory of our race, and in the welfare of the community shall we find the fulfilment and the justification of our lives.—H. B.

"Vital Peace, A Study of Risks." By Henry Wickham Steed. (Constable. 10s.)

OF the making of books about Peace there is no end, and, having read a very large number of them, I can never decide whether the value of getting the necessity of avoiding war discussed is worth the dangerous, war-making nature of most of these works.

Mr. Wickham Steed was born in 1871 and tells us that this book is the result of twenty years devotion to his subject. It seems doubtful whether those twenty years have been very well spent. The author is balanced and moderate, except when he happens to mention Fascism or National Socialism, these he does not understand, and they seem, therefore, to his failing vision and closed brain, to be wrong, because they embrace ideals and principles which he cannot be expected to grasp. A life spent in Fleet Street and in what the British Press is pleased to call "diplomatic journalism," is hardly a preparation for suddenly meeting at this advanced age statesmen who actually mean what they say and do what they say they will do.

Mr. Steed, therefore, quotes speeches by Mussolini which he considers favourable to war, but omits to quote speeches like Mr. Baldwin's "Our frontiers are the Rhine." This is a far more aggressive statement than either of the great national leaders would have dreamt of making. The hard-worked phrase, "collective security," still seems to mean much to the author, though he successively blames, though very mildly, Wilson, Chamberlain, Stresemann, Lloyd George, and every other European statesman who has not been blindly pro-French for their handling of League problems.

I should like to say I had discovered some new thing or original suggestion in this weighty tome, but it proves nothing, except that times have changed since the author was an authority upon world affairs.—N.S.O.

Shows Seen

THEATRES

THE LADY OF LA PAZ, at the Criterion Theatre, is the only play which I have the opportunity of reviewing this week. It is a sweet, odd little story, with its tolerances and intentions all mixed up with religious views and the inexperience of youth. Lilian Braithwaite plays the Comtesse Victoria, the lady of la Paz, who owns some acres of coffee plantation, has a reputation for having outlived three husbands, and has several grandchildren scattered in England and America. Of these we are immediately concerned with only two, Felicia, who at seventeen has already acquired a husband, and Ana, who at sixteen wishes to renounce the world and its pleasures for the peace of convent life. The Comtesse Victoria's business seems to be to safeguard the present and future of Felicia, a girl of spun glass. Felicia's marriage to a Spaniard with pronounced views about the place of the women of his household, belies her vigorous ancestry; but the ensuing complications are not too difficult for the Comtesse Victoria, with a large holding in the surrounding country, and a hand illegitimately in local politics.

The onerous part of Felicia makes a great demand upon the ability of the young actress, Nova Pilbeam, who, since her early success, has been thrust into parts of increasing emotional intensity, all of which seem a little too passionate for her youth and comparative inexperience.

ROYAL OPERA HOUSE, COVENT GARDEN.

THE dancers of the Ballets Russes are magnificently smooth, and their work now is beautifully co-ordinated. A performance of "Les Cent Baisers," with Baronova and Lichine, scored an immense success, while "La Boutique Fantasque" came splendidly to perfection when Danilova and Massine danced. These two ballets are harmonious, amusing, and delightful.

A scene from "Choreartium" at Covent Garden

In "Les Presages" the choreographer seeks to interpret the profound melancholy and majesty of the Fifth Symphony of Tchaikovsky in balletic form. It seems to me that attempts to interpret the more majestic music in terms of drama or mime usually fail. The two seem irreconcilable. It is unfortunate, as the choreographer attempts in "Les Presages," to interpret the baser passions in the form of an insect-like miming buffoon, nor is the gaiety of life adequately to be expressed by a lady, elegantly dressed. Music is interpreted by each individual person in a different way, in a manner which expresses his own mood and his own passion or madness. In the music of sweet sentiment an opportunity is found for balletic interpretation "Les Sylphides," for instance, wind themselves perfectly into the music of Chopin's waltzes, but in "Les Presages" the choreographer seeks to interpret profound melancholy and majesty. The Symphony has been considered to be Fascist in thought and conception. The ballet built upon it presents all the conventional figures of man struggling with destiny, and finally with the passion of war.

As far as one may comment upon the choreography of Massine, the interpretation of Brahms's Fourth Symphony in "Choreartium" seems to fail in exactly the same way as "Les Presages." What seems to be the bitter complaint of the music is not adequately interpreted by the slowly moving file of dark red figures making a pliez across the stage. All very slight tonal changes have their painstaking and to me superficial interpretation in immediate minute changes of step.

FILMS

THROUGH whatever changes in entertainment tastes, and though Empires crumble and Leagues fail, Right still triumphs in the American cinema world, and Big Bill still goes riding the rugged trail to the log hut where the horse thieves are holding up his girl. The two American films reviewed here are of this incredibly naïve kind, with tough cowboys and bouncing young women, hold-ups, and bank robberies, unorthodox shootings, and primitive tortures, and marches through trackless forests, where pools are so crowded with alligators that the intrepid marchers walk over their backs to the other side; there is the hoary old man and the headstrong young one, who is just too innocent to know what he is doing.

"A MESSAGE TO GARCIA"
REGAL (American)

PRESENTED by Fox, this claims to show an incident in the Spanish-American War of 1898, when the President of the United States, wishing to send a message to General Garcia, leader of the Cuban forces, chooses for the onerous task one Andrew S. Rowan, a lieutenant in the United States Army. Sergeant Dory is the mercenary deserter with whom he falls in on his way, and Senorita Raphaelita Maderos is the lovely lady filled with a consuming patriotism. John Boles, Barbara Stanwyck, and Wallace Beery play these colourful parts; but they are just John Boles, Barbara Stanwyck, and Wallace Beery to you and me.

Herbert Mundin, a traveller in tinware in the Cuban jungle, has rather the air of the Dame at the pantomime, whom one is not at all surprised to find in the most extraordinary places, and who turns up with equal inappropriateness in the heroine's grimy kitchen or the hero's sumptuous hall.

I have not read Mr. Elbert Hubbard's article from which this fanciful film is said to have been taken. I cannot believe, however, that such an orthodox plot can have been conceived anywhere outside the studio, and this film bears so strongly the imprint of Hollywood's mass production plot that one cannot see the film for the players.

"THE CALL OF THE PRAIRIE"
(American)

JUST a roughneck fiction of the early Bill Hart period; and though Bill has become Hopalong Cassidy with an urge to paternity, the mixture is there just as before. Johnny Nelson falls among thieves, who shoot his partner and rob a bank. Johnny is suspected by Hopalong Cassidy, the gentleman with fatherly instincts and a swift gun. There are stirring incidents—for the most part on horseback—before we leave Johnny in the arms of his lady (whose father, the leader of the thieves, is comfortably expiring on the floor by her side). William Boyd as Hopalong Cassidy shows his really delightful personality.

"THOROUGHBRED"

THE form of this Australian-made picture is also familiar. It is true that one has seen it played with less naïve sincerity than Wardour Films have done it. The hero, and the most delightful thing in it, is the lovely horse, Stormalong, and the picture is very well worth seeing for its racing shots, and for its harsh, clear Australian angles. Helen Twelvetrees appears in this picture with John Longden. One can only wonder why the closing scene of an otherwise good film is marred by its brutal ending—a brutality quite inconsistent with the light gaiety with which the film has followed its course.

"THE PETRIFIED FOREST."

A REMARKABLE feat has been achieved here, for "The Petrified Forest" is not so much a film as a photographed play, and such entertainments generally fall flat. There is certainly shooting and so on, but the action lies mainly in the dialogue as true drama should.

The scene is an Arizona garage-café; the characters, an ancient prospector who adores "real killers"; his waitress granddaughter who reads François Villon and longs for art and civilisation amid the dust of the desert; a rugger hearty; a defeatist English intellectual hiking for the Pacific; a Yankee business man and his wife, a rebel against "respectability"; and a gang of desperadoes with its leader, a notorious killer.

Scene from "The Petrified Forest." Bette Davis and Leslie Howard

Under the killer's gun, souls take off their clothes and stand disrobed of reticence and inhibition. Before the abyss of infinite darkness, they deal in facts and not in words. The miracle is that the dramatist has succeeded, or all but succeeded, in touching this psychological bedrock, even with the added unreality of a translation into celluloid to contend with. It must have been a magnificent play in flesh and blood, and one can say that it "purges the soul with pity and terror" according to the true canon of tragic art.

The acting is very good. Miss Bette Davis can give us the half-inarticulate yearnings of the "flower born to blush unseen and waste its sweetness on the desert air" as convincingly as she recently gave us the Cockney trollop. Mr. Leslie Howard rises to grandeur as the spirit-weary intellectual who "sees or thinks he sees" civilisation dying; what a pity he so closely resembles Allen of Hurtwood in appearance and sometimes in utterance! The killer is played by Mr. Humphrey Bogart, who can make your flesh creep and yet enlist your liking.

It is greatly to be hoped that this film will be a public success, for it is not only first-class entertainment but fine art, and that is something we had almost ceased to hope for.—J. A. M.

"OURSELVES ALONE"
LONDON PAVILION

THIS is the British picture of the week, and probably for many weeks. It is a story of opposing forces which takes the side of neither force, and shows events as they happen and men as they are. The opening scenes are some of the most touching which the cinema has given us, and the heartbreaking chant of Irish melody in a public house as the women hide the guns gives the motif. It is a story of Ireland in the days of the rebellion, when the whole of Ireland was divided against itself, and your immediate neighbour was the most probable spy. John Lodge, Antoinette Cellier, and John Loder take the chief parts; but it is excellently built up upon a strong cast, and not the least feature deserving congratulation is the authentic Irish accent which never once falls into the lamentable attempt at accent which is so often heard in British films. The producers are, I think, trying to teach the folly of war, and they picture civil war, which is the greatest folly of all. Although it follows the well-trodden path of plot and counter-plot with a slightly romantic plot running alongside, it is a fine picture which should be seen.

"FATAL LADY."

THE Plaza this week is presenting the touching little legend of Mary Stuart, who, when she is upon the threshold of fame as a singer in each of three capitals separately, becomes the central figure in a murder case, and finds herself so notorious that she can no longer hope for recognition of her genius in that sphere and under her own name. Between mysterious incident and malevolent circumstance, upon trans-continental trains and in restaurants, Mary Ellis as Mary Stuart manages to sing excerpts from several operas, and to exploit a personality which, they say, is in each case the cause of a fatality.

The picture is mildly entertaining and quite unconvincing. Mary Ellis has a clear and sweet voice; but one cannot help wondering where lay the promise of her ultimate virtuosity. Necessarily from several young and personable possible murderers, the old singer and teacher is the final scapegoat who, we are assured, murdered the lady's suitors to preserve her "art" for the world.—A. C.

ANTOINETTE CELLIER, who appears in the British Film "Ourselves Alone"

THE BIRTH OF THE SURREALIST

By JOHN MONTAGUE

THE strange figure reeked of sulphur, his black depthless eyes reflected everything in the wide modernly furnished studio. Paul Milger lay in bed quaking, he seemed to feel a hard sinewy hand about his heart. If he did not obey the intruder who stood above him so menacingly, that grip would tighten. He felt cold, his teeth chattered, the whole room was bathed in an unholy unnatural light. It glimmered from the chromium bed-rails and flashed back to the steel mirror, as though signalling indecipherable messages. He was afraid to look again into those two evil eyes, but he could feel them as they peered searchingly into his brain. He noticed the stranger had a hand missing —yes, of course, it was inside him holding his heart.

"Get up!" commanded the intruder beckoning with a long fore-finger—"get up."

Paul Milger threw back the coverlet, but could do no more.

"Let go my heart please, I cannot move," he pleaded. The stranger laughed mockingly, terribly, deeply it rolled round the room and echoed in the street then at the

back of the house, and was followed by the weird howling of a frightened dog.

"Why, most certainly dear friend," he said suavely—"of course you are my friend?"

"Yes, yes," agreed the frightened artist, "of course I am—of—of course."

The tightening round his heart loosened and then went—the stranger's hand appeared in its rightful position.

MILGER jumped out of bed and gave a howl. "Look! you are burning my carpet." He pointed to the thin spirals of smoke curling up from the stranger's feet. "My apologies sir—a thousand pardons, excuse me." His visitor produced a sheet of asbestos from nowhere in particular and placing it on the floor moved and stood upon it until the heat of his feet died down. His two fiery footprints remained, however, scorched deeply into the axminster, the faint wisps of smoke subsided and then died.

"You know who I am?" questioned the nocturnal visitor—"No?" he asked, upon receiving no reply.

"Well, Paul Milger, I am the devil—no, don't jump, don't be alarmed—calm yourself, I am quite harmless"—then his eyes flashed again, a cracking flash which struck the chromium mirror with a resounding bang—"Harmless, so long as I find you friendly and willing."

"Oh!" replied the other shaking—"Oh!"

The devil saw his obvious discomfiture and went on.

"You are an artist, shall I say an unsuccessful artist—right?"

"Er—yes," replied the frightened man, barely able to stand.

"Why are you unsuccessful?—No!—I will tell you. Of course you have heard of Turner, Constable, Corot, Whistler, Landseer, Rembrandt, Reubens, Delacrois"—he waved his hand—"and countless others, you've heard of them all. Artists whose names are famous in the pages of mortal history—inspired men—you, my friend, have so far failed. Why?" The devil paused dramatically. "Because you have never known inspiration. You are vainly chasing artistic fame blindly, doggedly, obstinately, and failing miserably to catch even the hem of that elusive lady's dress. Nothing can be more pathetic than a futile chase after artistic fame. You will die a disappointed, heartbroken man, unknown and unmourned."

"Do you really think so?" whispered the artist in an awed voice.

"Yes, I know so. I can guess what the future holds if you continue as you have been for the last five years."

A DISTANT church clock struck two melancholy notes, and a faint breeze stirred the trees outside. These mortal sounds reassured Milger—he felt a little less frightened, but although he dared not look at the other's face, he felt the awful power of those eyes. They still seemed to be probing his brain. The sulphurous smell seemed stronger; he coughed a little as it caught his throat.

"Well," said the devil, "since you are not marked out for fame as an artist in the real sense of the word, what do you propose to do?"

"I don't know" spluttered the other, "I really don't know; give up the chase I suppose." His fear was almost gone as no harm had come to him yet, nevertheless he felt distinctly uncomfortable.

"You need not," urged the devil coaxingly. "You certainly need not."

"What do you mean?" Milger asked curiously.

"Well, my friend," said the other softly, "I can show you how you can make a name for yourself—of a kind."

"In art?" asked Milger eagerly.

"Yes." The devil moved towards the studio door and beckoned him to follow. "Come, my friend."

Inside he paused at a picture and pointed at it. "Now, Milger," he said "What is this?"

The artist felt annoyed, for his visitor was ridiculing a piece of work he had fondly considered his finest. He felt it best, however, to humour his grim visitor, for though he appeared to be criticising in a friendly way Milger knew well enough that should the fit seize him he could be terrible. He would not risk annoying him.

"Oh! that," he answered in the airiest manner possible under such awkward circumstances, "that represents fairies at a woodland stream."

"Ho! Ho! Ho!" roared the devil. "Ho!" His terrible laughter resounded through the house and set the dog howling again in terror. "Fairies at a woodland stream"—he ceased his awesome laughter and turned suddenly upon the artist, who, catching a bare glimpse of his terrible eyes was unable to move. "Do you believe in fairies?" he snapped.

"Er—No—No—I don't."

"Why paint them then; how can you expect to reproduce that in which you do not believe?"

"It's silly—ridiculous," agreed the artist in an attempt to mollify his visitor.

"Of course it is," agreed the other now more gently. "You are a little fool."

"Yes, yes, I am."

"That's better—now I have something to tell you, and you are going to believe me —come we will go back to the bedroom."

MILGER followed meekly.

"I am about to give you a much-needed lesson in art, real art, not the weak-kneed reproduction of natural objects and scenery, but something inhuman. It will make you famous."

They were now back in the bedroom and Milger sat on the side of the bed. The devil stood with his back to the artist, admiring his fiery countenance in the steel mirror.

"My unsuccessful friend," he began presently, "you are not unacquainted with the post-war rise of another school of thought, that ever-growing school which aims to portray all the hideosities of which the human mind, if allowed to follow riotous excesses, is capable. Neurotical development is the ideal of this rapidly growing sect. Please do not interrupt me," he said menacingly, for he saw Milger's lips move as if to speak. He went on—"When I fell out of Heaven the hideous was first born, infantile as is anything young, but rapidly growing. With careful cunning hands I tended its growth. As civilisation marched over the world so my monstrosity grew. It thrived on hate, war, jealousy, bestiality. I gave it these, but all the time its opposite grew, the beautiful child born of Heaven.

"Just as my ward relished rape and murder, slaughter and bloodshed, so did this other child creep into the gentler nature of mankind, giving it a love and affection for the more beautiful sides of life—love, honour, respect, and discipline. My child was content at first with a minor percentage of mankind's devotion, but civilisation was beginning to rear its head menacingly, religion began to imbue into the minds of men the meaning of right and wrong. No good to my child. It was beginning to ail under the effects of ill-nourishment. It was being eclipsed by the child beautiful. Something had to be done.

"Right—throw the world into chaos, set men tearing at each others' throats, turn mankind into a chaotic screaming mob. Let the wicked take charge and wickedness would then be the watchword. The war known to mankind as the Great War was the last of a wonderful series, wonderful and very nourishing. My child was silent for a few years, its gluttony was appeased, but gradually the better side of man is emerging from the ashes, emerging with speed and clear-cut precision. Nations are beginning to follow leaders, who by sheer personality and brilliance are cutting away all that is rotten, and disciplining their nations. By their untiring labours they are setting up the basis of a new civilisation. Occasionally they are ruthless, this pleases the child, but this ruthlessness is not wrong, it is merely a step towards right. I have realised that. The position is getting bad I must fight it. I conceived an idea, subtle and simple, which will surely bring the world at my heel again." The devil turned from the mirror after his long lecture, and, facing Milger, said firmly: "You are one of the chosen and are going to help."

THE artist was momentarily nonplussed, his amazement gave way to fear, but he managed to jerk out, "And if I don't?"

The devil writhed and shook, then ground his teeth, turned his terrible eyes upon the artist, who felt himself shrivelling up beneath that awful gaze.

"If you don't," he said mockingly, "you will never find that which you seek—fame."

Milger shook visibly, "But—I do not see how my assisting you has any bearing upon that artistic future of mine which you seem to despise. How can I reconcile my art with your wishes? It does not seem in any way possible."

"No," replied the devil, "because you have not had it fully explained. Listen intently." He again turned his back to the artist and proceeded.

"Just now I mentioned why you were a failure."

"Yes."

"Through lack of inspiration."

"Yes."

"I mentioned the new post-war school of thought."

"Yes."

"Now, what does that school embrace?" He went on. "Literature, music, art, architecture, sculpture. It embraces everything that has any influence upon the culture of the people. It is the dry rot of civilisation. It suits my purpose and is but the means to an end. Turn man's mind from the channels of good sense and average respectability and collapse is inevitable. I foster this school and my influence is behind all its works. Its devotees are no longer satisfied with life the beautiful, but must experiment with the evil, with the undisciplined sub-conscious imaginings peculiar to these people comes their inspiration. They do not know why, they merely serve a lower call; they are not charlatans, but firm believers in their works." He laughed, then carried on. "Fame is theirs and money, for, like the glacier, they gather others on their downward fall. But it is a glorious fall, and none of them realise they are slipping." He suddenly shot a question at Milger, "Have you seen 'Omega'?"

"Why, yes—yes, I have," replied the artist.

"That, my dear friend, is a perfect example."

"But," argued Milger, "Stunckenbloch is an inspired man, a genius; his work is world famous."

"I know, I know," interrupted the devil, "he is working to plan, my plan, perhaps consciously, perhaps unconsciously, nevertheless, he is of the school."

"Oh!" said the other, and relapsed into silence.

"What he can do in sculpture you can do in painting—that can be arranged—but you'll never be a Landseer or a Whistler, my friend."

"No?"

"No—but in years to come you will be famous as one of the earliest exponents of that New Art. To-morrow you will awaken and remember nothing; you will be a different man; your inspiration will have begun. You will have the urge to take up brushes immediately and set to work with a will. You will find many of your friends will scoff, your past work you will destroy, and Paul Randolph Milger will at last have his feet set upon the road to fame."

The artist rubbed his eyes. "Perhaps, after all, this is a nightmare," he thought. "Shall I challenge him?" he asked himself. He decided not to, but sat silent.

A SOLITARY taxi skirred by. The wind still whispered through the trees; he wondered if he would ever see the light of a new day—perhaps he had died in his sleep and was the ghost of himself. He remembered having read of spirits leaving the sleeping mortal body and unable to return. He put his hand behind him and felt the bed. No, his body was not there. He was not a spirit left the body then. Presently he plucked up sufficient courage to look up, and behold the devil had gone. He rushed to the window, but then realised that anything capable of disappearing so silently and suddenly would not walk down the street. His bedroom door was open; he stepped out to the landing and stood by the banisters. Nothing to be seen. Presently, however, as he stood there wondering what had possessed him during that awful visitation, he heard the melancholy howling of a dog. Shuddering, he rushed into his room, slammed the door with a resounding bang, and, jumping into bed, pulled the clothes over his head. He was soon in a deep, dreamless sleep.

⊘ ⊘ ⊘

PYGMALION HALL, Burton-street, Mayfair, was the scene of belated activity. An endless procession of vehicles pulled up outside and disgorged examples of humanity which no novelist would dare to describe. He would be accused of over-characterisation. The Press had found this exhibition of New Art useful material. Sensation oozed from every picture and reporters did their level best to add to it.

A tall commissionaire stood at the entrance, grim of countenance, a pillar of solid reliability. With short, clipped words he ruled the hordes of excited petty people, and they obeyed his instructions implicitly. Presently, from out of a large red roadster, Paul Randolph Milger appeared, accompanied by a large chinchilla cat on a lead. He stopped by the commissionaire and wished him a tender good morning. After its gruff return, the artist entered the exhibition and made his way to Gallery 3. He looked neither right nor left as he made

his way through the crowds of curious people, but presently stopping before a huge picture entitled "Soul of an Ice-Cream Sundae," he called the gallery attendant and asked for a chair. The attendant brought one. "There, sir," he said, "the cat looks well this morning."

"He's very well, thank you," replied the artist, and sitting on the chair, he lifted the cat to his lap, where it settled down and purred contentedly. So he sat, occasionally fondling the animal, absent-mindedly, but his gaze never leaving the picture.

Many people asked curious questions concerning the strange man with the white cat, and the duty of an attendant, after all said and done, is to answer questions to the best of his ability. He did.

"That, sir, or madam," he would reply, "is Paul Randolph Milger, the famous New Idea artist."

"Really!" people would say, "so that's Milger. What a peculiar person."

"Oh, well!" the attendant would reply, "he is inspired"; and then he would whisper, "One must make allowances, you know. Why, that picture of his there is priced at five hundred pounds."

Edited by A. C. FINDLEY

LAWN TENNIS

The Davis Cup

IT is to be an all-Empire match in the Davis Cup Challenge Round, which will be played on the Centre Court at Wimbledon next Saturday, Monday, and Tuesday.

Australia, half-crippled, beat Germany, also half-crippled, in the fourth match. McGrath, who came into the team in place of Quist, who had twisted his ankle on Saturday, beat Henkel, who was still recovering from a chill. Von Cramm did not seem to have properly recovered from the muscle he pulled in the final against Perry. The only fit man of the regular teams was apparently Crawford.

On Saturday Henkel had to retire after the second set against Crawford. This made little difference, as we did not expect Henkel to win, anyway.

Then came a terrific duel between Adrian Quist and Gottfried von Cramm. In the second set Quist fell and damaged his ankle. Various attendants ran to his assistance, and certain officious officials, who ought to have known better, galloped on to the sacred turf in ordinary shoes. Had any of them seen a member of the public put a toe on a court he (the official) would have nearly screamed his head off.

A Great Match

AFTER a short pause Quist resumed, and it was obvious that his ankle was either not hindering him at all, or was actually spurring him on, for I have never seen him so active.

Von Cramm was listless at times, but in the final set both men played superb tennis. Their volleying was amazing. The last twelve games were extraordinary. Von Cramm had at least ten match points and Quist at least three before von Cramm finally won the great match.

I mean no reflection on Quist when I say that had not von Cramm been quite obviously still suffering from the trouble in his leg, he would have won far more easily. The Germans deserve sympathy for their misfortunes, as also do the Australians. The result of the tie was unsatisfactory to both sides. However, both teams are young and will, with any luck, meet again next year in full vigour and with no casualties. Then we can be sure of seeing magnificent lawn tennis.

On Monday Henkel had recovered somewhat, but naturally lacked practice on grass. Quist's ankle had stiffened and he was unable to play. McGrath stepped in and played so brilliantly that Australia won comfortably.

On Tuesday McGrath, by beating Henkel, covered himself with glory and earned for Australia the right to challenge Britain.

Contrary to my expectations there was quite a big crowd on Saturday. I can only suppose this was due to my note last week, and the extra crowd was made up of "Action" readers.

The Challenge Round

BRITAIN were beaten by America in a friendly match at Eastbourne last week. No significance need be attached to this match as the team were merely practising. Last year Britain were beaten easily by Australia in a similar practice match and then went on to beat America in the challenge round by five matches to nil.

It is very doubtful if Quist will be fit enough for the match. Whether he is or not I do not think for a moment that Australia can beat our team so long as they remain whole.

MOTOR RACING

The Belgian 24 Hours

BRITISH cars were to the fore in the Belgian 24 hours race, which finished at 4 p.m. on Sunday, July 5, at Spa.

The one Lagonda, driven by R. J. B. Seaman and F. E. Clifford, won its class, and the Delahayes won the under 4-litre class. An Aston Martin was first in the 1,500 c.c. class, and a Singer was second in the 1,100 class.

The Alfa Romeo, driven by Raymond Sommer and Severi, had an easy task in the supercharged class, and averaged 86.81 miles per hour for the twenty-four hours—the highest speed of the race.

Of the thirty-six starters, only seventeen finished. The race was run through intermittent rain.

The exciting moments were when de la Fontaine's Chrysler caught fire at the pits, and when Rangani's Fiat was ditched opposite the grand stand. Fortunately no injury was sustained by either driver, although the Chrysler was put out of the race. The Fiat was got back on the road, but was later excluded for not keeping up the necessary average speed.

Cornet's S.S. Jaguar also visited a ditch at Eau Rouge, was extricated, but was forced out later with a broken piston.

While working on his Singer by the roadside, the American driver, Collier, was struck on the head by the bonnet of his car, which was disturbed by the air rush of a passing machine.

The Aston Martins at one time seemed certain to win the team prize, the King's Cup; but the new 2-litre machine, driven by MacRobert and Elwes, broke a fuel pipe when ahead of the other competitors in its class, and lost its petrol some miles away from the pits.

A second Aston Martin was leading the 1,500 section, but lost all gears except top after nineteen hours' running. It continued to cruise around and finished second in its class.

The five cars covering the greatest distance were the "blown" Alfa Romeo, two Delahayes, the Lagonda, and one Aston Martin. The latter car outdistanced all the 2-litre cars, and all but two of the 4-litre machines—a great tribute to the British 1,500 c.c. engine.

HOW TO DO IT

GAMES AND EXERCISE

MANY people think that too much time is devoted to sport, games, and all physical exercise. Pause for a moment and think of the great influence of all forms of active games upon the race, and the lessons they have to teach. What a different race we should be without them, physically and morally!

Physical exercise is absolutely essential, but it must not be overdone. It not only develops the body but the mind, and the influence of mind over matter is well known! Healthy exercise teaches one, first of all, to respect the body. It develops a clean spirit, tones the character, gives that alertness and decision, endurance, well-being, while games promote unselfishness, tolerance, and fearlessness. A sport in every sense of the word is always a likeable person.

The varied forms of passive recreation amuse, distract, and are necessary pastimes, but they certainly do not recreate the mind and emotions such as active sports, and physical training. Exercise is necessary to keep fit; it has a wonderful effect upon those who suffer through leading sedentary lives; remedial exercise has done a tremendous amount of good.

The mental strain of the past years (and, indirectly, we are still suffering from the effects of the Great War), has, without doubt, affected the nervous system, so that fitness must be our aim, and not overdeveloped arm and leg muscles. More symmetrical development is needed, especially the strengthening of the abdominal and chest muscles. Before undertaking any form of exercise, the position should be studied first of all. Few walk and stand well. You have only to watch passers-by, and note carriage. Generally, you find eyes downcast, drooping shoulders, a shuffling gait, as though the body were too heavy to carry.

Observe, also, the position in which people stand; first lolling on one side, then over to the other, which, from the back, resembles lateral curvature of the spine; the latter often develops through standing on one leg. Great attention, therefore, must be paid to the position of the body.

Stand in front of a long glass, in your usual position. Now draw your shoulders back, crushing in the shoulder blades (without strain). This very movement will naturally thrust the chest forward. You will then be able to breathe more freely and deeply than with the chest contracted. This alone is invaluable. Now, with the shoulders slightly back, and the chest forward, lift up your head a little, at the same time draw in the chin. You will then notice that you are in a healthy position; the weight of your body will no longer be pressing on your stomach and chest. You will get an even balance. Study these simple things very well to get your position correct before setting out for a walk or march; you will walk more gracefully and keep your position quite easily if you fix your eyes on an object, imaginary or otherwise, just a little higher than your own eyes.

When once you have mastered your weakness of stooping you will then be able to undertake deep breathing and other beneficial exercises, bearing in mind that no exercise must cause, or be likely to cause, undue effort or strain.

A simple movement, and certainly one of the best for round shoulders, can be done every morning in front of the glass to see the effect; i.e., clasp the hands together behind, in the small of the back, then straighten and lower arms, as though you were trying to touch the back of the knees; the chest will expand at the same time: Pause for a moment, stretching well, then relax, and continue six or twelve times. Breathe in through the nostrils as you lower the arms, exhale through the mouth as you relax.

JIU-JITSU

By A. G. Woodgate

IT is not sufficiently recognised that jiu-jitsu, apart from its value as a means of defence and offence, is an excellent medium of physical training. Yet it is, in fact, the only form of sport in which some set of muscles, or some part of the body, is not used to a greater degree than any other, and it is this fact that makes jiu-jitsu an exercise that helps all other forms of bodily activity. Then, too, it is a sport in which sheer muscular strength and weight is at a premium, and the smallest and lightest of men can upset the biggest.

The first essentials in the jiu-jitsu exponent are perfect suppleness, the ability to take a fall without damage to oneself, and the art of thinking and moving simultaneously and as quick as lightning. The first two may be attained by exercise; the second, if not inherent, will come with continued practice in jiu-jitsu, so our first two lessons will consist of a few simple exercises.

1. For suppleness.—Lie flat on the back with the legs slightly bent at the knees. Then, keeping both shoulders flat on the floor, pass the right foot over as far to the left as possible without straining. Without lifting the right leg, draw the left leg sharply through, and the moment it is clear throw it well over to the right, accompanying the movement with a sharp screw of the hips. As the left foot touches the ground, repeat with the right, and so on. Remember the shoulders must be kept flat and all the work of twitching the hips from side to side must devolve on the muscles of the lower part of the body.

BOXING

By "Tommy" Moran

DRAWING an opponent and countering his leads as described last week needs constant concentration on the job in hand and a continual shifting of position to prevent him taking the initiative of attack. The right cross counter is another blow which can be used after first of all inducing your opponent to lead with his left. In this case, when he leads, drop your head to the left, which allows his left to pass over your shoulder. Then punch hard with your right hand, hooking it over the top of his left arm and striking the side of his head. Follow this with a short arm jab with your left into his solar plexus, to be followed immediately by a right uppercut as you step back. By this method you land three very substantial punches.

Upon stepping back, do not dance yards away from him, but just out of reach, watch him intently, and you will very soon recognise if your blows have had any effect. They certainly should have done so, and now get up on to your toes and crash into him with what is described as a one-two punch. You lead with the left, followed immediately by a straight right. The two punches are moving together and should strike home a split second after each other. In delivering this attack, draw up your body to your full height and hurl yourself at him. The left is in this case not a very weighty blow, but the right should have your full weight behind it.

A point here worth stressing is the fact that all these blows have been delivered as a direct result of moving your head inside a left lead. You will realise the necessity for keeping the neck muscles in perfect condition.

Far too many boxers cannot or will not move the head alone. They sway the body from the waist instead, which, in a case like this, is completely wrong.

Another very important matter is to switch your attack from head to body and vice versa. A man is naturally inclined to shift his defence to cover that part of himself which last received a hard blow. That is, he will raise his guard to his head if you land a solid punch on his face, so that you will generally find his body undefended if you switch your attack to it quickly enough. Of course, reverse the order if you have drawn his guard down through body punching. Then go for his head.

I think I have given a brief description of enough punches to keep you going until next week. If you have mastered all I have described up to the current issue, then you have enough knowledge to be considered very useful. Do keep yourself fit at all times. Never permit a single day to pass without at least half an hour's exercise and shadow boxing. Only a fit and healthy man can carry through these manoeuvres successfully.

SWIMMING

By K. G. Greene

THIS week we end our course, and I trust that all those who have taken the trouble to study and follow my advice, have received some benefit.

We now find ourselves left with only the final details to examine and master. There are many ways for the novice-cum-intermediary to improve upon his or her present standard, not by book or tutorial coaching, but simply by allowing their own common sense to guide them. Above all avoid the fatal lapse into the strait-jacket of stereotyped rules and regulations, and let your latent swimming instincts find their own expression in natural movements and easy motion.

Be natural, cultivate original development. The real cause for so much failure in the swimming world is, in my opinion, not so much from lack of orthodox technique, but lack of individual originality. I have in these short series of instructional articles only undertaken to initiate the learner into the elementary basic principles underlying the separate strokes, knowing well the impossibility of being able to do more. The ultimate development and perfection of style and speed rests entirely in the hands of the aspirant.

BEHIND THE NEWS

Edited by J. A. Macnab

The "Daily Herald" As Prophet

ON July 7 the "Daily Herald" informed us: "Chancellor Schuschnigg is convinced that no settlement is now possible, following failure of negotiations to effect Austro-German reconciliation."

On July 11 the Austro-German agreement came into being. Perhaps the "Herald" will explain that their first statement was just another "myth," like the one we exposed about the Negus's millions. ("Action," July 9.)

The difficulty of the public when reading the financial-democratic Press is to distinguish the information from the myth-information.

More Mythology

LORD SNELL, Socialist chairman of the L.C.C., told the delegates to the Seventh International T.U. Congress on July 8: "In this country we have complete freedom of speech and opinion. *No visitor need fear the imposition of sanctions* for what he feels it right to say."

We can forgive His Proletarian Lordship for having done nothing so vulgar as attend a Fascist meeting where his own Socialist supporters have used bricks and bottles to deny free speech to their fellow-countrymen. But has he forgotten that Signor Marconi was refused the use of the wireless he himself invented the day after the B.B.C. had allowed the broadcasting of Abyssinian propaganda?

Fascist Peacemakers—How Unfair!

THE following comments on the Austro-German agreement from "Reynolds News" and the "Sunday Referee" respectively are amusing:

"*Hitler's new alliance with Austria represents a triumph over Mussolini.*"

"*The Duce's determination to defend Austria from German aggression forced Hitler to accept these terms.*"

It must have been difficult for these financial-democratic organs to decide which of the Fascist leaders each paper disliked most. In the end the Socialist "Reynolds" chose Mussolini to belittle, while the Gaumont-Jewish "Referee" chose Hitler.

It never occurred to either paper that two great statesmen and national leaders were quietly arranging to keep the peace of Europe.

Patriarch Sounds Tocsin

FROM an East London paper of July 11:

"*Abyssinian Speaks at Poplar Peace Meeting.*

"*Mr. Emmanuel Abrahams, secretary of the Abyssinian Legation, made a moving appeal. . . .*

"*All Ethiopians worthy of the name would fight to the end and would not rest until they had driven the invader from the soil. They were only waiting for the rainy season to begin the fight again.*"

When is a Peace Council not a Peace Council? When it wants to renew a war that is over, on behalf of Mr. Abrahams and his slave-trading friends. To assist in the anti-aircraft defences of London, however, is militarism of the most brutal nature. Thus speaks democracy.

Lord Beaverbrook: A Little Late

DOWN in the Fleet-street forest something has stirred. Eleven months after the British Union's "Mind Britain's Business" compaign began, the "Daily Express" of July 15 remarks:

"*Who comes well out of this Locarno Conference? We do not know. Who comes out badly? Britain. Britain's motto should be: Mind Britain's Business.*"

We seem to have seen and heard those three words before.

War for Peace

THE "Battle Scarred Veteran," Sir Walter Citrine, speaking at the International Trade Union Congress last week, made one or two interesting statements. One rather subtle remark was when he advocated "War only for Peace"; another, "Resolute efforts must be made to destroy Fascism."

We rather wonder whether there is any connection between the two. He went on to say: "We do not admit that the aggressor has won—we will do all that lies in our power to prevent the aggressor attaining his aims and gathering the spoils of war." Sir Walter still hopes—so does Mr. Selassie.

League Ignores Non-Fascist Aggression

WHEN the League of Nations was founded, the Hedjaz was one of the original members. To-day the Hedjaz does not exist, and Hussein is no longer King Hussein.

The kingdom of Hedjaz was destroyed by the aggression of Ibn Saud in 1925.

Does the general public know anything about this? No. Does the general public care? No. Why not? Because the big propaganda organs of Fleet-street have not bothered to work up an agitation.

Has the League taken or called for action to defend this member of the League against aggression? No. Has the League of Nations Union got excited and demanded sanctions. No. Has the League refused to "recognise" Ibn Saud's conquest? No.

Why is the answer "No" to all these questions? Answer (very easy): Because the State that attacked a member of the League was not a Fascist State. The purpose of the League is not to prevent aggression, but to down Fascism.

What Toryism Is Proud Of

IN a leading article of July 8, the "Daily Telegraph" pooh-poohs this talk of malnutrition. "A Better Nourished Nation" reads the headline, and the following are extracts:—

"*The recently-issued L.C.C. reports show that of 189,000 (children) medically examined in London, 94 per cent. were satisfactorily nourished . . . . only 152, or .08 per cent. of the under-nourished, showed definite pathological malnutrition.*

"*How can it be said in the light of such figures that 'there is widespread malnutrition' in London?*

"*Though in certain black spots—the special or distressed areas—malnutrition is more rife than in London, no sweeping indictment can stand. It is contradicted by all the vital statistics which Sir Kingsley Wood marshalled with his customary skill.*"

Well, what were the vital statistics? We turn to the "Telegraph's" own Parliamentary report of the same day, and we read:

"*Sir Kingsley . . . . found, however, evidence of physical deterioration in the large number of recruits rejected by the army, and in the conclusions of Sir John Orr that 4,500,000 people had incomes too low to provide the minimum standard of food necessary according to the British Medical Association, and that 9,000,000 were only just on that level.*"

So Lord Camrose, Lord Kemsley, Lord Iliffe, and the other big business men who dictate the policy of the "Telegraph," can see in Sir John Orr's terrible figures, which Sir Kingsley Wood did not dispute, nothing but a contradiction of any sweeping indictment of the Government. Only 4½ million below the starvation line! Only nine million on the border-line of starvation! The Tory idea of "A Better Nourished Nation."

It is noteworthy that the leading article carefully presented the London figures, which Sir Kingsley did not quote, and which support the "Telegraph" argument, while omitting the national figures which he did quote, and which demolish that argument.

Tories' Real Objective

ON July 3 the City of London Conservative Association held a dinner attended by Mr. Baldwin. The chairman, Mr. Vivian Smith, stated during his speech that "one had only to look at the rise which had taken place in the price of leading industrial shares to realise that an enormous improvement had been effected in the industrial conditions of the country."

Further Decline in Trade

THE following figures for the first half-year of 1936 require no comment:

Decline in coal exports compared with 1935—£1,700,000.

Decline in cotton textile exports compared with 1935—£700,000.

Decline in exports of cotton piece-goods *to India alone*—89,100,000 sq. yd.

Increase in imports of grain and flour—£4,568,000. Much of this could have been grown here.

Increase in imports of dairy produce—£3,766,000. All of this could have been grown here.

Increase in imports of Argentine beef—69,000 cwt. All of this could be grown here.

Loss of British trade with Italy owing to sanctions—£8 million.

The New Patriotism

A WOMAN reader of a Southend paper recently got into touch with one of its correspondents who signed herself "True Patriot," on the natural assumption that a patriot was a person loving Britain, pledged to defend the Monarchy against sedition and the land against attack, and an upholder of British Nationalism.

She got back a letter from an organisation called a Women's Committee against Fascism, accompanied by another circular from the Communist Party. A "supporter's card" was also enclosed, containing declarations to be signed expressing opposition to Nationalism, support of total disarmament, and demand for the liberation of prisoners in foreign countries.

Evidently many of the letters against patriotism that appear in local and provincial papers over a patriotic nom-de-plume are contributed by Moscow-financed and affiliated subversive societies of this kind. We are accustomed to the contradictions of Communism; a creed built on the fantastic theories of Marx's distorted brain could hardly be consistent; but "patriots" who oppose nationalism are a new kind of animal, of which even Marx himself would hardly have approved, since he described patriotism as a bourgeois vice like the family and religion, to be exterminated by "the proletarian revolution."

The New Defenders of the Faith

NO less surprising is the discovery that Communism is the guardian of religious liberties. We are evidently expected to believe that the Bolshevik murder of 8,631 priests was an unfortunate slip, for in a recent speech at Hampstead Town Hall Mr. William Gallacher, Communist M.P., declared that

"*the Communists would fight for the Irish Catholics there (in Scotland) in the same way as they fought for the Jews in London.*"

Mr. Gallacher's memory is short. Doesn't he remember that visit he paid to Dublin on April 12? The Irish Catholics, for whom he is so keen to fight, stoned him in the streets, crying, "Down with Communism!"

Impartiality of Hampstead Council

THE Hampstead Town Hall has more than once been refused by the local Council to the British Union, a patriotic body pledged to support the Empire and maintain the Crown. Yet it was let to the King's enemies. That the Communist Party are indeed the King's enemies, pledged to depose the Royal Family and institute the vile Red Terror as in the Soviet was made abundantly clear by Mr. Dooley, of the Hampstead Communist Party, who stated:

"*There is no easy constitutional method to reach the goal attained by Russia, and the workers will have to take the same road to reach the grand success that country now enjoyed.*"

We are therefore entitled to conclude that the Hampstead Council thinks it right and proper to allow the use of the Town Hall to those who wish to depose the King, destroy the Empire, and substitute the Red Flag for the Union Jack, while they think it right and proper to refuse the hall to those who are sworn to maintain King, Empire, and Flag. This is called the democratic right of free speech.

How British Union Runs Meetings

IF you want truth, go to the paper that has no financial axe to grind and takes no orders from financier or politician. Anyone reading the "National" Press would imagine that Fascist meetings consist of "battle, murder, and sudden death." Here is an impartial account from the "Ilford Recorder" of July 9:

"*It was one of the quietest and most businesslike political meetings ever held in the town. . . . There never has been a political meeting more orderly. . . . Whatever you may think of the Fascists and their policy, you have to admit that they can give the older parties lessons in conducting meetings. No time was wasted by the chairman's thanks or any of the padding which is such a boring feature of most meetings. Sir Oswald was alone on the platform. He went into his speech without preliminary humming and hawing, and the meeting closed exactly an hour and fifty minutes after it began.*"

Political Bias of Co-op. Press

A CORRESPONDENT recently wrote to the "Co-operative News," expressing disgust that a Co-op. hall in Kent had been let to the British Union.

The Press officer of the Union wrote in reply, pointing out that the "Co-operative News" itself had recently reported the speeches of Mr. Tomlinson, manager of the Co-operative Wholesale Publicity, in which he showed what great benefits had come to the Co-operative movement under Hitler and Mussolini; and mentioning that the British Union policy was the only policy that guarantees the Co-operative movement against the unfair competition of the chain stores.

The "Co-operative News" refused to print this letter, merely eating its own words in "Answers to Correspondents" by the brief and eloquent note:

"*The articles (reports) you refer to have been contradicted in these pages by greater authorities on Italian and German co-operation than the lecturer you mention.*"

The Co-operative movement is being perverted, just as the trade unions have been, by being used as instruments of political advancement for Socialist politicians. But fancy being driven to call a leading officer of one's own organisation "a lecturer" in order to pretend that one's own movement is being badly treated in a foreign country when really, in the words of Mr. Tomlinson, in Italy and Germany, the Co-operative movement "sits in the seat of the mighty." Even the success of their own movement under Fascism abroad must be kept from British Co-operators, lest they, too, "should believe and be saved"! Then, of course, the Socialist politicians would lose the fleshpots, and that would be a terrible thing.

TELLING THE WORLD

Ha! Ha!

"BUCHMANISM is unconsciously part of the Fascist movement."—"New Statesman and Nation," July 18.

Remarks That Don't Ring True

"TALKING to the Red Army in 1935, Stalin severely criticised those who failed to have due regard for the value of human life."—Rev. L. Schiff in the "Church Times," July 17.

"Conventional Christianity can have no quarrel with Communism on account of the methods that have been employed to create the community."—Rev. B. C. Plowright in "Christ, Community, and Church."

Object of Democratic Government

"I AM told the Cabinet is actually considering the banning of political uniforms. Debates in the House of Commons are still worth something."—"Manchester Guardian," July 17.

Provocative?

"AT the corner of Shaftesbury-avenue there was a sharp scuffle between a demonstrator and a newspaper seller who replied to anti-Fascist cries with 'God Save the King.'"—"Daily Mirror," July 20.

"We Conservatives Surrender"

"I AM a Conservative. I have addressed many Conservative meetings on Sunday evenings at Finsbury Park. I can honestly say there is no difference between the way Conservative meetings are invariably attacked by the Socialists and the way in which the Fascist demonstration on Sunday was attacked, except that we Conservatives surrender to violence, whereas the Fascists refuse to be bullied."—Mr. Richard Glover in the "Islington and Holloway Press," July 4, 1936.

Little Dinosaur, You've Had a Busy Day!

"PERHAPS, like the dinosaurs, we have had our day; perhaps the future is for other species of animals. Their minds may in time become better than ours are now. . . .

"We think the dinosaurs large, brutal, and stupid. Will that be the verdict of our successors on us?"—Bertrand Russell in "Sunday Referee," June 12.

Printed by ARGUS PRESS, LTD., Temple Avenue and Tudor Street, London, E.C.4, England, and published by ACTION PRESS, LTD., Sanctuary Buildings, Gt. Smith Street, London, S.W.1, England. Telephone: Victoria 9084 (5 lines).

ACTION, October 17, 1936.

No. 35 [REGISTERED AT THE G.P.O. AS A NEWSPAPER] "BRITAIN FIRST" OCTOBER 17, 1936

FOR KING AND PEOPLE

PUBLISHED EVERY THURSDAY. R.S.35

MOSLEY: SPECIAL ARTICLE

See Page 9

BRITAIN IS CALLING

MARCH

WITH

MOSLEY

The World, The Flesh— and Financial Democracy

A Weekly Review of Men and Events

By WILLIAM JOYCE

LAST week I dealt with the monstrous incitement which preceded October 4 and produced those disgraceful scenes which culminated in the surrender of the Government to organised Red violence. My article was concerned entirely with the legal aspects of the case, and although there was more than adequate evidence to prove that the disorder was Jewish in its conception, and while police court proceedings show that it was largely Jewish in execution, I did not unnecessarily emphasise the Hebraic character of the successful assault made upon law and order. In view, however, of certain Press

Two Red Demonstrators

comments which have since been made, it is desirable to pursue more closely an examination of the part played by Jews in abasing and stultifying the Home Office and the police force.

Before reviewing any statements from the Press it is necessary to remind the public, with the heaviest emphasis, that during the disorder in question nearly 100 policemen were injured, some of them very seriously. It has not been suggested by anybody that these injuries were inflicted by Blackshirts; it is known, on the contrary, that these criminal assaults were made by Red demonstrators. This personal, physical, violent attack upon the representatives of the Law must be one of the gravest and most important features of the case, for every man or woman who has the least respect for the public peace and the magnificent police force which is entrusted with the duty of preserving it.

Jewry's Joy

VERY few examples of the cant, hypocrisy, and insolence of our opponents will suffice. Turn to the issue of the *Jewish Chronicle* for October 9, and we see a large headline: "Mosley Receives His Marching Orders." Another slogan reads: "The People Said NO." Why the word "chosen" was omitted from this sentence it is difficult to understand. An illuminating comment from the main report on the disorder reads: "*The Home Office refused to interfere, and thousands of police were there to ensure his (Mosley's) safe conduct, but neither the march nor the meetings took place. They were stopped by the people of the East End.*" Then follows a calumny on the police force: "*After many baton charges the Commissioner of Police had to admit that his task was impossible. Popular feeling was too great.*" To suggest that the constabulary were incapable of dispersing the Red fringe consisting of a few thousand hooligans, most of them Oriental, is an intolerable and insulting reflection upon a thoroughly competent force, but it is a reflection which brings out in the clearest relief the Jewish appreciation of violence as a political argument.

The article continues: "'He Shall Not Pass' was the constant chant of the crowd, and many of them risked their lives ensuring that the pledge was kept." To risk one's life in opposing the police is a felony, but it is a felony which seems to have the most enthusiastic endorsement of Jewish opinion. The report continues: "*The police fired warning shots on the ground.*" Strange as may be the accounts which we have read in some newspapers it was left for the *Jewish Chronicle* to imply that the police carried firearms. The *Chronicle* continues: "*They sang popular songs and chanted the heroic words, 'They shall not pass!' Other slogans less dignified, but equally pointed, were: 'Rats, rats, we must get rid of the rats!' and 'One, two three, four, five—we want Mosley dead or alive!'*"

Jewish Admission of Guilt

WE are at last beginning to approach an understanding of the Jewish conception of dignity; but the article does show clearly the distorted sense of humour of which the Hebrew mind is capable. Witness the following passage: "*As a 'Jewish Chronicle' representative was standing at one street corner a Jew came up to him and said: 'We're putting up a great fight to-day, aren't we?' Another Jew, who overheard this, remarked: 'Don't forget our brother non-Jews.'*" And yet there are still a few purblind people in our island who find it hard to believe that the violent assaults made upon the Blackshirts are mainly of Jewish origin.

But the full significance of the Jewish attitude towards the law cannot be grasped by anyone who has failed to read this amazing sentence: "*The police had been doing their job; the people had been doing theirs, each according to their lights. Now that it was over there was no ill-will.*" We wonder whether this statement is quite true as applied to the thirty-four police officers from Leman-street who were injured by the "people" who were doing their job according to their lights. It is impossible not to recall Gilbert's famous song:

"When a felon's not engaged in his employment—employment,
Or maturing his felonious little plans,
His capacity for innocent enjoyment—enjoyment,
Is quite as great as any honest man's."

It is hardly necessary to quote any more of the *Jewish Chronicle's* report on the events of October 4. Whether or not the editor, on reflection, will think it prudent to employ a less ingenious reporter is a matter for the Board of Deputies to consider, but it would have been a pity to deprive my readers of an opportunity to appreciate the Jewish attitude towards the crimes which were committed, as clearly stated in the article to which I have referred. Editorial sophism will in no way detract from the meaning, the implications, or the effect of this eulogy on crime.

The "Morning Post"

INSPIRED by the style of the essay which we have just been examining, I would take up the refrain, "Do not forget our brother non-Jews"; and so we turn to the *Morning Post* of Thursday, October 8. Of all the canting, whining, niddering nonsense which has ever appeared in a "National" newspaper it would be difficult to find anything to surpass the Editorial of this issue. This sickly effusion of pusillanimous verbiage pretends that Fascism and Communism must be placed in the same category. "Neither Fascism nor Communism is of any serious consequence in Britain," the learned editor declares. "*The peace is most often broken when the Communists or Fascists demonstrate on any considerable scale.*" Here is an unfortunate mistake, for the Communists have held hundreds of demonstrations without any interference merely because, unlike them, the Blackshirts do not interfere with their opponents' meetings; and the vast majority of Blackshirt demonstrations during the last four years have been free from violence or disorder, but where violence or disorder has occurred they have always been organised deliberately by the Red Front.

The custodian of the Oriental legacy which Disraeli left to Britain in the form of a Conservative Party, is constrained to describe Fascism as an alien doctrine. Most amazing of all, however, is the editor's contention that interference with Conservative meetings is a negation of freedom. "*Such incidents are a clear negation of freedom, and can leave the Authorities in no doubt as to what should be done.*" But on the other hand there follows the observation: "*It is not only of such incidents as these that the present trouble is made. That trouble arises from the importation of alien doctrines, each of which is based on force and, therefore, is most likely to cause force to be used.*"

Vale

NOW I have no desire to waste time in dissecting the crumbling corpse of the *Morning Post*, but among my friends it has a number of readers. I have read it for years, not because I can accept its politics, but because at one time, except in relation to German National Socialism, it did show some indication of fairness in comment. It is an organ sustained almost entirely for the moral solace of extreme Conservatives, who, at least, for all their faults, have no love of Communism. Let such people note that their editorial mentor now refuses to distinguish between the Reds and the only Movement which has actively and vigorously opposed them in this country; the only Movement which has refused to permit its meetings to be broken up by Red violence.

This request I make seriously because it is important for the extreme Conservative to know why his newspaper should be unwilling to distinguish between the Communists and their opponents.

I am not so sure as to the number of non-Jewish brothers who are interested in the conduct and policy of the *Morning Post*, which we had better leave at that point of disintegration whereat it is about to fall into the dust, which can be sprinkled over the tomb of the Government which surrendered, in practice, as the *Morning Post* surrenders in theory, to Red violence—to the weapons of the gutter and the ghetto; for there can be no viler insult to inflict upon the men who have devoted their lives to fighting Communism than to place them in the same category with their sub-human enemies.

WHO ARE THE PERSECUTED?

Constructive Suggestions on Palestine

By Capt. R. Gordon-Canning, M.C.

EVENTS in Palestine since the inauguration of the Mandate have advanced steadily to the predestined goal to which such a policy was undoubtedly bound to lead. A series of spontaneous but partial rebellions, terminating in 1936 in one complete and patriotic rising, culminating in conditions of actual warfare as a last despairing gesture to the British peoples. To such a pass has the iron control of Jewry over the British Government brought the British nation that, on behalf of political Zionism and international Jewry, Arab kills Briton, and the latter must retaliate in force, slaying scores of Arabs.

That order must be restored is essential; but merely a restoration of order will not bring with it the re-establishment of British authority. The crushing of a community whose numbers do not exceed 900,000 by the forces of the greatest Empire in history can bring neither glory nor authority. That such a method has to be employed is in itself an admission of grave errors in justice and administration.

In a few days' time there will be a force of 20,000 British soldiers, armed in the most modern and efficient manner, concentrated in Palestine, which will cost considerable sums of money both to the inhabitants of Palestine and to the people of Great Britain.

If the "National" Government of this country was free of Jewish influence it would have taken a similar step to that of the Governments of 1921 and 1929 (*), which was to stop further Jewish immigration until an official report had been made on the causes of Arab revolts. On each occasion, especially by the commission of 1929, excessive immigration had been found to have been the reason for Arab action. In fact, the Shaw Report, pages 97-98 and 123, followed up by Sir John Hope-Simpson's and also Mr. French's reports, are incontrovertible evidence in support of Arab arguments. The Zionists, knowing full well the bankruptcy of their arguments, have decided on this occasion to gamble on an attempt to force the Arab into open hostility against the British Government; and then, with the power of the Jewish community in the national Press and in Government, to create a "barrage" of propaganda about the banditry and murders committed by uncultivated Arabs, which shall alienate the sympathy of the British public. The Jewish mind is seldom at a loss to discover some means whereby Truth will be submerged by waves of repeated falsehoods.

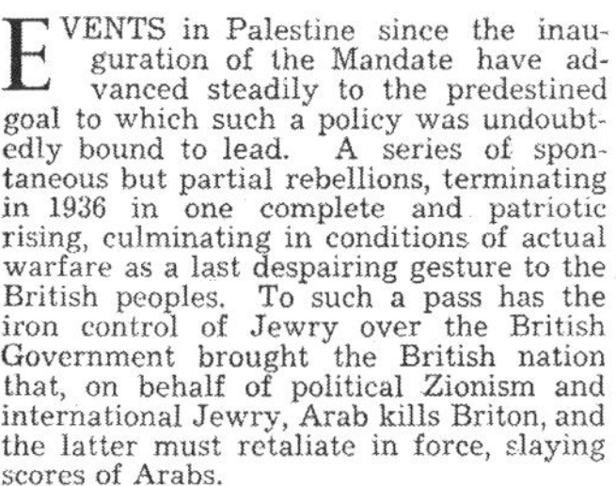

An Arab village being blown up in Palestine

What Can the Arab Expect?

THE obvious result of the present situation will be the crushing of Arab resistance; the arrival of the Royal Commission at Jerusalem; the report of this Commission confirming the reports of former Commissions; a White Paper implementing this report; a Jewish protest; a Government recantation; a new flood of Jewish immigrants; a new Arab revolt a few years later.

Before proceeding with the present situation and offering a constructive proposal, I shall recapitulate the main points of the Palestine Mandate and the manner of its administration, which, in themselves, will show (1) the contradiction in purpose, and (2) the partiality in execution.

1. The Mandate.

(a) It is contradictory to Articles 20 and 22 of the Covenant of the League of Nations.

(b) The Balfour Declaration stated: "A national home *in* Palestine, not *of* Palestine, which is the proclaimed aim not only of the extreme Zionists led by Jabotinsky, but also of the so-called moderate element led by Weizmann.

(c) Palestine is a mandated area "A," and should possess its own Government and local autonomy. The Zionists have placed every obstacle in the way of this autonomy.

(d) Under Articles 2 and 6 of the Mandate, the rights of the existing community take precedence of the undertaking to facilitate Jewish immigration.

2. British Government's undertaking to King Hussein and to the Arabs as a whole.

(a) From Sir Henry McMahon to King Hussein, October 25, 1915.

(b) From Lord Balfour to King Hussein in 1918, confirming previous pledges.

(c) The Anglo-French declaration, November 7, 1918.

(d) Mr. Lloyd George in Conference at Downing-street, September 19, 1919.

(e) The Secretary of State for the Colonies in the House of Commons, June 14, 1921.

3. Statistics (approximate).

(a) 1918—600,000 Arabs.
53,000 Jews.
1935—900,000 Arabs.
400,000 Jews.

(b) Jews own 425,000 acres, about *half* of the total area of *fertile* land in Palestine.

(c) Imports: 1935—£18,000,000.
Exports: 1935— £4,000,000.

This is the prosperity of the Jews. The exports are still mainly soap and citrus, articles exported long before the arrival of Zionists.

(d) Jews on the land, in spite of over 140,000 immigrants in the last five years, have diminished by 4 per cent.

(e) Minimum requirements of an Arab family, except in very fertile country, thirty-five acres. In 1930 average Arab holding twenty-two acres. Since that date Jewry has acquired a further 125,000 acres.

4. Examples of discrimination.

(a) While facility is given to East European Jews to emigrate to Palestine, permission is refused to any of the forty thousand Arabs from Palestine who migrated to the United States to return to their native country

(b) The Arab National Anthem and flag are not permitted to be sung or carried; while the Hatikvah is played (the High Commissioner stands up if present) and the Jewish flag is hoisted next to the Union Jack.

(c) The Jews are allowed to designate Palestine as "the land of Israel."

(d) No case of collective punishment had been enforced against a Jewish community up to July, 1936.

Our Abject Government

TO return to the situation of to-day, the Government has at the same time as ordering the dispatch of a division of troops to Palestine issued a statement of policy (September 7, 1936). Certain points of this statement are described by the Higher Arab Committee as incorrect, particularly that dealing with the negotiations of General Nuri Pasha-es-Said. The Higher Arab Committee had been prepared to call off the strike when Nuri Pasha had given the Committee to understand that in the event of this the British Government would prohibit further Jewish immigration until after the findings of the Royal Commission. Mr. Ormsby-Gore, Colonial Under-Secretary (who, when previously holder of this office, 1924-1929, displayed particular interest in political Zionism), issued a denial of any such undertaking, and said Nuri Pasha was acting entirely on his own.

The Arab Higher Committee also refuse to accept the Colonial Secretary's interpretation of the manifesto issued by them on August 31. In fact the Government has, as in nearly all its Imperial and foreign activities, never possessed a clear-cut policy since the situation developed into a patriotic revolution in Palestine last April. At moments wavering before the justice of the Arab claims, at moments cowed by their Jewish overlords into acts of heartless repression. For the benefit of fourteen million alien Jews, British blood is being endangered and British money being utilised. For the safeguarding of ghetto populations and Communistic revolutionaries, who are themselves intensely and fanatically opposed to the British Empire, we are crushing a friendly and virile population in its own land, and estranging the loyalty of one hundred million Muslims, citizens of the British Empire, besides creating in other Islamic and Arab countries a deep and lasting hatred.

Jews at the Wailing Wall in Jerusalem

The Future

WHAT, then, should be the policy of the British Union towards this Palestinian problem in which the Jew-controlled "democratic" Governments have involved the British people?

There are two unofficial proposals for a solution of Arab-Jewish differences. (a) Cust's proposals of a system of cantonisation (which is an elaboration of a scheme outlined by myself in 1929); (b) Mr. Neville Barbour's outlined in *The Times*, September 9, 1936. Neither of these are satisfactory, but there are many points from both which might be utilised, and assist towards a temporary settlement until a Fascist Government enters into power and will give definite assurances to the Arab population in Palestine.

Fascist Policy

(a) An assurance to the Arab world that the Zionists would never be given an opportunity to dominate, politically or economically, in Palestine.

(b) The deportation of all Zionist immigrants from foreign countries who were either economically unstable or had been convicted of political or civil crimes. Cessation of immigration except British Jews.

(c) There would then be room for the entry of British Jews.

(d) The effective participation of Arabs in Government, and the participation of Arabs in the exploitation of the country's resources. At the present time the Rutenburg Electric Power Concession is being run for the benefit of its Jewish shareholders and against the interests of the Arab population.

(e) The restitution of certain fertile lands to the Arabs.

(f) The closing down of the Jewish Agency in London.

By its own excesses Zionism stands condemned. The British Government might possibly have been able to implement its illegal promise of "a national home *in* Palestine;" but never "*of* Palestine," for which political Zionism aims. Never content Jewry shrieks and whines alternately, "persecution," even though he may have gained under this regime of "persecution" a million pounds sterling on half the fertile land of Palestine.

The problem of Palestine, similar to so many other post-war problems, is of no great complexity, and if dealt with purely on the grounds of strict justice could be dispensed with in one hour. However, not to mitigate international disputes, but to intensify them, is the policy of international Jewry, and for this policy and for the rapaciousness of so many of his race the reasonable Jew and the moderate Zionist must suffer. Not yet has Jewry learnt that anti-semitism is the logical offspring of semitism and that political Zionism in Palestine proclaims the death-knell of Zionism in that country.

On September 27 the Viceroy received a deputation of Indian Muslims led by Sir Muhammad Yakub. It came before him to express the anxieties felt by the Indian followers of the Islamic religion at the measures of repression exercised by the British Government against their co-religionists in Palestine.

The Viceroy, with much equivocation and tergiversation, replied that the conflict was essentially political and racial in Palestine, and he refuted the claim that the operation of the Mandate had been prejudicial to the economic status of the Arab population. Such statements are in direct conflict with the evidence of various Commissions appointed by H.M. Government to inquire the reason of Arab grievances.

The Viceroy, before making such statements, must have known, or not having done so should have known, what Sir John Hope Simpson stated about the economic position of the Arab fellah in his 1930 Report, followed up by another on the same lines by Mr. French.

The Viceroy well knows that British Governments have failed to implement the suggestions made by these two reports, and that the civil and religious rights of the Arabs have been more and more endangered by the excessive immigration of East European Jews. That a man in the position of Viceroy of India should lend himself to such mis-statements of fact and that he should support the demands of non-British Jewry in face of the opposition of 70 millions of British subjects in India is one of the most lamentable features of the present system of British financial democratic government.

Arab Strike Ended

THE six-month Arab strike, in which nearly 500 lives and much property have been lost, terminated on Monday before the superior armed forces of Great Britain and on the advice of the neighbouring Arab rulers. The latter, after consultation with representatives of the British Government, have, no doubt, been assured that the grievances of the Arabs in Palestine will be carefully investigated by the Royal Commission and removed by immediate legislation.

It is extremely doubtful whether the Government will be permitted to redress the Arab grievances under the menaces of its Jewish overlords. At least for fifteen years various Governments have not possessed the power to do so.

In Palestine, in all Arabia, the fair name of Britain has been tarnished and become synonymous for broken faiths all because of international Jewry.

Let it at least be hoped that there will now be a suspension of alien immigration into Palestine until after the findings of the Royal Commission.

* This does not mean that these Governments were free of Jewish influences; these were not then so concentrated on Zionism.

THE BRITISH COUNTRYSIDE

JUST DRIFTING

THE FATE OF BRITISH AGRICULTURE

(By Our Agricultural Correspondent.)

WHAT a sad thing it is to watch a great industry drifting slowly to destruction.

Yet this is what is happening to British agriculture, and the drift is fast increasing in pace.

We had all hoped to see better times for our farmers by now, for many have been the promises made by responsible statesmen, and many are the Boards that have been set up.

While there is plenty to criticise in the operations of such Boards, yet undoubtedly they are doing all in their power to put some stabilisation of prices into the industry, but their best efforts are doomed to fail, so long as the problem of foreign imports is left unsolved.

But the "hidden influence" has so far been successful, and only futile efforts to check imports are allowed to be made.

No long-term policy has even been put before the N.F.U. to discuss, and as we understand it, Mr. Elliot will be in no position to enunciate one until the autumn of 1937!

Yet another year of aimless drifting for hard-pressed farmers, many of whom will be hard put to it to keep afloat until then.

Disagreements Within the Industry

IT is a pity that at such a time there should be any disagreement within the industry itself, but we are faced with the childish squabble between the Pig Boards, with the result that even at this late hour nothing definite has been decided regarding the 1937 bacon contracts, yet these very Boards were set up to do away with uncertainties and quarrels and to arrange the bacon business amicably.

Most of us understand the difficulties which confront the Pigs Marketing Board, and now these difficulties are greatly enhanced by the rise in the price of feeding stuffs.

This rise has alarmed pig producers and poultry farmers, for when operations are based on certain costs of feeding materials (always allowing a little latitude each way) and such costs go up in an alarming fashion, producers cannot be blamed if they do not enter upon contracts.

Danger Ahead

HOWEVER, we *must* remember that should the Bacon Pig Scheme collapse *now*, our pig industry will be in a far worse plight than before it started. There is a regular wave of bacon pig production sweeping the Continent, and as the curtailment of imports depends upon the successful continuation of the Bacon Pig Scheme, we realise—or should realise—what a flood of imported bacon would pour in here at once unchecked.

That is why I see such danger ahead for our industry by this delay in coming to some settlement of the 1937 contract prices, and so allow producers to complete their breeding plans.

Again in the Sugar Beet industry, and in the poultry world things are not running as smoothly as one could wish.

Some farmers want a Board to run the Sugar Beet industry, others (and they seem to us to have a good case) can see no useful purpose in a new creation, so an investigation has been held and now we are awaiting a statement.

Poultry farmers have to let the Minister of Agriculture know whether they do, or do not, want a scheme; here too, opinions are very much divided, but in the main, I believe, poultry men would much rather be fully protected by a drastic tariff on all imported foreign eggs, and a slight duty on eggs from the Dominions.

Is it realised that in August this year we imported close on two million great hundreds of eggs in shell, or some 200,000 great hundreds more than in the same month of 1935?

Yet some tell us the state of agriculture is improving! Not amongst poultry farmers, I should think! Personally I know only too many who are being ruined by imports and are now faced with the serious position of rising costs of feeding stuffs.

Reflections

I HAVE recently been watching—in various parts of the country—demonstrations of power farming.

It is really remarkable what time can be saved and how much more work can be accomplished by means of power propelled implements and machines.

It would be easy, here, to point out that mechanisation lends itself to displacement of labour on the land, but while so doing it doubles or trebles productive powers.

Is it not a terrible reflection that while we have the means of production doubled and production itself doubled, yet there are some who believe in the restriction of production while thousands of our fellow creatures are trying to exist on a starvation diet?

[Photograph by A. Chamberlain

On a Sussex farm. Stacking the 1936 hay crop

MORE FREE SPEECH

THE *Bath Chronicle and Herald* reports that the police handled a Fascist meeting with tact. When it was obvious that some of the crowd had come prepared for some form of entertainment of a vigorous kind, Superintendent Tom Ashworth, who was in charge of a large body of police, "handled the situation in a persuasive manner, with the result that the meeting was called off."

With the result that some hundreds of Bath citizens were deprived of an opportunity to hear the Fascist case—dictated to by hooligans. But the occurrence will make honest citizens think.

A PLEA FOR THE STREET TRADER

Small Salesmen Are Being Driven from the Street—says *ANNE CUTMORE*

THE recent proposal to close the Caledonian Market is yet another blow to London's street traders, who during the past years have increasingly to compete with large multiple shops whose scope, size, and power grows with the ruin of the small trader. On its heels, however, comes more vicious legislation yet, closing main London streets to the street trader.

A scene in the Caledonian Market

Each year conditions become more difficult for the street trader and the costermonger. Rules of trading are more and more rigidly enforced by the police, and each year—even each month—sees a greater proportion of prosecutions by the police, and a greater proportion of the trader's earnings paid in fines for obstruction—an obstruction which is, in many cases, more nominal than real. Men have been arrested several times in one day, and often a week's earnings, and more, have disappeared in fines in the police court.

This most recent Government edict closes to the street trader all the principal West End streets, which have naturally become his most profitable trading place. Although ostensibly this is an attempt to straighten London's traffic problem, the effect will be to throw some 1,250 men out of work without compensation, for these men are not eligible for unemployment benefit, while the effect upon the increasingly difficult question of congestion will be negligible.

This arbitrary action appears to the men as yet another blow at them by authorities which favour the large multiple stores, which are everywhere closing down the small trader, whether in his shop or on the street.

Other Solutions

LONDON'S traffic problem admits of other solutions than this criminal one of ruining the street trader. Huge vans, many of them from those very multiple stores, now obstruct the traffic, carrying goods which our unused railway lines might carry as easily. Great charabancs, sometimes taking up two lines of traffic, carry passengers from place to place about our crowded thoroughfares, repeating the route already covered by the railway lines, which, running through country, or underground, are empty of passengers. Horse vans, the worst form of street obstruction, are to be seen in the streets in hundreds. Great drays, many of them drawing trailers, hold up two lines of traffic for hours, while their noise and petrol smell are at least as great a nuisance as the waste in time to the motorist and legitimate traveller on the road. Each of these vehicles forms an obstruction a hundred times greater than that of the street trader, with his small barrow pushed against the kerb.

If the Government were to remove the huge furniture vans, the provincial vans carrying produce, and the charabancs from the roads of London, compensation would, of course, have to be paid to the large and sometimes financially powerful firms for whom these vehicles ply. The small costermonger can, however, be driven from the streets to unemployment and the prospect of starvation, without compensation and almost without protest—so small a voice can the poor raise in defence of their right to live. What right has a rich and powerful country to drive its working people into bitter poverty by taking away their livelihood without any attempt at replacement?

No Compensation

MUCH vicious legislation has been passed by this Government, but there have been few more barbaric measures than this which, after persecution of these men, drives them off the streets which have been their trading ground for generations, to beggary without any effort at compensation—apparently without even the thought that compensation was necessary and right.

If a man is willing to work, he has a right to expect that the country which bore him shall give him work to do. If it cannot, then his right to live is just as great as that of the man who, by perhaps a more fortunate chance, is able to earn his living. If the country deliberately deprives a man of work which he has been doing for years, its failure to compensate the man, or offer him other employment, is criminal in its neglect of responsibility.

THE WORLD OF LABOUR

By JOHN EMERY

SOCIALIST FLUMMERY

Party Could Have Been Saved By Ten Just Men

IN the year 1924 I finally decided that the Labour Party was corrupt, and dishonest, and would never do anything for the workers of Britain.

I had been in it since I was a boy, but until 1924 I had been so busy working for it that I had never seen my leaders at close quarters. I saw them in 1924. I saw them flushed with victory, and many of them with something else, at the first great reception in the Park Lane Hotel, London. The sight of that gathering was bad enough, but there was something worse, for during the whole of that evening there was never a reference as to why and how Labour had got to office, or what they were going to do now they were there.

The countless men and women who had toiled and sacrificed to make a Labour Government possible were forgotten. They had served their purpose. They had allowed a group of political adventurers and careerists to get to power on their backs.

There were not ten men in the whole of the Parliamentary Labour Party who genuinely disapproved of the flunkeyism and the sycophancy displayed by the Labour leaders in that year. What is more, some who disapproved in 1924 began to feel that the whole thing was a racket and they might as well be in it. You who have read your Bibles will remember that Sodom and Gomorrah could have been saved had they been able to produce ten righteous men. The requisite number could not be found, and the cities had to go. Had Labour been able to produce ten righteous men in 1924 it, too, might have been saved; but after Edinburgh it is now generally accepted that Labour must inevitably receive the same fate as the two corrupt cities of the plain.

Party Squabble

I AM not here asserting that there were not ten honest men in all the Labour Party. I knew more than ten myself, but honesty in the case of a great movement was not enough. Courage also was wanted. There were many decent fellows who deplored the flummery and mummery of 1924, but they did all their deploring in private. And when the Whips were against those who had courage, the honest ones joined in the hunt.

When the late Arthur Cook, James Maxton, and the late John Wheatley started their crusade in the year 1928 to try to save the soul of the Labour movement, what happened? There were not ten Labour M.P.s who did not show more violent hatred to these three than they had shown against Mr. Baldwin or Mr. Neville Chamberlain.

In my Socialist and near Socialist journals these days I read the most vile and stupid attacks on Sir Oswald Mosley. But in all these screeds I have never found one of the writers yet who had stopped to ask himself the question—Why did Mosley leave the Labour Party? If they did they would be bound to give the answer that he left because the Labour Party had betrayed its own principles and broken its pledges to the poorest of the poor.

The Last Labour Government

LET me refresh your memory. During the term of the last Labour Government poverty was rampant in Britain. The world had had four years of enormously increased production, and every world market was stocked with food and machinery to make goods. That was the time when the Labour Government decided that we must economise.

The pledge to give the unemployed at least enough to eat was broken, and a Bill called an Anomalies Bill was introduced which struck thousands of working people off the live register. Do you know that that Bill was considered such a perfect Bill that every die-hard Tory Peer supported it in the House of Lords. Not a single Peer voted against it, and in the House of Commons only the I.L.P. members and Sir Oswald Mosley with two Liberals voted against it.

As a protest against the Labour Party's betrayal on this and other questions, Mosley left the Government. All he had done was to try, as Mr. Maxton was trying, to save the soul of the Labour movement. What was the result of his efforts? He was denounced as a traitor by practically every Labour M.P. When the unemployment figures stood at nearly 3,000,000, the Labour Government and the Party stopped all its normal activities in order to run a special campaign against him. And now, seven years later, Labour people and Left Wing writers are deploring that the soul of the movement has gone. Dr. Salter on the Right Wing and Mr. H. N. Brailsford on the Left are saying this, and all that they have found in 1936 is something some of us saw years ago. When we protested, the Salters and the Brailsfords were our most bitter opponents. Next time they feel like denouncing Oswald Mosley, they should remember that he left the Labour Party for precisely the same reason as they would leave it now had they the pluck.

Farce at Edinburgh

I AM not going to weary you this week with an analysis of what happened at Edinburgh. There is not the remotest reason why I should. Everything that happened there was so transparently stupid and dishonest that there is no need to point out the defects. They stand out so conspicuously that even newspaper men, who hitherto have only seen the surface of the thing, are at last able to see right into the rotten, corrupt body itself.

Rather this week would I write of the motives and the spirit of the leaders which made the Edinburgh fiasco inevitable. And I am writing this for the younger men in the hope that when they come to choose leaders they will be able to distinguish between the gold and the dross.

Every blundering move at Edinburgh was caused entirely by the fact that no question is ever considered as to whether it is right or wrong. The one consideration is, will it secure votes? On the Labour Party Executive are men who, to put it quite bluntly, are almost stupid. They are there through a process of bargaining with the block votes of their Union. The late Mr. Henderson once had to remind some of them that they could do Executive business better if they came to the meeting sober. These ones, however, are harmless. It is the cool, calculating, sober ones who do the real damage.

Sleight of Hand

DON'T imagine for one moment that trickery is something new in Labour politics. They have been like that since those two past masters, Mr. MacDonald and Mr. Henderson, assumed control. The only difference is that Mr. MacDonald had been playing the political game so long that acrobatics and evasion had become second nature to him.

Don't forget that Mr. MacDonald's first essay in politics was to go to Southampton in the hope of being adopted as Liberal candidate. The Liberals chose another man, so Mr. MacDonald got himself adopted as Socialist candidate. And don't forget that Mr. Henderson was Liberal election agent at Barnard Castle and would have liked to be Liberal candidate. The Liberals here, too, adopted their own man, and Mr. Henderson became Labour candidate whilst still a Liberal. A party guided by two such men was automatically doomed to follow a tortuous and winding path, before it finally fell in its own twisted tracks.

The two counterparts of these two illustrious statesmen in the Labour politics of to-day are Mr. Herbert Morrison and Dr. Hugh Dalton. It is not without interest that Mr. Morrison was a handmaiden to Mr. MacDonald, while Dr. Dalton thought his best interests lay in being handmaiden to Mr. Henderson.

Mr. MacDonald and Mr. Henderson, it should be explained, disliked each other intensely and had many serious quarrels, but, when troubled by the Left Wing, they had the sense enough to know that if they did not hang together they would probably hang separately. Dr. Dalton and Mr. Morrison have not quite that sense, nor the skill and dexterity of their two masters. But the intention and the purpose are precisely the same—each is fighting for his own hand.

Shifty-Eyed

A FORTNIGHT ago I predicted in these notes that the quarrel between these two would be made public. I was right, and now I will tell you why they quarrelled.

If you ever get to close quarters with these two, try this on them. Look them straight in the eye and you will find both will be unable to return you a straight look. Dr. Dalton's shifty gaze is an acquired habit, Mr. Morrison's is a natural defect. That shifty look of each is reflected in every political move they make. Like Mr. MacDonald it is utterly impossible for them to look straight or think straight.

Dr. Dalton

The framing of that crazy resolution on armaments is the perfect illustration of my point, and also my point that they act like their former masters, but with just something lacking. Had Mr MacDonald and Mr. Henderson been asked to draft that resolution, they would have produced one just as stupid, but it would have passed. Mr. MacDonald, you see, had been so long at the game, that without any conscious effort at all he could pour out the most wonderful cloud of words, so utterly meaningless, and so beautifully jumbled that delegates, quite unable to understand the words themselves, thought the whole meaning must be very profound. That was the difference between the old gang and the new. Mr. MacDonald could not help thinking and talking in circles. Mr. Morrison and Dr. Dalton were trying to imitate them and failed. Mr. MacDonald's wordy nonsense was produced as the result of a natural gift, which is always better than even the best apprenticeship.

In trying to get a true appreciation of the two apprentices who now think they are journeymen, you must quite clearly understand that neither man ever had, and has not now, a streak of idealism in all their bodies. The Labour movement to each is a place for a career. At one time Mr. Morrison was content that it should be a place to earn a living, but that was long ago. This open quarrel between the two is not over any question of principle whatever. Each has taken a different line on armaments merely as a step towards the leadership of the Labour Party, and I will now explain what has led up to it.

Feuds

THIS immediate feud dates from the Labour Conference last year. That, you will remember, was the first conference at which the big bosses of the unions plainly intimated that they intended to be bosses of the Labour Party also. It was the conference when the union leaders wished to declare war on Italy in the belief that the war would be fought at the safe distance of the Suez Canal. Spain, being much nearer, they decided this year to be neutral.

George Lansbury was publicly kicked out of the leadership and then our two heroes began to work. Mr. Morrison, with his Cockney impetuosity, jumped in too soon. Dr. Dalton went about his job in a more laborious and better calculated manner. It was alleged last year that, on the eve of the appointment of the new leader, Mr. Morrison was holding little group meetings to boost his chances, just as Mr. MacDonald did in 1922. This time the unions were suspicious, and Herbert was badly defeated. Mr. Attlee was appointed instead.

Dr. Dalton, knowing that leadership just now is a thankless task, decided to wait. Both knew, however, that the power of the union bosses had increased enormously. Mr. Morrison, since then, has been swinging to the Left. He saw that he was not the idol of the big bosses, but only their servant, to be used for attacking the Reds. His one hope, therefore, was to get Left and Pacifist support in the hope of curbing the big bosses before it was too late.

Dr. Dalton took exactly the opposite line. He saw that his one hope was to speak the mind of the big bosses, and armaments provided the opportunity. Dr Dalton knew that the union bosses wanted rearmament, not particularly to fight anybody, but simply as a means of providing work for their members and subscriptions for their unions. Dr. Dalton was the first man to ask the Labour Party to break from its traditional policy of voting against armaments when in opposition and voting for them when in office. He did it because it was the policy of the unions. And so, when you re-examine the spectacle of Mr. Morrison saying the conference resolution means that Labour M.P.s will oppose armaments in the House, and Dr. Dalton saying quite the opposite, make up your minds it means neither. All it means is the manoeuvres of these two men trying to capture the Labour machine.

Dr. Dalton, for the first time, has become the official spokesman of the union bosses. For the first time in history Mr. Morrison refuses to be official spokesman against Communist affiliation. Dr. Dalton is trying to get leadership by support of the Right. Mr. Morrison by the support of the Left. But neither are yet aware that there are underfed men, women, and children in Britain.

Labour Sneers at British Workers

IN the "Decline and Fall of the Labour Party," John Scanlon states that after 1923, the Labour Party entered into a new era—the era of the boiled shirt and the silk hat.

Judging by the remarks of Mr. Toole (Lord Mayor-Elect of Manchester) at the Labour Party Conference it has never passed from that era.

Referring to the Manchester plain clothes march held by the British Union some time ago, he stated that he agreed to the banning of uniforms in order that the people could see the Fascists without them. "You never saw such a motley lot," he said amidst laughter, "and I believe it convinced the people that the future of this country could not be trusted to such a crew."

A large number of the men on this march were ex-Service men. Between 1914 and 1918 they were trusted with the job of making this country safe for people like Mr. Toole. The working class were the people who believed in the promises made by Mr. Toole and his friends, only to find that after they had voted them into power, all the promises were forgotten.

Apparently when Mr. Toole agreed to the banning of uniform he did it, not with the intention, as was stated at the time, of preventing disorder, but in order that a certain section of the Manchester population should be given an opportunity of jeering at people not so well dressed as some of the pompous little men who belong to the Labour Party.—H. S.

RADIO FLASHES

B.B.C. BOYCOTT BREAKS

By "BLUEBIRD"

THE gap which appeared momentarily in the Popular Front on Sunday week, when the news-finch was allowed to give Sir Oswald Mosley's statement on the Communist riots in full, has closed up, and the B.B.C. is back in line.

Blackshirt activities in this country have increased to such an extent that it has been quite impossible to omit news of them altogether. Therefore the B.B.C. has fallen back on its old trick—the old, old trick of all democratic institutions—of news distortion and mere abuse. All through the week we have heard of Blackshirt riots, mayors and corporations petitioning one another or anybody else to stop Blackshirt meetings.

The result of all this has had exactly the opposite effect to that intended. Blackshirt meetings all over the country have been crowded—in many cases the people have come deliberately to scoff, and in many cases have remained to praise. In other cases people have come to see and hear what it is all about. The result of this has been many conversions to the Fascist cause.

For the past two years the B.B.C., in common with other news-diffusing concerns, have, ostrich-like, refused to mention British Fascism. Mosley's great meetings in London and all over the country have been completely ignored. As the B.B.C. find they can do this no longer they now go in for abuse. And it seems that many people are of the opinion that abuse from the B.B.C. is the best possible praise.

"Eye-Witness"

LAST Sunday evening in particular the accounts of the Communist rabble were certainly not by any means according to the facts. The B.B.C. raked up their old friend, "An Eye-Witness," who gave all sorts of lurid accounts of what had been going on. He said that gangs of youths had been wrecking shops and shouting out slogans, and that the inference was that they were Fascists because they carried black handkerchiefs!

Whoever heard of such nonsense? And who has ever heard of a Blackshirt carrying a black handkerchief? Possibly the handkerchiefs carried by Fascists are not all snowy white, but then many of them have not the same laundry facilities as have the news-finches and their friend, "Eye-Witness." If the B.B.C. have not got the courage to give the name of this eye-witness, they have no right whatever to give weight to his statements. By doing so they are proving themselves to be willing agents of the anti-Fascist front.

Later on the same evening I tuned in to Athlone and heard a very much fairer account of the proceedings.

The B.B.C.'s account later the same evening on the affairs of Spain rather led one to believe that there was stalemate and that the insurgents were being held up by the so-called "Government" forces. Athlone, on the other hand, gave quite a different account of things, and it is obvious from the positions of the opposing forces that Athlone's account was much nearer the truth than was that of the B.B.C.

Hearing the Truth

ANOTHER item of news to which we were treated was an account of a speech by Sir Thomas Inskip, the Minister for Defence, who blamed the microphone for the existence of dictators, and said that "wireless was a contributory factor to the unsettled state of the world."

Apparently, what worried our would-be dictator, Sir Thomas Inskip, was the fact that, because of the invention of the microphone, a statement could now be addressed personally to the whole of the inhabitants of a country by its leader so that he could tell them personally exactly what was happening; whereas in a democratic country, in which there is a so-called free Press, a politician makes a speech and then the various newspapers cut it up, alter it, and edit it to fit their own particular views.

It has been clearly demonstrated, both in Italy and Germany, that by the use of radio the Prime Minister of the country could unite the whole of that country for its own good. I admit that in a democratic country like our own radio can and does do a tremendous lot of harm by spreading false doctrines and subversive propaganda, but that is not quite what Sir Thomas meant.

Certainly it is all to the disadvantage of such politicians as Sir Thomas that radio is in existence, and the coming of television will be still worse. Anybody who has seen the film made by Sir Thomas Inskip, in which he drivels a lot of platitudes with set and expressionless face, will agree that sound radio and television are never likely to do him and others of similar kidney any good whatever. Not until the British Union comes into power in this country is radio likely to be used for the real benefit of the State.

Flowers

AND now, strangely enough, we have a few bouquets to present to the B.B.C.

The general standard of entertainment this week has been far higher than at any time since the Jubilee celebrations. The outstanding event was the presentation of "Cavalcade." I saw neither the play nor the film of this, neither did I hear its previous broadcasts; but it certainly impressed me very much, just as it must have depressed Mr. Siepmann of the B.B.C. and his gang, who have shown such a dislike of Imperial sentiment.

The cast throughout was brilliant, and the whole cavalcade of scenes was made to live. Particularly good was the scene in the theatre when an act was stopped and the manager rushed on to the stage and announced the relief of Mafeking. The gasp of the audience, followed by the swelling cheering, coming with realisation, was one of the finest dramatic moments I have ever heard on the radio. The final scene, in which Mrs. Marryott drinks the famous toast that "This country which we love so much shall find dignity, peace, and greatness once again," must have found a sympathetic echo in many Fascist homes.

This broadcast has already been given four times. It might well be repeated on Armistice Sunday, as it would be difficult to find a more suitable Sunday evening broadcast for such an occasion.

Interesting People

ON Saturday evening "In Town To-night" was revived for the fourth year. Let us hope that they will keep up the standard which was set for this first broadcast, and on many occasions exceed it. I realise that the success of this item depends on getting hold of important people and interesting people who happen to be in town, and they must be there to be got.

I would suggest that the B.B.C. might get hold of some of the Blackshirt speakers who have been talking all over the country, and particularly in the East End of London, and ask them to recount their experiences in standing up as Britons in the streets of Britain. But, perhaps, Mr. Siepmann would not like this.

What we want to avoid is having simpering film stars giving cheap advertisements for their films. Let us, in this new series, have really interesting people and not mere nonentities who have their script obviously written for them by the B.B.C.

New Serial

A NEW form of serial began on Saturday, which is far more satisfactory than those we have previously heard, in that each item is complete on its own, though there is to be a thread of continuity joining them all. It is called "The Palaver Is Finished," and is adapted from the Edgar Wallace stories of Mr. Commissioner Sanders and Lieutenant Bones, which were among the best and most famous of all Edgar Wallace's stories. If the remainder are up to the standard of Saturday night this will be an item to which everybody will listen.

"Music Hall" came on last week rather later than usual, from 9.20 to 10.20, immediately following the third news. This innovation is to be commended because recently the Saturday programmes have petered out into dullness by about half-past nine. What we want on Saturday is a sustained programme from about four o'clock to midnight, and last Saturday we certainly got it.

Outstanding in this "Music Hall" programme, I thought, were Elsie and Doris Waters, who are always topical and always funny.

Henry Hall, in his hour, for the third time introduced Oliver Wakefield into his programme. I strongly recommend everybody to listen to him; he is certainly one of the funniest comedians that one ever hears on the radio or anywhere else.

ANOTHER CONSERVATIVE OFFICIAL TURNS FASCIST

Mrs. Whinfield, for many years chairman of the Alton Women's Branch of the East Hants Conservative and Unionist Association, has resigned from the party and joined the British Union.

In a letter to the association announcing her resignation, she wrote that she no longer could see her way to support a Government whose policy was international in everything but name.

LANCASHIRE BUSINESS MEN'S LUNCHEON

Important Statement by SIR OSWALD MOSLEY

MANCHESTER, the city which, according to its City Council, finds the black shirt worn by members of the British Union provocative, gave the Union's Leader, Sir Oswald Mosley, a splendid reception last week, writes our Northern Correspondent. I wonder if the City Council's deputation, which is to meet the Home Secretary next week and urge legislation against the wearing of the black shirt, will tell Sir John Simon anything about the luncheon at the Victoria Hotel last Friday, when two hundred Lancashire business men met Sir Oswald and vigorously applauded his eloquent and outspoken reply to criticisms of the British Union.

The company at the luncheon was much more representative of Manchester and its people than the puppet politicians on its City Council, and to argue that the black shirt is provocative in Manchester is, in face of such a gathering, nothing but a wilful misrepresentation of the facts.

Some of the Business Men at Manchester. The arrow shows Sir Oswald Mosley.

Who Causes Disorder?

IN his speech at the luncheon, Sir Oswald stressed the fact that disorder only takes place at a very small percentage of the Union's meetings.

"I say without fear of contradiction," he declared, "there has never been any disorder at a public meeting of ours unless that disorder has been deliberately organised.

"It is not the public who make the disorder. In Leeds and London on the last two Sundays men were brought from all over Great Britain by train and by motor-coaches for the express purpose of attacking our meetings.

"It is now becoming a commonplace to have stone-throwing, and, beyond that, to have the use of catapults, which, at short range, are as dangerous as the use of bullets; to have the use of iron bars and the use of scythes.

"And our men are forbidden to use anything but their bare fists in their defence.

"The men imported to create disorder at our meetings," he continued, "bear names utterly foreign and alien to Great Britain. Printed incitements to violence are circulated as a preliminary to such attacks.

"Suppose the members of the British Union acted like that in regard to one of Mr. Neville Chamberlain's meetings. How long should we be out of gaol? Not for twenty-four hours! Yet the Socialist and Communist forces of this country have a free charter to do any of these things, and deliberately, like a military operation, with maps published in their newspapers, show how to attack the meeting by organised violence on British citizens."

In the past, said Sir Oswald, their opponents had ridiculed the black shirt. Now they spoke of it as a wicked and provocative thing.

The Choice of Clothes

"ARE we really to have it laid down in Great Britain that a man might not wear the clothes he wishes to wear? If that is the view of Parliament, then let Parliament have the courage to translate its opinion into law. Meantime, a Socialist has no more right to throw a brick at a Fascist whose clothes he dislikes than I have to throw one at Alderman Joseph Toole because I find his appearance unpleasant and provocative; or to deliver a heavy blow on the jaw of Mr. Baldwin for wearing, in Downing-street the detestable top-hat and frock-coat that symbolises a Victorian mugwumpery offensive to any decent-thinking Englishman.

"Why should Sir John Simon or Mr. Joseph Toole imply, though they do not say it directly, that, because we wear clothes the Socialists do not like, they are entitled to assault us, and that the blame is on us for wearing those clothes?"

Sir Oswald answered a large number of questions dealing with the subject of organised opposition at British Union meetings, and also on the Blackshirt policy for India and the Lancashire trade. When the luncheon concluded, it was obvious that the majority of the guests were favourably impressed with Sir Oswald's speech and many requests were made for literature and further information.

The luncheon, arranged many weeks ago, could not have occurred at a more opportune time to give the lie to the allegations of Blackshirt provocation in the cotton capital.

MUSICAL ESSAY IN THE MACABRE

BEECHAM and BERLIOZ

THE programme of Sir Thomas Beecham's concert at the Royal Opera House, Covent Garden, on Sunday afternoon, included Berlioz's Fantastic Symphony, "Episode in the Life of an Artist."

This work, conceived in an age of emotional extravagance, has found in Beecham its ideal interpreter. For those unacquainted with the Symphony, it will be useful to recall that it is the outcome of Berlioz's passion for Henrietta Smithson, the celebrated Shakespearean actress of the early nineteenth century.

It was the young composer's original intention to honour the lady with this work, but before it was begun she rejected him. Berlioz thereupon executed a complete *volte face*, and the Symphony was designed "to accomplish her discomfiture." In this form it was first performed. Miss Smithson recanted and became Mme. Berlioz, and the Symphony was recast as a paean in her praise.

Nevertheless, it remains an essay in the macabre with the "Artist" tortured by doubts and nightmares, and terrified by a march to the scaffold, and a witches' sabbath.

Beecham revelled in the work, and the London Philharmonic Orchestra responded by curdling our blood and entrancing us by turns. The ballroom scene can scarcely ever have been better played. Great music though it is, this Symphony requires the interpretative powers of a Beecham if it is to be kept in shape.

Ovation For British Composer

EARLIER in the afternoon we had heard, during the course of a generous programme, a new Oboe Concerto by the modern Italian Ticciati, and the Suite "Façade" by the modern Englishman, William Walton.

The Concerto, a slight and agreeable work, was played by Leon Goossens, while the trenchant wit of Mr. Walton's Suite was subtly underlined by Beecham—the man whom nothing escapes.

"Façade" is a succession of parodied dance forms. After ten years it loses none of its freshness; its sharp tang lingers on the palate, and each hearing leaves one somewhat bewildered by the demonic cleverness of Mr. Walton. The composer was present and received an ovation.

It has been stated that a concert by Sir Thomas Beecham is unique among Europe's music-making. Music lovers will be glad to know that Beecham concerts will be given at Covent Garden on most Sunday afternoons during the winter, and admission may be obtained from as little as one shilling.—S. W.

EAST LONDON REPLIES TO RED INVASION

Margaret Collins describes last Sunday's Stirring Events

OUTSIDE THE PARK

On every corner and for a mile along Grove-road the pavements were lined with indignant British workers. Tens of thousands of hands shot up in the Fascist salute as the Jewish Red procession was greeted with "Hail, Mosley!" and the National Anthem

FOLLOWING the ban of the Mosley march on October 4, the Communist Party announced its intention of holding a "victory" march in East London, to celebrate the denial of free speech.

The comrades, with red flags flying, marched down from Tower Hill to Victoria Park, E. They had a quiet passage through their native areas of Whitechapel, but when they reached the British East End their reception was very different. A crowd of many thousands lined the pavements near Victoria Park. Nearly everyone was wearing red, white, and blue ribbons in their buttonholes, and many people carried Union Jacks.

While they waited for the contingent, the crowd exchanged good-humoured chaff with the police. The men in blue knew they were safe with this crowd—British workers do not build barricades and attack the police with iron bars.

There was a sound of drums, and a motley throng poured over the bridge. One could hardly see the demonstrators for police, and scores of police-cars and mounted policemen guarded them at every step.

Behind the police was the oddest assortment ever let loose on British streets. It seemed as though every Jew from Whitechapel was there, and the rest of the contingent consisted of niggers, low-grade white women, and the ineffectuals from Bloomsbury who minced along, their lily white hands raised in the Communist salute.

Insulting the Flag

AT first the crowd was amiable, but the next minute their temper was roused. Four Union Jacks appeared, carried by four greasy aliens, who raised their hands in the Communist salute when they heard the white people singing patrotic songs. Behind the British flag waved the Red flag of Moscow.

The expression on the faces of the demonstrators was instructive—apart from the natives of Whitechapel (who know the feelings of British workers in East London) —the majority of the crowd had obviously never been in the East End. They had always been told that it was their stronghold, but their experience proved different as they straggled through massed ranks of British workers, whose reception gave them a clear idea of their unpopularity. Not one hand was raised in the Red-Front salute, not a cheer echoed from the thousands present: instead, there was one roar of condemnation, and above all rang out the strains of 'Rule, Britannia!"

Pawnbrokers' Heroes

AFTER a short time, the Red Front gave up in despair and proceeded to waddle out of the park, amid the derisive laughter of East End workers. Particularly noticeable were the young Jews (some not older than twenty-five) wearing medals. This is becoming so much of a farce that a Northern paper remarked the other day that youths of about twenty had been seen wearing Boer War and Crimea medals.

Another point that struck East London as funny was the presence of smart young women in leopard-skin coats, who raised expensively-gloved hands in the Moscow salute, chanting, "Workers of the world unite." East London took one look at these "workers" and burst into roars of laughter. The comparison between these luxuriously-dressed "workers" and the East End women, ill-clad, their voices raised in cries of "God Save the King!" was striking.

As they shuffled out of Bethnal Green the workers of the East End gave them a last derisive cheer. The Communists—whose usual practice is to straggle as wide apart as possible, to give an impression of numbers—crowded up together, terrified at being left by themselves. As they huddled together, escorted by hundreds of police, East London gave them a warm send-off:

"Don't come here again! You're not wanted in Bethnal Green!"

"Why don't you fight for Palestine?—and bring our boys back from there?"

The Gutter Flag

ONE significant fact was the capture of a red flag by a British boy. This Moscow flag was dragged through the gutter, amid the cheers of the crowd.

Later in the evening there was slight trouble in the East End. This, though regrettable, was understandable in view of the fact that the news had come through that three young British fellows had been slashed with Jewish razors. Even, then, this was nothing when one remembers the faces of the East End workers as they had to watch the insults to their King and country, and saw the Red rabble allowed to march through their own British streets.

But in spite of this great provocation, the British workers restrained themselves. It is against their tradition to copy the tactics of the Reds, who last Sunday were assaulting policemen and this Sunday were cowering behind police protection.

BRITISH UNION HEADQUARTERS SET ON FIRE

Grave Danger to Sleeping Family

Shortly before three o'clock on Tuesday morning, while the residents of Green-street were asleep, a call of "Fire!" from the street awakened them to find that a deliberate attempt had been made to set fire to the local headquarters of the British Union.

A girl, who was an eye-witness, says she was awakened by a screech of brakes and saw a car drawn up outside the British Union headquarters.

"I saw two men jump out, and as they seemed to be intent on breaking into the building I ran down shouting for help.

"The men threw something from a can and with a sudden roar a sheet of flame jumped up from the pavement. I ran in front of the car, trying to see its number, but they jumped in and started up the motor and I had to jump back as they shot forward."

Another resident who was awakened by the commotion endeavoured to jump on the running-board of the car, but was hit on the head with a heavy spanner.

The entrance to the Headquarters is through a wooden door leading through a little alley to the premises. Above is the bedroom of Mr. R. Cenci, who was asleep with his wife and three-years-old son; when they awoke they found a solid wall of flame licking round the window.

In an all-night café opposite a young man saw the men set fire to the door and he dashed across the road, forced his way into Mr. Cenci's house, and helped the frightened couple to escape. He carried the little boy down into the street and vanished into the crowd which had collected.

Other eye-witness accounts have been given to police officers who are investigating the matter and to Mr. E. G. Clark, the local officer of the British Union.

The men, who are believed to have been Jews, drove up in a dark green Ford. They attempted to smash their way through the door leading to the headquarters. But when disturbed smashed a can of petrol on the door and set fire to it, before making their escape.—H. G.

SOME SPECIMENS

Here are a few random photographs of the Red marchers. The procession was overwhelmingly alien and proved the British Union contention that without the Jews there would be no Communist Party in Britain

EDITORIAL OFFICES—
SANCTUARY BUILDINGS,
GREAT SMITH STREET,
LONDON S.W.1.
Telephone: Victoria 9084 (five lines)
Editor: JOHN BECKETT

THE YELLOW PRESS

WHATEVER decency and sobriety the national Press ever possessed have been completely submerged in their accounts of the happenings in East London during the last two week-ends. Last Sunday's papers, particularly the *Sunday Express* and the *Referee*, carried stories of East London which not only were outrages upon public decency, but relied entirely upon the hope that their readers would be incapable of remembering from one day to another what had occurred. In these articles we read of the Fascist terror in East London, and of the hideous atrocities which Blackshirt sympathisers were committing upon a peaceful and orderly Jewish population.

This in spite of the fact that on the previous Sunday rioting had occurred in East London in which nearly one hundred policemen were injured and without a Blackshirt being anywhere near the occurrences. Out of fifty-three arrests made by the police, no fewer than thirty-eight of the people charged with disorder possessed Jewish names.

On Sunday, October 4, the Jews of East London, aided by thousands of imported hooligans, tore up streets, overturned motor-cars, and created a condition of civil riot in which the police were admittedly unable to secure the peaceful progress of a procession of British people to a British political meeting. By Wednesday we were being regaled in our newspapers with blood-curdling accounts of the way the poor Jews were being treated, and the Jewish Socialist Mayoress of Stepney was petitioning for more policemen to be sent into East London.

Comment seems to be superfluous. These peaceful Jewish people terrorise the district, treat the policemen who are sent to protect them as Aunt Sallies, and then wail pitifully for increased police protection.

The whole thing is a contemptible ramp, and anyone who knows the history of Jewish-Communist violence and terrorism over the past few years may well wonder what sinister influences are at work to compel the national Press to attempt to cover it up in this way.

OCTOBER 11

LAST Sunday the "heroes" of October 4 held a "Victory" demonstration, in which they boasted that they would show that they could have an orderly procession over the same route that the British Union had not been allowed to cover. In other words, the people who had created the disorder the previous Sunday proposed to give occular demonstration that when they themselves were marching there was no Fascist terror such as they have alleged to exist.

They held their march, and there was not one single instance of violence being offered to them or to their police escort, in spite of the fact that, except when they were in the Mile End Ghetto, their route was lined with thousands of indignant British workers.

Here, if anywhere, was the most intense provocation. On October 4 a predominantly Jewish crowd refused British people the right to walk through the streets of the capital. On October 11 they had the impudence to hold a "Victory" march in which those same Jews who had refused British citizens the right to pass, paraded the streets.

The public cannot be cursed with such a short memory that it will not distinguish between the behaviour of the two races.

THE "VICTORY" PROCESSION

WE personally had the pleasure of seeing the Communist march. It is a very conservative underestimate to say that at least 65 per cent. of the marchers were unmistakably Jewish. The chief proof the march afforded was that if the Jewish people were denied the privilege of interfering in British politics, then there would be no Communist party in this country.

Probably the most outrageous statement made in the Monday morning newspapers was that of the *Daily Telegraph*. The proprietors of the *Daily Telegraph* claim to produce a dignified, moderate, Conservative newspaper, yet they say in their account of the demonstration that it was headed by 3,000 ex-Servicemen carrying Union Jacks.

At the parade in Royal Mint-street and at different parts of the route, we paid particular attention to the ex-Servicemen's contingent marching with "an Oriental attempt at a military swagger" in the front of the procession. The entire assembly was computed by the police to be under 5,000 and the so-called ex-Servicemen's contingent was not very much more than thirty strong.

A military officer of many years' experience who surveyed them at the beginning writes to say that it was the strangest collection of ex-Servicemen he ever saw in his life. "Most of them, even quite young boys, were wearing war ribbons. In one case, the Indian General Service Medal, with the 1919 class, was being worn in front of the 1914-15 Star. In another case, a rosette was being worn on the ribbon of the 1914-15 Star, although the medal beneath it had no class."

In two cases we noticed personally that war ribbons were being worn upside down, with the 1914 ribbon on the wrong side of the chest. We say advisedly that half these medals came from the pawnbrokers, and that the names on them never matched the picturesque name of the gentlemen who were wearing them.

Tens of thousands of patriotic British workers watched this motley procession carrying the Union Jack and the Red Flag in insulting proximity. Right through the British section of the route the marchers were greeted with the singing of the National Anthem, and thousands of hands raised in the Fascist salute.

Yet the newspapers would have us believe that there is no difference between Communism and Fascism.

AN OVERLOADED PROFESSION

I am a young unemployed teacher, one of a band whose numbers grow greater year by year.

Many of us have spent four or five years at the university risking and, by virtue of hard work, passing exams. We have had little money, but plenty of hope that we would find some-sort of employment in the teaching profession at the end of our course.

Now, in this year of grace, we find the door has been slammed on us. The reasons for this are:—

(1) Democratic Governments are flooding the universities every year with hundreds of fresh students. These Governments pay no regard to the small demand which will be made on this overwhelming supply of teachers when they are through their course.

(2) Many Local Education Authorities are corrupt. Influence with governors of schools and members of committees count for more than a high academic degree—a thing which has to be experienced to be believed.

(3) The competition for degrees resultant on the great supply of students, means that otherwise quite fair L.E.A.s can call the tune. Only graduates with a high academic degree are considered, and the rest, however efficient as teachers, can go to the dogs.

Was it not intellectual unemployed who gave democracy its final push over the precipice in Germany?

Democracy will surely fall in Britain, too. Because:—

(1) It is inefficient and sloppy. It talks instead of getting on with the job (vide any history of education!).

(2) It has no plan, no organised method of attack on acute problems.

(3) It has no sense of responsibility.

(4) It has no leader capable of inspiring youth.

(5) It is expensive.

Will Mosley sweep away these puppets at Westminster before they make an irretrievable mess of things?

I would be interested to know if there is any other reader of *Action* in the same position as myself.

FIRST CLASS HONOURS (Lond.).

CORRESPONDENCE

THE GOVERNMENT'S SURRENDER

I heard with utter astonishment, on the wireless on Sunday, the decision of the Commissioner of Police to ban the march of the British Union of Fascists which was to have taken place earlier in the day. It would appear that to leave the final decision in regard to the march to the Commissioner of Police was the only way out for the Government to satisfy the craving of the Jews and Communists and their alien associates and leaders to stifle one of the very few remaining traditions of the British people, namely, the freedom of speech.

The pleas of the various deputations to the Home Office and local mayors were never intended to be disregarded by the present pseudo-National Government, and although the Home Office apparently dare not show the country that they were in agreement with the Russian theory of preventing one's opponent from stating his case, they knew they had a trump-card in the Commissioner of Police, and thus the march would be banned in accordance with Jewish wishes.

Truly, the decay of England is setting in rapidly.

Where it is the wish of the Jews, who, numerically speaking, are a minority of the population, that the Englishman shall be deprived of his rights, the Government cannot, or dare not, say "No!"

We are taught, through the medium of our daily papers, which you have so admirably shown to be Jewish controlled, that the annihilation of opposition is common to German and Italian Fascism only, and that it is one of the birthrights of the British people to be able to express their opinions on any matters, openly and freely, subject always to the operation of the laws of libel, slander, and sedition.

Are we now to expect an announcement to the effect that this privilege has at last been withheld from all Britons? I think not.

The position at the present time indicates that this state of affairs virtually exists, although we shall probably be led to believe that this right may still be exercised. This will certainly be true in a measure, but such a statement will have to be qualified by the remark that the privilege is to be enjoyed only by the Jews and their allies, the Communists.

I must say that the statement issued by the British Union of Fascists shortly after the banning of the meeting was an excellent one, and its message should have a stirring effect on true Britons.

What would the great national heroes of the days of our grandfathers and great-grandfathers think of the Empire to-day—the Empire for which, in a number of cases, they laid down their lives? The battles they fought and won have, quite unbeknown to them, resulted, not in the advancement of the welfare of the British people, but in the glorification of the Jew.

Why is the Briton always subordinate in the eyes of those in authority to the foreigner? Will nothing ever be done by the ruling party from time to time to give preference to Britons?

E. CLARKE.

RED BRUTALITY

In to-day's issue of *Action* mention is made of a car charging into our procession last Sunday afternoon when we were returning to headquarters. One of our Blackshirts was injured in the process.

I should like to point out that one of our women members, a very young and very pretty child, up for the march from, I think, Southampton, also was injured and bleeding quite freely from a head wound. Being extremely brave, she made scarcely any fuss about the whole matter, and together we staunched the bleeding with handkerchiefs. Her bearing and courage were admirable all through, and I should like to draw the attention of the British Union to this gallant young victim of Communist violence.

(Mrs.) HASTINGS BONORA.
14, Queen's-gate, S.W.7.

ONWARD

I think that Sir Philip Game, as Chief Commissioner of the Metropolitan Police, acted in the best of interests on Sunday, but, of course, it just "shows up" the weakness of the present British Government.

Only a few weeks ago Trafalgar-square witnessed some terrible speeches made on behalf of the Spanish Reds, and the London Police allowed a procession which was composed of many foreigners, so-called English Jews, and wasters to march through the capital of King Edward's fine city.

If the British Government would act in a straightforward manner and clear all the foreigners out of the East End of London they would be highly praised by every true Englishman.

You will win in the end because all loyal citizens are behind you and watch your progress with great interest.

Germany, Italy, and other countries had to fight for freedom from the Jews, and to-day they are clean, law-abiding countries.

The British Government are making England look cheap in Palestine to-day, and all the good work done by Colonel Lawrence and Lord Allenby is being ruined—just for the sake of the Jews. The Arab is a good man and a friend of Britain, but we are told he must give up some of his land to the Jews.

Some say it will mean a world war against the coloured races.

Fascism can stop it. Amalgamate with Hitler and Mussolini. Shake hands with Germany and turn Mr. Haile Selassie out of England.

Let us be British, for God's sake. We want another great man like Kitchener.

Onward, Christian Soldiers!

Hendon. E. ROBSON.

"ACTION" FOR FASCIST NEWS

I would like to congratulate you and your staff on the excellence of this week's issue of your paper, *Action*. News of Fascism in Great Britain is always welcome to those who are interested in the welfare of their country—and I am certain that this week all readers must be more than satisfied.

Sunday's march and subsequent happenings gives much credit to the Blackshirts, and surely police court convictions in connection with the anti-Fascist rally have proved even to the most apathetic of English people, to what race these Communists and real enemies of the British people belong. The good wishes of hundreds of thousands of sincere patriots go with you to your final triumph.

A. R. H

HAIL! MOSLEY

I witnessed the events in the East End where I went to hear Sir Oswald Mosley state his case. I was dumbfounded when I heard that his meetings had been banned, notwithstanding they had been announced many weeks beforehand.

I was also baffled to see processions of Jews and Communists, who later on held meetings which were planned about one day after as a counter-demonstration. I heard the rabble threaten "that Mosley was not going to hold his meeting," and that they were going to prevent it. I saw them throw stones at the few Fascists who went to the pitches to explain that there was going to be no meeting.

But I have yet to know why your meeting was not, and the Communists were, allowed. I will not say that the mob rules in England, but I have an impression that it did on that memorable October 4.

I trust that Sir Oswald Mosley will go ahead and organise other meetings. I am sure it will not dismay him to have suffered such terrible injustice. At any rate, from now on he has my sympathy!

F. L. SLAVENBURY.

B.B.C. COMMUNIST PROPAGANDA

I attach hereto a reply that I have received from the B.B.C. to a letter of mine objecting to the Red propaganda contained in the play, "The Sailors of Cattaro," which I described as "an insult to His Majesty the King on the eve of his Coronation."

It is, perhaps, significant that, while I was formerly a fairly frequent broadcaster, as my sympathies with the B.U.F. have become known I have received no contract since last May.

You are at unrestricted liberty to make whatever use you like of this letter and enclosure.

CUTHBERT REAVELY.

Dear Sir,—Sir John Reith has asked me to thank you for your recent letter about "The Sailors of Cattaro." No doubt you heard the microphone announcement, which on both occasions preceded the broadcast of this play, and in which our reasons for including the work in our programme were given. I am afraid that we have little to add to this announcement, except perhaps to emphasise that it was certainly not our intention to broadcast the play for any purpose of propaganda. The play was selected purely on its artistic merits.

We are sorry, however, that this broadcast should have displeased you.—Yours faithfully,

THE BRITISH BROADCASTING CORPORATION
(*signed*) R. W. P. Cockburn,
for Controller (Public Relations).

ILL-MANNERED JEWS

The exceptionally noticeable rude and ill-mannered behaviour of Jews is well-illustrated by the following conversation which I overheard in a Jew barber's in Richmond.

The barber asked the customer, an elderly gentleman, if he would like a shampoo. The customer said he was sorry he hadn't time, and added, as an afterthought, "By the way, what is the time?"

The Jew promptly replied, "Vell, vat time do you vant it to be?" After asking the Jew whether he always spoke to his clients like that, the customer got up and left, and I don't suppose he will go back.

The Jews, by their rude, pushing, and uncivil behaviour, have been asking for trouble for years, and, while I do not advocate violence, the present time is an unusually opportune one for a concerted movement to put them in their place.

Richmond. ACTIONARY.

TRY THEM FOR TREASON

Congratulate you sincerely on your most excellent issue of October 10, consequent on the Bolshevik display at Tower Hill.

Can't we arrest the "leaders" of the Moscow rabble, try them for treason, and punish according to law?

T. ERNEST HILL.
13, Fernhurst-road, Croydon.

TRUST

When the first Lord Swaythling (formerly . . . adopted name Montagu) died, after a parliamentary career and an amassed fortune made possible by too trusting British citizens, it was found that his will disinherited any of his children who married Christians.

Another parliamentary Jew millionaire, Sir Charles Henry, who married one of the Lewisohns, and came into the House of Commons with the two Brunners, Alfred Mond, the two Schwanns, and others in 1906, went one better than Swaythling. A Christian turned Jew to marry Swaythling's son, so Sir Charles Henry made a will disinheriting any children of his who married anyone not born in the Jewish faith.

BELL-THE-CAT.

TAKE ACTION

I am writing this letter in lieu of filling in the questionnaire which you published in last week's *Action*.

I have discussed the matter with several friends, and we are all agreed that it would be difficult to improve a most excellent publication—which it is now.

In our opinion the motto should be "Carry on with the good work as heretofore," and the "castles" of Socialism and Financial Democracy will collapse from the sheer lack of defences.

In passing, permit me to congratulate Sir Oswald Mosley on his lucid explanation of the "franc racket," and no less for his almost uncanny forecast of the state of affairs in connection with it, so early as June last.

We suspected there was a "catch" in it somewhere when we read of the formidable array of international financiers who engineered the business.

Kindly note that my name is not for publication. Need I enumerate the reason?

SALFORD.

SPREADING THE GOSPEL

I have just wired for a quire of this week's *Action;* everyone of these will be posted to prominent people. About ten copies will go overseas.

J. P. J. CHAPMAN.

THE TRUTH EMERGES

BOYCOTT AND VIOLENCE DEFEATED

OSWALD MOSLEY SUMS UP AN HISTORICAL FOUR YEARS

FOUR years of struggle lie behind us; four years of Blackshirt heroism surmounting every material force the old world could muster. The fifth year begins and our enemies rage. *The measure of their fury is the measure of our advance.* Just over four years ago this Movement consisted of some forty men meeting in a small upstairs room. We had neither Press, money, nor resources. We had nothing but the spirit within us and the will to save Britain. Such was that spirit and such was that will that to-day we alone are the challenger for Power and all the Old Parties are huddled together in the same camp with but one object—to avert our victory. They have used every weapon in their corrupt armoury to stem our advance. They have followed the classic course of Financial-Democratic parties in the struggle to resist Fascism and National Socialism in all countries. They began with ridicule and affected contempt. They said Britain was no place for the creed of the modern world. Other nations might be active, but it was the eternal prerogative of Britain to be lazy. Other nations might be modern, but it was our character to be obsolete. Every country on earth might adopt the method and absorb the spirit of the new world, but Britain would cling ever to the old world. To the spiritual appeal of a new and mighty age Britain alone was immune.

An orderly march of Blackshirts with their colour party carrying the Union Jack. The old parties consider that this is provocative

THE politicians aptly described their own character, but they libelled the character of the British people and belied the history of a dynamic nation. So in the first phase their propaganda shrieked that any attempt to get anything done in Britain was merely ridiculous. Our force and our faith to them was contemptible; as contemptible as the British Army was in the eyes of the Kaiser in 1914. In particular, our novel methods of propaganda, which have been so largely responsible for public attention to our case and the rapidity of our subsequent advance, were derided in the early phase as an absurdity which would never attract any following in Britain. The black shirt, which to-day is a symbol of heroism and sacrifice to so many thousands of British people, was to be treated as a joke. The idea of wearing it was held to be fatal to our already slight prospects of success. It is a commentary on the psychological errors of our opponents that their jest of yesterday is now held to be such a menace to their system, and indeed is represented by them as such a danger to the stability of the State that they contemplate immediate legislation to repress it!

A Smile That Slipped

THE grin at any rate soon faded from the sickly features of Financial Democracy. The second phase of their attack was equally characteristic and followed the same classic course of Financial Democratic futility. The second phase was the boycott, and in Parliament and Press the simple rule was followed that Fascism must not be mentioned. So the school-girl giggle was succeeded by the mute hostility of the old gentleman who finds retreat into the stilted dignity of silence a safer course than argument and the battle of wits. They attempted the eternal but ever futile answer of senescence to victorious youth. Again the boycott broke down because thousands of British people flocked to our meetings to hear a new case with an appeal which pierced complacency and roused both memory and prospect of national greatness.

So the third phase began which brands with indelible disgrace the hypocrisy of Financial Democracy. Red violence was let loose with Conservative connivance. The simple plan of action was adopted which I long ago described as: "The Reds do the fighting and the Tories do the lying." Red hooligans attacked our meetings with organised violence, and Red violence was overcome by Blackshirt discipline. But Conservatives, who were familiar with that violence because they had long before surrendered to it, suddenly ceased to condemn it. When disorder took place at Blackshirt meetings because Reds attacked them, Conservatives were at pains to explain that it was all the fault of the Blackshirts. Fascists were stated to hold meetings only for the purpose of provoking trouble. Halls were hired and were filled with thousands of the British public only for the purpose of assaulting the lot of them. We held meetings not to convert our fellow-countrymen, but solely for the strange pleasure of "beating them up." Again, our opponents fell into a psychological error. In the first place, they failed to note that in the course of time hundreds of thousands of the British people had witnessed for themselves exactly what happened at our meetings.

Failure of Falsehood

THEY had seen audiences assemble in their thousands to hear our case and they had seen Reds assemble in their dozens to prevent them hearing that case. They had applauded when these hooligans were ejected from the hall. In the second place, our Conservative opponents had been encouraged by the success of some of their past propaganda to ignore the fact that some lies are too gross to be believed. The average Englishman replies to the charge of Fascist "provocation," that any man who really hired a hall and filled it with an audience merely for the purpose of provoking and assaulting them is a lunatic. Any mind so deranged would be certified immediately by any two competent doctors and Democracy's problem would thus be easily resolved!

It was too tall a story to ask the Public to believe that Fascists were guilty of deliberately creating disorder at their own meetings. Further the Public were aware that at the vast majority of British Union meetings no disorder occurred at all. In fact, disorder never has occurred at our meetings except when it has been highly organised in complete defiance of the existing law of the country which has never yet been enforced by Government when Fascists were the victims of violence deliberately incited by criminals whose identity was clear.

Such have been the three phases of Financial Democratic attack on the new faith of a new age: (1) Ridicule; the grin soon faded. (2) Boycott; their silence soon broke into angry yelps. (3) Red violence and blue lies; they have so far thought of no better methods than the last but they lose the game.

The only method they have never tried is to meet argument with argument, fact with fact, and reason with reason. They have never tried that method because they dare not and they cannot. Who doubts that our case would have been answered if it could be answered? Who, among our opponents, has even attempted to meet our case in argument? Why dare none of their Leaders meet us in public debate? Are all of them even incapable of replying from their own platforms in detailed refutation of the argument we urge? What answer have they ever given to the British Union case or to the Blackshirt spirit except the brickbat and the razor of red violence supported by the unctuous hypocrisy of a Conservatism which declares that to be assassinated is to be provocative?

What is Provocation ?

WHEREIN does our provocation consist? We have greatly dared to say to our fellow countrymen that a necessity for action in Britain exists. We have dared to say that poverty is unnecessary in an age wherein science has solved the problem of production and endowed mankind with potential wealth. We have dared to contend that the British Empire was a heritage handed to us by heroism, not for neglect or surrender but for retention and development. We have greatly dared to expose the corrupt interests which prevent that development. We have advanced a National policy for National salvation. We have appealed to the British people to be themselves and again to "dare to be great." So great are our crimes, and worthy only of the razor and judicial rebuke. But greater now is the disillusion of our enemies. For they believed that all of the people can be fooled all the time. They thought that any lie their millionaire Press cared to tell would be believed always by the people. Because the great toleration of the British people has permitted this vast corruption so long to exist they deluded themselves that they could get away with anything for ever. They are wrong, because there is a limit even to the good humour of the English. They are wrong because they seek to trick not only an intelligent but a brave and determined people. They will fail because they are faced at last by a spirit they can neither comprehend nor combat. They are faced by a reincarnation of the spirit that has taken a conquering race forth from this small island to fill the world with its name and its glory. For in dark hours the best and finest of the British spirit has always risen from the dust and marched against

Mosley watching his Blackshirts marching to a great East London meeting

great odds to the ever greater expression and achievement of the British race.

Such is the history of the Blackshirt Movement which reflects and embodies the history of the British people. So with history behind it and destiny within it, this mighty movement gathers strength from tempest and marches on to the triumph which high Fate ordains for men and women who care only for their country.

Mosley, at Leeds, addressing a huge crowd on Holbeck Moor. He had to contend with a crowd of imported Red hooligans armed with catapults, knives, razors, and other weapons, who objected to the doctrine "Britain First"

UNDER THE CONTROL TOWER

JEAN BATTEN'S RECORD

But She Should Not Cross the Tasman Sea

By BLACKBIRD

CONGRATULATIONS to Miss Jean Batten on her magnificent feat in flying from England to Australia in five days twenty-one hours, thereby beating the record for the quickest solo flight between the two countries.

Actually, the record for the fastest time was made by Scott and Black in 1934, during the Australian race, when they covered the distance in just under two days. Scott's record will take a lot of beating, and is likely to stand for a long time; but the solo record is one that appeals to the imagination of many people, because it is usually attempted on an ordinary type of touring machine which can be bought "off the peg" so to speak, whereas Scott's record was done on a specially built racing machine.

A Sensible Ban

SOME time ago the Australian authorities very sensibly frowned on single engine aeroplanes making this hazardous flight. Many lives have already been lost in attempting this crossing, so that it is hoped that Miss Batten will not be allowed to risk her life on so foolish an adventure. She has proved her courage and her ability as an aviator by her magnificent flight. No possible good to herself or aviation generally would be attained by her proposed hazardous flight.

It is proving nothing to fly across 1,100 miles of sea in a single engined land machine unequipped with wireless. When this route is opened as a commercial position, which it will be no doubt soon, it will be operated by multi-engined flying boats equipped with wireless. Under such conditions it should be perfectly safe. If Miss Batten were to attempt the flight and were to fail it would do untold harm to aviation, for she has already become a public figure and her loss would only impress people with the dangers of aviation, and her success could only be looked upon as a stunt.

Miss Jean Batten's Percival Gull in which she has broken the England—Australia record

The solo record was "invented" by the late Bert Hinkler. In 1920, when the Australian route was full of hazards, Bert Hinkler astonished the world by announcing that he was going to attempt the flight on a 35 h.p. Baby Avro. He flew, on his first lap, from London to Turin non-stop.

First Low-powered Flight

THIS flight, which was easily a record at the time, opened people's eyes to the possibilities of long-distance flights on low-powered machines. However, on this occasion, he got no further than Rome because trouble had broken out in Irak, through which he had to pass, and the British Government banned all civil flights over the route.

It was some years before he tried again, and in 1928 he started off on an Avro Avian, with an 80 h.p. Cirrus engine, on a record flight to Australia.

The existing record at that time was twenty-eight days which was made by Ross and Keith Smith in 1920. Bert Hinkler succeeded in reducing this to fifteen days. Since then various other people have been lopping off days and hours, and last year Mr. Broadbent reduced it to six days, twenty-one hours.

Miss Batten flew a Percival Gull, with a cruising speed of about 155 m.p.h., and it is a wonderful feat of endurance that enabled her to put up the very fine show that she did, and to break a record which has worn out many a mere male. She is now flying on across Australia, and when she reaches Sydney, it is her present intention to carry on across the thousand odd miles of the stormy Tasman Sea to New Zealand.

Where the Sparks Come From

WHENEVER any big flight of any sort is made I always find that I get a little reminder from Mr. Leonard Morgan, of K.L.G. plugs, to tell me that the flight was made with K.L.G. sparking plugs. Miss Batten used them, Scott used them in his Johannesburg flight, Swain used them when he beat the height record. I am thinking of writing to Mr. Morgan, telling him he would save himself an awful lot of trouble if he would write to me only when an important flight is accomplished on some other plug.

This firm really has a wonderful record. Every single King's Cup race has been won on K.L.G.s, every record flight to Australia, to the Cape, and so far as I know, every British flight and a good many foreign ones across the Atlantic have also been done with this same ignition unit.

The whole of the aviation side of this concern has been built up since the war, and its success is very largely due to the push and personal likeability of Mr. Morgan, who is known on every aerodrome in Great Britain and at many on the Continent.

MOTORING NOTES

BEFORE THE SHOW

By LYNX

THE air is thick with catalogues and announcements from every manufacturer, and the competition to get a preliminary boost in before the show started has been even more intensive than in previous years. At the moment Captain Black, of the Standard Company, seems to have tucked all his British rivals under the seat for the coming year. In addition to a fine and comprehensive programme, he now announces a 20 h.p. 8-cylinder saloon at £349. It does a real 80 m.p.h., and gets from rest to 50 m.p.h. in 12 seconds. (The 21 h.p. Morris time is 24.4 sec.) It is also an extremely handsome looking car and carries everything on it except the kitchen dresser.

While I consider the Standard people by far the most go ahead of the big British manufacturers, and cannot understand why anybody who wants to buy a British car at a low price ever buys the slow churning specimens that better-known manufacturers fob off on the public, I am still not quite sure about this new model.

It makes the very fair claim that it can compete with the big American cars in their own market, but we must remember that the big Americans only compete in the English market under a very substantial tax handicap; yet, even then, they succeed in giving practically as good a performance as the new Standard at considerably lower prices. The real way to judge car value is at the door of the factory, and you have only to read the advertisements of Chrysler, Buick, Chevrolet, etc., in the American papers to realise that at the factory door their products have got the British manufacturer knocked into a cocked hat.

While in this country we may indulge our patriotism and get a better equipped car by buying a Standard, this does not help in the colonial market. The South African, the Australian, and the New Zealander have got to have a big, strong, fast car, and the vast majority of them have got to have it cheap. There is no doubt that the new Standard is practically the only big British car which can give them anything like the performance and strength they desire for their price; but I should like to have seen it possible for them to be offered the same models less a few refinements at a considerably lower price. British visitors to the Dominions might then feel a little prouder of the British motor industry than they do at the present time.

Other Foreign Competition

WHILE I hope that every reader of these columns will buy a British car if at all possible, two very interesting new Italian models are now on the market which cannot escape notice. The first is a new Lancia called the "Aprilia" 12 h.p. developing 46-brake horse-power, and selling at £345. There have been many imitations of the Lancia unique suspension and frame-building, but there is still a feeling about handling one of these cars which I have never found in any other make.

The more interesting model, however, is the new 6 h.p. Fiat selling at £120, with a two-door convertible body. The tax on this car is only five guineas and it does as near 50 m.p.g. as makes no difference. In driving the car it is almost impossible, up to 50 m.p.h., to believe that there is not a far bigger power-unit under the bonnet. Acceleration up to 40 m.p.h. is better than any other Baby Car except the 8 h.p. Ford, the car cruises cheerfully at 45 m.p.h. and has a maximum of just over 50 m.p.h. For the man of very limited means who does not require to cover very heavy mileages in a day, this sturdy little model from a good stable seems to fill a niche which is quite vacant as far as the British car range is concerned.

On the Road

MR. Hibbert Binney, of Ashford, Kent, has earned the first copy of "The Greater Britain." He writes me a most interesting letter containing his experiences with a 1936 Hillman "Minx."

The "Minx" has now done 4,000 miles without any trouble, and he finds it "difficult to speak of its performance without using superlatives." He has touched 67 m.p.h., but unfortunately does not say whether this was the speedometer reading or a time test. (Readers might note that I do

The new 6 h.p. Fiat

not know of a single car on the market whose speedometer is not optimistic.) Mr. Binney praises the efficient and smooth-acting brakes and says, "the steering is a real joy." He does not give acceleration figures but believes them to be at least as good as the 10 h.p. Ford and far better than the Wolseley, Austin, or Morris cars of similar horsepower. He claims a petrol consumption of 29 m.p.h. and practically no oil consumption, and has very great praise for the comfort and leg room. The only criticisms are the complete inadequacy of the box spanners supplied to remove the sparking plugs, and the contortions required to lubricate steering nipples or springs.

The writer's experiences bear out to a considerable degree my own impressions of this model. The "Minx" is a good car, well thought out, sturdy, and excellent value at its power and price. At the same time I think Mr. Binney has rather exaggerated his acceleration claims. According to *The Autocar,* the figure from 0 to 50 m.p.h. is 31 seconds, and on the several models I have driven I have found a definite lag going upwards after about 33 m.p.h. Of course, their figures are far better than those of similar Austin or Morris models, but I am by no means sure that they are better than the Wolseley, and quite certain that they do not touch the 10 h.p. Ford figures.

With regard to his complaints my idea of paradise would be to see Mr. Rootes changing 100 sparking plugs with his own spanners and also Mr. Ford starting up 50 of his 10 h.p. cars and cutting his hand on the fender and number plate of each one.

FASCISM ENTERS "LITTLE MOSCOW"

IN the debate of the Rhondda Urban district Council on whether or not to subscribe public funds to the unemployed men's march on London, Mr. G. Maslin said he was sorry to find remnants of Fascism in Tylorstown, which was looked upon as a "little Moscow."

Another Communist member, Comrade F. J. Morton, said that if the Council had paid over the money quicker they would have averted an injunction.

Not wishing to risk a surcharge on their own pockets the Council decided to abide by the injunction restraining it from contributing public money to the march.

NATIONAL SOCIALIST WINTER AID

Ministers and Generals Collect for Poor

(From our Special Correspondent in Berlin)

THE spectacle offered by the appearance of dozens of generals, a Prime Minister, and hundreds of Ministers, mayors, and other high officials collecting coppers at the street corners is probably unique in the world's history.

It is repeated every year in Germany, where, since the National Socialists came to power, the whole nation combines to relieve the needs of the poor.

In the next few days the great Winter Aid campaign in Germany will be reopened. This campaign is of special interest. It is hardly unusual for important men of State to give an address on the subject of relieving the poor. On the contrary, in all countries and under every form of Government, "big pots" make a point of talking about assistance for the poor. But that is generally the alpha and omega. In National Socialist Germany, the talking takes place, too, but it is only the introduction, so to speak. Action follows.

Millions for the Poor

I ESTIMATE that this year's Winter Aid Fund will bring in about 400,000,000 marks—which is equal to £20,000,000 at par and in purchasing power. Last winter's total was 370 millions, and the previous year's 367½ millions.

The money is collected in voluntary contributions. Of course these contributions have a certain moral pressure behind them, for Mr. A. would feel ashamed to send the list back without an entry when his neighbour, Mr. B., is sure to see it afterwards, for one list is passed in each house, for example. But there is no official compulsion of any kind. I have been present at the house-to-house collections. When any householder stated that he had not much himself, the collector smiled, and told him that if he needed assistance himself, he could apply to the Winter Aid Bureau. If, as happened at one flat, the lady of the house says "No, thank you!" a dash is entered after her name. That is all. But, of course, the lady next door sees the dash, and assumes her neighbours are too poor to help.

It is interesting to see how the money is collected. Last year, 83,161,682 Winter Aid badges and plaquettes were sold—to a population, including children and the poor themselves, of some 67,000,000. A number of public-spirited persons must have purchased two or more. The fact is that only about 73,000,000 badges and plaquettes were made—and the demand was too great. So 10,000,000 from previous years, which had remained unsold, were extracted from the storeroom! The money thus obtained was used for relieving areas suffering from particular distress. Of course, unemployment was simultaneously reduced slightly, for persons who would otherwise be unemployed were engaged in manufacturing the badges.

Jews also Relieved

JEWS in Germany are not asked to contribute to the Winter Aid Fund. But they have copied the National Socialist plan, and started a "Winter Aid" of their own. When, however, any person of Jewish extraction, who is not relieved by his co-religionists, or who is a Jew by race but not by religion, is in need, the National Socialist Winter Aid will help him. My personal opinion is, however, that very few Jews are in need of assistance. They are not so rich as formerly, but still quite comfortably off.

At Christmas, fruit, nuts, flour, Christmas trees, and many other articles are distributed.

The Winter Aid has nothing to do with Poor Relief. It is granted in addition to this, and the Relieving Officers are not allowed to take it into consideration. But the main form of aid is made in briquettes, which are used for heating the homes instead of coal, and potatoes. Germans are great potato eaters, consuming just one pound per head per day.

Now and again the police, postal officials, and military collect. Military bands play on the open squares, and disabled men also take part.

Not Only For Unemployed

ONE of the first questions I put when I recently interviewed the responsible authorities was: "Why is more money required for Winter Aid since the unemployed figure has dropped by five millions?"

I was informed that not only the unemployed, of whom there are still about a million (as against six or seven four years ago), but also widows with small pensions, and others whose means are only just sufficient for absolute necessities, are assisted. But I was not content with the official answer alone. I at once paid a private call on several old ladies whom I know slightly. One was the grandmother of an acquaintance. I explained that I was interested to know what the Winter Aid had sent her. She reeled off a long list. It included extras for Yuletide, a Christmas tree, two books (her income does not run to these), additional briquettes—coupons enabling her to purchase fat at a reduced price, and tickets for cheaper fish. There were some other items. This lady is living on about 25s. per week, and the help gave her the opportunity of enjoying a few luxuries. Two other calls had more or less similar results.

But the main factor is that the receipt of Winter Aid has no social disadvantage. It is not "a scandal" to obtain fish or fat at reduced prices. The "Winter Aid" is on a level with an increase of pension (without any additional taxation) or with a present from the State. It can be taken with honour.

Poverty, so long as it is not the result of refusing to work, is not a crime under National Socialism. No German sleeps on the Spree Embankment—or anywhere else in the open, unless he is on holiday in summer, and does so for the benefit of his health. National Socialism has abolished paupery, and the poor are called "Minderbemittelte," which, translated literally, means "persons with lower means." And Minderbemittelte can "look the whole world in the face," for neither slur nor dishonour attaches to them. They are, however, not pampered. Little extra luxuries are for older people. The healthy, able-bodied poor, so far as they are workless, are supplied with the means of sustaining life without privations, with adequate clothing, and hygenic housing. But, I should add, "Winter Aid" is regarded in Germany as a bridge between past and future times. National Socialists are looking forward to the time when the last unemployed man can be given work, and the lowliest citizen's income is sufficient to include modest luxuries. And the Four Years' Plan proclaimed at Nuremberg at the Party Congress should do much to realise this hope.

Dr. Goebbels and Gen. Goering taking a street collection in Berlin

Red Terror in Liverpool

BLACKSHIRTS DEFEAT JEWISH-COMMUNIST ALLIANCE

IT is nearly midnight on Sunday yet the streets of Liverpool are still crowded.

I have just walked along a mile of pavements and seen many arrests made. Less than an hour ago Reds smashed in the window of a shop and police had to charge loot-seeking hooligans. In the region of the Tunnel entrance I saw policemen menaced by an ugly crowd as they arrested a howling man. The main streets are littered with bricks, broken glass, and pieces of pottery.

For five hours Red hooliganism has reigned. The Reds, arrogant in their knowledge of toleration by a weak Government, have created serious disorder in the centre of the city. Hundreds of mounted and foot police have had to do what they could to remedy Government delinquency and meet Red rowdyism with batons.

Outside I can hear the yells of a group of Reds.

Contrast

THE scenes in Liverpool's streets are in striking contrast to the stadium where Sir Oswald Mosley spoke. In the streets, where the Government should see order maintained, is nothing but chaos and danger for innocent persons. In the Stadium, Liverpool Blackshirts have held a great and orderly meeting and I have heard their Leader make a magnificent speech broken only by frequent bursts of tumultuous applause.

From seven o'clock bands of shouting and yelling hooligans, sweepings of the lowest quarters of the city, assisted by imported Communists and Jews, have rushed about the streets near the Stadium preventing hundreds from proceeding to the meeting place. For a long time before Sir Oswald was due to speak, and during the meeting, the telephone at the Stadium was constantly ringing. People unable to reach the meeting were ringing up the organisers explaining their difficulty and expressing their regret.

Ordered Discipline and Red Rabble

THE Blackshirt march to the Stadium, somewhat curtailed at the request of the police, was witnessed by thousands. At certain points along the route groups of Reds attempted to create serious trouble and police baton charges were made. Missiles were thrown, including bricks and glass, and an attempt was made to overturn a Blackshirt coach containing women members. Three policemen were injured, Blackshirts were struck by the flying stones, and one was so badly hurt that he had to be carried into the Stadium by his companions.

Throughout the meeting the scenes continued in the streets, and when the Blackshirts were leaving, at a late hour, the coaches were attacked by a howling, stone-throwing mob. Another policeman was struck on the head with a brick and had to be taken to hospital. Windows in the Stadium vestibule were smashed with a piece of lead piping. A woman saw a youth, who expressed sympathy with the Blackshirts, attacked by a gang of hooligans in Lime-street and left lying on the ground. Passers-by attended to his injuries.

THE CLENCHED FIST. A red at Liverpool being arrested.

In a statement to the Press, Mr. A. K. Wilson, Chief Constable of Liverpool, said: "No doubt there was a certain element of the crowd who were bent on disturbing the procession, and having been prevented from so doing vented their disappointment on the police. The latter have acted throughout with considerable restraint."

GREAT BLACKSHIRT MEETING AT HAMMERSMITH

RED TACTICS FOILED

SPONTANEOUS applause greeted Mr. William Joyce, Director of Propaganda, when he spoke in the crowded Hammersmith Town Hall on Friday, October 9.

The phrase "They shall not pass," written on the walls in Aldgate, was used as a theme. He told the audience that it was an appropriate signature of the Jew, when an Englishman wanted a job.

Loud applause followed when the speaker exposed the Jewish Red Terror and Jewish finance as the real controllers of the Democratic Government, which he proved by pointing to the incidents on Sunday, October 4.

He then went on to expound the Fascist policy. Dealing with unemployment, he explained that keeping out foreign imports from our markets and replacing them by goods made within Great Britain and the Empire would give employment to thousands of British workers.

He proved the fallacy that freedom existed to-day under a Democratic system, and that whereas the people to-day lived under a financial tyranny where finance was the boss of the nation, Fascism would revolutionise Capitalism to make it the servant of the people. One law for rich and poor, quoted Mr. Joyce, and any financier who broke the law would find himself in a concentration camp, he continued, amid applause.

Wild enthusiasm reigned in the hall after the speaker proclaimed that Mosley was the only Leader, and would lead Britain out of the chaos and ineptitude of to-day to the Greater Britain of to-morrow.

The meeting ended with the National Anthem and the Fascist marching song, to which the entire audience stood at attention.

Many remarks were heard from members of the audience on leaving that it was the best policy they had ever heard.

The Hammersmith people showed their disgust at the tactics of a few hooligans that had collected outside to shout and show their loyalty to the Jewish Soviet Government, and their hate to the British flag.—C. P.

SOCIALISTS JOIN THE BRITISH UNION

LOCAL PAPER GOES FASCIST

A sensation has been caused in Swansea, reports the *Swansea Guardian*, by the astonishing news that an unemployed association has been taken over by the Swansea district of the British Union.

The organisation concerned is the Ffynone Unemployed Association, who first published a Socialist paper called the *Ffynone Free Press*, the paper was continued under a title of *The New Leasure* but has ceased publication on the members joining the B.U.F.

The *Swansea Guardian* states that the new members were very much in evidence on the Fascist platform at a meeting on Tuesday last.

Books  Read

"Trial and Error." By A. J. L. Ball (Faber and Faber. 7s. 6d.)

IN case it is said that Mr. Ball might have resorted to other and more orthodox means to obtain a hearing for this effort to extricate himself from the charge of complicity in the Leopold Harris fire conspiracies, he describes the circuitous route by which "facilities" for petitioning the Crown are granted, and their inadequacy. He concludes: "I had long since realised the futility of petition, and had come to the conclusion that the only successful appeal that I could hope to make must be submitted to public opinion. It is the vital interest of every member of the community to protect every fellow-member from the perpetration of an act of injustice, and to my fellow-countrymen this, the only petition likely to obtain a sympathetic hearing, is therefore submitted."

The least result which can be hoped from such a book is that the procedure of mass trials be abandoned. The method is one which a merely superficial glance shows to be open to error. "No counsel, however able, could conduct without confusion the prosecution of sixteen people simultaneously; no individual could muster the entire case and still less could a common jury be expected fully to grasp the many points at issue." Early in the trial Mr. Loughborough Ball had been cross-examined for a whole day, and the case against him was generally considered to have been disproved; yet at the end of the trial, sixteen other cross-examinations had taken place, and the possible innocence of one of the defendants no longer remained in the mind of the jury.

The restraint with which the author writes makes the possibility of an injustice in his case all the more real. The mere possibility of the imprisonment of an innocent man for three years should have been enough to justify a retrial in this case; yet not only was a separate trial not granted, but petitions to the Home Office were also ignored.

Quite apart from the disturbing possibility of unjust imprisonment, which is shown as existing in the Courts of England, the book is extremely interesting in its account of prison life. It seems not impracticable to suggest that if a dietician were employed at each of the country's prisons, the physical health of the men could be guarded and improved without considerable expense. It would cost no more to provide exact quantities of the right food than it does to provide a minimum amount of food without particular dietic value, and make it as unpalatable as possible.

A paragraph upon Leopold Harris himself after he became King's evidence, sheds a curious light upon the method of insurance companies. "I must . . . convey an impression of Leopold Harris's activities at Maidstone after he had placed his vast knowledge of the frauds disclosed and to be disclosed, at the disposal of the Crown. His cell in the hospital was like an office; he had a work-table and ample facilities for writing. . . . He, the scourge of the insurance companies, had become their devoted servant, . . . he told me that his advice upon a case had been sought by the general manager of the company interested." In comparative luxury, therefore, a prisoner convicted of felony served his sentence in Maidstone jail, in constant communication with the outside world, and enjoying privacy which was allowed to no other inmate.

It is not possible, in the scope of a short review, to give any of the points with which the author seeks to substantiate his innocence. It is only possible to say that the circumstances of the trial and the facts which Mr. Loughborough Ball reveals in his book call loudly for examination and a retrial of his case.—A. C.

"The Seas Were Mine." By Capt. Howard Hartman.

"Sentenced to Adventure." By Serge Zolo. (Both, Harrap. 8s. 6d.)

THESE two volumes should make a pair on the shelves of all readers who tire of the esoteric and the exotic (Bloomsbury brand), and still smother an enormous call to wander. Behind the prim frontage of most of us office wallahs the call "for to admire and for to see" still makes drastic demand for appeasement. Short of setting out on the lone trail I can think of no better solace than Capt. Hartman and Mr. Zolo provide. I do not know what the commercial angle of publishing this sort of book is but Messrs. Harrap deserve to make a packet out of them, and I sincerely hope they do.

In "The Seas Were Mine" the hero, from good Pennsylvanian Dutch stock, takes to the sea at sixteen, gets adopted by the famous General Sir Godfrey Howard, and takes us through twenty-five years of the most amazing, but seemingly authentic wanderings. Capt. Hartman writes well and has a delightful sense of humour. China, at its most interesting, the Boer War, whale fishing, Samoa, adventures in India, and early aviation. His book is crowded with good things. It is not possible to feel the same affection for Mr. Zolo which one unconsciously acquires for the author of "The Seas Were Mine." "Sentenced to Adventure" is good reading, and it covers almost as many interesting travel phases, but the author is mannered and the book a self-conscious one. It is a pity that an extremely ill-mannered story of Amy Mollison comes right at the end of the book and leaves a nasty taste in the mouth which nothing else in the story justified.—N. S. O.

"Matabele Thompson." Edited by Nancy Rouillard. (Faber and Faber. 12s. 6d.)

THIS autobiography, written by a man who was closely associated with Cecil Rhodes in his scheme for opening Africa to financial interests, is designed to throw some light upon the character and ambitions of the explorer, and incidentally upon the men who surrounded him and in subsidiary ways helped his achievement. That it is in many ways a harsh and unflattering light is a result of the difficulty of the mission and the necessarily ruthless natures of the men who pioneered.

Francis Robert Thompson, son of a Yorkshire settler, earned his nickname in the successful conduct of the mission to King Lobengula to obtain a grant from the King for the mining rights of Matabeleland—a mission which resulted finally in the political origin of Southern Rhodesia. He describes vividly his sojourn of many dangerous months alone with unfriendly, suspicious Matabele natives, while Rhodes formed the Chartered Company in London, and tells with strong effect of the difficulties encountered, both from the natives and the white men of shady antecedents, who also surrounded the King in the hope of obtaining mining concessions. He is obviously impressed by the character and intelligence of the King.

At the end of 1888, the mission successfully accomplished, he returned to Oxford, and it is interesting to read his next short and bitter comment upon the expedition. "Only once did I again visit Rhodesia. It was in 1904, as a member of the South African Native Affairs Commission. I was standing on the railway platform at Figtree, when I was accosted by one of Lobengula's Indians. 'Ou Tomoson,' he said. 'How have you treated us after all your promises, which we believed?'

"I had no answer."

Thompson relates as a joke a conversation which took place between Cecil Rhodes and Barney Barnato, who was the hief controller of the diamond mines which Rhodes wished to purchase. Conditionally upon their purchase, Barnato suggested that he must be made life governor of the de Beers Consolidated Mines, a member of the Cape Parliament, and a member of the Kimberley Club. Rhodes replied: "I agree to the first condition because you have a million interest in the mines; *I agree to the second because it is fitting that with a million at stake in the country you should have a just ambition to be in the councils of the country;* but I shall have to see about the third."

Thompson has complete belief in Rhodes of the wide vision and unselfish patriotism. "He told me . . . that he had but one ambition—to paint the map red from the Cape to Egypt and to federate the world under the aegis of the British Empire. This was the Rhodes of the wide vision, the humane temper, and the unselfish ambition. . . . The other Rhodes with an entourage of fawning sycophants did not appeal to me, and I do not think to him either."

He describes the distress of Rhodes at the Jameson Raid. "'Look, Thompson, look what that damn fool Jameson has done!' . . . the sharp falsetto voice went on, over and over again. "But tell me, why did he do it?'"

Thompson, who earlier in his career was appointed British Resident and Chief Inspector of Native Reserves in Griqualand West and carried out the Amnesty of 1878, describes his efforts to maintain peace. "I visited all the locations and succeeded in inducing the people to conform to the order and immediately surrender their arms. Some twelve hundred or fifteen hundred guns were handed in, each two men being promised a plough in return. This was done at my suggestion, and on the written authority of the Governor; but I regret to say that the ploughs were never supplied. . . . To the best of my knowledge this is the only instance in South Africa of a completely peaceful disarmament of natives."

Although the book is for the most part concerned with an account of the hazardous expedition to Matabeleland, it contains also an account of the inauguration by Thompson of the Compound System at the de Beers diamond mines at Kimberley, where natives are segregated in an attempt to stop the illicit buying and smuggling of diamonds stolen by native workers.

The author begins with an account of the attack upon his home by natives, in which his father was killed and he himself seriously wounded. His own comment upon his work is of sufficient interest to be quoted here. "Land has always been to me among the first of the things of this life. It is also, I think, the safest of all assets. I am glad to know that when my task is done my sons will have this stake in South Africa."

As an autobiography of an early settler, this book is very interesting. As a participant's account of events and times too near our own to be widely understood, it is arresting and vivid.—A. C.

"Four Days' War." By S. Fowler Wright. (Robert Hale. 7s. 6d.)

SINCE the days of Jules Verne, excursions into the future destruction of the world have been a source of profitable concentration for many writers. H. G. Wells, Olaf Stapledon, and others, have prophesied our annihilation through plague, war, giant insects, red snow that destroys the propagatory capacities, palæolithic monsters, dawn and dusk men, spiders as big as the Queen Mary, choking weeds: all sorts of horrible things, utterly delightful to read because they make the world seem a really jolly place.

Fowler Wright, author of this book, leads a double life. He alternately puzzles out ingenious methods of murder and plans destruction on a larger scale. He revived the theory of a flat world and showed us the Puritans' "Beyond the Rim" of the Antarctic. He jumped us half a million years into the future to greet our descendants, who do everything by thought—even to crossing ravines on a thought bridge—and who grow their own fur coats on them. He is also responsible for the "Deluge," which drowned us all, and has translated Dante's "Inferno." It will be seen that Mr. Wright has ingenious and fantastic ideas.

Now he has excelled himself. He has worked out plans for the destruction of the Empire and Western Europe, in four days, through a Germano-Russian pact to dominate the globe! Interesting? And fantastic!—H. G.

"Old Heart Goes on a Journey." By Hans Fallada. (Putnam. 7s. 6d.)

WITH the naive comment that he intends to continue this story in another volume, the author of "Little Man What Now" has written an ingenious fairy story worthy of the Brothers Grimm, for all the world as though he were presenting a credible account of everyday events.

Did the bad old habit of attaching farm hands as bondsmen to their masters still exist in Germany in 1912? Hans Fallada illustrates it in all its abuse.

It is impossible to take this novel seriously. It is a story for children, written with all the strength one expected from its author, but presenting no clearly cut character and no action which touches reality. There is Good and Evil, and a war waged between them, precisely in the manner of legend. Not even the old professor, quite catches the sympathy of the reader because of the half light in which they exist.

Outside the plot the book has some vivid and delightful descriptions of German farm life and the circumscribed minds of the country people. For this it is interesting, but it is a very long way from "Little Man What Now" both in subject and treatment, and one is led to regret the pen of the reformer.—D. H.

Shows Seen

CINEMAS

THE GORGEOUS HUSSY

American
Empire

ALL history offers to the novelist, playwright, and dramatist inexhaustible material from which to draw tragedy or comedy. The thin lips of the historian cannot tell with so poignant an effect the story of the fall of dynasties, the rise of nations, or a people's awakening. He cannot tell with any subtlety of appreciation of the reign of courtesans or the effect upon a people of influences behind a throne.

America is so young in development that the story of her discovery, colonisation, and building can barely be considered history, and it is this newness, this sense of a nation feeling its way to adult life not far from our own genefation, which gives almost any film of early American colonisation its warmth and reality.

Before she became the uncontrollable playground of the gangster and the racketeer, Amercia retained in her people enough of the manners of her parent stock to take the rougher edges from the time. It was gracious time, diffident and coltish, and Joan Crawford in the character of Margaret Timberlake is well representative of it.

The picture itself is well mannered, as all these pictures are, and it does no violence to the events of history. It gives a fairly authentic account of President Jackson's fight for the United States.

The title of the picture is perhaps a little extravagantly inapt for this period piece with its rather plainly beautiful heroine and the dim early Georgian sets. It is odd, but not undesirable a precedent, to find the President of the United States correcting his Ministers and dismissing them from office for indulging in idle gossip.

Lionel Barrymore as the President has the necessary roughness of speech, but he lacks the Presidential weight and authority. Robert Taylor appears decoratively, but briefly. His place in the romantic scene is filled by Mr. Franchot Tone, returned from musical comedy.

What an oddly complicated picture of history will go down to posterity with the

Joan Crawford and Robert Taylor in "The Gorgeous Hussy"

motion pictures. With characteristic resource the film magnates choose any reign or period, and finding attached to it any slight or merely imaginary romance, distort and enlarge that romance until it becomes the pivot of the time, the frame and background of the canvas instead of an isolated dim incident in a corner. We would have given all the flutterings of Nell Gwynn's heart to hear her announcement to the angry crowd that she was the Protestant whore, or to follow the King throughout the whole of a day in his council chamber.
—A. C.

SAVOY HOTEL 217

Curzon

I SAW this film four months ago in the local cinema of a small middle-German market town, where the local film-show was an event of historic importance. Wednesday was "People's Evening," when a hundred splendid young men from the local labour camp paraded smartly in their earth-brown uniforms before the cinema, and two hundred students from the neighbouring Hochschule flocked to see Hans Albers breaking women's hearts in some new exotic adventure. It is not surprising that this bulky middle-aged hero should be the cinematic idol of Hitler's young Germany, for he is superbly blonde and the embodiment of the super-Nordic virtues. Even the tinge of salacity in his conduct is heavily Aryan.

Now this film, after many months, has reached Mayfair's luxury cinema; but for me it was not half so entertaining, sunk in the deep cushions of the Curzon, as it was then, sitting on a hard wooden form among a crowd of enthusiastic young Germans for whom Hans Albers was practically everything they wanted to be. Perhaps the film does not bear seeing twice. There is nothing very original in the plot, and the acting is sometimes very harrowing in its over-strain. Tsarist-Russia — with the sleigh-bells tinkling, and vodka and rich furs—makes an exciting background for passion and adventure. Yes, it is worth seeing! Some scenes will remain with you vividly. Especially the dramatic incidents in the doss-house, towards the end, which show acting and direction of unusual quality.—E. D. R.

THEATRES

THE NIGHT OF JANUARY 16th

Phoenix Theatre

ONE can only assume that American murder trials do not resemble our own in the appeals which witnesses are allowed to make to the pity of the jury. Such a play as this, with its actors performing on both sides of the footlights, should be superbly acted if it is not to fall into monotony, for many of the characters

The heroine in "The Night of January 16th"

on the stage make no movement during the whole of its course.

A little unorthodox as a murder trial perhaps, the play is very interesting, although the verdict is a foregone conclusion. Incidentally, these cases of millionaires who, through a miscalculation, lose their millions and in their fall bring down thousands of small men, seem to evoke no comment from justice.

The actors have a double job of work. They must act so that their deception, while apparent to the audience, is not apparent to the Court which ostensibly tries the case, and, since the audience knows even less of this case than the Court, they have an extremely difficult, if not impossible, task. It is the failure of some of the actors to convey these subtle differences which makes the verdict of the improvised jury a foregone conclusion, and lessens accordingly the interest and power of the play.

NIGHTMARE ?—OR VISION ?

SAM HIBBS HAD A DREAM— AND AFTER THE DREAM CAME THE AWAKENING

SAM HIBBS flung himself irritably into his armchair and felt for another fag. Loud wails of protest rose from his youngest boy just finishing breakfast. "Ow, Dad . . . get up . . . you're sittin' on my w——wig-wams!"

"Oh, for Heaven's sake, Elsie, shut the kid up . . . ought to be off to school, he did. Nice state of things when a chap can't have five minutes' peace in his own home."

Womanly hands, neither white nor well tended but very capable, led Hibbs junior, still howling, into the kitchen and shut the door on him. A moment later she reappeared with a small tray and papers.

"You needn't be so cross with the poor kid, Sam. After all—he spent hours last night at that model—wanted it to show his teacher . . . and now you've gone and squashed it."

"Well, damn it all, woman, how was I to know. He shouldn't have left it in my chair."

Elsie Hibbs was too wise to argue with her lord and master in that mood, but pushed the pot of freshly made tea towards him. "Get that down you and you'll feel better. Here's your *Clarion* and another paper—what's it called—oh, *Action*—a new one on me—that a Blackshirt left last night."

"Bung it in the stove, then," growled Hibbs. "Don't bring it near me."

Mrs. Hibbs took the offending periodical and withdrew in silence to the kitchen.

⊘ ⊘ ⊘

THERE was plenty of excuse for Sam Hibbs. He had been up all night on a temporary job with a lorry—he'd got very wet and tired—the job was none of his choice, but it was that or nothing.

If nothing, there'd be no cash for the instalment on the new furniture hire-purchased a year ago, and which had proved such a great disappointment. Rickety muck he called it. Somehow it had looked very different in Isaacstein's palatial showrooms. Nor would there be the monthly five bob for the wireless, nor the half a crown for Ted's bike (the latest model, he suspected, from Tokio).

Hibbs swigged noisily at his tea and scanned the headlines of the *Daily Clarion* through eyes half-shut with fatigue. "Hitler hailed by Nazis," he muttered, "and, oh lor', here's Musso on the warpath again. Those chaps'll get bumped off one day and serve 'em darn well right." Then he mused

Story by

F. E. HAYES

sleepily but complacently on the part he had taken in ragging a local Fascist speaker last Saturday. He'd shown him what was what, by the Lord, he had . . . he'd shown him what the British worker thought of such goings-on. Why, the fool hadn't been able to make himself heard! No dictators in this country . . . no blurry Blackshirts here . . . "Britons—never—never—shall—be—slaves." . . . His querulous murmurings died into silence broken only by an occasional snore.

He was driving a new lorry somewhere in the north. The locality seemed familiar to him yet there was something unusual about the highway itself. Very wide and even, with no cross-roads and restricted obviously to motor traffic only. Gosh, but this gave points to the other old track! They'd been mighty quick about it . . . funny he'd never seen the men on the job. Anyhow, it was a good piece of work—hats off to the Minister of Transport—and the lorry sped smoothly along at a good fifty.

Drawing up for a snack at a roadside hostelry, his eyes rested appreciatively on the bordering fields now whitening for the harvest. A real credit, he thought, and as for those farm buildings yonder, well, they were a vast improvement on ramshackle old barns. Very clean, very modern in line. Now he came to think about it, it had been the same all through the Midlands. Who was the fool who said farming didn't pay. It evidently did—to judge by the look of the farmer who had just parked his car by the lorry and was coming in for a drink.

Hibbs sat on a low stool outside the inn and enjoyed the smoke for which his soul had craved. He felt decidedly pleased with himself—he hardly knew why. . . He had reasonable hours and good pay. There was no need for tick these days—he jingled some coins significantly—and there was always something over after Elsie and the kids had been provided for. Yes, England, not Russia was the paradise for the worker.

⊘ ⊘ ⊘

THE lorry took to the road again and ate up the miles. Further ahead, he passed one of the mighty hydrogenation plant structures that had revitalised British coalfields. Building of workmen's houses was still going on apace, he was glad to see, and the miserable grey hovel of the miner seemed to be a thing of the far distant past. Soon he arrived at his destination, a well known town in Lancashire. The last time he'd been up this way he had seen half-starved men loafing about the ill-kept streets, silent mills, protest marches, red flags, riots and baton charges. Evidently the crisis was over. Quick work that. The people looked healthy, happy, and prosperous, and many greeted their friends with a salute strange to him yet he had a vague idea of seeing it somewhere before.

After a good square meal, thoroughly deserved and enjoyed Hibbs went sight-seeing. Several things struck him as peculiarly new. A thousand or more young factory workers doing physical jerks in their grounds. A poster outside a Workers' Theatre advertising the performance of a well known play by the Bankside Mills Company with tickets at ridiculously low charges.

Cinemas of a new design . . . Gaumont seemed to have gone out of business . . . but the Corporate and United British were billed everywhere . . . funny he'd never heard of *them*. A company of young men swung down the road bound, so he was told, for a year's training at some moorland camp. Camps seemed very popular . . . he remembered passing dozens on the way up. Oh, undoubtedly education had improved since his time. Who was the Education Minister now? . . . good man whoever he was for these youngsters were a credit to any race. He thought of his own boy and took from his wallet for the third time that day the holiday vouchers that ensured him and his family a fortnight in the Workers' Holiday Hotel at Bournemouth. He was getting it very reasonably, he thought . . . very satisfying not to be diddled by some shark of a landlady.

As Hibbs neared his hostel, a small silver plane roared overhead and nose-dived, but not before its pilot had jumped clear with his parachute. The street seemed strewn with the wreckage. An officer was quickly on the scene to take the luckless airman's name and address. "Stunting over towns *must* be stopped," he reminded him firmly. The crash had given Hibbs a considerable shock . . . it had been too close a shave for his liking. A few yards nearer and—there would have been no holiday in Bournemouth. Dazed, he leaned against a tree to recover his senses. What *was* the matter with his head now . . . ?

⊘ ⊘ ⊘

A TALL, well-built man with greying hair, clad in the strangely ubiquitous black uniform (now *where* had he seen it before?) looked at him keenly. "Feeling ill? Can I get you anything?" he asked.

Hibbs looked at him vacantly . . . his eyes rested on the flash and circle brassard. Something snapped in his brain. "I must have gone dotty," he muttered, "wh—what's happened? . . . things seem different somehow."

"Different!" the Blackshirt threw back his head and laughed loud and long.

"Of course there's a difference after ten years of corporate government. What else would you expect? Fifteen years ago I lost my job when I joined the Union, but I've lived to see my first faith justified . . ." his eyes glowed. "Isn't it marvellous what the Fascist spirit has done for our people . . . 'a race reborn,'" he quoted.

"Fascist spirit?" repeated Hibbs weakly, "my brain's gone clean. . . I *am* in England, arn't I?"—appealingly.

"You certainly are . . . in the thirteenth year of King Edward VIII."

Hibbs made calculations with a bewildered brain. "But who has done all this?"—he waved his arms vaguely. "Baldwin or Chamberlain or——?"

The Blackshirt seemed to loom very large and his voice rang jubilantly. "*MOSLEY* has led Britain for ten years . . . the new, the Greater Britain. Mosley—whose men you howled down and insulted. Who else but Mosley *could* have done it?"

"*MOSLEY*," shrieked Hibbs, thoroughly awake at last. "No dictators here . . . no Mosleys."

⊘ ⊘ ⊘

"WAKE up, Sam. Go up to bed, do . . . you'll get all cramped in that chair."

Hibbs blinked owlishly at his wife.

"You've had bad dreams, old man, shouting like mad, you were. Better have two aspirins and clear off upstairs." She looked at him anxiously, but he waved her away.

"No thanks, old girl. I'm all right—only fagged out." Sam rose stiffly and went towards the door. "If that young fool with the papers calls to-day—that Blackshirt, I mean—ask him in. I want to ask him a few things." And she heard him muttering as he shuffled along the passage, "Maybe he would do it . . . maybe he would."

CONTENTED BRITAIN—(2)

"To-day we meet in an atmosphere of such happiness and contentment as has not been seen since the War."

Mr. Neville Chamberlain, addressing the British Bankers' Association in 1935.

A SERIES OF LETTERS FROM H. J. GIBBS

The Secretary,
The Middletown Discussion Group.
THE DEMOCRATIC CHAOS.

Dear Sir,—You will remember that last week we discussed the trials of existence, and arrived at the conclusion that although we possess as many facilities for prosperity and peace as any other nation we have not attained either.

How has this occurred? History shows we were the first industrialised nation. Our Industrial Revolution was achieved by such men as Watt, the inventor of the steam-machine, Crompton, George Stephenson, Arkwright, Sir Humphrey Davy, and others.

Britain had a great opportunity in those days. You will remember the words of Macaulay to the House of Commons:

> "Our fields are cultivated with a skill unknown elsewhere, with a skill which has extracted rich harvests from moors and morasses. Our houses are filled with conveniences which the kings of former times might have envied. Our bridges, our canals, our roads, our modes of communication fill every stranger with wonder. Nowhere are manufactures carried to such perfection. Nowhere does man exercise such a dominion over matter."

We had no competitors worthy of consideration. In fact, a number of bankers—the Huths, Speyers, Rothschilds, etc.—came to London from Eastern Europe to capitalise our industry.

The political parties were swept up in the rush of industrialisation and followed the lead of industrialists and merchant bankers. The Liberal Party found favour through the policy of exporting anything anywhere in any quantities.

This theory was knocked on the head when other countries began their own industries. The bankers assisted them, by exporting capital and credit, in the probable belief that they would obtain higher profits; Europe had a lower standard of living and goods could be produced at a lower price there than in Britain: there were no freightage charges to be borne. The industrialists helped by exporting skilled mechanics and operatives to show foreign workers how to use machinery.

That is how we find British money in South America, France, Holland, China, Japan, America, and elsewhere, producing the same things we make in Britain. Even last year a number of Lancashire cotton operatives went to Japan to demonstrate the use of cotton machinery.

I don't think this very sensible, do you?

It means that countries with a lower standard of living than ours, or operating with a cheaper currency (as France will now the franc is devalualised), are able to sell goods cheaper than we can.

Japanese cotton-piece goods displace Lancashire cotton-piece goods in the Empire. Argentine meat is cheaper than English meat. European dairy produce is cheaper than British—and will be even more so now Holland and Switzerland have followed France in devalualising their currency. American iron and steel supplants the output of our own foundries.

British workers lose their jobs to foreigners, because, in world markets, foreign goods are cheaper.

British industry and capital following the path of Liberalism, and assisted along that path by the Tories, took the wrong turning

Last week we agreed that, in these times, it was "every man for himself and the Devil take the hindmost."

Now, the United Kingdom market is one of the largest consuming markets in the world. Supposing you had money invested in, say, Argentine meat ranches, would you not try to exercise some influence over political parties, in order to prevent them banning imports of Argentine meat into Great Britain? Would you not support the democratic system of government which permits Argentine meat to be sold in Britain?

According to your experience, this is the form which "every man for himself" takes. Therein lies your justification, for, under such circumstances, you would not support any organisation which stated it would ban Argentine meat.

If, however, it can be shown that your actions in such circumstances will bring about your own doom, I presume you will stop them.

That is what such actions are doing: in order to maintain profits in a world which is cheapening its currencies and its standards of living—bringing about a decreased consumption of goods—the only outcome of such activities will be to lower the standard of living and cheapen the currency of those whose capital is invested abroad.

That is what is happening

British workers are forced to accept lower wages in order that British goods can compete with the cheap labour of foreign countries. In cutting wages, the government and the bankers cut down the consumption of goods. If you cut down wages again, why, that starts the whole business over again, doesn't it?

The Fascist method of preventing this insane business from going on indefinitely I shall detail later, but, briefly it is this: to maintain high wages, whereby British workers can increase their consumption of the goods they make themselves or are made in the Empire. We could all increase our purchases of these goods to-morrow if we had the money. We haven't got it. To get it we must employ ourselves in making the goods we consume.

That should be the basis of a practical economic existence. The theory which is in practice to-day is obviously wrong. Trade with foreign countries on competitive terms, as is in practice now, should form but a minor part of economics, if it forms any part at all.

It is definitely stupid to let the whole of our trade be based upon this devalualisation system with its continual downwards movement. As a 'bus conductor said to me the other day, "If you haven't got money, you can't breathe." That is true and it is the outcome of the chaos of muddled competition based on false values.

I don't think we can disagree about that, do you?

LONDON TAKES 'ACTION'

" THE SELLERS "

I MADE my way down Kingsway to the Strand and trod the familiar pavement towards Charing Cross, thinking of many things amid the busy atmosphere of the crowded street thronged with late workers and early theatre-goers. Then I became conscious of something else, something which pierced my reverie sharply, bringing me up alert; there was unusual activity on each street corner and an air of vitality about groups of young men who stood selling a paper called *Action*. Some were in mufti, with red arm-bands displayed, others in black uniform. Rather smart, I thought; and one thing impressed me favourably—they looked fresh, athletic Englishmen, no Asiatic countenances were to be seen amongst them.

I walked on down the Strand to Charing Cross, every fifty yards or so passing more of these sellers. They impressed me with their organisation and keenness. Two alien-looking Jews came along and deliberately spat at the feet of one young man in uniform; I saw the blaze in his eyes, but he took no notice.

That decided me. I went and bought a paper; four other people who had seen the incident did the same. I stood and chatted to the young man for a few moments. "There are a lot of you out to-night." "Every main street in the West and East End has sellers to-night," he replied.

"What is the object of your Party?"

"To establish a functional Government of the British people not tied to alien financial and vested interests," was the reply.

How right, I thought, as I recalled the peculiar activities of the big foreign investment house in the City where I, along with other Englishmen, slaved for a miserly 35s. a week in order that the wheels of high finance might revolve.

I asked the young Blackshirt for the address of the nearest branch. He gave it to me. I wished him good luck and went home thinking about "Britain for the British."—W. M.

FACTS FOR YOUR FILE

Compiled by GEORGE SUTTON

Justice for Seamen at Last

IMPORTANT changes in the hours of duty of seamen in ocean-going vessels, involving the abolition of the traditional two-watch system of four-hour watches, and a reduction in the working time of deck hands from eighty-four to sixty-four hours a week without loss of pay, are made by an agreement ratified by the Sailors' and Firemen's Panel of the National Maritime Board on August 19, 1936. (*Ministry of Labour Gazette*, September, 1936).

Japan's Textile Progress

FOR three successive years Japan has sold more cotton cloth than any other country. The record exports of 1935 amounted to 2,715,000,000 square yards, as against the 1,946,000,000 square yards of Great Britain, Japan's chief competitor. Japan's rayon output in 1927 was ten and a half million lb. By 1935 Japan was running the United States a close second in the race for rayon leadership, producing 224,000,000 lb. as against America's 256,700,000. Ever since 1929 there has been a downward trend in wages in the Japanese textile industry, while at the same time there has been a growth in efficiency, in output per operative. More work can be done with fewer labourers. For instance, it took 56.2 male workers to operate 10,000 spindles in 1929. In 1935 only 22.5 operatives were needed for the same number of spindles. In the case of women, the number required to tend 10,000 spindles declined from 206 to 160.2 during the same period. The number of male workers per 100 looms during the same time diminished from 12.5 to 5.8 and the number of women from 50.2 to 37.5.

At the same time the average daily wage for men workers in the cotton industry was reduced from 1.59 yen to 1.34 yen, while for women the decrease was from 1.14 yen to 73 sen. The daily wage expenditure per 10,000 spindles was reduced more than 50 per cent. from 323.90 yen to 147.57 yen. (*Current History*, New York, Sept., 1936).

The Decline of Cotton

THE extent of the decline in our cotton goods exports from 1913 to 1935 is portrayed vividly in an article in the current *Board of Trade Journal*. Here are some figures illustrating the effects of foreign competition and local industrialisation:

	1913.	1935.
Total exports (linear yds.)	7,075,252,000	2,013,429,000
British India	3,057,305,600	497,803,500
China, Japan, and Hong Kong, etc.	773,241,800	17,840,200
Dutch East Indies, Ceylon, Straits Settlements, etc.	539,217,300	82,795,500
South America	582,146,000	279,963,300
Mexico, Central America, and West Indies	167,577,400	86,142,100
United States and Canada	157,064,500	70,220,000
Europe (excepting Balkans)	388,930,100	199,610,900
Balkans, Near and Middle East	477,604,100	94,900,900
North Africa ..	357,387,300	78,311,400

The only bright spots are our exports to West Africa and South and East Africa, shown respectively:

West Africa ...	243,160,900	235,677,900
South and East Africa	120,872,700	178,321,400

Rationalisation in Steel Industry

IN the year 1923 we produced 8,482,000 tons of steel in Great Britain and employed 161,000 workers for the purpose. In 1935 we produced 9,800,000 tons with only 124,000 persons. Output per person averaged 52.7 tons in 1923. Output per person in 1935 averaged 79 tons. An increase of approximately 50 per cent.

Empire and Wool Production

NEARLY half the wool produced in the world last year, which totalled 3,668 million lb., was grown in the British Empire. Australia's 963 million lb. was the largest output of any single country. The United Kingdom is the world's largest user of wool, accounting last year for 670 million lb., while the U.S.A. came second with 651 million lb. These figures are from the annual survey of wool production and trade issued by the Imperial Economic Committee for the year 1935-36.—*Daily Express*, 18.9.36.

Yet Great Britain imported last year nearly 150 million lb. of foreign wool.

Unproductive Land

THE total land area of Great Britain and Ireland is about 76,500,000 acres, of which some 65,500,000 acres are under cultivation, pasture, and rough grazings, while the total area under different types of forest amounts to practically 3,000,000 acres. By far the largest proportion of the 65,500,000 acres given as under cultivation is in reality under pasture and rough hill grazings. Relatively a small proportion of these lands may be termed productive, and it was recently stated by that eminent authority, Professor R. G. Stapledon, C.B.E., that in round figures there were 16,250,000 acres of land in England and Wales in a more or less neglected condition, and much more of it absolutely derelict, but that every acre in this vast area, amounting to 43 per cent. of the total land surface of England and Wales, is capable of radical improvement.—*Daily Dispatch*, 28.9.36.

Shipping and Coal

OF the 302,080 tons of merchant shipping launched from the shipbuilding yards of the world last year only 277,704, or 21.4 per cent., was built to depend exclusively on coal for propulsion. There were launched 812,956 tons of motor ships and 200,000 tons of steamers fitted to burn oil fuel under the boilers.—*Daily Herald*, 5.2.36.

Greater Food Production Possible

AT Glasgow recently Mr. Elliot gave figures showing that home production had increased by an average of 20 per cent. in the last five years. He instanced wheat with an increase of 65 per cent., sugar beet nearly 100 per cent., bacon 70 per cent., and beef and veal 13 per cent. Yet the June 4 returns showed that there were 76,600 fewer acres used for agriculture than in the previous year, and that is a feature with which we have become familiar in the last few years. There is something very satisfactory in an increased production from a smaller acreage, because it shows not only what we can do with the most modern aids, but also (which seems at the moment much more important) what we could do in an emergency. There is no doubt that we could in this country produce a vastly greater proportion of the food the nation needs within a year if we were to bend all our energies and summon all our resources to the task. British agriculture cannot be expected to produce at a loss, and until the Government takes measures to safeguard it and give it full confidence there will be no more progress towards strengthening the Food Front of National Defence than is needed for the defence of the personal and profit-and-loss account.

Decline

SIR GEOFFREY CLARKE, the president, speaking on October 1 at the autumn conference of the Association of British Chambers of Commerce at Cardiff, stated that: "From 1928 to 1935 the value of exports had declined from £844,000,000 to £426,000,000, and the imports from £1,196,000,000 to £757,000,000.

"The proportion of British to world tonnage had fallen from 43.4 per cent. in 1913 to 31 per cent. in 1936. Purely United Kingdom tonnage had been reduced in five years by no fewer than 3,000,000 tons, and we were steadily losing our carrying trade to other countries owing to the assistance given by them to their own shipping."

Referring to what used to be our great industry, the coal trade, this had been declining steadily since the war. Since 1913 the total exports had declined from 94,000,000 tons to 53,000,000 tons (these figures include bunker coal).

Millions For Homes

ACCORDING to a statement by Mr. D. W. Smith, deputy general manager of the Halifax Building Society, last Thursday, British Building Societies have advanced £1,000,000,000 since the war, largely for the erection and purchase of homes.

Praise for B.U.F. Discipline

ON the question of Fascist parades, Alderman Rowland Winn, chairman of the Leeds Watch Committee, stated: "The privilege of free speech is entitled to protection. I must say this, too, in fairness to the Fascists. They have been amenable to suggestions made to them. They have shown willingness to consult with the police. The other night they were going to hold a parade in a certain quarter of Leeds, but after friendly consultation with the police they abandoned the idea."—*Daily Telegraph*, Oct. 10, 1936.

BEHIND THE NEWS

Edited by J. A. Macnab

Sane Finance in Italy

ACCORDING to Senator Bevione, an economic and financial authority, Italy has come out of the Abyssinian war with more gold reserve than she had when she entered it. The drain on the gold reserves has been more than met by the sacrifices of the people, personal ornaments having produced 930 million and converted foreign holdings 2,000 million lire.

And now Italy, with more gold than before, "devalues" her currency. Why? asks the ordinary man, unless he has realised that gold is not wealth and is only useful for ornament or the more obsolete forms of dentistry.

Italy has, in fact, a managed currency, and her gold is only used for purposes of international trade, Italy not being a self-supporting unit as the British Empire could be. The amount of money the Italian Government issues is the amount necessary for the people to buy as much goods as there is available for consumption. The currency is not arbitrarily restricted and people made to starve, simply because there is only so much of this idiotic metal in some dungeon.

Finance Subordinate to the State

THE details of the Fascist financial laws are quoted by the *Morning Post* in a recent article. It is with some distaste that the *Post*, high priest of Tory capitalism, mentions the existence of a State which does not allow itself to be ruled by finance:

"'*The gold requirements of Italy,*' he (Bevione) says, '*will de determined in relation to Italy's international trade requirements, and to the admininstration of international accounts. When the regulation of these accounts is completed, then gold will have lost a great part of those imperative demands upon which the attention of bankers and industrialists is too much fixed. The more the citizens confront the necessity of national production the less necessary gold becomes.*'

"*This exposition of the Italian attitude,*" the article continues, "*of course, is only applicable to a State in which special laws, such as those passed by the Fascist Government, apply. The main characteristic of the Fascist financial laws can be summed up as follows:*

"1.—*The financial system ceases to be independent of the State, and can no longer be dominated by private groups working for their own ends or indirectly for other groups.*

"2.—*The system becomes national in so far as there are no international influences or interests moving within it. The series of special restrictive laws prevents this.*

"3.—*The Corporations Ministry co-ordinates and controls the complete national productive system.*

"4.—*There is complete State control of savings.*

"5.—*The system really rests on what may be called the credit of the nation and not on the gold reserve.*"

Finance the servant of the State and not the master of statesmen—elimination of international financial influences—impossibility of sectional interests combining to work against the national interest—credit based on real wealth and not on idle metal. A perfect system—except for the international usurer.

And the *Morning Post* tells us that this can only be obtained under Fascism. A striking tribute from the enemy!

"Fascism—a Popular Movement"

THE *News Chronicle*, a paper which does not support Fascism very strongly, reports a statement of the Spanish President Azaña, to the effect that "this struggle is not a struggle between democracy and Fascism, for Fascism is a movement with popular support, whereas the present rebels represent a small privileged class determined to retain its privileges at all costs."

For the popular support of the anti-Red armies, see hundreds of current photographs of cheering crowds as they enter towns taken from the Reds. But we thank the "Popular Front" for the admission that Fascism is dependent on mass support, which cuts away the ground from under the Popular Front's own chief argument.

Negus Gives £15 Tips

IS this ex-Negus a poverty-stricken refugee or a runaway plutocrat after all? The *Daily Herald* first told us he had millions, then that their own story to that effect was a "myth." He seems to be able to do himself pretty well at South-Coast resorts, with an occasional flip over to Geneva to see that the League of Nations is doing its stuff all right. Now we get a little further information about his finances—at least as far as loose change is concerned—from the excellent paper, *Flight*, which is, or ought to be, well known to all of our air-minded readers. The following is extracted from the issue of October 1:

"*While on the subject of gold, there were the very large coins which the Emperor of Ethiopia presented, one apiece, to the crew of the special machine which conveyed him to Paris (for Geneva), whither he travelled in order to study the hop, skip, jump, and dither tactics of the Vacillations Sub-Committee—or something—which was mumbling over the Abyssinian question. The Emperor remarked to Captain Jennens, the pilot, and Mr. Martin, the wireless operator, that the coins were not of great value, but might form small souvenirs of*

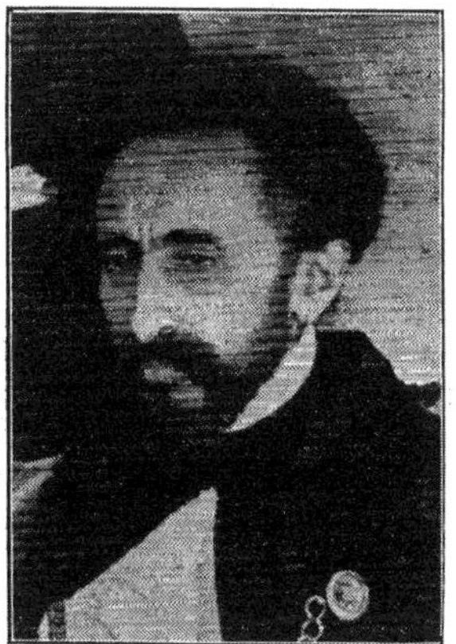

The Ex-Emperor

the occasion. They looked a bit dingy, but when examined proved to be pure gold and worth around fifteen pounds each."

Another oppressed "worker," driven into penury by Fascist oppression!

The Jewish Press recently recounted how Mr. James de Rothschild's butler used to present him, on evenings when he was to dine out, with a salver on which were ten sovereigns, for his tips to such Englishmen as might be privileged to wait upon him during the course of the evening.

The House of Rothschild has nothing on the House of Selassie.

An Athlete on "Living Like Athletes"

DEMOCRACY does not give opportunities for those who reject corruption to influence national politics, appreciably, and Lord Burghley, M.P., is better known as a famous hurdler than for any small contribution to national service that his position as a Tory back-bencher has enabled him to make.

As an athlete he can speak with authority which is denied by Party Whips to the political rank and file, and he had something important to say on the New Germany at a recent Liverpool meeting.

"The time has come for an intensive drive by the Government to improve the physical health of the nation," he declared, adding that during his recent stay in Germany he was greatly impressed by the physical standard of the people, who were being transformed into a physically A1 nation.

Poor Lord Burghley! Does he really believe that the Government of Baldwin, Chamberlain, and Eden is capable of an *intensive drive* about anything?

In the Fascist State *expert opinion* and *informed comment* alone have the right to be heard, and when a world-famous athlete speaks on physical fitness, and tells us what to do, his words shall be translated into immediate action. What a pity that Lord Burghley should adhere to a party that allows 13,500,000 Britons to suffer from underfeeding, whose stunted bodies are denied the right even to attempt to match the physical perfection of the Germans and himself.

Agriculture Sinking Fast—

IN these notes for August 20, we called attention to the fact that 73,000 have left the land in the last three years. Fresh figures are now available showing the position as at June 4, 1936, and these (the "Preliminary Statement of the Agricultural Returns for England and Wales") show a further decline during the past twelve months of 33,100. One-third of 73,000 is 24,333, so that the decline is not merely being maintained, but accelerated, and that at a time when unemployment figures in general are lower than at any time since the bottom of the last slump. From that slump some trades have made a partial and temporary recovery: agriculture has merely gone from bad to worse. Cultivated acreage declined, also, by 76,000.

—And Tories Congratula te Them selves

SUCH being the state of the most honourable industry in the world, the annual conference of the Midland Union of the National Society of Conservative and Unionist Agents, meets at Dudley. (A good, windy democratic title, is it not, rather like Kipling's "*Here is a mouth-filling song of a race that was run by a Boomer*"?) And what did the Tory election agents think of the countryside and themselves? That staunch squire, Mr. D. B. Joel, M.P., supplies the answer. He said:

"*Prosperity is steadily going on through the country, but there is yet wide scope for expansion, and I do not think we have yet reached saturation point in either the industrial or the agricultural field.*

"*Nothing can check our progress except war. I dismiss the thought of Fascism, for while you gentlemen continue to do your jobs there is no fear of that in this country.*"

Nothing can check their progress, evidently, while they are still allowed by the British people to drive 30,000 farm workers off the land each year in order that City lending houses may continue to draw the interest on foreign loans in the form of foodstuffs that ruin the British farmer.

What a chuckle the shades of old Solly Joel and Barney Barnato must have had to hear the Tory Party being congratulated on its yeoman service to Jewish finance!

Heroic Leadership

FROM the *East End News*, October 6:

"*P.C. Webb said about 10.15 p.m. on Friday he was one of a number of officers who were escorting a procession of 200 to 300 Communists along the Mile End-road towards Stepney Green. At the corner of Burdett-road a girl dressed in Blackshirt uniform was selling 'The Blackshirt' newspaper. The members of the crowd rushed towards her and attempted to get hold of her, but several police officers ranged themselves round her and protected her. Jacobs, who was the leader of the Communists, was shouting, 'Lynch her! Lynch her!'*"

80 per cent. Prosperity

MR. NEVILLE CHAMBERLAIN says we enjoy 80 per cent. of our former prosperity.

1936 is half-way between the last slump trough—1931—and the next, which may be expected in 1940-41. It is thus at the crest of the boom. Employment, we are told, is higher than ever. Stock-Exchange shares (perfect Tory barometer!) are soaring. Yet Lancashire starves, and why? Here is the answer:

	1913.	1935.
Cotton exports, total (in linear yards) ...	7,075,252,000	2,013,429,000
Ditto, to India alone	3,057,305,600	497,803,500

The foreign trade figures are even worse than the Indian, but I omit them because Fascism does not rely on foreign markets where it is necessary to meet coolie competition.

There are 100,000 unemployed in Lancashire, preponderantly in the textile industry. 80,000 cotton operatives could go back to work at once if Mosley's policy were adopted and colonial and Indian markets reserved for British industry—let alone the Dominion markets which could be secured by barter trading agreements through taking only Empire raw materials.

Our Guests

WHEN Mosley on October 4 was to march with other patriotic Englishmen bearing the Union Jack through the streets of the English capital to explain his provocative "Britain First" policy to those who wished to hear it, the "British workers" protested. They barricaded the streets and injured thirty-seven policemen in the execution of duty. Those who could be identified have been charged and punished for breaking the law. Out of fifty-five charged here are some of their names:

Hyman Tannerbaum	Michael Becow
Jack Schuckman	Israel Becow
Moisha Ben Aron	Benjamin Becow
Jack Utah	Alfred Lipman
Harry Bravitz	Maurice Remer
Sidney Kramer	Hyman Kersch
Jack Feldman	George Morris
Reuben Vicker	Alfred Guiver
Harry Dorfman	Keith Goldstein
Wilf Franks	Sally Sass
Lionel Chersin	Josef Yoselvitch
Sidney Goldstein	Miller Bloom
Jack Richman	Philip Goldberg
Jack Masters	Bennett Benjamin
Harry Jacobs	Keva Izbitsky
Jack Jacobs	Israel Spielberg
Aaron Rothzeig	Charles Goodman
Samuel Jacobs	Alfred Kofkin
Benjamin Burgess	Morris Goldstein

Quotations to Remember

"We mean to put on the Statute Book a law which will make people in this country citizens of the world before being citizens of this country."—Major C. A. Attlee, M.P., *Daily Herald* and *Manchester Guardian*, 3.10.34.

"I think in the present condition of the world we are bound in duty to those whom we represent to tell them that they cannot get Socialism without tears. I think that we have got to face the fact that, even if we are returned with a majority, we shall have to fight all the way, that we shall have another crisis at once."—Major Attlee (cited by Lord Elton), *The Times*, 1.11.35.

"My complaint against the general Labour Party is that it is too hesitant to take the plunge for a better and higher standard of living, freedom, and peace. Soviet Russia is a good example of what can be done, and if England would only follow, other countries would very soon do the same."—Sir Stafford Cripps, Dursley, 7.9.34.

"We must be prepared to take steps far more forceful than were taken at the time of the Ulster rebellion. We have got to face up to the realities of what definite Socialism means. We should not allow ourselves to be blinded to the real nature of the conflict which is bound to come."—Sir Stafford Cripps, Oxford, 27.5.34.

Printed by ARGUS PRESS, LTD., Temple Avenue and Tudor Street, London, E.C.4, England, and published by ACTION PRESS, LTD., Sanctuary Buildings, Gt. Smith Street, London, S.W.1, England. Telephone: Victoria 9084 (5 lines).

No. 40 [REGISTERED AT THE G.P.O. AS A NEWSPAPER] “BRITAIN FIRST” NOVEMBER 21, 1936

FOR KING AND PEOPLE

PUBLISHED EVERY THURSDAY. R.S.40

BRITISH UNION PROSPECTIVE CANDIDATES

See Page 7

MARCHERS WHO MATTER

After four years of scoffing at uniforms, Parliament is now devoting days of its time to a Bill to make them illegal. Sights like the above will be banned from our streets, but the wailing red banner-straggles are to continue. Mr. Aneurin Bevan, M.P. (Labour), and Mr. Harry Pollitt (Communist) congratulated the Hunger Marchers on having ruined the Armistice Day Ceremony and threatened to organise a similar march against the Coronation. The Press does not report this and Parliament does nothing about it.

BALDWIN'S BIGGEST BLUNDER—READ MOSLEY *ON PAGE 9*

The World, The Flesh—and Financial Democracy

A Weekly Review of Men and Events

By WILLIAM JOYCE

A Motley Crew

MOST of the creatures who have been forced to the front of the Socialist mob are uninteresting. Their pronouncements are pedestrian, and even the hiss of hatred which they emit against National Socialism is too constant and invariable to be capable of evoking any longer the sensation of sound. In truth, they are a drab and melancholy crew,

Sir Stafford (Chameleon) Cripps

whose sordid mediocrity is relieved only by one figure in particoloured raiment, always capable of executing the most fascinating somersaults in front of his admirers. Without Sir Stafford Cripps the whole wretched mob would fade into an undistinguished greyness.

Sir Stafford is reported in the *Daily Express* as having, at Stockport, where he held a meeting, urged opposition to conscription. Some deluded fool asked him what he thought about "the menace of Germany." The reply, which ought to be recorded and remembered, was that he did not believe that it would be a bad thing for the British working class if Germany did defeat us. Here we must pause and draw several deep breaths.

Fools Rush In

THE British Union has been assailed and stigmatised, slandered and persecuted merely for having advocated an honourable friendship with the German people, but it was not inappropriately left for a leader of the Socialist Party to venture the opinion that it might not be a bad thing for the British workers to be placed under a German National Socialist regime.

Perverse to the end, the gallant Sir Stafford will die in the last ditch to prevent the establishment of a British National Socialist Government, but so all-embracing, so capacious, so universally radiant is the warmth of his internationalism that he is prepared to present to the workers of Britain a solution which must draw prolonged shudders from the adipose superstructure which conceals the soul of Pritt.

Unscrupulous Journalism

SIR OSWALD MOSLEY and those who assist him have long since grown accustomed to the misrepresentation by the minions of Financial Democracy of all that they say, and when we consider the power, the experience, and the acumen of those who conduct the Daily Press we may be tempted to think that their ingenuity in suggesting the false and suppressing the true could not be excelled. This impression is incorrect.

The most astonishing perversion of Blackshirt utterances have been decisively capped by a certain journal which has a circulation in Cambridge, and which, in its treatment of a speech which I recently made there at a University dinner indicates the utmost limit of turpitude to which unscrupulous journalism may advance. In the report there occurs this amazing passage:—

"He won the sympathy of the meeting by appealing to his audience us the educated upper class. 'I could not speak like this to a worker, a miner, or a technician,' he declaimed. 'It is only people of our kind who sense the problem of what is right for us, as individuals, to do.' No miner, or technician, or any worker could envisage a proper objective for his energies, but an educated man could and did, and would not fail to achieve it."

This complete distortion is much too serious to remain unchallenged, and the argument from which it proceeds may well be repeated here.

Philosophic Doubt

I SHOWED that the so-called educated classes, and particularly the Universities, were assailed by a loathsome disease which some have described as "philosophic doubt." The ordinary worker, whether he be farmer, miner, or cotton-spinner, need not be treated for the disease. It was unnecessary to appeal to him to adopt a positive standard of moral values, since there was no reason to suppose that he had lost the power to distinguish between right and wrong.

Leadership indeed he required and sought, but the more privileged and comfortable members of the community, enjoying the amenities and imbibing the poisons of false philosophy at the Universities, were reduced to a condition of paralysis. Thousands of young men were to-day desirous of doing right, but so thoroughly had their minds been poisoned and their characters undermined that they knew not what right was.

If the masses of the people required leadership, those who aspired to responsibility for the culture of the nation required a revolutionary moral reconditioning. Their tragedy was that they could not be satisfied because they did not know what they wanted, nor could they know what they wanted if their standards of judgment had been warped and twisted by the casuistry and the fallacies of Democratic philosophy. Such was the substance of my remarks.

The enemies of National Socialism are now so frightened of its valid policy that they resort to the last and the foulest means of opposing it; namely, by putting into the mouths of its advocates statements diametrically opposed to those which they utter. There could be no greater tribute to the convincing nature of Fascist argument than that its enemies should consider their only defence to lie in preventing it from becoming known.

"An Honourable Man"

"Stanley thou shalt not from oblivion pass,
Arise, thou monumental brass."

Dryden's lines on Titus Oates may well be modified to describe the brazen integrity of the most honourable man that Financial Democracy had produced. Mr. Baldwin most cunningly remarks that Democracy must always be two years behind Dictators. It seems also that Financial Democratic honesty must always be two years late. Now at last the secret of the sealed lips is revealed. Mr. Baldwin claims that he would not tell the truth two years ago lest in the telling he lost an election.

Quite right, indeed, was his surmise that the people then had no desire for war with Germany; but if his honest nature permits him to face facts of any kind, he must realise to-day that people will not tolerate war with Germany. At the thousands of meetings which the British Union has held, the people have come to know that the security of Europe depends upon friendship with Germany.

However, it would be tedious and unpleasant to examine Mr. Baldwin's statement of the purpose of eliciting from it any valuable principles relating to foreign policy.

The Limpets

THE cardinal fact is that the people were deceived and the reason for their deception was the desire of Honest Stanley and his almost equally honest friends to perpetuate their tenure of office.

This little essay in the theology of false impression must now be applied to Sir John Simon's statement that the British Union receives money from foreign sources. Since there is no higher standard of honesty in the Cabinet than that represented by Mr. Baldwin himself, Sir John may say in two years' time that if he had told the truth the chances of the Government remaining in power would have been destroyed, and this explanation would have one of the most solid precedents in Parliamentary history. If it is right to mislead the nation in one respect, it must, of course, be right to mislead them in another; and if for the sake of Parliamentary advantage the Prime Minister is capable of deceiving, there can be no reason at all why the Home Secretary should not resort to similar tactics against the Fascist Movement on the eve of a debate in which representatives of Jewish international finance are to be arrayed against the freedom to express his case which the Fascist claims.

Fortunate, indeed, it is that the people have come to measure Parliamentary truth by Mr. Baldwin's standards. With this safe yardstick in their possession they will know how to deal with Sir John Simon.

Laughing Last

AS I write it is too early to discuss the debate on Public Order Bill in the House of Commons. Opposition to it, whether or not effective, has arisen in some curious quarters.

The Council of Civil Liberties entertains an unholy dread lest the police should enable the promoters of a public meeting to take legal action against those who have conspired to break it up.

But the most plaintive wail of all comes from the ultra-montane Jews. At a meeting of the Jewish People's Council the Bill was condemned because it does not contain provisions specifically forbidding reference in public to the Sacred Beast of Financial Democracy.

These Jews know that the measure has been conceived and drafted at their instigation. They cannot be unaware that in their interests the Government is making this futile gesture and that Sir John Simon has been wished by them into the unenviable position of Canute on the occasion of the latter's least successful public ceremony.

A Luckless Hebrew

BUT from this little congregation of the faithful there is something to learn. One luckless Hebrew asked the conference to concentrate entirely on fighting anti-Semitism and to ignore Fascism altogether. He may have thought that the best way of countering Fascist policy is to pretend that it does not exist. However, his little stratagem was sharply rejected. The resolution was passed, declaring that the fight must be not only against anti-Semitism, but also against Fascism.

Here is one more testimony to the justice of the attitude which Sir Oswald Mosley has adopted. He realised full well two years ago that the Jewish community was determined to oppose Fascism in all circumstances.

Not being able to visualise with complacency a financial system which would terminate their career of exploitation the Hebrews were determined to prevent National Socialism from arising in this land, and had the movement not taken up the challenge it would have deserved to perish, just as by responding in a manner worthy of the British people it has gained the strength which renders it invincible to-day and will render it supreme to-morrow.

An Interesting Publication

SOME of my readers may be interested in a magazine which makes its first appearance this month. It is the *Anglo-German Review*. Among the contributors to the first issue are: Lloyd George, Lord Redesdale, and Bruce Bairnsfather.

The periodical is very well produced and is full of interest. It cannot be regarded as a political document, and is indeed almost entirely concerned with social aspects of German life. It maintains a not very commendable silence as to the Jewish architects of ill-will, and for this reason must be regarded as suggestive rather than educational.

The promoters of this very interesting little magazine may feel that it is unwise to expose the influence of international Jewry on politics; but if such be their feeling now, they must eventually learn that the plainest speaking is needed. Nevertheless, this first number is full of interest, and with the reservation herein made, I can commend it to our readers.

The Conscientious Objector

The "MOORISH" TROOPS of FRANCO

Capt. Gordon-Canning describes Life in Morocco with the Inhabitants.

A GREAT many words have been written about the employment of "Moorish" troops in the Spanish Civil War by many writers who, probably to begin with, do not appreciate the general meaning of the word "Moorish," and, secondly, know nothing whatsoever of the history and daily existence of these mountain tribesmen, now fighting to win Spain for Christianity and save this country from atheistic Communism.

I, by some unknown fate, was destined to pass many weeks in the very heart of their country and to visit certain localities which, even in the twentieth century, within a few miles of Gibraltar, had rarely, if ever, entertained the presence of a European, at least for several hundred years, except here and there as a prisoner. For days on end I have lived in intimate association with these "Moors," walked their hills and spent nights in their huts listening first to their endless stories by the light of Price's flickering candles, and, later, to their stentorous breathing, as a dozen or more stalwart hillsmen, weary from a twelve-hour march over their tortuous mountain tracks, stretched themselves out on the bare earth for a well-earned rest. I have faced them as a stranger with no credentials and as an honoured guest of their leaders.

Photograph of Capt. Gordon-Canning in Moroccan Arab dress on journey November, 1924

I have studied their history and their association with Spain from the eighth century onward, and, therefore, can be said to know, perhaps, a little more about these "Moors" than the many journalists who write so glibly at the behest—so frequently—of their Jewish overlords, who themselves are not fit, in many cases (for all their material culture), to shake the hands of these hardy and courageous mountaineers. There is a Riffian saying: "It is small comfort to be alive when brave men are dead." Hardly applicable to our international financiers.

Moor

THIS word includes the several races or admixtures of race in Morocco. The two main being Berber, the original inhabitants, and by which two-thirds of the Spanish zone in Morocco is occupied, and the Arab, who invaded and emigrated to Morocco in the seventh and eleventh centuries. Here and there, but especially in the south, and not infrequently in the Riff, one finds considerable trace of negro blood originating from the great numbers of Central African slaves who, through the centuries, came to this country across the Sahara. There are also the Moroccan Jews in the towns, but there is no vital Jewish question as, on the whole, they live a separate existence in their mellahs.

The Spanish zone is inhabited, then (i) by the Riff tribes, under which can be included the Ghomara and Senhaja sections, with their own language and decidedly Nordic in head, hair, eyes, nose, etc., details of which are to be found in Dr. Carleton Coon's brilliant work, in a series of African studies for the Peabody Trust in Harvard University, entitled "The Riff Tribes," which was published in 1931. The Riffian is, in many cases, perhaps more frequently than not, fairer in colour than the southern Italian or Spaniard; and (ii) by the Arab tribes of the Djebala, who, admittedly, are by no means the highest type of Arab, and who have always been regarded by the pure Riff tribesmen as inclined to licentiousness and as being untrustworthy. However, in the two towns of Tetuan and Chaoun there are direct descendants living to-day of the great Moorish families of Granada, Cordova, Seville, etc. and who, it is reputed, still retain the keys of their old houses in Spain.

The greater number of General Franco's forces are made up from the tribesmen of the Riff, who, as they proved during the 1921-26 campaigns, are the first among warriors. These men, for all the characteristics of mountaineers hardy, individualistic and somewhat wild, proved, when given a leader and a cause, to be amenable to discipline, reliable, and not given to perpetrate tortures or to indiscriminate massacre against their defeated enemies. General Franco, during his many years service in Morocco, has proved to be a leader, and has endeared himself to these mountaineers. It would be a thousand times safer to fall into the power of these men than it would be to find oneself a captive of the Ogpu, the leaders of the C.N.T., or of the Anarcho-Iberian party.

Moors in Spain

SINCE A.D. 711, when Tarik, at the head of 7,000 Berbers and Arabs, landed at Tarifa Point, the histories of Morocco and Spain have been closely interwoven. From 711, until the fall of Granada in 1492, there were the Moorish or Arab kingdoms in Spain. During much of this period there existed the highest civilisation and the greatest toleration in Europe.* Spaniards, Arabs, and Berbers inter-married, and the whole of Spain from Toledo southward and eastward is full of Arabic and Moorish monuments of exquisite art. Many of the Spanish words to-day are derived from Arabic roots, and there is a great similarity between Spanish and Arabic music.

In 1492 Ferdinand and Isabella, staunch Catholics, expelled a large number of the Muslims then residing in Spain, and Philip III., in 1610, ordered the final expulsion of all remaining Muslim elements.

During the reign of Isabella (1859 to 1868) there was much fighting around Tetuan and Melilla in 1860, and again in 1895, while from 1911 onward there was a more or less continuous war between the Spanish forces occupying their zone in Morocco and the various tribes, which culminated into the large-scale war between the years 1921 and 1926, ending in the capitulation of Abd-el-Krim.

Some of the greatest glories in Spain to-day at Toledo, Cordova, Granada, and Seville are the results of the Moorish kingdoms in Spain which have been the subject for many historical books of the first order, such as "The History of the Moors in Spain," by Lane Poole, and the "History of the Muslims in Spain," by the Dutch author Dozy; and the famous tale of Washington Irving, called the "Conquest of Granada."

* See Renan.

To-day

THEREFORE, it is in no way surprising that General Franco, who has had intimate experience of these "Moorish" tribesmen in the Spanish zone, should employ these men as soldiers to defend the Spanish culture and the Spanish nation. Although, throughout the centuries, there has been intense rivalry between the Islamic and Catholic creeds, it is not to be wondered at to-day that the soldiers of these two religions should be found in the same ranks, fighting against the atheistic creed of Communism and against those who wantonly destroy holy relics, churches, and representatives, whether they be of the Catholic or of the Islamic faith.

There is infinitely more reason to be found on behalf of General Franco for his employment of these Riffian tribesmen in the Spanish Civil War than there is to be found on behalf of the French Government in employing the Central African negroes, the Senegalese especially, on the European battle fronts during the Great War, 1914-18, and, worse still, the French employment of these Senegalese troops during the occupation of the Ruhr.

The ways of fate are strange and if, as rumour has it at the moment, General Franco on completion of his task of overthrowing the Communistic and foreign elements in Spain will grant autonomy to the Riffian tribes, all what Abd-el-Krim was striving for and fought for between the years 1921 and 1926 will have been achieved, not by fighting against Spain, but by fighting on behalf of Spain, and what I came so near to achieve myself—the establishment of an autonomous Riff under Abd-el-Krim—and which was blocked by Spain in 1926—may now be offered with limits to the Riff by General Franco.

If this grant of autonomy proves to be a real fact, there is no doubt that the French zone in Morocco will be the scene of much internal trouble during the next few years.

Sidi M' Hamet, brother of the famous Abd-el-Krim, both now exiles in Reunion Island in charge of foreign negotiations for the Riff from 1921-1925.

The political situation in Morocco must always be an important question for the British Empire, commanding as it does the western portion of the Mediterranean route to the East.

Thus, not only may General Franco be able to restore to Spain her lost greatness and save her soul, but also to rekindle the spirit which once made the Moors leaders of civilisation and create stability in an area of high strategical significance to the British Empire.

THE SALENGRO AFFAIR

THE case of M. Salengro, Minister of the Interior, is exciting the same passion and controversy as did the Dreyfus Affair in the last century.

Evidently those who accuse M. Salengro of having, as a soldier, deserted his post in the presence of the enemy, are taking a fearful responsibility. As in the Dreyfus case, the parties of the extreme Right are said to be inspired by unworthy political motives in bringing forward such charges against an officer holding, on this occasion, a high post in the Government. The charge against such a large section of the public is absurd; no public would ruin the country's reputation for any political motive.

It would be more rational to suppose that many people are not convinced that the Arbitrary Commission, presided over by General Gamelin, re-established the reputation of the Minister of the Interior.

M. Salengro was in the cyclist corps of the 233 Infantry Regiment at the time of his disappearance in October, 1915. He explained that he crossed the parapet separating the French and German armies in order to secure some valuable papers from the body of a fallen comrade. He did not return. The cyclist Salengro, it was supposed, had died, but in November it appeared he was living, for he wrote to his *marraine de guerre* saying he had been captured "fighting like a lion," and that he was a prisoner in Germany.

Last Friday the President of the Council himself defended his Minister of the Interior in the Chamber of Deputies in answer to the interpellation of a Deputy.

On January 20, 1916, said M. Blum, a courtmartial was held at Versailles, which, judging by *contumace*, acquitted the cyclist Salengro by three votes against two. M. Blum considered this all the more remarkable since Salengro was not present. According to *Gringoire* the prisoner arrived in Switzerland in April, 1918, in a convoy of *grands blessés*.

After twenty years the Salengro case is revived. But an important report is missing, and the military records of the former cyclist have been deleted. It is also uncertain if the document recently required for the defence from the Ministry of Pensions will be forthcoming. *Gringoire*, a paper which M. Blum declares he would not touch, asserts that this important document has disappeared. So also did the first report on the disappearance of the cyclist Salengro.

FACTS THE PRESS DID NOT PRINT

Extracts from Herr Hitler's Speech at Nuremberg, September, 1936

THAT the German agricultural income would be higher than in any previous year of our peace period.

That the total national income of 41 milliards would show an annual rise to over 56 milliard Reichsmarks.

That the German harbour towns could no longer be compared with graveyards for dead ships, and that in 1936 alone ships would be constructed in the German ship-yards to the extent of over 640,000 tons.

That innumerable factories would not merely double the number of their employees, but treble and quadruple them, and that countless other factories would be reconstructed in just four years.

That the quiet automobile factories would not only thrive, but would be extended to an astounding degree, and that the production of cars would increase from the 45,000 in 1932 to about a quarter of a million.

That the deficit of our towns and counties would be balanced in four years, and that the Reich would receive an increased income tax of almost 5 milliards annually.

That the German Reich would have special auto-highroads such as have not yet been built on this scale of size and perfection, and that of this projected 7,000 km., 1,000 km. would be in use, and over 4,000 km. would be in process of construction after not quite four years.

That the German theatre would celebrate its revival in precisely the same manner as the productions of our German music.

But that the German nation would play a living part in this revolutionary intellectual revival, and all this, without any single Jew appearing in this intellectual guidance of the German nation!

What would they have said had I prophesied that Germany would have freed itself in these four years from the bondage of Versailles, that the Reich would adopt general conscription again, that as in peace time every German would serve two years for the freedom of the country, that a new navy to protect our coasts and our trade would be in the process of construction, and a powerful new air-force would guarantee the security of our towns, factories and workshops; that the Rhineland would be under the supremacy of the German nation again and that thereby the sovereignty of the Reich would be restored over the whole territory.

As Herr Hitler himself said: "If I had prophesied all these things four years ago, I should have been branded as mad with the ironic laughter of the whole world."

This restoration of Germany externally and internally has taken place at the expense of no other nation.—R. G. C.

THE BRITISH COUNTRYSIDE

ALWAYS A NEW CRISIS

THE FATAL LACK OF FORESIGHT

(By Our Agricultural Correspondent.)

I SUPPOSE that the ordinary business man must often ask himself why it is that he is now always hearing of some new crisis in agriculture, and why should such crisis be allowed, when, by a little prevision, a little practical planning, and the exercise of much sound common sense amongst those who rule they could be avoided.

During the last few days we have been hearing quite a lot regarding the new sugar beet contracts for the 1937 crop, and with good reason, for growers are faced crisis, but which is really something one expected would happen.

In such a season as we experienced last summer it is not too much to expect that much of the barley would be spoiled and thus only fit for grinding purposes, and that, comparatively speaking, the good malting samples were few and far between. I have heard some hard things said recently about the farmers for not producing malting barley, and the brewers for not buying it.

So far as I am any judge, I do not think either parties are to blame, for not one of us can con-

The British Countryside. A windmill, so many of which were once landmarks and are now disappearing as farming in Britain is allowed by the Government to perish.

with ever-increasing costs of production, and at the same time the price paid per ton for beet has not been leaving them a wide enough margin to show a small profit. That is why the N.F.U. have been pressing the Sugar Commission to fix the price at 38s. per ton, plus, of course, the usual extra payment for sugar content per unit over and above the basic 15½ per cent. As readers will remember, the Sugar Commission was called in to arbitrate on the deadlock that existed between the Sugar Beet Corporation and the Sugar Beet Committee of the N.F.U. For next season the price per ton has been fixed from 36s. to 37s. 6d., according to various factories, and this price is considered far from satisfactory by growers, for although they show an increase of price per ton, yet it is obvious that such an increase has not been sufficient to cover the extra cost of producing the crop. Not only have the prices of artificial manures risen, but there has been more difficulty in obtaining labour to lift the crop than in any year since we first commenced to grow it, and such labour as could be picked up had to be given higher wages than the crop could bear and yet remain an economic proposition.

Hence it is feared that the full acreage to obtain the 560,000 tons of sugar needed by the Government will not be obtained.

Once again we see a great industry, and one that has done much for agriculture, with its fate trembling in the balance, for no one can say that the handling of the industry by the Government from its very inception has been marked by brilliant methods.

The Brewers In a Flutter

FROM sugar beet to barley is not a very wide jump, for in the Eastern Counties so much of the beet land goes into barley afterwards. Now I learn the brewers are gravely concerned because they fear that there will not be enough really good malting barley home grown to meet their demands.

So we are faced by what some folk would probably call a barley trol the weather, and it is upon the weather that the success or failure of the barley crop depends. One shower at the right time may make all the difference between a good malting sample and a bad one, or one shower too much may spoil an excellent sample. Again, the condition of the land while the crop is growing may have more effect upon the grain than laymen would think.

I have also been told that in the Middle Ages nothing but good old English malt and hops went into the mash-tub, and there was then no question of good, bad, or indifferent malting samples.

The answer to this is that the beer brewed then and demanded by the consumer was vastly different from the tastes now obtaining, while, so far as I can gather, the laws and regulations concerning materials and specific gravity in the brewing were nothing like what they are to-day.

The ideal thing, of course, would be to grow all the barley needed for beer in this country, but climatic conditions are against that, and as I have so frequently pointed out ere this, while a straight tariff sounds the best way to deal with imported barley, yet the interests of the feeders have to be considered

Feeding Stuffs Too Dear

DOES it not seem as though almost every branch of agricultural industry are pulling in different directions, and this despite the efforts of the N.F.U. and other bodies to keep them together.

Much of the trouble to-day is owing to the fact that feeding stuffs are far too dear, and this has two effects upon commodities, it either renders their production so costly that no margin of profit is left, or it renders them (processed commodities and meat) too dear for the limited purchasing power of the ordinary person. Time was when the bulk of our feeding stuffs were produced at home, and processed at home, but now land has gone from under the plough and each year sees our

(Continued at foot of Col. 3.)

A Demand for Increased Home Production of Meat & Dairy Produce

THE possibilities of the improvement of the grasslands of Great Britain, and the potential increase in the amount of available productive grassland as against grassland offering a bare maintenance ration has been the subject of an article based upon recent investigations into the grasslands of Great Britain by Prof. R. G. Stapledon, Director, Welsh Plant Breeding Station.

It is estimated that no fewer than 16,000,000 acres of land in Great Britain can be turned into good pasture land by an expenditure of an amount varying from less than £3 to a maximum of £7 an acre.

At first this amount seems considerable, but compares favourably with £9 an acre spent by the Forestry Commission in fencing and planting land, from which there is no return for several years, whilst in the grassland improvement scheme for sheep and cattle there would be something to show for the money expended in a few months; furthermore, the Government takes little time to decide on granting a £10,000,000 loan to U.S.S.R.

Statistical figures for the import of butter and meat alone into this country are enlightening.

In 1933 we imported butter to the value of £10,000,000 from Denmark, £1,600,000 from Russia, £500,000 from Holland, £800,000 from Sweden, all countries outside the British Empire, and in the same year £2,000,000 worth of condensed milk from Holland.

The statistics for meat import show that of a total value of £77,796,000 worth of meat imported, £18,000,000 came from Argentina.

Prof. Stapledon comes very near the truth when he says, "From the national point of view, and having regard to the importance of food in times of crisis, to the importance of food at all times, and to the manifest need of the vigorous rural population, it seems almost incredible that such a state of affairs should be allowed to continue."

Under the present system of government, Prof. Stapledon's plan to increase agricultural production would be futile.

Only by following the Fascist policy, of an increased purchasing power of the people, and a maximum home production under the Corporate State, which would demand not only expert knowledge and experience, but scientific investigation in every corporation, would this project be possible.—J. W.

(Continued from Col. 2.)

wheat and oat acreage shrinking, to say nothing of barley.

Most of us can remember when the village mills scattered all over the country used to deal with our wheat and enable us to buy offals and bran direct from the mill, while it would also be kept busy grinding barley into meal, and crushing and grinding oats.

Those mills (which gave a lot of employment in a village) are now nearly all closed down, and the milling is done by huge firms in mills erected at the ports. One is inclined to think that as the small millers were crushed under, and their places taken by the big firms the prices of feeding stuffs have risen, and when one comes to consider it the milling industry to-day is in the hands of very few men.

Letters from Westminster

BY THE MEMBER FOR "ACTION"

NEVER has the Party system received such a shaking up as during last week. We began last Monday on a nice gentlemanly note, and everything looked as it always looks in the Mother of Parliaments.

There was Mr. Ted Williams, a miner from South Wales, pleading for justice for a retired General, and Mr. Garro-Jones, the Welsh Labour M.P. for Aberdeen, pleading for justice for public schoolboys in their frequent visits to the tuck shops. The elderly gentlemen on the Government Front Bench looked on approvingly at this manifestation of the unity of the classes.

On Monday night we talked about the condition of Britain for a long time, but there was very little interest in that, I must admit. The speeches always end in the same way. The Socialist speakers always demand to know what the Government is doing about it, and the answer is always—nothing.

The Conservatives, on the other hand, always demand to know what the Socialists did when they had the chance, and the answer always is—nothing. The M.P.s thoroughly enjoy this cut and thrust, although I gather it is being less and less appreciated in the country.

The Poverty Problem

IT was not until Tuesday that we really got down to business. That was the day on which all Parties who had solemnly pledged themselves to do something big and drastic for the poverty problem began the job. A private meeting had been held in the House of Commons at which the Popular Front was established. Leading members of the Cabinet were present and leaders from the Labour and Liberal Parties. At that meeting it was unanimously decided that the one great contribution which all Parties could make in establishing Jerusalem in England's green and pleasant land was to abolish the wearing of black shirts.

No Minister was prepared to say that this alone would abolish the distressed areas or obviate the necessity of nearly 2,000,000 people being fed by the relieving officers. But every Minister is convinced that if the virile Blackshirts stop demonstrating and talking about real politics, the House of Commons will be able to enjoy its afternoon nap in the smoke rooms in the winter and sun itself on the terrace in the summer.

The title should be "A Bill to Restore Tranquility in British Politics." The one humorous touch is that Mr. Gallacher, my Communist colleague, had asked for a Bill to suppress you, and now that he has got it he doesn't like it. He is wrong about this, though, as the Bill only applies to organisations which are likely to be a danger to the existing order in Parliament, and the Communist Party is never likely to be that.

Conditions in Central Africa

WELL, that kept us going all day on Tuesday. On Wednesdays and Fridays we are never expected to do much. These are the days when private members are allowed to introduce Bills or motions. As a rule they are talked out, as during the season members cannot be expected to abandon their social obligations for politics.

The condition of Britain, being what it is, the House had decided to spend Wednesday discussing a motion by Sir Graham-Little, calling attention to the condition of some of the tribes in Central Africa. But, alas, another enjoyable evening was wasted, because a number of hunger marchers had arrived in London and had actually asked to be allowed to speak. As Mr. Baldwin, himself, said, it might be taken as an admission that Parliament was unable to deal with the problems confronting the nation. At this we all girt up our loins, and none of us had the wit to see that if Parliament had been able to deal with the problems there would have been none to deal with, because the problem of unemployment is, roughly, the same age as Parliament itself.

But Labour believes there are votes in this hunger-marching business. Mr. Attlee demanded to know why Mr. Baldwin had put this insult on his people. He made a very good speech on this, and so did other Labour M.P.s, and then young Mr. Lennox-Boyd recalled that the Conservative Government of 1936 was following the procedure so carefully laid down by the Labour Government of 1931, of which the gallant Mr. Attlee was a member.

And it was true. Mr. MacDonald, Labour's Prime Minister in 1930, had police surrounding every approach to Downing-street. Neither Mr. Attlee, nor any Labour M.P., protested against that insult to the poor hunger marchers. They said then what the Conservatives say to-day. The march, they said, was a Communist move inspired and financed by Moscow to discredit Parliamentary institutions.

Baldwin's Amazing Admissions

IT was Thursday's debate which finally scattered the illusion that there was such a thing as decency and honesty in British public life. The debate was Defence. The Leader of the Opposition was brushed aside like a feather, his place taken by Mr. Winston Churchill.

We all know Mr. Churchill's insensate hatred of Germany. He cannot forgive Germany for recovering after he had fondly believed he had administered a knock-out blow in 1918. But, that apart, his indictment of the mess and muddle in our defence forces was devastating. His job was easy, for it is doubtful if at any time in history so many incompetent men have been gathered together in one Cabinet.

This Cabinet cannot possibly agree as to what is necessary for defence, because they have not yet agreed on what they have to defend. Mr. Baldwin says our frontier is the Rhine, and Sir Thomas Inskip says that anybody who says that is talking nonsense.

Mr. Churchill slashed about him unmercifully. He manfully admired Mr. Baldwin's candour in admitting in 1935 that he had been misinformed as to Germany's rearmament. Then, to everybody's surprise Mr. Baldwin, who had blamed Lord Londonderry for not giving correct information, now coolly informed the House that he knew all about this as far back as 1933.

To everybody's blank amazement he stated that if he had proceeded to rearm he would have lost the General Election, and so for three years, on his own confession, the entire British nation and the lives of men, women, and children throughout the Empire were jeopardised in order that the Conservative Party should be returned to power with he as Prime Minister.

Nothing that any Fascist could say on the rottenness of Party politics could be so terribly crushing as this appalling frankness of Britain's Prime Minister.

Every citizen has now a clear and immediate duty. Either Britain has to be rearmed or she hasn't. If she is to be rearmed, it should be done efficiently. But, above all, we should insist that no politician should be allowed to create the impressions that Germany is our enemy. Mr. Churchill is deliberately doing this. His policy is quite clear. He wants to encircle Germany in a hoop of steel. That is precisely the policy which Sir Edward Grey and Mr. Churchill pursued between 1910 and 1914.

THOSE JEWELS!

WHERE SOME OF THE SOCIALIST FUNDS ORIGINATED

By JOHN EMERY

THE Labour Party is in the doldrums. The stupid leadership is even making the most slavish idolaters rise in revolt. Last week Mr. Marchbanks (Sec., N.U.R.) openly derided the efforts of the professional careerists in his own Party.

That, following the slump at the municipal elections, has caused dismay at Transport House. They have known for some time that there were none so poor as to do them honour, and now they feel that there are none so rich as to go on subscribing for no return. And when the cash stops the machine stops, and a lot of men who couldn't earn their living at anything else may be thrown on the labour market.

Even before that happens the political bosses may pass through a bad time. Rich men, who used to subscribe to the secret Party funds, are leaving off, and, as a result, no money comes in at all except from the big unions. This leaves the union bosses with the power to crack the whip and sit back watching the professional politicians jump to each resounding crack.

When I see Labour politicians profess righteous indignation at the mere mention of foreign money, I cannot help but think it is a case of sour grapes. They know that the Communist Party is financed from Moscow and have issued scores of documents to prove it. But every one of us who has been close to the machine knows that the official Labour leaders have taken money from sources almost as alien to the British workers' cause as ever Moscow could possibly be.

Squeamishness

I CANNOT understand this new Labour and Communist squeamishness on foreign gold. There was a time when even the most kindly and Christian gentlemen in the Labour Party were actually proud to acknowledge it. I was in close touch with many of the early, romantic smugglings after the War, although I want to say here that I have never received a penny directly or indirectly from either the Communist Party or the Labour Party. But everybody in those adventures enjoyed them immensely.

There were two types in those affairs, as in most so-called "working-class" adventures — there were those who took risks because they believed in Communism, and those who saw a good profit in it. In every case the men who took the risks because they believed in something were working-class men; the men who did it for ten per cent. were the pseudo-Communist intellectuals from Bloomsbury.

Now that I am on the subject there is no reason why I shouldn't tell the story. In refusing to admit that they get foreign money, the Communist Party seems to forget that the late General Booth admitted he would take help from the Devil himself to carry on his good work. Nobody in Britain raised the slightest objection to the General's zeal, even with the certain knowledge that the Devil could not be a British subject.

In the early days of the Communist Party Mr. Francis Meynell, a former director of the *Daily Herald*, boasted that he had smuggled Russian crown jewels into this country. In case you should be inclined to doubt this I will let Mr. Meynell tell his story to you as he told it in *The Communist*:

After stating that he was abroad paper-buying, when a large quantity of pearls and diamonds came into his possession for conveyance to England, he said:

". . . I received warning that I was to be searched on my return to England. This news came to me on the very morning of my sailing, when the jewels were all hidden in my belongings. . . . I went to a sweet-shop and bought a box of chocolate creams. I took it back to my room . . . and pressed a diamond or a pearl into every chocolate in the lower layers. . . . I carried the box to the Post Office, addressed it to England, and posted it. When it arrived in London—the box was worth, perhaps, £10,000—my wife and I made ourselves rather sick through having to suck large quantities of chocolates in order to free the delicate jewels within them.

"On yet another occasion I was stopped at a British port . . . and my luggage was searched. I found it quite difficult, I remember, to talk at all intelligibly with three large diamonds in my mouth trying to rattle against my teeth.

"Months ago the whole of the Bolshevist jewel money was sent abroad and handed back to where it came from."

Meynell told a similar story to the *Evening News* of February 9, 1921, but, the *Evening News* said, he refused to state the total value of the jewels received, what portion was sold and the amount of money, or the value of any jewels returned.

He also refused to discuss whether *all* the jewels and *all* the money from jewels had been sent abroad, and whether the jewels were distinct from the £75,000 offered by the Bolshevists to the *Daily Herald*.

Offer by Russia

I KNOW some who smuggled jewels in here and did not receive a penny and did not want a penny of commission on the sales. But since those days Labour fell amongst thieves who did not have the courage of their craft. There was the famous offer of £75,000 from Russia to help finance the old *Daily Herald*, which the stolid trade unionists refused. They had by that time been converted by Mr. Ramsay MacDonald and Mr. Philip Snowden to the belief that if only they returned Labour men to Parliament all the workers' troubles would be over. Money was required for that, too, of course, and a new technique had to be invented, one which, if less romantic, would be more safe; but even at that there were gentle, kindly souls in the Labour movement who were all for accepting the Russian cash.

There was, for instance, the kindly and sincere Mr. Charles Roden Buxton. Mr. Buxton felt for all humanity. No native in Central Africa could develop a boil on his neck without Mr. Buxton becoming aware of it and doing something to reduce the swelling.

Well, when patriotic people objected to the *Daily Herald* receiving money from Russia, Mr. Buxton said:

". . . There was no reason why people should be horrified because a certain Russian party had offered the 'Daily Herald' £75,000. . . ."—*Daily Herald*, October 5, 1920.

I think Mr. Pollitt ought to have as much courage as the gentle Mr. Buxton.

Changed Technique

ALL the romance has gone from the running of Left revolts in Britain.

Mr. Walton Newbold, ex-Communist M.P., later supporter of Mr. J. H. Thomas and the National Government, has told publicly how the technique of the Communist Party changed. The Russians had evidently decided never again to cast pearls before swine, and, as Mr. Newbold said, he himself had seen the supplies of cash arrive in Britain in the Diplomatic bag.

The Labour Party, too, changed its technique. A mighty campaign had been proposed to compel the publication of all lists of party funds. Everybody knew, of course, that all the great gentlemanly parties of England had been financed by the sale of honours.

In these columns I have already quoted how a Yorkshire manufacturer had paid his cash but received no title. He sued in the British Courts for the return of his cash. Mr. Lloyd George, when challenged on how he accumulated his Political Fund, quite frankly stated that he raised the cash in the same way as it always had been raised in British politics. R. D. Blumenfeld, a former editor of the *Daily Express*, capped this by saying that in the good old days at Conservative headquarters there was a printed tariff. So much for a knighthood, still more for a baronetcy, and so on up or down the scale. Now you can understand why all the gentlemanly parties are gnashing their teeth—it is the terrible thought that there were sources of wealth which they had failed to tap.

"Purity" Campaign

WHEN the Labour Party discussed its purity campaign it was in an unfair position compared with its rivals. Mr. Lloyd George had already all the cash he wanted, and could finance the Liberal Party if it would accept his policy. The Conservatives were in power and could carry on the sales where Mr. Lloyd George had left off. Labour's chance to sell them seemed a long way off They were all for purity in public life.

The late Editor of "The Daily Express."

Then suddenly it looked as if Labour was to be in power. From that moment numbers of rich men began to claim old friendships with Labour leaders. Labour leaders who were poor in 1922 died rich men in less than ten years.

There are half a dozen men associated with *Action* now who know that the Labour Party had to set up two funds—one for publication and one for private purposes.

Control of this private fund was vested in one man now dead. Look again at the list of honours given by Mr. MacDonald. In that list you will find names who had no claim whatever for an honour, either for service to the nation or to the Labour movement. Some were, and still are, opponents of Labour. Purity in public life! Ugh!

Cash is King

NOW a party can survive for a long time in politics with poor leadership, or no leadership at all. The Conservative Party is a standing example of this, and not one person in a hundred could tell to-day who is leader of the Liberal Party. But there is one thing no party can do without, and that is cash.

That is Labour's dilemma. The trade unions, of course, still fork out very generously, and when the agreed-on contributions are all spent a private session at the Labour Party Conference can always be arranged to discuss finance.

The moment the union bosses feel like it they can agree on a special levy to keep the machines running.

But this, while helpful at the time, is bound to have serious effects on the future. It means that the careerists will have less and less say in party counsels the more they become solely dependent on trade union funds. That explains why in the recent hunger march gatherings it was the men of the Left who did all the exploiting of the marchers.

You can understand the terrible strain which that imposed on Mr. Herbert Morrison and Dr. Hugh Dalton. Every day much needed publicity was there for the asking, yet it had all to be refused.

The union bosses had said the march must not be recognised, and Mr. Morrison and Dr. Dalton obliged the bosses. Had the rich title hunters been pouring in their cash as in the palmy days from 1924 till 1929 the careerists would have retained a certain measure of independence. But those days are gone, and now, having taken money from open opponents of Labour, they go suddenly pious and righteous at the mere thought that anybody should take money from anything but the purest sources.

The cash may come back again, however, as the members of the Federation of British Industries are not so stupid as they look. If I were a member of the F.B.I. and really wanted to keep the workers in subjection, I would see that the present Labour and trade union leaders had enough money to keep them where they are until Father Time himself dismissed them.

DISTRIBUTION OF UNEMPLOYED

THERE are 12.4 per cent. of insured workers unemployed in Great Britain and Northern Ireland, or 1,689,715 out of a total of 13,058,000. These figures do not, of course, include agricultural workers.

The unequal distribution of this so-called "prosperity" is shown by a comparison of the figures for the London, South-Eastern, South-Western, and Midlands areas with the remainder of the country. The percentage unemployed in London is 6.3; in South-Eastern area 6.2; in South-Western area 8.2; in the Midlands area 8.7, an average of 7.3 per cent. Excluding these four areas, the average percentage unemployed in the remaining areas (North-Eastern with 12.8; North-Western with 16.1; the Northern with 21.0; Scotland with 17.7; Wales with 27.6; and Northern Ireland with 23.4) amounts to 19.8, or almost two and three-quarter times higher than in the southern half of the country.

In Wales approximately three in ten of the insured workers are without employment; in Durham one in four of the working population is out of a job, and in Cumberland even a higher proportion.

Yet there is no indication in the forecasts of the business of Parliament in the new Session of any action for the benefit of areas in which industrial depression still continues. Rearmament has had little effect, projected trading estates take a considerable time to develop; financial facilities for small undertakings under an Act recently passed leave the industrials cold. The Government smilingly refer to the improvement in the unemployment figures for the southern half of Britain and turn a disapproving eye when anyone mentions the remainder of the country.

RADIO FLASHES

HOIST WITH THEIR OWN PETARD

By " BLUEBIRD "

I HAVE been vastly amused during the past week, first of all by the loud cheers with which the B.B.C. greeted the first appearance of the Public Order Bill, and secondly by the screams and squeals of fear which we have had on most evenings after that, when the B.B.C. suddenly discovered that it might also refer to their friends as well as to the Blackshirts. First of all, the Young Socialists' League objected, then the Jewish People's Council, and then all sorts of others of similar mentality.

Apparently what the B.B.C. and its friends really want is just a Bill to prohibit Blackshirts only. It seems to be worrying them greatly to think that in future Socialists may not, perhaps, be allowed to throw bottles and slash Blackshirts about with razors. The real joke of the whole thing to my mind is that in the past the Blackshirts have always obeyed the law and have refrained from interfering with other people. The Press, the B.B.C., and all other little minds have been doing their best for years to try to make people believe that it is the Blackshirts that cause the trouble.

Now that a Bill is being promoted in order to prevent the Blackshirts doing all the things which they have been alleged to do, the screams and yells from the opposition parties who really used to do these things themselves and say it was the Blackshirts are too funny for words. Apart from everything else, the priggishness of their statements as broadcast by the B.B.C. must make people who are able to think for themselves (even very slightly) wonder why they are now screaming.

Shocking!

THE news-finch's song on Sunday night was most amusing. He started off with his little voice full of indignation by saying that there was a good deal of criticism of the way that Hitler had repudiated this final clause of the Treaty of Versailles. According to the news-finch protracted negotiations had been in progress and, he said, Hitler should have gone on with these negotiations.

It seems fairly obvious that these negotiations had been going on and on and on and on in the usual democratic manner, getting no nearer to the solution of the problem, so Hitler, in the true National Socialist manner, not wishing to waste any further time over futile negotiations, did what was wanted with a single stroke of the pen.

After that the finch went on to an account of the Socialist-Communist meeting in Trafalgar-square. Many points of Harry Pollitt's speech were reported. The finch finished up by saying that the crowds marched off singing the " Red Flag " and the " Internationale " (this in a very super-Parisian accent), amid cheering crowds.

The impression which the news-finch wished to convey was obviously that the whole of London had turned out to cheer this traitorous rabble. And yet when Mosley addresses those vast crowds which gather in the East End to hear and cheer the case for the Greater Britain, the B.B.C. does not even mention it. At the best it reports a riot and anything else it can to put the Blackshirt case in the wrong.

Red Bias

IF this is not an exhibition of bias by the B.B.C. I do not know what is. I am quite sure that the staff of the news department of the B.B.C. is manned (if that can be the right word to use in connection with this department) entirely with red-hot Socialists.

In describing the race of the Old Crocks to Brighton we were told that this was to celebrate the abolition of " the man with the red flag." Unfortunately " the man with the red flag " is still with us, and there seem to be many of him in the B.B.C.

Finally there was an item to the effect that the Archbishop of Canterbury, speaking on Christianity, had said that we had got to unite against the anti-Christian forces which were gaining strength daily in Europe. Christianity in this country, he said, was not dying out, it was merely being passed over.

I am very glad to hear that the Archbishop is beginning to see things in their true perspective.

In Italy and Germany the coming of Fascism resulted in a rout of the anti-Christian forces. If the Socialist - Communist element should ever get into power in this country, Christianity would suffer the fate that it has suffered in Russia. Most people wish that the Archbishop and his clerical colleagues would leave politics alone altogether, and not oppose the Christian element in politics.

Historical Drama

ON Sunday evening from 5.30 to 7 there was a presentation of the famous play "L'Aiglon," by Rostand. It was produced by Peter Cresswell, which, in itself, is sufficient for us to know in advance that the play would be worth hearing.

But how clever of Mr. Siepmann, the new programme planner, to have arranged for L'Aiglon to come on at the same time as the Johann Strauss play on the other wavelength. It is sheer brilliance to put on the only two highspots at the same time so one could not hear both. Mr. Siepmann is even cleverer than his predecessor, Mr. Wellington.

I do not know how many people care about these historical plays. They sound deadly dull when you see them in the programme, but for those who like beautiful words and fine acting they are well worth hearing. My own knowledge of history is painfully weak, so I do not know how historically accurate these plays are, but I do suggest to the B.B.C. that they should not produce such plays unless they are historically accurate, as many people will take them as being accurate and add them to their mental store of history.

I suppose that my own lack of knowledge of history is due to the fact that I could never summon up any interest in this subject at school. Therefore, in order to repair this deficiency I routed out one of my old school history books. On reading it, I discovered why it was I took no interest in this subject. History in the average school book is presented in the most unutterably dull fashion.

I believe that it is the intention of the B.B.C. to present plays of this sort as history lessons during the school broadcasts. If they can get Peter Cresswell to produce them, the coming generation should learn far more about history than their predecessors.

On Saturday afternoon we had a broadcast from Dunstable on Gliding. According to the official B.B.C. announcement, " The B.B.C. Outside Broadcast Director, Mr. Joly de Lotbinière, ever on the look-out for new ideas, has proceeded to Dunstable Downs personally to test the entertainment possibilities of gliding."

Now wasn't that jolly for Mr. de Lotbinière? You notice that a B.B.C. official does not merely go to Dunstable Downs like you or I —he *proceeds* there. Doesn't it conjure up a wonderful vision of some pompous official surrounded by underlings and hirelings.

Featureless

LATER on the same afternoon, we had the much heralded musical comedy, " Money For

(Continued in next column.)

(Continued from previous column)

Jam," featuring Bobby Howes. In its way it was a light amusing little comedy, but Bobby Howes was wasted and the play failed to put over his personality. Bobby Howes is a big personality on the stage, and that is not entirely due to his antics and facial expression.

But any comparatively competent B.B.C. singer or actor could have done as well as did Bobby Howes in " Money For Jam," and I sincerely hope that the next time the B.B.C. includes him in their programme he will be given the type of part which can put over his personality.

The " Music Hall " programme was quite good on the whole. Will Hay, as usual, was himself, and that would have compensated one if the rest of the programme had been thoroughly bad. Which in fact it was not.

On Sunday night, happening to tune in to Hilversum at a quarter to ten in the evening, I heard twenty minutes of Sophie Tucker. I gather that this lady and the B.B.C. recently had a little argument about what the B.B.C. thought was her monetary value, and I gather that the B.B.C. thought that this was not so great as Miss Tucker thought it was. Having heard this twenty minutes I am inclined for once to agree with the B.B.C.

Tail Piece

ON Monday evening a talk was given on " Party Politics " by a gentleman named A. Mess. He seems a very suitably-named person to talk on such a subject.

British Election Union Funds

BY the time this article appears in print the powers that be will have wasted valuable time on a matter of " Uniforms " in an attempt to prove to the public that they are provocative in so far as the British Union is concerned.

They have more important matters requiring their immediate attention which will be side-tracked for the Public Order Bill.

A daily paper came out on Saturday with a startling front-page headline: " Baldwin betrays his convictions for votes," and the subsequent article contains many points awkward for Mr. Baldwin.

The British Union is a Patriotic Movement, putting King and Empire first, and in these times it pains us to notice those members of a Cabinet stand bareheaded beside their King, paying saintly homage to our glorious dead, when their deliberations in Westminster and elsewhere suggest other things.

Can they conscientiously swear before that shrine they have done one iota since the first armistice to make this country a fit place for heroes to live in? The answer in parliamentary language is in the negative.

Look around you to-day and all you can see is not what has been done for the well-being of the people, but the reverse.

We are no movement of buffoonery, as our opponents would have you to believe, but serious-minded Britons, sure that in the long run we will make the public realise their own danger, and that of our country, in following the so-called " lead " of the present Government.

You are already giving us valuable help by reading our paper, and we ask you to give us practical help by sending a subscription to our Election Fund.

HELP FOR GERMAN JEWS

The Council for German Jewry, which has been at work for nine months, has issued an interim report, which shows that up to the end of October £719,592 had been contributed in Great Britain alone towards the Council's activities, and a further £40,000 is expected from collections in Australia, New Zealand and Belgium.
—*The Times*, 13-11-'36.

MORE SOCIALIST MEANNESS

Southall Blackshirts Pay Tribute To The Fallen

ON Sunday Southall Blackshirts paid homage, in a simple ceremony, to the men who fell in the War by placing a wreath at the Southall war memorial. Behind that simple act, however, is a story—a story of petty spite and contemptible meanness that is so typical of Socialist Councils all over the country.

Nearly two months ago arrangements were being made for this year's Armistice ceremony, and various political, religious and other organisations were invited to join in a procession and service. This invitation was also extended to and accepted by the local Blackshirts. The organiser of the whole proceedings, the leader of the Southall Salvation Army, expressed his delight at the prospect of including the Blackshirt Corps of Drums in the procession.

A contingent of Southall Blackshirts at the Southall War Memorial

A few days before the event the Southall Blackshirts were informed that it had been decided to exclude them from the procession, but if they wished they could take part in the service alone. The local organiser, Mr. F. I. Green, naturally refused to accept this insufferable attempted snub from the Socialist Council, who in common with the rest of the Internationale clique do not even let the remembrance of our fallen dead interfere with their spiteful pursuance of a political vendetta.

Mr. Green, therefore, decided to lay the wreath independent of the local bigwigs, and on Sunday morning a column of Blackshirts, preceded by the London Corps of Drums led by Mr. Pothecary, went to the Southall war memorial.

The Ceremony

AS the middle of the column reached the memorial the Blackshirts halted, and the colour party detached itself and followed Mr. Denmark, who carried the wreath to the foot of the memorial and placed it among the other floral tributes, while the colours were dipped. There was silence, and the colour party saluted the dead as Mr. Pothecary sounded the Last Post followed by the Reveille.

The last note died away and the simple act of remembrance was over; devoid of any meaningless clap-trap and stodgy flummery, yet all the more impressive because of its very sincerity and simplicity.

That the action of the Socialist Council was not approved by the people of Southall was evidenced by the crowd which had collected after the arrival of the Blackshirts. Bareheaded people stood and observed the silence, wondering perhaps why a patriotic organisation should be banned from taking part with civic bodies by a bunch of international Socialists who despise patriotism and glory in " pacifism " in a national act of remembrance. It must be borne in mind, moreover, that the Southall Blackshirts did not themselves ask to take part in this public function but were invited by the organisers to do so. It was only at the last hour that as a result of pressure by the Council this invitation was revoked.

Such despicable action is only to be expected from a Council which has banned the Blackshirts from Southall Park, while allowing every other political organisation to hold meetings there.

Affairs in this country have indeed reached a sorry pass, when a body of loyal Englishmen has to suffer insults at the hands of democratic busibodies, many of them " conchies " during the war, whose only loyalty is to the Red Internationale of class-hatred.
—A. L.

HACKNEY WAR MEMORIAL SERVICE

The report of the proceedings at this War Memorial last week should have stated that the ceremony was organised by the Central Hackney District, and that both South and Central Hackney Districts took part in the proceedings.

THESE "HONOURABLE" MEN!

The representatives of financial democracy are much more keen to become " worthies " of their country rather than heroes of their country. Nobody exemplifies this in a more befitting manner than the present Prime Minister, Mr. Baldwin. It would be well, however, to bring to Mr. Baldwin's notice the following quotation from one of the greatest of English writers, Thomas Hardy:

" He should be as cold blooded as a fish and as selfish as a pig to have a good chance of being one of his country's worthies."

The above description might be applied to other well-known political figures during the last decade, as well as to Mr. Baldwin, notably, Ramsay MacDonald Thomas, Snowden, and many Trade Union leaders.

OUR FRONT PAGE

The two pictures at the top of the front page are (left) the Southall District Blackshirts and (right) East Ham District Blackshirts marching on Armistice Sunday to their local War memorials.

The other pictures were taken in Yorkshire, Norfolk, and Sussex.

PROSPECTIVE BRITISH UNION PARLIAMENTARY CANDIDATES

The first Twelve with their Prospective Constituencies—the remainder of the First Hundred will be published in groups in "Action" each week. They will all be announced by the end of the year

CHELSEA.—Sir Lionel Berkeley Holt Haworth, K.B.E.

Space does not permit even the mention of the majority of the important positions held by, or the distinctions received by, this member of the British Union.
Sir Lionel entered the Indian Foreign Political Department in 1901, and held important appointments in India, Persia, and Arabia. He has been Consul-General at Meshed, in Khorasan, Political Resident in the Persian Gulf, and H.M. Consul-General for Fars Khuzistan.
He retired in 1929 and until two years ago took an active interest in the Conservative Party. Finding that Imperial patriotic and social ideals received no satisfaction he made a study of British Union policy, and has since been a well-known member.

EVESHAM.—John Dowty.

Born in Evesham fifty years ago, Mr. Dowty was educated at Worcester Grammar School and trained in his father's chemist shop in Pershore. He served with the Queen's Royal West Surrey Regiment and has been in the Malay States Rifles. He is a member of the National Farmers' Union and of the County Executive and the Parliamentary Committee and the Fruit and Vegetable Committee. Mr. Dowty owns a fruit and vegetable farm of twenty acres, does his own canning and preserving, and was the originator of roadside trading.
In addition to his many agricultural activities, he has found time to be an active and respected member of the British Union.

GORTON.—Thomas Davies.

Ex-labourer and then miner, Mr. Davies, who is forty years of age, has been a member of the British Union almost since its beginning. He was born at Ardwick, in Manchester, and served with the 3rd Manchester Regiment for the duration of the war. When he came out of the Army he realised that some hard thinking had to be done in order to get the land that he had fought for fit for heroes to live in.
This search for social justice took him into the Labour Party, and then for two years into the Communist Party, where he was a group leader. A spell of unemployment sent him into the National Unemployed Workers' Movement, where he acted as a branch secretary for some time.

HULME.—R. T. Parkyn.

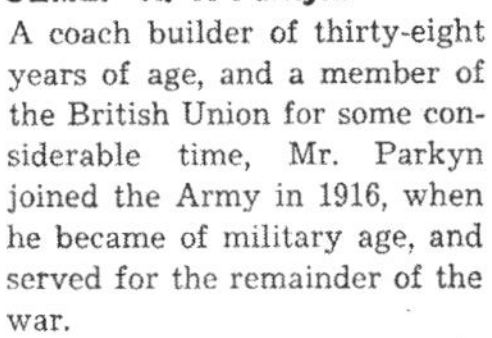

A coach builder of thirty-eight years of age, and a member of the British Union for some considerable time, Mr. Parkyn joined the Army in 1916, when he became of military age, and served for the remainder of the war.
He has spent two and a half

years in the Civil Service, taken a degree at Manchester University, and was in Persia for ten years.
Mr. Parkyn previously took no active part in politics, but had strong Socialist inclinations before joining the British Union.

LEEDS, W.—Bertram F. Lister.

A motor engineer, thirty-three years of age, Mr. Lister has one of the longest records of service in the country as a British Union district officer. Although born at Leeds he was educated and has spent the whole of his business life in Harrogate. From the beginning of the British Union has organised and been in charge of the work in that town.
Before he heard Mosley's call, he had been an active member of the Conservative Party, and assisted that Party in a number of elections.

LEWISHAM, W. — Lieut.-Col. James Walsh, D.S.O.

Enlisted in the King's Liverpool Regiment at the age of nineteen and, after eleven years in the ranks, rose to the rank of Regimental Sergeant-Major and was

commissioned in the field. He was rapidly promoted to Lieutenant-Colonel and Battalion Commander, Mentioned in Despatches four times, and made a member of the Distinguished Service Order.
He retired from the Army in 1924 and is now occupying an important commercial position.
He was for two years President of the Boxing Committee of the London Territorials, is an active British Union speaker, and has a record of self-sacrificing and unassuming service to Fascism.

LINCOLN.—Eric Herbert Adams.

Mr. Adams is thirty-five years of age, at present employed as a railway clerk. He enlisted in the Royal Air Force, but was too late for active service in the war. Afterwards served in the Coldstream Guards at home and in Turkey until 1923.
He has been an active member and propagandist for the British Union for nearly three years.

MERTHYR.—Thomas P. Moran.

A working engineer, Mr. Moran was one of the earliest members of the British Union. Before that he had been an officer of the Newcastle West Labour Party. Was educated at a Roman Catholic School in Newcastle, apprenticed to Armstrong-Whitworth and Co., and served in the Navy during the war and after as engine-room artificer. During this time won the cruiser-weight boxing championship of the combined Fleets.
Mr. Moran is responsible for organisation in South Wales, and has made a great reputation as an exponent of Fascism in industrial districts.

NORTHAMPTON.— Mrs. Norah Elam.

Was one of the leaders of the Woman's Suffrage movement in pre-war days, served three terms of imprisonment and endured several hunger strikes. On the outbreak of hostilities placed her services at the disposal of the Government. Mrs. Elam had a distinguished war record—recruiting in "Red" South Wales, working in a munition factory, and was a member of several important Government Committees.
In 1919 she contested Richmond, Surrey, as an independent Candidate, was then for a short time in the Conservative Party, but joined the British Union almost at its inception.
She is a popular and well-known Fascist propagandist.

NORFOLK, S.W.—Miss L. M. Reeve.

One of the many professional women who have seen in Fascism a hope for Britain's future, Miss Reeve has done yeoman work for the British Union in Norfolk.
She started life in domestic service in London, saved and borrowed sufficient money to pay for a business training course, and after considerable experience in the City, became assistant to an estate agent in Norfolk. In 1927 she took over the agency and is now managing the complete estate of 1,100 acres. Miss Reeve is the only woman in the country managing an agricultural property of this size.

PORTSMOUTH CENTRAL. — Vice-Admiral G. B. Powell, C.M.G.

This distinguished sailor first saw active service as a Lieutenant in the Navy at the Relief of Pekin. He was severely wounded and Mentioned in Despatches in the Boer War, and specially promoted for services in North China.
During the last war he began as Chief of Staff to the Senior Naval Officer at Malta, was

Liaison Officer to the French Admiral in the Mediterranean, and Mentioned in Despatches. Commanded H.M.S. Devonshire in 1917, and at the end of the War was appointed to H.M.S. Monarch, when he was "noted at the Admiralty for valuable services rendered during the War." He is an Officer of the Legion of Honour, a Commander of the Crown of Italy, a holder of the Croix de Guerre, and a Companion of the Order of St. Michael and St. George.
Admiral Powell has been an active British Union member for several years and is now in charge of Portsmouth.

(Continued on page 8.)

EDITORIAL OFFICES—
SANCTUARY BUILDINGS, GREAT SMITH STREET, LONDON, S.W.1
Editor: JOHN BECKETT
Telephone: Victoria 9084 (five lines)

FOREIGN FUNDS LIE

As Oswald Mosley shows on the opposite page, the great "gas" offensive against the British Union has begun. It was too much to expect that a new Movement openly pledged to the destruction of hypocrisy and corruption should be allowed to grow from strength to strength without all the sinister weapons that Financial Democracy is so used to wielding being brought against them. Just as a Bill to deprive the organisation of that unique propaganda weapon, its Black Shirt, is being rushed through Parliament, sponsored by all three Parties and preceded by unrivalled calumny in the Press, Sir John Simon announces that "he has evidence which goes to show that the British Union's funds are supplemented from abroad."

It is not the first time that this eminent lawyer has come to the assistance of the system which has treated him so well. His pompous legal declaration against the Trade Unions in 1926, which was denounced in every law journal of any standing, was an example of the way this political trickster is prepared to place his legal wiliness at the disposal of his masters.

This case is, however, even more flagrant. If there is one man who knows the meaning of words it is the Home Secretary, but he would be hard put to explain the meaning of his own words. Those words have been taken as meaning that the British Union was subsidised by foreign Governments. Simon has been publicly and immediately challenged to produce the evidence on which he based his suggestion that the British Union is subsidised by foreigners, and that suggestion has been given the lie direct. The country will demand that he either produces his evidence or withdraws the allegation. If he refuses to produce any evidence in face of our challenge, no fair-minded person can draw any conclusion except that the statement is untrue, and that his motive in making it was to create prejudice, and thus to facilitate the passage of his Bill attacking Fascism.

These poisonous attacks are boomerangs which will do far more damage to the throwers than to the target. Like all financial democratic tactics, they are based on the belief that the people of this country can be fooled all the time. They have not calculated upon the dynamic propaganda effect which Sir Oswald and his associates are wielding in every street, in every town, city, and village of Britain.

WHO PAYS FOR POLITICS?

There is little wonder that the old Party machines are willing to believe that the great British Union efforts are supplemented from abroad. For years they have exploited every dirty and dishonourable trick for the purpose of financing their organisation and their candidatures. The personnel of the House of Lords to-day leaves no room for doubt in the minds of an honest observer. Since the war British aristocracy has been riddled and fouled by any business man prepared to pay into Party funds for a title.

This racket was not confined to the chief figures. Swarms of little officials in the Party machine have had their rake-off as the golden stream poured into the Party war-chests. The Maundy-Gregory case revealed a great deal, but Mr. Maundy-Gregory was merely the pawn of far more influential people, and while he paid a gilded penalty, his employers are still at work.

LABOUR PARTY PURISTS

The Conservative and Liberal Parties may, at any rate, plead that they have only very disheartedly denied the "honours" scandals. The slimy people in control of the Labour Party have been in this, as in everything else, among the worst specimens of politicians, because while playing exactly the same game they call loudly upon the world to admire their irreproachability. As John Emery tells us on page 5, the honours scandal went on just as happily under the Labour Government as it had previously.

The present Labour leaders remained members of that Government quietly drawing their salaries.

The Labour Party have the effrontery to claim that they are the only political party to publish a balance sheet. Will the Labour Party publish the details of their election funds between 1923-31? Will they deny the immense sums subscribed privately to the Party by the late Bernard Baron, the Jewish millionaire? Will they say on what balance sheet are shown these subscriptions to a Party which claims to be financed from the "pennies of the workers"? Will they explain the private and confidential letters sent out to every kind of person whom they believed had money before each election, and tell us who subscribed, how much, and how the money was disbursed?

When the Labour Party talks about secret Party funds they are talking about a subject they understand backwards, and their effrontery is the more amazing.

RUSSIAN SUBSIDIES

The Labour leaders are working up a spurious and false campaign against the British Union for using foreign funds. This is a lie and a contemptible lie, as we have shown elsewhere. But if it were the truth, how hypocritical it would still be for the Labour Party to attack us on this score.

No less a person than Viscount Snowden writes in his memoirs the following (he is referring to the disclosures in August, 1920, with regard to the financing of the *Daily Herald* by Moscow):—

"*The 'Daily Herald' indignantly denied that it had received any money from Bolshevik sources. However, three weeks later, when it was known that the police were making inquiries, the 'Herald' came out with a fantastic story that one of its directors, Mr. Francis Meynell, 'without the knowledge of his colleagues, had collected £75,000 to be held in trust for the Third International, and to be offered to the 'Daily Herald' if the need arose.' A week later the British Government issued a communiqué, which stated that M. Kameneff, the Soviet representative in London, had informed his Government that £40,000 worth of diamonds had in fact been sold, and that the proceeds had been paid over to the 'Daily Herald.' The communiqué further stated that the British Government had evidence that the statement that Mr. Meynell acted on his own initiative was incorrect, and that Mr. Edgar Lansbury, the son of Mr. George Lansbury, the Editor of the 'Daily Herald,' had, in fact, received part of the notes given for the jewels. When the transaction could no longer be denied, the Editor of the 'Daily Herald' asked his readers if the money should be accepted. The Trade Unions, who were financially supporting the paper, dissociated themselves from the whole affair, of which they had had no knowledge previous to the exposure. What became of the money has never been cleared up satisfactorily. The whole transaction was a very sordid business and left a very bad impression.*"

Many Labour and Trade Union leaders have enjoyed luxury tours to Russia, Spain, and other parts of the world where the presence of a meddlesome Member of Parliament was considered to be of use to the Third International. The next time you read in the papers of Labour leaders giving indignant interviews about the appalling conditions they discovered in Spain, or Patagonia, in South America or China, just wonder how these poverty-ridden servants of the workers can afford to be continually running round the world in search of everybody's troubles but our own.

CORRESPONDENCE

HISTORY REPEATS ITSELF

I have just read, for the third or fourth time, a book which compels admiration for the German Leader and the German Nation as a whole. This book is called "Germany's Hitler" (published by Hurst and Blackett, Ltd., at 12s. 6d.) and is written by Heinz A. Heinz. This book is a series of interviews with Hitler's earlier acquaintances. As I have said, I have read this book three or four times, but it was only just during this past week that I have discovered a striking comparison between the German Leader and our own Leader, Sir Oswald Mosley. Not only are the circumstances similar, but the B.U.F.N.S. is to-day encountering the same difficulties as confronted Adolf Hitler in 1923, and again in 1927-9.

I quote several passages from the authentic, human documents of the rise of National Socialism and its Leader.

From page 229, for example: "Through the pressure of public opinion in Bavaria, the interdict was lifted from Hitler, and in the March of 1927 once more his voice was welcomed with immense acclaim in Munich. The Party there made a great leap forward, but it was suppressed by the half Jewish, half Polish Chief of Police, Grzesinski. . . ." Is that not a striking comparison with that of the B.U.F.N.S. to-day?

Again is this not an omen for the future when I read on page 230 that "twelve representatives of the Party in the Reichstag"—almost at the first attempt. I am sure there will be more than 2 per cent. in the House of Commons after Mosley's first attempt.

I was then astounded to read that "The following year saw an enormous augmentation in the membership of the Party. . . . *In Berlin it had come to open fighting with the Communists, who erected barricades in the streets*". . . . Which only goes to prove that the exports of Hitler have found their filthy way to this country.

The so-called "National Government" of this country, led by Baldwin and Simon, also had its counterpart in the pre-National Socialist Germany. Run by Brüning and Grzesinski (I think I have mentioned their English counterparts), the Government in 1931 (one or two years before the National Socialist Revolution) *banned the Brownshirt.*' (pp. 231-2.)

To quote page 236, "Chancellor Brüning had scarcely counted on this advancement of Hitler and was dismayed by it. *He resorted to strange measures.* On April 13, 1932, he ordered the demobilisation of the S.A. (Sturm Abteilung) and the dispersal of the Movement known as the Hitler Youth. The homes and property of these organisations were destrained upon. But it was all in vain. . . ."

Now, in England, Baldwin and Simon are emulating Brüning and Chief of Police Grzesinski.

But it will all be in vain, because, as you say—Mosley will win!

D. H. MAHONEY.

UNIFORM SCARE

Apropos of the banning of uniforms Bill, surely the "Mother of Parliaments" can never have witnessed anything so undignified as is happening at the present moment. Sir Oswald, God bless him, has thrown the whole lot of them into such a state of panic as cannot have been known before.

From the extreme Communist to the most blue-blooded Tory Diehard there does not appear to be one dissentient, not one who has the guts to stand up and demand fair play for a chivalrous opponent. Even during the crisis in August, 1914, there was not the apparent unanimity, for we did have a few strange creatures such as Ramsay MacDonald. The undignified stampede of all the old Parties would be pathetic if it weren't so ludicrous, and it can only have the effect of creating widespread sympathy for our cause amongst decent people. God speed the day when the Blackshirts take over the reins of government. My great regret is that I am not able to render as much financial aid as I would like, but take this opportunity of adding £1 to your Election Fund "BEWDLEYITE."

NEXT WEEK'S 'ACTION' . . .

contains an article of special interest to Newsagents.

Readers are asked to see that their local Newsagents receive this issue.

FOR THE ELECTION FUND

Enclosed is a donation for the Election Fund.

The Government may ban uniforms, but it can't prevent me from giving up "the pictures" and putting the money in a little box for you instead. (Sorry to have to write anonymously.)

CLERK (Spinster).

What a poor gift this is! I hope to increase it tenfold when I get a job.

My local Press informs me that an inquiry has been held into the sources of Fascist funds. A statement is apparently to be made in Parliament very soon. The lies which will be told will be cast in the old mould of democratic hypocrisy.

They will not say that there are Britons who are prepared to deny themselves of luxuries to contribute to Fascist funds. "We shall triumph over the parties of corruption because our will is stronger than their will, our spirit is finer than their spirit, our cause is greater than their cause."

"OMAR KHAYYAM."

PROSPECTIVE CANDIDATES

(*Continued from Page 7.*)

Major-General J. F. C. FULLER, C.B., C.B.E., D.S.O.—Westminster St. George's.

Acknowledged to be one of the greatest military authorities in the world, General Fuller was born at Chichester and educated at Malvern and Sandhurst.

Space does not permit an account of his distinguished Army career. He served throughout the South African War and the Great War, was loaded with distinctions in both these campaigns, and achieved a place in history by his creation and brilliant organisation of the Tank Corps.

Has written over two dozen books, mainly on military subjects; has been an active member of the British Union for over two years and has written frequently for the *Fascist Quarterly* and for *Action* under the title of "Our Military Correspondent."

BRITISH UNION PERSONALITIES

No. 3—Mrs. ANNE BROCK GRIGGS

Women Administrative Officer (Southern)

Mrs. Brock Griggs is one of the most popular officers in the British Union, and gives good cause for her popularity. Tall and slim she epitomises in her appearance the finest characteristics of English womanhood, embodying a keen and active brain, a gift for speaking, and able powers of administration with an attractive physique. She combines the best type of intelligent woman with the motherhood of two charming children.

She first achieved fame as a speaker of outstanding merit, holding many outdoor meetings in London and the Home Counties, facing surging crowds, holding her own, and eventually quelling by the force of her personality and oratory the efforts of the "Red Front" to smash her meetings.

Early in 1935 she joined the staff of the British Union as Woman Propaganda Officer, and was able to devote her whole time to the development of propaganda among the women in the Movement, and the extension of women's meetings, and to express the voice of the women speakers for whose training she was responsible.

Later, with the rapid extension, due in no little part to her propagandist efforts, of the membership and organisation of the women's section of the British Union, she took complete charge of the administration of women's activities in the southern half of the country.

In this position she has shown her great administrative qualities, and has rapidly achieved the well-deserved popularity she now holds by her infinite tact and patience.

The many demands made upon her time by the manifold duties she has undertaken leave little leisure, but she is never so busy that she cannot spare a few moments to give helpful advice to women officers and members on the many difficulties which arise in the running of the women's section of the Movement, and that advice has been instrumental in smoothing out friction on many occasions.

It is for the recognition of the fact that Britain needs to use the services of such women as Anne Brock Griggs that the Blackshirt Movement is striving in its policy for women.

BALDWIN'S BIGGEST BLUNDER

"Plays into the hands of the British Union which he is trying to frame up" says OSWALD MOSLEY

MR. BALDWIN, in Parliament on Thursday last, dealt Financial Democracy a mortal blow at the very moment that all Parties had combined to defend it. This old humbug has thus unconsciously rendered his one conspicuous service to the State. No Fascist and National Socialist has ever produced a more damning indictment of the present system and its leaders than Mr. Baldwin produced in the Defence Debate on Thursday last.

He was obliging enough to make the biggest error of his inept career but three days after the Public Order Bill had been introduced with the corrupt connivance of all Parties in order to maintain the present system against its challengers by the suppression of some of the main principles on which British justice has been built.

The great "frame-up" of the British Union had been carefully prepared in Parliament and Press. Well timed falsehoods of the grossest character had been released to create the maximum prejudice and to obscure every issue before the Public. Behind a barrage of well calculated lies the slimy forces of Financial Democracy advanced to the attack. At this crucial moment their commander made a blunder which has thrown them into a confusion from which they will never finally recover.

For Mr. Baldwin informed the Nation that he had deliberately betrayed his country rather than risk the loss of an election. For two years he had delayed the rearmament which he believed to be necessary because Socialist Pacifists were winning by-elections and he feared the loss of the General Election if he stated his conviction.

WHEN the Prosecuting Counsel for Financial Democracy makes such a statement we need only say to the Jury of Public Opinion, "My case, gentlemen," and await the verdict with confidence. Mr. Baldwin has admitted that he put the fortunes of his Party and his own miserable skin above the fortunes of his country. No statement could more vividly illustrate the character of the Financial Democrat and the system which produces him. But he went far beyond any Fascist criticism of Democracy in implying that the people could not be trusted if they were told the truth. That is an implication which the National Socialist will never accept. The "Democrat" admits that he does not believe in the people, but our faith rests on belief in the people.

A great people will always follow if they are told the truth of a national emergency and given a clear and decisive lead. The only difficulty under Financial Democracy is to reach the people with the truth through the barrage of Press lies.

Financiers' Servant

BUT Mr. Baldwin had no such difficulty, because the Press is on his side and in fact belongs to the great vested interests whom his Party exists to serve. In this connection, again, Baldwin exposed the Financial Democratic system with a devastating admission in the same debate. Even now he says that Government will not straighten out the rearmament muddle with compulsory powers, because "I hardly dare to reckon how it might react upon finance." Thank you, Baldwin; thank you again, for every time you speak you perform a service to the British people by cutting your own throat like a swimming pig.

Could any Fascist make a more "provocative" statement against the present system than Mr. Baldwin's admission that national safety had to be sacrificed because a British Prime Minister "hardly dares to reckon how it might react upon finance." And this admission was made in a debate every speech of which stressed the immense strides made in German rearmament by a country which the Democrats inform us possesses no finance!

Because the rich and prosperous Britain of their boasts possesses "Finance" it cannot bear the burden of National Defence. Because the poor and circumscribed Germany of their denunciation possesses no "Finance," it can bear the burden of National Defence! Carry on, Mr. Baldwin, for you will set a lot of people thinking who have never thought before, Tories I mean!

But when you speak of rearmament do not say, as you did the other night, "Germany is rearming and we must rearm." The British people have fought Germany once in a British quarrel, and they will not fight her again in a Jewish quarrel. Say, rather, "I will not permit Britain to be the one unarmed country in an armed world. Britain must be in a position to defend herself against any country in the world that may attack her. Britons shall only fight again in defence of British soil, but in defence of our land every man and every industry of the nation must be ready to serve. Rather than leave my country at the mercy of the world I will risk my political life, and, if necessary, leave public life for ever." Say that and in national danger the whole nation will rally to the standard. But to say that, Baldwin, you would have to be something that you have never been; you would have to be a man!

The Lesson

THE lesson of all this will not be lost upon the public. The Democrats destroy themselves at the very moment they strive to destroy us, and are characteristically making a better job of destroying themselves than of destroying us.

The Bill they introduce under the misleading title of Public Order Bill has the amiable intention of putting me in gaol if they can. To do that they must get public opinion on their side; otherwise putting me in gaol merely rallies thousands to our cause. That is why they are at such pains to "frame-up" public opinion if they can.

Apart from the expected uniform provisions, the Bill, I am happy to say, does not in any way affect the ordinary member of the Movement. They are already forbidden to carry weapons and to do other things there forbidden, and they do not carry weapons or do these things.

But clause 2 provides that "any person who takes part in the control or management of the association" may get two years in gaol on the evidence of "persons appearing to be members or adherents" unless he can prove that these persons were not "members or adherents." In other words, this clause is the well-designed machinery of the "frame-up."

The Frame-up

ALL our opponents have to do is to put their agents into the organisation or even have their agents merely proclaim themselves as "adherents" in order to get the Leader convicted upon statements made by people whom he has never seen unless he achieves the impossible and proves that they were not even his self-professed adherents.

So every principle of British justice is set aside in order to permit the *agent provocateur* (familiar so far only in the most corrupt police systems of the world) to "frame-up" the challenger of Financial Democracy corruption.

But I thank "Soapy Simon" for his service to our cause as I have already thanked his "Bellwether" Baldwin. For he has just a little overdone it. If the "frame-up" had been a little less gross and blatant he might have got away with it. He has characteristically been clever in the small way of legal drafting, but stupid in the big way of political strategy. He has forgotten that you can't fool all the people all the time, and that he has still to deal with British public opinion and British juries. He has also forgotten a lesson which all British history should teach him that nothing so quickly brings success to a cause in this country than an obvious attempt to "frame-up" its leaders by methods the people can see are crooked.

So in this hour of ordeal I feel nothing but a serene confidence. For whatever befalls me can bring nothing but a speedier triumph to the cause for which I have given my life.

THE HOME SECRETARY

Our caricaturist catches the knight with the boiling blood in happy vein

THE FRAME-UP

This article was written before the Debate on Monday. Sir Oswald finds nothing new to reply to in that discussion.

THE SPEECH THEY DID NOT REPORT

Extracts from Cmdr. Bower, M.P. for Cleveland, during the debate on the Second Reading of the Public Order Bill.

Like another hon. Member who has spoken from these benches, I am very gravely concerned about the organised hooliganism and complete denial of free speech which take place up and down the country, and particularly, in my own experience, in the Northern industrial constituencies. I wish to make it clear that when I speak of organised hooliganism, I do not mean the heckling which any candidate must expect; I do not even mean the exuberance of young boys and girls who come out for a lark—I mean fully-organised, deliberate hooliganism: rowdyism, intimidation, violence, obscene abuse, and in some cases personal violence inflicted upon members of my party. Various hon. Members have said that this is common to all parties. They are right, but I have yet to learn that members of the party opposite in general have to put up with what we have to suffer. I have often thought it is a great pity that more Members on our Front Bench—and not only on the Front Bench, but Members on the back benches who are fortunate enough to be able to purchase safe seats—cannot experience what some of us in the North have to experience in the front-line trenches. Perhaps the most regrettable aspect of the matter is that these attacks are not confined to the candidates, but are extended to their womenfolk, not only the loyal working-class women who do such wonderful work for us in districts where they are in a minority but the women of all classes who go to the meetings and have to suffer the utmost indignities.

I think this Bill does not go far enough in protecting us against such things. Shortly after the last General Election, the right hon. Gentleman the Member for Wakefield (Mr. Greenwood) said that this rowdyism was largely due to the provocative attitude taken up by what, I think, he called inexperienced young Tory candidates. I must say that that was rather a disingenuous statement, because I think the House will agree with me that the right hon. Gentleman the Member for Wakefield is rather an artist in provocation himself—he holds belts and medals for it. But I think he has never had gangs going to his meetings in Wakefield and stamping, screaming, using obscene abuse, and kicking the shins of the womenfolk until they are black and blue, which has happened to my wife and others. That does not happen in the case of hon. Members opposite, but it happens in our case all over the North and North-East. I am one of the few who is able to say that in this House, because, unfortunately, it happens mostly in constituencies which we do not represent here.

All platform speaking must be, in a sense, provocative to one's opponents. Are we to be confined, for fear of being provocative, to dreary platitudes? Are we to follow the example of those Labour candidates to whom Lord Snowden referred the other day? Are we to forgo the wonderful opportunities that are given to us by hon. Members opposite of criticising their programme, such as it is, their lack of unity, their lack of leadership, and their peculiarly

(Continued on page 10, column 3)

Under the Control Tower

OLD CROCKS, GLIDING AND UNDERCARTS

By BLACKBIRD

I HOPE that my colleagues. "Lynx" and "Bluebird," will forgive me for trespassing on what is really their territory this week. But aviators love old crocks, and gliding on the radio concerns me as much as "Bluebird," so here goes.

On Sunday morning I wandered out on to the Brighton By-pass to have a look at the Old Crocks' race, which is run annually on or about November 14, to celebrate what is now called "Emancipation Day." On November 14, 1896, the Government of that day, greatly daring, decided that "horseless carriages," as the first motor-cars were called, should in future be allowed to travel on the road without a man walking in front and carrying a red flag. They were to be limited to a speed of twelve miles an hour, which then was considered to be dangerously reckless.

About fifty or so of these Old Crocks, varying in date of birth between 1896 and 1904, paraded at Westminster and set out for Brighton. I watched them as they came up the hill past Croydon Aerodrome (hence the excuse for including them in these notes), and puffed up the hill before the descent towards Purley.

The huge Handley Page "Harrow" bomber for the R.A.F. Old hands will note the superficial resemblance to the Fokker air-liner of ten years ago

Then and Now

NOW this hill is hardly noticed by the modern motorists. The average baby car with four people on board will take the gradient at a speed between forty and fifty m.p.h. on top gear. It was amusing to see the Old Crocks face this fearsome mountain. All honour to some of them who took it at a speed of about twenty-five m.p.h. But some of them had to shed passengers, and I saw one case in which everybody had to jump out and push to keep the thing going. I was amused at the impertinence of the driver of a 1936 "Rolls-Bentley" who sailed up the hill blithely, with a large lying label giving the date of its birth as 1895!

The worst feature of the race was the appalling lack of consideration shown by the drivers of modern and comparatively modern cars to the Old Crocks. Everybody who had a car seemed to have it on the Brighton road, and these poor old gentlemen of *circa* 1900 vintage found themselves mobbed and hustled by scores of modern upstarts with no manners, who prevented them from getting a clear run up the hill. At one time there was a solid, motionless block of cars the whole way from the aerodrome gates to Purley cross-roads, a distance of very nearly a mile. It hardly seemed fair to the Old Crocks to have to function under such conditions. Police control and traffic organisation were practically non-existent. Surely on such an occasion it might have been possible to divert traffic to one of the other routes to Brighton just for this one day.

When Young

WHEN these old gentlemen first took the road as dashing young "mashers," they could drive the whole way to Brighton without seeing another of their kind. But they were certainly not designed to creep along in traffic blocks. How they fared when they got to the narrow hill through Redhill, or farther on, I tremble to think.

However, apparently a good time was had by all. At any rate the weather was fine this year. Last year it rained in torrents the whole time, but I expect that at the subsequent party at Brighton everybody appeared happy, no matter what happened. I know these parties.

And the Old Crocks in their heyday had no Mr. Hore-Belisha, passover-crossings, or Israel lights to guide them. It is a great thought.

Sitting on the Wind

ON Saturday afternoon the B.B.C. broadcast for half an hour a commentary on the gliding from Dunstable. Knowing the place well I thoroughly enjoyed the whole broadcast from beginning to end. There was obviously a fine south-west wind blowing right up against the side of the hill, giving a wonderful lift. Apparently on that day anybody who could handle a joy-stick, no matter how little they knew about soaring, could not fail to find the up-current and sit on it for as long as they liked. The chief difficulty was to get down again, for in a really high wind from the right quarter when the air is full of lift, it is quite a job to put your machine down again on top of the hill. In fact, so far as I can gather, the glider which contained the B.B.C. commentator had to be put down at the foot of the hill somewhere near the club house.

A serious difficulty with gliding is that of obtaining a suitable site. What is required is a hill 500-600 feet high with a steep side facing the prevailing wind. The country below must be devoid of trees and there must be plenty of room to alight without damage to the glider or to growing crops. This sounds easy, but it is not so easy as all that. There are plenty of good sites in England. I can think of many on the North Downs and the South Downs which would be quite suitable, but unfortunately there are such a thing as landlords to be considered. These gentry seem to do everything they possibly can to discourage gliding. Apparently gliders would frighten their tame birds. By this I do not mean their lady friends so much as the pheasants, partridges, etc., which they are to shoot.

Gliding is a wonderful way of getting the youth of the nation air-minded comparatively cheaply and no patriotic person should allow private sport and enjoyment to interfere with an activity of such importance to the welfare of the nation.

Tommy Did Not Rise

I SEE that Tommy Rose has come to grief once again in his B.A. Double Eagle. You will remember that he set out with this machine to fly in the famous fiasco to Johannesburg. After various troubles comparatively soon after he started he was finally put out of the race by the

(Continued at foot of column 3)

(Continued from column 2)

failure of the retractable undercarriage to unretract. At Cairo he landed with the wheels still folded, which did not do the aeroplane any good.

Tommy then went on to the Cape and then flew back to Cairo to collect the repaired Double Eagle. On his way back he arrived at Vienna and once again found that the wheels had done it on him. This time he was not so lucky and the machine overturned on landing—fortunately without any damage to Tommy.

According to Press reports, when he got out of the machine he said he would "never fly the ——— thing again." And who is to blame him? After all, in this year of grace 1936 retractable undercarriages should not fail. They are working every day on air liners throughout the world, and on all sorts of private aeroplanes, so that there must be plenty of experience for almost any size of aeroplane. There seems to be little excuse, therefore, for such an occurrence.

The Speech They Did Not Report

(Continued from page 9)

inconsistent attitude on disarmament and foreign policy? Above all, are we not to use the wonderful ammunition which is put into our mouths by the hon. and learned Gentleman the Member for East Bristol (Sir. S. Cripps), who has just given us another wonderful speech to use.

I hope I may be forgiven if I speak closely to a brief on this question, but I would like to give a few examples, and I do not wish to say anything that I cannot fully substantiate. At the General Election in 1931, my meetings in the Tees-side area of my constituency were consistently broken up. When I say they were broken up, I do not mean that I was merely heckled, because I am prepared to meet heckling at any time; but, to give an illustration, I was faced in the Co-operative Hall at South Bank-on-Tees — a hall which holds from 700 to 800 people —with a howling and screaming mob of about 200 who had placed themselves in the front seats. From the moment I went on to the platform they were on their feet, shouting and screaming at the top of their voices, women, I am sorry to say, using expressions towards my wife and myself with which after twenty years in the Navy I was hardly familiar. They let off Roman candles and crackers all over the floor. The hon. Member for Altrincham (Sir E. Grigg) had come to speak for me, but neither he nor I got a word in edgewise. The most pathetic thing was that while that hooliganism was going on I could see behind the ruffians the strained faces of people listening and trying to hear what the speaker had to say. I know the ruffians very well, but I know my constituency very well: I know the names and addresses of a great number of people who were responsible for the hooliganism. The game is led by a number of Dukes of Plaza Toro, who keep themselves well in the background. When we left the meeting we were followed to the Unionist Club by a very hostile crowd who threw bottles through the windows.

The next day, when I asked the local co-operative people what was the damage, I had to pay for seventeen chairs and a large number of windows that had been broken. I ought to add that, on leaving the meeting, the section of the audience in front stormed the platform, and the last view I had was of a drunken woman dancing on the Union Jack on the table. That is the sort of meeting I have had in my constituency at every General Election. Apart from one occasion, I have never had a hearing in that particular place. The breaking up of meetings has been absolutely deliberate. Moreover, when we left the meetings, gangs were assembled outside. I noticed that if I walked out in a determined manner, being a rather large individual, they parted in front of me and then closed in behind and indulged in the rather safer pastime of kicking the shins of the women-folk who had been brave enough to come down with us. (Interruption.) It is true; every word is true. It is all very well for hon. Members opposite to go on like that, but I can prove it.

At the 1935 General Election, exactly the same thing occurred. I reduced my meetings to a minimum in order to avoid provocation as far as possible, but we suffered the same violence. One night a loud-speaker lorry on which I was speaking was attacked by the crowd; they tore the tail and side-boards off the lorry and the lid off the loud-speaker unit; a man jumped up and made an attack on me—I do not think he will do it again—and my wife was bombarded with clods of earth by a crowd led by a well-known woman supporter of the party opposite.

It is only fair that for one moment I should refer to what happens at my opponents' meetings. It is difficult to get local supporters to ask questions, because they fear persecution in these areas, so at the last election I employed a trained questioner to go round to my opponent's meetings with instructions to be very careful never to ask a question unless questions were invited by the chairman. The lady went to three meetings in one night. At the first meeting she asked her questions and received some sort of reply; at the second meeting my opponent complained bitterly that he was being persecuted; and at the third meeting she was quite illegally refused admission, as it was a public meeting. Almost thou persuadest me to become a Socialist, because it must be extremely pleasant to be able to hold one's meetings in such peace, and to complain if you have the same person questioning you at successive meetings, when all the time your opponent's meetings are being deliberately smashed up by organised gangs. I have said that I am speaking on behalf of a great many people who are not in a position to speak here because they were not elected, but there is one hon. Member who suffered from the same sort of thing in the vicinity, and that is the hon Member. for Hartlepools (Mr. Gritten). He was so severely attacked one night that he had to retire to bed for four days. Perhaps he is not so young and vigorous as I am, and therefore less able to defend himself.

Motoring Notes

EXPLANATION NEEDED

By LYNX

THE industrial trouble* at the Austin works is inexplicable and rather disturbing. Here we have a great new industry handsomely protected against foreign competition, and with all its leading figures making millions of money, yet in the works of one of its wealthiest magnates we find attempts being made to cut the wages of the workpeople.

Lord Austin's statement on Sunday appeared to mean very little, except that he intended to do as he liked in his own factory. We find a very sober union, such as the Amalgamated Engineering Union, talking about a ballot for strike action, as no satisfaction can be obtained by conference, and then proceeding to allege that "the firm had for years been cutting down the basic rates for many of the jobs previously done by skilled men," and going on to say that "while the officers were always prepared to negotiate, they were not prepared to see the wages of the skilled jobs reduced to the ridiculous figure in operation at Messrs. Austin Motors."

If there is any substance whatever for these grave statements then Lord Austin must be held personally responsible to the country as a whole, and to purchasers of motor cars in particular.

In this country we pay a preposterous price for our cars. The only correct way to judge the price of a car is to find out its price at the door of the factory. One need only see the prices of Italian and American motor cars as advertised in newspapers in their own country to realise that if it were not for the tariff on imported motor cars Lord Austin, far from being a millionaire, would hardly be able to sell motor cars at all.

Surely, when we allow these motor magnates to sell us expensive cars, when we allow them to make huge personal fortunes as a result of this, then we have a right to expect in return that they will set a splendid example as employers. For a millionaire motor car manufacturer on a rising market to attempt to impose wage cuts upon any of his employees is a grave matter which prospective purchasers of motor cars would do well to remember.

A Police Scandal

EVERY month several hundred motorists are summoned for exceeding the 30 m.p.h. speed limit in restricted areas. As every motorist knows, once summoned, however flimsy the police evidence, it is a hundred to one that conviction, a substantial fine, and endorsement of the driving licence will follow. The police force as a whole has not increased its reputation with the public since motoring offences became general, but in a number of cases of this kind reported recently the evidence upon which motorists have been convicted has been that of one policeman driving a police car and watching a speedometer at the same time.

Last week I made out some tests with a friend of mine over a five-mile stretch of fairly busy streets. I was driving a 12 h.p. Austin, and he drove a small 8 h.p. Ford. The result was that if we stopped at traffic lights my friend in the Ford went away with a flying start, and although he never exceeded 30 m.p.h., in order to catch him before the next traffic block my speedometer went as high as 40 m.p.h. Had I been a policeman not aware of the accelerating power of the Ford and not realising the slowness of my own car, I should certainly have sworn that my friend exceeded the speed limit.

The acceleration of the average police car is not comparable with that of a motor cycle or a small fast car, and I am certain that this discrepancy accounts for a great deal of the conflicting evidence heard in these cases.

While on the unpleasant subject of magistrates and police courts —why is it that the majority of Benches make no effort whatever to find out the income of the persons they are so speedily mulcting of fines? If the object of the fine is a deterrent against crime, it seems fairly certain that a wealthy man in a Rolls-Royce will not be deterred by fines of between 10s. and £5, whereas the small man, who is perhaps driving a cheap secondhand car because he has to in the course of his business, may receive the most severe punishment by being fined in this way.

[*Since the above was written the strike has been settled.—ED.]

I VISITED THE COMMONS

Parliamentary Methods are almost unbelievable—says Leonard Gichard

EVERY voter should be compelled to visit the Gallery of the House of Commons, and to remain there during the course of a debate. If after this the voter is still a true believer in Parliamentary Democracy, his or her brain must have been addled before or during the process!

The procedure for gaining admission is comparatively simple. During any time that the House is sitting any member of the public is entitled to enter by the Strangers' Entrance (about half-way along the main building). As one goes up to the steps a challenge is issued by one of the policemen on duty—when one's business has been explained, permission is granted to enter the first hall of the Old Palace of Westminster.

There, once again, the policeman on duty makes inquiries as to the business of the visitor, who, if he asks for permission to enter the Gallery and there is vacant room, is referred to a small office nominally attached to the department of the Serjeant-at-Arms. If, however, the gallery is full at the time the hall is used as a waiting room, and the policeman will shepherd the visitor to a stone seat around the hall. Visitors are generally allowed up in batches of three or four with passes, issued from the office referred to. These passes are filled in by the visitor, who gives his name and address and the time of admission. In signing the form the visitor undertakes to refrain from causing a disturbance in the Gallery. The pass is then stamped, and entry is at length gained to the Lobby of the House.

Safety First!

THE policeman on duty in the Lobby inspects the pass, and the visitor is shown the way to a staircase, a very narrow and badly planned corridor, which eventually opens out into another office, where the visitor is once again asked to sign his name and address, and to surrender the pass previously issued. The details on the pass are checked against those entered in the book and at length the way to the Gallery is open.

The Gallery itself consists of some half-dozen rows of benches arranged at a steep slope and giving a view into the well of the Chamber itself. About two-thirds of the benches are visible. The usher on duty here is generally quite helpful, and in a stage whisper will explain very briefly who is speaking and show one to the best available seat.

In the Presence

THE scene in the House below is most illuminating on an average evening, when only a sprinkling of members are visible. For example, one evening last week during a debate on the Labour Amendment to the Address in reply to the King's Speech, three back-bench Members and two front benchers were present on the Government side of the House out of a total of over 400! One Member was speaking, rambling on, and on, and on; a spate of words, badly articulated, with little coherence and only a very superficial knowledge of the subject under discussion. Except for an occasional interjection from the opposite benches no notice at all is taken of the speech, the Members spending their time chatting to one another or sleeping in corner seats.

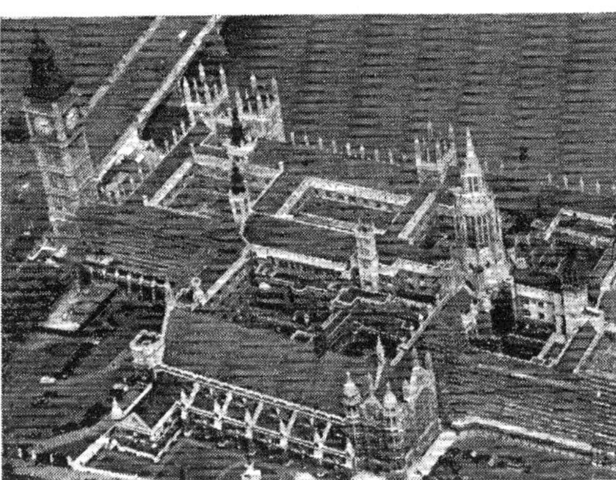

Thd Palace of Inertia

Those Members on the front benches on either side are particularly fortunate, as they can put their legs up on the table and go to sleep like that! Then when the speaking Member has exhausted his powers of endurance and finally sits down, the remaining Members (those of them that are sufficiently awake) stand in their places, and one of their number is called upon by the Speaker (that benign gentleman, who sits in lonely and solitary state at one end of the House, half-hidden by his wig), who, in a low tone, calls on one of the Members present to speak.

"But I Go on For Ever"

AND so the weary round goes on, minute after minute, hour after hour. Occasionally a Member will drop in on his way from one bar to another. Then the time for a division arrives, and a resounding bell echoes through the halls, rooms, and corridors, and ushers call loudly, "Division." Then, after a short interval, the Members flock in from their clubs, from the bars, from the reading rooms, from all over the House. They troop into the lobbies, marshalled by the Party Whips—entirely ignorant, for the most part, of the why and the wherefore of the case or amendment about which they are voting. The tellers then march, slow and in stately manner, down the floor of the House, and hand the number of "Ayes" and "Noes" to the Clerk to the House, who passes the slips to the Speaker, who gives out the result, amid cheers and counter-cheers.

Such is the beautiful system of Parliamentary Democracy which the Old Gangs are so anxious to preserve!

YOUNG ENGLAND AND THE BRITISH UNION

H. Sheppard, 20 years of age, and a member of the staff of "Action," tells why British Youth is turning Fascist

THE Press are continually sneering at the youthfulness of many members of the British Union. Why should the fact that British Youth is taking an active part in the future of its country arouse comment? If we do not do something, and do it very soon, the old politicians will lead the country to ruin and probably war. And Youth will pay the price.

Can we be expected to follow such men as Baldwin, Simon, Attlee, etc., or any of the old gang politicians? What do they know of modern conditions or the problems which confront modern Youth? They were brought up in the time when action was not expected, the time when discussions and debates were all the fashion. For a man to act according to his principles was a crime; always it must be the Party first, and the country a very bad second.

Do they think that we should be content with the fact that the so-called national Press publish at certain intervals reports that prosperity has returned, while all around us we see large numbers of unemployed, idle factories and mines, and large numbers of the population suffering from the effects of lack of food and clothing.

The Things That Matter

WHAT does a boom on the Stock Exchange matter to us? We see no signs of the nation as a whole benefiting by it. Only a few seem to gain and always the same few.

This great country and Empire belong to us. We are not going to stand by and allow our country to be made the laughing-stock of the world, because a few old men are afraid of the new creed which has arisen amongst the Youth and ex-Service men of all the great European Powers, and, therefore, do all they can to arouse a hatred of it by lies and distortions. We refuse to see large sections of our Empire given away in order that a few international financiers might be better off.

That is why we unite with the ex-Service men of this country—men who fought thinking that they were doing their bit in maintaining the greatness of Britain and the Empire—only to find they had been betrayed. Together in the British Union, under the leadership of a man who has suffered betrayal, but still understands the spirit of the new generation, we march onwards till the day comes when Britain will be great again, when all the peoples of the Empire will be united in one great brotherhood, and our King shall once again rule over an Empire of which he may be justly proud.

POLITICS AND RELIGION

"SPEAKING WITH OTHER TONGUES"

By Rev. H. E. B. NYE

IT is a common experience in most arguments to find people using the same words but attaching to them different meanings. This leads to endless discussion, but to no possible agreement. Those who have the privilege of being reported in the daily Press should be more careful. The Bishop of Chichester is reported to have said at a public gathering that "Fascism is a religion" and that "Communism is another." Mr. Stanley Baldwin, in the same paper, is reported to have informed the House of Commons that "Communism is a religion." The latter may be excused for not knowing the meaning of the word "religion," but a bishop should show more erudition. The only definition that I can find in my dictionary is: "Belief in a superhuman being or beings."

That is the usual sense in which the word is used, and to use it in any other is misleading. The good prelate is evidently at pains to prove that Fascism is a rival to Christianity, but in order to do that he should not misuse words. Fascists in Italy do not regard Mussolini as a god, and they can, therefore, be good Catholics and, at the same time, convinced Fascists. To imply that a man cannot be devoted to a great cause without renouncing his religion is pure nonsense.

"They Learn Nothing"

IT is this sheer inability to understand great mass movements which will eventually cause the undoing of these defenders of a lost cause. If bishops cannot distinguish between politics and religion they show a singular ineptitude for their job. And what on earth does Mr. Baldwin mean by "religion" if the atheist Communists are brought within the fold? Could confusion be worse confounded?

It could easily be proved that our public men are equally careless in the use of other words. This bemusing of the popular mind is dangerous. You can deceive up to a point, but with discovery comes loss of credit. It suits the convenience of unscrupulous or stupid statesmen to use the word "Fascism" in a sense divorced from its obvious meaning. An American writer, in a recent book, refers to "*those soft-thinking Liberal leaders who have sought to make of Fascism a synonym for all that is socially iniquitous, instead of a descriptive for a rational and workable social scheme to which they happen to be opposed.*"

What is Provocation?

THIS pernicious habit of misusing words introduces an entirely new vocabulary which makes complete chaos of speech. Thus it is "provocation" for peaceful and law-respecting Englishmen to march through their own streets, and "natural resentment" for mobs to hurl bricks, tear up paving stones, assault the police, and barricade the roads. A meeting of an enthusiastic multitude to hear and acclaim Sir Oswald Mosley in the East End becomes "indifference." An attempt to secure freedom of speech by ejecting persistent interrupters from a public meeting is defined as "brutality." Where will it all end?

Mr. Baldwin is a past master in the use of these equivocal expressions. He proclaims that the Fascists are not worth a snap of the fingers, and then (so rumour has it) contemplates a special Act of Parliament to deprive these "insignificant" patriots of the right to wear the clothes they prefer. Far be it from me to stigmatise these verbal inconsistencies as deliberate lies, or, even as the fastidious Churchill once expressed himself, as terminological inexactitudes, but they are certainly evidence of a fatal inability to see straight. This is a serious drawback for a statesman, if not for a politician.

The Spirit of Malice

THIS habit of speaking with other tongues has nothing in common with Pentecostal inspiration. The spirit that gives utterance is the spirit of ignorance or malice. Once the hearers are warned of this impediment to enlightenment they can safeguard themselves. The time has come when all speakers must be asked if they are using words in their natural or in their neo-democratic meaning. The public would then be able to form sane conclusions. That, however, is the last thing that politicians are likely to desire, so that Fascists must themselves defend not only English liberties, but the English language itself. In this struggle for exactitude the bishops should set a good example, and, as a first step, decide what they mean by the word "religion." They will then discover that Christians can be both good Christians and enthusiastic Blackshirts.

MONEY

WHAT IS IT?

THERE is nothing very complicated about money, once you get the hang of it.

What is complicated is the process of acquiring money. The present system makes that process difficult.

"A nation's wealth," say the upholders of the system, "is dependent upon its gold."

That is where they are wrong.

The true wealth of a nation is in its national resources, its labour, and its capacity to consume what it produces.

If gold were abolished to-morrow it would not be impossible to devise a new means of currency or exchange.

If food and raw materials were abolished to-morrow the nation would starve.

Yet, in spite of the obvious, a great mass of people still continue to accept the word of the finance racketeer that gold is the be-all and end-all of national economy. A new system is necessary.

We must remove "the stranglehold on production" of the present gold system.

Money should be issued according to the amount of goods produced and consumed. It should be the bill of exchange between those who want to buy and those who want to sell.

At present, those who want to sell cannot find the buyers. And those who want to buy cannot find the money.

We have the foodstuffs, the goods, the factories, and the men. When we remove money from its position as the all-powerful bullying boss we can use these resources to the full.

Books  Read

"From Heston to High Alps." By Douglas Fawcett. (Macmillan and Co. 6s.)

MANY people write books on how they learned to fly. Some of them have been well worth reading, some of them have not. Often I find much of interest in the difficulties of different pupils and their reactions to flying.

Douglas Fawcett was sixty-seven when he decided to learn to fly. He had been a well-known Alpine climber and had, apparently, got tired of walking up and down Alps to see the scenery. One day, in Switzerland, a friend suggested he should fly in an aeroplane and have a look at an Alp or two. He had never been up before, but thought it was quite a good idea. He discovered at once that the aeroplane could take all the tiring parts out of Alpine sports and give one views hitherto unobtainable, and so he decided at once to fly.

The first part of the book is devoted to his experiences at Heston, where he learned to fly an Avro Cadet under Captain V. H. Baker, known to hundreds of his pupils (who have still remained his friends in spite of this) as "Bake."

There is much good sense in his observations, and his experiences will be of interest not only to other pupils but also to experienced instructors.

The second part of the book describes various flights he made over the Alps after learning to fly, and the whole is illustrated with some magnificent photographs of the Alps, including some of the summit of Mont Blanc and the Matterhorn.—"BLACKBIRD."

THE DECLINE AND FALL OF THE ROMANTIC IDEAL

By F. L. LUCAS

(Cambridge. 8s. 6d.) *Reviewed by William Joyce*

MR. LUCAS takes what at first appears to be the charming course of appending an epilogue for the benefit of reviewers who have not the time to read the whole work. The device is by no means so simple as it sounds. I began with the epilogue This appendix, however, was so far from explicit that I felt bound to read the whole book in the hope of elucidating the problems which the epilogue posited. Having read the book I returned to the epilogue, and was no more edified than on the first reading.

The author bravely attempts to draw once again a line of demarcation between the classicals and the Romantics in literature. He displays a wealth of knowledge, much of which is misapplied. Indeed, it would be almost generous to diagnose his complaint as literary dyspepsia.

He has little time for the definition of Romanticism given by Wordsworth, who performed the somewhat doubtful service of founding the Nineteenth Century Romantic School. The Romantic is distinguished, we learn, not by the language of common men in the spontaneous overflow of powerful feelings excited by small celandines, but by a psycho-pathological taint of a nature to be revealed only by the notorious Professor Freud. Surely Mr. Lucas is a little hard. Strongly as I have adhered throughout many years to the classical school, and venomous as I have often felt to the more hazy Romantics, I cannot help thinking that Mr. Lucas might have spared them from the last degradation whereby the Jewish pornologist is introduced to explain their existence. Mr. Lucas's argument does apply in great measure to the so-called ultra-moderns, and as to the surrealists, there can be no doubt whatever.

If he wishes to clap Baudelaire into a psycho-pathological nursing home let him do so, but even this incarceration may be in some respects a travesty of justice. Again, that Coleridge was neurotic we need hardly question, but when we come to review Byron, Keats, and Shelley we must feel that the remedy is too drastic.

These poets were, in some respects, abnormal, but to say that the essence of their work is a release and operation of sub-conscious and largely inane processes is to betray a lack of proportion such as is manifested in the absurd political observations which quite unnecessarily are introduced. If a reason be sought for the downfall of the Romantic School, it will be found in the unhappy association between Romanticism and Financial Democracy. International plutocracy and gross materialism were dominant characteristics of the nineteenth century, and they would certainly suffice to kill a plant so delicate as the Romantic.

Towards the close Mr. Lucas makes a trip to Iceland, and parades his knowledge of old Norse literature. Even here the treatment is marred by the introduction of political prejudices. In the end we are left face to face with the conclusion that Mr. Lucas suffers from the usual disability of democratic philosophy. He does not know what he wants, and he is not sure what exists. The book would be without value if it did not show the relationship between Freudian theory and the excesses of the Romantic who steps across the bounds of sanity. Certainly the main interest of the work is to be found in its psychopathological aspect. It need not be read.

"I LEAP BEFORE I LOOK"

By DAVID HAIG THOMAS

(Putnam. 10s. 6d.)

HIS publishers introduce the author as a young man whose twenty-seven years have been full of incident. This is quite true. Mr. Haig Thomas begins his autobiography in the conventional manner, with an account of his adventures as a child of five. An accompanying photograph shows him seated demurely upon one leg, with clasped hands, curled hair, and the tolerant smile of the unbearable pre-War infant. After another short reminiscence of childhood, an uncomfortable story of the pheasants in Windsor Great Park, he sets out upon the adventures of his more mature years.

The narration is interesting, because the author has so obviously enjoyed doing the things he describes. It has the irresponsibility of the man who does not need to fear poverty, and for whom, to counteract shortage of money in any foreign country, "my income was always accumulating at home." A passion for shooting birds gives way to a no less consuming passion for photographing them, and, with Peter Scott, whose paintings of wild geese are well known, Mr. Haig Thomas has photographed birds of all kinds in all places. As a member of the winning boat-race crew, he went to Los Angeles when the Olympic Games were held there in 1932, and he later worked on the land in Canada. His description of the opening of the Games seems a little discourteous—but, indeed, the author seems more concerned with setting down his adventures as they occur, in the simplest possible language and without nice discrimination, than he does with making a coherent book. A. C.

"Hitler Over Russia." By Ernst Henri. (J. M. Dent. 8s. 6d. net.)

ERNST HENRI (I suspect the curvature of his nose) is the author of "Hitler over Europe," which was strongly recommended by Albert Einstein, Wickham Steed, and Bertrand Russell. That book I never read, and now that I have perused this one, I shall never read his next—"Hitler over Britain," which, presumably, is to complete this apoplectic, apocalyptic saga.

As a compendium of violent words it is unique. When he hears the word "Fascist" he falls into a priapic frenzy, and foaming in paroxysms of verbosity he proclaims such people to be "homosexuals, drug-fiends, and megalomaniacs."

As regards this cult in Germany, Hitler has ruined the peasants, he has degraded the unemployed "to outlawed pariahs," he has amputated "whole segments of society" by terror, and families have been "shipped off like cattle."

But when he turned to the Socialists and the Jews, he was stumped; for though "he could keep on arresting or murdering tens of thousands," he could not exhaust the stock!

The book opens with the extermination of Röhm and ends with the extermination of Hitler, and in between most of it reads like a modernised edition of some medieval black magical evocation. Thus, to quote the "Grimoire of Honorius" we have: "I conjure thee by the ineffable name of God, On, Alpha and Omega, Eloy, Eloym, Ya, Saday, Lux, etc., etc.," and in the Grimoire of Henri: "I exorcise thee by Zaharoff, Thyssen, Baltic Barons, Herrenklub, Perkonkrust, Tesz, Ustashi, Imro, Pow, Rows, Uno and Unr!"

And if you do not believe me read this book. Anyhow, it all ends happily like a Grimm's fairy tale, for the Hoffmann Plan (see the pentacle in the cover) goes phut, and no wonder, because it is "a reversion to the pre-Clausewitz epoch of European warfare—to the strategic school of Napoleon." Incidentally Clausewitz based his entire philosophy upon Napoleon; but never mind, the book ends happily: Göring's air army is wiped out, the imprisoned masses in Germany rise against the Fascist "gangsters and lunatics" who simultaneously destroy each other and "indivisible peace" descends upon the world! J. F.

"Why Aeroplanes Fly." By Arthur Elton and Robert Fairthorne. (Longmans. 2s. 6d.)

FOR those who want to learn something about elementary aerodynamics, Longmans, Green and Co. have produced what they call No. 1 of the "March of Time" series. Its purpose is to put the aeroplane into its historical perspective, to explain the first principles of flight and to discuss the social implications of the aeroplane in the modern world.

The book is written throughout in language easily understandable by the lay mind, and after reading it through the beginner can get a good idea of why an aeroplane or airship flies, how it is controlled, and what causes it to do the things it does.

There are some fine illustrations of every type of aeroplane from the early Montgolfier Balloon of 1783 to the very latest R.A.F. and civil aeroplane.

In addition, there are numerous diagrams showing such things as air streams and their effects on aerofoils.—"BLACKBIRD."

OF SPECIAL INTEREST—

"PILLARS OF CLOUD"

By JOHN SCANLON

(Chapman and Hall. 5s.)

NOBODY who read John Scanlon's book, "The Decline and Fall of the Labour Party," will want to miss his new book, which is written in the same slashing and humorous style.

It describes, year by year, the comic attempts of all the leading politicians to deal with the problem of poverty amid plenty since 1918. Mr. Scanlon has chosen for his title, "Pillars of Cloud." The foreword explains the book and the title. It reads:

"*In an earlier period of human history it was decided that a great pilgrimage should set out towards a new and fair land. The method chosen by the leaders to guide their followers was a pillar of cloud by day and a pillar of fire by night.*

"*In 1918 the leaders of thought in Britain and elsewhere decided that they, too, would conduct their followers to a new and fairer land, but in the interests of economy they thought it better to dispense with the fire, and conduct the pilgrimage entirely by cloud. No matter who happened to be the leader, the method was always the same.*

"*In 1936 the pilgrimage still continues, but many people believe it has become lost in the Pillars of Cloud.*"

The book has entailed considerable reading and research, but in order that everybody concerned with the future of Britain should be able to get it, the publishers are issuing it at the lowest price possible, 5s. It will be published on Monday, November 23. If you haven't 5s., order it from your library now as there is sure to be a rush.

Shows  Seen

LIBELLED LADY

American
Empire Cinema

AMERICA'S complicated divorce laws, once discovered and examined, offer almost unlimited scope for piquancy of plot. It seems that one must exercise a nice discrimination in the choice of a domiciliary state if one wishes to avoid contracting—quite innocently—a bigamous union. Thus, a marriage annulment valid in Yucatan may see you still tied in the strictest of marriage bonds in Ohio, and a New York paper. The American reporter, as all cinema audiences know, is attached to his paper as he is attached to no other thing, neither his dog nor his wife nor his child.

The underlying plot of "Libelled Lady" is very much the same as many pictures we have seen, in which the obscure young journalist obtains the lady, but its development and treatment is brilliantly different. It opens at once in swift movement and apparent confusion, rushes from press room to press room, finally picking out Mr. Spencer Tracy as a belligerent reporter, and Miss Jean Harlow, who sweeps brassily through

Myrna Loy and Spencer Tracy

Reno divorce may not serve you at all if you decide to live upon the Rocky mountains.

Miss Myrna Loy is the libelled lady of this picture's title, and the value of her reputation is assessed at five million dollars. The audience seemed inclined to join with Mr. William Powell in thinking it too high. Mr. Powell is the obscure journalist told off to make the libel real by compromising the lady, thus to save both the reputation and the existence of his a dusty press room clad in satin and orange blossom, complaining bitterly that she must always play second fiddle to the paper—a contention which seems amply justified. Mr. William Powell contracts with Miss Harlow a marriage of convenience which is far less convenient than he had expected, and not so very much of a marriage. It remains only for us to find Mr. Powell in amorous pursuit of Miss Myrna Loy for the picture to have swept into its stride as one of the most delightful light comedies which Hollywood has sent us for some time.

O'RILEY'S LUCK

American
Paramount

FRANCIS WALLACE'S football story, "O'Reilly of Notre Dame," translated into cinematic form, makes clean, straight entertainment about Americans, principally for Americans, but quite acceptable to British audiences. Paramount seem to believe in giving young actors plenty of opportunity, and Tom Brown, who plays O'Riley, justifies this policy—a young man to watch. Eleanore Whitney has to look pretty most of the time, but plays one or two tricky scenes very well. Most of the comedy lies in the capable hands of Benny Baker, who plays a stupid but lovable Dutch-American.

I have only one real criticism—Larry (late "Buster") Crabbe is much too nice to play a bumptious young cad, although he does it excellently.

By the way, don't worry about the change of players in mid-game—it's an old American custom.—M. C. W.

THE GAY DESPERADO

American
London Pavilion

THE Mary Pickford - Jesse Lasky combination, which produced as its first picture "One Rainy Afternoon," an abortive singing thing, all pseudo-Parisian boulevard, has done rather well in this second picture, again featuring Ida Lupino and again having pretensions to musicianship.

While banditry over the Mexican border may have nothing to offer in guile to the real American variety with which the cinemas have made us familiar, it seems vastly superior in courtesy and all the accredited graces of old-time outlawry. There is more than a touch of satire about "The Gay Desperado," which, in many ways, excuses the rather excessive length at which it is made.

If the Pickford-Lasky combination continues to improve at the rate which it is seen to do in these early pictures, we may possibly expect a very interesting development in future. While this, its latest production, is far from perfect, and, indeed, at times comes perilously near the fringe of boredom, it is an enormous improvement upon its first. It contains a delightful caricature of gangsterdom, and the charming English girl, Ida Lupino, does very well all that is necessary to support the voice of Tullio Carminati.

FREDLOS (Outcast)

Finnish
Academy

THE rather primitive story of the crazy and despotic Governor, whose power over his peasantry does not stop short at any usurpation of personal rights, is used here with Lapland and Finland as its setting. As the first Finnish picture seen in London, "Fredlös" is very interesting. It is made in an extremely beautiful natural setting of snow and ice and thawing waters, round the simple dwellings of Laplanders and Finlanders. Considered purely as a motion picture it can compare with any production, even the most finished and recent, which has been shown in recent years.

It is a picture of an enslaved people, driven by harsh and brutal laws to conduct the parallel of which would not be found even in the jungle. The very beautiful young girl heroine has a strong personality and is entirely unlike any beautiful young girl from the twentieth-century studios with which we are acquainted. This is an unusually beautiful production of a simple and moving story, well told and right in all its details.

WEDDING PRESENT

Paramount

PAUL GOLLIEO, who wrote the story of "Wedding Present," spent some years with the New York newspaper, *Daily News*, so we are able to presume he knows something of journalism in the States—if this is a true representation of it, when do American newspaper men work? Perhaps it explains why their newspapers use so much space for headlines.

As a comedy of almost slapstick variety this film is quite good fun. Drunken scenes on the stage, or in the cinema, are often slightly objectionable, but Richard Wallace, the director, is to be congratulated on that between the disappointed lover and the dyspeptic gangster. Cary Grant is much more attractive as a comedian than the rather solemn young man to whom we were first introduced some years ago, while Joan Bennett, as usual, upholds the honour of the Bennett family. Unlike Constance, she was never established in any groove or "type," with the result that her range is wider and her appeal more universal.

George Bancroft and Conrad Nagel have little to do, but do it well. It is a pity that actors of their ability cannot be given better parts.

See this film if you want to laugh, and, if you go, see if you recognise, in the part of the author's sister, Lois Wilson, star of "Covered Wagon," that grand old silent.—M. C. W.

DECREE NISI

Embassy

THE story of this play is, briefly, that the money-loving husband returns home unexpectedly to find his wife crying in the arms of an old friend of hers, who had come to see the new flat. When the husband discovers some letters written to her by the old friend divorce proceedings follow.

After a frame-up has been arranged, of false evidence against the two, the counsel for the wife, by a successful trick, wins the case—and the lady.

The chief fault is that the parts are so machine-made. There is the husband—domineering and possessive, absorbed in business and the job of getting on at all costs. In its more tense moments this part has a "Ha, fair maiden, I have you in my power" atmosphere, which makes it rather melodramatic.

Then there is the wife—sweet, suffering, and very chaste. An old nurse of the picture-book type completes this trio.

The cast acted smoothly and well, but the story lacks novelty.—M. M. C.

REASONABLE ENTERTAINMENT

A word might be said here about the little Court Cinema in Sloane-square, where sooner or later the finest films make their way. Last week this cinema was showing "Next Time We Live," an unusually mature production, well acted, and this week it shows Grace Moore in "On Wings of Song," for those people who find the feminine singing voice endurable. The price of seats in this little converted theatre is very moderate, and the films shown are always films of merit coming to it some time after their general release, and the programmes usually include a Silly Symphony or a Disney cartoon.

CLASSIFIED ADVERTISEMENTS

3 insertions for the price of 2
6 " " " " " 4
13 " " " " " 8

1/- ONLY
For 12 WORDS—Then 1d. per word

BOX NUMBERS
3D. EXTRA per insertion, which includes postage of replies.

Heavy Type
2D. per word, per insertion.

Your advertisement, together with remittance, should reach the ADVERTISEMENT MANAGER not later than Tuesday previous to publication date. Displayed Advertisements cannot be accepted for publication in "Action."

FOR SALE

A MAID—is a luxury! An Electric Cleaner a necessity! Newest models on specially low terms to members—Write for demonstration to Box 276, Action Press, Ltd., Sanctuary-buildings, Great Smith-street, Westminster. 5 per cent. of net sales to Election Fund. 40

CYCLE-DYNO SETS, British-made, fully guaranteed, including rear light, 13s. 9d., post free; makes ideal Christmas present.—Evershed and Company, 2, High-street, Bognor Regis. 44

FURNITURE; Agent offers Bedroom Suites, oak, walnut, mahogany, from 12 gns.; Oak Dining Room Suites from 8 gns.; 3-piece Tapestry Suites from 12 gns. Bedsteads, Bedding, Lino., and all Furnishing supplied. Monthly terms can be arranged as required.—Reply: J. Williams, Box 210, Action Press, Ltd., Sanctuary Bldgs., Great Smith-street, Westminster. 45

ITALIAN PIANO-ACCORDION, 21 keys, perfect condition; accept 30s. cash.—Box 278, Action Press, Ltd., Sanctuary-buildings, Great Smith-street, Westminster. 40

MASSAGE OIL for all athletes, 1s. 4d.—Meal, Masseur, Cross Hills, Halifax. 41

NEW BADGES.—Flash and Circle, chromium steel, safety-pin type, 1s. 6d. each.—Blackshirt Bookshop, 81, Stafford-street, Birmingham. 40

RADIO.—If dissatisfied with your present Foreign Reception, why not let us demonstrate one of our 1937 Short-Wave Models? No obligation!—Write, Box 275, Action Press, Ltd., Sanctuary-buildings, Great Smith-street, Westminster. 5 per cent. of net sales to Election Fund. 40

SOFT WATER SAVING—in Health, Time, and Money. 1937 model Water Softeners from 45s.—Write for free demonstration to Box 272, Action Press, Ltd., Sanctuary-buildings, Great Smith-street, Westminster. 5 per cent. of net sales to Election Fund. 40

FOR SALE

THE CORE OF THE JEWISH QUESTION. "Zionism," 6½d., post free; "An Analysis of Zionism," 2½d., post free; "Zionism and the Christian Church," 2½d., post free.—Write: Political Publications, 4, Stanhope-gardens, S.W.7. 40

VACUUM CLEANER, good make, complete with all accessories, perfect condition, little used: 39s. 6d.—Box 262, Action Press, Ltd., Sanctuary-buildings, Great Smith-street, Westminster. 40

XMAS PARTY Guests need Food! Food needs refrigeration! Latest models on lowest terms.—Write for free demonstration to Box 274, Action Press, Ltd., Sanctuary-buildings, Great Smith-street, Westminster. 5 per cent. of net sales to Election Fund. 40

YOUR WIFE—needs an Electric Washing Machine! Save your Laundry Bills! Demonstration without obligation.—Write, Box 275, Action Press, Ltd., Sanctuary-buildings, Great Smith-street, Westminster. 5 per cent. of net sales to Election Fund. 40

£12/10/-—MORRIS-COWLEY 4-Seater Saloon, excellent condition throughout.—Apply, 37, Cowslip-road, South Woodford. 41

£80 DOWN, balance weekly.—Facing Euston Station. Confectionery-Cigarette Shop, 7 rooms; rent £2; five rooms let furnished covering all outgoings; nice living for couple not afraid of work; well stocked; electric Frigidaire, auto scales, cash register, and furniture of the 5 furnished rooms; everything all at low price for quick sale. Owner having other business. No time-waster.—120, Shepherd's Bush-road, W.6. 40

LITERATURE

GERMANY'S desire for Peace and General Recovery—Read the facts; free literature in English from Dept. A. Deutscher Fichte-Bund, Hamburg 36, Jungfernstieg, 30. 47

TO LET

COMFORTABLE Bed-Sitting-room, near Chelsea, use bath, 15s., inclusive e.l.—Box 270, Action Press, Ltd., Sanctuary-buildings, Great Smith-street, Westminster. 41

BRICK-BUILT Bungalow, furnished, company's water, two bedrooms, one sitting room, one large kitchen.—Besbeech, Nipsells Chase, Maylandsea, Essex. 40

VICTORIA.—Bright furnished Top Flat, overlooking square, gardens; two rooms and bath, kitchen, £2 per week; refs.; view by appointment.—Box 269, Action Press, Ltd., Sanctuary-buildings, Great Smith-street, Westminster. 41

APARTMENTS WANTED

LADY requires two Rooms, unfurnished, good, quiet; terms moderate; central.—Box 279, Action Press, Ltd., Sanctuary-buildings, Great Smith-street, Westminster. 42

MISCELLANEOUS

COME AND BUY XMAS PRESENTS at the **BLACKSHIRT BAZAAR** (in aid of East End Election Fund), December 4 and 5, open 7-10 p.m., Saturday 12-10 p.m., at National Headquarters, Sanctuary-buildings, Great Smith-street, Westminster. Stalls: Perfumery, Flowers, Knitwear, Arts and Crafts, Toys, Cakes, Jams, Sweets, Sideshows. Fun for the children—Lucky Dip and Dancing. Entrance fee, 3d. Teas on Saturday, 9d. per head. **LADY MOSLEY** will open the Bazaar at 7 p.m. on December 4. **NON-MEMBERS INVITED.** 41

DO all insurances through British Union Member. Percentage to Funds.—Hill, 13, Fernhurst-road, Croydon. 40

SUPPORT PRIVATE ENTERPRISE.—Hand Laundry, 100 per cent. British is desirous of obtaining customers in the West End and District. For price list, 'phone Syd. 5684. Also lorry for hire. 40

YOUNG Englishman requires German lessons.—Box 257, Action Press, Ltd., Sanctuary-buildings, Great Smith-street, Westminster. 40

HOLIDAYS

BRIGHTON. GRESHAM HOTEL. Most central position facing sea; highly recommended; first-class cuisine; special winter terms. Tel.: 428911. 49

HOTEL QUELLENHOF, Arosa, Switzerland, 6,000 ft. a.s.l.; famous winter sports centre; moderate terms. English management. 52

HOLIDAYS IN SWITZERLAND.—Private party, organised by Fascist, leaving January, has vacancies, either sex; moderate cost.—Terms through Box 268, Action Press, Ltd., Sanctuary-buildings, Great Smith-street, Westminster. 41

ITALIAN RIVIERA.—Bordighera. Park Hotel; 100 rooms **first-class; best position. From 6s. daily.** 50

SITUATIONS WANTED

FASCIST (29) seeks responsible office or sales position. Experienced book-keeper; fluent French, German, Italian; good appearance and education; excellent references.—Box 266, Action Press, Ltd., Sanctuary-buildings, Great Smith-street, Westminster. 41

YOUNG Gentleman desires Situation.—BM/WSVK. 42

SITUATIONS VACANT

BOY wanted for cycle delivery; hours 8.30 to 6.30; Saturday early closing.—Kenya Coffee Co., 11, Henrietta-street, Oxford-street. 41

CAPABLE general maid wanted for Fascist family in Leicester.—Box 258, Action Press, Ltd., Sanctuary-buildings, Great Smith-street, Westminster. 40

EX-SERVICE MAN required, must be member of British Union, to sell Literature in a Midlands town; regular salary.—Write, Box 277, Action Press, Ltd., Sanctuary-buildings, Great Smith-street, Westminster. 42

IF you have had any selling experience and have personality, appearance, and guts, we can offer you a decently-paid job with unlimited prospects.—Write for interview, with full details, Box 271, Action Press, Ltd., Sanctuary-buildings, Great Smith-street, Westminster. 42

MALDON, ESSEX.—Capable cook-general; two in family; other help; good outings.—Apply, Box 243, Action Press, Ltd., Sanctuary-buildings, Great Smith-street, Westminster. 40

WANTED, experienced Furliner and Finisher; all-year-round job for good worker.—J. W. Higgs and Sons, The Real English Manufacturing Furriers, 368, London-road, Westcliff. Gentiles only. 42

YOUTH, good personality, for car and house; under 18; 10s. 6d. weekly, all found; substantial rise after first three months; previous knowledge not necessary.—Box 281, Action Press, Ltd., Sanctuary-buildings, Great Smith-street, Westminster. 40

FINANCIAL

In offers with Investment, readers are advised to make fullest inquiries before making the proposed investment.

MOTOR ENGINEER (M.I.M.T.) desires Partner, with capital, to found School of Motoring in busy West London district; main road premises available.—Box 267, Action Press, Ltd., Sanctuary-buildings, Great Smith-street, Westminster. 41

WANTED

WANTED, Parrots, anything. Exchange Cash, Wireless, Gongaphone, Canaries, Mains Cigarette Lighter.—65, Park-lane, Southend-on-Sea. 40

SHORT STORY

DEMOCRACY AND THE CRUISER

Another Lampoon on Democracy by

—F. A. S. SMITH—

THE last of the officers had gone overboard that morning, tied back to back, after the custom of the time, and with the accompanying ceremonies—representatives of the crew spitting over the stern as they sank, and so forth.

And now the elected committee had taken charge of the ship, and were assembled on the bridge. The battle cruiser San Democra was to be run on democratic lines: there were to be no more hasty actions; and the system would ensure that the best brains were always in charge.

At the moment the Starboard Watch held the majority of seats on the bridge. Not that there were more men in that Watch, but the system of election had worked in their favour.

"Ahem . . ." the chairman, Señor Stanlia, rose. "Señors . . . we have just received our instructions from Admiral Don Isaacs—very brief and to the point they are — 'Go where you like. Do what you like. But don't interfere with the interests of Financia.' . . . The admiral emphasises that Financia is the supreme power in these waters, and should any incidents occur there is bound to be trouble. . . . I may add that these instructions, received in code, are to be taken as sealed orders and must not be divulged to the ship's company."

The chairman continued his speech, presently coming to the question of what the San Democra should do and where she should go. The Starboard Watch Cabinet, he said, after carefully weighed consideration, had decided that the wise and sane policy was for them to hang about where they were, in their enviable position, until the crisis had passed.

For the opposition, Señor Attlia and Don Crippo spoke, and the discussion promised to be a lively one. Señor Attlia boldly proposed that all guns, rifles, torpedoes, etc., should be thrown overboard, as an example to other warships. Then no one would attack them, he said.

Don Crippo, in a forceful speech, declared their duty was to go to the assistance of the gallant Reds and blow the Blacks to hell. "If ever we are attacked," he concluded, "the men will strike! They will not fight! They will not stand for war!"

⊘ ⊘ ⊘

THE sea was calm and blue. No sound of guns reached them; no smell of cordite tainted the faint, warm breeze. Only two ships were sighted that day, the Monopolis and the Combinia, and, since they both belonged to Financia, no shot was fired by the San Democra. Two more Financian vessels passed next morning, the Importia and a sailing clipper, the Cutty Price, a ship which had long been in the service of Financia. But soon after midday, while the Commanding Committee was taking its siesta, a small torpedo boat was reported bearing down on the port bow.

Soon there came the Minister for Wireless to rouse the Cabinet and inform them that this torpedo boat, the Unity, was inquiring which side the San Democra was on, since she flew no flag other than that of the Starboard Watch.

This was an unforeseen circumstance! Señor Stanlia decided it was necessary to assemble the committee, to determine whose side they *were* on. Meanwhile, the Unity circled round a couple of miles away.

The discussion was formally opened. Starboard representatives seized upon the first side issue on which they could lay their hands, and launched out into exhaustive explanations revolving round the question of a halfpenny a day off the wages of flag makers. And when they had finished Port Watch members came up from the canteen and vigorously opposed any suggestion that might have been made, for the simple reason that they had been made by Starboard men. Eventually the matter was referred to a sub-committee.

⊘ ⊘ ⊘

BUT in the morning the Unity was still there. Capitan Axion, on her bridge lowered his glasses and remarked to his second in command: "There's something queer about that ship, Selva . . . and her damned funny wireless messages. . . ." He raised his glasses again. "Bah! . . . Awaiting report of sub-committee! It's a ruse of some kind! . . . Fire a shot across her bows."

The sun was low over the eastern horizon, as though it were joined to the end of its long flashing reflection. The Cabinet stumbled up to the bridge, one by one, half asleep, toppers awry, ties hurriedly tied, and trousers unpressed.

This was indeed a crisis. A call for decisive action. A representative rose pompously and moved a resolution that "The chairman and Commanding Committee of the battle-cruiser San Democra deplores the action of the torpedo-boat Unity and views with consternation the breach by the torpedo-boat Unity of paragraph nineteen of page fifty-three, sub-section B, section K4, of the third convention of the international covenant of February 30, nineteen hundred and four." The resolution was carried unanimously by the Starboard Watch members, and opposed unanimously by the Port Watch representatives. They maintained it should be paragraph four of page seventy-two of sub-section G.

⊘ ⊘ ⊘

THE resolution was wirelessed to the Unity, and as it was by now breakfast time, the Commanding Committee adjourned.

Capitan Axion received the message from his wireless officer. He read it three times, and each time he frowned harder.

"Chairman and Commanding Committee!" he ejaculated, "deplores my action! Do they, the——! . . . Breach of sub-section KBXY. Pah! ! Fire another shot at the silly ——s!"

The Commanding Committee had just started breakfast when the second shot screamed over. As they heard it every man stopped what he was doing, some with forks in the air, some with raised cups, some in the act of chewing. For a moment there was silence, and then mouths closed and cups and knives and forks were lowered to plates and saucers. The chairman looked gravely down the table. In his eyes this second shot was gross violation of paragraph nineteen. He completely overlooked the fact that he was originally at fault for not showing a flag. He saw it only as intolerable aggression. He called an urgent meeting of the Commanding Committee, and they returned to the bridge and took their seats.

⊘ ⊘ ⊘

THE chairman rose, looking dignified and solemn:

"Events," he said, in portentous tones, "have taken a very grave turn. . . . The only course now open to us is to await the decision of higher authorities. . . . As you are aware, señors, in time of war we are transferred from the command of Admiral Don Isaacs to the command of his compatriot, President of the Fleet, Señor Litvinoff Finkelstein. We await his instructions."

The instructions came through: "Attack Unity immediately. You have the moral support of the whole fleet behind you."

At that Señor Inskipio got up and moved the motion: (a) That shells, (1) high explosive, (2) shrapnel, shall be fired at the torpedo boat Unity by the battle-cruiser San Democra until the torpedo boat Unity be (1) sunk (2) surrender, (3) out of action. (b) That should the opportunity arise, torpedoes shall be fired by the battle cruiser San Democra at the torpedo boat Unity until she be (1) sunk, (2) surrender, (3) out of action. (c) That the flying machine of the battle cruiser San Democra shall be catapulted into the air, and shall proceed in the direction of, and fly over, the torpedo boat Unity, discharging bullets from its machine gun at the said vessel.† (†The aeroplane being a machine which did excellent service in the war of 1914-18, is not equipped with torpedoes or bombs.) (c) That rifles——" and so on.

Amendments and further proposals followed: "That gun crews shall not infringe union rules. . . . fixing of overtime rates. . . that the minimum of one hour be allowed each man for dinner. . . ." etc., etc.

The tactics of the San Democra absolutely mystified Capitan Axion. Never, in all his experience, had he met with such baffling strategy as this. But it was his duty to discover on which side the cruiser was: shortly before midday he fired another shot, this time directly at the San Democra.

He missed, but the spray of the shot touched the side of the cruiser. The only result he achieved was to make the Commanding Committee hurriedly transfer itself from the bridge to what were the officers' quarters.

As soon as the committee was assembled in safety the Cabinet asked for emergency powers, and their watch having the majority, they obtained them.

Señor Stanlia bravely went back to the bridge.

"Start shooting!" he commanded.

"We will put the matter in hand at once, señor," replied his secretary, and went to the telephone.

A moment later he came back to the chairman:

"The range officers, señor—they were pushed overboard!"

"What! Who did that?"

"Don Horr, señor, on your instructions."

"My instruc—— Shsss! . . . . Goodness me! Here's a mess. . . . Tell Don Horr it is his duty to accept full responsibility for this, and that he must resign on principle. . . . We can't have the men lose faith in their chairman at a time like this. . . . Tell him I'll give him another job in the Cabinet as soon as this has blown over. . . . And give him to understand if he doesn't accept my terms his administrative career is over."

"Very well, señor."

"And tell the men to point the guns as best they can—and better get the engines started up, too."

"Very well, señor."

⊘ ⊘ ⊘

THE guns began to move. One was fired, and then another, and so the ragged shooting started. Shells fell miles away from the torpedo boat. Some went out of sight; but now and then one would fall fairly close to the target.

The chairman watched the great barrels moving, and the black smoke bursting from their muzzles, and felt the vibration of the explosions.

"Aha, I think we have the situation well in hand," he remarked to his secretary, as he filled his pipe. "It won't— Hullo—" he noticed a group of men below him. "What are those men doing?"

"They are conscientious objectors, señor."

"Are they, indeed! Then have them put in irons at once."

The secretary said he would give the matter his personal attention. Soon he returned, told the chairman they were safe and went back to the telephone.

He had not been there a minute when, one by one, starting from the stern, the guns ceased firing. The chairman called him.

"The gunners, señor," explained the secretary. "They have struck . . . they have found a non-union man among them."

"Upon my soul!" The chairman was angry. "Then you had better get the ship round so the Starboard men can shoot."

"Very well, señor."

But he was back again in half a minute.

"The stokers, señor—they demand a special Battle Bonus."

"Well give it to them, man. We must get the engines going."

Meanwhile, Capitan Axion, even more puzzled by the strange shooting and the immobility of the cruiser, decided to retreat.

Within half an hour the dispute had been settled and the engines were going. Now the trouble was to steer the ship, but after a strange manoeuvre the chairman managed a landlubberly turn and started the cruiser in a drunken pursuit of the torpedo-boat.

⊘ ⊘ ⊘

CAPITAN AXION watched her through his telescope. The non-union man had been thrown overboard, and fairly regular, but hopelessly inaccurate, shooting came from the forward guns. Somehow he did not feel there was much danger. The strange behaviour of the San Democra had lit a spark of excitement in him. What if he, with his little torpedo-boat, could bag a battle-cruiser!"

And now real trouble was starting in the cruiser. The chairman received information from a committee agent that Don Crippo was organising a protest march of the Port Watch men to head a deputation to the chairman: and, as their ranks formed, rifles and cutlasses were issued to them. Soon another agent reported that the conscientious objectors had been released and were now, as special bomb throwing and machine gun sections, at the head of the protest march.

The chairman was perturbed. He called the other members of the Cabinet on to the bridge and spoke of "another unforeseen development," and it was proposed that the agitators leading the mutiny should be severely reprimanded. Ministers spoke of ". . . the nauseating and ungentlemanlike attitude taken up by certain members of the company at a time when the democratically elected committee most urgently needed their whole-hearted co-operation."

While they talked the protest marchers were forming fours: and all the time Capitan Axion watched the San Democra through his telescope.

Don Crippo received the reprimand. He tore it up and sent it back.

The chairman gravely received the pieces. "This can only mean, señors," he said in profound tones, "open, undemocratic, and anti-constitutional mutiny. . . Our only course is to instruct the loyal members of the crew to disarm the mutineers."

⊘ ⊘ ⊘

CAPITAN AXION watched the white column of water fall back to the sea where the last shell had fallen. He waited for the next. But no more came. The guns of the cruiser had ceased firing once more. He spoke to the officer in charge of the engine room.

"Bring the pressure up to bursting point!"

On board the cruiser loyal men were mustering to attack the mutineers. Soon the stokers and engineers came up to take sides. So again the water lapped against the steel sides of the great battle-cruiser, as she drifted.

As the crack of the first rifle shot came across the water the Unity acted. She turned sharply, turned until her bows pointed directly at the San Democra and then she shot forward, gathering speed with every second, straight at the doomed cruiser. On she came, her bows cleaving the water, a curved streak of spume flying to either side. Then, within sure range, she was broadside on to the stationary cruiser the torpedoes shot over her side.

Not until the survivors were picked up did Capitan Axion discover he had wasted twenty-four hours on what he could have done in the first five minutes.

CONTENTED BRITAIN—(7)

"To-day we meet in an atmosphere of such happiness and contentment as has not been seen since the war."

Mr. Neville Chamberlain, addressing the British Bankers' Association in 1935.

By H. J. GIBBS

The Secretary,
The Middletown Discussion Group.

THE PLIGHT OF THE WORKERS.

Dear Sir,—So far as we have looked at the confusion of tongues among those who are—let us never forget it!—employed by us to guide us through the difficulties of modern life.

Let us now realise where British workers stand in the midst of all this din and turmoil.

We know that the ground we stand upon is not very secure. The slightest dislocation of the franc or the dollar, a war in South America or China, a revolution in Spain or France, is sufficient—though Heaven alone knows why!—to set the ground beneath us shaking and trembling.

Our working conditions are extremely insecure—again, Heaven alone knows why.

Our hours of work are long. Most of us do at least forty-eight hours a week; the majority put in at least another six tidying things up for the next day. I reckon we all do sixty hours a week, don't you?

Business of Wages

Then there is the business of wages. Of all the maddest things in a mad world, wages give the clearest indication of the general insanity.

Do you know there are cities in Britain where people are dying solely because they haven't enough money to buy decent food in adequate quantities?

There are large towns and villages in the North where the majority of people cannot earn more than 35s. to 40s. a week. This, added to the long hours of toil deep down in the blackness of the coal-pits or amid the continual roar of our modern factories, is increasing the death-rate to an enormous extent, merely because the people do not get sufficient to eat in order to withstand the racket of industrial occupation.

There are continual trade disputes. Miners come out against wages, cotton operatives strike because of long hours and wages, 'bus drivers stop work because they refuse to work on schedules they hold to be unfair, office employees organise a stay-in strike in protest against other employees being sacked. At times thousands of men and women are idle round factory gates and pit-heads, waiting; waiting until their plea for a reconsideration of their dispute be heard.

Waste of Energy

What a wicked waste of energy! The men are not always to blame—the employers are not always to blame. Both are caught up in this futile catch-as-catch-can world of ours and are forced to adopt the attitudes they do—or lose business and working rights. And—I hope we shall agree on this—both have become so used to considering only their own side of affairs that they have lost a proper sense of perspective and are equally to be blamed on occasion.

Then there is the business of holidays. The last of the two-yearly Ministry of Health census to find out how many workers get holidays ascertained that only one worker in six (1,750,000 out of the 10,630,000 insured workers) gets holidays on pay.

There is the matter of the cost of living. Wages, we know, have definitely not risen. But the cost of living has.

The cost of all items has risen by 47 per cent. since July, 1914, food by 31 per cent. But that does not tell the whole story: the cost of food has risen by 9 per cent. since 1933!

What a stupid situation! Here are thousands of people wanting, indeed begging, food, yet the cost of it rises so that is is even further removed from them. Families all over the country would readily consume butter, cheese, British meat, more coal, more clothes, more household articles, ten thousand things; but, instead of devising a method whereby this demand can be supplied, all the Government does is to allow prices to rise so that consumption is even smaller than it would be normally.

What need is there for this situation to drag on? At this time of the year, with the long evenings making us only too ready to go home and enjoy our homes, or go out for an evening's pleasure, when presents have to be bought and we need new clothes and more substantial foods, there should be no poverty at all. There should be no deprivation. But there is—far too much, and we all experience it in some shape or another, don't we?

And, moreover, when we do buy goods, what do we buy? What are the cheapest goods? Those

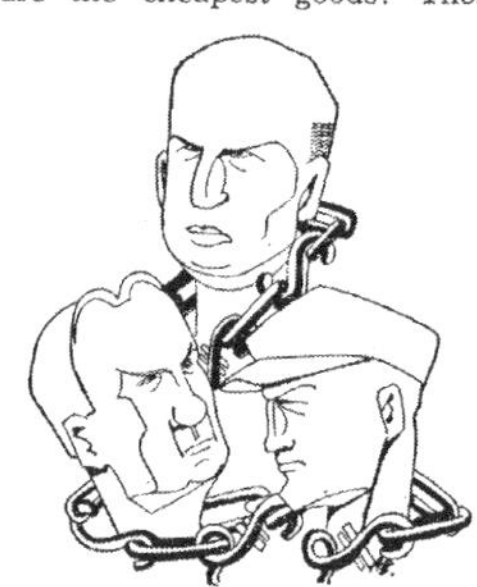

made in foreign countries—ask your wife. So that, instead of making sure of employing ourselves in making what we can, we are forced to employ foreigners to make things for us!

Finally, there is no adequate machinery to ensure that our protests—our much-vaunted "free speech"—shall be heard and acted upon.

Well, well! It certainly does seem mad, doesn't it?

But is there any need for it? Of course not.

We live in a world of greater actual and far greater potential plenty than has ever been known. We have all realised that elementary fact; but what we have not realised at all apparently is that we must make a determined and unafraid effort to organise our life so that we can get our share of this plenty: it's no use sitting down and waiting for it to come from the men in Parliament who have shown themselves incapable of solving the difficulty.

We could all assure ourselves of plenty to eat and drink, of food and clothing and shelter, of holidays on pay, and an end of these disruptive and purposeless trade disputes, if we got down to the business of studying the situation seriously and letting the problem indicate its own obvious remedies.

We could all have a forty-hour week, even less, if we tackled the job scientifically.

That reminds me of a comment made by an employer of labour in Bristol who has introduced the forty-hour week. You may have read it yourself; if not, here it is:

"The heart of the reduced working week principle is summed up by saying that science, planned production and the scientific management of distribution can enable mankind to enjoy an extended leisure. The next step is to arrange our house so that we may all have more time for leisure. If more goods and services are being made available year by year all parties should take a share in the resulting benefits."

(Mr. E. H. Taylor, managing director of Messrs. Joseph Lingford and Son, Ltd.)

That's not such a bad idea, is it? Now let's see how we can achieve it through Fascism.

FACTS FOR YOUR FILE

Compiled by GEORGE SUTTON

The Rich Get Richer

FOLLOWING on a recent note to the effect that the rise in the value of 365 representative securities from the bottom of the slump in 1932 to September, 1936, amounted to over £1,700,000,000, the *Bankers' Magazine* for November, 1936, reports a further rise on the month of £122,600,000 on the same securities.

The above news, combined with the information in the Press of a further increase in loans from the bank to individuals, indicates the extent of the speculators' paradise that now exists.

Unemployment

THE figures for unemployment in Great Britain on October 26 show a net reduction of 12,529 on the month, and now total 1,611,810.

Actually the number of persons "wholly unemployed" shows an increase on the month of about 23,000, and an increase in the category "persons normally in casual employment" of 3,300. The improvement is entirely in those "temporarily stopped" and amounts to 38,700.

Plight of a Cotton Town

MANCHESTER GUARDIAN has a special article on conditions in Darwen as an example of what is happening in parts of Lancashire. The town's population has been falling for nearly a generation; in 1911 it was 40,000, in 1921 38,700, in 1931 36,100, and in 1935 (on the Registrar-General's estimate) 33,700. It has a relatively low birth-rate and deaths between 1927 and 1935 exceed births by over 900.

In 1933 unemployment averaged 35 per cent. of the insured population; in 1934, 32 per cent.; in 1935, 30 per cent. Under-employment among weavers adds to the seriousness of the problem. Even now more than a quarter of the town's insured workers are unemployed, with the average for the country about 12.5 per cent. To judge from the available figures the number of persons now employed in Darwen is only two-thirds of what it was in 1929.

Cotton weaving claims one insured man in three and five insured women in every six. Fewer than half the sheds at work before the slump are now active. Everything indicates that most of those that are closed will never reopen. (*Manchester Guardian*, November 10, 1936.)

National Socialism and the Workers

MEASURES have been introduced by General Goering which would inspire a similar Government here, if we were fortunate to possess it. One of these measures compels firms in the metal and building industries with more than ten employees to take on an appropriate number of apprentices, the number to be decided by the Labour Office according to the circumstances of the business. It is also made compulsory for all business firms with ten or more employees to employ an appropriate number of persons over the age of forty on the ground that the Four-year Plan cannot be carried through unless all the labour resources of the German people are used. (Details from *The Times*, November 10, 1936.)

Communal Riots in India

MR. BUTLER, Under-Secretary for India, informed the House of Commons yesterday, in reply to a question, that 105 persons were killed and 516 injured in communal riots in various parts of India in 1935. (*Hansard*, November 9, 1936, col. 476.)

This number has considerably increased this year. Yet the supposed success of Government of India Act is dependent on peace between the religious sects.

Conservative M.P. and Anti-Semitism

MR. CROSSLEY, Tory M.P. for Stretford Division of Lancashire, stated in a speech in the House of Commons on Monday: "I am bound to say that one of the principal causes of anti-Semitism in the East End is that the furniture trade is practically entirely in Jewish hands at the moment. The hours they have to work are disgracefully long, and the wages they are paid are very low." (*Hansard*, November 9, 1936, col. 598.)

Inequitable

MR. RUNCIMAN stated in reply to a question that "The Canadian Customs duty on all types of United Kingdom furniture is 18 per cent. ad valorem. The duties imposed by the Union of South Africa are, generally, 20 per cent. ad valorem on metal furniture and 25 per cent. ad valorem on wooden furniture. Canadian and South African furniture enter the United Kingdom duty free." (*Hansard*, November 10, 1936, col. 665.)

Mr. Runciman Still Conscious?

"I AM very conscious of the competition from Japan, not only in these (rubber footwear) but in other things as well." (Mr. Runciman in the House of Commons, November 10, col. 667.) But he does nothing, so that we have grave doubts whether Mr. Runciman is really conscious!

Wisdom of the Ancients

"PARLIAMENTARY Government, in the long run, will stand or fall, not by academic considerations, but by its capacity to meet the burning problems of the day." (Mr. Dingle Foot, Lib., Dundee, House of Commons, November 9, 1936.)

"There is no real sense of security in the present prosperity boom." (Mr. Cartland, C., King's Norton, House of Commons, November 9, 1936.)

One-sided Trade With Russia

Captain Cazalet (U., Chippenham), speaking in the House of Commons last week, criticised the proposed credit (or loan) of £10,000,000 to Russia, and the existing trade agreement. It had been generally understood that there would be no loan to Russia unless or until some settlement had been reached about past debts. He stated that it is not too much to say that opinion in Moscow, commercial, journalistic, and official, was amazed at this action of our Government, and that this Government should have "sold the pass" in regard to the question of debts.

In 1934 our purchases from Russia amounted to something over £17,000,000, while Russia purchased from this country goods manufactured here valued at just over £3,500,000. In 1935 we bought from Russia £21,000,000, and they bought about £3,500,000 from us. During the first eight months of this year our purchases from Russia totalled £10,000,000, and Russia only bought £2,250,000.

We, however, kindly allowed Russia to count re-exports as exports, although much of these re-exports never entered this country. This concession was intended to benefit British shipping. The facts are that the number of British ships calling at Leningrad in 1934 was 140; in 1935 it was about fifty, and in the first six months of this year it was about seven.

Germany, however, arranged that all goods she purchased from Russia shall be carried in German ships, so that in Leningrad last year no fewer than 400 German ships called in that port.

Thus is proved our contention that only under a Fascist and National Socialist regime are the vital interests of our countrymen adequately safeguarded.

Japan Hits Yorkshire

India, one of Yorkshire's best markets for woollen piece goods, is fast becoming a Japanese preserve. In 1927-28 we exported to India 7,125,000 yards of woollen piece goods, while Japan sent only 1,414,000 yards.

In 1934-35 our exports dropped to 2,078,000 yards, and exports from Japan rose to 6,859,000 yards.

Anti-German Lies

MR. CROWDER, the Tory member for Uxbridge, asked the Chancellor of the Exchequer yesterday to make a statement as to the continued operation of the system of frozen credits in Germany, and whether, for the sake of British creditors, he will make further representations to the German Government to abandon what is practically a system of national default.

Lt.-Col. Colville, replying for the Government, stated that: "The frozen trade debts of Germany to this country which existed in 1934 have been liquidated in accordance with the provisions of the Anglo-German Payments Agreement of November 1, 1934. Interest is being paid in full to United Kingdom creditors in respect of the Dawes and Young Loans. The other German long-term loans, as also the short-term credits, are being dealt with in accordance with agreements reached between the German authorities and the representatives of the United Kingdom creditors concerned. (*Hansard*, November 9, 1936, col. 513.)

And so is exploded another anti-Fascist libel.

TWO VIEWS

Who Causes Anti-Semitism?

THE *Northamptonshire Evening Telegraph* says that Sir Oswald's Fascists are in no way perturbed by the fact that there will be introduced in Parliament the Bill to ban political uniforms. "Of course not," he says; "uniforms do not make the Movement; what makes the Movement is the Spirit of Fascism which no Government can ban."

The writer also says that Fascists "are confident that the Bill has been forced on the Government by the Labour and Jewish influence, but that, when passed, it will be impotent." It is good to know that some provincial papers are letting the cat out of the bag; unfortunately they do not comment on the astounding disclosure that a British Government is surrendering its governmental powers to Jewry. The spectacle of a National Government allowing the Jews to hold over it the big stick will make more Britishers wonder, make more Britishers think, and the inevitable result of this wondering and thinking will make them anti-Semitic. The Jews themselves are the cause of anti-Semitism.

The *Glasgow Evening Citizen*, in its comments on the Public Order Bill, says: "that hatred [between Fascists and Communists] will not be ended merely because the uniform of the Fascists has been proscribed. It is not the uniform, but the theory which it symbolises, that is the fundamental cause of the trouble. The Communists will, no doubt, continue to try to wreck Fascist meetings, just as they try to wreck Conservative, Liberal, and sometimes Socialist meetings."

Quite so; what is wanted is a firm hand on the aggressors and not on the victims. But the history of weak Democratic Governments shows that they are prone to take the supposed easier path of surrendering to force rather than do their duty by putting down disorder with a firm hand. History also demonstrates that by this easier path a Democratic Government commits hara-kiri.

BEHIND THE NEWS

Edited by J. A. Macnab

Non-Intervention

EXTRACT from latest speech of "La Pasionaria," woman Red leader in Spain:

"*Generous Spanish blood, aided by Soviet war equipment, is fighting for the welfare of the world's proletariat.*"—November 14.

Comment by the Russian delegate to the Non-intervention Committee would be interesting to read.

Youth Wants Action

AS some religious publications have recently taken it upon themselves to enter partisan politics for the purpose of slanging Fascism, which upholds religious toleration, it is refreshing to observe the following comments in the *New Chronicle of Christian Education* for November 12:

"*One of the best ways of understanding modern youth is by discovering what things are successfully appealing to it in the world to-day. None of the three political parties is setting fire to young people, but some things are—Fascism, Communism, National Socialism. And why do Mussolini, Hitler, and Mosley send young men marching clamorously about Europe in shirts of many colours? It is because these leaders are actually prepared to lead. They propose to do things and are getting them done.*"

The mention of Communism is interesting. It shows that the paragraph was not written by a Fascist sympathiser. And let it not be forgotten that many of the best National Socialists, both here and in Germany, have been people who had early been driven into the revolutionary camp in disgust with financial democracy, and embraced with enthusiasm the new revolutionary creed which offered them more than Communism could ever do, and yet preserved love of country, which is seldom utterly dead, and the right to worship God in freedom. He who is well satisfied with the present order is the worst curse in the country, and of all, the Liberal is the most reactionary, for he wishes to go back to the state of affairs that gave rise to the present crisis of the West.

Sam Hoare Scores a Century

IT was stated in Parliament on November 9 that during 1935 the number killed in communal riots in India was 105 and injured, 516.

The India Bill, which was sponsored by Sir Samuel Hoare, depends for any hope of success on peace between the religious sects. Every weakening of Central Government has brought increased disorder of this kind. The 1936 figures, when they are published, will show a still higher figure.

The Soviets need not bother to spend so much money on disruptive propaganda in the Indian Empire while we have patriotic Conservative politicians prepared to pass Acts that will achieve the same object.

Does Hoare Approve?

THE rate at which disruption of the British *raj* is proceeding is well illustrated by the news from Peshawar that Sir Ralph Griffith, Governor of the N.W. Frontier Province, in a farewell speech to the Legislative Council on November 10, welcomed the decision of the Redshirt party to participate in the forthcoming elections.

Only last year the Redshirt organisation was considered by the Indian Government to be a movement of violent revolution, having as its object to drive the British out of India by force. Twelve months later a provincial governor is instructed to fawn upon it.

Blackshirt Terrorism

HUMOUR is not infrequently to be extracted from the serious columns of the *Daily Mirror*. In its account of the Hyde Park mass meeting to demonstrate against the Means Test on November 8, we read:

"... the vast crowd—*estimated at* 250,000. . . .

"Some confusion arose towards the end, when a rumour went round that *two* Blackshirts were fighting with Communists. A mass of people rushed to the scene, and some women, taking fright, climbed over railings into the enclosures, lifting their children after them. There was *a rush for the gates, but the police kept order.*"

It is disgraceful that Sir John Simon should have allowed these two thugs to terrorise 125,000 people each. But perhaps they were "provoked," for the same account informs us that in the demonstration "each contingent was led by marchers in khaki shirts and red ties," and that the platform "was surrounded by red flags."

The platform, it need only be added, was occupied by Mr. Attlee, who denounced the Means Test which his own party had drafted in 1930. Mr. Attlee was the man who jumped at Mosley's £2,000-a-year job when Mosley resigned in disgust at the Labour Government's total failure to redeem its election pledges to the unemployed.

Doves of Peace

THIS Mr. Attlee doesn't regard the Communists' khaki shirts and red ties as one little bit provocative, because he knows the difference between their policy of peace and brotherhood and the wicked Blackshirts' warmongering. He remembers Mosley's bloodthirsty words, "British blood shall never again be shed in foreign quarrels"; and he contrasts the Soviet olive-branch of *Pravda*, the official Moscow newspaper:

"*The object is the erection of one world Soviet republic, consisting of subsidiary Soviet republics, set in what had once been the national countries of the former world of free individuals and free nations. . . . The world nature of our programme is not mere talk, but an embracing and blood-soaked reality. . . . Our ultimate aim is world-wide Communism, our fighting preparations are for world revolution, for the conquest of power on a world-wide scale, and the establishment of a world proletarian dictatorship.*"

Mr. Attlee is also reminded of the manner in which this desirable state of affairs is to be brought about. At the 15th Congress of the Russian Communist Party, as long ago as 1927, Stalin stated:

"*Do not forget the words of Lenin: he said that in our Socialist enterprise much depended on our ability to know how to postpone the date of the inevitable war with the capitalist world.*"

Hence the feverish League activity of Litvinoff, while the Red Army and Air Force doubles, trebles, and quadruples itself from year to year.

Correction

A PARAGRAPH on this page last week described Mr. Geoffrey Lloyd, M.P., as an employee of the *News Chronicle*. This is inaccurate: Mr. Lloyd's name was susbstituted for another by an error in transcription, and I regret having misled any of our readers who did not realise that a mistake had been made.

General Meeting of Ostrich Club

"BETRAYAL OF SPAIN" was the title given to a meeting held at Hendon Town Hall. Mrs. Marjorie Pollitt presided, and the speakers were Miss Isabel Brown, of the Spanish Medical Aid; Mr. Langdon Davies, a representative of the *News Chronicle*; the Rev. E. Iredell, of St. Clement's Church, Barnsbury (the vicar who had the "Internationale" played on the organ), who has recently returned from Spain; Mr. R. Stewart, a representative of the Catalan Government; and Mr. I. Edelman, of the Friends of the Soviet Union.

THE OSTRICH CLUB

Not Abyssinian After All.—"The irony is that Fascism and Naziism are almost entirely of Jewish origin."—Mr. A. C. Johnson, prospective Liberal candidate for Salisbury, in *Salisbury Times*, November 6.

"Sanctions Mean War."—"I believe Sir Anthony Eden (*sic*) is doing his best to keep the country out of any catastrophe that may take place in Europe.

"The only thing we can do is to trust the Cabinet, hoping that their wisdom will land us clear of trouble."—Rev. F. Humble, at a Brompton ex-Servicemen's dinner, November 7.

Simon the Storm-Trooper.—"The hope that the Government will ban the wearing of political uniforms is based on a misunderstanding of this Government in regard to Fascism, for, as I understand it, they are allies of Mosley."—Mr. W. Mellow, chairman of executive of Socialist League, at Whitechapel, November 1.

As in Russia, of course.—"I know some of you may say that we are associating with some pretty queer fish by supporting Communists, Anarchists and left-wing Socialists in Spain, but I am convinced that if the Spanish Government is successful in the war, out of the Communist dictatorship which will inevitably follow will come a Liberal Government."—Dr. Margaret Deas, addressing Hornsey Liberal Association.

Red-Front Geography.—"It is evident to all right-thinking people that Spain is not outside the orbit of the British nation."—Mrs. Pollitt, at Hendon, November 6.

MOSLEY CONFIRMED

GENEVA REPORTS INCREASED PRODUCTION, BUT NO RECOVERY OF TRADE

By A. Raven Thomson

THE report just issued by the International Labour Office at Geneva on the recovery of world production confirms in the most complete manner the whole National Socialist argument upheld by Sir Oswald Mosley since 1930. The Director, Mr. Harold Butler, reports as follows on world production and world trade:

"*According to this, the output of primary products is now slowly mounting to the level of 1929, while manufacturing production is above that level. The unemployed index for 1936 has shown a continued decline, but the quantum of world trade, which has fallen by nearly one-third, has not shown the same capacity to recover, being still nearly 20 per cent. short of the 1929 position.*

"*Every country, without exception, shows industrial production running at a higher level in 1936 than in the corresponding months of 1935. In most countries the gap between the cost of living and wholesale prices is gradually closing. The conclusion is drawn that in the great majority of countries industrial production is rapidly improving and unemployment is being reduced without any marked rise in prices. Recovery closely coincides with the adoption of expansionist measures. But unemployment has not been reduced to the extent that industrial production has recovered, nor is there any comparable improvement in international trade. To a great extent the improved production indices reflect an increase in the output of investment rather than of consumption goods. Agricultural income has risen in nearly all countries and for nearly all products, while the rise in selling prices exceeds the increased cost of production.*"

Conclusions

THE ensuing conclusions follow automatically from this:

(1) That recovery is entirely on account of improved home markets, as world trade still remains at 20 per cent. below the former level.

(2) Unemployment is still high on account of continued rationalisation.

(3) Improvement in agriculture has been the cause of recovery in most countries except Britain.

(4) Expansionist monetary experiments have been wholly successful.

All these proposals have been part of the Fascist policy from the outset and may be found in the following extracts from Mosley's resignation speech from the Labour Government in 1930.

On the export trade:

"*I submit that this hope of recovering our position through an expansion of our export trade is an illusion, and a dangerous illusion; and the sooner the fallacy is realised the quicker can we devote ourselves to a search for the real remedy. There are innumerable factors, beyond those which I have mentioned, militating against any increase of our export trade to that extent. There is the industrialisation of other countries for their own home markets; there is the industrialisation of countries which had no industries at all a few years ago.*"

On rationalisation:

"*I have been at some pains to examine the facts in trades which have at any rate partially rationalised, and I think we can take, as a criterion of a rationalised trade, those trades which, in a relatively short space of time, have greatly increased their production for a profitable market. I applied this criterion to trades of that character—four big groups of trades—and I found, between 1924 and 1929, an average increase in production of over 20 per cent., but an average decline in the insured workers in those trades of over 4 per cent. Over five years you have that immense increase in production—a very great achievement—and over the same long period a steady decline in the employment in those trades which were ever increasing their efficiency and expanding their markets. It would appear, therefore, on the evidence which exists, that rationalisation in itself is at any rate no short and easy cut to the solution of the unemployment problem.*"

On agriculture:

"*I had an estimate put to me that 500,000 men could thereby be put on the land. I believe that to be an exaggeration, but I am confident that a good many could be put on the land. It would lead directly to the rationalisation of trades like milling and baking, diverting all the energies of those engaged in those trades from speculation in wheat to the efficiency of their own industrial processes, and by those economies, and economies in freight and insurance, which we can deal with in other and more detailed debates, I believe the basis of a great agricultural policy can be laid.*"

Mosley Pointed the Way

MOSLEY pointed the way of recovery, which the old gang politicians then proceeded to make as difficult as possible by cutting down the standard of life of the people, ruining the home market, subsidising exports that were gone for ever and neglecting agriculture, the one mainstay of the economic system.

Yet recovery came despite them all; but equally another collapse and depression will follow. Already the report warns us:

"*To a great extent the improved production indices reflect an increase in the output of investment rather than of consumption goods.*"

This is the first symptom of coming crisis, when new capital investment floods the market with more unwanted goods. The system will soon flounder into another depression, and then it will be the Mosley they ridiculed in 1930 who alone will be capable of saving Britain.

Printed by ARGUS PRESS, LTD., Temple Avenue and Tudor Street, London, E.C.4, England, and published by ACTION PRESS, LTD., Sanctuary Buildings, Gt. Smith Street, London, S.W.1, England. Telephone: Victoria 9084 (5 lines).

THE COMPLETE EDITION PUBLISHED IN TEN VOLUMES

ACTION

1936-1940

Every edition of the weekly newspaper of the British Union Of Fascists published by Oswald Mosley from 1936 to 1940

A new resource for historians, sociologists, students of politics and international relations and general readers

A MAJOR NEW
THE WEEKLY NEWSPAPER OF T

Every single edition as published by Osw

- A facsimile edition of all 222 issues published in ten volumes
- The definitive primary reference source for historians, sociologists, students of politics and general readers
- An indispensable study guide to the rise and fall of fascism in the UK
- Reproduced from printer's originals; the only surviving complete set in existence
- A new insight into the politics and society of the UK in the 20th century

The study of the socio-political history of Nazi Germany and Fascist Italy is a highly developed field which is richly endowed with widely available primary source material.

The power and significance of the corresponding movement in thirties Britain is often overlooked. Very little primary source material is readily available for historians and scholars and as a consequence the study of the development and influence of this extreme movement which so closely mirrored its counterparts in Europe, has long been neglected.

Action was the weekly newspaper of the British Union Of Fascists. It was printed from February 1936 and actually continued in publication into June 1940; six months after the outbreak of World War II. Professionally printed and widely

UDY RESOURCE
: BRITISH UNION OF FASCISTS
Mosley from 1936 to 1940 in 10 volumes

distributed, Action took the Mosleyites into the mainstream. Each week for four years over 20,000 copies of Action were distributed with an estimated readership of 50,000.

Unlike many of the crude political pamphlets of the day Action was a sophisticated publication with a mainstream veneer which achieved a wide reach and carried an extreme political message much further into the public consciousness than is recognised or understood today.

For the first time a complete facsimile edition of all 222 editions of Action is being reprinted and made available to Universities, Colleges and indivual collectors. An invaluable primary reference source, this major publishing event opens up new avenues of understanding is of great value for students of 20th century politics, history and international relations.

Each of the 10 hard-back volumes contains 22 complete editions of Action. Together the 10 volumes form a complete primary resource which throws new light on the social and political landscape of Britain in the thirties and forties

"A prophet or an achiever must never mind an occasional absurdity, it is an occupational risk." OSWALD MOSLEY

Taken from the only surviving complete set in existence.

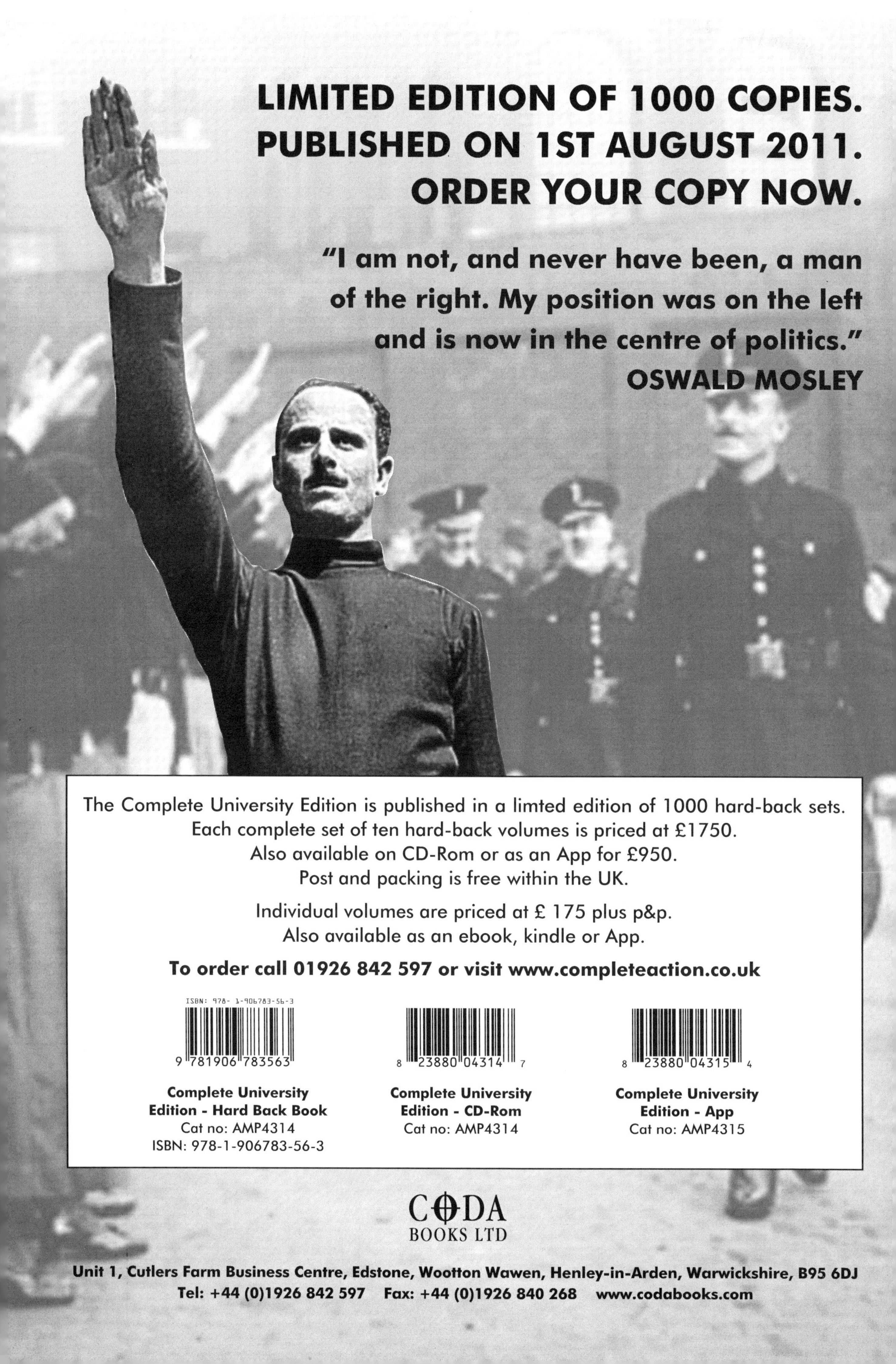

LIMITED EDITION OF 1000 COPIES.
PUBLISHED ON 1ST AUGUST 2011.
ORDER YOUR COPY NOW.

"I am not, and never have been, a man of the right. My position was on the left and is now in the centre of politics."
OSWALD MOSLEY

The Complete University Edition is published in a limted edition of 1000 hard-back sets.
Each complete set of ten hard-back volumes is priced at £1750.
Also available on CD-Rom or as an App for £950.
Post and packing is free within the UK.

Individual volumes are priced at £ 175 plus p&p.
Also available as an ebook, kindle or App.

To order call 01926 842 597 or visit www.completeaction.co.uk

Complete University Edition - Hard Back Book
Cat no: AMP4314
ISBN: 978-1-906783-56-3

8 23880 04314 7

Complete University Edition - CD-Rom
Cat no: AMP4314

Complete University Edition - App
Cat no: AMP4315

CODA
BOOKS LTD

Unit 1, Cutlers Farm Business Centre, Edstone, Wootton Wawen, Henley-in-Arden, Warwickshire, B95 6DJ
Tel: +44 (0)1926 842 597 Fax: +44 (0)1926 840 268 www.codabooks.com